Lynette Louis-Jacques

problems in american history

volume 1 / through reconstruction

edited by RICHARD W. LEOPOLD, ARTHUR S. LINK

problems in

Edmund S. Morgan, *Yale University*
Alden T. Vaughan, *Columbia University*
Max Savelle, *University of Illinois, Chicago Circle*
Merrill Jensen, *University of Wisconsin*
Clarence L. Ver Steeg, *Northwestern University*
Richard N. Current, *University of North Carolina*
Charles G. Sellers, *University of California at Berkeley*
Douglass C. North, *University of Washington*
Arthur Bestor, *University of Washington*
Eugene D. Genovese, *University of Rochester*
Kenneth M. Stampp, *University of California at Berkeley*
Thomas J. Pressly, *University of Washington*
John Hope Franklin, *University of Chicago*

AND STANLEY COBEN

american history *fourth edition*

volume 1 / through reconstruction

PRENTICE-HALL, INC.
Englewood Cliffs, N.J.

problems in american history   *fourth edition*

volume 1 / through reconstruction

edited by RICHARD W. LEOPOLD, ARTHUR S. LINK, AND STANLEY COBEN

© 1952, 1957, 1966, 1972 by PRENTICE-HALL, INC.
ENGLEWOOD CLIFFS, NEW JERSEY

All rights reserved.
No part of this book may be reproduced
in any form or by any means without
permission in writing from the publisher.

ISBN: 0-13-712935-1

Library of Congress Catalog Card Number: 78-39188

Printed in the United States of America

10 9 8 7 6 5 4 3 2 1

PRENTICE-HALL INTERNATIONAL, INC., London
PRENTICE-HALL OF AUSTRALIA, PTY. LTD., Sydney
PRENTICE-HALL OF CANADA, LTD., Toronto
PRENTICE-HALL OF INDIA PRIVATE LIMITED, New Delhi
PRENTICE-HALL OF JAPAN, INC., Tokyo

contents

problem 1
1. the sources of authority
EDMUND S. MORGAN

3.   **1. AUTHORITY FROM GOD**
Kings as God's Lieutenants upon Earth (*James I, March 21, 1609*); God Gives the Sword into the People's Hand (*Christopher Goodman, 1558*); The God-Given Authority of Elected Magistrates (*John Winthrop, 1645*); The Christian's Duty to Resist Tyrannical Rulers (*Jonathan Mayhew, 1750*); Kings Reign and Princes Decree Justice under the Authority of God (*Jonathan Boucher, 1775*)

12.   **2. AUTHORITY FROM THE KING**
The King Delegates Authority to the Massachusetts Bay Company (*Charles I, 1629*); Proprietary Authority in New Jersey (*Carteret Government, 1668; Middletown Town Meeting, 1669*); The Colonists Acknowledge Only the Authority of the King (*James Wilson, 1774*)

18.   **3. AUTHORITY FROM THE PAST**
An American Common Law (*John Winthrop, 1639*); The Earth Belongs to the Living (*Thomas Jefferson, 1789*); The Binding Power of the Past (*Abel P. Upshur, 1829*)

23.   **4. AUTHORITY FROM THE PEOPLE**
The Practical Necessity (*The Mayflower Compact, 1620; Dover, New Hampshire, Compact, 1640; Richard Henderson, 1775*); The Theoretical Justification (*John Locke, 1689*)

28.   **5. AUTHORITY FROM PRESTIGE**
Nature's Noblemen (*Henry Timberlake, 1765; James Adair, 1775; Cadwa'lader Colden, 1727*); A willing Submission to Eminence (*Petition to the Virginia Company, 1618*); Deference in Rebellion (*Andrew Beall, 1776*); Aristocratic Republicans (*John Adams, 1813*)

37.   **CONCLUSION**

problem 2
38. the character of colonial politics
ALDEN T. VAUGHAN

41. **1. WHO COULD VOTE, AND FOR WHICH OFFICES?**
Definitions of Freemanship (*Connecticut, 1769; South Carolina, 1838; Virginia, 1769*); Religious Restrictions (*Assembly of the Province of Maryland, 1759*); Mixed Government (*James Glen, 1761*); Town Meeting Democracy (*Fitchburg, Massachusetts, 1764*)

51. **2. WHO WON ELECTIONS, AND HOW?**
Patterns of Voter Response (*Jackson T. Main, 1966*); Swilling the Planters with Bumbo (*Charles S. Sydnor, 1952*); Encroachments on Voter Independence (*Duane Papers, 1768*)

62. **3. ROYAL GOVERNMENT IN AMERICA**
His Excellency, the Captain General and Governor-in-Chief (*Leonard Woods Labaree, 1930*); The Perils of Office (*Samuel Shute, 1723*)

69. **4. THE SPIRIT OF THE TIMES**
An Excess of Democracy (*Andrew Burnaby, 1760*); Not Enough Democracy (*New York City Broadside, 1770*); "The Most Perfect Society Now Existing" (*St. Jean de Crèvecoeur, 1782*)

74. **CONCLUSION**

problem 3
78. road to revolution
MAX SAVELLE

79. **1. THE UNDERLYING FACTORS**
The Economic Factor (*Daniel Dulany, 1765*); The Political Factor (*Thomas Pownall, 1765*); The Religious Factor (*Jonathan Mayhew, 1763*); The Social Factor (*St. Jean de Crèvecoeur, 1782*); The Psychological Factor (*Nathaniel Ames, 1758; Philip Freneau and Hugh H. Brackenridge, 1771*)

86. **2. THE AMERICAN CASE**
The Question of Representation (*James Otis, 1764*); The Question of the Royal Veto (*Patrick Henry, 1763*); The Question of Taxation: The Virginia Resolutions (*House of Burgesses, 1765*); The Question of Taxation: The Stamp Act Congress (*The Stamp Act Congress, 1765*); Self-Taxation: The Mainspring of Liberty (*John Dickinson, 1767–1768*); The Idea of a Federal Empire (*Rich-*

ard Bland, 1766; Samuel Adams, 1773; James Wilson, 1774; Thomas Jefferson, 1774); The English Liberals Defend America (John Wilkes, 1775; Richard Price, 1776; William Pitt, Earl of Chatham, 1775); The Final Statement of the American Case (Continental Congress, 1774)

106. 3. THE BRITISH CASE
Taxation of the Colonies (Soame Jenyns, 1765); The Ideal of a Unified Empire (Lord Mansfield, 1766); The Question of Sovereignty—William Blackstone (Sir William Blackstone, 1765–1769); An English Moderate Speaks (Edmund Burke, 1775); The American Tories Support the British National Ideal (Thomas Hutchinson, 1773; Samuel Seabury, 1774; Jonathan Boucher, 1797)

118. 4. THE RESORT TO INDEPENDENCE
The King Refuses to Compromise (George III, 1775); An Appeal to Common Sense (Thomas Paine, 1776); Independence Proclaimed (Continental Congress, July 4, 1776)

126. CONCLUSION

problem 4

128. the articles of confederation and the constitution of 1787
MERRILL JENSEN

130. 1. THE PROBLEM OF UNION, 1774–1777
The Defense of State Sovereignty (Thomas Burke, 1777)

134. 2. THE DEMAND FOR A STRONG CENTRAL GOVERNMENT, 1780–1786
Hamilton's Plan (Alexander Hamilton, 1780); The Annapolis Convention (Louis Guillaume Otto, 1786)

141. 3. THE OPPOSITION TO A STRONG CENTRAL GOVERNMENT, 1783–1785
Opposition to More Power for Congress (Fairfax County, Virginia, 1783); The Danger of Holding a Convention (Massachusetts Delegates, 1785)

145. 4. THE CONVENTION OF 1787
The Nationalist Position (Governor Edmund Randolph, 1787); The True Federalist Position (John Lansing and William Paterson, 1787)

151. 5. THE ARGUMENTS AGAINST THE CONSTITUTION
A National, Not a Federal, Government Is Proposed (Samuel Adams, 1787); The Federal Farmer (Richard Henry Lee, 1787); The Country Is in a Good Condition (Massachusetts Centinel, 1787); Answers to Federalist Arguments (New York Journal and Weekly Register, 1787); The Faults of the Constitution (Massachusetts Centinel, 1787)

164. **6. THE NATIONALIST DEFENSE OF THE CONSTITUTION**
The Benefits to be Derived from the Constitution *(American Herald, 1787)*; Defense of the Constitution *(James Wilson, 1787)*; The Necessity for Ratification *(Massachusetts Centinel, 1787)*

170. **CONCLUSION**

problem 5

172. launching the new government
   CLARENCE L. VER STEEG

173. **1. LAUNCHING THE SHIP OF STATE**
Setting the Course *(George Washington, 1788–1789)*; How Shall the Debt Be Paid? *(Alexander Hamilton, 1790; James Madison, 1790)*; Debating the Nature of the Constitution *(Alexander Hamilton, 1791; James Madison, 1791)*

190. **2. THE REVOLUTION OF 1800**
Background for Revolution: The Alien and Sedition Acts *(John Allen, 1798; Thomas Jefferson, 1798)*; A Change of Course? *(Thomas Jefferson, 1810)*

198. **3. CONTROVERSIES OF THE JEFFERSONIAN ERA**
The Republicans Attack the Judiciary *(William B. Giles, 1802; Archibald Henderson, 1802)*; A Change of Economic Policy? *(Thomas Jefferson, 1801; Alexander Hamilton, 1801)*; The Embargo Issue *(Albert Gallatin, 1808; Timothy Pickering, 1809)*

214. **CONCLUSION**

problem 6

216. foundations of foreign policy:
   beginning the great debate, 1776-1826
   RICHARD N. CURRENT

217. **1. ALLIANCE—OR DIPLOMATIC INDEPENDENCE?**
The French Alliance *(John Adams, 1778)*; A Declaration of Diplomatic Independence *(George Washington, September 17, 1796)*; Jefferson Considers an Alliance with Britain *(Thomas Jefferson, 1802)*

contents

225.   2. WAR FOR NEUTRAL RIGHTS?
Virtual Allies of Bonaparte *(John Randolph, 1812)*; Free Trade and Seamen's Rights *(Henry Clay, 1813)*; The Voice of the Commercial Interests *(Daniel Webster, 1814)*

233.   3. EUROPEAN LEAGUE—OR AMERICAN BALANCE?
The Holy Alliance *(John Quincy Adams, 1820)*; A New World "Counterpoise" *(Henry Clay, 1818, 1820)*

237.   4. AN ANGLO-AMERICAN DOCTRINE?
The Case of Cuba *(John Quincy Adams, 1823)*; England's Overture *(James Monroe, 1823; Thomas Jefferson, 1823)*; No Cock-boat *(John Quincy Adams, 1823)*; Monroe's Message *(James Monroe, 1823)*

246.   5. CRUSADE FOR FREEDOM?
American Interest in the Greek Cause *(Daniel Webster, 1824)*; Meddle Not with Greece *(Joel R. Poinsett, 1824; John Randolph, 1824; Alexander Smyth, 1824)*

253.   CONCLUSION

problem 7

255. jacksonian democracy
CHARLES G. SELLERS, JR.

256.   1. POLITICAL DEMOCRACY
The Ballot Demanded *(Nonfreeholders of Richmond, Virginia, 1829)*; Property over Numbers *(Benjamin Watkins Leigh, 1829)*; Romantic Democracy *(George Bancroft, 1835)*; Equality *(James Flint, 1822; Richard Flower, 1819; Sir Charles A. Murray, 1834–1836; Isaac Holmes, 1823; Frances Trollope, 1832)*; The Conservative Democrat *(James Fenimore Cooper, 1838)*

268.   2. THE JACKSONIAN PROGRAM: BANKING
The Monster of Chestnut Street *(Arthur M. Schlesinger, Jr., 1945)*; The Bank Veto *(Andrew Jackson, 1832)*; The Bank Defended *(Boston Daily Advertiser & Patriot, 1832)*; Reforming the State Banks *(Churchill C. Cambreleng, 1835)*; Dénouement *(Bray Hammond, 1947)*

281.   3. THE MEANING OF JACKSONIAN DEMOCRACY
To Restrain the Power of the Business Community *(Arthur M. Schlesinger, Jr., 1945)*; To Liberate Business *(Richard Hofstadter, 1948)*; To Restore the Ways of the Plain Republican Order *(Marvin Meyers, 1953)*

289.   CONCLUSION

problem 8

292. acceleration in economic growth
DOUGLASS C. NORTH

293. 1. THE UNDERLYING INFLUENCES
The Leveling Influence of Democracy (*Alexis de Tocqueville, 1835*); The Matrix (*Stanley Lebergott, 1964*)

301. 2. THE SOURCES OF ECONOMIC GROWTH
The Mainspring of Growth (*Adam Smith, 1776*); Attack on Mercantilism (*Adam Smith, 1776*); In Defense of Government Intervention (*Alexander Hamilton, 1827*)

308. 3. OBSTACLES TO EXPANSION
The Need for a Strong Central Government (*Alexander Hamilton, 1802*); Foreign Discrimination (*Thomas Jefferson, 1793*)

311. 4. THE LACK OF CAPITAL AND HIGH PRICE OF LABOR
(*Albert Gallatin, 1810*)

313. 5. ACCELERATION IN ECONOMIC GROWTH
Internal and Interregional Trade (*Douglass C. North, 1961*); Protection and Manufacturing (*Daniel Webster, 1828*); Human Capital and Manufacturing (*G. S. Gibb, 1950*); A British Appraisal (*Joseph Whitworth and George Wallis, 1854*)

325. CONCLUSION

problem 9

327. the ferment of reform
ARTHUR BESTOR

331. 1. REFORM AND REFORMERS: A CONTEMPORARY INTERPRETATION
Emerson on the Reform Movement (*Ralph Waldo Emerson, 1841*)

333. 2. ROOTS OF THE REFORM MOVEMENT
The Religious Inspiration of Reform (*Charles G. Finney, 1835*); Humanitarianism (*William Jay, 1842*); Reform as a Corollary of Democratic Principles (*Elizabeth Cady Stanton, 1848*); The Doctrine of Progress (*Horace Greeley, 1850*); Appeals from Disadvantaged Groups Themselves (*Manayunk Working People's Committee, 1833*)

contents

340. **3. VARIETIES OF PROPAGANDA**
Factual Indictment *(Theodore D. Weld, 1839)*; Tearful Sentimentality *(Emeline S. Smith, 1849)*; Outspoken Denunciation *(William Lloyd Garrison, 1852)*; Reasoned Argument *(Horace Mann, 1849)*

347. **4. PROPOSED ROADS TO REFORM**
Individualism *(Henry David Thoreau, 1847)*; Organized Movements *(Alexis de Tocqueville, 1840)*; Legislative Action *(Massachusetts House of Representatives, 1850)*; Reform Through Model Communities *(Albert Brisbane, 1843)*; Social Revolution *(Richard Realf, 1860)*

357. **5. THE REFORM MOVEMENT AS VIEWED BY ITS OPPONENTS**
Laissez Faire *(Francis Wayland, 1837)*; The Fanaticism and Irreligion of the Reform Movement *(Princeton Review, 1838)*; The Tyranny of Organized Mass Opinion *(William Ellery Channing, 1829)*

362. **6. THE ULTIMATE ACCOMPLISHMENT: A FEW LANDMARKS**
Constitutional Amendments *(Constitution of the United States, 1865, 1868, 1870, 1919, 1920, 1933)*; Legislative Action *(Norris-LaGuardia Anti-Injunction Act, 1932)*; Judicial Decision *(U.S. Supreme Court, 1937)*

367. **CONCLUSION**

problem 10

368. **the civilization of the slaveowning south**
    EUGENE D. GENOVESE

369. **1. THE ARISTOCRATIC LOW COUNTRY**
The Rice Coast *(Herbert Ravenal Sass, 1936)*; Rose Hill Plantation *(Duncan Clinch Heyward, 1937)*; Random Notes from a Great Southern Lady *(Mary Boykin Chesnut, 1862)*

386. **2. THE CHIVALRY AND ITS LADIES**
A Southern Planter *(Susan Dabney Smedes, 1889)*; What Manner of Men? *(Frances Anne Kemble, 1863)*; The Ladies *(Anne Firor Scott, 1970)*; The Virginians in the Southwest *(Joseph G. Baldwin, 1853)*; Gentlemen and Parvenus *(W. E. B. DuBois, 1962)*

409. **3. INSIDE VIEWS FROM THE OUTSIDE**
Bitter Words from a Non-Slaveholder *(Hinton R. Helper, 1857)*; An Ex-Slave Surveys the Plantation *(Frederick Douglass, 1892)*; Two Recollections *(Andrew Goodman, Mingo White, 1930)*

427. **CONCLUSION**

problem 11

429. what caused the civil war?
KENNETH M. STAMPP

431. 1. WAS IT THE AGGRESSIONS OF THE SLAVE POWER?
The Record of the Slave Power (*Henry Wilson, 1872–1877*); The Defensive South (*Chauncey S. Boucher, 1921*)

439. 2. WAS IT THE ISSUE OF STATE SOVEREIGNTY VS. NATIONALISM?
The Constitutional Interpretation (*Alexander H. Stephens, 1868*); The State Sovereignty Argument (*South Carolina Convention, 1860*); The Nationalist Argument (*Abraham Lincoln, 1861*)

445. 3. WAS IT ECONOMIC SECTIONALISM?
The Irrepressible Conflict (*Charles A. and Mary R. Beard, 1927*); Southern Grievances (*Robert Toombs, 1860*); Northern Grievances (*Joshua R. Giddings, 1844, 1846*)

453. 4. WAS IT THE WORK OF IRRESPONSIBLE AGITATORS?
A Blundering Generation (*James G. Randall, 1940*); A Needless War (*Charles W. Ramsdell, 1929*)

462. 5. WAS IT THE "MORAL URGENCY" OF SLAVERY ISSUE?
Slavery the "Single Cause" (*James Ford Rhodes, 1913*); "The Travail of Slavery" (*Charles G. Sellers, Jr., 1960*); The Inevitability of Violence (*Arthur M. Schlesinger, Jr., 1949*)

473. 6. WAS IT THE FAILURE OF DEMOCRACY?
The Civil War and the Democratic Process (*Avery Craven, 1950*)

476. CONCLUSION

problem 12

479. why did the union win the civil war?
THOMAS J. PRESSLY

481. 1. WAS THE OUTCOME OF THE WAR INEVITABLE?
"Inevitablist" Outlook (*Richard N. Current, 1960*); "Evitablist" Outlook (*David M. Potter, 1960*); Outlook of Contemporaries (*William Gilmore Simms, 1861, 1864; Mary Boykin Chesnut, 1862; George Templeton Strong, 1861, 1862; Lord Palmerston, 1862; Lord John Russell, 1862*)

491. 2. WAS THE OUTCOME OF THE WAR CAUSED BY CONFEDERATE MISMANAGEMENT?
Mrs. Chesnut Describes Arguments over Responsibility for Confederate Defeat (*Mary Boykin Chesnut, 1865*); Former Confederate Officials Dispute over Reasons for Confederate Defeat (*Joseph E. Johnston, 1874; C. G. Memminger, 1874*); The Confederate Collapse (*George A. Trenholm, 1874*); A Former Official of the Confederate War Department Explains Why the Confederacy Lost (*Robert G. H. Kean, 1865*)

499. 3. WAS THE OUTCOME OF THE WAR THE RESULT OF THE UNION'S LARGER ARMY?
Lee, Stephens, "Bill Arp," and the Size of the Union Army (*Robert E. Lee, 1865; Alexander H. Stephens, 1868, 1870; "Bill Arp," 1865*); General Grant Discounts the Effect of Larger Union Armies (*Ulysses S. Grant, 1865, 1885*)

504. 4. WAS THE OUTCOME OF THE WAR THE RESULT OF THE SUPERIOR CHARACTERISTICS OF THE UNION AS A SOCIETY?
Bancroft and Cox Extol the Union (*George Bancroft, 1866; Samuel S. Cox, 1885*); Jefferson Davis Praises the Principles of the Confederacy (*Jefferson Davis, 1881*)

508. CONCLUSION

problem 13

510. reconstruction
JOHN HOPE FRANKLIN

513. 1. CONFLICTING VIEWS REGARDING THE FUTURE OF THE SOUTH
(*Thaddeus Stevens, 1865; New York Times, 1865*)

515. 2. DID THE SOUTH ACCEPT THE VERDICT OF THE WAR?
The Vindictive South (*Carl Schurz, 1865*); The Repentant South (*Benjamin C. Truman, 1866*); White Southerners Speak Out (*James D. B. DeBow, 1866*); The Voice of the Negro (*Alexandria Convention, 1865*)

530. 3. RADICAL RECONSTRUCTION
A Leader of the Radicals (*Thaddeus Stevens, 1865*); The Joint Committee on Reconstruction Speaks Its Mind (*Joint Committee on Reconstruction, 1866*); Radical Reconstruction Condemned (*Andrew Johnson, 1867*)

537. 4. THE SOUTH IN TRAVAIL
The Southern Whites Protest (*Carolina Democratic Central Committee, 1868*); The Southern Whites Act (*Ku Klux Klan Investigation, 1872*); Negro "Domination" Condemned (*H. H. Chalmers, 1881*); Negro "Domination" Denied (*John R. Lynch, 1913*)

545. 5. THE END OF AN ERA
A Traditional Interpretation (*James Ford Rhodes, 1906*); A Revisionist Evaluation (*W. E. B. DuBois, 1910*)

550. CONCLUSION

preface

The enthusiastic response accorded the first three editions of Problems in American History *seems to justify the original expectations of the editors and contributors. By combining a problem framework with use of primary sources, prepared by distinguished experts who could draw upon their own research, we hoped to enrich the study of American history.*

Reflecting important changes in the teaching of United States history, ten new chapters have been added in the last two editions (1966 and 1972), and almost every other chapter has undergone significant revision. Among the problems prepared for the fourth edition, for example, are sections on twentieth-century feminism, on the development of a distinct Southern culture before the Civil War, and on the New Left. Chapters drastically revised include those on the Cold War (including a section dealing with Vietnam) and on racial conflicts since the 1950s.

The editors wish to express their appreciation to the contributors for undertaking, once again, and with renewed enthusiasm, the task of revision. We are indebted to Professors David B. Davis of Yale and Paul K. Conkin of the University of Wisconsin for their searching review of the entire work and for their many fruitful suggestions. We are also grateful to Robert Fenyo of Prentice-Hall, who shared many of the burdens connected with our task, and to countless teachers throughout the country whose classroom experience with Problems in American History *led them to send us recommendations which helped shape this fourth edition.*

STANLEY COBEN
RICHARD W. LEOPOLD
ARTHUR S. LINK

problems in american history

volume 1 / through reconstruction

1 EDMUND S. MORGAN

the sources of authority

Men, wherever we find them, live under the authority of government, and philosophers have long wondered why. What would happen, they ask, if a number of men found themselves on a desert island beyond the reach of any established government? How would they behave toward one another? Would they live together peaceably without the need for government, or would they submit themselves to one or more of their number? The philosophers have usually concluded that they would submit, and have described how and why and to whom.

American history is very much like this philosophical speculation but with one important difference: we do not have to imagine what happened after the people arrived on the island. America *was* the desert island—really a continent, of course, but a relatively isolated and deserted one. It is estimated that in the seventeenth century there were scarcely more than a million native inhabitants in the whole area now embraced by the United States, and only a small portion of them were on the east coast. The distance of the settlers from "home base" was three thousand miles, a long and hazardous journey that made control from the Old World sporadic and uncertain.

In examining the behavior of the people who migrated to America, we find, as we might expect, that different people acted differently. There were some who saw the desert island as a fine place to throw off the inhibitions of society. Thomas Morton and his friends, who settled at Mount Wollaston in Massachusetts in the 1620s, seem to have been of this character. They set up bachelor's quarters, invited the Indian maidens to join them, and went on one of the big sprees of American history. There were also men of a more sober nature, prototypes of the later frontiersmen, who thought their nearest neighbor too close if they could see the smoke from his campfire. When the Puritans settled at Boston, they found William Blackstone, a college man, living comfortably amidst the blueberry bushes on Beacon Hill. He stayed for a while but soon found the pious company too much and took himself off to Narragansett Bay, in much the same spirit as Henry Thoreau a couple of centuries later took himself off to Walden Pond.

Such men, although they appeal strongly to our sympathies, are always rare. Most people are frightened by the prospect of living where there is no authority to control them or their neighbors, and the people who came to settle in America were no exception. Before sailing they usually arranged for a government to rule them in the New World; and if for any reason the arrangements failed, they made new ones immediately upon arrival.

In creating governments these early Americans had to consider the nature and source of authority. On this problem they displayed a variety of opinions, with far-reaching implications for the future. Though they came mostly from England and generally settled under grants from the King of England, they were not content to rest authority entirely upon him. Englishmen had been quarreling about this subject for generations, and many came to America because they did not like the kind of authority claimed by the government at home. After their arrival the different circumstances in which they found themselves affected their ideas and increased the variety of their viewpoints.

The selections that follow are designed to illustrate this variety among both the original settlers and their descendants, for the problem of authority is a recurring one, which we can never wholly escape as long as we live with other people—witness the philosophical speculations about desert islands. It reappears whenever government does something we dislike, and in the history of the United States it arose also whenever settlers on the frontier moved beyond the reach of their old governments and had to create new ones of their own. In their march across the continent, Americans became so accustomed to considering and reconsidering the problem, to creating and abandoning authority, that they came to hold government in less awe than the peoples of most other countries do. In the course of time they have repudiated most sources of authority apart from the fourth one listed below, but it is well to remember that it was not always so, and it may be worth inquiring whether any of the other views presented here have any validity for our own time.

In reading them, the student should remember that they are not necessarily to be regarded as being mutually exclusive. It was possible to derive authority from all these sources simultaneously. On the other hand, it was possible to repudiate one source without repudiating the others, or to emphasize one at the expense of the others. Rebellion in politics, like heresy in religion, may come simply from a shift in emphasis.

1. AUTHORITY FROM GOD

At the time the first American colonies were founded, it was almost universally agreed that the ultimate source of authority (as opposed to mere naked force) was God. The question, of course, was how it came from God to man, for no one supposed that the Creator Himself would condescend to become a politician and govern His creatures in person. Did God hand authority in some private dispensation to a single individual and his heirs? Did He give it to a whole people and let them designate the man or men who should exercise it? In the latter case, was the authority of God transferred from the people to the elected governors during their term of office? Once given, could it be withdrawn? What did God require of governors? And of the governed? These were questions that agitated men in England and Europe and continued to agitate them in America. The different answers given at different times were usually elicited by a desire to enlist God on one side or the other in some struggle for power. The selections should make it clear that rebels could sometimes construct as persuasive a claim to His exclusive endorsement as kings could.

Kings as God's Lieutenants upon Earth

James the First of England was fond of assuring everyone of his close association with God. In the early seventeenth century some Catholic spokesmen claimed that God channelled all His authority through Rome. James, as the principal defender of the "divine right of Kings," took every possible occasion to explain that kings in general and he in particular received authority directly from on high, without the assistance of any intermediate dispenser. James was eager to establish this view not only against the Pope but also against his own subjects, who wished to restrict his authority through Parliament. The following passage is from a speech he made to Parliament on March 21, 1609.[1]

The state of monarchy is the supremest thing upon earth: for kings are not only God's lieutenants upon earth, and sit upon God's throne, but even by God himself they are called gods. . . .

Kings are justly called gods, for

[1] James I, *Works* (London, 1616), 529–31.

that they exercise a manner or resemblance of Divine power upon earth: for if you will consider the attributes to God, you shall see how they agree in the person of a king. God hath power to create, or destroy, make, or unmake at His pleasure, to give life, or send death, to judge all, and to be judged nor accountable to none: to raise low things, and to make high things low at His pleasure, and to God are both soul and body due. And the like power have kings: they make and unmake their subjects: they have power of raising, and casting down: of life, and of death: judges over all their subjects, and in all causes, and yet accountable to none but God only. They have power to exalt low things, and abase high things, and make of their subjects like men at the chess; a pawn to take a bishop or a knight, and to cry up, or down any of their subjects, as they do their money. And to the king is due both the affection of the soul and the service of the body of his subjects. . . .

But now in these our times we are to distinguish between the state of kings in their first original, and between the state of settled kings and monarchs that do at this time govern in civil kingdoms: for even as God, during the time of the Old Testament, spake by oracles, and wrought by miracles; yet how soon it pleased him to settle a church which was bought, and redeemed by the blood of his only son Christ, then was there a cessation of both; He ever after governing His people and church within the limits of His revealed will. So in the first original of kings, whereof some had their beginning by conquest, and some by election of the people, their wills at that time served for law; yet how soon kingdoms began to be settled in civility and policy, then did kings set down their minds by laws, which are properly made by the king only; but at the rogation of the people, the king's grant begin obtained thereunto. And so the king became to be *Lex loquens* [a speaking law], after a sort, binding himself by a double oath to the observation of the fundamental laws of his kingdom. . . . Therefore all kings that are not tyrants, or perjured, will be glad to bound themselves within the limits of their laws; and they that persuade them the contrary, are vipers, and pests, both against them and the Commonwealth. For it is a great difference between a king's government in a settled state, and what kings in their original power might do. . . . As for my part, I thank God, I have ever given good proof that I never had intention to the contrary: and I am sure to go to my grave with that reputation and comfort, that never king was in all his time more careful to have his laws duly observed, and himself to govern thereafter, than I.

I conclude then this point touching the power of kings, with this axiom of divinity, that as to dispute what God may do, is blasphemy; . . . so is it sedition in subjects, to dispute what a king may do in the height of his power; but just kings will ever be willing to declare what they will do, if they will not incur the curse of God. I will not be content that my power be disputed upon: but I shall ever be willing to make the reason appear of all my doings, and rule my actions according to my laws.

God Gives the Sword into the People's Hand

In 1558, eight years before James I was born, England was ruled by Mary Tudor, a Catholic queen from whom many leading Protestants fled to exile in Geneva, Switzerland. From this refuge they called to their fellow countrymen to rebel. One of the most persuasive appeals was Christopher Goodman's *How Superior Powers oght to be obeyd of their subjects: and Wherin they may lawfully by Gods Worde be disobeyed and resisted*. The passage which follows is taken from this work, published in 1558; it shows how God might be considered to have withdrawn His authority from a monarch and left it among the people. Goodman's ideas, which were common among English Protestants, became part of the heritage that American settlers carried with them to the New World fifty years later.[2]

And though it appear at the first sight a great disorder, that the people should take unto them the punishment of transgression, yet, when the magistrates and other officers cease to do their duty, they are as it were, without officers, yea, worse than if they had none at all; and then God giveth the sword into the people's hand, and he himself is become immediately their head (if they will seek the accomplishment of his laws) and hath promised to defend them and bless them.

And although the rebellion of the people, their ingratitude and contempt of God's laws hath been such at all times, that it is a rare thing to show their duty in this behalf, by any example: yet is there one fact of the Israelites worthy memory, and appertaining to this purpose, which is written in the book of the Judges, at what time they had no lawful magistrate in all Israel, who notwithstanding rose up wholly against the tribe of Benjamin in Gabaa (because of that shameful villainy, which the sons of Belial had done to the Levite's wife) . . . .

But you will say: it is another matter for the people to enterprise such an act being without a ruler, and when they have a ruler appointed unto them, without whom they may do nothing. To this I answered before, that it is all one to be without a Ruler, and to have such as will not rule in God's fear. Yea it is much better to be destitute altogether, than to have a tyrant and murderer. For then are they no more public persons, condemning their public authority in using it against the laws, but are to be taken of all men, as private persons, and so examined and punished. . . . Wherefore this zeal to defend God's laws and precepts, wherewith all sorts of men are charged, it is not only praiseworthy in all, but required of all, not only in abstaining from the transgression of the said laws, but to

---

[2] Christopher Goodman, *How Superior Powers oght to be obeyd of their subjects: and Wherin they may lawfully by Gods Worde be disobeyed and resisted* (Geneva, 1558), 185–91.

see the judgments thereof executed upon all manner of persons without exception. And that if it be not done by the consent and aid of the superiors, it is lawful for the people, yea it is their duty to do it themselves, as well upon their own rulers and magistrate, as upon other of their brethren, having the word of God for their warrant, to which all are subject, and by the same charged to cast forth all evil from them, and to cut off every rotten member, for fear of infecting the whole body, how dear or precious so ever it be. If death be deserved, death; if other punishments, to see they be executed in all.

For this cause have you promised obedience to your superiors, that they might herein help you; and for the same intent have they taken it upon them. If they will do so, and keep promise with you according to their office, then do you owe unto them all humble obedience. If not, you are discharged, and no obedience belongeth to them: because they are not obedient to God, nor be his ministers to punish the evil, and to defend the good. And therefore your study in this case ought to be, to seek how you may dispose and punish according to the laws, such rebels against God, and oppressors of your selves and your country; and not how to please them, obey them, and flatter them as you do in their impiety. Which is not the way to obtain peace and quietness, but to fall into the hands of the almighty God, and to be subject to his fearful plagues and punishments.

The God-Given Authority of Elected Magistrates

The officers of government in Massachusetts, known collectively as the magistrates, were elected annually, but they did not regard their authority as coming from the people who chose them. In 1645, when the representatives of the people, known as the deputies, attempted to impeach John Winthrop for some of his actions as deputy governor, he waited until they had thoroughly examined his conduct and found him guiltless. Then he treated them to the following "little speech," in which he explained why they ought not to have tried him originally. The people Winthrop was addressing would probably have agreed that his authority came from God, and Winthrop admitted that God gave it to him through their election. But did God leave any authority other than that of election in their hands? Could they displace a ruler at any other time than that regularly prescribed? If so, under what conditions? Winthrop gave his answer with quiet certainty. The reader may wish to compare it with the views of Christopher Goodman earlier and of Jonathan Mayhew and Jonathan Boucher later.[3]

I suppose something may be expected from me, upon this charge that is befallen me, which moves me to speak now to you; yet I intend not to intermeddle in the proceedings of the court, or with any of the persons concerned therein. Only I

[3] John Winthrop, *The History of New England,* James Savage, ed. (Boston, 1853), 2:279–82.

bless God, that I see an issue of this troublesome business. I also acknowledge the justice of the court, and, for mine own part, I am well satisfied; I was publicly charged, and I am publicly and legally acquitted, which is all I did expect or desire. And though this be sufficient for my justification before men, yet not so before the God who hath seen so much amiss in my dispensations (and even in this affair) as calls me to be humble. For to be publicly and criminally charged in this court is matter of humiliation, (and I desire to make a right use of it) notwithstanding I be thus acquitted. If her father had spit in her face, (saith the Lord concerning Miriam) should she not have been ashamed seven days? Shame had lien upon her, whatever the occasion had been.

I am unwilling to stay you from your urgent affairs, yet give me leave (upon this special occasion) to speak a little more to this assembly. It may be of some good use, to inform and rectify the judgments of some of the people, and may prevent such distempers as have arisen amongst us. The great questions that have troubled the country, are about the authority of the magistrates and the liberty of the people. It is yourselves who have called us to this office, and being called by you, we have our authority from God, in way of an ordinance, such as hath the image of God eminently stamped upon it, the contempt and violation whereof have been vindicated with examples of divine vengeance. I entreat you to consider, that when you choose magistrates, you take them from among yourselves, men subject to like passions as you are. Therefore when you see infirmities in us, you should reflect upon your own, and that would make you bear the more with us, and not be severe censurers of the failings of your magistrates, when you have continual experience of the like infirmities in yourselves and others.

We account him a good servant, who breaks not his covenant. The covenant between you and us is the oath you have taken of us, which is to this purpose, that we shall govern you and judge your causes by the rules of God's laws and our own, according to our best skill. When you agree with a workman to build you a ship or house, etc., he undertakes as well for his skill as for his faithfulness, for it is his profession, and you pay him for both. But when you call one to be a magistrate, he doth not profess nor undertake to have sufficient skill for that office, nor can you furnish him with gifts, etc., therefore you must run the hazard of his skill and ability. But if he fail in faithfulness, which by his oath he is bound unto, that he must answer for. If it fall out that the case be clear to common apprehension, and the rule clear also, if he transgress here, the error is not in the skill, but in the evil of the will: it must be required of him. But if the case be doubtful, or the rule doubtful, to men of such understanding and parts as your magistrates are, if your magistrates should err here, yourselves must bear it.

For the other point concerning liberty, I observe a great mistake in the country about that. There is a twofold liberty, natural (I mean as our nature is now corrupt) and civil or federal. The first is common to man with beasts and other creatures. By this, man, as he stands in relation to man simply, hath liberty to do what he lists; it is a liberty to evil as well as to good. This liberty is incompatible and inconsistent with authority, and cannot endure the least restraint of the most just authority. The exercise and maintaining of this liberty makes men grow more evil, and in time to be worse than brute beasts: *omnes sumus licentia deteriores* [We are all made worse by license]. This is that great enemy of truth and peace, that wild beast, which all the ordinances of God are bent against, to restrain and subdue it.

The other kind of liberty I call civil or federal, it may be also be termed moral, in reference to the covenant between God and man, in the moral law, and the politic covenants and constitutions, amongst men themselves. This liberty is the proper end and object of authority, and cannot subsist without it; and it is a liberty to that only which is good, just, and honest. This liberty you are to stand for, with the hazard (not only of your goods, but) of your lives, if need be. Whatsoever crosseth this, is not authority, but a distemper thereof. This liberty is maintained and exercised in a way of subjection to authority; it is of the same kind of liberty wherewith Christ hath made us free. The woman's own choice makes such a man her husband; yet being so chosen, he is her lord, and she is to be subject to him, yet in a way of liberty, not of bondage; and a true wife accounts her subjection her honor and freedom, and would not think her condition safe and free, but in her subjection to her husband's authority. Such is the liberty of the church under the authority of Christ, her king and husband; his yoke is so easy and sweet to her as a bride's ornaments; and if through forwardness or wantonness, etc., she shake it off, at any time, she is at no rest in her spirit, until she take it up again; and whether her lord smiles upon her, and embraceth her in his arms, or whether he frowns, or rebukes, or smites her, she apprehends the sweetness of his love in all, and is refreshed, supported, and instructed by every such dispensation of his authority over her. On the other side, ye know who they are that complain of this yoke and say, let us break their bands, etc., we will not have this man to rule over us.

Even so, brethren, it will be between you and your magistrates. If you stand for your natural corrupt liberties, and will do what is good in your own eyes, you will not endure the least weight of authority, but will murmur, and oppose, and be always striving to shake off that yoke; but if you will be satisfied to enjoy such civil and lawful liberties, such as Christ allows you, then will you quietly and cheerfully submit unto that authority which is set over you, in all the administrations of it, for your good. Wherein, if we fail at any time, we hope we shall be willing (by God's assistance) to hearken to good advice from any of you, or in any other way of God; so shall your liberties be preserved, in upholding the honor and power of authority amongst you.

The Christian's Duty to Resist Tyrannical Rulers

The views expressed by Christopher Goodman in 1558 were brought to America by the English Puritans and revived whenever the safety of the community seemed to be threatened by ungodly rulers. In 1689, for example, when

New Englanders ejected Governor Edmund Andros, the ministers did not hesitate to call God's blessing upon them for doing so. In 1750, the Reverend Jonathan Mayhew spelled out the philosophy of revolt to Bostonians in a sermon from which the following excerpts are taken. It was preached on the 101st anniversary of the execution of Charles I. The reader may wish to ask whether Mayhew differs at all from Goodman in his notion of when God will approve rebellion.[4]

The apostle's doctrine, in the passage thus explained [Romans, chapter XIII, verses 1–8], concerning the office of civil rulers, and the duty of subjects, may be summed up in the following observations, viz.

That the end of magistracy is the good of civil society, as such.

That civil rulers, as such, are the ordinance and ministers of God; it being by his permission and providence that any bear rule, and agreeable to his will that there should be in some persons vested with authority in society, for the well-being of it.

That which is here said concerning civil rulers extends to all of them in common: it relates indifferently to monarchical, republican, and aristocratical government, and to all other forms which truly answer the sole end of government, the happiness of society; and to all the different degrees of authority in any particular state; to inferior officers no less than to the supreme.

That disobedience to civil rulers in the due exercise of their authority, is not merely a political sin, but a heinous offence against God and religion.

That the true ground and reason of our obligation to be subject to the higher powers, is the usefulness of magistracy (when properly exercised) to human society, and its subserviency to the general welfare.

That obedience to civil rulers is here equally required under all forms of government which answer the sole end of all government, the good of society; and to every degree of authority, in any state, whether supreme or subordinate. From whence it follows:

That if unlimited obedience and non-resistance be here required as a duty under any one form of government, it is also required as a duty under all other forms, and as a duty to subordinate rulers as well as to the supreme.

And, lastly, that those civil rulers to whom the apostle injoins subjection are the persons in possession; the powers that be; those who are actually vested with authority.

There is one very important and interesting point which remains to be inquired into, namely, the extent of that subjection to the higher powers, which is here enjoined as a duty upon all Christians. Some have thought it warrantable and glorious to disobey the civil powers in certain circumstances, and in cases of very great and general oppression, when humble remonstrances fail of having any effect; and when the public welfare cannot be otherwise provided for and secured, to rise unanimously even against the sovereign himself, in order to redress their grievances; to vindicate their natural and legal

---

[4] Jonathan Mayhew, *A Discourse Concerning Unlimited Submission and Non-Resistance to the Higher Powers* (Boston, 1750), 9–13, 29–30.

rights; to break the yoke of tyranny, and free themselves and posterity from inglorious servitude and ruin. It is upon this principle that many royal oppressors have been driven from their thrones into banishment, and many slain by the hands of their subjects. It was upon this principle that Tarquin was expelled from Rome; and Julius Caesar, the conqueror of the world and the tyrant of his country, cut off in the senate-house. It was upon this principle, that King Charles I was beheaded before his own banqueting-house. It was upon this principle that King James II was made to fly that country which he aimed at enslaving; and upon this principle was that revolution brought about which had been so fruitful of happy consequences to Great Britain.

But, in opposition to this principle, it has often been asserted that the scripture in general (and the passage under consideration in particular) makes all resistance to princes a crime, in any case whatever. If they turn tyrants, and become the common oppressors of those whose welfare they ought to regard with a paternal affection, we must not pretend to right ourselves, unless it be by prayers and tears and humble entreaties. And if these methods fail of procuring redress, we must not have recourse to any other, but all suffer ourselves to be robbed and butchered at the pleasure of the Lord's annointed; lest we should incur the sin of rebellion and the punishment of damnation. For he has God's authority and commission to bear him out in the worst of crimes, so far that he may not be withstood or controlled. Now whether we are obliged to yield such an absolute submission to our prince; or whether disobedience and resistance may not be justifiable in some cases, notwithstanding anything in the passage before us, is an inquiry in which we are all concerned; and this is the inquiry which is the main design of the present discourse. . . .

I now add, further, that the apostle's argument is so far from proving it to be the duty of people to obey, and submit to, such rulers as act in contradiction to the public good,* and so to the design of their office, that it proves *the direct contrary*. For, please to observe, that if the end of all civil government be the good of society; if this be the thing that is aimed at in constituting civil rulers; and if the motive and argument for submission to government, be taken from the apparent usefulness of civil authority, it follows, that when no such good end can be answered by submission, there remains no argument or motive to enforce it; if, instead of this good end's being brought about by submission, a *contrary end* is brought about, and the ruin and misery of society effected by it, here is a plain and positive reason against submission in all such cases, should they ever happen.

And therefore, in such cases, a regard to the public welfare ought to make us withhold from our rulers, that obedience and submission which it would otherwise be our duty to render to them. If it be our duty, for example, to obey our king merely for this reason, that he

---

* This does not intend their acting so in *a few particular instances,* which the best of rulers may do through mistake, etc., but their acting so *habitually;* and in a manner which plainly shows that they aim at making themselves great by the ruin of their subjects [Mayhew's note].

rules for the public welfare (which is the only argument the apostle makes use of), it follows, by a parity of reason, that when he turns tyrant, and makes his subjects his prey to devour and destroy, instead of his charge to defend and cherish, we are bound to throw off our allegiance to him, and to resist; and that according to the tenor of the apostle's argument in this passage. Not to discontinue our allegiance, in this case, would be to join with the sovereign in promoting the slavery and misery of that society, the welfare of which we ourselves, as well as our sovereign, are indispensably obliged to secure and promote, as far as in us lies. It is true the apostle puts no case of such a tyrannical prince; but by his grounding his argument for submission wholly upon the good of civil society, it is plain he implicitly authorizes, and even requires us to make resistance, whenever this shall be necessary to the public safety and happiness.

Kings Reign and Princes Decree Justice under the Authority of God

When Jonathan Mayhew spoke the words in the preceding passage, he was not calling upon his listeners to revolt against the existing government, but his words, and others to the same effect, gained a lively pertinence in the next twenty-five years. While Mayhew and other ministers gave their blessing (and God's) to rebellion, a few, mostly from the Anglican Episcopal Church, affirmed vehemently that God gives authority only to rulers and never to the people. Jonathan Boucher of Maryland, one of those who took this position, was so unpopular that he sometimes preached with loaded pistols on his pulpit. In the following extracts from a sermon preached in 1775 shortly before his departure for England, he calls upon Americans to submit peaceably to the divine authority of government, whatever may be the result.[5]

The glory of God is much concerned that there should be good government in the world; it is, therefore, the uniform doctrine of the Scriptures that it is under the deputation and authority of God alone that kings reign and princes decree justice. Kings and princes (which are only other words for supreme magistrates) were doubtless created and appointed, not so much for their own sakes, as for the sake of the people committed to their charge; yet are they not, therefore, the creatures of the people? So far from deriving their authority from any supposed consent or suffrage of men, they receive their commission from Heaven; they receive it from God, the source and original of all power. However obsolete, therefore, either the sentiment or the language may now be deemed, it is with the

---

[5] Jonathan Boucher, *A View of the Causes and Consequences of the American Revolution* (London, 1797), 534, 545–46.

most perfect propriety that the supreme magistrate, whether consisting of one or of many, and whether denominated an emperor, a king, an archon, a dictator, a consul, or a senate, is to be regarded and venerated as the vicegerent of God. . . .

All government, whether lodged in one or in many, is, in its nature, absolute and irresistible. It is not within the competency even of the supreme power to limit itself, because such limitation can emanate only from a superior. For any government to make itself irresistible, and to cease to be absolute, it must cease to be supreme; which is but saying, in other words, that it must dissolve itself or be destroyed. If, then, to resist government be to destroy it, evey man who is a subject must necessarily owe to the government under which he lives an obedience either active or passive: active, where the duty enjoined may be performed without offending God; and passive (that is to say, patiently to submit to the penalties annexed to disobedience), where that which is commanded by man is forbidden by God. No government upon earth can rightfully compel any one of its subjects to an active compliance with anything that is, or that appears to his conscience to be, inconsistent with, or contradictory to, the known laws of God, because every man is under a prior and superior obligation to obey God in all things. When such cases of incompatible demands of duty occur, every well-informed person knows what he is to do; and every well-principled person will do what he ought, viz., he will submit to the ordinances of God, rather than comply with the commandments of men. In thus acting he cannot err, and this alone is "passive obedience," which I entreat you to observe is so far from being "unlimited obedience" (as its enemies wilfully persist to miscall it) that it is the direct contrary. Resolute not to disobey God, a man of good principles determines, in case of competition, as the lesser evil, to disobey man; but he knows that he should also disobey God, were he not, at the same time, patiently to submit to any penalties incurred by his disobedience to man.

2. AUTHORITY FROM THE KING

The English colonies in America were all founded by private individuals or groups, acting under the authority of the King as granted to them in royal charters. Initially the King simply transferred all his authority to the individual or group in question to exercise however they pleased. But beginning in Virginia as early as 1624, he began to resume control of colonial governments, and by 1776 he had taken over the government of all but four of the thirteen colonies. His authority operated in these colonies through governors whom he appointed to carry out his wishes. The authority of the government thus came to rest on the King's commission to his governor.

The fact that all authority was thus officially derived from the King did not, as far as the colonists were concerned, automatically validate all authority that was exercised in his name. If, for example, the King conferred authority on a man by charter to govern a particular territory, could that man transfer the authority again to another man? And if all authority came from the King, what obedience was due to the British Parliament? The documents that follow show how the King conferred authority by charter and what kind of difficulties might arise from the uncertainties just mentioned.

The King Delegates Authority to the Massachusetts Bay Company

The charter from which the following extract is taken incorporated twenty-six men in the year 1629 as the Massachusetts Bay Company and gave to them, and to anyone they should admit to join their company, the region from three miles north of the Merrimack River to three miles south of the Charles. The extract contains the portion in which the King empowers them to govern the territory (in much the same language that he used in empowering other corporations or individuals to govern other colonies). This passage is offered not only to illustrate the manner in which the King conferred authority to govern, but also for comparison with passages in the following and preceding sections where other sources of authority are given for the government of Massachusetts. Are the other passages consistent with this one?[6]

And we do of our further grace, certain knowledge and mere motion, give and grant to the said governor and company, and their successors, that it shall and may be lawful, to and for the governor or deputy governor, and such of the assistants and freemen of the said company for the time being as shall be assembled in any of their general courts aforesaid, or in any other courts to be specially summoned and assembled for that purpose, or the greater part of them (whereof the governor or deputy governor, and six of the assistants to be always seven) from time to time, to make, ordain, and establish all manner of wholesome and reasonable orders, laws, statutes, and ordinances, directions, and instructions, not contrary to the laws of this our realm of England, as well for settling of the forms and ceremonies of government and magistracy, fit and necessary for the said plantation, and the inhabitants there, and for naming and styling of all sorts of officers, both superior and inferior, which they shall find needful for that government and plantation, and the distinguishing and setting forth of the several duties, powers, and limits of every such office and

---

[6] Nathaniel B. Shurtleff, ed., *Records of the Governor and Company of the Massachusetts Bay in New England,* 5 vols. (Boston, 1853–54), 1:16–17.

place, and the forms of such oaths warrantable by the laws and statutes of this our realm of England, as shall be respectively ministered unto them for the execution of the said several offices and places; as also for the disposing and ordering of the elections of such of the said officers as shall be annual, and of such others as shall be to succeed in case of death or removal, and ministering the said oaths to the new elected officers, and for impositions of lawful fines, mulcts, imprisonment, or other lawful correction, according to the course of other corporations in this our realm of England, and for the directing, ruling, and disposing of all other matters and things, whereby our said people, inhabitants there, may be so religiously, peaceably, and civilly governed, as their good life and orderly conversation, may win and incite the natives of [the] country to the knowledge and obedience of the only true God and Saviour of mankind, and the Christian faith, which in our royal intention, and the adventurers' free profession, is the principal end of this plantation. Willing, commanding, and requiring, and by these presents for us, our heirs and successors, ordaining and appointing, that all such orders, laws, statutes and ordinances, instructions and directions, as shall be so made by the governor, or deputy governor of the said company, and such of the assistants and freemen as aforesaid, and published in writing, under their common seal, shall be carefully and duly observed, kept, performed, and put in execution, according to the true intent and meaning of the same. And these our letters patents, or the duplicate or exemplification thereof, shall be to all and every such officers, superior and inferior, from time to time, for the putting of the same orders, laws, statutes, and ordinances, instructions, and directions, in due execution against us, our heirs and successors, a sufficient warrant and discharge.

And we do further, for us, our heirs and successors, give and grant to the said governor and company, and their successors by these presents, that all and every such chief commanders, captains, governors, and other officers and ministers, as by the said orders, laws, statutes, ordinances, instructions, or directions of the said governor and company for the time being, shall be from time to time hereafter employed either in the government of the said inhabitants and plantation, or in the way by sea thither, or from thence, according to the natures and limits of their offices and places respectively, shall from time to time hereafter forever, within the precincts and parts of New England hereby mentioned to be granted and confirmed, or in the way by sea thither, or from thence, have full and absolute power and authority to correct, punish, pardon, govern, and rule all such the subjects of us, our heirs and successors, as shall from time to time adventure themselves in any voyage thither or from thence, or that shall at any time hereafter inhabit within the precincts and parts of New England aforesaid, according to the orders, laws, ordinances, instructions, and directions aforesaid, not being repugnant to the laws and statutes of our realm of England, as aforesaid.

Proprietary Authority in New Jersey

In 1664 King Charles II granted to the Duke of York all the territory from Connecticut to Maryland. The Duke sent Richard Nicolls to New York as his deputy to govern the area, and Nicolls in turn encouraged a number of New Englanders to settle in the New Jersey area by giving them a patent which allowed them to make their own laws in the towns they established. Shortly after they settled in New Jersey, the Duke of York granted the region to two friends, John Lord Berkeley and Sir George Carteret, who sent over Captain Philip Carteret as governor. It is doubtful that Nicolls had authority to grant settlers the privileges he did, but it is equally doubtful that the Duke of York had the right to transfer to Berkeley and Carteret his authority to govern. The result, indicated in the following documents, is that we find two different groups claiming authority to govern by virtue of grants which could both be traced back to the Duke of York and from him to the King. The first is an act of the Carteret government, dated 1668, demanding the submission of the settlers from New England. The second, written in 1669, is the reply given by the Middletown town meeting. The conflict was not wholly resolved until the King took over New Jersey in 1702 and sent his own governor to take charge.[7]

The Carteret Government

Whereas there was an act of General Assembly, passed the thirtieth day of May last, for a rate of thirty pounds to be raised upon the county for the defraying of public charge, equally to be laid upon the towns then in being, viz: the towns of Bergen, Elizabethtown, Newark upon Pishawack river, Woodbridge, Middletown and Shrewsbury, that is to say five pounds on each town. Now the major part of the inhabitants of Middletown and Shrewsbury, refusing to pay the same, contrary to the consent and act of their own Deputies, and likewise refuse to submit to the laws of this government. It is hereby enacted by the present General Assembly, that Mr. Luke Watson and Mr. Samuel Moore shall go and demand the aforesaid rate of five pounds from each town, together with forty shillings more from each of said towns, which is their just proportion of the rate of twelve pounds now made by this present General Assembly for the defraying of public charges, which if they refuse to pay, the said Luke Watson and Samuel Moore [are] to take by way of distress, together with the charges and expenses the country is and shall be at for their obstinate refusal of paying their just dues according to law, and for so doing, the General Assembly doth undertake to save them harmless. It is further enacted by the authority aforesaid, that Luke Watson and Samuel

[7] New Jersey Historical Society, *Proceedings*, second series (1872–74), 3:23–30.

Moore, aforesaid, do demand the positive resolution of the inhabitants, or the major part of them of the said towns, whether or no they will submit to the laws and government of this province, under the Right Honorable John Lord Berkeley and Sir George Carteret, Knight and Baronet, the absolute Lords Proprietors of the same, according to His Royal Highness, the Duke of York's grant, upon which answer the General Assembly will proceed accordingly.

The Town of Middletown

In a legal town meeting, the major part being present, it was this day put to the vote concerning answering the demand of Luke Watson and Samuel Moore, who were authorized by the General Assembly to demand our positive resolution of submission to the government of the absolute Lords proprietors, as saith the Act bearing date the seventh of November, it was unanimously resolved that this following act shall be our positive resolution, and shall be presented to the General Assembly, viz:

That if the oath of allegiance to our Sovereign Lord, the King, and fidelity to the Lords Proprietors' interest, be the submission intended in the act, this is our result: that as true loyal subjects to the King, we are ready at all demands either to engage, swear, or subscribe all true allegiance to his Royal Majesty of England, as in duty bound, either before the Governor, or any other minister of justice authorized by him to administer the same, without any equivocation or mental reservation, as true loyal subjects ought to do; and this we will perform absolutely. . . .

As to the Lords Proprietors' interest, it being a new, unheard of thing to us, and so obscure to us that at present we are ignorant what it is; yet as men not void of judgment, knowing right well that all oaths, engagements, or subscriptions ought to be administered in truth, in righteousness, and in judgment, upon which consideration we are not willing to swear to we know not what, . . . And should we submit to the interest so far as by swearing thereunto: having a propriety of land not only purchased from the Chief Proprietors of the Country: viz. the Indians: but also granted unto us by the Deputy to his Royal Highness the Duke of York (which appears under hand and seal) : it would be an act beneath the wisdom of the owners of such a patent: and herein we should appear to be self-violators of our patent ourselves. . . .

Notwithstanding for the future benefit and tranquility: and for the establishment of peace in the province: we shall be willing to submit to the Lords proprietors interest according to the late order provided that some secure way could be projected or some provision made by the Lords proprietors government which might secure us from destroying of ourselves by weakening this our interest which we so highly prize which indeed is the very foundation of our livelihood. If no secure way or course can be thought of or projected to secure our own interest, we are at present resolved not to intangle ourselves into any other interest appertaining to any men, but shall (by the assistance of God) stick to our patent, the liberties and privileges thereof which is our interest, which once was committed to us, not to betray, like treacherous men, who for filthy lucre's sake have been ready to betray themselves and others but to deal faithfully with it being a trust committed to us. And in so doing we conceive we need not fear what any man or power can do unto us.

The Colonists Acknowledge Only the Authority of the King

The fact that the authority of colonial governments derived from the King rather than Parliament led to grave difficulties when Parliament became—as it did in the eighteenth century—the most powerful part of the British government. In the course of a century and a half the colonists had become accustomed to having very little interference from England, for the King seldom exercised his authority over them except through the appointment of royal governors, whose powers were not extensive. The colonists were thus habituated to virtual self-government. When Parliament assumed authority to tax them, they regarded the move as a usurpation and insisted that the only authority of England over them rested in the King. Thus the American rebels who resisted Great Britain did so, until July 4, 1776, at least, in the name of the King. James Wilson, a Pennsylvania lawyer, explained their position in a pamphlet published in 1774, from which the following excerpt is taken.[8]

Those who launched into the unknown deep, in quest of new countries and habitations, still considered themselves as subjects of the English monarchs, and behaved suitably to that character, but it nowhere appears, that they still considered themselves as represented in an English parliament, or that they thought the authority of the English parliament extended over them. They took possession of the country in the *king's* name: they treated, or made war with the Indians by *his* authority: they held the lands under *his* grants, and paid *him* the rents reserved upon them: they established governments under the sanction of *his* prerogative, or by virtue of *his* charters:—no application for those purposes was made to the parliament: no ratification of the charters or letters patent was solicited from that assembly, as is usual in England with regard to grants and franchises of much less importance. My Lord Bacon's sentiments on this subject ought to have great weight with us. His immense genius, his universal learning, his deep insight into the laws and constitution of England, are well known and much admired. Besides, he lived at that time when settling and improving the American plantations began seriously to be attended to, and successfully to be carried into execution. Plans for the government and regulation of the colonies were then

---

[8] James Wilson, *Works*, James DeW. Andrews, ed. (Chicago, 1896), 2:537–39.

forming: and it is only from the first general idea of these plans, that we can unfold, with precision and accuracy, all the more minute and intricate parts, of which they now consist. "The settlement of colonies," says he, "must proceed from the option of those who will settle them, else it sounds like an exile: they must be raised by the *leave,* and not by the *command* of the *king.* At their setting out, they must have their commission, or letters patent, from the *king,* that so they may acknowledge their *dependency upon the crown* of England, and under his protection." In another place he says, "that they still must be subjects of the realm." "In order to regulate all the inconveniences, which will insensibly grow upon them," he proposes, "that the king should erect a subordinate council in England, whose care and charge shall be, to advise, and put in execution, all things which shall be found fit for the good of those new plantations; who, upon all occasions, shall give an account of their proceedings, to the king or the council board, and from *them* receive such directions, as may best agree with the government of that place." It is evident, from these quotations, that my Lord Bacon had no conception that the parliament would or ought to interpose, either in the settlement or the government of the colonies. The only relation, in which he says the colonists must still continue, is that of subjects: the only dependency, which they ought to acknowledge, is a dependency on the crown.

This is a dependence, which they have acknowledged hitherto; which they acknowledge now; and which, if it is reasonable to judge of the future by the past and the present, they will continue to acknowledge hereafter. It is not a dependence, like that contended for on parliament, slavish and unaccountable, or accounted for only by principles that are false and inapplicable: it is a dependence founded upon the principles of reason, of liberty and of law.

3. AUTHORITY FROM THE PAST

Habit is the monarch that rules us all, and perhaps there could never be an orderly society without it. Wise men have always known this, and some have therefore argued that the mere age of a custom or of a government is a reason for obeying it. The Americans who came from England during the colonial period had an extreme veneration for the authority of age, for this was the cornerstone of English liberty. England had no written constitution to guarantee popular rights, to guide Parliament in making laws, or to restrain the King. Instead the authority of age was called on to help defend or defeat every proposed measure and every claimed right. Furthermore the greatly revered English common law originated in custom and rested on the willingness of judges to follow the decisions of their predecessors.

The colonists brought with them both the common law and the propensity to rest their rights on ancient precedents. The propensity did not flourish in the New World, where institutions as well as men were tested not so much by their age as by their ability to get things done. According to Benjamin Franklin, Americans even admired their God "more for the Variety, Ingenuity, and Utility of his Handyworks, than for the Antiquity of his Family." Nevertheless, Americans have sometimes appealed to this source of authority and perhaps are ruled by it more than they realize. One may well ask, for example, whether their Revolution was not begun as an attempt to preserve ancient rights rather than to acquire new ones.

An American Common Law

John Winthrop, the first governor of the Massachusetts Bay Colony, had been trained in the English common law and had great respect for it. Although the laws of Massachusetts, in order to carry out the religious purposes of the colony's founders, must differ from those of England, Winthrop wanted them to take form gradually from judicial and executive decisions. The legislature, however, was unwilling to wait for time to hallow customs and decisions into laws. It wished to frame a complete code of law, which would direct the decisions of judges and magistrates, instead of allowing them to use their discretion to suit the case at hand. In the following passage, written in 1639, Governor Winthrop explains why he favored (though unsuccessfully) the other method.[9]

The people had long desired a body of laws, and thought their condition very unsafe, while so much power rested in the discretion of magistrates. Divers attempts had been made at former courts, and the matter referred to some of the magistrates and some of the elders; but still it came to no effect; for, being committed to the care of many, whatsoever was done by some, was still disliked or neglected by others. At last it was referred to Mr. Cotton and Mr. Nathaniel Ward, etc., and each of them framed a model which were presented to this general court, and by them committed to the governor and deputy governor and some others to consider of, and so prepare it for the court in the third month next. Two great reasons there were, which caused most of the magistrates and some of the elders not to be very forward in this matter. One was, want of sufficient experience of the nature and disposition of the people, considered with the condition of the country and other circumstances, which made them conceive, that such laws would be fittest for us, which should arise pro re nata upon occasions, etc., and so the laws of England and other states grew, and therefore the fundamental laws of England are called

---

[9] Winthrop, *The History of New England*, 1:388–89.

customs, consuetudines. 2. For that it would professedly transgress the limits of our charter, which provide, we shall make no laws repugnant to the laws of England, and that we were assured we must do. But to raise up laws by practice and custom had been no transgression; as in our church discipline, and in matters of marriage, to make a law, that marriages should not be solemnized by ministers, is repugnant to the laws of England; but to bring it to a custom by practice for the magistrates to perform it, is no law made repugnant, etc. At length (to satisfy the people) it proceeded, and the two models were digested with divers alterations and additions, and abbreviated and sent to every town, to be considered of first by the magistrates and elders, and then to be published by the constables to all the people, that if any man should think fit, that any thing therein ought to be altered, he might acquaint some of the deputies therewith against the next court.

The Earth Belongs to the Living

The past has undeniably been a source of authority, but whether it ought to be has been questioned, for it has often stood in the way of desirable reforms. In the following selection, Thomas Jefferson, writing from France in 1789, argues for a freedom from the past more complete than any country has been willing to endorse.[10]

The question whether one generation of men has a right to bind another, seems never to have been started either on this or our side of the water. Yet it is a question of such consequences as not only to merit decision, but place also, among the fundamental principles of every government. The course of reflection in which we are immersed here on the elementary principles of society has presented this question to my mind; and that no such obligation can be transmitted I think very capable of proof. I set out on this ground which I suppose to be self evident, *"that the earth belongs in usufruct to the living";* that the dead have neither powers nor rights over it. The portion occupied by any individual ceases to be his when himself ceases to be, and reverts to the society. . . . What is true of every member of the society individually, is true of them all collectively, since the rights of the whole can be no more than the sum of the rights of individuals. To keep our ideas clear when applying them to a multitude, let us suppose a whole generation of men to be born on the same day, to attain mature age on the same day, and to die on the same day, leaving a succeeding generation in the moment of attaining their mature age all together. Let the ripe age be supposed of 21 years, and their period of life 34 years more, that being the average term given by the bills of mortality to persons who

---

[10] T. Jefferson to James Madison, September 6, 1789, in Thomas Jefferson, *Writings*, Paul L. Ford, ed., 10 vols. (New York, 1892–99), 5:115–21.

have already attained 21 years of age. Each successive generation would, in this way, come on and go off the stage at a fixed moment, as individuals do now. Then I say the earth belongs to each of these generations during its course, fully, and in their own right. The 2d. generation receives it clear of the debts and incumbrances of the 1st., the 3d. of the 2d. and so on. For if the 1st. could charge it with a debt, then the earth would belong to the dead and not the living generation. Then no generation can contract debts greater than may be paid during the course of its own existence. . . .

What is true of a generation all arriving to self-government on the same day, and dying all on the same day, is true of those in a constant course of decay and renewal, with this only difference. A generation coming in and going out entire, as in the first case, would have a right in the 1st year of their self dominion to contract a debt for 33 years, in the 10th for 24, in the 20th for 14, in the 30th for 4, whereas generations changing daily, by daily deaths and births, have one constant term beginning at the date of their contract, and ending when a majority of those of full age at that date shall be dead. . . .

On similar ground it may be proved that no society can make a perpetual constitution, or even a perpetual law. The earth belongs always to the living generation. They may manage it then, and what proceeds from it, as they please, during their usufruct. They are masters too of their own persons, and consequently may govern them as they please. . . . Every constitution, then, and every law, naturally expires at the end of 19 years. If it be enforced longer, it is an act of force and not of right.

The Binding Power of the Past

In the following selection, Judge Abel P. Upshur of Virginia argues that the present generation cannot honorably repudiate some of the decisions and commitments of the past. He was appealing to the Virginia Constitutional Convention in 1829 to apportion representation in the state legislature on a basis of white population combined with property values. This would retain for the eastern slave-holding counties the majority which they had held under the old constitution. If representation were based simply upon white population, the western counties would have a preponderance; and since their slave holdings were small, they might shift the burden of taxes to the easterners by placing a heavy, perhaps a prohibitive, tax on slaves.[11]

Gentlemen have fallen into a great error both in their reasoning and in their conclusion, by considering the subject before us, as if we were now for the first time, entering into a social compact. If we stood in the nakedness of nature, with no rights but such as are strictly personal, we should all come together upon precisely equal ground. But

---

11 *Proceedings and Debates of the Virginia State Convention of 1829–30* (Richmond, 1830), 74.

such is not the case. We cannot now enter into a new compact upon the basis of original equality; we bring more than our fair proportion, into the common stock. For fifty-four years we have been associated together, under the provisions of an actual Government. A great variety of rights and interests, and a great variety of feelings dear to the heart and connected with those rights and interests, have grown up among us. They have grown up and flourished under a Government which stood pledged to protect them; that Government itself was but a system of pledges, interchangeably given among those who were parties to it, that all the rights and all the interests which it invited into existence, should be protected by the power of the whole. Under this system, our property has been acquired; and we felt safe in the acquisition, because under the provisions of that system, we possessed a power of self-protection. And by whom was that system ordained? Not indeed, by the same *men* who are now here assembled, but by the same *community*, which is now here represented. It was the *people of Virginia* who gave us these pledges; and it is the people of Virginia who now claim a right to withdraw them. Sir, can it be fair, or just, or honourable, to do this? The rights and interests which you are now seeking to prostrate, you yourselves invited into being. Under your own distributions of political power, you gave us an assurance that our property should be safe, for you put the protection of it into our own hands. With what justice or propriety then, can you now say to us, that the rights and interests which you have thus fostered until they have become the chief pillars of your strength, shall now be prostrated; melted into the general mass, and be re-distributed, according to your will and pleasure? Nay, Sir, you do not even leave us the option whether to come into your measures or not. With all these rights, and all these interests, and all these feelings, we are to be *forced,* whether willing or unwilling; we are to be *forced* by the unyielding power of a majority, into a compact which violates them all! Is there not, Sir, something of *violence* and *fraud* in this? . . .

I am sensible, Sir, that there is nothing in this view of the subject, unless the rights and interests to which I have alluded, are of a peculiar and distinctive character. What then are they? I purposely waive all subjects of minor importance, as too inconsiderable to give any rule. But a peculiar interest, and a great, and important, and leading interest, is presented in our slaves; an interest which predominates throughout the Eastern divisions of the State, whilst it is of secondary consequence West of the Blue Ridge. And what, let us now inquire, are its claims to consideration?

Will you not be surprised to hear, Sir, that the slave population of Virginia pays 30 per cent of the whole revenue derived from taxation? Did there ever exist in any community a separate and peculiar interest of more commanding magnitude? But this is not all. It affords almost the whole productive labor of one half of the Commonwealth. What difference does it make whether a certain amount of labor is brought into the common stock by four hundred thousand slaves, or four hundred thousand freemen? The gain is the same to the aggregate wealth; which is but another name for the aggregate power, of the State. And here permit me to remark, that of all the subjects of taxation which ever yet existed, this has been the most oppressively dealt with. You not only tax our slaves as property, but you also tax their labor. Let me illustrate the idea by an example. The farmer who derives his income from the labor of slaves, pays a tax for those slaves, considered as property. With that income so derived, he purchases a carriage, or a horse, and these again are taxed. You first tax the slave who makes the money; and then you tax the article which the money procures. Is not this a great injustice, a gross inequality? No such tax is laid upon the white laborer of the West, and yet the product of his labor is of no more importance to the general welfare than the same product from the labor of slaves. Here then, is a striking peculiarity in our property, a peculiarity which subjects it to double impositions, and which therefore demands a double security.

There is yet, Sir, another view of this subject which is not only of importance with reference to the immediate topic under consideration, but which furnishes a strong argument against the change which gentlemen contemplate. One eleventh of the power which we possess in the national councils is derived from slaves. We obtain that power by counting three-fifths of the whole number [of slaves], in apportioning representation among the several states. Sir, we live in times of great political changes. Some new doctrine or other is broached almost every day; and it is impossible to foresee what changes in our political condition a single year may bring about. Suppose a proposition should be made to alter the Constitution of the United States in the particular now under consideration; what could Virginia say, after embracing such a basis as gentlemen propose? Would she not be told by those who abhor this species of property, and who are restive under the power which it confers, "you have abandoned this principle in your own institutions, and with what face can you claim it, in your connexions with us?" What reply could she make to such an appeal as this? Sir, the moral power of Virginia has always been felt, and deeply felt, in all the important concerns of this nation; and that power has been derived from the unchanging consistency of her principles, and her invincible firmness in maintaining them. Is she now prepared to surrender it, in pursuit of a speculative principle of doubtful propriety, at best, and certainly not demanded by any thing in her present condition?

4. AUTHORITY FROM THE PEOPLE

The idea that authority comes from the people is not new. It is at least as old as the Greeks and has persisted from their time to ours. It has, however, meant different things at different times. Before the establishment of the American colonies it found expression principally in the kind of philosophical speculation mentioned earlier: in trying to determine where the authority of government originated, philosophers would imagine a "social compact" in which people hitherto unconnected assembled and gave their consent to be governed by some ruler under some particular form of government.

When settlers came to America, they usually carried authority with them in the form of royal charters, but occasionally they found themselves outside the designated territorial limits. In this situation they had recourse to social compacts of the kind the philosophers imagined. Thus practical necessity might make popular consent the basis of an actual government.

Even where government rested firmly on a royal charter or on divine decree, there might be recognition of the importance of popular consent. The New England Puritans, for example, frequently spoke of a social compact, or "covenant" as they preferred to call it, as the foundation of their government. John Winthrop, who claimed authority from God and from the King, also believed that the settlers who accompanied him to Massachusetts, by the very act of doing so, had entered into a covenant with one another. Later generations inherited this notion that both government and society begin in a social compact.

The idea was stated most persuasively for both Englishmen and Americans by the English philosopher John Locke, in two treatises written before, but published after 1688. For Englishmen, Locke's doctrine meant that they had been entitled to depose King James II and replace him with William III. But they were content to let subsequent kings reach the throne by heredity. Americans applied Locke's doctrine more extensively. On July 4, 1776, in words that echoed his, they repudiated the King entirely and turned to the people as the sole source of authority. They then created governments that constantly recurred to this source, governments in which all the rulers were replaced at regular intervals. Without specifically repudiating God or the past (there is no mention of God in the federal constitution), they succeeded in resting all authority on the supreme people. There it has remained.

The Practical Necessity

The kind of social compact that Americans adopted when they found themselves beyond the reach of established authority is illustrated in the following three examples. The first is the Mayflower Compact of 1620, described by Governor William Bradford, who was present at the event. The second is a compact formed by settlers of Dover, New Hampshire, in 1640, before that colony had any organized government. The third is a speech made by Richard Henderson before a convention at Boonesborough, Kentucky, May 1775, then within the boundaries of Virginia, but beyond the reach of existing governmental institutions.[12]

The Mayflower Compact

I shall a little return back and begin with a combination made by them before they came ashore, being the first foundation of their government in this place; occasioned partly by the discontented and mutinous speeches that some of the strangers amongst them had let fall from them in the ship—that when they came ashore they would use their own liberty; for none had power to command them, the patent they had being for Virginia, and not for New England, which belonged to another government, with which the Virginia Company had nothing to do. And partly that such an act by them done (this their condition considered) might be as firm as any patent, and in some respects more sure.

The form was as followeth: In the name of God, Amen. We whose names are underwritten, the loyal subjects of our dread sovereign Lord, King James, by the grace of God, of Great Britain, France, and Ireland king, defender of the faith, etc., having undertaken, for the glory of God, and advancement of the Christian faith, and honor of our king and country, a voyage to plant the first colony in the Northern parts of Virginia, do by these presents solemnly and mutually in the presence of God, and one of another, covenant and combine our selves together into a civil body politic, for our better ordering and preservation and furtherance of the ends aforesaid; and by virtue hereof to enact, constitute, and frame such just and equal laws, ordinances, acts, constitutions, and offices, from time to time, as shall be thought most meet and convenient for the general good of the colony, unto which we promise all due submission and obedience. In witness whereof we have hereunder subscribed our names at Cape Cod the 11 of November, in the year of the reign of our sovereign lord, King James of England, France, and Ireland, the eighteenth, and of Scotland the fifty-fourth. Anno Dom. 1620.

The Dover, New Hampshire, Compact

Whereas sundry mischiefs and inconveniences have befallen us, and more and greater may, in regard of want of civil government, his most gracious Majesty having settled no order for us to our knowledge: We, whose names are under written, being inhabitants upon the river Piscataqua, have voluntarily agreed to combine ourselves into a body politic, that we may the more comfortably enjoy the benefit of his Majesty's laws, together with all such laws as shall be concluded by a major part of the freemen of our society, in case they be not repug-

---

[12] William Bradford, *History of Plimoth Plantation* (Boston, 1899), 109–10; Nathaniel Bouton et al., eds., *Documents and Records Relating to the Province of New Hampshire*, 39 vols. (Concord, N.H., 1867–1941), 1:126; Lewis Collins, *History of Kentucky* (Covington, Ky., 1882), 2:502.

nant to the laws of England, and administered in behalf of his Majesty. And this we have mutually promised and engaged to do, and so continue till his excellent Majesty shall give other orders concerning us. In witness whereof, we have hereunto set our hands, October 22 [1640], in the 16th year of the reign of our sovereign Lord Charles, by the grace of God, King of Great Britain, France and Ireland, defender of the faith, etc.

Richard Henderson Before a Kentucky Convention

Our peculiar circumstances in this remote country, surrounded on all sides with difficulties, and equally subject to one common danger, which threatens our common overthrow, must, I think, in their effects, secure to us an union of interests, and, consequently, that harmony in opinion, so essential to the forming good, wise, and wholesome laws. If any doubt remain amongst you with respect to the force or efficacy of whatever laws you now, or hereafter make, be pleased to consider that all power is originally in the people; therefore make it their interest, by impartial and beneficial laws, and you may be sure of their inclination to see them enforced. For it is not to be supposed that a people, anxious and desirous of having laws made,—who approve of the method of choosing delegates, or representatives, to meet in general convention for that purpose, can want the necessary and concomitant virtue to carry them into execution.

Nay, gentlemen, for argument's sake, let us set virtue for a moment out of the question, and see how the matter will then stand. You must admit that it is, and ever will be, the interest of a large majority that the laws should be esteemed and held sacred; if so, surely this large majority can never want inclination or power to give sanction and efficacy to those very laws which advance their interest and secure their property. And now, Mr. Chairman and gentlemen of the convention, as it is indispensably necessary that laws should be composed for the regulation of our conduct, as we have a right to make such laws without giving offense to Great Britain or any of the American colonies, without disturbing the repose of any society or community under heaven; if it is probable, nay, certain, that the laws may derive force and efficacy from our mutual consent, and that consent resulting from our own virtue, interest, and convenience, nothing remains but to set about the business immediately, and let the event determine the wisdom of the undertaking.

The Theoretical Justification

One of the most influential descriptions of the formation of government is to be found in the writings of John Locke. It would be impossible within the scope of this problem even to suggest the many implications that Americans drew from the ideas expressed by Locke, but the student will examine many of them

the sources of authority

in subsequent problems. The following selections, taken from *An Essay concerning the true original, extent and end of civil government*, first published in 1689, should be compared particularly with the descriptions of Indian societies in the next section and with the Declaration of Independence in Problem Three.[13]

To understand political power aright, and derive it from its original, we must consider what estate all men are naturally in, and that is a state of perfect freedom to order their actions and dispose of their possessions and persons as they think fit, within the bounds of the law of nature, without asking leave, or depending upon the will of any other man.

A state also of equality, wherein all the power and jurisdiction is reciprocal, no one having more than another; there being nothing more evident than that creatures of the same species and rank, promiscuously born to all the same advantages of nature, and the use of the same faculties, should also be equal one amongst another without subordination or subjection, unless the Lord and Master of them all should by any manifest declaration of His will set one above another, and confer on him by an evident and clear appointment an undoubted right to dominion and sovereignty. . . .

Man being born, as has been proved, with a title to perfect freedom, and an uncontrolled enjoyment of all the rights and privileges of the law of nature, equally with any other man or number of men in the world, hath by nature a power not only to preserve his property— that is, his life, liberty, and estate— against the injuries and attempts of other men, but to judge of and punish the breaches of that law in others as he is persuaded the offence deserves, even with death itself, in crimes where the heinousness of the fact in his opinion requires it. But because no political society can be nor subsist without having in itself the power to preserve the property, and, in order thereunto, punish the offences of all those of that society, there, and there only, is political society, where every one of the members hath quitted this natural power, resigned it up into the hands of the community in all cases that exclude him not from appealing for protection to the law established by it. And thus all private judgment of every particular member being excluded, the community comes to be umpire. . . . Those who are united into one body, and have a common established law and judicature to appeal to, with authority to decide controversies between them and punish offenders, are in civil society one with another; but those who have no such common appeal, I mean on earth, are still in the state of nature, each being, where there is no other, judge for himself and executioner, which is, as I have before shown it, the perfect state of nature. . . .

Wherever, therefore, any number of men so unite into one society, as to quit every one of his executive

---

[13] John Locke, *Two Treatises of Government* (London, 1690), 220–21, 305–8, 316, 319.

power of the law of nature, and to resign it to the public, there, and there only, is a political, or civil society. And this is done wherever any number of men, in the state of nature, enter into society to make one people, one body politic under one supreme government, or else when any one joins himself to, and incorporates with, any government already made. For hereby he authorises the society, or which is all one, the legislative thereof, to make laws for him, as the public good of the society shall require, to the execution whereof his own assistance (as to his own decrees) is due. . . .

Men being, as has been said, by nature all free, equal, and independent, no one can be put out of this estate, and subjected to the political power of another, without his own consent, which is done by agreeing with other men to join and unite into a community, for their comfortable, safe, and peaceable living, one amongst another, in a secure enjoyment of their properties and a greater security against any that are not of it. . . .

Whosoever therefore out of a state of nature unite into a community must be understood to give up all the power necessary to the ends for which they unite into society, to the majority of the community, unless they expressly agreed in any number greater than the majority. And this is done by barely agreeing to unite into one political society, which is all the compact that is, or needs be, between the individuals that enter into or make up a commonwealth. And thus that which begins and actually constitutes any political society is nothing but the consent of any number of freemen capable of a majority to unite and incorporate into such a society. And this is that, and that only, which did or could give beginning to any lawful government in the world.

5. AUTHORITY FROM PRESTIGE

In the last analysis all authority rests on consent, on the willingness of some men to yield to others. They may yield out of a belief that God wants them to, out of habit or custom, out of fear or anarchy. But unless they yield willingly, whether to an hereditary king or to a town meeting, their society is not likely to survive for long.

There are many forces that can affect men's willingness to subject themselves to others. No one wishes to be ruled by a fool, by a child, by someone he considers weaker or less worthy than himself. In order to command obedience a man endowed with authority must also, in the long run, command respect. He may earn respect by his achievements, or by his character, wealth, dignity, age, strength, or social status. However he gets it, if he commands respect, he enjoys an informal authority that may be more powerful than any which can be conferred formally by public office. The most stable society is perhaps one where this informal

Nature's Noblemen

The desert island that became the United States was not quite deserted when the first European settlers arrived. Though the native inhabitants were few in number and lived in what seemed a primitive manner, they proved surprisingly tenacious of their primitive customs and habits. Europeans observing them, while dismayed at their refusal to accept the superiority of European ways, nevertheless found much to admire; and what Europeans admired most was the way in which authority, among most Indian tribes, was almost entirely informal, resting on personal prestige. Although tribal customs differed greatly from region to region, most Indian rulers could command obedience only while they commanded respect. The consent of the people was not given for life or for a prescribed term but only from moment to moment. Formal authority was all but dissolved into informal authority. In the first selection below, Henry Timberlake, a British soldier in the French and Indian War of 1754–1763, describes the Cherokee Indians; in the second, James Adair talks about government among all the southern tribes; in the third, Cadwallader Colden, governor of New York, speaks of the Iroquois.

Henry Timberlake

They have many of them a good uncultivated genius, are fond of speaking well, as that paves the way to power in their councils. . . . They seldom turn their eyes on the person they speak of, or address themselves to, and are always suspicious when people's eyes are fixed upon them. They speak so low, except in council, that they are often obliged to repeat what they were saying; yet should a person talk to any of them above their common pitch, they would immediately ask him if he thought they were deaf? . . .

Their government, if I may call it government, which has neither laws or power to support it, is a mixed aristocracy and democracy, the chiefs being chose according to their merit in war, or policy at home; these lead the warriors that chuse to go, for there is no laws or compulsion on those that refuse to follow, or punishment to those that forsake their chief: he strives, therefore, to inspire them with a sort of enthusiasm, by the war-song, as the ancient bards did once in Britain. These chiefs, or headmen, likewise compose the assemblies of the nation, into which the war-women are admitted. The reader will not be a little surprised to find the story of Amazons not so great a fable as we imagined, many of the Indian women being as famous in war, as powerful in the council.

The rest of the people are divided into two military classes, warriors and fighting men, which last are the plebeians, who have not distinguished themselves enough to be admitted into the rank of warriors. There are some other honorary titles among them, conferred in reward of great actions; the first of which is Outacity, or Man-killer; and the second Colona, or the Raven. Old warriors likewise, or war-women, who can no longer go to war, but have distinguished themselves in their younger days, have the title of Beloved. This is the only title females can enjoy; but it abundantly recompences them, by the power they acquire by it, which is so great, that they can, by the wave of a swan's wing, deliver a wretch condemned by the council, and already tied to the stake.[14]

James Adair

This leads me to speak of the Indian method of government.—In general, it consists in a federal union of the whole society for mutual safety. As the law of nature appoints no frail mortal to be a king, or ruler, over his brethren; and humanity forbids the taking away at pleasure, the life or property of any who obey the good laws of their country, they consider that the transgressor ought to have his evil deeds retaliated upon himself in an equal manner. The Indians, therefore, have no such titles or persons, as emperors, or kings; nor an appellative for such, in any of their dialects. Their highest title, either in military or civil life, signifies only a *Chieftain:* they have no words to express despotic power, arbitrary kings, oppressed, or obedient subjects; neither can they form any other ideas of the former, than of "bad war chieftains of a numerous family, who inslaved the rest." The power of their chiefs, is an empty sound. They can only persuade or dissuade the people, either by the force of good-nature and clear reasoning, or colouring things, so as to suit their prevailing passions. It is reputed merit alone, that gives them any titles of distinction above the meanest of the people. If we connect with this their opinion of a theocracy, it does not promise well to the reputed establishment of extensive and puissant Indian American empires. When any national affair is in debate, you may hear every father of a family speaking in his house on the subject, with rapid, bold language, and the utmost freedom that a people can use. Their voices, to a man, have due weight in every public affair, as it concerns their welfare alike. Every town is independent of another. Their own friendly compact continues the union. An obstinate war leader will sometimes commit acts of hostility, or make peace for his own town, contrary to the good liking of the rest of the nation. But a few individuals are very cautious of commencing war on small occasions, without the general consent of the headmen: for should it prove unsuccessful, the greater part would be apt to punish them as enemies, because they abused their power, which they had only to do good to the society. They are very deliberate in their councils, and never give an immediate answer to

---

[14] Henry Timberlake, *The Memoirs of Lieut. Henry Timberlake* (London, 1765), 54–55, 70–71.

any message sent them by strangers, but suffer some nights first to elapse. They reason in a very orderly manner, with much coolness and good-natured language, though they may differ widely in their opinions. Through respect to the silent audience, the speaker always addresses them in a standing posture. In this manner they proceed, till each of the headmen hath given his opinion on the point in debate. Then they sit down together, and determine upon the affair. Not the least passionate expression is to be heard among them, and they behave with the greatest civility to each other. In all their stated orations they have a beautiful modest way of expressing their dislike of ill things. They only say, "it is not good, goodly, or commendable." And their whole behaviour, on public occasions, is highly worthy of imitation by some of our British senators and lawyers.

Most of their regulations are derived from the plain law of nature. Nature's school contemns all quibbles of art, and teaches them the plain easy rule, "do to others, as you would be done by;" when they are able, without greater damage to themselves, than benefit to their creditor, they discharge their honest debts. But, though no disputes pass between them on such occasions, yet if there be some heart-burnings on particular affairs, as soon as they are publicly known, their red Archimagus, and his old beloved men, convene and decide, in a very amicable manner, when both parties become quite easy. They have no compulsive power to force the debtor to pay; yet the creditor can distrain his goods or chattels, and justly satisfy himself without the least interruption—and, by one of his relations, he sends back in a very civil manner, the overplus to the owner. These instances indeed seldom happen, for as they know each other's temper, they are very cautious of irritating, as the consequences might one day prove fatal—they never scold each other when sober—they conceal their enmity be it ever so violent, and will converse together with smooth kind language, and an obliging easy behavior, while envy is preying on their heart. In general, they are very punctual in paying what they owe among themselves, but they are grown quite careless in discharging what they owe to the traders, since the commencement of our destructive plan of general licences. "An old debt," is a proverbial expression with them, of "nothing."

There are many petty crimes which their young people are guilty of,—to which our laws annex severe punishment, but theirs only an ironical way of jesting. They commend the criminal before a large audience, for practising the virtue, opposite to the crime, that he is known to be guilty of. If it is for theft, they praise his honest principles; and they commend a warrior for having behaved valiantly against the enemy, when he acted cowardly; they introduce the minutest circumstances of the affair, with severe sarcasms which wound deeply. I have known them to strike their delinquents with those sweetened darts, so goodnaturedly and skillfully, that they would sooner die by torture, than renew their shame by repeating the actions.[15]

---

[15] James Adair, *The History of the American Indians* (London, 1775), 427-30.

Cadwallader Colden

Each Nation is an absolute Republick by its self, govern'd in all Publick Affairs of War and Peace by the Sachems or Old Men, whose Authority and Power is gain'd by and consists wholly in the Opinion the rest of the Nation have of their Wisdom and Integrity. They never execute their Resolutions by Compulsion or Force upon any of their People. Honour and Esteem are their Principal Rewards, as Shame and being Despised are their Punishments. They have certain Customs which they observe in their Publick Affairs with other Nations, and in their Private Affairs among themselves, which it is scandalous for any one not to observe, and draw after them publick or private Resentment when they are broke.

Their Generals and Captains obtain their Authority likewise by the general Opinion of their Courage and Conduct, and loose it by a Failure in those Vertues.

Their Great Men, both Sachems and Captains, are generally poorer than the common People, for they affect to give away and distribute all the Presents or Plunder they get in their Treaties or War, so as to leave nothing to themselves. If they should once be suspected of Selfishness, they would grow mean in the opinion of their Country-men, and would consequently loose their Authority.

Their Affairs of Great Consequence, which concern all the Nations, are Transacted in a General Meeting of the Sachems of every Nation. These Conventions are generally held at Onnondaga, which is nearly in the Center of all the Five Nations. But they have fixed upon Albany to be the Place for their Solemn Treaties with the English Colonies. . . .

As I am fond to think, that the present state of the Indian Nations exactly shows the most Ancient and Original Condition of almost every Nation; so I believe, here we may with more certainty see the Original Form of all Government, than in the most curious Speculations of the Learned; and that the Patriarchal, and other Schemes in Politicks are no better than Hypotheses in Philosophy, and as prejudicial to real Knowledge.[16]

A Willing Submission to Eminence

The English settlers of America never dared try so complete a reliance on informal authority as that which prevailed among the Indians. But the colonists did recognize the need to make formal authority coincide as closely as possible

---

[16] Cadwallader Colden, *The History of the Five Indian Nations* (New York, 1727), XV–XVII.

with informal. They carried with them habits of deference to their social superiors, and they recognized that government conducted by common men might lack the prestige needed to command obedience. When George Yeardley, a social upstart, was knighted and named governor of Virginia in 1618, succeeding to the office previously held by the noble Lord de la Warr, several of the earlier leaders of the colony, then in England, but planning to return to Virginia, were troubled. They expressed their views in the following petition to the Virginia Company.

Right Honorable and the rest of this Honorable Court: We doubt nothing, but you allow it an approved truth, that great actions are carried with best success by such commanders who have personal authority and greatness answerable to the action; [since] it is not easy to sway a vulgar and servile nature by vulgar and servile spirits; and surely in the raising of so happy a state, as is hoped, in the plantation of Virginia, [there will be some] whom only reverence of the commanders eminence or nobility (whereunto by nature every man subordinate is ready to yield a willing submission without contempt or repining) may easily persuade under those duties of obedience: which authority conferred upon a mean man, and of no better than selected out of their own rank, shall never be able to compel.

We urge not this as willing to derogate from the governor who now holds the place, and hath succeeded the thrice noble deceased Lord Lawarr, whose memory for this business be ever happy; unto whom we suppose, if another noble like himself might have risen up, this business would have found much willinger forwardness, and a great many old adventurers and planters, both here in England would have returned, together with many new of good worth set onwards; and many of the chief there, who are now ready to revolt and look home, would settle themselves with firmer alacrity.

If then it may be supposed an advancement to the colony, to have both such who have suffered many years in the early days of the business under his lordship the Lord Lawarr to return, and many voluntary forces to address them thither, as also to stay and fix such of the better sort as be ready to come away, and all for want of some eminent commander, we humbly beseech this honorable court to take into consideration this our only request (who otherwise finding themselves much disparaged and wronged are resolved to abandon and quit the country and action forever) that some either Noble, or little less in honor or dower may be maturely advised upon, to maintain and hold up the dignity of so great and good a cause.[17]

---

[17] Susan M. Kingsbury, ed., *The Records of the Virginia Company of London*, 4 vols. (Washington, D.C., 1906–33), 3:231–32.

Deference in Rebellion

Deference dies hard. In April 1776, as the embattled colonists moved toward independence, a Maryland militia company made clear that they shared some of the sentiments of their early Virginia forbears. They were ready to bear arms against the troops of the King of England, but only if led by the right sort of person. Their former captain explained their anxiety to the Maryland Council of Safety in the following letter.

Bladensburgh 18th April 1776

Gentlemen. It is with reluctance I take up my pen to address you on a matter I would wish to be silent on, was I not urged to do it by the strongest entreaties of a Company inferiour to none in the province, whom I respect, and who I have the highest satisfaction in obliging. My resigning has thrown the Company into great confusion and concern for fear M\ William Hamilton, my first Lieutenant, should take place as Captain, who they look upon not to be worthy, or in any respect proper for that office; but perhaps may be recommended by the Colonel through prejudice to me, as I would not condescend to serve under him; if it so happens that he should be appointed Captain, it will be the utter distruction of the Company, as they are determined not to serve under him. I would not willingly interfere with this Gentlemans private character, therefore shall only relate the matter to your Honours how he came to be appointed Lieutenant, which was, as he had been a soldier several years in the last war, I imagined he must have been better quallified than any other person I had the opportunity of getting at that time, however found myself much deceaved for he was as ignorant as those who had never seen a musket thrown in their lives, and surprizingly awkward in every respect, and still continues so. There are many young men in the company who are much better qualified in every respect, and I believe as many so as in any Company in the Province. M\ Hamilton is a poor man and has a wife and several children, and no person to work for them, but himself, therefore cannot make the appearance that an Officer ought to make, is a person of no Education, neither is he qualified in any respect whatever to keep company with the other Gentlemen Officers, which is a material objection by the Company, as they would not choose to serve under an officer who could not keep company with, and be looked upon by other officers but more particularly, as he is esteemed a very improper person in other respects, and of more consiquence to those under him. There are other objections which I do not choose to meddle with, yet I hope have said enough to evince to you, how very displeasing he is to the Company, and the ill consequences that might arise, in case of his appointment, and what I can with much truth and certainty assure would come to pass (i. e.) the breaking up of a Company of much consiquence. Relying on your Honours wisdom in not appointing a person so disagreeable (as nothing but my particular desire to have the Company kept together and to be satisfy'd, could have induced me to write in this manner) I remain with the utmost respect Gentlemen,

> Your mo. obed[t] hble. Serv[t]
> Andrew Beall[18]

Aristocratic Republicans

Since the coming of the Revolution no one has thought it appropriate to argue in America that noble birth should confer authority. In a government of the people, by the people, for the people, authority, whether formal or informal, is supposed to attach not to birth but to virtue and talent. Benjamin Franklin accordingly advised Europeans in 1782 that America was no place for a man who expected recognition because of high birth. Birth, he said "is a commodity that cannot be carried to a worse market than that of America." Thirty years later John Adams was not so sure. As he reminded Thomas Jefferson in the following passage, the personal authority that attached to members of prestigious families could not be abolished by the declaration that all men are created equal. In Virginia and Massachusetts alike, the new Americans were still prone to submit themselves to men of distinguished family.

We are now explicitly agreed, in one important point, vizt. That "there is a natural Aristocracy among men; the grounds of which are Virtue and Talents."

You very justly indulge a little merriment upon this solemn subject of Aristocracy. I often laugh at it too, for there is nothing in this laughable world more ridiculous than the management of it by almost all the nations of the Earth. But while We smile, Mankind have reason to say to Us, as the froggs said to the Boys, What is Sport to you is Wounds and death to Us. When I consider the weakness, the folly, the Pride, the Vanity, the Selfishness, the Artifice, the low craft and meaning cunning, the want of Principle, the Avarice, the unbounded Ambition, the unfeeling Cruelty of a majority of those (in all Nations) who are allowed an aristocratical influence; and on the other hand, the Stupidity with which the more numerous multitude, not only become their Dupes, but even love to be Taken in by their Tricks: I feel a stronger disposition to weep at their destiny, than to laugh at their Folly.

But tho' We have agreed in one point, in Words, it is not yet certain that We are perfectly agreed in Sense. Fashion has introduced an indeterminate Use of the Word "Talents." Education, Wealth, Strength, Beauty, Stature, Birth, Marriage, graceful Attitudes and Motions, Gait, Air, Complexion, Physiognomy, are Talents, as well as Genius and Science and learning. Any one of these Talents, that in fact commands or in-

---

[18] *Archives of Maryland* (Baltimore, 1892), 11:350–51.

fluences true Votes in Society, gives to the Man who possesses it, the Character of an Aristocrat, in my Sense of the Word.

Pick up, the first 100 men you meet, and make a Republick. Every Man will have an equal Vote. But when deliberations and discussions are opened it will be found that 25, by their Talents, Virtues being equal, will be able to carry 50 Votes. Every one of these 25, is an Aristocrat, in my Sense of the Word; whether he obtains his one Vote in Addition to his own, by his Birth Fortune, Figure, Eloquence, Science, learning, Craft Cunning, or even his Character for good fellowship and a bon vivant. . . .

If a descent from, pious, virtuous, wealthy litterary or scientific Ancestors is a letter of recommendation, or introduction in a Mans his favour, and enables him to influence only one vote in Addition to his own, he is an Aristocrat, for a democrat can have but one Vote. Aaron Burr had 100,000 Votes from the single Circumstance of his descent from President Burr and President Edwards. . . .

No Romance would be more amusing, than the History of your Virginian and our new England Aristocratical Families. Yet even in Rhode Island, where there has been no Clergy, no Church, and I had almost said, no State, and some People say no religion, there has been a constant respect for certain old Families. 57 or 58 years ago, in company with Col. Counsellor, Judge, John Chandler, whom I have quoted before, a Newspaper was brought in. The old Sage asked me to look for the News from Rhode Island and see how the Elections had gone there. I read the List of Wantons, Watsons, Greens, Whipples, Malbones etc. "I expected as much" said the aged Gentleman, "for I have always been of Opinion, that in the most popular Governments, the Elections will generally go in favour of the most ancient families." To this day when any of these Tribes and We may Add Ellerys, Channings Champlins etc are pleased to fall in with the popular current, they are sure to carry all before them. . . .

I see the same Spirit in Virginia, that you and I see in Rhode Island and the rest of New England. In New York it is a struggle of Family Feuds. A fewdal Aristocracy. Pensylvania is a contest between German, Irish and old English Families. When Germans and Irish Unite, they give 30,000 majorities. There is virtually a White Rose and a Red Rose a Caesar and a Pompey in every State in this Union and Contests and dissentions will be as lasting. The Rivalry of Bourbons and Noailleses produced the French Revolution, and a similar Competition for Consideration and Influence, exists and prevails in every Village in the World. . . .

Our Winthrops, Winslows, Bradfords, Saltonstalls, Quincys, Chandlers, Leonards, Hutchinsons, Olivers, Sewalls etc are precisely in the Situation of your Randolphs, Carters and Burwells, and Harrisons. Some of them unpopular for the part they took in the late revolution, but all respected for their names and connections and whenever they fall in with the popular Sentiments, are preferred, cetoris paribus to all others.[19]

---

[19] L. J. Cappon, ed., *The Adams-Jefferson Letters* (Chapel Hill n.c., 1959), 2:397–402. John Adams to Thomas Jefferson, November 15, 1813.

CONCLUSION

American history has been a continuous exploration of the meaning of authority. While authority came from God, it was easy to disagree about whom He gave it to; one man could claim access to Him about as easily as another. Even when the King was acknowledged as the immediate source of authority, there could be disagreement. When the people claimed authority themselves, the question still remained but in a different form, and it gave shape to the whole of our history.

Who *were* the people? Were they the people of the British Empire or were they the people of the American colonies? Were they the people of the United States or of a particular state? Were they the people who owned property or all the people? Could the people of one generation bind those of another by legislation or by contracts? How much authority could the people give their government? And how much did they give it? How could they withdraw it? What was left to the individual? How should the people of the United States deal with other people and with other governments whose authority perhaps did not come from the consent of their own people?

If Americans had agreed on these questions, our history would have been a highly peaceful and highly monotonous chronicle. Instead, it has been full of the problems with which the rest of this book is concerned. The problems range over many issues, and most of them could not have been solved simply by an agreement on the nature and sources of authority, but this issue does run through them all. They are problems in American history not merely because they happened here but because they happened in a country that accepted the people as the ultimate source of authority.

2 ALDEN T. VAUGHAN

the character of colonial politics

No part of the American experiment is more revered or more imitated than its form of government. Praises have been heaped on the Founding Fathers for their soundness of judgment and breadth of vision in devising a Constitution both durable and flexible. Yet the Founding Fathers would be the first to admit that their handiwork rested firmly on the colonial experience. James Madison, James Wilson, Benjamin Franklin, and the other architects of our national polity codified more than they originated, synthesized more than they invented. So too did those who in the 1770s and 80s framed the several state constitutions and those who kept in motion the organs of town and county government.

What was the experience on which they built? Colonial America had no single system of government. Although the monarch of Great Britain had nominal jurisdiction over all of England's empire, his mainland colonies exhibited a confusing variety of political systems. Even the usual textbook classifications are little help: of the thirteen colonies that wrenched free from the Empire in 1776, nine are usually referred to as royal, two as proprietary, and two as charter or corporate colonies. Yet this division is misleading. Massachusetts, ostensibly royal, nonetheless had a charter which spelled out the basic form of her government and the basic rights of her people—including the unique right of the lower house of the legislature to choose the upper house. Delaware, also partly royal, was so closely tied to neighboring Pennsylvania that she shared the same governor, selected by the Penn family but approved by the King's Privy

the character of colonial politics

Council. And on the local level, where the political system was of most importance in the daily lives of the people, the usual categories are meaningless; there the patterns of government owed more to geography and habit than to royal, proprietary, or corporate status. The New England colonies focused on town autonomy and used county government only for judicial and militia purposes; New York retained some vestiges of the semi-feudal patroonships established during the Dutch period; in Maryland the ancient units of "manor" and "hundred" could occasionally be found; while the Southern provinces administered local government chiefly through county courts. The structure of colonial politics seemed confusing even to those who watched it grow.

Yet the purely structural part of the English political heritage is relatively easy to identify. Far less so is another part of the English political heritage on which the new nation drew: political practices, as distinct from political forms. Here the letter of the law did not necessarily reveal the spirit of the law—in fact, much that was firmly entrenched in colonial American politics was based more on common usage than on written law. But written or not, the mundane political practices were important. Criteria of franchise eligibility, methods of campaigning, procedures of voting, usages of power and of patronage, and techniques of legislative and executive administration were as much a part of the colonial political experience as were the more ascertainable matters of form. And in political practice as in political form, there was great variety in the American colonies, not only from colony to colony but within each colony from town to town or county to county. There was variety as well in time: practices were often modified to suit the needs—perhaps even the whims—of those who had influence in government. As in any political system there was growth, erosion, and fluctuation in the methods by which the political needs of the people were served.

The franchise is a case in point. Every colony placed restrictions of some sort on eligibility to vote (as does every state today), but in many colonies the restrictions were altered by the legislature from time to time, and in any event they were often observed in the breach. So too was the manner in which the franchise could be exercised and the number and rank of the officials to whom it could be applied. Any study in depth of the colonial franchise becomes bewildering, and except for rather broad generalizations, inconclusive.

Similar dilemmas cloud the question of imperial relations. It is one thing to know that certain colonies had royal governors; it is quite another to know how much authority those governors actually wielded. Their power was never constant, varying not only with the personal characteristics of the incumbent and of the council and assembly with which he had to deal, but with the nature of the problems confronted (or avoided) and the trends of political growth that accompanied the political maturation of the American colonies.

And the problems of measuring political influence apply internally as well as externally. Which provincial offices had effective authority and which were figurehead positions? Which depended upon the ability of the man in office and which on the nature of the office itself? Answers to such questions go far toward an understanding not only of the political system of colonial America but also of the political system under which we live today.

One of the controversies that has of recent years intrigued many American and British historians is the extent to which the American colonies were democratic. Such a query has deep semantic pitfalls, for the term democracy has never—in either the eighteenth or twentieth century—lent itself to easy definition. We use it in at least two distinct but overlapping senses today: first as a *method* or form of government in which the will of the people is carried out by elected representatives on the local, state, and national levels; and second as an *attitude* or spirit of social and economic, as well as political, life—an atmosphere in which every man is judged on merit and the rights of all are respected. Institutionally, the former sense of democracy might be symbolized by the Constitution of 1787, the latter sense by the Bill of Rights.

Colonial Americans of course had little to say about the fundamental forms of their governments; these were established by charters, grants, and royal commissions. Most colonists were probably content with their "mixed governments," in which royalty in the person of the governor and other crown agents, aristocracy in the council, and the commonality through the elected assemblies joined hands to preserve stability and protect property while at the same time ensuring the personal liberties to which Englishmen were accustomed. Such a partnership made good theory, but it was bound to undergo important changes in a land where there was no titled aristocracy, no mass of ignorant commoners, and where the source of monarchical authority was three thousand miles away. Furthermore, as the ethnic composition of America changed and as the American experience increasingly diverged from that of the mother country, political institutions became more American. Thus, according to many observers, then and now, government in America became more democratic in both form and spirit than it had been in England or any other European nation. By 1750 there had emerged in most colonies what some historians call a "middle-class democracy" in which the franchise was broader by far than in England, elected officials generally reflected the interests and aspirations of the public, and royal officials often succumbed to the pressure of the populace and its chosen spokesmen.

But there is another way of looking at the American polity. The outward form in the royal colonies was at best only half democratic: the chief magistrates and council, except in Massachusetts, received appointments from the crown as did many subordinate officials. The governor and upper house of the proprietary colony of Maryland and the governor of Pennsylvania (it had no upper house) were the appointees of men who rarely were themselves residents of America and who cared more for the profits than they did for the privileges of their tenants. Further, the governments of all colonies, royal or not, tended to be led by relatively few families, and they were usually among the wealthiest. Clans such as the Hutchinsons and Olivers in Massachusetts, the Livingstons, Clintons, and Delancys in New York, the Lees, Byrds, and Carters in Virginia dominated the political life of their colonies. And where was the democracy in spirit? There were widespread assumptions, imported from the Old World, that the franchise should be limited, that social distinction merited political power, and that a sound government must not be at the complete mercy of the people. Few colonists demanded changes in the structure of government, and few objected to discriminations against religious, ethnic, or economic minorities—in fact they insisted on them.

The problem for the student who would understand the political structure and spirit of colonial America is thus twofold: he must decide on both absolute and relative terms the character of the governmental system as it existed in the eighteenth century. He must also probe the political atmosphere of the colonies for evidence on the attitude toward individual rights and the extent to which colonial Americans enjoyed what we today would call "a free society."

The readings that follow will of necessity sample only a few parts of the problem of understanding and evaluating a political system that bridged the Atlantic Ocean, that stretched from New Hampshire to Georgia, that changed and adjusted during a century and a half of uneven growth, and that involved tangibles and intangibles in no consistent proportions. But a reading of some of the documents and descriptions of colonial politics should lead to a better understanding of the structure that served as inspiration and example for the American republic.

1. WHO COULD VOTE, AND FOR WHICH OFFICES?

At first glance determining the size and composition of the electorate in eighteenth-century America would seem a simple matter. Most of the legislative records survive, and in them the qualifications for voting are carefully spelled out. Of course the franchise requirements varied somewhat from colony to colony and from time to time, but such variations should only make the task a bit more laborious. On closer inspection, however, apparent simplicity gives way to puzzling complexity.

Most of the American colonies extended the privilege of suffrage fairly broadly—for the eighteenth century. Yet excluded by the prevailing social philosophy were vast categories: women, slaves, indentured servants, and, of course, minors, vagabonds, and criminals. Such exclusions stemmed in part from social prejudice, but mainly from the traditional English assumption that ownership of property must be a prerequisite to political influence. In England a "forty-shilling freehold"—one earning forty shillings per year in rent or other income—served as the arbitrary minimum; in America that figure was often applied, though a wide variety of other kinds of property—town houses, ships, merchandise, money—increasingly found recognition in the colonies. And in land-abundant, labor-short America, most free men could own enough property of one kind or another to qualify for political franchise.

Not all colonies used exactly the same yardstick; Georgia demanded a freehold earning fifty shillings a year, while in some other colonies the criterion was expressed in acreage rather than in value. Furthermore, most of the colonies added options for those who lived in towns and cities, as did Virginia in 1736 when the General Assembly passed a provision which extended the franchise to town dwellers who owned a house and lot. Most colonies also imposed additional qualifications. The New England provinces often insisted that voters give evidence of good character; most of the Southern colonies added racial restrictions; while many of the colonies limited the franchise—on paper at least—to Protestant Christians, often excluding Catholics and Jews, sometimes even Quakers and Baptists.

The chief problem comes in discovering who met the various qualifications. Tax records, deeds, wills, and other documents offer important clues, but few final answers. And even if an accurate measure of property holdings could be made, there would still be doubt as to the real size of the electorate. Evidence is abundant that many men were allowed to vote who had less than the requisite amount of property or who failed to meet the stipulated standards of religious orthodoxy, length of residence, or of age. By the same token, some who met all qualifications were barred from voting by illegal but effective tactics on the part of election officials, rival candidates, or local pressure groups. Historians have differed widely in their estimates of the size of colonial electorates.

If we are to understand the character of colonial politics, we must also know which offices were filled by choice of the voters. The number of elective offices were as varied from colony to colony as were voting qualifications, though happily there is a much smaller problem of measurement. For example, we know that the Virginia voter cast his ballot for two men to represent his county in the House of Burgesses, the colony's lower legislative chamber. That was all. By contrast, the Rhode

the character of colonial politics

Islander voted on the provincial level for representatives to the lower house and the upper house, as well as for the governor, while through town meetings he voted on the local level for a vast array of public servants from constable to surveyor of fences.

The readings presented in this section of the chapter illustrate the problem of measuring the extent of the franchise and of evaluating the frequency with which it could be exercised.

Definitions of Freemanship

Because the basic structure of colonial government had been decreed by royal charters and instructions, American colonists rarely determined which offices would be filled by vote of the people. They had much to say, however, about who was entitled to vote, for within certain limitations each colony could extend or contract the franchise as it saw fit. All colonies accepted the ancient English custom of requiring a man to meet specified conditions of age, residence, and religion, and to have a material stake in society before he could qualify as a freeholder or be admitted as a freeman. Freemanship, in turn, was tantamount to suffrage.

Unfortunately for anyone trying to discover the extent of the colonial franchise, no two colonies had identical requirements, as the readings that follow will illustrate. Some, such as Connecticut, combined the forty-shilling property requirement with, among other things, a moral requirement of "quiet and peaceable behaviour." South Carolina, on the other hand, required its voters to have 50 acres of land or pay taxes that indicated an equivalent wealth, and also insisted that they be free, white, and Christian. Finally, Virginia's oath for freeholders could be taken only by those having 100 acres of unimproved land, or 25 acres "with a house and plantation on it," or a house and lot in town.[1]

Connecticut

Be it enacted by the Governor, Council, and Representatives, in General Court assembled, and by the authority of the same, that the town clerks in the several towns in this Colony, shall enroll in their respective offices, the names of all such persons in their respective towns as are, or shall be admitted freemen of this corporation: which enrollments shall be made by the direction of the authority and selectmen of the town, in the open freemen's meeting, legally assembled.

That no person, hereafter shall be admitted, and made free of this corporation, but in the open freemen's meeting of the town whereto he belongs, regularly assembled.

That all such inhabitants in this Colony as have accomplished the age

---

[1] *Acts and Laws of His Majesty's English Colony of Connecticut in New England* (New Haven, 1769), 80–81; Thomas Cooper, ed., *The Statutes at Large of South Carolina* (Columbia, S.C., 1838), 3:2–3; *The Acts of Assembly Now in Force in the Colony of Virginia* (Williamsburg, 1769), 104.

of twenty-one years, and have the possession of freehold estate to the value of forty shillings per annum, or forty pounds personal estate in the general list of estates in that year wherein they desire to be admitted freemen; and also are persons of a quiet and peaceable behaviour, and civil conversation, may if they desire it, on their procuring the selectmen of the town wherein such persons inhabit, or the major part of them, to certify that the said persons are qualified as abovesaid, be admitted and made free of this corporation, in case they take the oath provided by law for freemen: which oath any one assistant or justice of the peace is hereby impowred to administer in said freemen's meeting.

And all such persons admitted and sworn, as aforesaid, shall be freemen of this corporation; and their names shall be enrolled in the roll of freemen in the Town-Clerk's office of that town wherein they are admitted, as aforesaid. . . .

And that if any freeman of this corporation shall walk scandalously, or commit any scandalous offence, it shall be in the power of the Superiour Court in this Colony, on complaint thereof to them made, to disfranchise such freeman; who shall stand disfranchised till by his good behavior the said Superiour Court shall cause to restore him to his franchisement or freedom again: which the said Court is impowered to do.

South Carolina

Whereas, several disputes have arisen about the qualifications of such persons who shall be deemed capable to vote for or elect members of the Commons House of Assembly, and of the qualifications of such who shall be elected to serve as representatives in the said Commons House of Assembly, whereby the true intent and meaning of the above recited Act hath been wrongfully wrested and perverted; therefore, for the preventing of the same for the future,

I. Be it enacted by his Excellency John Lord Carteret, Palatine, and the rest of the true and absolute Lords and Proprietors of this Province, by and with the advice and consent of the rest of the members of the General Assembly, now met at Charlestown for the south and west part of this Province, and by the authority of the same, that every white man (and no other) professing the Christian religion, who has attained to the age of one and twenty years, and hath been a resident and an inhabitant of the parish for which he votes for a representative for the space of six months before the date of the writs for the election that he offers to give in his vote at, and hath a freehold of at least fifty acres of land, or shall be lyable to pay taxes to the support of this government, for the sum of fifty pounds current money, shall be deemed a person qualified to vote for, and may be capable of electing a representative or representatives to serve as a member or members of the Commons House of Assembly for the parish or precinct wherein he actually is a resident.

II. And be it further enacted by the authority aforesaid, that no apprentice or other covenanted servant for term of years, whether by indenture or by custom of the country, nor any searfaring or other transient man, who has neither freehold nor is liable to pay tax for a stock of fifty pounds current money towards the publick charge of this Province, within the parish he offers to give his vote for a representative or representatives as above directed, shall be deemed capable of voting or electing a representative; anything in the afore recited act contained to the contrary notwithstanding. . . .

Virginia

You shall swear that you are a freeholder in the County of _____ and have at least one hundred acres of freehold lands unseated, lying and being in the Parish of _____ in the County of _____ in your sole possession, or in the possession of your tenant or tenants for years; or that you have one-hundred acres of freehold lands unseated, lying and being in the Counties of _____ in your sole possession, or in the possession of your tenant or tenants for years; and that the greatest part of the said land doth lie in the County of _____ or that you are freeholder and sole owner of twenty-five acres of land, with a house and plantation upon it, lying and being in the County of _____ in your sole possession, or in the possession of your tenant or tenants for years; or that you are a freeholder and sole owner of a house and lot, or a house and part of a lot, in your own possession, or the possession of your tenant or tenants, lying and being in the City or Town of _____; and that such freehold estate hath not been made or granted to you fraudulently, on purpose to qualify you to give your vote; and that you have not been polled before at this election.

Religious Restrictions

As fundamental as the belief that the franchise must be restricted to men of some property was the belief that voters must also adhere to an acceptable religion. The tie between church and state was recognized in the colonial period as a cooperative one: the church supported the authority and stability of the state, while the state preserved the theological supremacy of the predominant sect. Again, there were many exceptions. The laws were often vague and often ignored by those responsible for their enforcement. But most of the governments had, at one time or another, laws designed to preserve the religious purity of the colony.

There is a touch of irony to the example that follows. Established as a haven for Roman Catholics, Maryland by 1717 was so firmly entrenched in the Protestant camp that its legislature could enact a franchise restriction against Catholics. The Calvert family had turned Protestant, the Catholics had rapidly lost their early dominance, and the crisis in England associated with the Glorious Revolution and the subsequent attempts to reestablish the Stuart line had branded the Catholic a political subversive as well as a religious heretic. Hence the enactment of a law designed to keep Catholic influence from undermining the state.[2]

Whereas notwithstanding all the measures that have been hitherto taken for preventing the growth of popery within this Province, it is very obvious, that not only profest Papists still multiply and increase in number, but that there are also too great numbers of others that adhere to and espouse their interest in opposition to the Protestant establishment: and being under just apprehensions (from what steps they have already taken) that if Papists should continue to be allowed their vote in electing delegates, they, with their adherents, and those under their influence, will make such a party at the elections of many of the counties within this Province, as well as the City of Annapolis, as to determine the choice in some of their great favourites and adherents, which if they should accomplish, how much it would tend to the discouragement and disturbance of his Lordship's Protestant Government, is not easy to imagine.... Therefore...

Be it enacted, by the authority aforesaid, by and with the advice and consent aforesaid, that all profest Papists whatsoever, be (and are hereby declared) uncapable of giving their vote in any election of a delegate or delegates within this Province, either for counties, cities or borroughs, unless they first qualify themselves for so doing by taking the several oaths appointed to be taken by an act of Assembly of this Province entitled *An Act for the Better Security of the Peace and Safety of his Lordship's Government and the Protestant Interest Within This Province,* and subscribe the Oath of Abjuration and Declaration therein mentioned.

And further, inasmuch as too many persons that are really Papists, or popishly inclined, act in disguise, and will not make any publick profession of their principles, for the better and more effectual carrying on their wicked and malicious designs, for the undermining and subverting of our present establishment:

Be it therefore further enacted, by the authority and consent aforesaid, that it shall and may be lawful for the sheriff or other judges of elections and such sheriff or other judges are hereby required, as often as any of them shall see needful (or upon the information of any other person duly qualified to vote) to tender and administer the oaths and subscriptions aforesaid, to any person or persons suspected to be Papists or popishly inclined; and upon their refusal, to set aside such vote or votes.

Provided always, that nothing in this act be construed to debarr or hinder any of the people called and generally reputed Quakers, from their votes in election, they being otherwise duly qualified.

[2] *Abridgement and Collection of the Acts of the Assembly of the Province of Maryland* (Philadelphia, 1759), 197.

Mixed Government

Regardless of how broad or how narrow the franchise of a colony might have been, there were some government officials for whom no colonist could vote. Such officers were scarce in the corporate colonies of Rhode Island and Connecticut and the proprietaries of Pennsylvania and Maryland. In the royal colonies, however, they comprised a large segment of the civil administration. The governor and council owed their appointments directly to the monarch (although they were actually appointed by the Privy Council), and they in turn had control of a sizeable army of provincial subordinates. These men were agents of the Crown, not of the inhabitants. Usually they were local men, and so their interests were not necessarily contrary to those of the people. Nor were they really free of popular manipulation: the assembly through its control of provincial finances could often dictate their selection and to a lesser extent direct their performance of duty. But in any event, the people were denied the opportunity to express their preference for the men who would fill certain offices; and the loyalties of the incumbents were sufficiently strong to make most of them side with the Crown at the outbreak of the Revolution.

The selection that follows illustrates the blend of democracy and autocracy that characterized the administration of royal colonies. The people had an assembly, and the people had a say in many other matters. But at the same time, a cumbersome overlay of royal officials, from governor down to customs collectors, served at the pleasure of the King. The selection is taken from a description of South Carolina written by its royal governor, James Glen, in 1761.[3]

The government of South Carolina is one of those called royal governments, to distinguish it I presume from the charter governments, such as Massachusetts-Bay, Connecticut, and Rhode-Island; and from the proprietary governments, such as Pennsylvania and Maryland. . . .

---

[3] Chapman J. Milling, ed., *Colonial South Carolina: Two Contemporary Descriptions* (Columbia, S.C., 1951), 39–42. Copyright © 1951 by the University of South Carolina Press. Reprinted by permission of the publisher.

The Governor is appointed by patent, by the title of Governor-in-Chief and Captain-General in and over the Province; he receives also a Vice Admiral's commission: but alas, these high sounding titles convey very little power, and I have often wished that Governors had more: I cannot, however, help making this disinterested remark, that though a virtuous person might be trusted with a little more power, perhaps there may be as much already given, as can safely be delegated to a weak or wicked person; and considering that such may in ill times happen to be employed, a wise and good prince will therefore guard against it.

The members of the Council are appointed by the King, under his Royal Sign Manual, and are twelve in number; to which number the Surveyor-General of the Customs must be added, he having a seat in Council in all the governments within his district.

The Assembly consists of forty-four members, elected every third year by the freeholders of sixteen different parishes; but the representation seems to be unequal; some parishes returning five, others four, three, two, or only one; and some towns which, by the King's instructions have a right to be erected into parishes, and to send two members, are not allowed to send any.

There is a Court of Chancery, composed of the Governor and Council, and there is a Master in Chancery, and a Register belonging to the said Court.

The Court of King's Bench consists of a Chief Justice appointed by his Majesty, and some assistant justices: the same persons constitute the Court of Common Pleas; there is a Clerk of the Crown, who is also Clerk of the Pleas; an Attorney-General, and a Provost-Marshal.

There is a Secretary of the Province, who is also Register, and pretends a right to be, and appoints, the Clerk of the Council; there is also a Clerk of the Assembly, a Surveyor-General of the Land, a Receiver-General of the Quit-Rents, a Vendue Master, and Naval Officer: all which officers are appointed by the crown.

There is a Court of Vice Admiralty; the Judge, Register, and Marshall thereof, are appointed by the Lords Commissioners of the Admiralty.

There is a Comptroller of the Customs; three collectors, one at each port, viz. Charles-Town, Port Royal, and Winyaw; there likewise are two Searchers at Charles-Town; and all these are appointed by the Commissioners of the Customs, or by the Lords Commissioners of the Treasury.

The Public Treasurer, the Country Comptroller, the Commissioners for Indian Affairs, and several other officers, are appointed by the General Assembly.

The clergy are elected by the people.

The Governor appoints justices of the peace, and officers in the militia, which are offices of no profit and some trouble, and therefore few will accept of them unless they are much courted.

Town Meeting Democracy

Nowhere in colonial America did the freemen have a greater role in selecting their rulers than in New England. Three of the four New England colonies had charters. Those of Connecticut and Rhode Island permitted almost the equivalent of dominion status: the people were free to choose all of their local and provincial officers although a few royal officials, such as naval and customs officers, did have authority to function within the colony. The charter of Massachusetts was not quite so generous, but that colony had a somewhat greater degree of self-government than prevailed in the other royal colonies in that its own popularly elected assembly selected the governor's council.

the character of colonial politics

But what distinguished government in New England from that in the other colonies was not so much its prevalence of charters or its method of electing governors and councils as its form of local government. Only in New England were towns the basic unit of settlement; counties existed but their political functions were few. Since each town was responsible only to the general assembly, it acted as a semi-autonomous political unit. The same, perhaps, could be said of county government in some of the Southern colonies, but there the officeholders were selected by the royal governor; in New England the people annually chose their own local public servants. As the legislature of Massachusetts Bay Colony put it in 1695: "it has been a continued practice and custom in the several towns within this province, annually to chuse select-men or towns-men, for the ordering and managing of the prudential affairs of such town, and other town officers, for the executing of other matters and things in the laws appointed by them to be done and performed." Accordingly, New Englanders enjoyed an exercise of the franchise on the local level that gave a strongly democratic bent to their society.

The following selection, taken from the records of Fitchburg, Massachusetts, illustrates the extent to which the inhabitants of the New England colonies employed the franchise through town meetings, not only in the selection of local officers but also in the determination of specific issues.[4]

At a legal meeting of the freeholders and other inhabitants of the Town of Fitchburgh qualified by law to vote in town affairs on **Monday the fifth day of March A.D. 1764** at the house of Captain S[a]muel Hunts in said Fitchburgh.

The town being assembled . . . voted and chose Mr. Amos Kimball moderator and

2ly Chose Ephraim Whitney town clark

3ly Chose Messrs.
   Amos Kimball
   David Goodridge
   Samuel Hunt
   Ephraim Whitney
   Ruben Gibson
   select men for Fitchburg

4ly Chose Mr. Ephraim Kimball town treasurer

5ly Chose Messrs. John White and Thomas Dutton wardens

6ly Chose Mr. John White constable

7ly Chose Messrs.
   John Fitch
   Ebenezer Bridge
   Phinehas Steward
   Kindal Boutall
   Thomas Dutton
   survayors of highways

8ly Chose Messrs. James Pool and Joseph Spafford tything m[e]n

9ly Chose Messrs. Soloman Steward and Isaac Gibson fence v[iew]ers

10ly Chose Mr. Soloman Steward serveyor of shingles and clabords

11ly Chose Mr. Jonathan Wood a culler of hoops and staves

12ly Chose Mr. Phinehas Steward and Thomas Gary hogg-reaves

13ly Chose Messrs. William Chadwick and Silos Snow deer reavs

14ly Chose Mr. William Steward sealer of leather

---

[4] *The Old Records of the Town of Fitchburg, Massachusetts* (Fitchburg, 1898), 1:4–10.

15ly Chose Messrs. Ezra Whitney and Hezekiah Hodgkins fierwards

16ly Chose Mr. David Goodridge a seveiar of wheat

17ly Voted the annual metting be for the future on the first Mondy of March.

18ly Voted that the constable or constabls for said town for the future warn all town meetings. . . .

At a legal meeting of the free holders and other inhabitants of the Town of Fitchburgh duly qualified by law to vote in town meetings at the new dwelling house of Captain Samuel Hunts in said Fitchburgh on Monday, the 26th day of March, 1764. The town being met voted and chose Mr. David Goodridge, moderator.

2ly Voted to raise forty pounds by a rate on the inhabitants and to mend high ways and that each of the inhabitants who work at the ways be allowed four pence per hour, and one shiling and four pence per day be allowed for a yoak oxen, for a cart and plough eight pence per day each.

3ly Voted that Kendall Boutall, Ruben Gibson, and Jonathan Wood be a committee to provide a surveyor and with his assistance find the center of the town.

4ly Amos Kimball layed his acounts for servise done the town in procureing the en[c]orporation of the town and some other articles, and voted by the town to pay him thirteen pounds and nine pence in discharge of his acount.

4ly [sic] Captain Samuel Hunt laid his acount befor the town, and voted by them to pay him eight shilings and eight pence in discharge of the same.

5ly Voted to pay Mr. John Fitch one pound, two shilings, and five pence to discharge his acount.

6ly Voted to pay Ephriam Whitney one pound, one shiling, and four pence in discharge of his acount.

7ly Voted to pay Mr. Jonathan Wood fifteen shilings in discharge of his acount.

8ly Voted that the inhabitants be taxd for the same sums which shall be collected according to law.

9ly Voted that eight pounds be raised by tax on the inhabitants to defray contingent charges that may arise.

10ly Voted that the hoggs may run at large the present year. . . .

At a legal meeting of the freeholders and other inhabitants of the Town of Fitchburgh, duely qualified by law to vote in town meetings at the new dwelling house of Captain Thomas Cowdins, in said Fitchburgh on Wensday, the twelf day of Septembr, 1764. The town being meet voted and chose Amos Kimball, moderator.

2ly Voted that there be two scools in said town and that Mr. John Fitch and Kindal Boutwell and their neighborurs shall have the benifitt of their scoole money in order to provide scooling amonge them selves.

3ly Voted that eight pounds be raised in order to provide a scoole master in said town.

4ly Voted Amos Kimball, Ephraim Whitney, and Thomas Dutton be a scoole comite.

5ly Voted that Amos Kimball, Ephraim Kimball, and Thomas Dutton be a commite to provide a bueering yard in said town. . . .

At a legal meeting of the freeholders and other inhabitants of the

the character of colonial politics

Town of Fitchburgh, quallified by law to vote in town meetings at the house of Captain Thomas Cowdins, in[n] holder, in said town, on Mondy, the 26 day of Novembr, 1764.

Firstly, voted and chose David Goodridge, moderator.

2ly Voted that they will have six Sabath days preching the winter insuing.

3ly Voted that Ephriam Whitney, David Goodridge, and Ephriam Kimball be the committee to provide preching for the present.

4ly Voted that Mr. Petter Whitney and Mr. Rusell be the genttlemen the committee apply them selvs to first for preaching in said town.

5ly Voted that the meeting be adjoyrnd for one ouer.

6ly Voted that the place for seting a meeting house be in a field called Captain Thomas Cowdin's whet yard nigh Decon Amos Kimball's mills in the most convenint place therein.

7ly Voted that they will be provideing stuff for the building of a meeting house in said town.

8ly Voted that the town have the benifit of providing of all nesesarys as to timbers etc. for the building of a meetin house in said town in such maner as the commite shall think proper.

9ly Voted that it be left to the committe to say what the hight of the meeting house shall be.

10ly Voted that [D]avid Goodridge, Ephriam Whitney, and Thomas Cowdin be a committee to manage and take the care of bulding the meeting house in said town.

11ly Voted and chose Ephriam Whitney, Amos Kimball, and Ephriam Kimball a committee to agree with Captain Thomas Cowdin for a conveniant plase for to seet a meeting house in said town, even the land above voted and made choice of, and to take secuerity of the land in behalf of the town.

12ly Voted that fifty pounds be raised for the bulding of a meeting house in said town.

13ly Voted to have the preaching in Captain Thomas Cowdin's house in said town.

2. WHO WON ELECTIONS, AND HOW?

The measure of a system of government can be taken in a number of ways. One is the size and character of its electorate; another is the range and character of its officeholders. Many societies throughout history have boasted of large electorates but have in fact limited the choice open to the voters to insignificant distinctions of background, economic status, or party affiliation. On the other hand, modern democracies rarely restrict the choice of the voters except to insist that candidates for office meet certain minimum standards of age and residence. Yet even democratic societies seldom pick true cross-sections of their own population, for most voters believe that the requirements of office call for something above the average in education (though not necessarily formal), intelligence, and training.

The pattern in colonial America was varied. Most colonies established a property qualification for officeholders, and although it was usually higher than the suffrage requirement, it was rarely high enough to disbar a significant portion of the citizenry. At the same time, the political life of the colonies seemed strongly dominated by members of the upper classes. The Virginia aristocracy may not have been as solid and as firmly entrenched as we once believed, but there is no doubt that certain Virginia families held disproportionate power in the Old Dominion. The electorate may have wanted it that way, as in more modern times it has often preferred to keep certain families in high office. More important is the extent to which the voter had a viable choice. Did he, in fact, freely choose the Livingstons, Lees, Hutchinsons, and Olivers, or did he take them in grudging preference to other entrenched families? Or, to phrase the problem somewhat differently, did deeply ingrained habits of deferring to one's social superiors largely offset the democratic potential of a broad electorate?

A question of this kind is difficult to answer, for there is little evidence on the political motives of the bulk of the voters. The readings that follow will, however, suggest the complexity and diversity of the problem of judging the composition of the officeholding class, and the methods by which it achieved positions of public trust.

Patterns of Voter Response

By studying the men who won election to colonial offices, historians of early American politics have been able to draw some tentative conclusions about the voting patterns of eighteenth-century Americans. Not all scholars read the results in the same light, however. Robert E. and Katherine Brown, for example, see more of the democratic impulse and less of the deferential in their studies of Massachusetts and Virginia than does Jackson Turner Main. The following excerpt is taken from a recent article in which Professor Main summarizes his findings.[5]

Truly democratic ideas, defending a concentration of power in the hands of the people, are difficult to find prior to about 1774. Most articulate colonials accepted the Whig theory in which a modicum of democracy was balanced by equal parts of aristocracy and monarchy. An unchecked democracy was uniformly

---
[5] Jackson T. Main, "Government by the People: The American Revolution and the Democratization of the Legislature," *William and Mary Quarterly*, third series, 23 (1966), 391–97.

condemned. For example, a contributor to the *Newport Mercury* in 1764 felt that when a state was in its infancy, "when its members are few and virtuous, and united together by some peculiar ideas of freedom or religion; the whole power may be lodged with the people, and the government be purely democratical"; but when the state had matured, power must be removed from popular control because history demonstrated that the people "have been incapable, collectively, of acting with any degree of moderation or wisdom." Therefore while colonial theorists recognized the need for some democratic element in the government, they did not intend that the ordinary people—the *demos*—should participate. The poorer men were not allowed to vote at all, and that part of the populace which did vote was expected to elect the better sort of people to represent them. "Fabricus" defended the "democratic principle," warned that "liberty, when once lost, is scarce ever recovered," and declared that laws were "made for the people, and not people for the laws." But he did not propose that ordinary citizens should govern. Rather, "it is right that men of *birth and fortune,* in every government that is free, should be invested with power, and enjoy higher honours than the people." According to William Smith of New York, offices should be held by "the better Class of People" in order that they might introduce that "Spirit of Subordination essential to good Government." A Marylander urged that members of the Assembly should be "ABLE in ESTATE, ABLE in KNOWLEDGE AND LEARNING," and mourned that so many "little upstart insignificant Pretenders" tried to obtain an office. "The *Creature* that is able to keep a little Shop, rate the Price of an Ell of Osnabrigs, or, at most, to judge of the Quality of a Leaf of Tobacco" was not a fit statesman, regardless of his own opinion. So also in South Carolina, where William Henry Drayton warned the artisans that mechanical ability did not entitle them to hold office. This conviction that most men were incompetent to rule, and that the elite should govern for them, proved a vital element in Whig thought and was its most antidemocratic quality. The assumption was almost never openly challenged during the colonial period.

Whether the majority whose capacity was thus maligned accepted the insulting assumption is another question. They were not asked, and as they were unable to speak or write on the subject, their opinions are uncertain. But the voters themselves seem to have adhered, in practice at least, to the traditional view, for when the people were asked to choose their representatives they seldom elected common farmers and artisans. Instead they put their trust in men of the upper class. In the colonies as a whole, about 30 per cent of the adult white men owned property worth £500 or more. About two thirds of these colonials of means had property worth £500 to £2,000; their economic status is here called *moderate*. The other third were worth over £2,000. Those worth £2,000 to £5,000 are called *well-to-do*, and those whose property was valued at more than £5,000 are called *wealthy*. The overwhelming majority of the representatives belonged to that ten per cent who were well-to-do or wealthy. Government may have been for the people, but it was not administered by them. For evidence we turn to the legislatures of New Hampshire, New York, New Jersey, Maryland, Virginia, and South Carolina.

In 1765 New Hampshire elected thirty-four men to its House of Representatives. Practically all of them lived within a few miles of the coast; the frontier settlements could not yet send deputies, and the Merrimack Valley towns in the south-central part of the colony, though populous, were allotted only seven. New Hampshire was not a rich colony. Most of its inhabitants were small farmers with property enough for an adequate living but no more. There were a few large agricultural estates, and the Portsmouth area had developed a prosperous commerce which supported some wealthy merchants and professional men; but judging from probate records not more than one man in forty was well-to-do, and true wealth was very rare. Merchants, professional men, and the like comprised about one tenth of the total population, though in Portsmouth, obviously, the proportion was much larger. Probably at least two thirds of the inhabitants were farmers or farm laborers and one in ten was an artisan. But New Hampshire voters did not call on farmers or men of average property to represent them. Only about one third of the representatives in the 1765 House were yeomen. Merchants and lawyers were just as numerous, and the rest followed a variety of occupations: there were four doctors and several millers and manufacturers. One third of the delegates were wealthy men and more than two thirds were at least well-to-do. The relatively small upper class of the colony, concentrated in the southeast, furnished ten of the members. They did not, of course, constitute a majority, and the family background of most of the representatives, like that of most colonials, was undistinguished. Probably nearly one half had acquired more property and prestige than their parents. In another age New Hampshire's lower house would have been considered democratic—compared with England's House of Commons it certainly was—but this was a new society, and the voters preferred the prosperous urban upper class and the more substantial farmers.

New York was a much richer colony than New Hampshire. Although most of its population were small farmers and tenants, there were many large landed estates and New York City was incomparably wealthier than Portsmouth. In general the west bank of the Hudson and the northern frontier were usually controlled by the yeomanry, as was Suffolk County on Long Island, but the east bank from Albany to the City was dominated by great "manor lords" and merchants. The great landowners and the merchants held almost all of the twenty-eight seats in the Assembly. In 1769 the voters elected only seven farmers. Five others, including Frederick Philipse and Pierre Van Cortland, the wealthy manor lords from Westchester, were owners of large tenanted estates. But a majority of New York's legislators were townspeople. Merchants were almost as numerous as farmers, and together with lawyers they furnished

the character of colonial politics

one half of the membership. The legislators were no more representative in their property than in their occupation. At most, five men, and probably fewer, belonged to the middle class of moderate means. At least 43 per cent were wealthy and an equal number were well-to-do. The members' social background was also exceptional. Ten came from the colony's foremost families who had, for the times, a distinguished ancestry, and two thirds or more were born of well-to-do parents. Taken as a whole the legislators, far from reflecting New York's social structure, had either always belonged to or had successfully entered the colony's economic and social upper class.

New Jersey's Assembly was even smaller than that of New York. The body chosen in 1761, and which sat until 1769, contained but twenty men. Half of these represented the East Jersey counties (near New York City) which were in general occupied by small farmers, but only three of the ten members came from that class. The others were merchants, lawyers, and large proprietors. Although several of these had started as yeomen they had all acquired large properties. West Jersey, which had a greater number of sizable landed estates, especially in the Delaware Valley region, sent the same sort of men as did East Jersey: three farmers, an equal number of large landowners, and an even larger number of prosperous townsmen, some of whom also owned valuable real estate. Merchants and lawyers made up one half of the membership. As usual, a considerable proportion—perhaps forty per cent—were self-made men, but the colony's prominent old families furnished at least 30 per cent of the representatives. Four out of five members were either well-to-do or wealthy.

In contrast to the legislatures of New Hampshire, New York, and New Jersey, Maryland's House of Delegates was a large body and one dominated by the agricultural interest. Like its northern equivalents, however, its members belonged to the upper class of the colony—in Maryland, the planter aristocracy. The 1765 House supposedly contained over sixty members, but only fifty-four appear in the records. About one half of these came from the Eastern Shore, an almost entirely rural area. Except for Col. Thomas Cresap who lived on Maryland's small frontier, the remainder came from the Potomac River and western Chesapeake Bay counties, where agriculture was the principal occupation but where a number of towns also existed. About one sixth of the Delegates belonged to the yeoman farmer class. Most of these lived on the Eastern Shore. Incidentally, they did not vote with the antiproprietary, or "popular," party, but rather followed some of the great planters in the conservative "court" party. As in the northern colonies, a number of the Delegates were *nouveaux riches,* but in Maryland's stable and primarily "Tidewater" society, fewer than one fifth had surpassed their parents in wealth. The overwhelming majority came from the lesser or the great planter class, and probably one third belonged to the colony's elite families. Four fifths were well-to-do or wealthy. Lawyers and merchants (among whom were several of the self-made men) furnished about one sixth of the principally rural membership.

Virginia's Burgesses resembled Maryland's Delegates, but they were even richer and of even more distinguished ancestry. The Old Dominion's much larger west helped to make the House of Burgesses twice as large a body, with 122 members in 1773. Small property holders, though they formed a great majority of the voters, held only one out of six seats. Half of the Burgesses were wealthy and four fifths were at least well-to-do. Merchants and lawyers contributed one fifth of the members, much more than their proper share, but most of them were also large landholders and the legislature was firmly in control of the great planters. Indeed the median property owned was 1,800 acres and 40 slaves. Virginia's social structure was quite fluid, especially in the newly settled areas, but between five sixths and seven eighths of the delegates had inherited their property. A roll call of the Burgesses would recite the names of most of the colony's elite families, who held nearly one half of the seats.

The planters of South Carolina, unlike the Virginians, were unwilling to grant representation to the upcountry, and its House of Commons was an exclusively eastern body. The colony was newer and its society may have been more fluid, for in 1765 between 20 and 40 per cent of the representatives were self-made men. The legislature also differed from its southern equivalents in Maryland and Virginia in that nearly half of its members were merchants, lawyers, or doctors. But these figures are deceptive, for in reality most of these men were also great landowners, as were almost all of the representatives; and prominent old families contributed one half of the members of the House. All were at least well-to-do and over two thirds were wealthy. The rich planters of South Carolina's coastal parishes held a monopoly of power in the Assembly.

These six legislatures, from New Hampshire to South Carolina, shared the same qualities. Although farmers and artisans comprised probably between two thirds and three fourths of the voters in the six colonies, they seldom selected men from their own ranks to represent them. Not more than one out of five representatives were of that class. Fully one third were merchants and lawyers or other professionals, and most of the rest were large landowners. Although only about 10 per cent of the colonials were well-to-do or wealthy, this economic elite furnished at least 85 per cent of the assemblymen. The mobile character of colonial society meant that perhaps 30 per cent had achieved their high status by their own efforts; but an even larger percentage were from prominent, long-established families.

Swilling the Planters with Bumbo

In any system in which offices are filled by the choice of the people, the techniques by which candidates woo the voter and earn his support are not tangential but central to the political process. The following selection from

the character of colonial politics

Charles S. Sydnor's little classic, *Gentlemen Freeholders,* describes the methods by which candidates to the Virginia House of Burgesses won their seats.[6]

It would be pleasant to think that voters were good and wise in the bright, beginning days of the American nation; that in Jefferson's Arcadia, to use a popular euphemism, the sturdy, incorruptible freeholders assembled when occasion demanded and, with an eye only to the public good and their own safety, chose the best and ablest of their number to represent them in the Assembly. It is true that the voters of early Virginia chose their representatives and that often they chose remarkably well; but it is an error to think that the voters were the only positive active force at work in elections. For good or ill, the candidates and their friends also played an important part by using many forms of persuasion and pressure upon the voters.

A play called *The Candidates; or the Humours of a Virginia Election,* written about 1770 by Colonel Robert Munford of Mecklenburg County, Virginia, provides valuable insight into the part played by candidates in the elections of eighteenth-century Virginia. In this play one of the former delegates to the Assembly, Worthy by name, has decided not to stand for reelection. The other, Wou'dbe, offers himself once more "to the humours of a fickle croud," though with reluctance, asking himself: "Must I again resign my reason, and be nought but what each voter pleases? Must I cajole, fawn, and wheedle, for a place that brings so little profit?" The second candidate, Sir John Toddy, "an honest blockhead," with no ability except in consuming liquor and no political strength except his readiness to drink with the poor man as freely as with the rich, looks for support among the plain people who like him because he "wont turn his back upon a poor man, but will take a chearful cup with one as well as another." Scorned by the leading men of the county, the other two candidates, Smallhopes and Strutabout, a vain, showy fellow, are adept in the low arts of winning the support of ignorant men.

Each of these candidates had some influence, following, or support which, in the language of that day, was known as his interest. It was common practice at this time for two candidates to join interests, as the phrase went, in hopes that each could get the support of the friends of the other. When Sir John suggests to Wou'dbe a joining of interests by asking him "to speak a good word for me among the people," Wou'dbe refuses and tells him plainly, "I'll speak a good word to you and advise you to decline" to run. Because Wou'dbe could not, from principle, join interests with any one of the three other candidates, he loses votes by affronting first one and then another of them. Just in the nick of time, Wou'dbe's colleague Worthy

---

[6] Charles S. Sydnor, *Gentlemen Freeholders: Political Practices in Washington's Virginia* (Chapel Hill, N.C., 1952), 39–59. Reprinted by permission of the University of North Carolina Press.

descends from the upper reaches of respectability and greatness to save Wou'dbe from defeat and political virtue from ruin. With stilted phrase Worthy denounces "the scoundrels who opposed us last election" and directs Wou'dbe to "speak this to the people, and let them know I intend to stand a poll." The good men of the county rally to the side of righteousness; Sir John (between alcoholic hiccoughs) announces "I'm not so fitten" as "Mr. Worthy and Mr. Wou'dbe"; Strutabout and Smallhopes looking as doleful as thieves upon the gallows, are ignominiously defeated; and Worthy and Wou'dbe are triumphantly reelected.

Among the more important of the unwritten rules of eighteenth-century Virginia politics, a rule which the candidates and their advisers often mentioned was the necessity for candidates to be present at the elections. Judge Joseph Jones, out of his ripe experience, wrote in 1785 to his young nephew James Monroe, "respecting your offering your service for the County the coming year, . . it would be indispensably necessary you should be in the County before the election and attend it when made." In 1758 several of Washington's friends wrote him to "come down" from Fort Cumberland, where he was on duty with his troops, "and show your face" in Frederick County where he was a candidate for burgess. One of his supporters warned him that "you being elected absolutely depends on your presence." Thanks to the hard work of his friends and the patriotic circumstances of his absence, Washington was elected, but it is evident that the absence of a candidate from the county before and during the taking of the poll was regarded as a distinct handicap. . . .

A sharp distinction must be made between election-day and pre-election behavior of the candidate toward the voter. The code of the times required that in the days before the election the candidate maintain a dignified aloofness from the voters; however, this rule was broken perhaps as often as it was observed. The tipsy Sir John Toddy, in *the Candidates,* assisted by his henchman Guzzle, tries unabashedly to work himself into the good graces of three freeholders named Prize, Twist, and Stern. As they and their wives are sitting on a rail fence, with other freeholders standing about, Sir John comes up to the group. At his shoulder stands Guzzle to whisper the names of the prospective voters to him.

Sir John. Gentlemen and ladies, your servant, hah! my old friend Prize, how goes it? how does your wife and children do?

Sarah. At your service, sir *(making a low courtsey.)*

Prize. How the devil come he to know me so well, and never spoke to me before in his life? *(aside.)*

Guzzle. (whispering to Sir John) Dick Stern.

Sir John. Hah! Mr. Stern, I'm proud to see you; I hope your family are well; how many children? does the good women keep to the old stroke?

Catharine. Yes, an't please your honour, I hope my lady's well, with your honour.

Sir John. At your service, madam.

Guzzle. (whispering [to] Sir John) Roger Twist.

Sir John. Hah! Mr. Roger Twist! your servant, sir. I hope your wife and children are well.

Twist. There's my wife. I have no children, at your service. . . .

the character of colonial politics

James Madison in his old age recalled that when he entered politics it was "the usage for the candidates to recommend themselves to the voters . . . by personal solicitation." Madison thoroughly disliked this practice. Shortly before the election of representatives to the first Congress of the United States he wrote from Philadelphia to George Washington:

I am pressed much in several quarters to try the effect of presence on the district into which I fall, for electing a Representative; and am apprehensive that an omission of that expedient, may eventually expose me to blame. At the same time I have an extreme distrust to steps having an electioneering appearance, altho' they should lead to an appointment in which I am disposed to serve the public; and am very dubious moreover whether any step which might seem to denote a solicitude on my part would not be as likely to operate against as in favor of my pretensions.

Colonel Landon Carter, writing in 1776, said that he had once been "turned out of the H. of B." because "I did not familiarize myself among the People," whereas he well remembered his "son's going amongst them and carrying his Election." The contrasting experiences of father and son suggest that going among the people was important to get a man elected. However, the son, Robert Wormeley Carter, lost his seat in an election in Richmond County in 1776 even though, according to his father, he had "kissed the —— of the people, and very seriously accommodated himself to others." With mounting anger the Colonel wrote: "I do suppose such a Circumstance cannot be parallelled, but it is the nature of Popularity. She, I long discovered to be an adultress of the first order." . . .

Many of the candidates may have been perfectly circumspect in their preelection behavior, but all of them, with hardly an exception, relied on the persuasive powers of food and drink dispensed to the voters with openhanded liberality. Theoderick Bland, Jr., once wrote with apparent scorn that "Our friend, Mr. Banister, has been very much ingaged ever since the dissolution of the assembly, in swilling the planters with bumbo." When he supplied the voters with liquor, Banister was in good company; it included Washington, Jefferson, and John Marshall.

The favorite beverage was rum punch. Cookies and ginger cakes were often provided, and occasionally there was a barbecued bullock and several hogs. The most munificent as well as democratic kind of treat was a public occasion, a sort of picnic, to which the freeholders in general were invited. George Washington paid the bills for another kind of treat in connection with his Fairfax County campaigns for a seat in the House of Burgesses. It consisted of a supper and ball on the night of the election, replete with fiddler, "Sundries etc." On at least one occasion he shared the cost of the ball with one or more persons, perhaps with the other successful candidate, for his memorandum of expenses closes with the words: "by Cash paid Captn. Dalton for my part of ye Expense at the Election Ball. £8.5.6." . . .

It was a common practice for candidates to keep open house for the freeholders on their way to the election, and it is a marvel where space was found for all to sleep.

When Littlepage heard that some of the voters who lived more than twenty-five miles from the courthouse were unwilling to ride so far in cold weather, he invited them to call at his house which was about five miles from the courthouse. Some ten of them came and were hospitably entertained, "though their entertainment was not more than was usual with him." Some of the company "were pretty merry with Liquor when they came" to his home. That evening "they chiefly drank Cider." "Some of them drank Drams in the Morning, and went merry to the Court House."

Candidates frequently arranged for treats to be given in their names by someone else. Lieutenant Charles Smith managed this business for George Washington during a campaign in Frederick County in 1758. Two days after the election, which Washington had not been able to attend, Smith sent him receipts for itemized accounts that he had paid to five persons who had supplied refreshments for the voters. . . .

On election day the flow of liquor reached high tide. Douglas S. Freeman calculated that during a July election day in Frederick County in the year 1758, George Washington's agent supplied 160 gallons to 391 voters and "unnumbered hangers-on." This amounted to more than a quart and a half a voter. An itemized list of the refreshments included 28 gallons of rum, 50 gallons of rum punch, 34 gallons of wine, 46 gallons of beer, and 2 gallons of cider royal. . . .

To avoid the reality as well as the appearance of corruption, the candidates usually made a point of having it understood that the refreshments were equally free to men of every political opinion. If a candidate's campaign was under investigation, it was much in his favor if he could show that among his guests were some who had clearly said that they did not intend to vote for him. Washington reflected an acceptable attitude when he wrote while arranging for the payment of large bills for liquor consumed during a Frederick County election: "I hope no Exception were taken to any that voted against me but that all were alike treated and all had enough; it is what I much desir'd." Washington seems to have followed this policy in subsequent elections. A young Englishman, who witnessed an election at Alexandria in 1774 when Washington was one of the two successful candidates, wrote:

The Candidates gave the populace a Hogshead of Toddy (what we call Punch in England). In the evening the returned Member gave a Ball to the Freeholders and Gentlemen of the town. This was conducted with great harmony. Coffee and Chocolate, but no Tea. This Herb is in disgrace among them at present.

Bountiful supplies of free liquor were responsible for much rowdiness, fighting, and drunkenness, but the fun and excitement of an election and the prospect of plentiful refreshments of the kind customarily consumed in that day helped to bring the voters to the polls. Thus in a perverse kind of way treating made something of a contribution to eighteenth-century democracy. Although one sometimes found a man who lived by the rule, "never to taste of a man's liquor unless I'm his friend," most of the voters accepted such refreshments as were offered. As they drank, they were less likely to feel that they were incurring obligations than that the candidate was fulfilling his obligation. According to the thinking of that day, the candidate ought to provide refreshments for the freeholders. His failure to fulfill this obligation would be interpreted as a sign of "pride or parsimony," as a "want of respect" for the voters, as James Madison found to his sorrow. . . .

Encroachments on Voter Independence

Probably no system of electoral politics can be totally free from corruption. This holds particularly true in the absence of secret ballots where the voter becomes vulnerable to reprisals as well as to the lure of bribes. Although most of the British Colonies adopted some form of secret ballot early in the eighteenth century, New York held out to the eve of the Revolution. The following list of charges against a candidate in 1768 reflects the variety of pressures to which a voter could be subjected.[7]

Charges Against Mr. Scott

1. To prove Mr. Scott offered George Clark a Taylor Money to take up his Freedom on Condition he would Vote for him and that he had favored him greatly in taking less Fees than was usual on the Account of his promising to Vote for him. . . .
2. To Prove some short Time before the Election Mr. Scott was at a Meeting with some Journeymen Carpenters Solliciting Votes and that he offered to give Money to their Box that they then refused it, but that he has given it since. . . .
3. To prove Mr. Scott sent up to Pumpton etc. to bring down Voters at 6/. per Day etc. . . .
4. To prove that Mr. Scott offered to give at his Expence to John Walters a Certificate of his Freedom if he would Vote for him. . . .
5. To prove Mr. Scott has in Solliciting Votes declared that he & Mr. Jauncey were in one Interest. . . .
6. To prove Thomas White had a Canoe offered him to Vote for Mr. Scott. . . .
7. To prove that Teunis Ryerson was offered a half Joe to Vote for Mr. Scott. . . .
8. To prove John Deboe a Hatter was offered to have his Deed made good in the Square if he would Vote for Mr. Scott & leave Mr. Jauncey out. . . .
9. To prove ———— offered one Crum a Carman a Dollar to Vote for Mr. Scott and that he refused it. . . .
10. To Prove that John Parsells of Long Island said he would not have Voted for Mr. Scott if he had not been paid for it. . . .
11. To Prove That one Colegrove a Hatter was threatened to be sued if he would not Vote for Scott. . . .
12. That William Young had a Quarters Rent forgiven him to Vote for Scott. . . .

---

[7] From the Duane Papers. Courtesy of the New York Historical Society.

3. ROYAL GOVERNMENT IN AMERICA

While much of the structure of American colonial politics was under the immediate control of the people, much was not. In royal colonies the governor, councillors (except in Massachusetts), and a host of minor placemen owed their appointments directly or indirectly to the crown. And in proprietary and corporate colonies, the long arm of royal authority could also be felt: naval officers, customs officers, surveyors of the King's woods, and numerous other functionaries reminded the colonist that he was a subject of the English monarch. A list of all the royal officials who served in America and of those who were in turn appointed by them would equal if it did not exceed a similar list of elected officials. Inevitably the character of colonial politics was shaped as much by the relationship within the empire as it was by the institutions of self-government.

At the same time it is clear that royal government, like provincial and local self-government, was not static. As the colonies grew in population and sophistication, royal authority increasingly found itself struggling against the determined men and institutions of elected government. Although the clash did not become critical until the 1760s, it had been making headway since the beginning of the century, and in some areas even earlier. The complaints of royal agents at all levels of the colonial service show clearly that those who labored for the crown had no easy task. In particular, the colonial assemblies, under the belief that they had inherited all of the prerogatives of Parliament, encroached upon the jurisdiction of governors, customs agents, and even the Privy Council. It is difficult, then, to measure with any surety the functions and powers of royal government in America. Yet an important part of judging the nature of colonial politics lies in evaluating the role and the effectiveness of royal authority in the American colonies. While the readings that follow deal only with the character and problems of royal governors, it should be borne in mind that lesser crown officials had parallel qualifications and parallel problems.

His Excellency, the Captain General and Governor-in-Chief

In all but four of the thirteen colonies that later became the United States, the chief executive officer received his appointment from the crown. Nominations usually came from the Secretary of State for the Southern Department or the Board of Trade, while final decisions lay with the King's Privy Council. The

the character of colonial politics

commission delivered to a new governor carefully spelled out his duties and the limits of his authority; armed with this document and with a set of confidential instructions the royal governor, designated usually as "Captain General and Governor-in-Chief" set sail for America—unless he happened to be one of the few native Americans who received gubernatorial appointments.

The character, background, and ability of the royal chief magistrates has long been open to debate. Since 1930, however, the standard account of the men who filled colonial governorships has been Leonard Woods Labaree's *Royal Government in America*, from which the following selection is taken.[8]

The royal governor was the most important agent of the home government in the administration of the colonies. His office was twofold in character, since he was both the guiding head of a local government and the central link in the chain which bound the colony politically to the mother country. He had, therefore, to hold in a nice balance the frequently dissimilar interests and needs of the two peoples. His was a task for no mere placeman. The problems which confronted an incumbent of the office were often perplexing enough to demand statesmanship of a high order. Writers on colonial history have often maintained that honesty, disinterestedness, and real political ability were seldom if ever found in the persons of the various royal appointees. Such a statement, however, cannot be reconciled with the facts. Bearing in mind the nature of the governorship, the frequently inadequate financial return, and the eighteenth-century idea that political office was a property right, one is rather led to wonder at the comparatively high quality of the men appointed. The British officials were more successful than might be expected in finding suitable men to fill these posts which required the exchange of the comforts of English life for the ruder, less cultured, more primitive society of a colonial capital, and in which the governor faced the almost certain prospect of a series of quarrels with a hostile assembly, should he fulfill his whole duty to the crown.

The men who were appointed to colonial governorships may be broadly divided into three groups. One included provincials—men who by birth or long residence in America had become familiar with colonial institutions and colonial problems and whose sincere attachment to the crown had been shown, often by years of devoted service. Many such appointments were in the nature of promotions. After holding office for years as a member of the governor's council, a man might advance to the senior position on the board, in which post, or through later appointment as lieutenant governor, he might temporarily administer the colony during the absence of the governor. Loyalty and ability proven by such service were more than once rewarded with appointment to the governorship of the same or some other province.

---

[8] Leonard Woods Labaree, *Royal Government in America: A Study of the British Colonial System Before 1783* (New Haven, 1930), 37–44. Reprinted by permission of the author; all rights reserved.

Such names as those of Christopher Codrington, Jr., governor of the Leeward Islands, and Sir Henry Moore, governor of New York, stand out among those of Americans who proved by the general success of their administrations the wisdom of their appointment from the colonial training school. But with other native governors, such as Thomas Hutchinson of Massachusetts Bay and Lewis Morris of New Jersey, their American background and earlier political associations were in themselves additional causes for antagonism and misunderstanding when duty forced the governors to oppose their fellow colonists.

A second group of colonial governors was composed of men who were primarily military or naval officers, who often held positions of civil authority chiefly to enable them better to maintain their military leadership or to repay them financially for the often unwelcome assignment of an American command. Throughout the troubled period of the Seven Years' War the governorship of Virginia was held in succession by two of the commanders in chief in America, the Earl of Loudoun and Sir Jeffrey Amherst. The only reason given by the Board of Trade for recommending Amherst's appointment was that it was "necessary and expedient" for the royal service that the commander in chief of his Majesty's forces in America be made governor of Virginia. Neither Loudoun nor Amherst ever exercised direct control of the civil government of Virginia, both of them leaving the colony in the hands of the lieutenant governor and simply drawing their share of the salary and perquisites of the office. Sometimes naval officers were appointed as governors or lieutenant governors of provinces which were strategically important. Four such men held office in Jamaica and the same number administered the affairs of Nova Scotia. In addition to such men a number of governors or lieutenant governors could be named whose chief service was in connection with the long series of wars which marked the colonial period. The civil administrations of these men were largely incidental to their military commands, or, more frequently, followed afterward as rewards for services rendered. . . .

But by no means all of those with previous service in the army or navy were appointed to colonial office primarily for military reasons. In a period marked by frequent wars, many officers naturally had been in the armed forces of Great Britain at some time in their careers. In fact, as far as accurate information can be had, about one half of the governors and lieutenant governors of the royal provinces appointed before 1783 had at one time or another held commissions in the army or navy. The service they had rendered might vary in extent and importance from that of the earl of Dunmore who had been a junior officer in the Third Footguards for three years during his young-manhood, to that of Guy Carleton, who began his military career in 1742, served in America throughout the Seven Years' War and in the American Revolution, rose through the various ranks to lieutenant general in 1777 and general in 1783, and was elevated to the peerage as Lord Dorchester in 1786. Nearly one half of these military officers held the rank of colonel or lieutenant colonel during their civil administrations. Military titles were very common among the royal governors.

The third and by far the largest group of governors was composed of Englishmen who owed their appointments to political connections at home. Many of the men with military histories actually belong in this category. The group was very largely made up of typical members of the officeholding class in England, neither better nor worse than the men who were carrying on the real administration of the mother country. Practically all such men viewed political office as a property right rather than as a public trust. Most of them looked upon the opportunity to head an American government as merely one step in the forward progress of their political or financial ambitions. Many men desired the governorship because it seemed to offer great money-making opportunities. Often such men's hopes were doomed to disappointment, especially in the smaller continental provinces where the salary was anything but munificent and the perquisites of office amounted to little. In other cases, especially when the individual was not too scrupulous in his methods of acquiring wealth, his hopes were better justified. A shrewd governor might build up a comfortable fortune through illegal trade, the operations of privateers, or the granting of improperly large tracts of land to himself and his friends. In the larger West India islands the salaries and other rewards of office were higher than in most of the continental colonies. The governorship of either Jamaica, Barbados, or the Leeward Islands was therefore considered a more desirable position than that of any other province, with the possible exception of Virginia. But in most of the royal colonies the real profits were quite uncertain.

The general level of those who were appointed to colonial governorships was relatively high. There were those, of course, who through unworthy motives or actions incurred the hatred of the colonists and whose names served as a reproach for years to follow. Such a man was Lord Cornbury, scion of the great house of Clarendon, whose peculations from the treasury of New York led the colonists to distrust the governors of the province for the next half century and thereby profoundly affected New York's political history. Such again was Daniel Parke of the Leeward Islands, who, in spite of a laudable personal courage, was attacked and killed by inhabitants of Antigua who had been embittered by the severity of his rule and the immorality of his private life. Against such names, however, must be placed those of men like Robert Hunter, who throughout his controversies with the New York assembly retained the friendship and esteem of its members and who later secured from the Jamaica assembly legislation which none of his predecessors had been able to obtain; Henry Grenville of Barbados, whose statue was erected at public expense in the town hall of Bridgetown upon his departure from the island; and Thomas Pownall, whose subsequent writings show him to have been one of the fairest and most discerning Englishmen to come in contact with the colonies. In general, the governors appointed by the crown compare not unfavorably in honesty and ability with the men now elected by the people of the several states of the union.

Of the slightly more than three hundred governors general, governors, lieutenant governors, and deputy governors appointed by the crown for the English colonies during the period from 1624 to 1783, approximately one in every four was a peer or the son of a peer or belonged to one of the lesser titled classes. Forty-five of the total had gained political experience as members of the House of Commons at Westminster prior to their appointment, and nine others entered parliament after their return from America. Forty-eight had matriculated at Oxford or Cambridge or at some other university or college in the British Isles, America, or the European continent. More than a score had been admitted to one or another of the Inns of Court. The Royal Society included fifteen governors in its membership. This group constituted a true cross-section of the British governing classes and was composed of men in every way characteristic of those who held office in Great Britain itself during this period. Those who criticize the British government for the sort of men sent over as provincial governors, should first become familiar with the types of those who filled the offices of equal standing in the mother country during the same period.

The Perils of Office

Despite the theoretical extent of his authority, a royal governor's best hope lay in his own ability tactfully to compromise the demands of the crown with the persistence of the provincial assembly. Many a new governor, even one such as Thomas Hutchinson who could claim a long American lineage, discovered that the instructions he was honor-bound to carry out were totally incompatible with the wishes of the people's representatives. The reading below comes from a report to the King by Governor Samuel Shute of Massachusetts.[9]

[Upon arrival in the Massachusetts Bay in October 1716] I soon called the General Assembly together. I found the House of Representatives, who are chosen annually, possessed of all the same powers of the House of Commons, and of much greater, they having the power of nominating once a year the persons that constitute your Majesty's Council, etc., and giving the salary of the governor and lieutenant-governor but from six months to six months; and likewise giving such only as is no way suitable to the rank of your Majesty's governor and lieutenant-governor, or to the known abilitys of the province, and this notwithstanding your Majesty's instruc-

---

[9] *Calendar of State Papers, Colonial Series, America and West Indies, 1722–1723* (London, 1934), 324–30. Reprinted by permission of the Controller of Her Britannic Majesty's Stationery Office.

tions. . . . The said House likewise appoint the salary of the treasurer every year whereby they have in effect the sole authority over that important office, which they often use in order to intimidate the treasurer from obeying the proper orders for issuing money; if such orders are not agreeable to their views and inclinations. By all which means the House of Representatives are in a manner the whole legislative, and in a good measure the executive power of the province. This House consists of about one hundred, who by an act of Assembly must be persons residing in the respective towns which they represent: whereby it happens that the greatest part of them are of small fortunes and mean education; men of the best sense and circumstances generally residing in or near Boston; so that by the artifice of a few designing members, together with the insinuations of some people in the town of Boston, the country representatives are easily made to believe that the House is barely supporting the privileges of the people, whilst they are invading the undoubted prerogatives of the Crown. Were it not for this act, the Assembly would certainly consist of men of much better sense, temper, and fortune than they do at present. The Assembly usually sit at Boston, the capital of this province, a large and populous town supposed to contain about 18,000 inhabitants, under no magistracy, by the want of which many of the inhabitants become too much disposed to a levelling spirit, too apt to be mutinous and disorderly, and to support the House of Representatives in any stepps they take towards encroaching on the prerogative of the Crown. That this is too much the prevailing temper in the majority of the inhabitants of this town is plain from hence, that if I have at any time, according to the known power vested in your Majesty's governor of that province, with the strongest reasons, given my negative to any person nominated to be of your Majesty's Council there, the said town have hardly ever failed to choose him their representative. Three negatived councellors are the present representatives of the town of Boston. This practice is so notoriously known and justified that it is a common maxim that a negatived councellor makes a good representative. The House of Representatives thus constituted and abetted, notwithstanding the many uncommon privileges they enjoy by virtue of their charter, far from being contented therewith, have for some years last past been making attempts upon the few prerogatives that have been reserved to the Crown; which for that reason, as well as from the obligation of my oath and the trust reposed in me by your Majesty, I have endeavoured to my utmost to maintain against all invasions whatsoever.

I would humbly beg leave to lay before your Majesty some instances in which they have endeavoured to wrest those prerogatives out of your royal hands. (1) The House of Representatives have denied your Majesty's right to the woods in the province of Main, contrary to the reservations in their charter, to an act of Parliament of Great Britain, and the instructions I received from your Majesty, etc. The said House having received an account of a great quantity of trees that were felled, and cutt into loggs in the county of York, many of them fit for masting the royal navy, voted that a committee of that House should be joyned with a committee of the Council to make inquiry into that affair, and to dispose of those loggs for the use of the province. To which the Council, at my instance, made the following amendment, viz., "saving to his Majesty his right." But the House of Representatives refused to agree to that amendment. After which, without either my consent or the Council's, they sent a committee of their own with orders to dispose of the said loggs for the use of the province. (2) The House of Representatives would have refused me the power of a negative on the choice of their Speaker, which I thought it necessary to make use of against Mr. Cooke when he was chosen to that office, he having publickly opposed your Majesty's known rights to those woods. And the said House, insisting on their choice notwithstanding the negative I had given it, I dissolved that Assembly and then made a representation of the whole matter to the right honorable, the Lords of Trade etc., who sent me the opinion of your Majesty's Attorney-General, that the power was vested in your Majesty's governor for the time being. And when they acquainted me at the next meeting of the House of Representatives by a message, that they had chosen Mr. Clarke for their Speaker, and I had returned them for answer that I approved their said choice, the House of Representatives sent me this message, viz., "that they did not send up the foregoing message for my approbation, but for my information only," and since that time, whenever the Speaker has been absent by sickness, or otherwise, they have never failed to choose the said Mr. Cooke Speaker *pro tempore*. (3) The House of Representatives voted a publick fast throughout your Majesty's said province, a thing never attempted by any of their predecessors; it being very well known that the power was always vested in and exercised by your Majesty's governor in that and all other colonies in America. (4) Though the royal charter has vested in the governor only the power of proroguing the General Assembly, yet the House of Representatives sent up a vote to the Council adjourning the General Assembly to the town of Cambridge; to which I refused to give my assent, and yet after this they adjourned themselves for several days without my consent or privity, and did not meet me on the day to which I had adjourned the General Assembly. (5) I had hoped that the House of Representatives, upon making due reflection on the several attempts they had unwarrantably made against these, your Majesty's undoubted prerogatives, and the constant opposition they had met with from me therein, would have desisted from any further attempts of this kind. But to my great surprize they have endeavored to wrest the sword out of your royal hands, as will appear by the following instances. Though the charter, as well as your Majesty's commission, gives the command of all the forts in the said province to your Majesty's governor, and the sole power of building and demolishing such forts; yet the House of Representatives voted that a committee of their House should go down to your Majesty's Castle William to take an account of all the stores there, and to take receipts from the officers for the same, without any application made to me for my leave, and in the same manner without asking my consent, ordered the treasurer that he should pay no more subsistence money to the officers and soldiers of Fort Mary at Winter Harbour; and directed him to take speedy care that the provisions of ordnance, arms, and ammunition, and all other stores of war at that fort, should be transported to Boston, and lodged with him. . . . (6) The House of Representatives voted that Mr. Moody, a major in your [Majesty's for]ces there should be suspended, and that even unheard; which vote they sent up to the [Council for their?] concurrence. But the Council nonconcurring the said House of Representatives ordered [the salary of Maj?] or Moody should be no longer paid. And upon my expostulating with the House on their proceeding against a major in your Majesty's service, so manifestly contrary to all rules of justice, they sent me a message justifying their proceedings against him, in terms that have not been usually given to one that has the honour of being your Majesty's governor in that province. . . . (7) The House of Representatives ordered a committee to command the officers at the eastern and western parts of the province to draw out their forces and muster them only under colour of an order signed by their Speaker. . . .

I would with humble submission, further lay before your Majesty, that upon my arrival I had good reason given to me to expect that they would allow me my salary, £1,500 per annum of the money currant there. But they gave me no more the first year than £1,200 of that money. At which time £160 there was equal in value to £100 sterling, and they did likewise continue the same allowance for two years after; and though provisions have been much dearer since, they have given me no more than £1,000 per annum of that money, which is now so much reduced in its value that £260 is but equal to £100 sterling, and therefore is now above a third less in value that when I first arrived there, so that £385 sterling per annum is all which they in reality now allow me. They vote me that sum by moietys at each session of their Assembly, which is once in six months, but even that they don't give me till I have passed the bills in the respective sessions, thereby to constrain me as far as they can to consent to any bills they lay before me. . . .

4. THE SPIRIT OF THE TIMES

A system of government is more than a matter of form and practice; it is as much a matter of spirit. A system that is at heart authoritarian can subvert the most democratic of structures, while a proper regard to the wishes of the people can mitigate, if it can not obviate, a polity with few democratic procedures. It is not enough, then, to know the size of the electorate, the method of choosing representatives, the backgrounds of the men vying for office, or the strength of royal government. We must know as well the extent to which the voice of the people was truly exercised, the extent to which the institutions of government were susceptible to influence by popular sentiment. This is difficult to measure, for it is largely subjective. A few scattered expressions of approval of the democratic tone of colonial politics may indicate nothing more than the optimism of the author or the peculiarities of a local situation. Descriptions of a monarchical or an aristocratic atmosphere are equally suspect.

Despite the range of judgments left to us by contemporaries, there is little doubt that the tone of colonial politics differed markedly from that of Europe. Friendly and hostile critics alike were in agreement that the American colonies exuded a spirit of equality that made the New World unlike the Old. The critics differed however, in their appreciation of the American political mood: some, like the Reverend Andrew Burnaby, condemned it, while others, such as Hector St. Jean de Crèvecoeur, author of the famous *Letters from an American Farmer,* viewed the relative equalitarianism of American society as an unqualified blessing. On the other hand, colonial politics had a healthy number of critics who saw aristocratic tendencies and declaimed loudly against them. There is material in the documentary record to support widely differing views of the spirit of colonial politics.

An Excess of Democracy

To many eighteenth-century minds, political democracy was a mixed blessing. It was all right to have some democracy; the "better sort" of people deserved a voice in government, and ever since the English nobility wrenched such a concession from King John, no right-thinking Englishman would deny it. But there must be a limit. Aristocracy and monarchy must not give way to vulgar mobocracy. Yet that is what some observers thought was happening in the corporate colonies of Connecticut and Rhode Island, where the people had almost complete control of the machinery of government. And in neighboring Massachusetts Bay, Governor Hutchinson complained that Boston was an "absolute democracy."

Among those who saw and deplored the growing democratic spirit (as well as form) of colonial politics was Andrew Burnaby, English clergyman, who visited the colonies from 1759 to 1760.[10] He comments here on Rhode Island.

The government of this province is entirely democratical, every officer, except the collector of the customs, being appointed, I believe, either immediately by the people, or by the general assembly. The people choose annually a governor, lieutenant-governor, and ten assistants, which constitute an upper house. The representatives, or lower house,

---

[10] Rufus Rockwell Wilson, ed., *Burnaby's Travels Through North America* (New York, 1904), 125–30.

are elected every half year. These jointly have the appointment of all other public officers (except the recorder, treasurer, and attorney-general, which are appointed likewise annually by the people), both military and civil, [and] are invested with the powers of legislation, of regulating the militia, and of performing all other acts of government. The governor has no negative, but votes with the assistants, and in case of an equality has a casting voice. The assembly, or two houses united, are obliged to sit immediately after each election; at Newport in the summer, and in the winter alternately at Providence and South Kingston in Narraganset: they adjourn themselves, but may be called together, notwithstanding such adjournment, upon any urgent occasion by the governor. No assistant, or representative, is allowed any salary or pay for his attendance or service.

There are several courts of judicature. The assembly nominates annually so many justices for each township, as are deemed necessary. These have power to join people in matrimony, and to exercise other acts of authority usually granted to this order of magistrates. Any two of them may hear causes concerning small debts and trespasses; and three may try criminals for thefts, not exceeding ten pounds currency. Appeals in civil causes are allowed to the inferior courts of common-pleas; in criminal ones to the sessions of the peace; and in these the determinations are final. The sessions are held in each county twice every year by five or more justices; they adjudge all matters relating to the preservation of the peace, and the punishment of criminals, except in cases of death. Appeals are allowed from this court, in all causes that have originated in it, to the superior one. The inferior courts of common-pleas sit twice every year in each county, and are held by three or more justices. They take cognizance of all civil causes whatsoever, triable at common law, and if any one thinks himself aggrieved here, he may appeal to the superior one, which is held also annually twice in each county, by three judges, and which exercises all the authority of a court of King's-bench, common-pleas, and exchequer. The dernier resort is to the King in council, but this only in cases of £300 value, new tenor. The people have the power of pardoning criminals, except in cases of piracy, murder, or high treason; and then it is doubted whether they can even reprieve. . . .

The character of the Rhode Islanders is by no means engaging, or amiable, a circumstance principally owing to their form of government. Their men in power, from the highest to the lowest, are dependent upon the people, and frequently act without that strict regard to probity and honour, which ought invariably to influence and direct mankind. . . . Their magistrates are partial and corrupt: and it is folly to expect justice in their courts of judicature; for he who has the greatest influence is generally found to have the fairest cause. Were the governor to interpose his authority, were he to refuse to grant flags of truce, or not to wink at abuses, he would at the expiration of the year be excluded from his office, the only thing perhaps which he has to subsist upon. Were the judges to act with impartiality, and to decide a cause to the prejudice or disadvantage of any great or popular leader, they would probably never be re-elected; indeed, they are incapable in general of determining the merits of a suit, for they are exceeding illiterate, and where they have nothing to make them partial, are managed almost entirely by the lawyers. . . .

[The colony] has also been loaded with taxes, and many of the people have been oppressed by the mode of collecting them: for, the assembly having determined the quota of each township, the inhabitants have been assessed by the town council, consisting of the assistants residing there, the justices of the town, and a few freeholders elected annually by the freemen; and these have been generally partial in their assessments, as must necessarily happen under a combination of such circumstances. . . .

Not Enough Democracy

If Reverend Burnaby saw too much democracy, some observers saw too little. From time to time protests were made in the several colonies against political practices which deprived the citizen of what he interpreted as his legitimate rights. Such protests sometimes took the form of petitions to the provincial assembly, sometimes appeared as political pamphlets, and sometimes merely as private commentary that never reached print. But most common of all was the broadside, a colonial device that had particular effectiveness in towns and cities.

The following excerpt from a New York City broadside of 1770 condemns the undemocratic implications of *viva voce* voting.[11]

To the Freeholders, and Freemen of the City and Province of New York

Gentlemen

The method of taking the suffrages of the people for places of trust, by ballot, is so manifestly conducive to the preservation of liberty that its opposer must necessarily be eyed with jealousy, unless it be excusable on the score of his folly, and then his opinion deserves only our contempt.

It is not in human power to devise a more effectual antidote to corruption than a law for elections by ballot, by which no man of opulence will be able to procure a seat in the Assembly by an undue influence upon the fears of the electors, nor find it worth his while to spend money which he can never be sure will have the wicked effects for which it was given.

Every patriotic heart must therefore exult on hearing of the late motion for a balloting law. A law which may be properly stiled, *An Act for the Redemption of the Poor, and the Establishment of the Liberties of the Colony.* A law friendly to all but such as are desirous of selling their birth-right for a mess of pottage, and the sons of wealth and ambition who thirst after the power of enslaving the rest of their countrymen.

---

[11] Broadside, 1770. Courtesy of New York Historical Society.

the character of colonial politics

Thanks to Heaven, that this salutary design is prosecuted when from our public virtues there is so much reason to think it will meet with success. This mode of election is practised in several of the plantations, and so is not subject to the lazy trite objection of novelty. Abundant experience has shewn its utility in Pennsylvania, the Carolinas, New-England, and several other colonies: and if the Assembly will push it with spirit, in a manner becoming its importance, exercise the means in their power, and intreat his Majesty's confirmation of a proper law for this glorious amendment of our constitution, there can be no reason to doubt of the royal concurrence. . . .

"The Most Perfect Society Now Existing"

The character of colonial politics can be measured against the political system of twentieth-century America. If so, its democratic trappings may seem unimpressive. If, however, comparison is made instead to other societies of the eighteenth century, the middle-class qualities that set America apart from Europe become more noticeable. The absence of a titled aristocracy, the relative weakness of royal control, and the solid economic underpinning that prevented extremes of wealth and poverty gave an equalitarian cast to American society that was often extolled by Americans at the time. None was so eloquent as the French immigrant and author, Hector St. Jean de Crèvecoeur, who delighted in contrasting America's society of opportunity with the static structure of the Old World.[12]

[The visitor from Europe] is arrived on a new continent; a modern society offers itself to his contemplation, different from what he had hitherto seen. It is not composed, as in Europe, of great lords who possess every thing, and of a herd of people who have nothing. Here are no aristocratical families, no courts, no kings, no bishops, no ecclesiastical dominion, no invisible power giving to a few a very visible one; no great manufacturers employing thousands, no great refinements of luxury. The rich and the poor are not so far removed from each other as they are in Europe. Some few towns excepted, we are all tillers of the earth, from Nova Scotia to West Florida. We are a people of cultivators, scattered over an immense territory, communicating with each other by means of good roads and navigable rivers, united by the silken bands of mild government, all respecting the laws, without dreading their power, because they are equitable. We are all animated with the spirit of an industry which is unfettered and unrestrained, because each person works for himself. If he travels through our rural districts he views not the hostile castle, and the haughty mansion, contrasted with the clay-built hut and miserable

---

[12] J. Hector St. Jean de Crèvecoeur, *Letters from an American Farmer* (New York, 1904), 49–53.

cabin, where cattle and men help to keep each other warm, and dwell in meanness, smoke, and indigence. A pleasing uniformity of decent competence appears throughout our habitations. The meanest of our loghouses is a dry and comfortable habitation. Lawyer or merchant are the fairest titles our towns afford; that of a farmer is the only appellation of the rural inhabitants of our country. It must take some time ere he can reconcile himself to our dictionary, which is but short of words of dignity, and names of honour. There, on a Sunday, he sees a congregation of respectable farmers and their wives, all clad in neat homespun, well mounted, or riding in their own humble waggons. There is not among them an esquire, saving the unlettered magistrate. There he sees a parson as simple as his flock, a farmer who does not riot on the labour of others. We have no princes, for whom we toil, starve, and bleed: we are the most perfect society now existing in the world. Here man is free as he ought to be. . . .

The laws, the indulgent laws, protect [the immigrants] as they arrive, stamping on them the symbol of adoption; they receive ample rewards for their labours; these accumulated rewards procure them lands; those lands confer on them the title of freemen, and to that title every benefit is affixed which men can possibly require. This is the great operation daily performed by our laws. From whence proceed these laws? From our government. Whence the government? It is derived from the original genius and strong desire of the people ratified and confirmed by the Crown. This is the great chain which links us all. . . .

CONCLUSION

Probably no major revolution in modern history has preserved so much of the political system against which it rebelled as did the American Revolution of 1776, for aside from royal control, Americans were largely content with their governments. Even in the twentieth century our system of politics owes a sizable debt to the forms, practices, and even to the spirit of colonial politics.

The franchise has, of course, been broadened considerably since the eighteenth century. Property qualifications have been almost entirely removed; only the poll tax lingers in some areas as an anachronistic vestige. Requirements of "good character" no longer apply unless disfranchisement of certain criminals serves as a remote parallel. Race, religion, and nationality are no longer legal restrictions, though extra-legal barriers unfortunately remain. And most significant of all, numerically at least, has been the enfranchisement of women: in 1920 a single Constitutional enactment theoretically doubled the size of the national electorate. (Many states of course had already extended the vote to women.) Even the restrictions of age and residence have undergone substantial change.

the character of colonial politics

The characteristics of the candidates, on the other hand, have not changed very much. Colonial society expected public office to be sought and achieved by members of the upper class, but imposed few barriers to men of whatever means. This is still true today, though to a lesser degree. We no longer impose a property qualification on candidates; yet the fiscal standing of today's officeholder is undoubtedly several cuts above the national average. Especially on the national level, wealth is a useful if not an essential aid to public office. At the same time, the colonial custom of expecting officials to serve without pay has been totally repudiated; if today's officeholder is not rewarded handsomely, he at least makes a living wage and therefore need not have a separate source of income. That, more than any other single reform in our political system, has broadened the range of candidates.

Another similarity between the colonial political system and our own is in election practices. The secret ballot is now almost universal, and new forms of mass media have added new dimensions to campaign methods, but at bottom the candidate still has to win the allegiance of the voters. "Swilling the planters with bumbo" is not so far removed from political banquets, barbecues, and the like. Now, as then, some voters succumb to rational reasoning, some to irrational loyalties, some to a dram of good—or bad—alcohol.

Royal and proprietary government disappeared, of course, with the Revolution. Out went the royal charters, the governors appointed in England, and the plethora of subordinate crown officials. Out too went the proprietary rights of the Penn and Calvert families. America was no longer ruled from England.

Yet in many significant respects the national polity which finally crystalized in the Constitution of 1787 substituted for the old imperial tie a new structure of quite similar purpose and form. It has, to be sure, many crucial differences—most obviously the difference in who created and who administers the central government. The Constitution of 1787 was of our own making and the polity it created is manned by men of our own choosing. Yet like the royal control of the colonial period, our modern central government exercises authority over all citizens of America in the interests of their security, prosperity, and well-being. Authority emanates from Washington instead of from London, and from an elected leader instead of a hereditary monarch, but it is significant that we kept the parts of the old system that seemed compatible with American experience. We kept a single executive, a two-house legislature, a system of national courts (though we chose to separate it from the other two branches), and we gave the national government a vast range of duties and powers which meshed with, but did not supplant, the organs of state and local administration.

At the same time, much of the form of colonial government survived on the state level. When the Revolution made their royal charters invalid, Connecticut and Rhode Island turned them into state constitutions by the substitution of a few words and phrases. The other former colonies also devised constitutions that changed very little of the structure of government on either the state or local levels. The top of the political hierarchy continued in most cases to consist of a governor and two-house legislature; the local units and their officials continued to vary in accordance with the experience of the several states: county-oriented in Virginia and most of the South, town-centered in New England. Thus the structure of colonial government formed an important part of America's political heritage on every level, but with modifications that stamped a distinctively American caste on our polity.

The spirit of our political society has changed too, but the change is more one of degree than of kind. We have broadened the meaning of democracy to include the economic and social spheres to an extent that would have amazed the American colonist of the eighteenth century, yet we still have much in common with the society observed by Crèvecoeur, Burnaby, and others. The spirit is much the same; its application has altered sharply.

From the perspective of the twentieth century it is clear that American colonial polity was neither all democratic nor all aristocratic. America had elements of both, and the proportions varied considerably from colony to colony and from time to time. New England had a remarkable degree of local democracy; Virginia and the rest of the South had very little. But on the provincial level all of the colonies enjoyed a fairly wide franchise—estimated by modern historians to have been as high in some colonies as eighty or ninety per cent of the adult free white males, while in England the figure may have been less than ten per cent. And the comments of some of America's most severe critics assure us that even royal government often gave way to the will of the people. Yet there were always present some unsavory (to the modern eye) aspects of colonial politics: the disfranchisement of women, non-Christians, Negroes, the propertyless, and the politically unorthodox. There was also a strong tendency in a few colonies for the political system to be dominated by a relatively small clique of provincial aristocrats. Finally, a powerful element of monarchy infused the American political system through the royal governors, their appointees, and the various officials sent out from London. The American political system offered a varied blend of monarchy, aristocracy, and democracy.

What is most important, however, is that the long-range trend was toward greater and greater democracy at the expense of the other two ingredients. This was not a steady development. In many colonies aristocratic elements grew more firmly entrenched with time, while some franchise laws became less liberal as the eighteenth century wore on. But overall the picture is an encouraging one. And when the break with

Great Britain came, and Americans could frame governments exactly as they chose, the new state and federal constitutions made clear that democracy, as a form and spirit of government, had won the day. That, more than anything else, gives the clue to the character of colonial politics.

3 MAX SAVELLE

road to revolution

The American Revolution was a product of long-accumulating forces which had been set in motion by the actual experience of American colonization. Indeed, the planting in the wilderness of many groups of Englishmen with English ideas of economic individualism, of Protestantism, and of representative institutions was only the first act in a drama which was to be marked by the development of those ideas along new lines. These new lines of development diverged widely, in America, from those followed by the evolution of these same ideas in England. The divergence eventually produced conflict; and the conflict reached its great climax in the Declaration of Independence, which was both a severing of the ties that had bound the colonies to the mother country and a statement of the causes that had led to the break.

Charles M. Andrews, one of the most distinguished of American historians, in an article published in January 1926, entitled "The American Revolution," said:

> The revolt of the colonies from Great Britain began long before the battles of Moore's Creek Bridge and Lexington; before the time of James Otis and the writs of assistance; before the dispute over the appointment of judges in North Carolina and New York; before the eloquence of Patrick Henry was first heard in the land; and even before the quarrel in Virginia over the Dinwiddie pistole fee. These were but the outward and visible signs of an inward and factual divergence. The separation from the mother country began just as soon as the mercantile system of commercial control, the governmental system of colonial administration, and the whole doctrine of the in-

ferior status of a colonial assembly began to give way before the pressure exerted and the disruptive power exercised by these young and growing colonial communities. New soil had produced new wants, new desires, new points of view, and the colonists were demanding the right to live their own lives in their own way. As we see it today the situation was a dramatic one. On one side was the immutable, stereotyped system of the mother country, based on precedent and tradition and designed to keep things comfortably as they were; on the other, a vital dynamic organism, containing the seed of a great nation, its forces untried, still to be proved. It is inconceivable that a connection should have continued long between two such yokefellows, one static, the other dynamic, separated by an ocean and bound only by the ties of a legal relationship.[1]

The American Revolution was thus no one-sided affair. As a deep running, bitter argument, for the settlement of which both sides eventually resorted to violence, it had, like all arguments, two sides—and there was great plausibility and deep conviction on the side of the English statesmen and their American "Tory" supporters who were willing to sacrifice home, property, friends, family, and even, on occasion, life itself, for their loyalty to England and for the ideal that England represented to them. Today, in the calm of Anglo-American friendship and neighborliness, it is possible to see the revolution as a conflict of economic, social, ideological, and political forces that, given the unwillingness of either side to surrender its position, could be resolved only by an appeal to war. To the sincere men of the eighteenth century who stood on the two sides, the picture of the conflict of forces was not so clear. The statements they made, therefore, while so obviously irreconcilable, were none the less entirely sincere and reasonable to them; for those statements voiced convictions that had for centuries grown and gathered force within them in the course of their experience, and the experiences of their forefathers.

1. THE UNDERLYING FACTORS

John Adams, one of the greatest leaders of the Revolution, said that the Revolution arose out of a "perpetual discordance between British principles and feelings and those of America," which, he said, "ought to be traced back for two hundred years, and sought in the history of the country from the first plantation in America."[2]

What were those basic principles and feelings?

---

[1] *American Historical Review*, 31:230-31. Used by permission of The American Historical Association.

[2] Charles F. Adams, ed., *The Works of John Adams*, 10 vols. (Boston, 1850-56), 10:284.

The habits and attitudes among the Americans that brought them to resist the legislative and administrative acts of the British government were derived from their experience during two centuries of growth and self-direction in the American wilderness. Practically, they had developed the habit of managing their own affairs; psychologically, they had arrived at a state of mind that simply assumed the right to self-direction without outside interference from anyone. It was a rude shock to them, therefore, to discover, after 1763, that Britain accepted no such practice and no such principle, as shown by the successive efforts to force the colonies to accept Parliamentary rule.

The Economic Factor

At the very base of the controversy was the vague but mounting discontent of the Americans over the regulation of their economic life by the mother country. True, they had acquiesced, with a mixture of resignation, criticism, and nullification, in the regulation of American commerce exercised for over a century by the mother country under the system of Navigation Laws and Acts of Trade; but they had acquiesced partly because they had grown up under the system of regulation, and partly because the system was in fact only very ineffectively enforced, while it did confer certain marked encouragements and protections to the colonial economy. It was not until the passage of the Revenue Act of 1764, which marked a new and aggressive inclination on the part of England to enforce the system, that Americans became genuinely alarmed by the implications of British control over their commerce.

Yet certain Americans had seen these implications earlier, and had realized that the very nature of the economic development of the colonies was driving them in directions that must inevitably conflict with the general principles of British mercantilistic colonial policy. As early as 1751 Benjamin Franklin had recognized the fundamental economic divergence of the colonies from the mother country, and had pointed out the unwisdom of the old system of British control of American trade.

One of the clearest statements of the importance of the economic factor in the colonial system, in regard to the generally held American theory of commercial relationships, was that of Daniel Dulany of Maryland, written in 1765 as a part of his protest against Parliamentary taxation. Like Franklin, Dulany recognized that economic divergence was inherent in the nature of things and that allowing the colonies a large degree of economic freedom would enlarge, not reduce, the profits derived by the mother country. Dulany put it as follows.[3]

---

[3] Daniel Dulany, *Considerations on the Propriety of Imposing Taxes in the British Colonies, for the Purpose of Raising a Revenue, by Act of Parliament*, 2nd ed. (Annapolis, 1765).

It must be acknowledged, that the Balance of Trade between *Great-Britain* and her Colonies, is considerably against the latter, and that no Gold or Silver Mines have yet been discovered in the old *American* Settlements, or among the *Treasures* of the new Acquisitions. How then is this Balance to be discharged? The former Trade of the Colonies, which enabled them to keep up their Credit with *Great-Britain*, by applying the Balance they gained against Foreigners, is now so fettered with Difficulties, as to be almost prohibited. In order therefore to reduce the Balance against them upon the Trade, between the Colonies and *Great-Britain*, this Trade must be contracted, so as to bring the Scales to an Equilibrium, or a Debt will be incurred that can't be paid off, which will distress the Creditor as well as the Debtor, by the Insolvency of the latter. . . .

I confess that I am one of those who do not perceive the Policy in laying difficulties and Obstructions upon the gainful Trade of the Colonies with Foreigners, or that it even makes any real Difference to the *English* Nation, whether the Merchants, who carry it on with Commodities *Great-Britain* will not purchase, reside in *Philadelphia, New-York* or *Boston, London, Bristol,* or *Liverpool,* when the Balance gained by the *American* Merchant in the Pursuit of that Trade, centers in *Great-Britain*, and is applied to the Discharge of a Debt contracted by the Consumption of *British* Manufactures in the Colonies, and in this to the Support of the national Expense.

The Political Factor

Another major factor in the divergence of the colonies from the mother country lay in the actual growth of political institutions and ideals in the colonies that differed sharply and in many ways from the corresponding institutions and ideals in England. By the middle of the eighteenth century American ideas and practices relative to political representation, the qualifications for the suffrage, the nature and the operation of the law, the proper constitutional relationships between the various functions of government, the nature of the colonial and the imperial constitutions, and a host of other matters had come to differ widely from the original English concepts from which they were derived. The question that now appeared and demanded answer with almost terrifying urgency was that of the demarcation line between the rights of the British government, derived from the ancient British experience and institutions, and the new American rights derived from the colonists' experience in the New World. This question had never been seriously studied, much less answered.

The fact of the political divergence of the colonies had been dimly realized in the first half of the eighteenth century by men such as Governor William Keith of Pennsylvania, Archibald Kennedy of New York, Benjamin Franklin, Governor Thomas Pownall of Massachusetts, and others. Pownall was one of the most objective and thoughtful of English observers. In his book, *The Administra-*

tion of the Colonies, published in 1765, he recognized the fact that a new constitutional problem had appeared with the development of the colonial governments, and that this problem must be solved. His volume passed through several revisions; the fourth edition, published in 1768, restated the problem, recognizing the legitimate contentions of the Americans, and offered several suggestions for resolving the problem, the chief of which called for the creation of a Secretaryship of State for the colonies (a suggestion that was realized in 1768), and the formation of a grand imperial union governed by a "senate" or Parliament, in which all the parts of the Empire, including the American colonies, would be represented.[4]

The fact is [he said] that the constitution of the government of England, as it stood at that time, founded upon, or built up with the feudal system, could not extend beyond the realm. There was nothing in the nature of the constitution providing for such things as colonies, or provinces. Lands without or beyond the limits of the realm could not be the property of the realm, unless by being united to the realm. But the people who settled upon these lands in *partibus exteris,* being the King's liege subjects, the king, as sovereign Lord, assumed the right of property, and of government. Yet the people being entitled to the rights, privileges, etc. of freemen, the King established by his commission of government, or charters, these colonies as free states, subordinate according to such precedents or examples as his ministry thought suitable to the present case; and the county palatine of Durham became this precedent, and the model of this constitution as to the *regalia.* This was the actual state of circumstances of our colonists at their first migration, and of the colonies at their first settlement; and had nothing further intervened, would have been their constitution at this day. . . .

The Religious Factor

The developing divergence of the colonies from the mother country was considerably deeper than the economic and political factors would indicate. The vast majority of Americans were "dissenters," or non-Anglicans, and the notion that the earliest settlers had fled to America to escape religious persecution was already a powerful element in the nascent American self-consciousness. The dissenters distrusted and criticized the Anglican Church, especially in colonies like Virginia where that church was "established"; Americans generally were moving in the direction of the complete separation of the church from all official connection with the state.

---

[4] Thomas Pownall, *The Administration of the Colonies,* 4th ed. (London, 1768), 14–19:33–36, 51, 56, 59–60, 69, 97, 163.

road to revolution

For this reason there was strong American opposition to anything that looked like an extension of the political power of the Anglican Church in the colonies, and when a movement arose to establish an Anglican bishopric in America the opposition became very articulate and even, in a literary sense, violent. One of the most persuasive and most influential protesting clergymen was the radical Reverend Jonathan Mayhew of Boston. In a pamphlet, entitled *Observations on the Charter and the Conduct of the Society for the Propagation of the Gospel in Foreign Parts,* Mayhew gave voice to the apprehension of his fellow-Americans.[5]

When we consider the real constitution of the church of England; and how aliene her mode of worship is from the simplicity of the gospel, and the apostolic times: When we consider her enormous hierarchy, ascending by various gradations from the dirt to the skies: When we consider the visible effects of that church's prevailing among us to the degree that it has: When we reflect on what our Forefathers suffered from the mitered, lordly SUCCESSORS *of the fishermen of Galilee,* for nonconformity to a non-instituted mode of worship; which occasioned their flight into this western world: When we consider that, to be delivered from their unholy zeal and scepter'd tyrants, they threw themselves as it were into the arms of Savages and Barbarians: When we reflect, that one principal motive to their exchanging the fair cities, villages, and delightful fields of Britain for the then inhospitable shores and desarts of America, was, that they might here enjoy, unmolested, God's holy word and ordinances, without such heterogeneous and spurious mixtures as were offensive to their well-informed consciences: When we consider the narrow, censorious, and bitter spirit that prevails in too many of the episcopalians among us; and what might probably be the sad consequence, if this growing party should once get the upper hand here, and a major vote in our houses of *Assembly:* (in which case the church of England might become the established religion here; *tests* be ordained, as in England, to exclude all but conformists from posts of honor and emolument; and all of us be taxed for the support of *bishops* and their *underlings:*) When we consider these things, and too many others to be now mentioned, we cannot well think of that church's gaining ground here to any great degree, and especially of seeing bishops fixed among us, without much reluctance—Will they never let us rest in peace, except *where all the weary are at rest?* Is it not enough, that they persecuted us out of the old world? Will they pursue us into the new to convert us here?—*compassing sea and land to make* US *proselytes,* while they neglect the heathen and heathenish plantations! What other new world remains as a sanctuary for us from their oppressions, in case of need? Where is the COLUMBUS to explore one for, and pilot us to it, before we

---

[5] Jonathan Mayhew, *Observations on the Charter and the Conduct of the Society for the Propagation of the Gospel in Foreign Parts* (Boston, 1763).

are consumed by the flames, or deluged in a flood of episcopacy? . . .

One of our Kings, it is well known, excited his Scotch subjects to take up arms against him, in a great measure, if not chiefly, by attempting to force the English liturgy upon them, at the instigation of the furious episcopal zealots of that day; by whom he was wheedled and duped to his destruction. But GOD be praised, we have a KING, whom Heaven long preserve and prosper, too wise, just, and good to be put upon any violent measures, to gratify men of such a depraved turn of mind.

The Social Factor

Still another factor of profound importance in the disaffection of the colonies stemmed from the rapid increase of population. During the eighteenth century hordes of immigrants arrived from the continent, and the admixture of these non-English stocks inevitably produced a large body of people who had never known Britain nor felt any particular loyalty to it. Moreover many of these newcomers had pushed into the back country beyond the Alleghenies where the land titles were in dispute. They were quick to resent English efforts to prevent the occupation of the West either by the Proclamation of 1763 or by other measures. In their protests they were joined by speculators along the seaboard.

The changing nature of American society, and the appearance of a "new man," "the American," was remarked by St. Jean de Crèvecoeur, a Frenchman who lived for a time in Pennsylvania, and who in 1782 published his famous observations on colonial society entitled *Letters from an American Farmer*.[6]

Whence came all these people? They are a mixture of English, Scotch, Irish, French, Dutch, Germans, and Swedes. From this promiscuous breed, that race now called Americans have arisen. . . .

The Americans were once scattered all over Europe; here they are incorporated into one of the finest systems of population which has ever appeared, and which will hereafter become distinct by the power of the different climates they inhabit. The American ought therefore to love this country much better than that wherein either he or his forefathers were born. . . .

What attachment can a poor European emigrant have for a country where he had nothing? The knowledge of the language, the love of a few kindred as poor as himself, were the only cords that tied him: his country is now that which gives him land, bread, protection, and consequence: *Ubi panis ibi patria*, is the motto of all emigrants. What then is the American, this new man? He is either an European, or the descendant of an European; hence that strange mixture of blood, which you will find in no other country. . . . *He* is an American, who leaving behind him all his ancient

---

[6] W. P. Trent, ed., *Letters from an American Farmer* (New York, 1945), 48–49, 51–53.

prejudices and manners, receives new ones from the new mode of life he has embraced, the new government he obeys, and the new rank he holds. He becomes an American by being received in the broad lap of our great *Alma Mater.* Here individuals of all nations are melted into a new race of men, whose labours and posterity will one day cause great changes in the world. Americans are the western pilgrims, who are carrying along with them that great mass of arts, sciences, vigour, and industry, which began long since in the east; they will finish the great circle. . . . The American is a new man, who acts upon new principles; he must therefore entertain new ideas, and form new opinions. From involuntary idleness, servile dependence, penury, and useless labour, he has passed to toils of a very different nature, rewarded by ample subsistence.—This is an American.

The Psychological Factor

Any study of the background of the American Revolution would be incomplete without alluding to the growth of national self-consciousness among the colonists. Despite divisions among themselves, and often without clearly realizing it, Americans were moving toward a belief that they were different from the British people. They came to feel a pride in being Americans and a loyalty to a tradition and an ideal uniquely American. This loyalty began as a devotion of the individual to his own province but by the third quarter of the eighteenth century had expanded into a sense of the magnificent future of all North America. Common ideals and common aspirations transcended provincial boundaries. Even before the crisis with the mother country arose, this sense of destiny was expressed by Nathaniel Ames, a Boston publisher. An extract from the 1758 edition of his *Astronomical Diary* is given as the first selection below.[7]

This consciousness of the differentness and the glorious destiny of America found expression in the work of numerous literary figures, such as William Smith of Pennsylvania, William Livingston of New York, and others. A good example is "Poem on the Rising Glory of America," written by Philip Freneau and Hugh H. Brackenridge on the occasion of the Princeton commencement of 1771. An extract is given as the second selection below.[8]

Ames

The Curious have observ'd, that the Progress of Humane Literature (like the Sun) is from the East to the West; thus has it travelled thro' Asia and Europe, and now is arrived at the Eastern Shore of *America.* As the Cœlestial Light of the Gospel was directed here by the Finger of GOD, it will doubtless, finally drive the long! long! Night of Heathenish Darkness from *America:*—So Arts

---

[7] Nathaniel Ames, *Astronomical Diary* (Boston, 1758).

[8] *Poem on the Rising Glory of America* (Philadelphia, 1772).

and Sciences will change the Face of Nature in their Tour from Hence over the Appalachian Mountains to the Western Ocean; and as they march thro' the vast Desert, the Residence of wild Beasts will be broken up, and their obscene Howl cease for ever;—Instead of which, the Stones and Trees will dance together at the Music of *Orpheus,*— The Rocks will disclose their hidden Gems,—and the inestimable Treasures of Gold & Silver be broken up. Huge Mountains of Iron Ore are already discovered; and vast Stores are reserved for future Generations: This Metal more useful than Gold and Silver, will employ millions of Hands, not only to form the martial Sword, and peaceful Share, alternately; but an Infinity of Utensils improved in the Exercise of Art, and Handicraft amongst Men. Nature thro' all her works has stamp'd Authority on this Law, namely, "That all fit Matter shall be improved to its best Purposes."—Shall not then those vast Quarries, that team with mechanic Stone,—those for Structure be piled into great Cities,—and those for sculpture into Statues to perpetuate the Honor of renowned Heroes; even those who shall now save their Country,—*O! Ye unborn Inhabitants of America! Should this Page escape its destin'd Conflagration at the Year's End, and these Alphabetical Letters remain legible, —when your Eyes behold the Sun after he has rolled the Seasons round for two or three Centuries more, you will know that in* ANNO DOMINI *1758, we dream'd of your Times.*

Freneau and Brackenridge

This is thy praise America thy pow'r
Thou best of climes by science visited
By freedom blest and richly stor'd with all
The luxuries of life. Hail happy land
The seat of empire the abode of kings,
The final stage where time shall introduce
Renowned characters, and glorious works
Of high invention and of wond'rous art,
While not the ravages of time shall waste
Till he himself has run his long career; career;
Till all those glorious orbs of light on high
The rolling wonders that surround the ball,
Drop from their spheres extinguish'd and consum'd,
When final ruin with her fiery car
Rides o'er creation, and all natures works
Are lost in chaos and the womb of night.

2. THE AMERICAN CASE

All the economic, political, social, religious, and emotional factors must be kept in mind in any approach to the question of why thirteen of the thirty-odd British colonies in America seceded from the Empire in 1776. The great common denominator among them was the determination of the Americans to be masters in their own house. Their case was a strong one; yet the British case against such a high degree of autonomy as the self-governing colonies were demanding was also highly plausible, at

road to revolution

least to the leaders on the British side and the Tories in America. As the argument advanced, step by step, the British became more adamant in their position while, step by step, the Americans were led to abandon their hope for autonomy within the Empire and to adopt, at long last, the resort to revolution and complete independence.

The first outspoken challenges to British authority in the colonies, foreshadowing the conflict that was to follow, took place in the widely separated colonies of Massachusetts and Virginia in the midst of the Seven Years War. In the North, young James Otis questioned the authority of the British government or its agents to issue general search-warrants, or "writs of assistance," to stamp out smuggling. In the South, young Patrick Henry disputed the right of the King to veto a law passed by the Virginia assembly. Both these challenges were hurled at accepted administrative practices as old as the colonies themselves. It was the mood of challenge, and the new constitutional practices implied in it, that were new.

The Question of Representation

The issue over the "writs of assistance" arose in 1761 when the British government ordered colonial judges to issue these general search warrants in order to stamp out smuggling and, particularly, the illicit trade with France. As might have been expected, the Americans engaged in such traffic protested strenuously, and they were supported by a public opinion alarmed by an apparent violation of the constitutional rights of Englishmen. James Otis, a young Boston lawyer, was foremost among those who demanded that the courts declare these writs invalid.

When these pleas went unheeded and when England proceeded to tighten its economic control through new taxes, Otis published in 1764 a pamphlet entitled *The Rights of the British Colonies Asserted and Proved*. Otis argued that Parliament could not tax the colonies unless they were represented in that body. He accepted that legislature as the supreme lawmaking body for the Empire but insisted that colonial delegates sit in it. At the same time he believed that the colonies should continue to have their own representative assemblies to administer local affairs. He did not envisage the possibility of a clash between the two bodies. A selection from the Otis pamphlet follows.[9]

The sum of my argument is, that civil government is of God: that the administrators of it were originally the whole people: that they might have devolved it on whom they pleased: that this devolution is fiduciary, for the good of the whole; that by the British constitution, this

[9] James Otis, *The Rights of the British Colonies Asserted and Proved* (Boston, 1764).

devolution is on the King, lords and commons, the supreme, sacred, and uncontroulable legislative power, not only in the realm, but thro' the dominions: that . . . His Majesty George III is rightful king and sovereign, and with his Parliament, the supreme legislative of Great Britain, France, and Ireland, and the dominions thereto belonging: that this constitution is the most free one, and by far the best, now existing on earth: that by this constitution, every man in the dominions is a free man: that no parts of His Majesty's dominions can be taxed without their consent: that every part has a right to be represented in the supreme or some subordinate legislature: that the refusal of this would seem to be a contradiction in practice to the theory of the constitution: that the colonies are subordinate dominions, and are now in such a state, as to make it best for the good of the whole, that they should not only be continued in the enjoyment of subordinate legislation, but be also represented in some proportion to their number and estates, in the grand legislature of the nation: that this would firmly unite all parts of the British empire, in the greatest peace and prosperity; and render it invulnerable and perpetual.

The Question of the Royal Veto

At almost the same time that the dispute over writs of assistance was reaching a climax in Massachusetts, a comparable dispute was flaring up in Virginia over the right of the King to veto a law enacted by the local legislature. In 1755, and again in 1758, a law had fixed the value of the tobacco then paid to the ministers of the churches as their salaries. The parsons, who had lost money thereby, had appealed to England against this law, and in 1759 the King had vetoed it. When one of the parsons then sued his parish to recover his losses, a young lawyer from the west named Patrick Henry led the defense. In his argument against the parson's claim, Henry insisted that the law was a good law and that, since it was made by the Virginia legislature, it represented the will of the people of the colony. Then he created a sensation by claiming that the King had no right to veto such a law, since such an act would nullify the expressed will of the people. By its very nature, therefore, the royal veto was a violation of the constitution or social compact, the fundamental law of society. The following is a summary of Henry's December 1763 speech by the Reverend James Maury, one of the clergymen involved in the case.[10]

Mr. Henry, mentioned above (who had been called in by the defendant, as we suspected, to do what I some time ago told you of), after Mr. Lyons had opened the cause, rose and harangued the jury for near an hour. This harangue turned upon points as much out of his own depth, and that of the jury,

---

[10] Moses C. Tyler, *Patrick Henry* (Boston, 1887), 47–49.

as they were foreign from the purpose,—which it would be impertinent to mention here. However, after he had discussed those points, he labored to prove "that the Act of 1758 had every characteristic of a good law; that it was a law of general utility, and could not, consistently with what he called the original compact between the king and people . . . be annulled." Hence he inferred, "that a king, by disallowing acts of this salutary nature, from being the father of his people, degenerated into a tyrant, and forfeits all right to his subjects' obedience. . . . When he came to that part of it where he undertook to assert "that a king, by annulling or disallowing acts of so salutary a nature, from being the father of his people, degenerated into a tyrant, and forfeits all right to his subjects' obedience,"

the more sober part of the audience were struck with horror. Mr. Lyons called out aloud, and with an honest warmth, to the Bench, "that the gentleman had spoken treason," and expressed his astonishment, "that their worships could hear it without emotion, or any mark of dissatisfaction." At the same instant, too, amongst some gentlemen in the crowd behind me, was a confused murmur of "treason, treason!" Yet Mr. Henry went on in the same treasonable and licentious strain, without interruption from the Bench, nay, even without receiving the least exterior notice of their disapprobation. One of the jury, too, was so highly pleased with these doctrines, that, as I was afterwards told, he every now and then gave the traitorous declaimer a nod of approbation.

The Question of Taxation: The Virginia Resolutions

Many Americans soon realized that representation in Parliament was impracticable and might even prove to be a two-edged sword that could be turned against them. Distances were too great for effective participation, while American representation in Parliament might lead to the abolition of the colonial assemblies. Finally, the Americans would probably always be outvoted at Westminster. Hence the demand for representation in Parliament was allowed to die a quiet death.

Meanwhile the English government proceeded with its program to reorganize the Empire. In 1764 Parliament passed the Sugar Act and a companion law severely restricting the issuance of colonial paper money. Both these measures excited protest among the merchants, but the great majority of the people did not appreciate at once all the implications of British control of the colonies' commerce. Much more direct in effect was taxation, and it is not surprising that the Stamp Act of 1765 led to widespread denunciation, and even resistance.

When news of the Stamp Act reached the colonies, legislature after legislature asserted that its members alone had the right to levy taxes. One of the most far-reaching statements of this right of colonial self-taxation was drafted by Patrick Henry and enacted by the Virginia legislature in 1765. These Virginia resolutions follow.[11]

Resolved, That the first Adventurers and Settlers of this his Majesty's Colony and Dominion of *Virginia* brought with them, and transmitted to their Posterity, and all other his Majesty's Subjects since inhabiting in this his Majesty's said Colony, all the Liberties, Privileges, Franchises, and Immunities, that have at any Time been held, enjoyed, and possessed, by the people of *Great Britain.*

Resolved, That by two royal Charters, granted by King *James* the First, the Colonists aforesaid are declared entitled to all Liberties, Privileges, and Immunities of Denizens and natural Subjects, to all Intents and Purposes, as if they had been abiding and born within the Realm of *England.*

Resolved, That the Taxation of the People by themselves, or by Persons chosen by themselves to represent them, who can only know what Taxes the People are able to bear, or the easiest Method of raising them, and must themselves be affected by every Tax laid on the People, is the only Security against a burthensome Taxation, and the distinguishing Characteristick of *British* Freedom, without which the ancient Constitution cannot exist.

Resolved, That his Majesty's liege people of this his most ancient and loyal Colony have without Interruption enjoyed the inestimable Right of being governed by such Laws, respecting their internal Polity and Taxation, as are derived from their own Consent, with the Approbation of their Sovereign, or his Substitute; and that the same hath never been forfeited or yielded up, but hath been constantly recognized by the Kings and People of Great Britain.

The Question of Taxation: The Stamp Act Congress

The sentiments of Virginia on the subject of taxation were shared by most of the other colonies. There existed, however, no mechanism through which the colonies could take a common stand or express their discontent with a common voice. The first step in this direction came in 1765, when Massachusetts called for a Congress of all the colonies to meet at New York and agree upon common procedures in the face of the threat to their liberties. Nine colonies sent delegates to this so-called Stamp Act Congress, which met in New York in the fall of 1765.

The Stamp Act Congress wrote the then generally accepted American argument into a Declaration against Parliamentary taxation. It also sent petitions to King George III, the House of Lords, and the House of Commons, asking

---

[11] John P. Kennedy, ed., *Journals of the House of Burgesses of Virginia, 1761–1765,* 33 vols. (Richmond, 1907), 4:359–60.

for the repeal of the obnoxious Act. The American argument, as outlined in the Declaration, is presented in the selection that follows.[12]

The members of this Congress, sincerely devoted, with the warmest sentiments of affection and duty to his majesty's person and government, inviolably attached to the present happy establishment of the protestant succession and with minds deeply impressed by a sense of the present and impending misfortunes of the British colonies on this continent, having considered as maturely as time would permit, the circumstances of the said colonies, esteem it our indispensable duty to make the following declarations, of our humble opinion respecting the most essential rights and liberties of the colonists, and of the grievances under which they labor, by reason of several late acts of parliament.

1st. That his majesty's subjects in these colonies owe the same allegiance to the crown of Great Britain, that is owing from his subjects born within the realm, and all due subordination to the august body, the parliament of Great Britain.

3d. That it is inseparably essenjects in these colonies are entitled to all the inherent rights and privileges of his natural born subjects within the kingdom of Great Britain.

3d. That it is inseparably essential to the freedom of a people, and the undoubted rights of Englishmen, that no taxes should be imposed on them, but with their own consent, given personally, or by their representatives.

4th. That the people of these colonies are not, and from their local circumstances, cannot be, represented in the House of Commons in Great Britain.

5th. That the only representatives of the people of these colonies, are persons chosen therein, by themselves; and that no taxes ever have been, or can be constitutionally imposed on them, but by their respective legislatures.

6th. That all supplies to the crown, being free gifts of the people, it is unreasonable and inconsistent with the principles and spirit of the British constitution, for the people of Great Britain to grant to his majesty, the property of the colonies. . . .

8th. That the late act of parliament, entitled, An act for granting and applying certain stamp duties, and other duties in the British colonies and plantations in America, etc. by imposing taxes on the inhabitants of these colonies, and the said act, and several other acts, by extending the jurisdiction of the courts of admiralty beyond its ancient limits, have a manifest tendency to subvert the rights and liberties of the colonists. . . .

12th. That the increase, prosperity, and happiness of these colonies depend on the full and free enjoyment of their rights and liberties, and an intercourse with Great Britain, mutually affectionate and advantageous. . . .

Lastly, That it is the indispensable duty of these colonies to the best of sovereigns, to the mother

---

[12] *Niles' Weekly Register* (1812), 2:340–41.

country, and to themselves, to endeavor by a loyal and dutiful address to his majesty, and humble application to both houses of parliament, to procure the repeal of the act for granting and applying certain stamp duties [and] of all clauses of any other acts of parliament, whereby the jurisdiction of the admiralty is extended as aforesaid, and of the other late acts for the restriction of the American commerce.

Self-Taxation: The Mainspring of Liberty

Resolutions on the right of self-taxation were not the only colonial reply to the Stamp Act. More effective were agreements among the merchants of the seaboard cities to import no goods from England as long as the levy was in force. These nonimportation agreements dealt the British mercantile interests a devastating blow; and it was the consequent petitions from Englishmen rather than from Americans that were probably most decisive in the repeal of the Stamp Act in 1766.

In abandoning the Stamp Act, however, Parliament asserted its right in the Declaratory Act to legislate for the colonies "in all cases whatever." Most Americans, jubilant over the repeal of the law of 1765, ignored this assertion, but there were some who saw that it posed a constitutional question in unequivocal terms, and that sooner or later the issue would have to be faced.

The issue, in fact, flared up immediately. In 1767 Parliament passed the Townshend duties upon American imports, as another means of raising in the colonies a revenue to defray the cost of imperial protection. At nearly the same time a Secretaryship of State for the Colonies was created, the machinery to enforce the Navigation Acts was tightened, and the New York legislature was suspended for disobeying an act of Parliament. This series of events aroused colonial anger and resistance anew. Many Americans were prepared to move from their earlier denial of the right of Parliament to tax the colonies internally to the position that import duties were also taxation and that, therefore, Parliament had no right to tax them in any way whatever.

The most lucid and effective expression of this new argument was contained in John Dickinson's *Letters from a Farmer in Pennsylvania*, printed in 1767–1768. In these letters, selections from which are given below, Dickinson rejected the distinction between "internal" and "external" taxes, condemned as unconstitutional the suspension of the New York Assembly, denied the principles of the Declaratory Act, and insisted Parliament could not legislate for the colonies in any cases involving taxation. On the other hand, he did agree that Parliament could pass regulations for the empire as a whole. In all his criticisms of the mother country Dickinson rested his argument upon the exclusive right of the colonies to tax themselves; if Parliament were allowed to seize this power, it would be able to impose its will upon the colonial legislatures in any matter whatsoever; and if that ever happened, the liberty of the colonies would be completely submerged under Parliamentary tyranny.[13]

With a good deal of surprize I have observed, that little notice has been taken of an act of parliament, as injurious in its principle to the liberties of these colonies, as the *Stamp-Act* was: I mean the act for suspending the legislature of *New-York*. . . .

There is one consideration arising from this suspension, which is not generally attended to, but shews its importance very clearly. It was not *necessary* that this suspension should be caused by an act of parliament. The crown might have restrained the governor of *New-York*, even from calling the assembly together, by its prerogative in the royal governments. This step, I suppose, would have been taken, if the conduct of the assembly of *New-York* had been regarded as an act of disobedience *to the crown alone;* but it is regarded as an act of disobedience to the authority "of the BRITISH LEGISLATURE." This gives the suspension a consequence vastly more affecting. It is a parliamentary assertion of the *supreme authority* of the *British* legislature over these colonies, in *the point of taxation,* and is intended to COMPEL *New-York* into a submission to that authority. It seems therefore to me as much a violation of the liberty of the people of that province, and consequently of all these colonies, as if the parliament had sent a number of regiments to be quartered upon them till they should comply. For it is

evident, that the suspension is meant as a *compulsion;* and the *method* of compelling is totally indifferent. . . .

The parliament unquestionably possesses a legal authority to *regulate* the trade of *Great-Britain,* and all her colonies. Such an authority is essential to the relation between a mother country and her colonies; and necessary for the common good of all. He, who considers these provinces as states distinct from the *British Empire,* has very slender notions of *justice,* or of their *interests.* We are but parts of a *whole;* and therefore there must exist a power somewhere to preside, and preserve the connection in due order. This power is lodged in the parliament; and we are as much dependent on *Great-Britain,* as a perfectly free people can be on another. . . .

That we may legally be bound to pay any *general* duties on these commodities relative to the regulation of trade, is granted; but we being obliged *by the laws* to take from *Great-Britain,* any *special* duties imposed on their exportation *to us only, with intention to raise a revenue from us only,* are as much *taxes,* upon us, as those imposed by the *Stamp-Act.* . . .

What but the indisputable, the acknowledged exclusive right of the colonies to tax themselves, could be the reason, that in this long period of more than one hundred and fifty years, no statute was ever passed for the sole purpose of raising a revenue on the colonies? And how clear, how cogent must that reason be, to which

---

[13] *Memoirs of the Historical Society of Pennsylvania* (Philadelphia, 1895), 14:308, 310, 312, 317, 335, 364, 400.

every parliament, and every minister, for so long a time submitted, without a single attempt to innovate? . . .

No free people ever existed, or can ever exist, without keeping, to use a common, but strong expression, "the purse strings," in their own hands. Where this is the case, *they have a constitutional check* upon the administration, which may thereby be brought into order *without violence:* But where such a power is not lodged in the *people,* oppression proceeds uncontrouled in its career, till the governed, transported into rage, seek redress in the midst of blood and confusion. . . .

Let these *truths* be indelibly impressed on our minds—*that we cannot be* HAPPY, *without being* FREE— that we cannot be free, *without being secure in our property*—that *we* cannot be secure in our property, *if, without our consent, others may, as by right, take it away*—that *taxes imposed on us by parliament,* do thus take it away—that *duties laid for the sole purpose of raising money,* are taxes—that *attempts* to lay such duties *should be instantly and firmly opposed*—that this opposition can never be effectual, *unless it is the united effort of these provinces*—that therefore BENEVOLENCE *of temper towards each other,* and UNANIMITY *of councils,* are essential to the welfare of the whole—and lastly, that for this reason, every man amongst us, who in any manner would encourage either *dissension, diffidence,* or *indifference,* between these colonies, is an enemy to *himself,* and to his *country.* . . .

The Idea of a Federal Empire

Just as American pamphleteers had been compelled to reject the distinction between "internal" and "external" taxes, so did they finally come to realize that any law passed by Parliament affecting domestic affairs of a colony must involve taxation in some form or other. It thus followed that no valid line could be drawn between "taxation" and "legislation," and that the colonies must logically renounce the power of Parliament to legislate upon any matter affecting their internal concerns.

As early as 1766 Richard Bland of Virginia, in *An Inquiry into the Rights of the British Colonies,* argued that the colonies were new societies, separate from the mother country, and that their claim to complete internal self-government rested upon the Lockean concept of the social compact. Benjamin Franklin was impressed by Bland's reasoning, and a year later expressed similar views in a letter to Lord Kames. This thorough-going claim was genuinely revolutionary in that it was based upon the idea that sovereignty may be divided, that each colony was sovereign within itself, and that, therefore, the British Empire was a confederation of sovereign societies.

By 1773 the debate between the colonists and the mother country no longer centered around representation in Parliament or taxation, internal or external. The central issue had become the limits between the authority of Parliament over the colonies and the degree of self-government to be enjoyed by them as a matter of right. And by 1773 most Americans had accepted the Bland-Franklin position that the colonies were new, separate societies, and that, accordingly, Parliament's authority extended only to their boundaries and no farther.

The first of the three following selections, which illustrate this idea of federal empire, is an extract from Richard Bland's *An Inquiry into the Rights of the British Colonies*.[14] The second is an excerpt from the reply in 1773 of the Massachusetts legislature, led by Samuel Adams, to a criticism of its behavior by the royal governor.[15] The third is taken from a systematic exposition of the American argument by James Wilson of Pennsylvania in his *Considerations on the Nature and Extent of the Legislative Authority of the British Parliament*, published in 1774.[16] The fourth extract is from Thomas Jefferson's *Summary View of the Rights of British America*, originally written in 1774 as instructions for the Virginia delegates to the First Continental Congress.[17]

Bland

Men in a State of Nature are absolutely free and independent of one another as to sovereign Jurisdiction, but when they enter into a Society, and by their own Consent become Members of it, they must submit to the Laws of the Society according to which they agree to be governed; for it is evident, by the very Act of Association, that each Member subjects himself to the Authority of that Body in whom, by common Consent, the legislative Power of the State is placed: But though they must submit to the Laws, so long as they remain Members of the Society, yet they retain so much of their natural Freedom as to have a Right to retire from the Society, to renounce the Benefits of it, to enter into another Society, and to settle in another Country; for their Engagements to the Society, and their Submission to the publick Authority of the State, do not oblige them to continue in it longer than they find it will conduce to their Happiness, which they have a natural Right to promote. This natural Right remains with every Man, and he cannot justly be deprived of it by any civil Authority. . . .

Now when Men exercise this Right, and withdraw themselves from their Country, they recover their natural Freedom and Independence: The Jurisdiction and Sovereignty of the State they have quitted ceases; and if they unite, and by common Consent take Possession of a new Country, and form themselves into a political Society, they become a sovereign State, independent of the State from which they separated. If then the Subjects of England have

---

[14] Richard Bland, *An Inquiry into the Rights of the British Colonies* (Williamsburg, 1766), 9–10, 16, 20.

[15] James K. Hosmer, *The Life of Thomas Hutchinson* (Boston, 1896), 380–96.

[16] James D. Andrews, ed., *The Works of James Wilson*, 2 vols. (Chicago, 1896), 2:501–43.

[17] Julian P. Boyd, ed., *The Papers of Thomas Jefferson* (Princeton: Princeton University Press, 1950–), 1:121–37.

a natural Right to relinquish their Country, and by retiring from it, and associating together, to form a new political Society and independent State, they must have a Right, by Compact with the Sovereign of the Nation, to remove into a new Country, and to form a civil Establishment upon the Terms of the Compact. . . .

From this Detail of the Charters, and other Acts of the Crown, under which the first Colony in North America was established, it is evident that "the Colonists were not a few unhappy Fugitives who had wandered into a distant Part of the World to enjoy their civil and religious Liberties, which they were deprived of at home," but had a regular Government long before the first Act of Navigation, and were respected as a distinct State, independent, as to their *internal* Government, of the original Kingdom, but united with her, as to their *external* Polity, in the closest and most intimate LEAGUE AND AMITY, under the same Allegiance, and enjoying the Benefits of a reciprocal Intercourse.

Samuel Adams

Your Excellency tells us, "you know of no line that can be drawn between the supreme authority of Parliament and the total independence of the colonies." If there be no such line, the consequence is, either that the colonies are the vassals of the Parliament, or that they are totally independent. As it cannot be supposed to have been the intention of the parties in the compact, that we should be reduced to a state of vassalage, the conclusion is, that it was their sense, that we were thus independent. "It is impossible," your Excellency says, "that there should be two independent Legislatures in one and the same state." May we not then further conclude, that it was their sense, that the colonies were, by their charters, made distinct states from the mother country? Your Excellency adds, "for although there may be but one head, the King, yet the two Legislative bodies will make two governments as distinct as the kingdoms of England and Scotland, before the union." Very true, may it please your Excellency; and if they interfere not with each other, what hinders, but that being united in one head and common Sovereign, they may live happily in that connection, and mutually support and protect each other? Notwithstanding all the terrors which your Excellency has pictured to us as the effects of a total independence, there is more reason to dread the consequences of absolute uncontrolled power, whether of a nation or a monarch, than those of a total independence. . . .

After all that we have said, we would be far from being understood to have in the least abated that just sense of allegiance which we owe to the King of Great Britain, our rightful Sovereign; and should the people of this province be left to the free and full exercise of all the liberties and immunities granted to them by charter, there would be no danger of an independence on the Crown. Our charters reserve great power to the Crown in its Representative, fully sufficient to balance, analogous to the English constitution, all the liberties and privileges granted to the people. All this your Excellency knows full well; and whoever considers the power and influence, in all their branches, reserved by our charter, to the Crown, will be far from thinking that the Commons of this province are too independent.

Wilson

All men are, by nature, equal and free: No one has a right to any authority over another without his consent: all lawful government is founded on the consent of those who are subject to it: Such consent was given with a view to ensure and to encrease the happiness of the governed, above what they could enjoy in an independent and unconnected state of nature. The consequence is, that the happiness of the society is the first law of every government. . . .

What has been already advanced will suffice to show, that it is repugnant to the essential maxims of jurisprudence, to the ultimate end of all governments, to the genius of the British constitution, and to the liberty and happiness of the Colonies, that they should be bound by the legislative authority of the parliament of Great Britain. . . .

I am sufficiently aware of an objection, that will be made to what I have said concerning the legislative authority of the British parliament. It will be alleged, that I throw off all dependence on Great Britain. . . . I shall take some pains to obviate the objection, and to show that a denial of the legislative authority of the British parliament over America is by no means inconsistent with that connection, which ought to subsist between the mother country and her colonies, and which, at the first settlement of those Colonies, it was intended to maintain between them; but that, on the contrary, that connection would be entirely destroyed by the extension of the power of parliament over the America plantations. . . .

From this dependence, abstracted from every other source, arises a strict connection between the inhabitants of Great Britain and those of America. They are fellow-subjects; they are under allegiance to the same prince; and this union of allegiance naturally produces a union of hearts. It is also productive of a union of measures through the whole British dominions. To the King is intrusted the direction and management of the great machine of government. He therefore is fittest to adjust the different wheels, and to regulate their motions in such a manner as to co-operate in the same general designs. He makes war: he concludes peace: he forms alliances: he regulates domestic trade by his prerogative, and directs foreign commerce by his treaties with those nations, with whom it is carried on. He names the officers of government; so that he can check every jarring movement in the administration. He has a negative on the different legislatures throughout his dominions, so that he can prevent any repugnancy in their different laws. . . .

After considering, with all the attention of which I am capable, the foregoing opinion—that all the different members of the British empire are distinct states, independent of each other, but connected together under the same sovereign in right of the same crown—I discover only one objection that can be offered against it. But this objection will, by many, be deemed a fatal one. "How, it will be urged, can the trade of the British Empire be carried on, without some power, extending over the whole, to regulate it? The legislative authority of each part, according to your doctrine, is confined within the local bounds of that part: how, then, can so many interfering interests and claims, as must necessarily meet and contend in the commerce of the whole, be decided and adjusted?"

Permit me to answer these Questions by proposing some others in my turn. How has the trade of Europe—how has the trade of the whole globe, been carried on? Have those widely extended plans been formed by one superintending power? Have they been carried into execution by one superintending power? Have they been formed—have they been carried into execution, with less conformity to the rules of justice and equality, than if they had been under the direction of one superintending power?

Jefferson

Remind him [the King] that our ancestors, before their emigration to America, were the free inhabitants of the British dominions in Europe, and possessed a right, which nature has given to all men, of departing from the country in which chance, not choice has placed them, of going in quest of new habitations, and of there establishing new societies, under such laws and regulations as to them shall seem most likely to promote public happiness. . . . That settlements having been thus effected in the wilds of America, the emigrants thought proper to adopt that system of laws under which they had hitherto lived in the mother country, and to continue their union with her by submitting themselves to the same common sovereign, who was thereby made the central link connecting the several parts of the empire thus newly multiplied. . . .

That the exercise of a free trade with all parts of the world, possessed by the American colonists as of natural right, and which no law of their own had taken away or abridged, was next the object of unjust incroachment. . . . History has informed us that bodies of men as well as individuals are susceptible of the spirit of tyranny. A view of these acts of parliament for regulation, as it has been affectedly called, of the American trade, if all other evidence were removed out of the case, would undeniably evince the truth of this observation. . . .

That we shall at this time also take notice of an error in the nature of our landholdings, which crept in at a very early period of our settlement. . . . From the nature and purpose of civil institutions, all the lands within the limits which any particular society has circumscribed around itself, are assumed by that society, and subject to their allotment only. This may be done by themselves assembled collectively, or by their legislature to whom they may have delegated sovereign authority: and, if they are allotted in neither of these ways, each individual of the society may appropriate to himself such lands as he finds vacant, and occupancy will give him title. . . .

That these are our grievances

which we have thus laid before his majesty with that freedom of language and sentiment which becomes a free people, claiming their rights as derived from the laws of nature, and not as the gift of their chief magistrate. . . . Open your breast, Sire, to liberal and expanded thought. . . . Let no act be passed by any one legislature which may infringe on the rights and liberties of another. This is the important post in which fortune has placed you, holding the balance of a great, if a well poised empire. This, Sire, is the advice of your great American council, on the observance of which may perhaps depend your felicity and future fame, and the preservation of that harmony which alone can continue both to Great Britain and America the reciprocal advantages of their connection. It is neither our wish nor our interest to separate from her. We are willing on our part to sacrifice every thing which reason can ask to the restoration of that tranquility for which all must wish. On their part let them be ready to establish union on a generous plan. Let them name their terms, but let them be just. Accept of every commercial preference it is in our power to give for such things as we can raise for their use, or they make for ours. But let them not think to exclude us from going to other markets, to dispose of those commodities which they cannot use, nor to supply those wants which they cannot supply. Still less let it be proposed that our properties within our own territories shall be taxed or regulated by any power on earth but our own. The god who gave us life, gave us liberty at the same time: the hand of force may destroy, but cannot disjoin them.

The English Liberals Defend America

As the American case against the mother country gradually developed, the Americans discovered that they were not entirely without sympathizers and supporters in England. There were, in fact, a number of distinguished Englishmen who understood what it was that the Americans were demanding, and who, therefore, were prepared to grant it—at least in a certain degree. Such men were William Pitt, Earl of Chatham; the Earl of Shelburne; John Wilkes; and Richard Price. The sympathy and varying degrees of support given by such English leaders greatly encouraged the Americans. It may, indeed, have been one of the decisive factors influencing the Americans to hold their ground when the final test came.

The most active and boisterous English opposition to the Parliamentary program came from the advocates of Parliamentary reform, led by John Wilkes. Along with other radicals, Wilkes, a member of the House of Commons and later Lord Mayor of London, espoused the American cause. Like his associates, however, he was more interested in promoting reform at home than in furthering a genuine understanding of the American concept of the federative Empire. As Lord Mayor of London in the critical year 1775, Wilkes presented a petition to the King for the dismissal of the ministers whose inept leadership had brought about the imperial crisis. The first selection that follows consists of the petition.[18]

Of all the Englishmen who debated the American issue, only the Earl of Shelburne and a few of his followers, like Granville Sharp and Richard Price, understood and accepted the logic of the colonial demand for recognizing that a federative Empire did exist. It was Price who wrote what was perhaps the most penetrating and significant explanation of this position in a pamphlet entitled *Observations on the Nature of Civil Liberty, the Principles of Government, and the Justice and Policy of the War with America*, published in London in 1776. The second selection printed below contains an extract from Price's work.[19]

William Pitt, Earl of Chatham, who was certainly the most distinguished English statesman of his generation, sympathized with the American demand for self-taxation, on the ground that this was an inalienable right enjoyed by all Englishmen. Pitt never did grasp fully the American concept of the federated Empire, however, and he would never have accepted this part of the American ideology. The third selection below is from one of Chatham's speeches in the House of Lords demanding the withdrawal of English troops from America at the moment of crisis in 1775.[20]

Wilkes

We, your Majesty's dutiful and loyal subjects, the Lord Mayor, Aldermen, and Livery of the City of *London,* beg leave to approach the Throne, and to declare our abhorrence of the measures which have been pursued, and are now pursuing, to the oppression of our fellow-subjects in *America.* These measures are big with all the consequences which can alarm a free and commercial people; a deep, and, perhaps, fatal wound to Commerce; the ruin of Manufactures; the diminution of the Revenue, and consequent increase of Taxes; the alienation of the colonies; and the blood of your Majesty's subjects.

But your Petitioners look with less horrour at the consequences, than at the purpose of those measures. Not deceived by the specious artifice of calling despotism dignity, they plainly perceive that the real purpose is, to establish arbitrary power over all *America.*

Your Petitioners conceive the liberties of the whole to be inevitably connected with those of every part of an Empire founded on the common rights of mankind. They cannot, therefore, observe, without the greatest concern and alarm, the Constitution fundamentally violated in any part of your Majesty's Dominions. They esteem it an essential,

---

[18] Peter Force, ed., *American Archives,* 4th Series, I, 1853–1854.

[19] Richard Price, *Observations on the Nature of Civil Liberty, the Principles of Government, and the Justice and Policy of the War with America* (London, 1776), 1–65.

[20] *The Parliamentary History of England,* 18:149–56.

an unalterable principle of liberty, the source and security of all constitutional rights, that no part of the Dominion can be taxed without being represented. Upon this great leading principle, they most ardently wish to see their fellow-subjects, in *America,* secured in what their humble petition, to your Majesty, prays for—Peace, Liberty, and Safety. Subordination in Commerce, under which the Colonies have always cheerfully acquiesced, is, they conceive, all that this country ought, in justice, to require. From this subordination such advantages flow, by all the profits of their commerce centring here, as fully compensate this Nation for the expense incurred, to which they, also, contribute, in Men and Money, for their defence and protection, during a general war; and, in their Provincial wars, they have manifested their readiness and resolution to defend themselves. To require more of them would, for this reason, derogate from the justice and magnanimity which have been hitherto the pride and character of this country.

It is, therefore, with the deepest concern that we have seen the sacred security of Representation, in their Assemblies, wrested from them; the Trial by Jury abolished, and the odious powers of Excise extended to all cases of Revenue; the sanctuary of their Houses laid open to violation, at the will and pleasure of every Officer and Servant in the Customs; the Dispensation of Justice corrupted, by rendering their Judges dependent, for their seats and salaries, on the will of the Crown; Liberty and Life rendered precarious, by subjecting them to be dragged over the Ocean, and tried for treason or felony here; where the distance, making it impossible for the most guiltless to maintain his innocence, must deliver him up, a victim to Ministerial vengeance. Soldiers and others, in *America,* have been instigated to shed the blood of people, by establishing a mode of trial which holds out impunity for such murder; the capital of *New England* has been punished with unexampled rigour, untried and unheard, involving the innocent and the suspected in one common and inhuman calamity; Chartered Rights have been taken away, without any forfeiture proved, in order to deprive the people of every legal exertion against the tyranny of their rulers; the Habeas Corpus Act, and Trial by Jury, have been suppressed, and *French* Despotick Government, with the Roman Catholic Religion, have been established, by law, over an extensive part of your Majesty's Dominions, in *America;* dutiful Petitions for redress of those grievances, from all your Majesty's *American* subjects, have been fruitless. . . .

Your Petitioners are persuaded that these measures originate in the secret advice of men who are enemies, equally, to your Majesty's title, and to the liberties of your people. That your Majesty's Ministers carry them into execution by the same fatal corruption which has enabled them to wound the peace and violate the Constitution of this country; thus they poison the fountain of publick security, and render that body, which should be the guardian of liberty, a formidable instrument of arbitrary power.

Your Petitioners do, therefore, most earnestly beseech your Majesty to dismiss, immediately and forever, from your Councils, these Ministers and advisers, as the first step toward a full redress of those grievances which alarm and afflict your whole people. So shall peace and commerce be restored, and the confidence and affection of all your Majesty's subjects be the solid supporters of your Throne.

Price

Our Colonies in NORTH AMERICA appear to be now determined to risque and suffer every thing, under the persuasion, that GREAT BRITAIN is attempting to rob them of that Liberty to which every member of society, and all civil communities, have a natural and unalienable right. The question, therefore, whether this is a reasonable persuasion, is highly interesting, and deserves the most careful attention of every *Englishman* who values Liberty, and wishes to avoid staining himself with the guilt of invading it. . . .

From what has been said it is obvious, that all civil government, as far as it can be denominated *free,* is the creature of the people. It originates with them. It is conducted under their direction; and has in view nothing but their happiness. All its different forms are no more than so many different modes in which they chuse to direct their affairs, and to secure the quiet enjoyment of their rights.—In every free state every man is his own *Legislator.*—All *taxes* are free gifts for public services.—All *laws* are particular provisions or regulations established by COMMON CONSENT for gaining protection and safety.—And all *Magistrates* are Trustees or Deputies for carrying these regulations into execution. . . .

Let us think here of what may be practicable in this way with respect to *Europe* in particular.—While it continues divided, as it is at present, into a great number of independent kingdoms whose interests are continually clashing, it is impossible but that disputes will often arise which must end in war and carnage. It would be no remedy to this evil to make one of these states supreme over the rest; and to give it an absolute plenitude of power to superintend and controul them. This would be to subject all the states to the arbitrary discretion of one, and to establish an ignominious slavery not possible to be long endured. It would, therefore, be a remedy worse than the disease; nor is it possible it should be approved by any mind that has not lost every idea of Civil Liberty. On the contrary.—Let every state, with respect to all its internal concerns, be continued independent of all the rest; and let a general confederacy be formed by the appointment of a SENATE consisting of Representatives from all the different states. Let this SENATE possess the power of managing all the *common* concerns of the united states, and of judging and deciding between them, as a common *Arbiter* or *Umpire,* in all disputes; having, at the same time, under its direction, the common force of the states to support its decisions.—In these circumstances, each separate state would be secure against the interference of foreign power in its private concerns, and, therefore, would possess *Liberty;* and at the same time it would be secure against all oppression and insult from every neighbouring state.—Thus might the scattered force and abilities of a whole continent be gathered into one point; all litigations settled as they rose; universal peace preserved; and nation prevented *from any more lifting up a sword against nation.* . . .

But ought there not, it is asked, to exist somewhere in an *Empire* a supreme legislative authority over the whole; or a power to controul and bind all the different states of which it consists?—This enquiry has been already answered. The truth is, that such a supreme controuling power ought to exist no-where except in such a SENATE or body of delegates as that [already] described . . . ; and that the authority or supremacy of even this senate ought to be limited to the common concerns of the *Empire*.—I think I have proved that the fundamental principles of Liberty necessarily require this.

In a word. An *Empire* is a collection of states or communities united by some common bond or tye. If these states have each of them free constitutions of government, and, with respect to taxation and internal legislation, are independent of the other states, but united by compacts, or alliances, or subjection to a Great *Council,* representing the whole, or to one monarch entrusted with the supreme executive power: In these circumstances, the Empire will be an Empire of Freemen.

Chatham

When I urge this measure of recalling the troops from Boston, I urge it on this pressing principle, that it is necessarily preparatory to the restoration of your peace, and the establishment of your prosperity. It will then appear that you are disposed to treat amicably and equitably; and to consider, revise, and repeal, if it should be found necessary, as I affirm it will, those violent acts and declarations which have disseminated confusion throughout your empire. . . .

Property is private, individual, absolute. Trade is an extended and complicated consideration: it reaches as far as ships can sail or winds can blow: it is a great and various machine. To regulate the numberless movements of its several parts, and combine them into effect, for the good of the whole, requires the superintending wisdom and energy of the supreme power in the empire. But this supreme power has no effect towards internal taxation; for it does not exist in that relation; there is no such thing, no such idea in this constitution, as a supreme power operating upon property. Let this distinction then remain for ever ascertained; taxation is theirs, commercial regulation is ours. As an American I would recognize to England her supreme right of regulating commerce and navigation: as an Englishman by birth and principle, I recognize to the Americans their supreme unalienable right in their property; a right which they are justified in the defence of to the last extremity. To maintain this principle is the common cause of the Whigs on the other side of the Atlantic, and on this. " 'Tis liberty to liberty engaged," that they will defend themselves, their families, and their country. In this great cause they are immoveably allied: it is the alliance of God and nature—

immutable, eternal—fixed as the firmament of heaven. . . .

To conclude, my lords; if the ministers thus persevere in misadvising and misleading the King, I will not say, that they can alienate the affections of his subjects from his crown; but I will affirm, that they will make the crown not worth his wearing—I will not say that the King is betrayed; but I will pronounce,—that the kingdom is undone.

The Final Statement of the American Case

The American case now rested upon a concept of the British Empire as a federation of quasi-sovereign states, bound together by allegiance to a common Crown. But the British government could not envisage any such empire, and the ministry had determined to discipline the colonies in order to impress upon them a due sense of their subservient position. Events now piled up until, after the Tea Act of 1773 and the disciplinary "Intolerable Acts" of 1774, the colonies felt the time had come again to unite in a common front to meet what they regarded as Parliamentary tyranny. Thus representatives of the colonies met again in the fall of 1774 at Philadelphia, to consider ways and means of meeting the crisis. The temper of this congress was still relatively conciliatory, and a plan proposed by Joseph Galloway to meet the constitutional problem by the creation of an American Parliament coordinate with the British Parliament failed of adoption by only one vote.

The Continental Congress, however, firmly protested against Parliament's policies; in a series of declarations and petitions directed to the American people, the King, Parliament, and the people of Great Britain, it based its protests upon the idea that the colonies were autonomous governmental units within an Empire held together by loyalty to a common sovereign. The Congress admitted that the legislative powers of Parliament extended to the regulation of intercolonial and external relations, but it insisted that the powers of Parliament did not extend into the internal affairs of any colony. These ideas appear most clearly in the so-called *Declaration and Resolves* of the Congress, adopted on October 14, 1774.[21]

Resolved, N. C. D.

1. That [the people of America] are entitled to life, liberty, & property, and they have never ceded to any sovereign power whatever, a right to dispose of either without their consent.

2. That our ancestors, who first settled these colonies, were at the time of their emigration from the mother country, entitled to all the rights, liberties, and immunities of free and natural-born subjects,

---

21 W. C. Ford, ed., *Journals of the Continental Congress*, 34 vols. (Washington: Library of Congress, 1904–1937), 1:63–73.

within the realm of England. . . .

4. That the foundation of English liberty, and of all free government, is a right in the people to participate in their legislative council: and as the English colonists are not represented, and from their local and other circumstances, cannot properly be represented in the British parliament, they are entitled to a free and exclusive power of legislation in their several provincial legislatures, where their right of representation can alone be preserved, in all cases of taxation and internal polity, subject only to the negative of their sovereign, in such manner as has been heretofore used and accustomed. But, from the necessity of the case, and a regard to the mutual interest of both countries, we cheerfully consent to the operation of such acts of the British parliament, as are bona fide, restrained to the regulation of our external commerce, for the purpose of securing the commercial advantages of the whole empire to the mother country, and the commercial benefits of its respective members; excluding every idea of taxation, internal or external, for raising a revenue on the subjects in America, without their consent.

5. That the respective colonies are entitled to the common law of England, and more especially to the great and inestimable privilege of being tried by their peers of the vicinage, according to the course of that law. . . .

7. That these, his majesty's colonies, are likewise entitled to all the immunities and privileges granted & confirmed to them by royal charters, or secured by their several codes of provincial laws. . . .

9. That the keeping a Standing army in these colonies, in times of peace, without the consent of the legislature of that colony, in which such army is kept, is against law.

10. It is indispensably necessary to good government, and rendered essential by the English constitution, that the constituent branches of the legislature be independent of each other; that, therefore, the exercise of legislative power in several colonies, by a council appointed, during pleasure, by the crown, is unconstitutional, dangerous, and destructive to the freedom of American legislation. . . .

In the course of our inquiry, we find many infringements and violations of the foregoing rights, which, from an ardent desire, that harmony and mutual intercourse of affection and interest may be restored, we pass over for the present, and proceed to state such acts and measures as have been adopted since the last war, which demonstrate a system formed to enslave America. . . .

To these grievous acts and measures, Americans cannot submit, but in hopes that their fellow subjects in Great-Britain will, on a revision of them, restore us to that state in which both countries found happiness and prosperity, we have for the present only resolved to pursue the following peaceable measures: . . . 1st. To enter into a non-importation, non-consumption, and non-exportation agreement or association. 2. To prepare an address to the people of Great-Britain, and a memorial to the inhabitants of British America, & 3. To prepare a loyal address to His Majesty; agreeable to resolutions already entered into.

3. THE BRITISH CASE

When the question of the constitutional nature of the British Empire was raised by American resistance to Parliamentary legislation, there was only one possible answer to most Englishmen and American Tories: The British Empire was a nation, an integral unity, of which every English man was a member. Its supreme legislature was Parliament, and every subject of the British Crown, no matter where he was, was also subject to the acts of Parliament. Certain English liberals, like William Pitt, Earl of Chatham and the Earl of Camden, were willing to admit the right of the colonies to be taxed by none but themselves, thus placing a limit upon the powers of Parliament; others, like Edmund Burke, were prepared to waive doctrinaire principles and preserve the peace and mutual affection between the parts of the Empire by making concessions on the grounds of expediency. But even Chatham was never willing to surrender the essential principle of the integral, national Empire. They differed from the ministry and the King only as to ways and means of implementing their concept of the Empire and making it work.

The Empire, in the view of those who were responsible for British policies, had always been thus. The resistance of the colonies to Parliament, and their eventual contention that the Empire was a federation of separate states, bound together only by loyalty to a common King, was to them new and revolutionary in the extreme. They thus thought of themselves as defending the old institutions and ideals against the subversive innovations of the Americans. The Britith Empire represented to these Englishmen, as to the American Tories, a national ideal that would be shattered and utterly destroyed if the revolutionary ideas of the American radicals should be allowed to establish themselves. For these Englishmen, the preservation of the integrity of the Empire, as they knew it, was a kind of crusade.

Taxation of the Colonies

The English cause possessed a strong champion in Soame Jenyns, a thoughtful—and somewhat facetious—poet, essayist, and member of Parliament. In a pamphlet entitled *The Objection to the Taxation of our American Colonies by the Legislature of Great Britain Briefly Considered,* and published in 1765, Jenyns contended that the American argument against Parliamentary taxation was unfounded and indefensible.

As a matter of historical fact, Jenyns was right. Parliament had, on occasion, legislated upon the internal affairs of the colonies. It had taxed them and regulated their internal trade and had set terms to many of the provincial "constitutions." And as for representation, there was much truth in the fact that large areas and groups in England itself were as completely without delegates in Parliament as the colonists. A selection from the Jenyns pamphlet follows.[22]

The great capital argument, which I find on this subject, and which, like an elephant at the head of a Nabob's army, being once overthrown, must put the whole into confusion, is this: that no Englishman is, or can be taxed, but by his own consent: by which must be meant one of these three propositions; either that no Englishman can be taxed without his own consent as an individual; or that no Englishman can be taxed without the consent of the persons he chuses to represent him; or that no Englishman can be taxed without the consent of the majority of all those, who are elected by himself and others of his fellow-subjects to represent them. Now let us impartially consider, whether any one of these propositions are in fact true: if not, then this wonderful structure which has been erected upon them, falls at once to the ground, and like another Babel, perishes by a confusion of words, which the builders themselves are unable to understand.

First then, that no Englishman is or can be taxed but by his own consent as an individual: this is so far from being true, that it is the very reverse of truth, for no man that I know of is taxed by his own consent; and an Englishman, I believe, is as little likely to be so taxed, as any man in the world.

Secondly, that no Englishman is, or can be taxed, but by the consent of those persons, whom he has chose to represent him; for the truth of this I shall appeal only to the candid representatives of those unfortunate counties which produce cyder, and shall willingly acquiesce under their determination.

Lastly, that no Englishman is, or can be taxed, without the consent of the majority of those, who are elected by himself, and others of his fellow-subjects, to represent them. This is certainly as false as the other two; for every Englishman is taxed, and not one in twenty represented: copyholders, leaseholders, and all men possessed of personal property only, chuse no representatives: Manchester, Birmingham, and many more of our richest and most flourishing trading towns send no members to parliament, consequently cannot consent by their representatives, because they chuse none to represent them; yet are they not Englishmen? or are they not taxed?

I am well aware, that I shall hear Locke, Sidney, Seldon, and many other great names quoted, to prove that every Englishman, whether he has a right to vote for a representative or not, is still represented in the British parliament; in which opin-

---

[22] Charles N. Cole, ed., *The Works of Soame Jenyns*, 4 vols. (London, 1790), 2:189–204.

ion they all agree: on what principle of common sense this opinion is founded I comprehend not, but on the authority of such respectable names I shall acknowledge its truth; but then I will ask one question, and on that I will rest the whole merits of the cause: Why does not this imaginary representation extend to America, as well as over the whole island of Great Britain? If it can travel three hundred miles, why not three thousand? if it can jump over rivers and mountains, why cannot it sail over the ocean? If the towns of Manchester and Birmingham sending no representatives to parliament, are notwithstanding there represented, why are not the cities of Albany and Boston equally represented in that assembly? Are they not alike British subjects? are they not Englishmen? or are they only Englishmen when they solicit for protection, but not Englishmen when taxes are required to enable this country to protect them? . . .

One method indeed has been hinted at, and but one, that might render the exercise of this power in a British parliament just and legal, which is the introduction of representatives from the several colonies into that body; but as this has never seriously been proposed, I shall not here consider the impracticability of this method, nor the effects of it, if it could be practiced; but only say, that I have lately seen so many specimens of the great powers of speech, of which these American gentlemen are possessed, that I should be much afraid, that the sudden importation of so much eloquence at once, would greatly endanger the safety of the government of this country; or in terms more fashionable, though less understood, this our most excellent constitution. If we can avail ourselves of these taxes on no other condition, I shall never look upon it as a measure of frugality; being perfectly satisfied, that in the end, it may be much cheaper for us to pay their army, than their orators.

The Ideal of a Unified Empire

The implications in colonial discontent, however, were deeper than Soame Jenyns realized. Though he disposed of the American argument to his own satisfaction, he failed completely to consider the fundamental constitutional nature of the British Empire. This question was faced more directly by Lord Mansfield, chief justice of the court of King's Bench, in the debate in the House of Lords in 1766 over the repeal of the Stamp Act. Mansfield emphasized the idea that Parliament was the supreme legislature for the whole empire. Like Jenyns, he conceded that Parliament did not personally represent anyone. It was, however, the lawmaking body for all Britons, who collectively constituted an indivisible nation. For Mansfield it was unthinkable that Englishmen anywhere could challenge the authority of Parliament to pass any law it deemed right and proper. An extract from his speech constitutes the selection below.[23]

---

[23] *The Parliamentary History of England*, 16:172–77.

What has been wrote by those who have treated on the law of nature, or of other nations, in my opinion, is not at all applicable to the present question. . . .

I deny the proposition that parliament takes no man's property without his consent: it frequently takes private property without making what the owner thinks a compensation. If any lord makes objection to any part of the proposition, he ought to confine himself in his argument to the part he objects to, and not run into matters which do not relate to such objection. . . .

The proposition before your lordships has unhappily been attended with a difference of opinion in England. I shall therefore use my endeavours, in what I have to offer your lordships on this occasion, to quiet men's minds upon this subject.

In order to do this, I shall first lay down two propositions:

1st, That the British legislature, as to the power of making laws, represents the whole British empire, and has authority to bind every part and every subject without the least distinction, whether such subjects have a right to vote or not, or whether the law binds places within the realm or without.

2nd, That the colonists, by the condition on which they migrated, settled, and now exist, are more emphatically subjects of Great Britain than those within the realm; and that the British legislature have in every instance exercised their right of legislation over them without any dispute or question till the 14th of January last.

As to the 1st proposition:

In every government the legislative power must be lodged somewhere, and the executive must likewise be lodged somewhere.

In Great Britain the legislative is in parliament, the executive in the crown.

The parliament first depended upon tenures. How did representation by election first arise? Why, by the favour of the crown. And the notion now taken up, that every subject must be represented by deputy, if he does not vote in parliament himself, is merely ideal. . . .

No distinction ought to be taken between the authority of parliament, over parts within or without the realm; but it is an established rule of construction, that no parts without the realm are bound unless named in the act. And this rule establishes the right of parliament; for unless they had a right to bind parts out of the realm, this distinction would never have been made. . . .

As to the second proposition I laid out,

It must be granted that they migrated with leave as colonies, and therefore from the very meaning of the word were, are, and must be subjects, and owe allegiance and subjection to their mother country.

The Question of Sovereignty—William Blackstone

Carried to its logical conclusion, this argument over the authority of Parliament versus the rights and powers of the colonial assemblies became one about the bedrock, fundamental nature of sovereignty. For the English statesmen, sovereignty in any state is one and indivisible, and was centered, in the British Empire, in King, Lords, and Commons. The American argument, as presented by Richard Bland and others, was that sovereignty was divisible: that King, Lords, and Commons were, indeed, sovereign in matters pertaining to foreign relations, interdominion affairs, and in other questions pertaining to the general welfare, but that the internal government of any colony was sovereign, with the King, in matters pertaining exclusively to the internal affairs of that colony.[24] The classic expression of the English ideal of imperial sovereignty is that explained by Sir William Blackstone, Professor of Law at Oxford University, in his *Commentaries on the Laws of England* (1765–1769).

Blackstone

Besides these adjacent islands, our more distant plantations in America, and elsewhere, are also in some respects subject to the English laws. Plantations, or colonies in distant countries, are either such where the lands are claimed by right of occupancy only, by finding them desart and uncultivated, and peopling them from the mother country; or where, when already cultivated they have been either gained by conquest, or ceded to us by treaties. And both these rights are founded upon the law of nature, or at least upon that of nations. But there is a difference between these two species of colonies, with respect to the laws by which they are bound. For it hath been held, that if an uninhabited country be discovered and planted by English subjects, all the English laws then in being, which are the birthright of every subject, are immediately there in force. . . .

The power and jurisdiction of parliament, says Sir Edward Coke, is so transcendent and absolute, that it cannot be confined, either for causes or persons, within any bounds. . . . It hath sovereign and uncontrollable authority in making, confirming, enlarging, restraining, abrogating, repealing, reviving, and expounding of laws, concerning matters of all possible denominations, ecclesiastical, or temporal, civil, military, maritime, or criminal: this being the place where that absolute despotic power, which must in all governments reside somewhere, is entrusted by the constitution of these kingdoms. All mischiefs and grievances, operations and remedies, that transcend the ordinary course of the laws, are within the reach of this extraordinary tribunal. It can regulate or new model the succession to the crown; as was done in the reign of Henry VIII and William III. It can alter the established religion of the land; as was done in a variety of instances, in the reigns of King Henry VIII and his three children. It can change and create afresh even the constitution of the kingdom and of parliaments themselves; as was done by the act of union, and the several statutes for triennial and septennial elections. It can, in short, do every

[24] This idea of divided sovereignty, which anticipates the philosophy of the later United States Constitution, may be said to have been one of the most significant ideological inventions of the Revolutionary era.

thing that is not naturally impossible; and therefore some have not scrupled to call its power, by a figure rather too bold, the omnipotence of parliament. True it is, that what the parliament doth, no authority upon earth can undo. So that it is a matter most essential to the liberties of this kingdom, that such members be delegated to this important trust, as are most eminent for their probity, their fortitude, and their knowledge; for it was a known apothegm of the great lord treasurer Burleigh, "that England could never be ruined but by a parliament": and, as Sir Matthew Hale observes, this being the highest and greatest court, over which none other can have jurisdiction in the kingdom, if by any means a misgovernment should any way fall upon it, the subjects of this kingdom are left without all manner of remedy. . . .

It must be owned that Mr. Locke, and other theoretical writers, have held, that there remains still inherent in the people "supreme power to remove or alter the legislative, when they find the legislative act contrary to the trust reposed in them: for when such trust is abused, it is thereby forfeited, and devolves to those who gave it." But however just this conclusion may be in theory, we cannot adopt it, nor argue from it, under any dispensation of government at present actually existing. For this devolution of power, to the people at large, includes in it a dissolution of the whole form of government established by that people; reduces all the members to their original state of equality; and, by annihilating the sovereign power, repeals all positive laws whatsoever before enacted. No human laws will therefore suppose a case, which at once must destroy all law, and compel men to build afresh upon a new foundation; nor will they make provision for so desperate an event, as must render all legal provisions ineffectual. So long therefore as the English constitution lasts, we may venture to affirm, that the power of parliament is absolute and without control.

An English Moderate Speaks

Some Englishmen, while devoted to the idea of an integral Empire, strongly opposed the ministerial policies of both taxing the colonies and using force to coerce them. The constitutional arguments of these English compromisers at times resembled the early arguments of the Americans. It must be remembered, however, that their basic concept was essentially that of Mansfield and the American Tories.

One of the greatest of these friends of America in England, and surely the most eloquent, was Edmund Burke, the ablest orator in Parliament and, eventually, the greatest English political philosopher of his generation.

Burke acknowledged the supreme legislative function of Parliament for the whole Empire, but he was impatient of all fine-spun constitutional or logical distinctions. He felt that the decisive factor in British policy ought to be expediency—an expediency based upon the long historical evolution of British institutions and ideals. The selection that follows, from his "speech on conciliation with America," written in 1775, illustrates his point of view.[25]

The proposition is peace. Not peace through the medium of war; not peace to be hunted through the labyrinth of intricate and endless negotiations; not peace to arise out of universal discord, fomented from principal, in all parts of the empire; not peace to depend on the juridical determination of perplexing questions, or the precise marking the shadowy boundaries of a complex government. It is simple peace, sought in its natural course and in its ordinary haunts. It is peace sought in the spirit of peace, and laid in principles purely pacific. I propose, by removing the ground of the difference, and by restoring the *former unsuspecting confidence of the colonies in the mother country,* to give permanent satisfaction to your people,—and (far from a scheme of ruling by discord) to reconcile them to each other in the same act and by the bond of the very same interest which reconciles them to British government. . . .

My idea, therefore, without considering whether we yield as matter of right or grant as matter of favor, is, *to admit the people of our colonies into an interest in the Constitution,* and, by recording that admission in the journals of Parliament, to give them as strong an assurance as the nature of the thing will admit that we mean forever to adhere to that solemn declaration of systematic indulgence. . . .

This competence in the colony assemblies is certain. It is proved by the whole tenor of their acts of supply in all the assemblies, in which the constant style of granting is, "An aid to his Majesty"; and acts granting to the crown have regularly, for near a century, passed the public offices without dispute. Those who have been pleased paradoxically to deny this right, holding that none but the British Parliament can grant to the crown, are wished to look to what is done, not only in the colonies, but in Ireland, in one uniform, unbroken tenor, every session. . . .

My hold of the colonies is in the close affection which grows from common names, from kindred blood, from similar privileges, and equal protection. These are ties which, though light as air, are as strong as links of iron. Let the colonies always keep the idea of their civil rights associated with your government,—they will cling and grapple to you, and no force under heaven will be of power to tear them from their allegiance. But let it be understood that your government may be one thing and their privileges another, that these two things may exist without any mutual relation,— the cement is gone, the cohesion is loosened, and everything hastens to decay and dissolution. As long as you have the wisdom to keep the sovereign authority of this country as the sanctuary of liberty, the sacred temple consecrated to our common faith, wherever the chosen race and sons of England worship freedom, they will turn their faces towards you. The more they multiply, the

---

[25] Edmund Burke, *The Works of Edmund Burke,* 12 vols. (Boston, 1894), 2:99–186.

more friends you will have; the more ardently they love liberty, the more perfect will be their obedience. Slavery they can have anywhere. It is a weed that grows in every soil. They may have it from Spain, they may have it from Prussia. But, until you become lost to all feeling of your true interest and your natural dignity, freedom they can have from none but you. This is the commodity of price, of which you have the monopoly. This is the true Act of Navagation, which binds to you the commerce of the colonies, and through them secures to you the wealth of the world. Deny them this participation of freedom, and you break that sole bond which originally made, and must still preserve, the unity of the empire. Do not entertain so weak an imagination as that your registers and your bonds, your affidavits and your sufferances, your cockets and your clearances, are what form the great securities of your commerce. Do not dream that your letters of office, and your instructions, and your suspending clauses are the things that hold together the great contexture of this mysterious whole. These things do not make your government. Dead instruments, passive tools as they are, it is the spirit of the English communion that gives all their life and efficacy to them. It is the spirit of the English Constitution, which, infused through the mighty mass, pervades, feeds, unites, invigorates, vivifies every part of the empire, even down to the minutest member.

The American Tories Support the British National Ideal

Many thoughtful men in the colonies shared the national ideal of British thinkers like Burke. These men, conservatives in temperament and by conviction, gave their supreme loyalty to the ideal of an integral and indivisible English nation, of which, they thought, the Americans were inseparable members. In addition to this basic loyalty, however, they reasoned that both the rationalistic philosophy of natural rights and the social compact as the origin of the body politic, and the concept of the British Empire as a federation of autonomous societies of Englishmen formed by such compacts, were erroneous and likely to lead the Americans to disaster.

Such "Tory" thinkers were Thomas Hutchinson, Governor of Massachusetts, Rev. Samuel Seabury, an Anglican minister of New York, and Rev. Jonathan Boucher, an Anglican minister of Annapolis, Maryland. The selections that follow present the main arguments of the American Tories. The first is an extract from a speech by Hutchinson to the Massachusetts legislature in 1773; the second is from a pamphlet by Seabury published in 1774; the third is taken from one of Boucher's sermons delivered on the eve of the Revolution but not published until 1797.[26]

---

[26] James K. Hosmer, *The Life of Thomas Hutchinson* (Boston, 1896), 363–428; Samuel Seabury, *A View of the Controversy Between Great Britain and Her Colonies* (New York, 1774), 6–33; Jonathan Boucher, *A View of the Causes and Consequences of the American Revolution* (London, 1797), 348, 359–60, 363–64, 514, 515–16, 545–54.

Hutchinson

So much . . . of the spirit of liberty breathes through all parts of the English constitution, that, although from the nature of government, there must be one supreme authority over the whole, yet this constitution will admit of subordinate powers with legislative and executive authority, greater or less, according to local and other circumstances. Thus we see a variety of corporations formed within the kingdom, with powers to make and execute such by-laws as are for their immediate use and benefit, the members of such corporations still remaining subject to the general laws of the kingdom. We see also governments established in the plantations, which, from their separate and remote situation, require more general and extensive powers of legislation within themselves, than those formed within the kingdom, but subject, nevertheless, to all such laws of the kingdom as immediately respect them, or are designed to extend to them; and, accordingly, we, in this province have, from the first settlement of it, been left to the exercise of our Legislative and Executive powers, Parliament occasionally, though rarely, interposing, as in its wisdom has been judged necessary. . . .

If what I have said shall not be sufficient to satisfy such as object to the supreme authority of Parliament over the plantations, there may something further be added to induce them to an acknowledgement of it, which, I think, will well deserve their consideration. I know of no line that can be drawn between the supreme authority of Parliament and the total independence of the colonies; it is impossible there should be two independent legislatures in one and the same state; for, although there may be but one head, the King, yet the two legislative bodies will make two governments as distinct as the kingdoms of England and Scotland before the union. If we might be suffered to be altogether independent of Great Britain, could we have any claim to the protection of that government, of which we are no longer a part. Without this protection, should we not become the prey of one or the other powers of Europe, such as should first seize upon us? Is there any thing which we have more reason to dread than independence? I hope it never will be our misfortune to know, by experience, the difference between the liberties of an English colonist, and those of the Spanish, French, or Dutch.

We all profess to be the loyal and dutiful subjects of the King of Great Britain. His Majesty considers the British empire as one entire dominion, subject to one supreme legislative power; a due submission to which, is essential to the maintenance of the rights, liberties, and privileges of the several parts of this dominion. We have abundant evidence of his Majesty's tender and impartial regard to the rights of his subjects; and I am authorized to say, that "his Majesty will most graciously approve of every constitutional measure that may contribute to the peace, the happiness, and prosperity of his colony of Massachusetts Bay, and which may have the effect to shew to the world, that he has no wish beyond that of reigning in the hearts and affections of his people."

Seabury

The [Continental] Congress, Sir, was founded in sedition; its decisions are supported by tyranny; and is it *presumption* to controvert its *authority?* In your opinion, they "are *restless Spirits,*"—"enemies to the natural rights of mankind" who shall dare to speak against the *Congress,* or attempt to "diminish the influence of *their* decisions: while *they* are friends to America, and to the natural rights of mankind, who shall traduce and slander the sovereign authority of the nation; contravene and trample under foot the laws of their country." ...

In every government there must be a supreme, absolute authority lodged somewhere. In arbitrary governments this power is in the monarch; in aristocratical governments, in the nobles; in democratical in the people; or the deputies of their electing. ...

Upon supposition that every English colony enjoyed a legislative power independent of the parliament; and that the parliament has no just authority to make laws to bind them, this absurdity will follow —that there is no power in the British empire, which has authority to make laws for the whole empire; i.e. we have an empire, without government; or which amounts to the same thing, we have a government which has no supreme power. All our colonies are independent of each other: Suppose them independent of the British parliament,—what power do you leave to govern the whole? None at all. You split and divide the empire into a number of petty, insignificant states. This is the direct, the necessary tendency of refusing submission to acts of parliament. Every man who can see one inch beyond his nose, must see this consequence. And every man who endeavours to accelerate the independency of the colonies on the British parliament, endeavours to accelerate the ruin of the British empire.

To talk of being liege subjects to King George, while we disavow the authority of parliament is another piece of whiggish nonsense. I love my King as well as any whig in America or England either, and am as ready to yield him all lawful submission: But while I submit to the King, I submit to the authority of the laws of the state, whose guardian the King is. The difference between a good and a bad subject, is only this, that the one obeys, the other transgresses the law. The difference between a loyal subject and a rebel, is, that the one yields obedience to, and faithfully supports the supreme authority of the state, and the other endeavours to overthrow it. If we obey the laws of the King, we obey the laws of the parliament. If we disown the authority of the parliament, we disown the authority of the King. There is no medium without ascribing powers to the King which the constitution knows nothing of:—without making him superior to the laws, and setting him above all restraint. These are some of the ridiculous absurdities of American whiggism. ...

I will here, Sir, venture to deliver my sentiments upon the line that ought to be drawn between the supremacy of Great-Britain, and the dependency of the colonies. And I shall do it with the more boldness, because, I know it to be agreeable to the opinions of many of the warmest advocates for America, both in England and in the colonies, in the time of the stamp-act.—I imagine that if all internal taxation be vested in our own legislatures, and the right of regulating trade by duties, bounties, etc. be left in the power of the Parliament; and also the right of enacting all general laws for the good of all the colonies, that we shall have all the security for our rights, liberties and property, which human policy can give us: The dependence of the colonies on the mother country will be fixed on a firm foundation; the sovereign authority of Parliament, over all the dominions of the empire will be established, and the mother-country and all her colonies will be knit together, in one GRAND, FIRM, AND COMPACT BODY.

Boucher

It can, I think, admit of no dispute, that an accommodation between the Colonies and the Mother Country, on almost any terms, is infinitely more to be desired by both countries than even the most signal successes in war. In the latter way, to succeed is to become a separate people; not as Abram and Lot became a separate people, whilst yet they continued to be friends; but having no longer any community either of interest or affection, as perfect aliens to each other, and, in short, as totally distinct and separate nations. There seems no possibility of any middle course. . . .

Were the question to be determined by present expediency, it is possible the arguments in favour of a separation might be found to be the strongest. But, as such a separation would be a new thing in the world, . . . and as also there are in this vast continent many thousands of respectable men, who, considering allegiance [to the British crown] as a duty, find it impossible to bring themselves to retain or relinquish it just as a mere convenience may seem to suggest, we hope at least to be permitted to pause before we determine.

There is an objection of no ordinary magnitude at the very threshold of this novel proposal. It has never been proved, nor, in my humble opinion, can it ever be proved, that the Parent State can do what is asked; that is to say, can, without a breach of the Constitution, voluntarily withdraw or forbear it's [sic] government over America. Allegiance and protection are not merely reciprocal duties, entirely dependent the one on the other. Each duty continues to be equally obligatory, and in force, whether the other be performed or not. . . .

The only rational idea of civil liberty, or (which is the same thing) of a legitimate and good government . . . is, when the great body of the people are trained and led habitually to submit to and acquiesce in some fixed and steady principles of conduct. It is essential, moreover, to Liberty, that such principles shall be of power sufficient to controul the arbitrary and capricious wills of mankind; which, whenever they are not so controuled, are found to be dangerous and destructive to the best interests of society. The primary aim, therefore, of all well-framed Constitutions is, to place man, as it were, out of the reach of his own power, and also out of the power of others as weak as himself, by placing him under the power of law. To counteract that aim (and to do so is the object of all self-constituted assemblies) is to carry back social man to his supposed original independence, and to throw him once more into what has been called a state of Nature. In our own case, it is violently pulling down an old, well-poised Constitution, arbitrarily to introduce, in its stead, what, if it be no anarchy, must at best be a democracy. Now, it ought never to be out of the recollection of mankind, that democracies, even when established without either tumult or tyranny, and by the very general though perhaps not unanimous consent of the community, not contended with an equality of rights, in theory at least, naturally aim at an equality of possessions. . . .

This popular notion, that government was originally formed by the consent or by a compact of the people, rests on, and is supported by, another similar notion, not less popular, nor better founded. This other notion is, that the whole human race is born equal; and that no man is naturally inferior or, in any respect, subjected to another; and that he can be made subject to another only by his own consent. . . . Man differs from man in every thing that can be supposed to lead to supremacy and subjection, *as one star differs from another star in glory.* . . . A musical instrument composed of chords, keys, or pipes, all perfectly equal in size and power, might as well be expected to produce harmony, as a society composed of members all perfectly equal to be productive of harmony and peace. If (according to the idea of the advocates of this chimerical scheme of equality) no man could rightfully *be compelled to come in* and be a member even of a government to be formed by a regular compact, but by his own individual consent; it clearly follows, from the same principles, that neither could he rightfully be made or compelled to submit to the ordinances of any government already formed, to which he has not individually or actually consented. On the principle of equality, neither his parents, nor even the vote of a majority of the society . . . can have any such authority over any man. . . . The same principle of equality that exempts him from being governed without his own consent, clearly entitles him to recall and resume that consent whenever he sees fit; and he alone has a right to judge when and for what reasons it may be resumed.

All government, whether lodged in one or in many, is, in its nature, absolute and irresistible. . . . Without some paramount and irresistible power, there can be no government. In our Constitution, this supremacy is vested in the King and the Parliament; and, subordinate to them, in our Provincial Legislatures. If you were now released from this constitutional power, you must differ from all others "of the human race," if you did not soon find yourselves under a necessity of submitting to a power no less absolute, though vested in other persons, and a government differently constituted.

4. THE RESORT TO INDEPENDENCE

Down to the beginning of 1776 the American "Whigs" (those most violently critical of the mother country), had scarcely contemplated the possibility of secession from the British Empire. They protested, with complete sincerity, that all they wanted was the preservation of what they believed to be their rights of self-government as Englishmen. But they had been forced to define those rights in terms that amounted to nothing less than a demand for complete autonomy within their own provincial boundaries—a kind of quasi-sovereignty in their internal affairs. This was equivalent to a demand for a recognition by England that the Empire was not in fact an integral and indivisible "nation" of Englishmen everywhere, governed by one supreme Parliament, but, rather, a federation of autonomous republics in which Parliament had full power to regulate affairs of common interest, but no power whatever over the internal concerns of any colony.

The King Refuses to Compromise

It would have required too much of human nature to expect King George and his ministers to accept the American proposition, even had they really understood it, which they evidently did not. In their minds there could be no intermediate position between their concept of the Empire and complete, sovereign independence for the colonies. According to their own lights, and given their loyalty and responsibility to the Empire, they could not concede, or even seriously consider, a proposition that seemed so clearly to mean the complete dissolution of the Empire. They were convinced that the measures they had regretfully taken toward America were absolutely necessary for the preservation of the Empire they were sworn to preserve, and of the ideals that Empire represented. The Americans had resisted the enforcement of the Parliamentary laws; they had begun to accumulate military stores with the obvious intention of resorting to force, and now, in the spring of 1775, they had fired upon British soldiers on the village green at Lexington. Clearly, in the minds of the king and his ministers, they were in rebellion, and must be disciplined if the Empire were to be preserved.

King George still attributed the American resistance to the vicious machinations of a few evil men; he completely failed to comprehend the American point of view; and he still believed this was a rebellion, to be handled firmly but generously! The King, like the vast majority of his contemporaries in England, could envisage no imperial structure but that of the inviolable, indivisible,

road to revolution

unitary whole. He, like they, was apparently incapable of seeing, much less understanding, the historic processes at work in America. In their failure to comprehend, these men were compelled by their own obtuseness to preside over the very catastrophe they most feared—the dissolution of the Empire.

It was this mood that prompted the King to refuse—on the ground that the Continental Congress was an "illegal body"—to receive the "Olive Branch petition" that the Congress presented to him in the summer of 1775 in a last desperate effort to get Parliament to establish a basis for conciliation by renouncing its claim to unlimited sovereignty over the colonies. It was this mood, also, that prompted the language of the King's speech to Parliament in October 1775, after a spring and summer of actual armed conflict. This speech represented the thought of the King and of the ministry, as well as that of a clear majority in Parliament.[27]

The authors and promoters of this desperate conspiracy have, in the conduct of it, derived great advantage from the difference of our intention and theirs. They meant only to amuse, by vague expressions of attachment to the parent state, and the strongest protestations of loyalty to me, whilst they were preparing for a general revolt. On our part, though it was declared in your last session that a rebellion existed within the province of the Massachuset's Bay, yet even that province we wished rather to reclaim than to subdue. The resolutions of parliament breathed a spirit of moderation and forbearance; conciliatory propositions accompanied the measures taken to enforce authority, and the coercive acts were adapted to cases of criminal combinations amongst subjects not then in arms. I have acted with the same temper, anxious to prevent, if it had been possible, the effusion of the blood of my subjects, and the calamities which are inseparable from a state of war; still hoping that my people in America would have discerned the traitorous views of their leaders, and have been convinced, that to be a subject of Great Britain, with all its consequences, is to be the freest member of any civil society in the known world.

The rebellious war now levied is become more general, and is manifestly carried on for the purpose of establishing an independent empire. I need not dwell upon the fatal effects of the success of such a plan. The object is too important, the spirit of the British nation too high, the resources with which God hath blessed her too numerous, to give up so many colonies which she has planted with great industry, nursed with great tenderness, encouraged with many commercial advantages, and protected and defended at much expense of blood and treasure.

It is now become the part of wisdom and (in its effects) of clemency, to put a speedy end to these disorders by the most decisive exertions. For this purpose I have increased my naval establishment, and greatly augmented my land forces;

---

[27] *Parliamentary History of England,* 18:695–97.

but in such a manner as may be the least burthensome to my kingdoms. . . .

When the unhappy and deluded multitude, against whom this force will be directed, shall become sensible of their error, I shall be ready to receive the misled with tenderness and mercy: and in order to prevent the inconveniences which may arise from the great distance of their situation, and to remove, as soon as possible, the calamities which they suffer, I shall give authority to certain persons upon the spot to grant general or particular pardons and indemnities, in such manner, and to such persons as they shall think fit; and to receive the submission of any province or colony, which shall be disposed to return to its allegiance. It may be also proper to authorize the persons so commissioned to restore such province or colony so returning to its allegiance, to the free exercise of its trade and commerce, and to the same protection and security, as if such province or colony had never revolted.

An Appeal to Common Sense

Meanwhile, in America, the leaders of dissent were moving in desperation toward an acceptance of the hitherto dreaded idea of secession from the Empire. Thomas Paine, a recent immigrant from England, seized upon this moment to galvanize American opinion into a decision to throw off the British yoke entirely and forever. Paine's pamphlet, Common Sense, published early in 1776, declared that the time for argument and conciliation was now past: Every circumstance of nature and of reason proclaimed that the time had come for the continent and the island to part. Let Americans cease quibbling and protesting their subservience to the British King; let them accept the inevitable, and depart.[28]

Volumes have been written on the subject of the struggle between England and America. Men of all ranks have embarked in the controversy, from different motives, and with various designs; but all have been ineffectual, and the period of debate is closed. Arms as the last resource decide the contest; the appeal was the choice of the king, and the continent has accepted the challenge. . . .

By referring the matter from argument to arms, a new area for politics is struck—a new method of thinkings hath arisen. All plans, proposals, etc. prior to the nineteenth of April, i.e. to the commencement of hostilities, are like the almanacks of the last year; which though proper then, are superceded and useless now. Whatever was advanced by the advocates on either side of the question then, terminated in one and the same point, viz. a union with Great Britain; the only difference between the parties was the method of effecting it; the

---

[28] Moncure D. Conway, ed., *The Writings of Thomas Paine*, 4 vols. (New York, 1902), 1:69–120.

one proposing force, the other friendship; but it hath so far happened that the first hath failed, and the second hath withdrawn her influence. . . .

But Britain is the parent country, say some. Then the more shame upon her conduct. Even brutes do not devour their young, nor savages make war upon their families; wherefore, the assertion, if true, turns to her reproach; but it happens not to be true, or only partly so, and the phrase *parent* or *mother country* hath been jesuitically adopted by the King and his parasites, with a low papistical design of gaining an unfair bias on the credulous weakness of our minds. Europe, and not England, is the parent country of America. This new world hath been the asylum for the persecuted lovers of civil and religious liberty from *every part* of Europe. Hither have they fled, not from the tender embraces of the mother, but from the cruelty of the monster; and it is so far true of England, that the same tyranny which drove the first emigrants from home, pursues their descendants still. . . .

The next war may not turn out like the last, and should it not, the advocates for reconciliation now will be wishing for separation then, because neutrality in that case would be a safer convoy than a man of war. Every thing that is right or reasonable pleads for separation. The blood of the slain, the weeping voice of nature cries, 'TIS TIME TO PART. Even the distance at which the Almighty hath placed England and America is a strong and natural proof that the authority of the one over the other, was never the design of Heaven. The time likewise at which the continent was discovered, adds weight to the argument, and the manner in which it was peopled, encreases the force of it. The Reformation was preceded by the discovery of America: As if the Almighty graciously meant to open a sanctuary to the persecuted in future years, when home should afford neither friendship nor safety. . . .

Every quiet method for peace hath been ineffectual. Our prayers have been rejected with disdain; and hath tended to convince us that nothing flatters vanity or confirms obstinacy in Kings more than repeated petitioning—and nothing hath contributed more than that very measure to make the Kings of Europe absolute. Witness Denmark and Sweden. Wherefore, since nothing but blows will do, for God's sake let us come to a final separation, and not leave the next generation to be cutting throats under the violated unmeaning names of parent and child. . . .

Small islands not capable of protecting themselves are the proper objects for government to take under their care; but there is something absurd, in supposing a Continent to be perpetually governed by an island. In no instance hath nature made the satellite larger than its primary planet; and as England and America, with respect to each other, reverse the common order of nature, it is evident that they belong to different systems. England to Europe: America to itself.

I am not induced by motives of pride, party, or resentment to espouse the doctrine of separation and independence; I am clearly, positively, and conscientiously persuaded that it is the true interest of this continent to be so; that everything short of *that* is mere patchwork, that it can afford no lasting felicity,—that it is leaving the sword to our children, and shrinking back at a time when a little more, a little further, would have rendered this continent the glory of the earth. . . .

A government of our own is our natural right: and when a man seriously reflects on the precariousness of human affairs, he will become convinced, that it is infinitely wiser and safer, to form a constitution of our own in a cool deliberate manner, while we have it in our power, than to trust such an interesting event to time and chance. If we omit it now, some Massanello may hereafter arise, who, laying hold of popular disquietudes, may collect together the desperate and the discontented, and by assuming to themselves the powers of government, finally sweep away the liberties of the Continent like a deluge. Should the government of America return again into the hands of Britain, the tottering situation of things will be a temptation for some desperate adventurer to try his fortune; and in such a case, what relief can Britain give? Ere she could hear the news, the fatal business might be done; and ourselves suffering like the wretched Britons under the oppression of the Conqueror. Ye that oppose independence now, ye know not what ye do: ye are opening a door to eternal tyranny, by keeping vacant the seat of government. There are thousands and tens of thousands, who would think it glorious to expel from the continent, that barbarous and hellish power, which hath stirred up the Indians and the Negroes to destroy us; the cruelty hath a double guilt, it is dealing brutally by us, and treacherously by them.

Ye that tell us of harmony and reconciliation, can ye restore to us the time that is past? Can ye give to prostitution its former innocence? neither can ye reconcile Britain and America. The last cord now is broken, the people of England are presenting addresses against us. There are injuries which nature cannot forgive; she would cease to be nature if she did. As well can the lover forgive the ravisher of his mistress, as the Continent forgive the murders of Britain. The Almighty hath implanted in us these unextinguishable feelings for good and wise purposes. They are the Guardians of his Image in our hearts. They distinguish us from the herd of common animals. The social compact would dissolve, and justice be extirpated from the earth, or have only a casual existence were we callous to the touches of affection. The robber and the murderer would often escape unpunished, did not the injuries which our tempers sustain, provoke us into justice.

O! ye that love mankind! Ye that dare oppose not only the tyranny but the tyrant, stand forth! Every spot of the old world is overrun with oppression. Freedom hath been hunted round the globe. Asia and Africa have long expelled her. Europe regards her like a stranger, and England hath given her warning to depart. O! receive the fugitive, and prepare in time an asylum for mankind.

Independence Proclaimed

Through the winter of 1775–1776, as fighting between the colonies and the mother country spread from one end of the seaboard to the other, as England closed the colonies to trade with all the world and began to enforce the blockade, and as the sentiment of independence began to run like wildfire among the people, the individual colonies took step after step in directions that made it almost impossible for them ever to return to their old position in the Empire. One colony after another set up governments that were "extra-constitutional," formulated by conventions that had no official sanction or legal status, and proclaimed new constitutions and "bills of rights" that could never have received the approval of the mother country. And these governments, wherever they could, seized upon the properties and revenues of the Crown. Meanwhile, the Continental Congress had created a committee to seek aid from foreign countries, especially France; and it had already sent agents for this purpose abroad. Practically, independence was already a fact.

The last few steps toward independence were swift and sure. In the spring of 1776 Virginia instructed its delegates in the Continental Congress to introduce a motion for complete separation from the mother country. Such a resolution was introduced by Richard Henry Lee on June 7, 1776; and on June 10, the Congress appointed a committee, composed of Benjamin Franklin, John Adams, Thomas Jefferson, Roger Sherman, and Robert R. Livingston, to prepare a formal Declaration of Independence in case Congress approved Lee's resolution. On July 2 the Congress adopted the resolution as revised:

> That these United Colonies are, and of Right, ought to be Free and Independent States; that they are Absolved from all Allegiance to the British Crown, and that all political connection between them and the State of Great Britain, is and ought to be totally dissolved.

Two days later, July 4, 1776, the formal Declaration of Independence, to be presented to all the world, was laid before the Congress and approved.

It had taken the Americans a decade and a half to become convinced that they could no longer remain in the British Empire and be either free or happy. Having arrived at this conclusion, they could not recede. They could go only forward—and the only step forward was to move out of the Empire into the world of independence and sovereignty. It would require seven years of bitter war to make good their independent position; but the step out of the Empire into that position was taken in the Declaration of Independence.[29]

---

[29] *Journals of the Continental Congress*, 5:510–15.

The Unanimous Declaration of the Thirteen United States of America

When, in the Course of human events, it becomes necessary for one people to dissolve the political bands which have connected them with another, and to assume, among the Powers of the earth, the separate and equal station to which the Laws of Nature and of Nature's God entitle them, a decent respect to the opinions of mankind requires that they should declare the causes which impel them to the separation.

We hold these truths to be self-evident, that all men are created equal, that they are endowed by their Creator with certain unalienable Rights, that among these are Life, Liberty, and the pursuit of Happiness. That, to secure these rights, Governments are instituted among Men, deriving their just Powers from the consent of the governed. That, whenever any form of Government becomes destructive of these ends, it is the Right of the People to alter or to abolish it, and to institute new Government, laying its foundation on such Principles, and organizing its Powers in such form, as to them shall seem most likely to effect their Safety and Happiness. Prudence, indeed, will dictate that Governments long established should not be changed for light and transient causes; and, accordingly, all experience hath shewn, that mankind are more disposed to suffer, while evils are sufferable, than to right themselves by abolishing the forms to which they are accustomed. But, when a long train of abuses and usurpations, pursuing invariably the same Object, evinces a design to reduce them under absolute Despotism, it is their right, it is their duty, to throw off such Government, and to provide new Guards for their future Security. Such has been the patient sufferance of these Colonies; and such is now the necessity which constrains them to alter their former Systems of Government. The history of the present King of Great Britain is a history of repeated injuries and usurpations, all having in direct object the establishment of an absolute Tyranny over these States. To prove this, let Facts be submitted to a candid world.

He has refused his Assent to Laws the most wholesome and necessary for the public good.

He has forbidden his Governors to pass Laws of immediate and pressing importance, unless suspended in their operation till his Assent should be obtained; and when so suspended, he has utterly neglected to attend to them.

He has refused to pass other Laws for the accommodation of large districts of People, unless those People would relinquish the right of Representation in the legislature; a right inestimable to them and formidable to tyrants only. . . .

He has dissolved Representative Houses repeatedly, for opposing, with manly firmness, his invasions on the rights of the People. . . .

He has endeavoured to prevent the Population of these States; for that purpose obstructing the Laws of Naturalization of Foreigners; refusing to pass others to encourage their migrations hither, and raising the conditions of new Appropriations of Lands.

He has obstructed the Administration of Justice, by refusing his Assent to Laws for establishing Judiciary Powers.

He has made Judges dependent on his Will alone, for the tenure of their offices, and the amount and payment of their salaries.

He has erected a multitude of New Offices, and sent hither swarms of Officers to harass our People, and eat out their substance.

He has kept among us, in times of Peace, Standing Armies, without the Consent of our legislatures. . . .

He has combined with others to subject us to a jurisdiction foreign to our constitution, and unacknowledged by our laws; giving his Assent to their Acts of pretended Legislation:

For quartering large bodies of armed troops among us:

For protecting them, by a mock Trial, from Punishment for any Murders which they should commit on the Inhabitants of these States:

For cutting off our Trade with all parts of the world:

For imposing Taxes on us without our Consent:

For depriving us, in many cases, of the benefits of Trial by Jury:

For transporting us beyond Seas to be tried for pretended offences:

For abolishing the free System of English Laws in a neighbouring province, establishing therein an Arbitrary government, and enlarging its Boundaries, so as to render it at once an example and fit instrument for introducing the same absolute rule into these Colonies:

For taking away our Charters, abolishing our most valuable Laws, and altering fundamentally the Forms of our Government:

For suspending our own Legislatures, and declaring themselves invested with Power to legislate for us in all cases whatsoever.

He has abdicated Government here, by declaring us out of his protection, and waging War against us. . . .

In every stage of these Oppressions, We have Petitioned for Redress, in the most humble terms: Our repeated Petitions, have been answered only by repeated injury. A Prince, whose character is thus marked by every act which may define a Tyrant, is unfit to be the ruler of a free People.

Nor have We been wanting in attentions to our British brethren. We have warned them from time to time of attempts by their legislature to extend an unwarrantable jurisdiction over us. We have reminded them of the circumstances of our emigration and settlement here. We have appealed to their native justice and magnanimity, and we have conjured them by the ties of our common kindred, to disavow these usurpations, which, would inevitably interrupt our connexions and correspondence. They too have been deaf to the voice of justice and of consanguinity. We must, therefore, acquiesce in the necessity, which denounces our Separation, and hold them, as we hold the rest of mankind, Enemies in War, in Peace Friends.

We, therefore, the Representatives of the united States of America, in General Congress assembled, appealing to the Supreme Judge of the World for the rectitude of our intentions, do, in the Name, and by Authority of the good People of these Colonies, solemnly publish and declare, that these United Colonies are, and of Right, ought to be Free and Independent States; that they are Absolved from all Allegiance to the British Crown, and that all political connexion between them and the State of Great Britain, is and ought to be totally dissolved; and that, as Free and Independent States, they have full Power to levy War, conclude Peace, contract Alliances, establish Commerce, and to do all other Acts and Things which Independent States may of right do. And for the support of this Declaration, with a firm reliance on the protection of divine Providence, we mutually pledge to each other our Lives, our Fortunes, and our sacred Honour.

CONCLUSION

The American Revolution was one of the great tragic events of human history. Two societies, each led by a body of able and sincere men, and each motivated by the highest ideals it knew, came to an impasse over the question of the true nature of the Imperial constitution. When they finally arrived at this impasse, neither side could retreat without the sacrifice of its highest political ideal. It is difficult to imagine a more colossal example of the tragic consequences of sheer misunderstanding and stubborn unwillingness, in the name of principle, to compromise.

On the American side, the leaders of Whig opinion were deeply and sincerely convinced that the colonies had always been autonomous, that it was their right as Englishmen to be so, that autonomy had been granted them in their original charters, and that Parliament, by its program of taxation and control instituted in 1763, was introducing a new, revolutionary idea and practice into the long-established and accepted *status quo*. In this sense the Whigs thought of themselves as conservatives, fighting against the "tyrannical" innovations of Parliament for the way of life they had always known. Though their history may have been faulty, and their contention, unconsciously, essentially new, the important thing was that they believed, with deadly earnestness, that they were right.

On the British side, almost all Englishmen, even Chatham and Burke, embraced the theory that the British Empire and nation were one and indivisible, and that Parliament was the supreme and entirely sovereign legislature for the whole. Liberals like Chatham and Burke and Pownall were willing to make certain compromises, in the name of expediency, it is true. But the ministers and the King would not compromise on any essential point. Either the Americans were loyal British subjects, citizens in the integral British nation, or they were not. There could be no middle ground. To these sincere, if shortsighted and doctrinaire, British patriots, including the American Tories, it was the Americans who were advancing new, subversive, and revolutionary doctrines that could not fail to destroy the integrity of the Empire they were sworn to defend and to preserve. For them, as for the Americans, the argument became a contest, and the contest became a conflict, over the preservation of an old, long-established, and inviolable ideal. They, too, looked upon themselves as defending the conservation of the only way of life they had ever known.

In the face of these two doctrinaire positions, it was obvious that either one side must give in or the issue must be decided by force of arms. And since neither side would give in, it was inevitable that the decision be reached by armed conflict.

On the surface, then, the American Revolution appears to have been an ideological war—a war fought for the enforcement of one or the other of two rival political theories. Beneath the surface, however, it was much more than that. For, as John Adams said, the real Revolution was over before the shots were fired at Lexington and Concord. The real Revolution lay in the fact, almost unknown to the Americans themselves, that in the course of their economic, social, political, religious, and psychological evolution they had grown away from the mother country. In every one of these aspects of their group life, the American colonies differed from the mother country in practice, in institutions, and in ideals. In the course of building their new societies in America, Americans had also built a new way of life and a new outlook. That new outlook was symbolized for them in the word "liberty"—and the implementation of liberty, its administration and its defense, was embodied in the institutions, particularly the political institutions, that they regarded as their own.

Thus the true causes of the Revolution lay far beneath the surface argument over the constitution of the Empire. It lay, as Adams said, in the hearts of men. The constitutional argument was only the words and the symbols used to articulate and defend a much deeper meaning and a much more significant fact in human history: The appearance in the world of a new society, or group of societies, with a way of life that was its own.

In the time that has elapsed since the American Revolution a curious paradox has been revealed. Time has been on the side of the Americans of 1776, and the principle of sovereign government by consent and participation of the governed has become one of the dominant political ideas of the modern world. Yet in another sense time worked against the Americans. For as the American states, once independent, advanced down the road toward "a more perfect union," they came to be dominated, in the persons of a Hamilton, a Webster, and a Lincoln, by the very concept of the integral nation, bound, in every individual, to the sovereignty of a "national" government, against which the Americans had struggled, and from which they had severed themselves, in the name of natural rights, in 1776. It took a great and tragic civil war to impose the idea of the integral nation upon the southern states that had assisted in its original rejection in 1776.

4

MERRILL JENSEN

the articles of confederation and the constitution of 1787

From the American Revolution to the present day, Americans have debated the question of the division of power between the government of the United States and the governments of the individual states making up the union. Before the adoption of the Declaration of Independence, Americans insisted on the rights of the legislatures of the individual colonies as opposed to the government of Great Britain. After 1776 colonial rights became "states rights" and down to the present day the idea of "states rights" is a real factor in American political life.

The United States has had but two constitutions: The Articles of Confederation from 1781 to 1789, and the Constitution of 1787, since 1789. Each constitution is short and simply written, but Americans have never been able to agree as to the precise meaning of either of them. Interpretations without number have been written by historians, politicians, and judges. But the debate still goes on. One side holds that the central government is and should be a strictly federal government, that it should possess and use strictly delegated and sharply limited powers, and that it should follow the letter of a written constitution. All other powers of government should be held and used by the separate states. The other side argues that the central government is and should be a truly national government; that the written constitution should be interpreted loosely so that any power, whether in the constitution or not, can be used by the central government if it chooses; and finally, that the central government should not and cannot be limited by ideas of "states rights" or "state sovereignty."

This debate over the kind of government the nation should have began in the First Continental Congress in 1774. It became heated during the discussion over the Articles of Confederation in 1776 and 1777. It continued through the rest of the war and without letup during the years of the Confederation. The Convention of 1787 considered at length the question of whether a "national" or a "federal" government was best for the United States, and came out with a compromise between the two. When the Constitution of 1787 was submitted to the people for ratification, one of the main charges against it was that it had replaced the "federal" Articles of Confederation with a "national" constitution. An equally important argument against the new Constitution was that it did not have a bill of rights protecting individuals against the power of the government.

The debate was vigorous, and in the end the supporters of the Constitution were forced to agree that a bill of rights would be provided, once the new government was organized. The first Congress under the new government proposed a Bill of Rights in the form of amendments to the Constitution, and ten of these were soon adopted by the states. The Tenth Amendment included the essence of the second article of the Articles of Confederation. It declared that "The powers not delegated to the United States by the Constitution, nor prohibited by it to the States, are reserved to the States respectively, or to the people."

These amendments, and provisions of the Constitution itself, thus left the way open for future generations to debate the nature of the government provided for by the Constitution. In all these debates the participants have constantly referred back to what the "founding fathers" said or are supposed to have said about the nature of the history of the period and of the Articles of Confederation and the Constitution of 1787. Some of these appeals to "history" have been sincere, and some have not. In any case, it is worthwhile to go back to see what the founding fathers actually did say.

One striking fact is that very little new has been said since the eighteenth century. The documents which follow show that most of the ideas with which we are familiar today were expressed by leaders of the Revolutionary generation. They stated the issues as clearly as they have ever been stated. Furthermore, they were in as sharp disagreement about those issues as Americans have ever been since then. Mixed in with statements of fundamental conviction about the nature of government there is, of course, much that today would be called propaganda. The argument sounds familiar. The party out of power insists that the country will collapse unless it gets in; the party in power says the country will collapse unless it stays in.

The documents given here are but samples of a vast literature. By 1789 the United States had nearly a hundred newspapers and all of them were taking sides in politics. Men were writing pamphlets and political histories by the dozen. Politicians were writing letters and giving speeches by the hundred. Few though these samples may be, they illustrate the great variety of conflicting opinions held concerning the nature and purpose of the government of the United States.

1. THE PROBLEM OF UNION, 1774–1777

In the spring of 1774 the British Parliament passed a series of laws punishing Massachusetts for the Boston "Tea Party" of December 1773. These acts, which the Americans called the "Intolerable Acts," led to the calling of the First Continental Congress, which met at Philadelphia in September 1774. As soon as the Congress met, it split into two groups or "parties," which were a reflection of the internal political conflicts that had existed in the various colonies for many years. One party was composed of men who had been "radical" leaders in opposition to British colonial policies after 1763. Simultaneously, they had also won popular support by attacking the political aristocracies that had long ruled the colonies. These "radical" or "popular" leaders denied that the British Parliament had any right to legislate for the colonies. They insisted that Parliament did not have the right to tax them and by 1774 they had come close to denying that Parliament had any right to regulate their trade. They insisted that the elected legislature of each colony was the only legislature which could pass laws for the citizens of a colony. In essence they believed in "states rights" as the idea has been called since the American Revolution.

The conservative party in the First Congress was composed largely of men who were members of the ruling aristocracies of the colonies. Since 1763 they had opposed the popular leaders in colonial politics. It was not that the conservatives liked British policies: they did not. But they did oppose the violent means of opposition that the popular leaders had encouraged. By 1774 these conservative leaders were afraid that the popular leaders would either drive or lead the colonies into declaring independence; and the conservative leaders did not want independence. Therefore in the First Congress they offered a plan for the creation of a central government over the colonies. They hoped that this plan would settle disputes between the colonies and England and, at the same time, keep the colonies within the British Empire. The conservatives believed that a strong central government over the colonies was necessary: to regulate trade; to settle boundary disputes between colonies; to maintain order within individual colonies. In offering his plan for such a central government, Joseph Galloway summed up the ideas of the conservatives:

"In every government, patriarchal, monarchical, aristocratical, or democratical, there must be a supreme legislature. . . . There is a necessity that an American legislature should be set up, or else that we should give the power to Parliament or King."

The Galloway plan provided for an American Parliament elected by the colonial legislatures, with a president-general appointed by the King. Each colony was to retain its "constitution" and control over its "internal police," but the American Parliament was given wide power over the colonies. It was to "hold and exercise all the legislative rights, powers, and authorities necessary for regulating and administering all the general police and affairs of the colonies in which Great Britain and the colonies, or any of them, the colonies in general, or more than one colony, are in any manner concerned, as well civil and criminal as commercial." Legislation for the colonies might originate in either the British or the American Parliament, but both must pass it before it could go into effect.

The radical party would have none of this plan, and they managed to defeat its adoption. On top of this, they erased all record of it from the journals of the Congress.

By the time the Second Continental Congress met in May 1775, war had begun at Lexington and Concord, Massachusetts. The radical leaders in the Congress at once began working for independence, in fact if not in name. The conservative leaders tried to block every radical move; tried to reach some settlement which would avoid a complete break with Great Britain. By the spring of 1776, the conservatives realized that independence could not be avoided. Therefore they tried to delay a declaration of independence until a central government could be created. The radicals were more interested in independence than in a constitution, but they did agree to a compromise. On the same day that Congress appointed a committee to write a declaration of independence, in June 1776, it appointed a committee to draft articles of confederation.

The first draft of the first constitution of the United States was laid before Congress shortly after the Declaration of Independence was adopted in July 1776. It was largely the work of John Dickinson, who had been a leading opponent of independence. Dickinson's draft provided the legal foundation for a strong government over the new United States. The only guarantee of the rights of the states was a provision that they should have control over their "internal police," but even this guarantee was limited by the provision that such control must not interfere with the Articles of Confederation. On the other hand, the only restriction on the power of Congress was that it was not to levy duties or tariffs except to maintain a post office.

The radical or "states rights" leaders of the Revolution would have none of this. They did not want a central government in America that would interfere in any way with the independence of each of the states.

They had denied that the British government had any right to do so, and they were not going to give such power to the new central government of the United States.

The radicals won a complete victory. The Articles of Confederation provided for a strictly federal government. The members of Congress were elected by the state legislatures. Each state had one vote in Congress. Congress had no power over the states or the citizens of the states. It could not tax them, regulate their trade, nor interfere with the internal affairs in any way whatsoever. The states were declared to be sovereign, and all powers not specifically delegated to Congress were retained by the states. The two letters of Thomas Burke which follow are a clear statement of the radical or "states rights" conception of what a central government should be.

The Articles of Confederation were submitted to the states for ratification in the fall of 1777 and went into effect in March 1781 after the necessary ratification by all thirteen of the states. They served as the constitution of the United States until March 1789, when a new government under the present Constitution of the United States began to operate.

The Defense of State Sovereignty

The following two letters of Thomas Burke of North Carolina were written during the final stages of the debate over the Articles of Confederation. Burke expresses clearly the ideas of the radicals. He led in the successful movement to write into the Articles of Confederation a declaration of the sovereignty of the states and a statement that all powers not expressly delegated were retained by the states. The letters, dated March 11, 1777, and April 29, 1777, are addressed to the governor of North Carolina.[1]

March 11, 1777

The more experience I acquire, the stronger is my conviction that *unlimited power can not be safely trusted* to any man or set of men on earth. No men have undertaken to exercise authority with intentions more generous and disinterested than the Congress and none seem to have fewer or more feeble motives for increasing the power of their body politic. What could induce individuals blest with peaceable domestic affluence to forego all the enjoyment of a pleasing home, to neglect their private affairs, and at the expense of all their time and some part of their private fortunes, to attend public business under many insurmountable difficulties and inconveniences? What but a generous zeal for the public? And

[1] *Letters of Members of the Continental Congress*, 2:294–96, 345–46.

what can induce such men to endeavor at increasing the power with which they are invested, when their tenure of it must be exceedingly dangerous and precarious and can bring them individually neither pleasure or profit? This is a question I believe cannot be answered but by a plain declaration that power of all kinds has an irresistible propensity to increase a desire for itself. It gives the passion of ambition a velocity which increases in its progress, and this is a passion which grows in proportion as it is gratified. . . . Great part of our time is consumed in debates, whose object on one side is to increase the power of Congress, and on the other to restrain it. The advocates do not always keep the same side of the contest. The same persons who on one day endeavor to carry through some resolutions, whose tendency is to increase the power of Congress, are often on another day very strenuous advocates to restrain it. From this I infer that no one has entertained a concerted design to increase the power; and the attempts to do it proceed from ignorance of what such a being ought to be, and from the delusive intoxication which power naturally imposes on the human mind. . . .

These and many other considerations make me earnestly wish that the power of Congress was accurately defined and that there were adequate check provided to prevent any excess. I am also exceedingly desirous to have particular instructions relative to some heads which I shall enclose to you to be laid before the assembly. One thing now embarrasses me very much. It is this. Whenever any matter wherein the jurisdiction or authority of Congress is contested is debated, it is usual to lay it over undetermined. By the rule of secrecy you know, Sir, I am not at liberty to communicate anything before it is determined and therefore cannot consult the state upon it. In these cases all our time is lost, for nothing is entered on the Journals, and nothing therefore can give testimony hereafter that such points were contested, and even reject[ed] by a majority as is indeed the usual case. . . .

I enclose you an abstract of the debates in Congress on every question of any consequence that has been determined in Congress since my last. . . . The last matter in the abstract will show you that even thus early, men so eminent as members of Congress are willing to explain away any power that stands in the way of their particular purposes. What may we not expect some time hence when the seat of power shall become firm by habit and men will be accustomed to obedience, and perhaps forgetful of the original principles which gave rise thereto. I believe Sir the root of the evil is deep in human nature. Its growth may be kept down but it cannot be entirely extirpated. Power will sometime or other be abused unless men are well watched, and checked by something they cannot remove when they please.

April 29, 1777

At present, nothing but executive business is done, except the Confederation, and on mere executive business there are seldom any debates; (and still more seldom any worth remembering). We have agreed to three articles: one containing the name; the second a declaration of the sovereignty of the States, and an express provision that they be considered as retaining every power not expressly delegated; and the third an agreement mutually to assist each other against every enemy. The first and latter passed without opposition or dissent, the second occasioned two days debate. It stood originally the third article; and expressed only a reservation of the power of regulating the internal police, and consequently resigned every other power. It appeared to me that this was not what the States expected, and, I thought, it left it in the power of the future Congress or General Council to explain away every right belonging to the States and to make their own power as unlimited as they please. I proposed, therefore an amendment which held up the principle that all sovereign power was in the States separately, and that particular acts of it, which should be expressly enumerated, would be exercised in conjunction, and not otherwise; but that in all things else each state would exercise all the rights and power of sovereignty, un-controlled. This was at first so little understood that it was some time before it was seconded, and South Carolina first took it up. The opposition was made by Mr. Wilson of Pennsylvania, and Mr. R. H. Lee of Virginia. In the end, however, the question was carried for my proposition, eleven ayes, one no, and one divided. The no was Virginia, the divided, New Hampshire. I was much pleased to find the opinion of accumulating powers to Congress so little supported, and I promise myself, in the whole business I shall find my ideas relative thereto nearly similar to those of most of the States. In a word, Sir, I am of opinion the Congress should have power enough to call out and apply the common strength for the common defence, but not for the partial purposes of ambition. We shall next proceed to the structure of the common councils; and here, I think, we shall meet with difficulties of the most arduous nature. The inequality of the States, and yet the necessity of maintaining their separate independence, will occasion dilemmas almost inextricable.

2. THE DEMAND FOR A STRONG CENTRAL GOVERNMENT, 1780–1786

The supporters of a strong central government were defeated in the writing of the Articles of Confederation, but they did not give up. Most of them were out of power in the states during the first part of the Revolution, but by 1780 they began winning elections, and by 1781 were in control of a majority of the states, and hence of Congress. They were aided in this return to power by the disasters of 1780 which threatened defeat of the American cause. Runaway inflation wiped out the paper money used to finance the first part of the war. The British army was moving north from South Carolina, and it looked as if it could not be stopped. Practically everyone agreed that desperate measures were necessary.

the articles of confederation and the constitution of 1787

Conservative revolutionary leaders argued that the most important thing to do was to increase the power of Congress. Some went so far as to argue for the appointment of Washington as a dictator and of vice-dictators for each of the states. Others argued that a convention should be called to write a new constitution, even before the Articles of Confederation were ratified. The conservatives in Congress tried to amend the Articles so as to give Congress more power and an independent income. In 1783 some conservatives even thought there was a chance of uniting the army and the public creditors in a military revolt which would throw out Congress and set up a strong central government. They said that the war could not be won unless something drastic was done.

But peace came in 1783 without the adoption of any revolutionary measures. Nevertheless, the conservative leaders continued to demand that the central government be strengthened, and predicted chaos unless it was done. In 1782 the New York legislature passed resolutions, written by Alexander Hamilton, asking for a constitutional convention. Washington pleaded repeatedly in 1783 for a strong central government. In 1785 the Massachusetts legislature instructed its delegates in Congress to persuade that body to summon a convention, but the delegates refused to do so. Then, early in 1786, the Virginia legislature issued a call for a meeting of state representatives at Annapolis, Maryland, to discuss adding commercial powers to the Articles of Confederation. The invitation was accepted by only a few states. There was considerable suspicion of the motives of the Virginians on the part of northern merchants. Such men agreed that Congress should have the power to regulate trade, but they did not believe that the Virginians were sincere since they were not interested in commerce and were "aristocrats."

The Annapolis Convention met and issued a call for a general convention at Philadelphia in the spring of 1787. Congress pigeonholed the report in the autumn of 1786 and most of the states ignored it as well. Then occurred an event which alarmed the entire country: Shays's Rebellion in Massachusetts. Conservative leaders well knew that their great opportunity had arrived.

The documents that follow are examples of the thinking of the conservative spokesmen of the Revolutionary period concerning the kind of central government they wanted.

Hamilton's Plan

This portion of a letter by Alexander Hamilton to James Duane on September 3, 1780, is a clear statement of the ideas and the demands of those men in the United States who wanted a strong central government. It is important because it shows that by 1780 the program of those who were later to call themselves the Federalist Party had been definitely formulated.[2]

The fundamental defect is a want of power in Congress. It is hardly worth while to show in what this consists, as it seems to be universally acknowledged; or to point out how it has happened, as the only question is how to remedy it. It may, however, be said that it has originated from three causes: an excess of the spirit of liberty, which has made the particular states show a jealousy of all power not in their own hands; and this jealousy has led them to exercise a right of judging in the last resort of the measures recommended by Congress, and of acting according to their own opinions of their propriety, or necessity; a diffidence in Congress of their own powers, by which they have been timid and indecisive in their resolutions: constantly making concessions to the states, till they have scarcely left themselves the shadow of power; a want of sufficient means at their disposal to answer the public exigencies, and of vigor to draw forth those means; which have occasioned them to depend on the states individually, to fulfill their engagements with the army; the consequence of which has been to ruin their influence and credit with the army, to establish its dependence on each state separately, rather than *on them*, that is, rather than on the whole collectively.

It may be pleaded that Congress had never any definite powers granted them, and of course, could exercise none, could do nothing more than recommend. The manner in which Congress was appointed would warrant, and the public good required, that they should have considered themselves as vested with full power *to preserve the republic from harm*. They have done many of the highest acts of sovereignty, which were always cheerfully submitted to: The Declaration of Independence; the declaration of war; the levying of an army; creating a navy; emitting money; making alliances with foreign powers; appointing a dictator, etc., etc. All these implications of a complete sovereignty were never disputed, and ought to have been a standard for the whole conduct of administration. Undefined powers are discretionary powers, limited only by the object for which they were given; in the present case, the independence and freedom of America. . . .

But the Confederation itself is defective, and requires to be altered. It is neither fit for war nor peace. The idea of an uncontrollable sovereignty, in each state, over its internal police, will defeat the other powers given to Congress, and make our union feeble and precarious. There are instances without number where acts, necessary for the general good, and which rise out of the powers given to Congress, must interfere with the internal police of the states; and there are as many instances in which the particular states, by arrangements of internal police, can effectually, though indirectly, counteract the arrangements

---

[2] John C. Hamilton, ed., *The Works of Alexander Hamilton*, 7 vols. (New York, 1850–51), 1:150–53, 154, 157–58, 161, 167.

of Congress. You have already had examples of this, for which I refer you to your own memory.

The Confederation gives the states, individually, too much influence in the affairs of the army. They should have nothing to do with it. The entire formation and disposal of our military forces ought to belong to Congress. It is an essential cement of the union: and it ought to be the policy of Congress to destroy all ideas of state attachments in the army and make it look up wholly to them. For this purpose, all appointments, promotions, and provisions whatsoever, ought to be made by them. It may be apprehended that this may be dangerous to liberty. But nothing appears more evident to me than that we run much greater risk of having a weak and disunited federal government than one which will be able to usurp upon the rights of the people. . . .

The forms of our state constitutions must always give them great weight in our affairs, and will make it too difficult to bend them to the pursuit of a common interest; too easy to oppose whatever they do not like: and to form partial combinations subversive of the general one. There is a wide difference between our situation and that of an empire under one simple form of government, distributed into counties, provinces, or districts, which have no legislatures, but merely magistratical bodies, to execute the laws of a common sovereign. Here the danger is that the sovereign will have too much power, and impress the parts of which it is composed. In our case, that of an empire composed of confederated states; each with a government completely organized within itself, having all the means to draw its subjects to a close dependence on itself; the danger is directly the reverse. It is that the common sovereign will not have power sufficient to unite the different members together, and direct the common forces to the interest and happiness of the whole.

The Confederation, too, gives the power of the purse too entirely to the State Legislatures. It should provide perpetual funds, in the disposal of Congress, by a land tax, poll tax, or the like. All imposts upon commerce ought to be laid by Congress, and appropriated to their use. For, without certain revenues, a Government can have no power. That power which holds the purse-strings absolutely, must rule. This seems to be a medium which, without making Congress altogether independent, will tend to give reality to its authority. . . .

The first step must be to give Congress powers competent to the public exigencies. This may happen in two ways: one, by resuming and exercising the discretionary powers I suppose to have been originally vested in them, for the safety of the states; and resting their conduct on the candor of their countrymen, and the necessity of the conjuncture: the other, by calling immediately a Convention of all the states, with full authority to conclude finally upon a General Confederation; stating to them, beforehand, explicitly, the evils arising from a want of power in Congress and the impossibility of supporting the contest on its present footing; that the delegates may come, possessed of proper sentiments, as well as proper authority, to give efficacy to the meeting. Their commission should include a right of vesting Congress with the whole, or a proportion, of the unoccupied lands, to be employed for the purpose of raising a revenue: reserving the jurisdiction to the states by whom they are granted.

The first plan, I expect, will be thought too bold an expedient by the generality of Congress; and indeed, their practice hitherto has so riveted the opinion of their want of power that the success of this experiment may very well be doubted.

I see no objection to the other mode that has any weight, in competition with the reason for it. The Convention should assemble the first of November next. The sooner the better. Our disorders are too violent to admit of a common or lingering remedy. The reasons for which I require them to be vested with plenipotentiary authority are, that the business may suffer no delay in the execution; and may, in reality, come to effect. A Convention may agree upon a Confederation: the states, individually, hardly ever will. We must have one at all events, and a vigorous one, if we mean to succeed in the contest and be happy hereafter. As I said before, to engage the states to comply with this mode, Congress ought to confess to them, plainly and unanimously, the impracticability of supporting our affairs on the present footing, and without a solid coercive union. I ask that the Convention should have a power of vesting the whole, or a part, of the unoccupied lands in Congress; because it is necessary that body should have some property as a fund for the arrangements of finance; and I know of no other kind that can be given them.

The Confederation, in my opinion, should give Congress complete sovereignty; except as to that part of internal police which relates to the rights of property and life among individuals, and to raising money by internal taxes. It is necessary that everything belonging to this should be regulated by the state legislatures. Congress should have complete sovereignty in all that relates to war, peace, trade, finance; and to the management of foreign affairs; the right of declaring war; of raising armies, officering, paying them, directing their motions in every respect; of equipping fleets, and doing the same with them; of building fortifications, arsenals, magazines, etc., etc.; of making peace on such conditions as they think proper; of regulating trade, determining with what countries it shall be carried on; granting indulgencies; laying prohibitions on all the articles of export, or import; imposing duties; granting bounties and premiums for raising, exporting, or importing, and applying to their own use the product of these duties; only giving credit to the states on whom they are raised, in the general account of revenues and expenses; instituting Admiralty Courts, etc.; of coining money; establishing banks on such terms, and with such privileges, as they think proper; appropriating funds, and doing whatever else relates to the operations of finance; transacting everything with foreign nations; making alliances, offensive and defensive; treaties of commerce, etc., etc.

The Confederation should provide certain perpetual revenues, productive, and easy of collection; a land tax, poll tax, or the like; which, together with the duties on trade, and the unlocated lands, would give Congress a substantial existence, and a stable foundation for their schemes of finance. What more supplies were necessary should be occasionally demanded of the states, in the present mode of quotas. . . .

If a Convention is called, the minds of all the states, and the people, ought to be prepared to receive its determinations by sensible and popular writings, which should conform to the views of Congress. There are epochs in human affairs when *novelty* even is useful. If a general opinion prevails that the old way is bad, whether true or false, and this obstructs or relaxes the operations of the public service, a change is necessary, if it be but for the sake of change. This is exactly the case now. 'Tis a universal sentiment that our present system is a bad one, and that things do not go right on this account. The measure of a Convention would revive the hopes of the people, and give a new direction to their passions, which may be improved in carrying points of substantial utility. The eastern states have already pointed out this mode to Congress: they ought to take the hint and anticipate the others.

The Annapolis Convention

This account of the Annapolis Convention was written on October 10, 1786, by Louis Guillaume Otto, the French consul in New York to Count Vergennes, the French Foreign Minister. Otto, a sophisticated foreign observer, was sympathetic with the aims of the men who wanted a stronger central government.[3]

The commissioners appointed by various states to propose a general plan of commerce, and to give to Congress the powers necessary to execute it, assembled at Annapolis in the course of last month. But five states alone being represented, they did not think it best to enter into the main question, and confined themselves to addressing to Congress and the different legislatures a report which characterizes the present spirit of the politics of this country.

In translating this report I have not merely taken the pains to put it into French, but to render it intelligible. The effort was made to give to the original an obscurity which the people will penetrate with difficulty, but which the strong and enlightened citizens will not fail to turn to account.

For a very long time, my lord, the necessity of imparting to the federal government more energy and vigor has been felt, but it has also been felt that the excessive independence granted to the citizens, as regards the states, and to the states as regards Congress, is too dear to individuals for them to be deprived of it without great precautions.

The people are not ignorant that the natural consequences of an increase of power in the government would be a regular collection of taxes, a strict administration of jus-

---

[3] George Bancroft, *History of the Formation of the Constitution of the United States of America*, 2 vols. (New York, 1883), 2:399–401.

tice, extraordinary duties on imports, rigorous executions against debtors—in short, a marked preponderance of rich men and of large proprietors.

It is, however, for the interest of the people to guard as much as possible the absolute freedom granted them in a time when no other law was known but necessity, and when an English army, as it were, laid the foundations of the political constitution.

In those stormy times it was necessary to agree that all power ought to emanate only from the people; that everything was subject to its supreme will, and that the magistrates were only its servants.

Although there are no nobles in America, there is a class of men denominated "gentlemen," who, by reason of their wealth, their talents, their education, their families, or the offices they hold, aspire to a preeminence which the people refuse to grant them; and, although many of these men have betrayed the interests of their order to gain popularity, there reigns among them a connection so much the more intimate as they almost all of them dread the efforts of the people to despoil them of their possessions, and, moreover, they are creditors, and therefore interested in strengthening the government, and watching over the execution of the laws.

These men generally pay very heavy taxes, while the small proprietors escape the vigilance of the collectors.

The majority of them being merchants, it is for their interest to establish the credit of the United States in Europe on a solid foundation by the exact payment of debts, and to grant to Congress powers extensive enough to compel the people to contribute for this purpose. The attempt, my lord, has been vain, by pamphlets and other publications, to spread notions of justice and integrity, and to deprive the people of a freedom which they have so misused. By proposing a new organization of the federal government all minds would have been revolted; circumstances ruinous to the commerce of America have happily arisen to furnish the reformers with a pretext for introducing innovations.

They represented to the people that the American name had become opprobrious among all the nations of Europe; that the flag of the United States was everywhere exposed to insults and annoyance; the husbandman, no longer able to export his produce freely, would soon be reduced to extreme want; it was high time to retaliate, and to convince foreign powers that the United States would not with impunity suffer such a violation of the freedom of trade, but that strong measures could be taken only with the consent of the thirteen states, and that Congress, not having the necessary powers, it was essential to form a general assembly instructed to present to Congress the plan for its adoption, and to point out the means of carrying it into execution.

The people, generally discontented with the obstacles in the way of commerce, and scarcely suspecting the secret motives of their opponents, ardently embraced this measure, and appointed commissioners, who were to assemble at Annapolis in the beginning of September.

The authors of this proposition had no hope, nor even desire, to see the success of this assembly of commissioners, which was only intended to prepare a question much more important than that of commerce. The measures were so well taken that at the end of September no more than five states were represented at Annapolis, and the commissioners from the northern states tarried several days at New York in order to retard their arrival.

The states which assembled, after having waited nearly three weeks, separated under the pretext that they were not in sufficient numbers to enter on business, and, to justify this dissolution, they addressed to the different legislatures and to Congress a report, the translation of which I have the honor to enclose to you.

In this paper the commissioners employ an infinity of circumlocutions and ambiguous phrases to show to their constituents the impossibility of taking into consideration a general plan of commerce and the powers pertaining thereto, without at the same time touching upon other objects closely connected with the prosperity and national importance of the United States.

Without enumerating these objects, the commissioners enlarge upon the present crisis of public affairs, upon the dangers to which the Confederation is exposed, upon the want of credit of the United States abroad, and upon the necessity of uniting, under a single point of view, the interests of all the states.

They close by proposing, for the month of May next, a new assembly of commissioners, instructed to deliberate not only upon a general plan of commerce, but upon other matters which may concern the harmony and welfare of the states, and upon the means of rendering the federal government adequate to the exigencies of the union.

In spite of the obscurity of this document, you will perceive, my lord, that the commissioners were unwilling to take into consideration the grievances of commerce, which are of exceeding interest for the people, without at the same time perfecting the fundamental constitution of Congress.

It is hoped that new commissioners will be appointed, with ample powers to deliberate on these important objects, and to place Congress in a position not only to form resolutions for the prosperity of the union, but to execute them.

3. THE OPPOSITION TO A STRONG CENTRAL GOVERNMENT, 1783–1785

By the end of the Revolution virtually all of the supporters of the Articles of Confederation were convinced that it needed strengthening. They wanted, however, to go slowly and see how things would work out in peacetime. Furthermore, they had been much alarmed by the program of the conservatives who had controlled Congress from 1781 to 1783, and particularly by the financial measures of Robert Morris, the superintendent of finance.

Thus, while they agreed that the Articles should be amended, they wanted to make sure that the fundamental federal structure of the government was not altered. From 1783 to 1786 they supported two additions to Congressional powers: One, the right to collect a five per cent duty on all imports for a twenty-five year period until the national debt was paid; the other, the right to regulate trade. The impost proposal was on the point of success in 1786, by which time twelve states had agreed. Only New York held out, but even New York gave partial approval to the idea. The power to regulate trade was defeated by the Southern states whose leaders feared their section would be exploited by the North. During the summer of 1786, however, Congress worked out a series of amendments to the Confederation, which would have added strength to the government, while retaining the federal structure; but these amendments were lost sight of as the movement for the Convention of 1787 got under way.

Underlying the thinking of the men who wanted to add a few specific powers to the Confederation was the fear that their political opponents would seize upon any opportunity to create what had been called, since the beginning of the Revolution, a "consolidated" government, and what was to be called, in the Convention of 1787, a "national" government. That fear had a solid foundation, for the "nationalists" had been perfectly frank about their desire to have a central government which could act coercively upon the states and individual citizens of the states. The documents which follow are examples of the thinking of those men who believed in maintaining the Articles of Confederation, but who were willing to add specific powers to that Constitution if that could be done without altering its basic character.

Opposition to More Power for Congress

The following are instructions of Fairfax County, Virginia, to the county's representatives in the Virginia legislature. The citizens of Fairfax County objected to a permanent revenue for Congress. Furthermore, they feared that land companies from other states which laid claims to lands within Virginia might use any increase in power of the central government—something these companies had long urged—to validate their claims. The instructions are dated May 30, 1783.[4]

We desire and instruct you strenuously to oppose all encroachments of the American Congress upon the sovereignty and jurisdiction of the separate States; and every assumption of power, not expressly vested in them, by the Articles of Confederation. If experience shall

---

[4] Kate Mason Rowland, *The Life of George Mason*, 2 vols. (New York, 1892), 2:50–51.

prove that further powers are necessary and safe, they can be granted only by additional articles to the Confederation, duly acceded to by all the States; for if Congress, upon the plea of necessity, or upon any pretence whatever, can arrogate powers not warranted by the Articles of Confederation, in one instance, they may in another, or in an hundred; every repetition will be strengthened and confirmed by precedents.

And in particular we desire and instruct you to oppose any attempts which may be made by Congress to obtain a perpetual revenue, or the appointment of revenue officers. Were these powers superadded to those they already possess, the Articles of Confederation, and the Constitutions of Government in the different States would prove mere parchment bulwarks to American liberty.

We like not the language of the late address from Congress to the different States, and of the report of their committee upon the subject of revenue, published in the same pamphlet. If they are carefully and impartially examined, they will be found to exhibit strong proofs of lust of power: They contain the same kind of arguments which were formerly used in the busines of ship money, and to justify the arbitrary measures of the race of Stuarts in England. And the present king and council of Great Britain might not improperly adopt great part of them, to prove the expediency of levying money without consent of Parliament. After having reluctantly given up part of what they found they could not maintain, they still insist that the several States shall invest *the United States in Congress assembled with a power to levy,* for the use of the United States, the following duties, &c., and that the revenue officers shall be amenable to Congress. The very style is alarming. The proposed duties may be proper, but the separate States only can safely have *the power of levying taxes.* Congress should not have even the appearance of such a power. Forms generally imply substance, and such a precedent may be applied to dangerous purposes hereafter. When the same man, or set of men, holds both the sword and the purse, there is an end of liberty. As little are we satisfied with the resolution of Congress of the 10th of October, 1780, lately renewed, engaging that *the unappropriated lands* "that may be ceded or relinquished to the United States by any particular States, shall be disposed of for the common benefit of the United States." Who is to judge of the quality and legality of pretended appropriations? And will this vague resolution be a sufficient bar to Congress against confirming the claims under Indian purchases, or pretended grants from the Crown of Great Britain, in which many of their own members are interested as partners, and by which great part of the ceded lands may be converted to private, instead of public purposes? The intrigues of the great land companies, and the methods by which they have strengthened their interest are no secret to the public. We are also at a loss to know whence Congress derives the powers of demanding cessions of lands and of erecting new States before such powers have been granted them by their constitutents.

The Danger of Holding a Convention

In 1785 the Massachusetts legislature instructed its delegates in Congress to introduce a resolution calling for a constitutional convention. The delegates refused to do so. They replied on September 3, 1785, that any commercial powers given to Congress should be temporary until it could be seen how such powers would work. Their basic objection, however, was that a convention might be used to alter the structure of government set up by the Articles of Confederation.[5]

If an alteration, either temporary or perpetual, of the commercial powers of Congress, is to be considered by a Convention, shall the latter be authorized to revise the Confederation *generally,* or only for express purposes? The great object of the Revolution was the establishment of good government, and each of the states, in forming their own, as well as the federal constitution, have adopted republican principles. Notwithstanding this, plans have been artfully laid, and vigorously pursued, which had they been successful, we think would inevitably have changed our republican governments into baleful aristocracies. Those plans are frustrated, but the same spirit remains in their abettors. And the institution of the Cincinnati, honorable and beneficent as the views may have been of the officers who compose it, we fear, if not totally abolished, will have the same fatal tendency. What the effect then may be of calling a Convention to revise the Confederation generally, we leave with your Excellency and the honorable Legislature to determine. We are apprehensive and it is our duty to declare it, that such a measure would produce thro'out the Union, an exertion of the friends of an aristocracy to send members who would promote a change of government, and we can form some judgment of the plan which such members would report to Congress. But should the members be altogether republican, such have been the declamations of designing men against the Confederation generally; against the rotation of members, which perhaps is the best check to corruption, and against the mode of altering the Confederation by the unanimous consent of the Legislatures, which effectually prevents innovations in the Articles by intrigue or surprise, that we think there is great danger of a report which would invest Congress with powers that the honorable legislature have not the most distant intention to delegate. Perhaps it may be said this can produce no ill effect because Congress may correct the report however exceptionable, or if passed by them, any of the states may refuse to ratify it. True it is that Congress and the states have such powers, but would not such a report affect the tranquility and weaken the government of the Union? We have already considered

---

[5] *Letters of Members of the Continental Congress,* 8:208–9.

the operation of the report as it would respect Congress; and if animosities and parties would naturally arise from their rejecting it, how much would these be increased if the report approved by Congress and some of the states, should be rejected by other states? Would there not be danger of a party spirit's being thus more generally diffused and warmly supported? Far distant we know it to be from the honorable legislature of Massachusetts to give up a single principle of republicanism, but when a general revision shall have proceeded from their motion, and a report which to them may be highly offensive, shall have been confirmed by seven states in Congress, and ratified by several Legislatures, will not these be ready to charge Massachusetts with inconsistency in being the first to oppose a measure which the state will be said to have originated? Massachusetts has great weight and is considered as one of the most republican states in the Union; and when it is known that the legislature have proposed a general revision, there can be no doubt that they will be represented as being convinced of the necessity of increasing generally the powers of Congress, and the opinion of the state will be urged with such art as to convince numbers that the Articles of the Confederation are altogether exceptionable. Thus, whilst measures are taken to guard against the evils arising from the want in one or two particulars of power in Congress, we are in great danger of incurring the other extreme. "More power in Congress" has been the cry from all quarters, but especially of those whose views, not beng confined to a government that will best promote the happiness of the people, are extended to one that will afford lucrative employments, civil and military. Such a government is an aristocracy, which would require a standing army and a numerous train of pensioners and placemen to prop and support its exalted administration. To recommend one's self to such an administration would be to secure an establishment for life and at the same time to provide for his posterity. These are pleasing prospects, which republican governments do not afford, and it is not to be wondered at that many persons of elevated views and idle habits in these states are desirous of the change. We are for increasing the power of Congress as far as it will promote the happiness of the people, but at the same time are clearly of the opinion that every measure should be avoided which would strengthen the hands of the enemies to a free government. And that an administration of the present Confederation with all its inconveniences, is preferable to the risk of general dissensions and animosities which may approach to anarchy and prepare the way to a ruinous system of government.

4. THE CONVENTION OF 1787

The call of the Annapolis Convention in September 1786 was at first ignored by Congress and by most of the states. Then came Shays's Rebellion. Men in every state were alarmed by the news. It caused many who had not been greatly concerned hitherto to take an interest in a stronger central government, while political leaders who had long been working for such a government realized that the alarm created might be used to their advantage. In February 1787 Congress issued a call for a convention to meet in Philadelphia the following May for the purpose of revising and amending the Articles of Confederation. All the states except Rhode Island elected delegates.

When the Convention met its members expressed fear at what they called the excesses of democracy. By democracy they meant the political structure that was the result of the American Revolution. The majorities in most state legislatures were checked neither by governors nor by supreme courts, while Congress could not interfere as the British government had done before 1776. As a result, by 1786 seven of the states had issued paper money or established state loan offices for the relief of debtors and taxpayers. Others had passed laws delaying the collection of debts and taxes. When the Massachusetts legislature refused any such relief, Shays's Rebellion was the result. Farmers in other states threatened similar action. All this caused real fear among conservative-minded Americans. After the Constitution of 1787 was written, James Madison declared that the "mutability" of state laws was so serious an evil that it contributed far more to the "uneasiness" that produced the Convention than did the inadequacy of the Articles of Confederation.

The majority of the Constitutional Convention at once agreed that the remedy was to replace the "federal" government with a "national" government. Therefore they decided to ignore their instructions to revise and amend the Confederation. When the question was asked as to the difference between the two kinds of government, Gouverneur Morris, according to James Madison, "explained the distinction between a *federal* and a *national, supreme* government; the former being a mere compact resting on the good faith of the parties; the latter having a complete and *compulsive* operation."

The extreme nationalists wanted to reduce the states to mere administrative units. They proposed to escape from state control by having members of Congress, and even the executive, elected by popular vote. This, however, was politically unrealistic. The representatives from the small states were still afraid of what the large states would do, while the proponents of a strictly federal government were opposed to so drastic a change. But most important, it was doubtful that the states would accept such an open revolution.

The Constitution that was evolved was, therefore, a compromise. As Madison pointed out in *The Federalist,* it was both national and federal in character. The states were checked, not openly, as proposed by Edmund Randolph, but by constitutional limitations. They were forbidden to make anything but gold and silver legal tender in payment of debts, or interfere with contracts. The Constitution itself, and all treaties, were declared to be the supreme law of the land. Finally, the nationalists looked to the creation of a federal court system as the ultimate bulwark against state action.

The documents which follow illustrate the broad differences of opinion rather than the innumerable debates on the specific details of the Constitution itself.

The Nationalist Position

On May 29, 1787, Governor Edmund Randolph of Virginia gave the opening speech of the Convention. It was a clear statement of the convictions of the nationalists. The speech was followed by a series of resolutions to serve as the basis for a new constitution, known as the Virginia Plan.[6]

Governor Randolph opened the business of the convention. He observed that the Confederation fulfilled *none* of the objects for which it was framed. . . .

1st. *It does not provide against foreign invasion.* If a state acts against a foreign power contrary to the laws of nations or violates a treaty, it cannot punish that state, or compel its obedience to the treaty. It can only leave the offending state to the operations of the offended power. It therefore cannot prevent a war. If the rights of an ambassador be invaded by any citizen, it is only in a few states that any laws exist to punish the offender. A state may encroach on foreign possessions in its neighborhood and Congress cannot prevent it. Disputes that respect naturalization cannot be adjusted. None of the judges in the several states under the obligation of an oath to support the Confederation, in which view this writing will be made to yield to state constitutions.

Imbecility of the Confederation equally conspicuous when called upon to support a war. The journals of Congress a history of expedients. The states in arrears to the federal treasury. . . .

What reason to expect that the treasury will be better filled in future, or that money can be obtained under the present powers of Congress to support a war. Volunteers not to be depended on for such a purpose. Militia difficult to be collected and almost impossible to be kept in the field. Draughts stretch the strings of government too violently to be adopted. Nothing short of a regular military force will answer the end of war, and this only to be created and supported by money.

2. *It does not secure harmony to the states.* It cannot preserve the particular states against seditions within themselves or combinations

---

[6] Charles C. Tansill, ed., "Notes of James McHenry, May 14, 1787," *Documents Illustrative of the Formation of the Union of the American States* (Washington, 1927), 923–25.

against each other. What laws in the Confederation authorize Congress to intrude troops into a state. What authority to determine which of the citizens of a state is in the right, the supporters or the opposers of the government, those who wish to change it, or they who wish to preserve it.

No provision to prevent the states breaking out into war. One state may, as it were, underbid another by duties, and thus keep up a state of war.

3. *Incapable to produce certain blessings.* The benefits of which we are *singly incapable* cannot be produced by the union. The 5 per cent impost not agreed; a blessing Congress ought to be enabled to obtain.

Congress ought to possess a power to prevent emissions of bills of credit.

Under this head may be considered the establishment of great national works—the improvement of inland navigation—agriculture—manufactures—a freer intercourse among the citizens.

4. *It cannot defend itself against encroachments.* Not an animated existence which has not the powers of defense. Not a political existence which ought not to possess it. In every Congress there has been a party opposed to federal measures. In every state assembly there has been a party opposed to federal measures. The states have been therefore delinquent. To what expedient can Congress resort to compel delinquent states to do what is right. If force, this force must be drawn from the states, and the states may or may not furnish it.

5. *Inferior to state constitutions.* State constitutions formed at an early period of the war, and by persons elected by the people for that purpose. These in general with one or two exceptions established about 1776. The Confederation was formed long after this and had its ratification not by any special appointment from the people, but from the several assemblies. No judge will say that the Confederation is paramount to a state constitution.

Thus we see that the Confederation is incompetent to any one object for which it was instituted. The framers of it wise and great men; but human rights were the chief knowledge of the times when it was framed so far as they applied to oppose Great Britain. Requisitions for men and money had never offered their form to our assemblies. None of those vices that have since discovered themselves were apprehended. Its defects therefore no reflection on its contrivers.

Having pointed out its defects, let us not be afraid to view with a steady eye the perils with which we are surrounded. Look at the public countenance from New Hampshire to Georgia. Are we not on the eve of war, which is only prevented by the hopes from this convention.

Our chief danger arises from the democratic parts of our constitutions. It is a maxim which I hold incontrovertible, that the powers of government exercised by the people swallows up the other branches. None of the constitutions have provided sufficient checks against the democracy. The feeble Senate of Virginia is a phantom. Maryland has a more powerful senate, but the late distractions in that state have discovered that it is not powerful enough. The check established in the constitution of New York and Massachusetts is yet a stronger barrier against democracy, but they all seem insufficient.

The True Federalist Position

The following selection consists of extracts from speeches by John Lansing and William Paterson on June 16, 1787 in defense of the Paterson, or New Jersey, plan. This plan has often been called the "small states" plan, but it was that only in part. More important, it represented the opinions of those who wanted to maintain the federal structure of the Articles of Confederation, but who at the same time wanted to add real power to the central government.[7]

Mr. Lansing . . . observed that this system is fairly contrasted with the one ready to be reported—the one federal, and the other national. In the first, the powers are exercised as flowing from the respective state governments; the second, deriving its authority from the people of the respective states—which latter must ultimately destroy or annihilate the state governments. To determine the powers on these grand objects with which we are invested let us recur to the credentials of the respective states and see what the views were of those who sent us. The language is there expressive. It is, upon the revision of the present Confederation, to alter and amend such parts as may appear defective, so as to give additional strength to the union. And he would venture to assert that had the legislature of the state of New York apprehended that their powers would have been construed to extend to the formation of a national government, to the extinguishment of their independency, no delegates would have here appeared on the part of that state. This sentiment must have had its weight on a former occasion, even in this house, for when the second resolution of Virginia, which declared in substance that a federal government could not be amended for the good of the whole, the remark of an honorable member of South Carolina, that by determining this question in the affirmative their deliberative powers were at an end, induced this house to waive the resolution. It is in vain to adopt a mode of government which we have reason to believe the people gave us no power to recommend—as they will consider themselves on this ground authorized to reject it. See the danger of exceeding your powers by the example which the requisition of Congress of 1783 afforded. They required an impost on all imported articles; to which, on federal grounds, they had no right unless voluntarily granted. What was the consequence? Some, who had least to give, granted it; and others, under

---

[7] Tansill, "Notes of Robert Yates, June 16, 1787," *Documents Illustrative of the Formation of the Union of the American States*, 770–73.

various restrictions and modifications, so that it could not be systematized. If we form a government, let us do it on principles which are likely to meet the approbation of the states. Great changes can only be gradually introduced. The states will never sacrifice their essential rights to a national government. New plans, annihilating the rights of the states (unless upon evident necessity) can never be approved. I may venture to assert that the prevalent opinion of America is, that granting additional powers to congress would answer their views; and every power recommended for their approbation exceeding this idea will be fruitless.

Mr. Paterson.—As I had the honor of proposing a new system of government for the union, it will be expected that I should explain its principles.

1st. The plan accords with our own powers.

2d. It accords with the sentiments of the people.

But if the subsisting confederation is so radically defective as not to admit of amendment, let us say so and report its insufficiency and wait for enlarged powers. We must, in the present case, pursue our powers, if we expect the approbation of the people. I am not here to pursue my own sentiments of government, but of those who have sent me; and I believe that a little practical virtue is to be preferred to the finest theoretical principles which cannot be carried into effect. Can we, as representatives of independent states, annihilate the essential powers of independency? Are not the votes of this convention taken on every question under the idea of independency? Let us turn to the 5th article of Confederation—in this it is mutually agreed that each state should have one vote. It is a fundamental principle arising from confederated governments. The 13th article provides for amendments; but they must be agreed to by every state—the dissent of one renders every proposal null. The Confederation is in the nature of a compact; and can any state, unless by the consent of the whole, either in politics or law, withdraw their powers? Let it be said by Pennsylvania, and the other large states, that they, for the sake of peace, assented to the Confederation; can she now resume her original right without the consent of the donee?

And although it is now asserted that the larger states reluctantly agreed to that part of the Confederation which secures an equal suffrage to each, yet let it be remembered that the smaller states were the last who approved the Confederation.

On this ground representation must be drawn from the states to maintain their independency, and not from the people composing those states.

The doctrine advanced by a learned gentleman from Pennsylvania, that all power is derived from the people and that in proportion to their numbers they ought to participate equally in the benefits and rights of government, is right in principle, but unfortunately for him, wrong in the application to the question now in debate.

When independent societies confederate for mutual defence, they do so in their collective capacity; and then each state for those purposes must be considered as *one* of the contracting parties. Destroy this balance of equality and you endanger the rights of the *lesser* societies by the danger of usurpation in the greater.

Let us test the government intended to be made by the Virginia plan on these principles. The representatives in the national legislature are to be in proportion to the number of inhabitants in each state. So far it is right upon the principles of equality when state distinctions are done away, but those to certain purposes still exist. Will the government of Pennsylvania admit a participation of their common stock of land to the citizens of New Jersey? I fancy not. It therefore follows that a national government, upon the present plan, is unjust, and destructive of the common principles of reciprocity. Much has been said that this government is to operate on persons, not on states. This, upon examination, will be found equally fallacious, for the fact is, it will, in the quotas of revenue, be proportioned among the states, as states; and in this business Georgia will have one vote and Virginia sixteen. The truth is, both plans may be considered to compel individuals to a compliance with their requisitions, although the requisition is made on the states.

Much has been said in commendation of two branches in a legislature, and of the advantages resulting from their being checks to each other. This may be true when applied to state governments, but will not equally apply to a national legislature, whose legislative objects are few and simple.

Whatever may be said of Congress, or their conduct on particular occasions, the people in general are pleased with such a body, and in general wish an increase of their powers for the good government of the union.

5. THE ARGUMENTS AGAINST THE CONSTITUTION

Opposition to the Constitution began during the Convention itself. Robert Yates and John Lansing of New York and Luther Martin of Maryland were conspicuous examples of men who left the Convention before it was over and went home and explained to the people of their states the reasons for their opposition. George Mason of Virginia and Elbridge Gerry of Massachusetts refused to sign the Constitution, as did Edmund Randolph of Virginia. Randolph's motives were never clear, but Mason objected because there was no bill of rights and Gerry feared that civil war would arise out of the controversy over ratification, especially in Massachusetts.

As soon as the Constitution appeared in the newspapers in September 1787, it shocked the supporters of the Articles of Confederation. Apparently few of them had realized that the Convention would ignore their instructions and create what seemed like an entirely different government. In the debate over its ratification, the opponents of the Constitution stressed two main points—that the Constitution contained no bill of rights and that it created a national and not a federal government. In addition they objected to many of the specific details of the Constitution.

Despite their objections, most of the opponents of the Constitution agreed that the central government should be strengthened, particularly as regards the regulation of trade and the collection of revenue. Many of them were willing to accept the document if a bill of rights was attached. Others demanded that a new convention be called in order to amend the work of the Philadelphia Convention. Such a movement began to grow and was regarded as a serious threat by the supporters of the Constitution. Eventually in three crucial states, Massachusetts, Virginia, and New York, the supporters of the Constitution promised that once the new government was established, amendments would be submitted to the states for ratification. It is probable that ratification was obtained in these states only because of this promise, for the majorities in their ratifying conventions were at first opposed to the Constitution.

A National, Not a Federal, Government Is Proposed

This letter of December 3, 1787, to Richard Henry Lee expresses the views of Samuel Adams on the new Constitution. Eventually he was induced to support ratification, largely because of the promise that a bill of rights would be added to the Constitution.[8]

I confess, as I enter the building I stumble at the threshold. I meet with a national government, instead of a federal union of sovereign states. I am not able to conceive why the wisdom of the Convention led them to give the preference to the former before the latter. If the several states in the union are to become one entire nation, under one legislature, the powers of which shall extend to every subject of legislation, and its laws be supreme and control the whole, the idea of sovereignty in these states must be lost. Indeed I think, upon such a supposition, those sovereignties ought to be eradicated from the mind; for they would be *imperia in imperio* justly deemed a solecism in politics, and they would be highly dangerous, and destructive of the peace, union, and safety of the nation. And can this national legislature be competent to make laws for the *free* internal government of one people, living in climates so remote and whose "Habits & particular Interests" are and probably always will be so different. Is it to be expected that general laws can be adapted to the feelings of the more eastern and the more southern parts of so extensive a nation? It appears to me diffi-

---

[8] William V. Wells, *The Life and Public Services of Samuel Adams*, 3 vols. (Boston, 1866), 3:251–53.

cult if practicable. Hence then may we not look for discontent, mistrust, disaffection to government and frequent insurrections, which will require standing armies to suppress them in one place and another where they may happen to arise. Or if laws could be made, adapted to the local habits, feelings, views, and interests of those distant parts, would they not cause jealousies of partiality in government which would excite envy and other malignant passions productive of wars and fighting. But should we continue distinct sovereign states, confederated for the purposes of mutual safety and happiness, each contributing to the federal head such a part of its sovereignty as would render the government fully adequate to those purposes and *no more,* the people would govern themselves more easily, the laws of each state being well adapted to its own genius and circumstances, and the liberties of the United States would be more secure than they can be, as I humbly conceive, under the proposed new constitution. You are sensible, Sir, that the seeds of aristocracy began to spring even before the conclusion of our struggle for the natural rights of men, seeds which like a canker worm lie at the root of free governments. So great is the wickedness of some men, and the stupid servility of others, that one would be almost inclined to conclude that communities cannot be free. The few haughty families think *they* must govern. The body of the people tamely consent and submit to be their slaves. This unravels the mystery of millions being enslaved by the few!

The Federal Farmer

The following is a selection from the first of Richard Henry Lee's "Letters from a Federal Farmer to a Republican," one of the ablest and most effective series of essays written in opposition to the Constitution. It is dated October 8, 1787.[9]

The present moment discovers a new face in our affairs. Our object has been all along to reform our federal system, and to strengthen our governments—to establish peace, order, and justice in the community—but a new object now presents. The plan of government now proposed is evidently calculated totally to change, in time, our condition as a people. Instead of being thirteen republics, under a federal head, it is clearly designed to make us one consolidated government. Of this, I think, I shall fully convince you in my following letters on this subject. This consolidation of the states has been the object of several men in this country for some time past. Whether such a change can ever be effected, in any manner; whether it can be effected without convulsions and civil wars; whether such a change will not totally destroy the liberties of this country—time only can determine.

---

[9] E. H. Scott, ed., *The Federalist and Other Constitutional Papers* (Chicago, 1894), 842–44, 845–47.

To have a just idea of the government before us, and to show that a consolidated one is the object in view, it is necessary not only to examine the plan, but also its history, and the politics of its particular friends.

The Confederation was formed when great confidence was placed in the voluntary exertions of individuals, and of the respective states; and the framers of it, to guard against usurpation, so limited and checked the powers that, in many respects they are inadequate to the exigencies of the union. We find, therefore, members of Congress urging alterations in the federal system almost as soon as it was adopted. It was early proposed to vest Congress with powers to levy an impost, to regulate trade, &c., but such was that known to be the caution of the states in parting with power, the vestment even of these was proposed to be under several checks and limitations. During the war the general confusion and the introduction of paper money infused in the minds of people vague ideas respecting government and credit. We expected too much from the return of peace, and of course we have been disappointed. Our governments have been new and unsettled; and several legislatures, by making tender, suspension, and paper money laws, have given just cause of uneasiness to creditors. By these and other causes, several orders of men in the community have been prepared, by degrees, for a change of government; and this very abuse of power in the legislatures, which in some cases has been charged upon the democratic part of the community, has furnished aristocratical men with those very weapons, and those very means, with which in great measure they are rapidly effecting their favorite object. And should an oppressive government be the consequence of the proposed change, [posterity] may reproach not only a few overbearing, unprincipled men, but those parties in the states which have misused their powers.

The conduct of several legislatures, touching paper money and tender laws, has prepared many honest men for changes in government which otherwise they would not have thought of—when by the evils, on the one hand, and by the secret instigations of artful men, on the other, the minds of men were become sufficiently uneasy, a bold step was taken which is usually followed by a revolution or a civil war. A general convention for mere commercial purposes was moved for—the authors of this measure saw that the people's attention was turned solely to the amendment of the federal system; and that, had the idea of a total change been started, probably no state would have appointed members to the convention. The idea of destroying ultimately the state government and forming one consolidated system could not have been admitted. A convention, therefore, merely for vesting in Congress power to regulate trade was proposed. This was pleasing to the commercial towns, and the landed people had little or no concern about it. September, 1786, a few men from the middle states met at Annapolis and hastily proposed a convention to be held in May, 1787, for the purpose, generally, of amending the Confederation. This was done before the delegates of Massachusetts and of the other states arrived. Still not a word was said about destroying the old constitution and making a new one. The states still unsuspecting and not aware that they were passing the Rubicon, appointed members to the new convention, for the sole and express purpose of revising and amending the Confederation—and, probably not one man in ten thousand in the United States till within these ten or twelve days, had an idea that the old ship was to be destroyed, and he put to the alternative of embarking in the new ship presented, or of being left in danger of sinking. The States, I believe, universally supposed the convention would report alterations in the Confederation which would pass an examination in Congress, and after being agreed to there, would be confirmed by all the legislatures, or be rejected.

Virginia made a very respectable appointment and placed at the head of it the first man in America. In this appointment there was a mixture of political characters; but Pennsylvania appointed principally those men who are esteemed aristocratical. Here the favorite moment for changing the government was evidently discerned by a few men, who seized it with address. Ten other states appointed, and tho' they chose men principally connected with commerce and the judicial department, yet they appointed many good republican characters—had they all attended we should now see, I am persuaded, a better system presented. The nonattendance of eight or nine men who were appointed members of the convention, I shall ever consider as a very unfortunate event to the United States. Had they attended, I am pretty clear that the result of the convention would not have had that strong tendency to aristocracy now discernible in every part of the plan. There would not have been so great an accumulation of powers, especially as to the internal police of this country, in a few hands as the constitution reported proposes to vest in them—the young visionary men and the consolidating aristocracy would have been more restrained than they have been. Eleven states met in the convention and after four months close attention presented the new constitution, to be adopted or rejected by the people. The uneasy and fickle part of the community may be prepared to receive any form of government; but I presume the enlightened and substantial part will give any constitution presented for their adoption a candid and thorough examination; and silence those designing or empty men who weakly and rashly attempt to precipitate the adoption of a system of so much importance. We shall view the convention with proper respect—and, at the same time that we reflect there were men of abilities and integrity in it, we must recollect how disproportionately the democratic and aristocratic parts of the community were represented. Perhaps the judicious friends and opposers of the new constitution will agree that it is best to let it rely solely on its own merits, or be condemned for its own defects.

In the first place I shall premise that the plan proposed is a plan of accommodation—and that it is in this way only, and by giving up a part of our opinions, that we can ever expect to obtain a government founded in freedom and compact. This circumstance candid men will always keep in view in the discussion of this subject.

The plan proposed appears to be partly federal, but principally, however, calculated ultimately to make the states one consolidated government.

The first interesting question, therefore, suggested is, how far the states can be consolidated into one entire government on free principles. In considering this question extensive objects are to be taken into view, and important changes in the forms of government to be carefully attended to in all their consequences. The happiness of the people at large must be the great object with every honest statesman, and he will direct every movement to this point. If we are so situated as a people as not to be able to enjoy equal happiness and advantages under one government, the consolidation of the states cannot be admitted.

There are three different forms of free government under which the United States may exist as one nation; and now is, perhaps, the time to determine to which we will direct our views. 1. Distinct republics connected under a federal head. In this case the respective state governments must be the principal guardians of the people's rights, and exclusively regulate their internal police; in them must rest the balance of government. The Congress of the states, or federal head, must consist of delegates amenable to, and removable by the respective states. This Congress must have general directing powers; powers to require men and monies of the states; to make treaties; peace and war; to direct the operations of armies, &c. Under this federal modification of government the powers of Congress would be rather advisory or recommendatory than coercive. 2. We may do away [with] the federal state governments and form or consolidate all the states into one entire government, with one executive, one judiciary, and one legislature, consisting of senators and representatives collected from all parts of the union. In this case there would be a complete consolidation of the states. 3. We may consolidate the states as to certain national objects, and leave them severally distinct independent republics, as to internal police generally. Let the general government consist of an executive, a judiciary, and balanced legislature, and its powers extend exclusively to all foreign concerns, causes arising on the seas to commerce, imports, armies, navies, Indian affairs, peace and war, and to a few internal concerns of the community; to the coin, post-offices, weights and measures, a general plan for the militia, to naturalization, *and, perhaps to bankruptcies,* leaving the internal police of the community, in other respects, exclusively to the state governments; as the administration of justice in all causes arising internally, the laying and collecting of internal taxes, and the forming of the militia according to a general plan prescribed. In this case there would be a complete consolidation, *quoad* certain objects only.

Touching the first, or federal plan, I do not think much can be said in its favor. The sovereignty of the nation, without coercive and efficient powers to collect the strength of it, cannot always be depended on to answer the purposes of government; and in a congress of representatives of foreign states there must necessarily be an unreasonable mixture of powers in the same hands.

As to the second, or complete consolidating plan, it deserves to be carefully considered at this time by every American. If it be impracticable, it is a fatal error to model our governments, directing our views ultimately to it.

The third plan, or partial consolidation, is, in my opinion, the only one that can secure the freedom and happiness of this people. I once had some general ideas that the second plan was practicable, but from long attention and the proceedings of the convention, I am fully satisfied that this third plan is the only one we can with safety and propriety proceed upon. Making this the standard to point out, with candor and fairness, the parts of the new constitution which appear to be improper, is my object. The convention appears to have proposed the partial consolidation evidently with a view to collect all powers ultimately in the United States into one entire government; and from its views in this respect, and from the tenacity of the small states to have an equal vote in the Senate, probably originated the greatest defects in the proposed plan.

Independent of the opinions of many great authors, that a free elective government cannot be extended over large territories, a few reflections must evince that one government and general legislation alone never can extend equal benefits to all parts of the United States. Different laws, customs, and opinions exist in the different states, which by a uniform system of laws would be unreasonably invaded. The United States contain about a million of square miles, and in half a century will probably contain ten millions of people; and from the center to the extremes is about 800 miles. . . .

The Country Is in a Good Condition

The following selection from a Boston newspaper of August 22, 1787, is a denial of the "hard times" arguments. It was written during the Convention, and is an answer to the propaganda describing the country as being on the verge of economic chaos. Many similar answers appeared during the ratification controversy.[10]

Was an intelligent foreigner, unacquainted with the real situation of this country . . . to come into one of our principal towns and be immediately presented with the newspapers published in these states the last two years, and to have no information but what he obtained from them, he would conceive us to be a poor, miserable, distracted people, distressed and suffering almost for the necessaries of life— without order or government—in anarchy and confusion. Was he then to be attended to one of our public assemblies, like that of commencement—a ball—the celebration of our independence, as at Boston or Philadelphia—or other public occasions, there to behold the whole assembly clothed in all the brilliant

---

[10] *The Massachusetts Centinel,* August 22, 1787.

show of gaudy fashion, in the rich silks, the fine cloths and costly manufactures of the remoter parts of the world, with scarcely an article of American production on a single individual, except possibly that some of the men might have American shoes and hats; and was he then to be told that the people throughout the country in their public assemblies in like manner appear all clothed in the manufactures of other countries—he would be struck with astonishment, and be apt to reason thus with himself: Is it possible that I am among the people whose newspapers I have been reading? How can this appearance be consistent with the complaints of the distress and hard times I have read of in their papers? Surely, if this people make this brilliant appearance in public, with the labor of my poor industrious countrymen beyond the Atlantic, the furniture of their houses must be somewhat in proportion—they must have other articles to a great amount, the manufactures of those countries, who have thus, by their labor and industry furnished them with the rich profusion of clothing I now behold. But I was told this morning at breakfast that tea, to an astonishing amount, the growth of the East Indies, at so many thousand miles distant; coffee, sugar, and chocolate, all articles of importation, are not only used in all the seaport towns, but in most families throughout the country. This being the case, I must conclude that this country is much more rich and fertile than any I am acquainted with in the old world, to allow its inhabitants the importation and use of so many foreign goods, or that they import and use more than they can pay for: If the latter, though it will account for the complaints of distressing hard times, decay of trade, etc., yet it shows a degree of folly and unreasonableness which I am sorry to discover. Their papers are full of violent language and indecent abuse of their governments, to that degree that one would think, instead of being under the mild and genial influence of republics, that their tempers were soured and their feelings irritated by the severe exercise of arbitrary sway. Instead of the kind soothing language of mildness and conciliation to persuade each other to do what is right and just with regard to their public and private debts—to retrieve and make the best of wrong measures—to introduce manufactures, agriculture, industry, frugality, and economy, so necessary for the good of the country —and totally prohibiting foreign frippery, they seem to be whetting up each other's resentments, endeavoring to excite a general dissatisfaction, without knowing the causes from whence their uneasinesses spring, or having any fixed object in view—inattentive to the fatal consequences of such conduct, that tends to civil commotion and disturbance, the hydra of all evil. Unhappy people! Insensible of the blessing they enjoy, superior in all respects to those of most other countries in the world—attributing that to the forms of their government, which in general are the best on earth, that ought to be attributed only to their folly and extravagance in an undue use of foreign gewgaws, and the importation and use of goods that they ought to manufacture themselves.

Answers to Federalist Arguments

Many Federalist writers argued that the Constitution should be adopted because of the high character of the members of the Convention. They also insisted that anarchy would follow if the Constitution were not adopted. The following selection, dated November 8, 1787, is one of the ablest answers to such arguments.[11]

I have read with a degree of attention several publications which have lately appeared in favor of the new Constitution; and as far as I am able to discern—the arguments (if they can be so termed) of most weight which are urged in its favor may be reduced to the two following:

1st. That the men who formed it were wise and experienced; that they were an illustrious band of patriots and had the happiness of their country at heart; that they were four months deliberating on the subject, and therefore it must be a perfect system.

2nd. That if the system be not received, this country will be without any government, and of consequence, will be reduced to a state of anarchy and confusion, and involved in bloodshed and carnage; and in the end a government will be imposed upon us, not the result of reason and reflection, but of force and usurpation.

As I do not find that either Cato or the Centinel, Brutus, or the Old Whig, or any other writer against this Constitution, have undertaken a particular refutation of this new species of reasoning, I take the liberty of offering to the public, through the channel of your paper, the few following animadversions on the subject; and the rather because I have discovered that some of my fellow citizens have been imposed upon by it.

With respect to the first it will be readily perceived that it precludes all investigation of the merits of the proposed constitution, and leads to an adoption of the plan without enquiring whether it be good or bad. For if we are to infer the perfection of this system from the characters and abilities of the men who formed it, we may as well determine to accept it without any enquiry as with. A number of persons in this as well as the other states, have, upon this principle, determined to submit to it without even reading or knowing its contents.

But supposing the premises from which this conclusion is drawn to be just, it then becomes essential, in order to give validity to the argument, to enquire into the characters of those who composed this body, that we may determine whether we can be justified in placing such unbounded confidence in them.

It is an invidious task, to call in question the characters of indi-

---

[11] *The New York Journal and Weekly Register,* November 8, 1787.

viduals, especially of such as are placed in illustrious stations. But when we are required implicitly to submit our opinions to those of others from a consideration that they are so wise and good as not to be liable to err, and that too in an affair which involves in it the happiness of ourselves and our posterity; every honest man will justify a decent investigation of characters in plain language.

It is readily admitted that many individuals who composed this body were men of the first talents and integrity in the union. It is at the same time well known to every man who is but moderately acquainted with the characters of the members, that many of them are possessed of high aristocratic ideas, and the most sovereign contempt of the common people; that not a few were strongly disposed in favor of monarchy; that there were some of no small talents and of great influence, of consummate cunning, and masters of intrigue, whom the war found poor, or in embarrassed circumstances, and left with princely fortunes, acquired in public employment, who are at this day to account for many thousands of public money; that there were others who were young, ardent, and ambitious, who wished for a government corresponding with their feelings while they were destitute of that experience which is the surest guide in political researches; that there were not a few who were gaping for posts of honor and emolument; these we find exulting in the idea of a change which will divert places of honor, influence and emolument into a different channel, where the confidence of the people will not be necessary to their acquirement. It is not to be wondered at that an assembly thus composed should produce a system liable to well founded objections, and which will require very essential alterations. We are told by one of themselves [Mr. Wilson of Philadelphia] the plan was a matter of accommodation; and it is not unreasonable to suppose that in this accommodation principles might be introduced which would render the liberties of the people very insecure.

I confess I think it of no importance what are the characters of the framers of this government, and therefore should not have called them in question if they had not been so often urged in print, and in conversation, in its favor. It ought to rest on its own intrinsic merit. If it is good it is capable of being vindicated; if it is bad, it ought not to be supported. It is degrading to a freeman, and humiliating to a rational one, to pin his faith on the sleeve of any man, or body of men, in an affair of such momentous importance.

In answer to the second argument, I deny that we are in immediate danger of anarchy and commotions. . . .

The country is in profound peace, and we are not threatened by invasion from any quarter. The governments of the respective states are in the full exercise of their powers; and the lives, the liberty, and property of individuals are protected. All present exigencies are answered by them. It is true, the regulation of trade and a competent provision for the payment of the interest of the public debt is wanting; but no immediate commotion will rise from these; time may be taken for calm discussion and deliberate conclusions. Individuals are just recovering from the losses and embarrassments sustained by the late war; industry and frugality are taking their station and banishing from the community idleness and prodigality. Individuals are lessening their private debts, and several millions of the public debt is discharged by the sale of western territory. There is no reason, therefore, why we should precipitately and rashly adopt a system which is imperfect or insecure; we may securely deliberate and propose amendments and alterations. I know it is said we cannot change for the worse; but if we act the part of wise men we shall take care that we change for the better. It will be labor lost if after all our pains we are in no better circumstances than we were before.

If any tumults arise they will be justly chargeable on those artful and ambitious men who are determined to cram this government down the throats of the people before they have time deliberately to examine it. All the measures of the leaders of this faction have tended to this point. In Congress they attempted to obtain a resolution to approve the Constitution without going into an examination of it. In Pennsylvania the chiefs of the party who themselves were of the convention that framed this system, within a few days after it dissolved, and before Congress had considered it, indecently brought forward a motion in their general assembly for recommending a convention; when a number of respectable men of that legislature withdrew from the house, refusing to sanction with their presence a measure so flagrantly improper, they procured a mob to carry a sufficient number of them by force to the house, to enable them to proceed on the business.

In Boston the printers have refused to print against this plan and have been countenanced in it. In Connecticut papers have been handed about for the people to sign, to support it, and the names of those who declined signing it have been taken down in what was called a black list, to intimidate them into a compliance, and this before the people had time to read and understand the meaning of the constitution. Many of the members of the convention who were charged with other public business have abandoned their duty and hastened to their states to precipitate an adoption of the measure. The most unwearied pains has been taken to persuade the legislatures to recommend conventions to be elected to meet at early periods before an opportunity could be had to examine the constitution proposed; every art has been used to exasperate the people against those who made objections to the plan. They have been told that the opposition is chiefly made by state officers who expect to lose their places by the change, though the propagators of this falsehood know that very few of the state offices will be vacated by the new constitution, and are well apprized that should it take place it will give birth to a vast number of more lucrative and permanent appointments, which its principal advocates in every state are warmly in the pursuit of. Is it not extraordinary that those men who are predicting that a rejection of this Constitution will lead to every evil which anarchy and confusion can produce, should at the same moment embrace and pursue with unabating industry every measure in their power to rouse the passions, and thereby preclude calm and dispassionate enquiry? It would be wise in them, however, to reflect in season that should public commotion take place, they will not only be answerable for the consequences, and the blood that may be shed, but that on such an event it is more than probable the people will discern the advocates for their liberties from those who are aiming to enslave them, and that each will receive their just deserts.

The Faults of the Constitution

The following article, dated November 21, 1787, and written by an officer of the Continental Army, is typical of the opposition aroused by the lack of a bill of rights and by various particular details of the Constitution.[12]

The following objections made to the new Constitution you are requested to publish for the consideration of the public at this all-important crisis. Yours, Anonymous.

The objections that have been made to the new Constitution are these:

1. It is not merely (as it ought to be) a Confederation of States, but a Government of Individuals.
2. The powers of Congress extend to the lives, the liberties, and the property of every citizen.
3. The sovereignty of the different states is *ipso facto* destroyed in its most essential parts.
4. What remains of it will only tend to create violent dissensions between the state governments and the Congress, and terminate in the ruin of the one or the other.
5. The consequence must therefore be, either that the union of the states will be destroyed by a violent struggle, or that their sovereignty will be swallowed up by silent encroachments into a universal aristocracy; because it is clear that if two different sovereign powers have a coequal command over the purses of the citizens, they will struggle for the spoils, and the weakest will be in the end obliged to yield to the efforts of the strongest.
6. Congress being possessed of these immense powers, the liberties of the states and of the people are not secured by a bill or DECLARATION OF RIGHTS.
7. The sovereignty of the states is not expressly reserved; the form only, and not the substance of their government, is guaranteed to them by express words.
8. TRIAL BY JURY, that sacred bulwark of liberty, is ABOLISHED IN CIVIL CASES, and Mr. W[ilson], one of the convention, has told you that not being able to agree as to the form of establishing this point, they have left you deprived of the substance. Here are his own words—the subject was involved in difficulties. The convention found the task too difficult for them and left the business as it stands.
9. The liberty of the press is not secured and the powers of Congress are fully adequate to its destruction as they are to have the trial of libels,

---

[12] *The Massachusetts Centinel,* November 21, 1787.

or pretended libels, against the United States, and may be a cursed abominable stamp act (as the Bowdoin administration has done in Massachusetts) preclude you effectually from all means of information. Mr. W[ilson] has given you no answer to these arguments.

10. Congress have the power of keeping up a standing army in the time of peace, and Mr. W[ilson] has told you that it was necessary.

11. The legislative and executive powers are not kept separate as every one of the American constitutions declares they ought to be; but they are mixed in a manner entirely novel and unknown, even to the constitution of Great Britain; because,

12. In England the king only has a nominal negative over the proceedings of the legislature, which he has never dared to exercise since the days of King William, whereas by the new Constitution both the President General and the Senate, two executive branches of government, have that negative, and are intended to support each other in the exercise of it.

13. The representation of the lower house is too small, consisting only of sixty-five members.

14. That of the Senate is so small that it renders its extensive powers extremely dangerous. It is to consist only of twenty-six members, two-thirds of whom must concur to conclude any treaty or alliance with foreign powers. Now we will suppose that five of them absent, sick, dead, or unable to attend, twenty-one will remain, and eight of these (one-third and one over may prevent the conclusion of any treaty, even the most favorable to America. Here will be a fine field for the intrigues and even the bribery and corruption of European powers.

15. The most important branches of the executive department are to be put into the hands of a single magistrate who will be in fact an elective king. The military, the land and naval forces are to be entirely at his disposal, and therefore:

16. Should the Senate, by the intrigues of foreign powers, become devoted to foreign influence, as was the case of late in Sweden, the people will be obliged, as the Swedes have been, to seek their refuge in the arms of the monarch or President General.

17. Rotation, that noble prerogative of liberty, is entirely excluded from the new system of government, and great men may and probably will be continued in office during their lives.

18. Annual elections are abolished and the people are not to reassume their rights until the expiration of two, four, and six years.

19. Congress are to have the power of fixing the time, place, and manner of holding elections, so as to keep them forever subjected to their influence.

20. The importation of slaves is not to be prohibited until the year 1808, and slavery will probably resume its empire in all the states.

21. The Militia is to be under the immediate command of Congress, and men conscientiously scrupulous of bearing arms, may be compelled to perform military duty.

22. The new government will be expensive beyond any we have ever experienced, the judicial department alone, with its concomitant train of judges, justices, chancellors, clerks, sheriffs, coroners, escheators, state attorneys and solicitors, constables,

etc., in every state and in every county in each state, will be a burden beyond the utmost abilities of the people to bear, and upon the whole.

23. A government partaking of monarchy and aristocracy will be fully and firmly established, and liberty will be but a name to adorn the short historic page of the halcyon days of America.

These, my countrymen, are the objections that have been made to the new proposed system of government; and if you read the system itself with attention, you will find them all to be founded in truth.

6. THE NATIONALIST DEFENSE OF THE CONSTITUTION

The arguments for a strong central government began long before the Convention of 1787, and continued during the Convention. Newspapers pointed to the distresses of the country, and particularly to its economic distress. As soon as the Constitution appeared, its supporters took the name Federalist and labeled all opponents Anti-Federalists. This was a charge which was denied, and it was insisted that whatever they were, the Federalists did not believe in a federal government. Moreover, the writing of *The Federalist Papers* fixed, for posterity at least, the idea that believers in a national government were Federalists and that the Constitution of 1787 provided for a federal government.

The movement in behalf of ratification took many forms. The appearance of the Constitution was greeted by glowing newspaper accounts. Washington and Franklin, in particular, were praised, and the country was told that the Constitution should be adopted without question because these two men had helped to draft it. Criticism of the Constitution was so immediate and so specific, however, that the Federalists had to resort to an elaborate defense. They argued at length that a bill of rights was unnecessary. They insisted that the Constitution was "federal" and not "national." They denied that the Convention had intended to reduce the states to "mere corporations." They repeated again and again the argument that only adoption of the Constitution could save the country from economic chaos and anarchy.

The Federalists, too, engaged in personal abuse. They accused every opponent of the Constitution of being a Daniel Shays. Over and over again they charged that the leading opponents of the Constitution were either state officeholders who were afraid they would lose their jobs, or men with "mean minds" and "narrow views." The Federalists even said that opposition to the Constitution was anti-Christian.

The ablest exposition of the Constitution came from the pens of James Madison, Alexander Hamilton, and John Jay, who united to write *The Federalist Papers*. No material has been included from these essays because they are readily available, but they should be read in connection with the following documents.

The Benefits to Be Derived from the Constitution

This article is typical of the praise which greeted the Constitution when it first appeared. It was printed in a Boston newspaper on September 30, 1787.[13]

The result of the Federal Convention has at length transpired after a profound secrecy being observed by the members who composed it; which, at least, has done honor to their fidelity, as we believe that scarcely another example can be adduced of the same caution among so large a number of persons. This country, singular in everything: in her rise, progress, extent of jurisdiction, in her emancipation and liberty, we flatter ourselves, is going to exhibit a new instance of a government being firmly indissolubly established, without the arts, violences, and bloodshed which have disgraced the annals of the Eastern hemispheres. Its acceptance will enroll the names of the Washingtons and Franklins of the present age with those of the solons and numas of antiquity. The military virtues of the former and the philosophic splendor of the latter will be obscured by the new lustre they will acquire as the legislators of an immense continent. Illustrious Chieftain! immortal sage! ye will have the plaudit of the world for having twice saved your country! You have once preserved it against the dangers and misery of foreign domination; you will now save it from the more destructive influence of civil dissension. The unanimity you have secured in your deliberations is an auspicious omen of our future concord and felicity. We anticipate with pleasure the happy effects of your wisdom. The narrow, contracted politics, the sordid envy, the mean jealousy of little minds; the partial views and the local prejudices which have so long retarded the growth of this people will be now annihilated. In their place a more enlightened and dispassionate legislation, a more comprehensive wisdom, and a plain manly system of national jurisprudence will be happily substituted. America, which has sunk in reputation from the operation of these causes, will arise with renewed splendors when the clouds, which have so long obscured her fame, shall be thus dissipated. By considering what we have already suffered by an opposite policy we may the more easily conceive what we must necessarily obtain from the adoption of this new Constitution. We shall indeed have but little to fear and everything to hope. The true interests of the several parts of the Confederation are the same. They only differ in points which are fictitious and imaginary. We shall distinguish our friends, and punish our enemies. Our distance from the fatal vortex of European politics will

---

[13] *The American Herald,* September 30, 1787.

secure us from the dangers of war. The canvas of these states will whiten the ocean; instead of being any longer neglected, our friendship will be prized and courted by all. A new era will commence and this country will be said to be in existence, but from the moment when the plan submitted to the people shall be generally adopted. The distinctions of state councils will be lost in the stronger ties by which the citizens of America will be connected to one another. As yet everything looks fair and the voice of opposition scarcely heard in whispers; may [it] then perish; and may peace, unanimity and happiness become perpetual throughout America.

Defense of the Constitution

The following consists of selections from one of the ablest short defenses of the Constitution against the attacks upon it. James Wilson's speech in the State House Yard in Philadelphia in October 1787 was published widely and many other Federalist writings were based upon it. It was also the subject of many articles written in opposition to the Constitution.[14]

It will be proper . . . before I enter into the refutation of the charges that are alleged, to mark the leading discrimination between the State constitutions and the constitution of the United States. When the people established the powers of legislation under their separate governments, they invested their representatives with every right and authority which they did not in explicit terms reserve; and therefore upon every question respecting the jurisdiction of the House of Assembly, if the frame of government is silent, the jurisdiction is efficient and complete. But in delegating federal powers, another criterion was necessarily introduced, and the congressional power is to be collected, not from tacit implication, but from the positive grant expressed in the instrument of the union. Hence, it is evident, that in the former case everything which is not reserved is given; but in the latter the reverse of the proposition prevails, and everything which is not given is reserved.

This distinction being recognized, will furnish an answer to those who think the omission of a bill of rights a defect in the proposed constitution; for it would have been superfluous and absurd to have stipulated with a federal body of our own creation, that we should enjoy those privileges of which we are not divested, either by the intention or the act that has brought the body into existence. For instance, the liberty of the press, which has been a copious source of declamation and opposition—what control can proceed from the Federal government to shackle or destroy that sacred palladium of national freedom? If, indeed, a power similar to

---

[14] John Bach McMaster and Frederick D. Stone, *Pennsylvania and the Federal Constitution, 1787–1788* (Philadelphia, 1888), 143–49.

that which has been granted for the regulation of commerce had been granted to regulate literary publications, it would have been as necessary to stipulate that the liberty of the press should be preserved inviolate, as that the impost should be general in its operation. With respect likewise to the particular district of ten miles, which is to be made the seat of federal government, it will undoubtedly be proper to observe this salutary precaution, as there the legislative power will be exclusively lodged in the President, Senate, and House of Representatives of the United States. But this could not be an object with the Convention, for it must naturally depend upon a future compact, to which the citizens immediately interested will, and ought to be, parties; and there is no reason to suspect that so popular a privilege will in that case be neglected. In truth, then, the proposed system possesses no influence whatever upon the press, and it would have been merely nugatory to have introduced a formal declaration upon the subject—nay, that very declaration might have been construed to imply that some degree of power was given, since we undertook to define its extent.

Another objection that has been fabricated against the new constitution, is expressed in this disingenuous form—"The trial by jury is abolished in civil cases." I must be excused, my fellow citizens, if upon this point I take advantage of my professional experience to detect the futility of the assertion. Let it be remembered then, that the business of the Federal Convention was not local, but general—not limited to the views and establishments of a single state, but co-extensive with the continent, and comprehending the views and establishments of thirteen independent sovereignties. When, therefore, this subject was in discussion, we were involved in difficulties which pressed on all sides, and no precedent could be discovered to direct our course. The cases open to a trial by jury differed in the different States. It was therefore impracticable, on that ground, to have made a general rule. The want of uniformity would have rendered any reference to the practice of the States idle and useless; and it could not with any propriety be said that, "The trial by jury shall be as heretofore," since there has never existed any federal system of jurisprudence, to which the declaration could relate. Besides, it is not in all cases that the trial by jury is adopted in civil questions; for cases depending in courts of admiralty, such as relate to maritime captures, and such as are agitated in courts of equity, do not require the intervention of that tribunal. How, then was the line of discrimination to be drawn? The Convention found the task too difficult for them, and they left the business as it stands, in the fullest confidence that no danger could possibly ensue, since the proceedings of the Supreme Court are to be regulated by the Congress, which is a faithful representation of the people; and the oppression of government is effectually barred, by declaring that in all criminal cases the trial by jury shall be preserved.

This constitution, it has been further urged, is of a pernicious tendency, because it tolerates a standing army in the time of peace. This has always been a topic of popular declamation; and yet I do not know a nation in the world which has not found it necessary and useful to maintain the appearance of strength in a season of the most profound tranquility. Nor is it a novelty with us; for under the present articles of confederation, Congress certainly possesses this reprobated power, and the exercise of that power is proved at this moment by her cantonments along the banks of the Ohio. But what would be our national situation were it otherwise? Every principle of policy must be subverted, and the government must declare war, before they are prepared to carry it on. Whatever may be the provocation, however important the object in view, and however necessary dispatch and secrecy may be, still the declaration must precede the preparation, and the enemy will be informed of your intention, not only before you are equipped for an attack, but even before you are fortified for a defence. The consequence is too obvious to require any further delineation, and no man who regards the dignity and safety of his country can deny the necessity of a military force, under the control and with the restrictions which the new constitution provides.

Perhaps there never was a charge made with less reasons than that which predicts the institution of a baneful aristocracy in the federal Senate. This body branches into two characters, the one legislative and the other executive. In its legislative character it can effect no purpose, without the cooperation of the House of Representatives, and in its executive character it can accomplish no object without the concurrence of the President. Thus fettered, I do not know any act which the Senate can of itself perform, and such dependence necessarily precludes every idea of influence and superiority. But I will confess that in the organization of this body a compromise between contending interests is discernible; and when we reflect how various are the laws, commerce, habits, population and extent of the confederated States, this evidence of mutual concession and accommodation ought rather to command a generous applause, than to excite jealousy and reproach. For my part, my admiration can only be equalled by my astonishment in beholding so perfect a system formed from such heterogeneous materials.

The next accusation I shall consider is that which represents the federal constitution, as not only calculated, but designedly framed, to reduce the State governments to mere corporations, and eventually to annihilate them. Those who have employed the term corporation upon this occasion are not perhaps aware of its extent. In common parlance, indeed, it is generally applied to petty associations for the ease and convenience of a few individuals; but in its enlarged sense, it will comprehend the government of Pennsylvania, the existing union of the States, and even this projected system is nothing more than a formal act of incorporation. But upon what pretence can it be alleged that it was designed to annihilate the State governments? For I will undertake to prove that upon their existence depends the existence of the Federal plan. For this purpose, permit me to call your attention to the manner in which the President, Senate, and House of Representatives are proposed to be appointed. The President is to be chosen by electors, nominated in such manner as the legislature of each State may direct; so that if there is no legislature there can be no electors, and consequently the office of President cannot be supplied. . . .

The power of direct taxation has likewise been treated as an improper delegation to the federal government; but when we consider it as the duty of that body to provide for the national safety, to support the dignity of the union, and to discharge the debts contracted upon the collected faith of the States for their common benefit, it must be acknowledged that those upon whom such important obligations are imposed, ought in justice and in policy to possess every means requisite for a faithful performance of their trust. But why should we be alarmed with visionary evils? I will venture to predict that the great revenue of the United States must, and always will, be raised by impost, for, being at once less obnoxious and more productive, the interest of the government will be best promoted by the accommodation of the people.

The Necessity for Ratification

The following essay is characteristic of the demand for immediate ratification of the Constitution, and outlines the benefits to be derived from the new government. It was printed in a Boston newspaper on October 20, 1787.[15]

Let every well-wisher to his country carefully consider the following questions and answer then according to the feelings which his particular situation has excited, without having recourse to those abstract reasonings and jealousies which are rather calculated to confound than inform. Let him reflect for a moment whether the surmises of persons whose personal interest and importance are likely to be affected, ought to be put in competition with the deliberate, cool, dispassionate determination of men selected by the several states, for the sole purpose of forming a federal constitution, whose interests as men, and as citizens, are at least of equal consequence with those who wantonly carp at their productions. Let it then be asked:

1. Whether in the present situation of public affairs it is not *absolutely necessary* that some form of government should be immediately established for the United States, distinct from that which is formed by the Confederation?

2. Whether it is possible that any plan or form of government devised by men can be perfect and entirely pleasing to every state in the union, and to all the inhabitants of each state?

3. Whether the Constitution framed by the late Convention ought not to be adopted by the several states as the only means of extricating the people from the distresses which they at present labor under, especially as it contains a provision for amending any defects which may be discovered therein?

4. Whether, if the Constitution now offered should be refused, there is any probability of obtaining another more generally acceptable?

5. What will be the consequence of a refusal of this Constitution? What will become of our public

---

[15] *The Massachusetts Centinel,* October 20, 1787.

creditors? How will our commerce be regulated, our people employed, and poverty, and extreme distress be prevented? Will not anarchy take place, and the people, driven to despair, seize upon each other's property, and at length submit to some aspiring chief, who, by taking advantage of our situation, will become a king or a tyrant?

6. Will the distresses of the people be much longer submitted unto, that men who are feeding upon the public property, and who do not partake of their sufferings, may amuse themselves in speculations about government, whilst they are indifferent to the calamities they thereby occasion?

7. Are not the amazing number of writs and executions returnable to every court, and the trifling sums for which valuable real estates are sold by the sheriff, alarming proofs of our ruinous situation?

8. Does the proprietor of houses and lands although his rents are reduced below what they were in the cheapest times, receive them regularly, and are not his tenants, from the general distress frequently two and three quarters, and sometimes a whole year in arrear, and do they not afterwards often remove without being able to pay anything?

9. What are the profits arising from trade and commerce, and whence happens it that so many of the respectable class of citizens who seek their living thereby become bankrupts?

10. Upon what do the widows and orphans subsist whose property is immersed in the public funds, and whose husbands and fathers gave up their all to save their country?

11. Ye tradesmen, who formerly by your diligence and industry were enabled to enjoy the comforts as well as the necessaries of life; say, how many of you do now find as much employment as will produce a bare subsistence for your apprentices —and even of this pittance, how many of your employers are able to pay you with punctuality?

12. Ye laborers, recount the many days which you spend in idleness "because no man giveth you to work" and that in the season of the year when most is to be done, and from which you have been accustomed to lay up fuel and other necessaries for an approaching winter?

13. Where is the man, be his fortune what it may, unless he partakes of the *public stock,* who does not experience the effects of this general calamity?

CONCLUSION

Once the Constitution was adopted, Americans divided into parties seeking to control the new government. From the first elections in 1788 down to the present day they have continued to follow a party system and to interpret the nature of the government provided for by the Constitution. In the beginning the Federalists, who were believers in a national government, upheld national power and a broad interpretation of the Constitution. The Anti-Federalists, who were really federalists, demanded a strict construction of the Constitution, and broad powers for the states. They insisted that the central government could do only what the Constitution said specifically it had the power to do, and no more. They called themselves Democratic-Republicans and were soon organized behind the leadership of Thomas Jefferson. As a party they supported the idea of "states rights" as opposed to the nationalist ideas of the Federalists.

After the Democratic-Republicans gained power in 1801 they soon stretched the interpretation of the Constitution as broadly as any nationalist. They did so to justify the purchase of Louisiana from France. On the other hand, the Federalists, who were bitterly opposed to the acquisition of Louisiana, now argued for a strict construction of the Constitution and insisted that the central government had no such power. By the time of the War of 1812 they were as vigorous in their support of "states rights" as Jefferson had been in the 1790s, and before the war was over, they were threatening secession from the Union.

From 1815 to 1860 the argument became increasingly heated, until debate yielded to the clash of arms. One basic cause of the Civil War was the disagreement between the North and the South as to the nature of the union of the states. Southern leaders argued that it was a compact among sovereign states, that the states might nullify a law of Congress, and that, failing all else, a state had the right to secede from the Union. Northern leaders insisted that the Union was older than the Constitution, that the central government was sovereign, and that a state could never secede.

A bloody, four-year war settled the issue of whether a state could secede. Soon thereafter, Supreme Court decisions backed up the nationalist view. But the idea of "states rights" could not be killed. It was used by first one group and then another. Businesses regulated by state governments appealed to the federal courts, which exercised a judicial veto. When the national government passed regulatory laws, business again appealed to the federal courts and escaped control for a time on the ground that they were local businesses.

With the advent of the New Deal in 1933, parties once more shifted position. The Democrats, who had been "states righters" while the Republicans were in power, now adopted a sweeping nationalistic interpretation of the Constitution to justify New Deal measures. The Republicans, who had been nationalists most of the time since their foundation in the 1850s, now embraced "states rights" theories to oppose the New Deal, and tried to steal Thomas Jefferson from the Democrats.

The Second World War added vastly to the power of the national government, but the idea of "states rights" is still a vital force in American political life. The Constitution has not been finally interpreted despite more than a century and a half of argument.

5 CLARENCE L. VER STEEG

launching the new government

Students too often assume that with the adoption of the Constitution the new government automatically sprang into full operation. They tend to see the national government through twentieth-century eyes—Congress conducting its legislative business according to established procedures; the President in his full executive capacity suggesting legislation, making appointments, and carrying on foreign policy; and federal courts passing on the validity of Congressional and state enactments. Of course, upon reflection most readers recognize that the Constitution, magnificent as it was, only outlined the structure of government; in a sense, it was a blueprint for a building that still needed to be constructed.

It is no wonder, therefore, that the first decades following the ratification of the Constitution are often called "the formative years." Measures were passed that influenced the course of our government for generations; precedents were established that reach through the years to the present day; and political traditions developed that run throughout our history. It was during these years, for example, that the two party system, now such an integral part of our political life, developed. It was also the period that marked the beginning of the "Hamiltonian" and "Jeffersonian" traditions in American politics, the establishment of a national system of taxation, the working out of procedures in Congress, and the setting of countless precedents ranging from how the President should be addressed to how the President should carry on foreign affairs.

Of course, many parts of the Constitution itself needed definition. To take a single example, the Constitution solemnly declared: "The Judicial

Power of the United States shall be vested in one Supreme Court, and in such inferior courts as the Congress may from time to time ordain and establish." But how was this statement to be interpreted? How many justices should comprise the Supreme Court? Would the existing courts operate as the "inferior" courts within the federal system? Or should special "inferior" courts be created? Such questions needed to be debated—and decided.

All the questions raised were, in reality, part of a fundamental question: What course should the national government pursue under the new Constitution? In this problem an attempt has been made to provide a representative sampling of the answers given by contemporaries covering the formative years, 1789–1809. As one would expect, strong difference of opinion is to be found in the selections that follow; but it is interesting that, almost without exception, all groups claimed the Constitution as the touchstone for their position, asserting that the measures or procedures they advocated would best carry out the spirit of that basic document. It is also worth noting that each group was essentially concerned with the welfare of the nation, but differed as to how that important objective could be achieved.

1. LAUNCHING THE SHIP OF STATE

Many of the leading supporters of the Constitution feared that those forces which had opposed ratification would obtain control of the new government in the first election and thwart the intentions of the framers. No less a person than Washington wrote: "There will . . . be no room for the advocates of the Constitution to relax in their exertions. If they should be lulled into security, appointments of Anti-Federal men may probably take place, and the consequences, which you so justly dread, be realized." But such fears proved groundless. In the elections of 1788, the supporters of the Constitution not only registered an overwhelming victory, but Washington himself was elected President of the United States by a unanimous electoral vote.

The nation looked to the President for leadership when Congress met in its historic first session in the spring of 1789, and those who rallied to his side became the first organized party in our history—the Federalists. The Federalists dominated the first decade under the new government, recognizing, as Hamilton stated it, that "it is to little purpose to have *introduced* a system, if the weightiest influence is not given to its firm *establishment,* in the outset." The measures and policies that they introduced touched every phase of American political and economic life; in fact, the force of these policies extended to the Constitution itself.

Opposition to Federalist policies developed during Washington's administration, often from leading supporters of the Constitution such as Madison, who claimed that the intent of the framers was not being fulfilled. Differences arose over diplomatic policy, taxation, the national debt, and, most important, over the basic meaning of the Constitution.

In the following pages, the direction of Washington's leadership will be examined together with two of the pre-eminent issues that arose during his administration. In each selection the views of the Federalists and those who opposed the Federalists are presented; the reader will wish to note where there was agreement as well as disagreement.

Setting the Course

What did the representatives who gathered in New York City expect from their new government? And what was the attitude of those individuals and groups who had opposed the Constitution? The answers to these questions varied almost as much as the individuals assembled.

Some Anti-Federalists carried their opposition directly into the new government; others supported the movement for a convention to revise the Constitution immediately; still others almost reversed themselves. Elbridge Gerry, for example, an articulate critic of the Constitution, declared in the early weeks of the first session that "the salvation of America depends on the establishment of this government. . . . If the Constitution . . . should not be supported, I despair of having a government of these United States."

The most significant index to Federalist ideas came from George Washington, whose leadership markedly influenced the events of the next decades. Indeed, Washington's role as our first President has not always been appreciated. Because Washington was reserved and often reluctant to commit himself in public pamphlets or private letters for fear of being misunderstood, he has been slighted in favor of Alexander Hamilton, his precocious, colorful Secretary of the Treasury. Yet during these years it was the Virginian who stood at the helm. No policies were advocated without his consent; no measures were passed without his support. It is necessary, therefore to look to Washington, the leader of the new government, to anticipate the direction which that government would take.

The following selection, although labeled Washington's "First Inaugural Address," is, in fact, a composite of excerpts from a proposed address he never gave, from the inaugural address he actually delivered on April 30, 1789, and from letters to Sir Edward Newenham and Thomas Jefferson in the winter and spring of 1788–1789.[1] The writer has taken the liberty of assembling these

---

[1] John C. Fitzpatrick, ed., *The Writings of George Washington*, 39 vols. (Washington, D.C., 1931–44), 30:72, 83, 291–96, 299–308.

documents, which embody the ideas of Washington on good government, instead of relying exclusively on the first President's actual inaugural, for Washington hesitated to include suggestions in his formal address which would encourage any protest against excessive use of executive power. As a result, his actual inaugural speech contained no advice to Congress concerning legislation.

Fellow Citizens of the Senate and the House of Representatives. . . .

By the article establishing the Executive Department, it is made the duty of the President "to recommend to your consideration, such measures as he shall judge necessary and expedient." The circumstances under which I now meet you, will acquit me from entering into that subject, farther than to refer to the Great Constitutional Charter under which you are assembled; and which, in defining your powers, designates the objects to which your attention is to be given. It will be more consistent with those circumstances, and far more congenial with the feelings which actuate me, to substitute, in place of a recommendation of particular measures, the tribute that is due to the talents, the rectitude, and the patriotism which adorn the characters selected to devise and adopt them. In these honorable qualifications, I behold the surest pledges, that as on one side, no local prejudices, or attachments; no separate views, nor party animosities, will misdirect the comprehensive and equal eye which ought to watch over this great assemblage of communities and interests: so, on another, that the foundations of our National policy will be laid in the pure and immutable principles of private morality; and the pre-eminence of a free Government, be exemplified by all the attributes which can win the affections of its Citizens, and command the respect of the world.

I dwell on this prospect with every satisfaction which an ardent love for my Country can inspire: since there is no truth more thoroughly established, than that there exists in the economy and course of nature, an indissoluble union between virtue and happiness, between duty and advantage, between the genuine maxims of an honest and magnanimous policy, and the solid rewards of public prosperity and felicity: Since we ought to be no less persuaded that the propitious smiles of Heaven, can never be expected on a nation that disregards the eternal rules of order and right, which Heaven itself has ordained: And since the preservation of the sacred fire of liberty, and the destiny of the Republican model of government, are justly considered as *deeply,* perhaps as *finally* staked, on the experiment entrusted to the hands of the American people. . . .

The mind is so formed in different persons as to contemplate the same object in different points of view. . . . Although the agency I had informing this system, and the high opinion I entertained of my Colleagues for their ability and integrity may have tended to warp my judgment in its favour; yet I will not pretend to say that it appears absolutely perfect to me, or that there may not be many faults which have escaped my discernment. I will only say, that, during and since the Session of the Convention, I have attentively heard and read every oral and printed information of both sides of the question that could readily be procured. This long and laborious investigation, in which I endeavoured as far as the frailty of nature would permit to act with candour has resulted in a fixed belief that this Constitution, is really in its formation a government of the people; that is to say, a government in which all power is derived from, and at stated periods reverts to them, and that, in its operation, it is purely, a government of Laws made and executed by the fair substitutes of the people alone. . . . Hence I have been induced to conclude that this government must be less obnoxious to well-founded objections than most which have existed in the World. And in that opinion I am confirmed on three accounts: *first,* because every government ought to be possessed of power adequate to the purposes for which it was instituted; Secondly, because no other or greater powers appear to me to be delegated to this government than are essential to accomplish the objects for which it was instituted, to wit, the safety and happiness of the governed; and thirdly because it is clear to my conception that no government before introduced among mankind ever contained so many checks and such efficatious restraints to prevent it from degenerating into any species of oppression. . . .

It is true, that, for the want of a proper Confederation, we have not yet been in a situation fully to enjoy those blessings which God and Nature seemed to have intended for us. But I begin to look forward, with a kind of political faith, to scenes of national happiness, which have not heretofore been offered for the fruition of the most favoured Nations. The natural political, and moral circumstances of our Nascent empire justify the anticipation. We have an almost unbounded territory whose natural advantages for agriculture and Commerce equal those of any on the globe. In a civil point of view we have unequalled privilege of choosing our own political Institutions and of improving upon the experience of Mankind in the formation of a confederated government, where due energy will not be incompatible with unalienable rights of freemen. To complete the picture, I may observe, that the information and morals of our Citizens appear to be peculiarly favourable for the introduction of such a plan of government as I have just now described.

Whether the Constitutional door that is opened for amendments in ours, be not the wisest and apparently the happiest expedient that has ever been suggested by human prudence, I leave to every unprejudiced mind to determine. . . .

. . . I can say, there are scarcely any of the amendments which have been suggested, to which I have *much* objection, except that which goes to the prevention of direct taxation; and that, I presume, will be more strenuously advocated and insisted upon hereafter, than any other. I had indulged the expectation, that the New Government would enable those entrusted with its Administration to do justice to the public creditors and retrieve the National character. But if no means are to be employed but requisitions, that expectation was vain and we may as well recur to the old Confœderation. If the system can be put in operation without touching much the Pockets of the People, perhaps, it may be done; but, in my judgment, infinite circumspection and prudence are yet necessary in the experiment. It is nearly impossible for anybody who has not been on the spot to conceive (from any description) what the delicacy and danger of our situation have been. Though the peril is not past entirely; thank God! the prospect is somewhat brightening. . . .

It might naturally be supposed that I should not silently pass by the subject of our defence. . . . Seperated as we are from them, by intervening Oceans, an exemption from the burden of maintaining numerous fleets and Armies must ever be considered as a singular felicity in our National lot. It will be in our choice to train our youths to such industrious and hardy professions as that they may grow into an unconquerable force, with out our being obliged to draw unprofitable Drones from the hive of Industry. As our people have a natural genius for Naval affairs and as our Materials for Navigation are ample; if we give due encouragement to the fisheries and the carrying trade; we shall possess such a nursery of Seamen and such skill in maratime operations as to enable us to create a Navy almost in a moment. But it will be wise to anticipate events and to lay a foundation in time. Whenever the circumstances will permit, a grand provision of warlike stores, arsenals and dock-yards ought to be made. . . .

A well organized Militia would constitute a strong defence; of course, your most serious attention will be turned to such an establishment. . . .

The complete organization of the Judicial Department was left by the Constitution to the ulterior arrangement of Congress. You will be pleased therefore to let a supreme regard for equal justice and the inherent rights of the citizens be visible in all your proceedings on that important subject. . . .

. . . Notwithstanding the embarrassments under which our trade has hitherto laboured, since the peace, the enterprising spirit of our citizens has steered our Vessels to almost every region of the known world.

In some distant and heretofore unfrequented countries, our new Constellation has been received with tokens of uncommon regard. An energetic government will give to our flag still greater respect. . . . But an internal commerce is more in our power. . . .

Notwithstanding the rapid growth of our population, from the facility of obtaining subsistence, as well as from the accession of strangers, yet we shall not soon become a manufacturing people. . . .

Many articles, however, in wool, flax, cotton, and hemp; and all in leather, iron, fur, and wood may be fabricated at home with great advantage. If the quantity of wool, flax, cotton and hemp should be encreased to ten-fold its present amount (as it easily could be, I apprehend the whole might in a short time be manufactured. Especially by the introduction of machines for multiplying the effects of labour, in diminishing the number of hands employed upon it. But it will rest with you to investigate what proficiency we are capable of making in manufactures, and what encouragement should be given to particular branches of them. . . .

It remains for you to make, out of a Country poor in the precious metals and comparatively thin of inhabitants a flourishing State. But here it is particularly incumbant on me to express my idea of a flourishing state with precision; and to distinguish between happiness and splendour. The people of this Country may doubtless enjoy all the great blessings of the social State: and yet United America may not for a long time to come make a brilliant figure as a nation, among the nations of the earth. . . . We shou'd not, in imitation of some nations which have been celebrated for a false kind of patriotism, wish to aggrandize our own Republic at the expence of the freedom and happiness of the rest of mankind. . . .

It belongs to you especially to take measures for promoting the general welfare. It belongs to you to make men honest in their dealings with each other, by regulating the coinage and currency of money upon equitable principles; as well as by establishing just weights and measures upon an uniform plan. Whenever an opportunity shall be furnished to you as public or as private men, I trust you will not fail to use your best endeavors to improve the education and manners of a people; to accelerate the progress of arts and Sciences; to patronize works of genius; to confer rewards for inventions of utility; and to cherish institutions favourable to humanity. Such are among the best of all human employments. Such exertion of your talents will render your situations truly dignified and cannot fail of being acceptable in the sight of the Divinity. . . .

Having thus imparted to you my sentiments, as they have been awakened by the occasion which brings us together, I shall take my present leave; but not without resorting once more to the benign parent of the human race, in humble supplication that since he has been pleased to favour the American people, with opportunities for deliberating in perfect tranquility, and dispositions for deciding with unparallelled unanimity on a form of Government, for the security of their Union and the advancement of their happiness; so his divine blessing may be equally *conspicuous* in the enlarged views the temperate consultation, and the wise measures on which the success of this Government must depend.

How Shall the Debt Be Paid?

Almost everyone agreed with Washington that some action should be taken with respect to the public debt incurred by the central government during the Revolution, but few agreed on precise measures; and, though the Constitution stated that all debts contracted before the adoption of the Constitution were "valid," no one was quite certain what this phrase meant. Congress, therefore, asked the Secretary of the Treasury, Alexander Hamilton, to submit a report on the public credit which could guide them in proposing legislation. He complied on January 14, 1790, with his famous "Report on the Public Credit," which recommended payment at face value of the depreciated government certificates and the assumption of the revolutionary debts of the states by the federal government. By these measures Hamilton hoped to bind all monied and creditor groups firmly to the new government.

His proposals stirred up a hornet's nest of criticism. Congressmen led by James Jackson of Georgia complained that speculators would receive enormous profits, and some years later John Taylor of Virginia issued several pamphlets, condemning the program with what he called its "paper junto," its "pernicious" policies, and its "usurpations upon constitutional principles." In contrast, Oliver Wolcott of Connecticut asserted that he would consider the rejection of the plan to assume the state debts as an "overthrow of the national government," while the *United States Gazette*, a partisan newspaper, warned its readers that the want of "a prosperous funding system" would make the national government "but a shadow."

It was almost inevitable that these far-reaching economic measures of the Federalists should arouse deep-rooted antagonisms, for one section or group thought it was being exploited to the advantage of the other. Certainly the Hamiltonian recommendations on funding the public debt marked the beginning of a concerted opposition to measures of the Federalist party. They were also important because Hamilton and Madison, two of the leading supporters of the Constitution, parted company.

The selections that follow include their areas of agreement as well as disagreement. The first selection is taken from the above-mentioned report that Hamilton communicated to Congress.[2] The second selection includes excerpts from the speeches Madison delivered in Congress on February 11 and 24, 1790.[3]

Hamilton

. . . If the maintenance of public credit, then, be truly so important, the next inquiry which suggests itself is, By what means is it to be effected? The ready answer to which question is, by good faith; by a punctual performance of contracts.

[2] John C. Hamilton, ed., *The Works of Alexander Hamilton*, 7 vols. (New York, 1850–51), 3:1–45.

[3] Gaillard Hunt, ed., *The Writings of James Madison*, 9 vols. (New York, 1900–10), 5:441–45, 458–61. Used by permission of G. P. Putnam's Sons, publisher.

States, like individuals, who observe their engagements, are respected and trusted, while the reverse is the fate of those who pursue an opposite conduct.

Every breach of the public engagements, whether from choice or necessity, is, in different degrees, hurtful to public credit. . . . Those who are most commonly creditors of a nation, are, generally speaking enlightened men; and there are signal examples to warrant a conclusion, that, when a candid and fair appeal is made to them, they will understand their true interest too well to refuse their concurrence in such modifications of their claims as any real necessity may demand.

While the observance of that good faith, which is the basis of public credit, is recommended by the strongest inducements of political expediency, it is enforced by considerations of still greater authority. There are arguments for it which rest on the immutable principles of moral obligation. . . .

Having now taken a concise view of the inducements to a proper provision for the public debt, the next inquiry which presents itself is, What ought to be the nature of such a provision? This requires some preliminary discussions.

It is agreed, on all hands, that that part of the debt which has been contracted abroad, and is denominated the foreign debt, ought to be provided for according to the precise terms of the contracts relating to it. The discussions which can arise, therefore, will have reference essentially to the domestic part of it, or to that which has been contracted at home. It is to be regretted that there is not the same unanimity of sentiment on this part as on the other.

. . . It involves this question: Whether a discrimination ought not to be made between original holders of the public securities, and present possessors, by purchase? Those who advocate a discrimination, are for making a full provision for the securities of the former at their nominal value; but contend that the latter ought to receive no more than the cost to them, and the interest. And the idea is sometimes suggested, of making good the difference to the primitive possessor.

The Secretary, after the most mature reflection on the force of this argument, is induced to reject the doctrine it contains, as equally unjust and impolitic; as highly injurious, even to the original holders of public securities; as ruinous to public credit.

It is inconsistent with justice, because, in the first place, it is a breach of contrast—a violation of the rights of a fair purchaser. . . .

The impolicy of a discrimination results from two considerations: one, that it proceeds upon a principle destructive of that quality of the public debt, or the stock of the nation, which is essential to its capacity for answering the purposes of money, that is the security of transfer; the other, that . . . it includes a breach of faith, it renders property in the funds, less valuable, consequently, induces lenders to demand a higher premium for what they lend, and produces every other inconvenience of a bad state of public credit. . . .

But there is still a point of view, in which it will appear perhaps even more exceptionable than in either of the former. It would be repugnant to an express provision of the Constitution of the United States. This provision is, that "all debts contracted, and engagements entered into, before the adoption of that Constitution, shall be as valid against the United States under it, as under the Confederation"; which amounts to a constitutional ratification of the contracts respecting the debt, in the state in which they existed under the Confederation. And, resorting to that standard, there can be no doubt that the rights of assignees and original holders must be considered as equal. . . .

The Secretary, concluding that discrimination between the different classes of creditors of the United

States cannot with propriety, be made, proceeds to examine whether a difference ought to be permitted to remain between them and another description of public creditors—those of the States, individually. The Secretary, after mature reflection on this point, entertains a full conviction, that an assumption of the debts of the particular States by the Union, and a like provision for them, as for those of the Union, will be a measure of sound policy and substantial justice.

It would, in the opinion of the Secretary, contribute, in an eminent degree, to an orderly, stable, and satisfactory arrangement of the national finances. . . .

The principal question, then must be, whether such a provision cannot be more conveniently and effectually made, by one general plan, issuing from one authority, than by different plans originating in different authorities? In the first case, there can be no competition for resources; in the last, there must be such a competition. . . .

If all the public creditors receive their dues from one source, distributed with an equal hand, their interest will be the same. And, having the same interests, they will unite in the support of the fiscal arrangements of the Government—as these, too, can be made with more convenience where there is no competition. These circumstances combined, will insure to the revenue laws a more ready and more satisfactory execution.

If, on the contrary, there are distinct provisions, there will be distinct interests, drawing different ways. That union and concert of views, among the creditors, which in every Government is of great importance to their security, and to that of public credit, will not only not exist, but will be likely to give place to mutual jealousy and opposition. . . .

Persuaded, as the Secretary is, that the proper funding of the present debt will render it a national blessing, yet he is so far from acceding to the present position, in the latitude in which it is sometimes laid down, that "public debts are public benefits"—a position inviting to prodigality, and liable to dangerous abuse—that he ardently wishes to see it incorporated, as a fundamental maxim, in the system of public credit of the United States, that the creation of debt should always be accompanied with the means of extinguishment. This he regards as the true secret for rendering public credit immortal. And he presumes that it is difficult to conceive a situation in which there may not be an adherence to the maxim. At least he feels an unfeigned solicitude that this may be attempted by the United States, and that they may commence their measures for the establishment of credit with the observance of it.

Madison

It has been said, by some gentlemen, that the debt itself does not exist in the extent and form which is generally supposed. I confess, sir, I differ altogether from the gentlemen who take that ground. Let us consider, first, by whom the debt was contracted, and then let us consider to whom it is due. The debt was contracted by the United States, who, with respect to that particular transaction, were in a national capacity. The Government was nothing more than the agent or organ, by which the whole body of the people acted. The change in the Government which has taken place has enlarged its national capacity, but it has not varied the national obligation, with respect to the engagements entered into by that transaction. . . .

The only point on which we can deliberate is, to whom the payment is really due; for this purpose, it will be proper to take notice of the several descriptions of people who are creditors of the Union, and lay down some principles respecting them, which may lead us to a just and equitable decision. As there is a small part of the debt yet unliquidated, it may be well to pass it by and come to the great mass of the liquidated debt. It may here be proper to notice four classes into which it may be divided:

First. Original creditors, who have never alienated their securities.

Second. Original creditors who have alienated.

Third. Present holders of alienated securities.

Fourth. Intermediate holders, through whose hands securities have circulated.

The only principles that can govern the decision on their respective pretensions, I take to be, 1. Public Justice; 2. Public Faith; 3. Public Credit; 4. Public Opinion.

With respect to the first class, there can be no difficulty. Justice is in their favor, for they have advanced the value which they claim; public faith is in their favor, for the written promise is in their hands; respect for public credit is in their favor, for if claims so sacred are violated, all confidence must be at an end; public opinion is in their favor, for every honest citizen cannot but be their advocate.

With respect to the last class, the intermediate holders, their pretensions, if they have any, will lead us into a labyrinth, for which it is impossible to find a clew. This will be the less complained of, because this class were perfectly free, both in becoming and ceasing to be creditors; and because, in general, they must have gained by their speculations.

The only rival pretensions then are those of the original creditors, who have assigned, and of the present holders of the assignments.

The former may appeal to justice, because the value of the money, the service, or the property advanced by them, has never been really paid to them.

They may appeal to good faith, because the value stipulated and expected, is not satisfied by the steps taken by the Government. The certificates put into the hands of the creditors, on closing their settlements with the public, were of less real value than was acknowledged to be due; they may be considered as having been forced, in fact, on the receivers. They cannot, therefore, be fairly adjudged an extinguishment of the debt. They may appeal to the motives for establishing public credit, for which justice and faith form the natural foundation. They may appeal to the precedent furnished by the compensation allowed to the army during the late war, for the depreciation of bills, which nominally discharged the debts. They may appeal to humanity, for the sufferings of the military part of the creditors can never be forgotten, while sympathy is an American virtue. To say nothing of the singular hardship, in so many mouths, of requiring those who have lost four-fifths or seven-eights of their due, to contribute the remainder in favor of those who have gained in the contrary proportion.

On the other hand, the holders by assignment, have claims, which I by no means wish to depreciate. They will say, that whatever pretensions others may have against the public, these cannot effect the validity of theirs. That if they gain by the risk taken upon themselves, it is but the just reward of that risk. That as they hold the public promise, they have an undeniable demand on the public faith. That the best foundation of public credit is that adherence to literal engagements on which it has been erected by the most flourishing nations. That if the new Government should swerve from so essential a principle, it will be regarded by all the world as inheriting the infirmities of the old. Such being the interfering claims on the public, one of three things must be done; either pay both, reject wholly one or the other, or make a *composition* between them on some principle of equity. To pay both is perhaps beyond the public ability; and as it would far exceed the value received by the public, it will not be expected by the world, nor even by the creditors themselves. To reject wholly the claims of either is equally inadmissible; such a sacrifice of those who possess the written engagements would be fatal to the proposed establishment of public credit; it would moreover punish those who had put their trust in the public promises and resources. To make the other class the sole victims is an idea at which human nature recoils.

A composition, then, is the only expedient that remains; let it be a liberal one in favor of the present holders, let them have the highest price which has prevailed in the market; and let the residue belong to the original sufferers. This will not do perfect justice; but it will do more real justice, and perform more of the public faith, than any other expedient proposed. The present holders, where they have purchased at the lowest price of the securities, will have a profit that cannot reasonably be complained of; where they have purchased at a higher price, the profit will be considerable; and even the few who have purchased at the highest price cannot well be losers, with a well-funded interest of six per cent. The original sufferers will not be fully indemnified; but they will receive, from their country, a tribute due to their merits, which, if it does not entirely heal their wounds, will assuage the pain of them. I am aware, that many plausible objections will lie against what I have suggested, some of which I foresee and will take some notice of. It will be said, that the plan is impracticable; should this be demonstrated, I am ready to renounce it; but it does not appear to me in that light. I acknowledge that such a scale as has often been a subject of conversation, is impracticable.

The discrimination proposed by me, requires nothing more than a knowledge of the present holders, which will be shown by the certificates; and of the original holders, which the office documents will show. . . .

I acknowledge that I cannot subscribe to all the reasons which some gentlemen urge. I am far from thinking that the assumption of the state debts will be the means of keeping the debts dispersed through out the states. The assumption of those debts will give them, immediately, the character of debts of the United States; they will be embarked in the same bottom; they will take the same course, and, of consequence, will arrive at the same place where it is acknowledged the domestic debts of the United States, by degrees, have assembled. Whether they will remain in this place, or flow out of the United States altogether, is a question which time will decide. I look for such a revolution of the debt as will place the greatest part of it in foreign hands. . . .

Some gentlemen have made the passage of this resolution a condition of providing for the acknowledged debt of the United States. I think this a preposterous condition, and a language improper to be held, after the decision which has taken place. In priority of time and obligation, we ought to provide for the acknowledged debt. Before we determine to enter into a new obligation, we should see how far we are able to discharge those positively due by us. The connexion between these resolutions is not such as to require or justify the condition. The plan of the Secretary draws a distinction between the two debts.

If we are to make a common stock of the debts of the States, not yet discharged, it can only be justified by securing provision for those which are discharged; with this view, therefore I will now move to add to the resolution these words: "the effectual provision be, at the same time made for liquidating and crediting to the States, the whole of their expenditure during the war, as the same hath been or may be stated for the purpose: and, in such liquidation, the best evidence shall be received that the nature of the case will permit." . . . The limitation act has already barred a great number of equitable claims of one State; perhaps there are other States in the same predicament . . . if adequate provision is not made on this head, a great deal more injustice will be done than by a refusal to assume the State debts.

I hope I shall be excused for connecting these provisions; because I think it impossible to separate them, in justice or propriety. If, by providing for the first, we can secure a provision for the last, we may do great honor to the councils of America, and establish its character for equity and justice. If we do not wish to decide precipitately on the question, I shall be content to delay it; and perhaps gentlemen may be impressed with the propriety of doing so till they take a view of the funds which are in contemplation, and see how effective and adequate they are likely to prove.

Debating the Nature of the Constitution

On December 13, 1790, Alexander Hamilton, Secretary of the Treasury, submitted a report to Congress recommending the establishment of a national bank. This proposal brought up two important questions: the first involved extensive powers over the economic and financial life of the nation, and the second involved the issue of constitutionality.

launching the new government

In the Congressional debate over the economic effect of such a bank, strong voices issued strong opinions. Fisher Ames, a devoted Federalist, found the proposed bank "almost essential to revenue, and . . . little short of indispensably necessary in times of public emergency." Indeed, he continued, "This new capital will invigorate trade and manufactures with new energy." Those who opposed this view were equally vocal. James Jackson of Georgia was convinced that the Bank would "benefit a small part of the United States, the mercantile interest only," and Representative Stone of Maryland went a step further and stated that the Bank would "raise in this country a moneyed interest at the devotion of the government," a prospect that scarcely pleased the agricultural South and the small farmers.

Important as this side of the debate was, the Constitutional question eventually became decisive. Did the government enjoy powers not explicitly granted to it by the Constitution? In answering this fundamental question, the foremost supporters of the Constitution disagreed and disagreed violently. The first selection that follows is taken from Hamilton's memorandum of February 23, 1791, written at the request of Washington, expounding the doctrine of implied powers or what is often called the "loose" interpretation of the Constitution.[4] The second selection is taken from a speech delivered in Congress on February 2, 1791, by James Madison, often called the "father of the Constitution."[5] He argued for a "strict" interpretation of Constitution. It is something of an irony to see these leading statesmen, who jointly wrote essays in support of ratification, now on opposite sides of the issue, but it demonstrates, beyond anything else, how fundamental was the question of interpretation. It is wise to remember, although it is not necessarily true in the case of Hamilton and Madison, that the "constitutional position" of many leaders depended upon their interests. Those who would be helped by a national bank would be inclined to search the Constitution for some phrase or clause to authorize it while those not helped would, of course, do the opposite.

Hamilton

The Secretary of the Treasury having perused with attention the papers containing the opinions of the Secretary of State and Attorney-General, concerning the constitutionality of the bill for establishing a National Bank, proceeds, according to the order of the President, to submit the reasons which have induced him to entertain a different opinion. . . .

Now it appears to the Secretary of the Treasury that this *general principle* is *inherent* in the very *definition* of government, and *essential* to every step of the progress to be made by that of the United States, namely: That every power vested in a government is in its nature *sovereign*, and includes, by *force* of the *term*, a right to employ all the means requisite and fairly appli-

---

[4] *The Works of Hamilton*, 4:104–38.

[5] *Writings of Madison*, 6:30–36.

cable to the attainment of the *ends of such power,* and which are not precluded by restrictions and exceptions specified in the Constitution, or not immoral, or not contrary to the essential *ends* of political society.

This principle, in its application to government in general, would be admitted as an axiom; and it will be incumbent upon those who may incline to deny it, to prove a distinction, and to show that a rule which, in the general system of things, is essential to the preservation of the social order, is inapplicable to the United States. . . .

If it would be necessary to bring proof to a proposition so clear, as that which affirms that the powers of the federal government, as to *its objects,* were sovereign, there is a clause of its Constitution which would be decisive. It is that which declares that the Constitution, and the laws of the United States made in pursuance of it, and all treaties made, or which shall be made, under their authority, shall be the *supreme law of the land.* The power which can create the *supreme law of the land* in *any case,* is doubtless *sovereign* as to such case.

This general and indisputable principle puts at once an end to the *abstract* question, whether the United States have power to erect a *corporation;* that is to say, to give a *legal* or *artificial capacity* to one or more persons, distinct from the *natural.* For it is unquestionably incident to *sovereign power* to erect corporations, and consequently to *that* of the United States, in *relation* to the *objects* intrusted to the management of the government. The difference is this: where the authority of the government is general, it can create corporations in *all cases;* where it is confirmed to certain branches of legislation, it can create corporations *only* in those cases. . . .

It is not denied that there are *implied,* as well as *express powers,* und (sic) that the *former* are as effectually delegated as the *latter.* And for the sake of accuracy it shall be mentioned, that there is another class of powers, which may be properly denominated *resulting powers.* . . .

To return:—It is conceded that *implied powers* are to be considered as delegated equally with *express ones.* Then it follows, that as a power of erecting a corporation may as well be *implied* as any other thing, it may as well be employed as an *instrument* or *mean* of carrying into execution any of the specified powers, as any other *instrument* or *mean* whatever. The only question must be, in this, as in every other case, whether the mean to be employed, or in this instance, the corporation to be erected, has a natural relation to any of the acknowledged objects or lawful ends of the government. . . .

It leaves, therefore, a criterion of what is constitutional, and of what is not so. This criterion is the *end,* to which the measure relates as a *mean.* If the *end* be clearly comprehended within any of the specified powers, and if the measure have an obvious relation to that *end,* and is not forbidden by any particular provision of the Constitution, it may safely be deemed to come within the compass of the national authority. There is also this further criterion, which may materially assist the decision: Does the proposed measure abridge a pre-existing right of any State or of any individual? If it does not, there is a strong presumption in favor of its constitutionality, and slighter relations to any declared object of the Constitution may be permitted to turn the scale. . . .

It is presumed to have been satisfactorily shown in the course of the preceding observations:

1. That the power of the government, *as* to the objects intrusted to its management, is, in its nature, sovereign.

2. That the right of erecting corporations is one inherent in, and inseparable from, the idea of sovereign power.

3. That the position, that the government of the United States can exercise no power but such as is delegated to it by its Constitution, does not militate against this principle.

4. That the word *necessary,* in the general clause, can have no *restrictive* operation derogating from the force of this principle; indeed, that the degree in which a measure is or is not *necessary,* cannot be a *test of constitutional right,* but of *expediency only.*

5. That the power to erect corporations is not to be considered as an *independent* or *substantive* power, but as an *incidental* and *auxiliary* one, and was therefore more properly left to implication, than expressly granted.

6. That the principle in question does not extend the power of the government beyond the prescribed limits, because it only affirms a power to *incorporate* for purposes *within the sphere* of the *specified powers.*

And lastly, that the right to exercise such a power in certain cases is unequivocally granted in the most *positive* and *comprehensive* terms. To all which it only remains to be added, that such a power has actually been exercised in two very eminent instances; namely, in the erection of two governments; one northwest of the River Ohio, and the other southwest—the last independent of any antecedent compact. And these result in a full and complete demonstration, that the Secretary of State and Attorney-General are mistaken when they deny generally the power of the national government to erect corporations. . . .

A hope is entertained that it has, by this time, been made to appear, to the satisfaction of the President, that a bank has a natural relation to the power of collecting taxes—to that of regulating trade—to that of providing for the common defence—and that, as the bill under consideration contemplates the government in the light of a joint proprietor of the stock of the bank, it brings the case within the provision of the clause of the Constitution immediately respects the property of the United States.

Under a conviction that such a relation subsists, the Secretary of the Treasury, with all deference, conceives, that it will result as a necessary consequence from the position, that all the specified powers of government are sovereign, as to the proper objects, that the incorporation of a bank is a constitutional measure; and that the objections taken to the bill, in this respect, are ill-founded. . . .

Madison

. . . The essential characteristic of the Government, as composed of limited and enumerated powers, would be destroyed, if, instead of direct and incidental means, any means could be used, which, in the language of the preamble to the bill, "might be conceived to be conducive to the successful conducting of the finances, or might be conceived to tend to give facility to the obtaining of loans." He [Madison] urged an attention to the diffuse and ductile terms which had been found requisite to cover the stretch of power contained in the bill. He compared them with the terms necessary and proper, used in the Constitution, and asked whether it was possible to view the two descriptions as synonymous, or the one as a fair and safe commentary on the other.

If, proceeded he, Congress, by virtue of the power to borrow, can create the means of lending, and, in pursuance of these means, can incorporate a Bank, they may do any thing whatever creative of like means. . . .

The doctrine of implication is always a tender one. The danger of it has been felt in other Governments. The delicacy was felt in the adoption of our own; the danger may also be felt, if we do not keep close to our chartered authorities.

Mark the reasoning on which the validity of the bill depends! To borrow money is made the end, and the accumulation of capitals implied as the means. The accumulation of capitals is then the end, and a Bank implied as the means. The Bank is then the end, and a charter of incorporation, a monopoly, capital punishments, etc., implied as the means.

If implications, thus remote and thus multiplied, can be linked together, a chain may be formed that will reach every object of legislation, every object within the whole compass of political economy.

The latitude of interpretation required by the bill is condemned by the rule furnished by the Constitution itself.

Congress have power "to regulate the value of money"; yet it is expressly added, not left to be implied, that counterfeiters may be punished.

They have the power "to declare war," to which armies are more incident than incorporated banks to borrowing; yet the power "to raise and support armies" is expressly added; and to this again, the express power "to make rules and regulations for the government of armies"; a like remark is applicable to the powers as to the navy.

The regulation and calling out of the militia are more appertinent to war than the proposed Bank to borrowing; yet the former is not left to construction.

The very power to borrow money is a less remote implication from the power of war, than an incorporated monopoly Bank from the power of borrowing; yet, the power to borrow is not left to implication.

It is not pretended that every insertion or omission in the Constitution is the effect of systematic attention. This is not the character of any human work, particularly the work of a body of men. The examples cited, with others that might be added, sufficiently inculcate, nevertheless, a rule of interpretation very different from that on which the bill rests. They condemn the exercise of any power, particularly a great and important power, which is not evidently and necessarily involved in an express power. . . .

From this view of the power of incorporation exercised in the bill, it could never be deemed an accessory or subaltern power, to be deduced by implication, as a means of executing another power; it was in its nature a distinct, an independent and substantive prerogative, which not being enumerated in the Constitution, could never have been meant to be included in it, and not being included, could never be rightfully exercised.

He here adverted to a distinction, which he said had not been sufficiently kept in view, between a power necessary and proper for the Government or Union, and a power necessary and proper for executing the enumerated powers. In the latter case, the powers included in the enumerated powers were not expressed, but to be drawn from the nature of each. In the former, the powers composing the Government were expressly enumerated. This constituted the peculiar nature of the Government; no power, therefore, not enumerated could be inferred from the general nature of Government. Had the power of making treaties, for example, been omitted, however necessary it might have been, the defect could only have been lamented, or supplied by an amendment of the Constitution.

But the proposed Bank could not even be called necessary to the Government; at most it could be but convenient. Its uses to the Government could be supplied by keeping the taxes a little in advance; by loans from individuals; by the other Banks, over which the Government would have equal command; nay greater, as it might grant or refuse to these the privilege (a free and irrevocable gift to the proposed Bank) of using their notes in the Federal revenue. . . .

With all this evidence of the sense in which the Constitution was understood and adopted, will it not be said, if the bill should pass, that its adoption was brought about by one set of arguments, and that it is now administered under the influence of another set? and this reproach will have the keener sting, because it is applicable to so many individuals concerned in both the adoption and administration.

In fine, if the power were in the Constitution, the immediate exercise of it cannot be essential; if not there, the exercise of it involves the guilt of usurpation, and establishes a precedent of interpretation levelling all the barriers which limit the powers of the General Government, and protect those of the State Governments. If the point be doubtful only, respect for ourselves, who ought to shun the appearance of precipitancy and ambition; respect for our successors, who ought not lightly to be deprived of the opportunity of exercising the rights of legislation; respect for our constituents who have had no opportunity of making known their sentiments, and who are themselves to be bound down to the measure for so long a period; all these considerations require that the irrevocable decision should at least be suspended until another session.

It appeared on the whole, he concluded, that the power exercised by the bill was condemned by the silence of the Constitution; was condemned by the rule of interpretation arising out of the Constitution; was condemned by its tendency to destroy the main characteristic of the Constitution; was condemned by the expositions of the friends of the Constitution, whilst depending before the public; was condemned by the apparent intention of the parties which ratified the Constitution; was condemned by the explanatory amendments proposed by Congress themselves to the Constitution; and he hoped it would receive its final condemnation by the vote of this House.

2. THE REVOLUTION OF 1800

The opposition created initially by the economic policies of the Federalists was nourished during the following decade by differences over a number of issues: the nature of the Constitution, the whiskey insurrection, the sharply contested elections of 1796, the position of the judiciary in the federal government, the contrasting views on foreign policy, and the clash over the Alien and Sedition Acts. In foreign affairs, for example, the Federalists looked to Great Britain for security in the continuous series of international crises after 1789, while the opposition, led by Jefferson, looked to France. On the one hand, Hamilton condemned Madison and Jefferson for being positively "womanish" about France; on the other, the two Virginians saw the Secretary of the Treasury constantly "betraying" his sentiments as an Anglophile. When the Jay Treaty was negotiated with Great Britain in 1794, the opposing points of view were clearly revealed. Jefferson and Madison denounced the Treaty, while Hamilton, under the pen name "Camillus," defended every clause.

As early as 1792, Hamilton perceived that those groups who opposed the measures of the administration were assuming the appearance of a party and with the emergence of the Republicans as a second major party by 1798 any lingering doubts evaporated. Two years later, in a bitterly contested campaign, the Republicans gained enough support to win control over the executive and legislative branches of the government. Although their margin of victory was slim, their ranks were strengthened during the ensuing years, giving them the fullest opportunity to mold the new government according to their beliefs.

The following selections emphasize the political transition taking place from 1798 to 1800, which had a significant effect upon the formative years under the new government.

Background for Revolution: The Alien and Sedition Acts

The passage of the Alien and Sedition Laws in the early summer of 1798 brought the political pot to a boil. The Alien Law gave the President extensive powers to expel suspicious foreigners—and the word "foreigners" was given a broad interpretation—while the Sedition Law was so inclusive that criticism of the administration or its measures constituted a criminal offense.

These enactments were deemed essential by some Federalists because of the crisis with France; but many, if not most, members of the party supported the measures as a weapon to thwart the power of the emerging Republican party. The Republicans denounced the acts as a crisis in freedom and used them as a rallying cry for the party. The vigorous enforcement of the Acts and the sweeping interpretation given them by the Federalist judiciary strengthened the Republicans and weakened the Federalists. This development helped to clear the way for a Republican victory in 1800.

The first selection taken from the bitter debates over the bill was delivered on July 5, 1798 by Congressman John Allen, Federalist of Connecticut, and illustrates the point of view of those who strongly supported the measure.[6] The second includes excerpts from Jefferson's finished draft of the celebrated Kentucky resolutions which were written in November 1798 as a protest against the Acts.[7]

Allen

Mr. Allen.—I hope this bill will not be rejected. If ever there was a nation which required a law of this kind, it is this. Let gentlemen look at certain papers printed in this city and elsewhere, and ask themselves whether an unwarrantable and dangerous combination does not exist to overturn and ruin the Government by publishing the most shameless falsehoods against the Representatives of the people of all denominations, that they are hostile to free Governments and genuine liberty, and of course to the welfare of this country; that they ought, therefore, to be displaced, and that the people ought to raise an *insurrection* against the Government. . . .

But, sir, in the same speech the people are instructed that opposition to the laws, that insurrection is a duty, whenever they think we exceed our Constitutional powers; but, I ask the gentleman, who shall determine that point? I thought the Constitution had assigned the cognizance of that question to the Courts, and so it has. But the attempt here is to evince, and the doctrine we know is openly avowed by members of this House, that each man has the right of deciding for himself, and that as many as are of the opinion that the law is unconstitutional, have a right to combine and oppose it by force. The people I venerate; they are truly sovereign; but a section, a part of the citizens, a town, a city, or a mob, I know them not; if they oppose the laws, they are insurgents and rebels; they are not the people. The people act in their elections by displacing obnoxious Representatives, and by the irresistible force of their opinions; when the people wills, the Government is convinced and obeys. It is too manifest to admit of doubt or denial that the intention and tendency of such

---

[6] *Annals of Congress*, 8:2093–2101.

[7] *The Writings of Jefferson*, 17:379–91.

principles, are to produce divisions, tumults, violence, insurrection, and blood; all which are intended by the fashionable doctrine of modern times, which the gentleman terms "a recurrence to first revolutionary principles," from which may God preserve us. Do we want another revolution in this country? But, sir, that a revolution is intended, I hope to convince you before I sit down. In the Aurora, of last Friday, we read the following:

"The period is now at hand when it will be a question difficult to determine, whether there is more safety and liberty to be enjoyed at Constantinople or Philadelphia?"

This, sir, is faithfully pursuing the system of the gentlemen in announcing to the poor deluded readers of the factious prints, the rapid approach of Turkish slavery in this country. Who can doubt the existence of a combination against the real liberty, the real safety of the United States I say, sir, a combination, a conspiracy against the Constitution, the Government, the peace and safety of this country, is formed, and is in full operation. It embraces members of all classes; the Representative of the people on this floor, the wild and visionary theorist in the bloody philosophy of the day, the learned and ignorant. And the paper from which I have so often read, with three or four others, furnish demonstrations without number of the truth of the accusation. Each acts its part: but all are in perfect unison. Permit me to read a paragraph from "The Time-Piece," a paper printed in New York:

When such a character attempts by antiquated and exploded sophistry, by Jesuitical arguments, to extinguish the sentiment of liberty, 'tis fit the mask should be torn off from this meaner species of aristocracy than history has condescended to record; where a person without patriotism, without philosophy, without a taste for the fine arts, building his pretensions on a gross and indigested compilation of statutes and precedents, is jostled into the Chief Magistry, by the ominous combination of old Tories with old opinions, and old Whigs with new, 'tis fit this mock Monarch, with his Court, composed of Tories and speculators, should pass in review before the good sense of the world. Monarchies are seen only with indignation and concern; at sight of these terrible establishments, fears accompany the execrations of mankind; but when the champion of the wellborn, with his serene Court, is seen soliciting and answering Addresses, and pronouncing anathemas against France, it shall be my fault if other emotions be not excited; if to tears and execrations be not added derision and contempt.

Gentlemen contend for the liberty of opinions and of the press. Let me ask them whether they seriously think the liberty of the press authorizes such publications? The President of the United States is here called "a person without patriotism, without philosophy, and a mock monarch," and the free election of the people is pronounced "a jostling him into the Chief Magistracy by the ominous combination of old Tories with old opinion, and old Whigs with new."

If this be not a conspiracy against Government and people, I know not what to understand from the "threat of tears, execrations, derision, and contempt." Because the Constitution guarantees the right of expressing our opinions, and the freedom of the press, am I at liberty to falsely call you a thief, a murderer, an atheist? Because I have the liberty of locomotion, of going where I please, have I a right to ride over the footman in the path? The freedom of the press and opinions was never understood to give the right of publishing falsehoods and slanders, nor of exciting sedition, insurrection, and slaughter, with impunity. A man was always answerable for the malicious publication of falsehood; and what more does this bill require?

In Aurora, of last Tuesday, is this paragraph:

"Where a law shall have been passed in violation of the Constitution, making it criminal to expose the crimes, the official vices or abuses, or the attempts of men in power to usurp a despotic authority, is there any alternative between an abandonment of the Constitution and resistance?"

The gentleman (*Mr. Livingston*) makes his proclamation of war on the Government in the House on Monday, and this infamous printer (Bache) follows it up with the tocsin of insurrection on Tuesday. While this bill was under consideration in the Senate, an attempt is made to render it odious among the people. "Is there any alternative," says this printer, "between an abandonment of the Constitution and resistance?" He declares what is unconstitutional, and then invites the people to "resistance." This is an awful, horrible example of "the liberty of opinion and freedom of the press." Can gentlemen hear these things and lie quietly on their pillows? Are we to see all these acts practised against the repose of our country, and remain passive? Are we bound hand and foot that we must be witnesses of these deadly thrusts at our liberty? Are we to be the unresisting spectators of these exertions to destroy all that we hold dear? Are these approaches to revolution and Jacobinic domination, to be observed with the eye of meek submission? No, sir, they are indeed terrible; they are calculated to freeze the very blood in our veins. Such liberty of the press and of opinion is calculated to destroy all confidence between man and man; it leads to a dissolution of every bond of union; it cuts asunder every ligament that unites man to his family, man to his neighbor, man to society, and to Government. God deliver us from such liberty, the liberty of vomiting on the public floods of falsehood and hatred to everything sacred, human, and divine! If any gentleman doubts the effects of such a liberty, let me direct his attention across the water; it has there made slaves of thirty millions of men.

Jefferson

1. *Resolved,* that the several States composing the United States of America are not united on the principle of unlimited submission to their general government; but that by compact under the style and title of a Constitution for the United States and of amendments thereto, they constituted a general government for special purposes, delegated to that government certain definite powers, reserving, each State to itself, the residuary mass of right to their own self-government; and that whensoever the general government assumes undelegated powers, its acts are unauthoritative, void, and of no force: That to this compact each

State acceded as a State, and is an integral party, its co-States forming, as to itself, the other party: That the government created by this compact was not made the exclusive or final judge of the extent of the powers delegated to itself; since that would have made its discretion, and not the Constitution, the measure of its powers; but that as in all other cases of compact among parties having no common judge, each party has an equal right to judge for itself, as well of infractions as of the mode and measure of redress. . . .

III. *Resolved,* that it is true as a general principle, and is also expressly declared by one of the amendments to the Constitution that "the powers not delegated to the United States by the Constitution, nor prohibited by it to the States, are reserved to the States respectively or to the people"; and that no power over the freedom of religion, freedom of speech, or freedom of the press being delegated to the United States by the Constitution, nor prohibited by it to the States, all lawful powers respecting the same did of right remain, and were reserved to the States, or to the people: That thus was manifested their determination to retain to themselves the right of judging how far the licentiousness of speech and of the press may be abridged without lessening their useful freedom, and how far those abuses which cannot be separated from their use should be tolerated rather than the use be destroyed; And thus also they guarded against all abridgment by the United States of the freedom of religious opinions and exercises, and retained to themselves the right of protecting the same, as this State, by a law passed on the general demand of its citizens, had already protected them from all human restraint or interference. And that in addition to this general principle and express declaration, another and more special provision has been made by one of the amendments to the Constitution which expressly declares, that "Congress shall make no law respecting an establishment of religion, or prohibiting the free exercise thereof, or abridging the freedom of speech, or of the press," thereby guarding in the same sentence, and under the same words, the freedom of religion, of speech, and of the press: insomuch, that whatever violates either throws down the sanctuary which covers the others, and that libels, falsehoods, defamation, equally with heresy and false religion, are withheld from the cognizance of Federal tribunals. That, therefore . . . [the Sedition Act], which does abridge the freedom of the press, is not law, but is altogether void and of no force. . . .

VI. *Resolved,* that the imprisonment of a person under the protection of the laws of this Commonwealth, on his failure to obey the simple *order* of the President to depart out of the United States, as is undertaken by the said act entitled "An act concerning aliens," is contrary to the Constitution, one amendment to which has provided, that "no person shall be deprived of liberty without due process of law," and that another having provided "that in all criminal prosecutions, the accused shall enjoy the right to a public trial by an impartial jury, to be informed of the nature and cause of the accusation, to be confronted with the witnesses against him, to have compulsory process for obtaining witnesses in his favour, and to have the assistance of counsel for his defense," the same act, undertaking to authorize the President to remove a person out of the United States, who is under the protection of the law, on his own suspicion, without accusation, without jury, without public trial, without confrontation of the witnesses against him, without having witnesses in his favour, without defense, without counsel, is contrary to these provisions also of the Constitution, is therefore not law, but utterly void and of no force. That transferring the power of judging any person who is under the protection of the laws, from the courts to the President of the United States, as is undertaken by the same act concerning aliens, is against the article of the Constitution which provides that "the judicial power of the United States shall be vested in courts, the judges of which shall hold their offices during good behavior," and that the said act is void for that reason also. And it is further to be noted, that this transfer of judiciary power is to that magistrate of the General Government who already possesses all the Executive, and a negative in all the legislative powers. . . .

VIII. . . . In questions of power, then, let no more be heard of confidence in man, but bind him down from mischief by the chains of the Constitution. That this commonwealth does therefore call on its co-States for an expression of their sentiments on the acts concerning aliens, and for the punishment of certain crimes herein before specified, plainly declaring whether these acts are or are not authorized by the federal compact. And it doubts not that their sense will be so announced as to prove their attachment unaltered to limited government, whether general or particular. And that the rights and liberties of their co-States will be exposed to no dangers by remaining embarked in a common bottom with their own. That they will concur with this commonwealth in considering the said acts as so palpably against the Constitution as to amount to an undisguised declaration that the compact is not meant to be the measure of the powers of the general government, but that it will proceed in the exercise over these States, of all powers whatsoever: That they will view this as seizing the rights of the States, and consolidating them in the hands of the general government, with a power assumed to bind the States (not merely in cases made Federal) . . . but in all cases whatsoever, by laws made, not with their consent, but by others against their consent: That this would be to surrender the form of government we have chosen, and to live under one deriving its powers from its own will, and not from our authority; and that the co-States, recurring to their natural right in cases not made Federal, will concur in declaring these acts void and of no force, and will each take measures of its own for providing that neither these acts nor any others of the General Government not plainly and intentionally authorized by the Constitution, shall be exercised within their respective territories. . . .

A Change of Course?

At the time of his election in 1800, Jefferson was convinced that the nation had been rescued from the disaster of continued Federalist control. He compared the country to a ship that had nearly foundered in a fierce storm. "Her strength has stood the waves into which she was steered, with a view to sink her," Jefferson wrote to John Dickinson. "We shall put her on her republican tack, and she will now show by the beauty of her motion the skill of her builders." And what about the Constitution? "The Constitution on which our Union rests," Jefferson wrote, "shall be administered by me according to the safe and honest meaning contemplated by the plain understanding of the people of the United States, at the time of its adoption—a meaning to be found in the explanations of those who advocated, not those who opposed it." Republican newspapers compared their victory in the elections as equal in importance to the American Revolution.

Most Federalists expected a decided change under the new administration. *The Gazette of the United States,* a Federalist newspaper, asserted that there was nothing to fear from the conduct of one or two individuals. But, "it is the general ascendency of the worthless, the dishonest, the rapacious, the vile, the merciless, and the ungodly, which forms the principal ground of alarm. . . . They already proclaim in their appropriate jargon, that the 'reign of terror' has ceased, and that the triumph of democratical and republican principles, over a tyrannical aristocracy, is commencing. . . . It is fallacious, therefore, to imagine that we shall experience only a change of men."

In this light it is especially interesting and instructive to read the following selection, taken from Jefferson's first inaugural of March 4, 1810.[8] It might help to clarify the meaning of the Revolution of 1800, for the ideas, the simplicity, and the sensitive shadings combine to help make Jefferson's address one of the most distinguished presidential messages in American history as well as a summary of Republican hopes in 1801.

. . . During the contest of opinion through which we have passed, the animation of discussion and of exertions has sometimes worn an aspect which might impose on strangers unused to think freely and to speak and to write what they think; but this being now decided by the voice of the nation, announced according to the rules of the constitution, all will, of course, arrange themselves under the will of the law, and unite in common efforts for the common good. All, too, will bear in mind this sacred principle, that though the will of the majority is in all cases to prevail, that will, to be rightful, must be reasonable; that the minority possess their equal rights, which equal laws

---

[8] *The Writings of Jefferson,* 3:317–23.

must protect, and to violate which would be oppression. Let us, then, fellow citizens, unite with one heart and one mind. Let us restore to social intercourse that harmony and affection without which liberty and even life itself are but dreary things. . . . But every difference of opinion is not a difference of principle. We have called by different names brethren of the same principle. We are all republicans—we are all federalists. If there be any among us who would wish to dissolve this Union or to change its republican form, let them stand undisturbed as monuments of the safety with which error of opinion may be tolerated where reason is left free to combat it. I know, indeed, that some honest men fear that a republican government cannot be strong; that this government is not strong enough. But would the honest patriot, in the full tide of successful experiment, abandon a government which has so far kept us free and firm, on the theoretic and visionary fear that this government, the world's best hope, may by possibility want energy to preserve itself? I trust not. I believe this, on the contrary, the strongest government on earth. I believe it is the only one where every man, at the call of the laws, would fly to the standard of the law, and would meet invasions of the public order as his own personal concern. Sometimes it is said that man cannot be trusted with the government of himself. Can he, then, be trusted with the government of others? Or have we found angels in the forms of kings to govern him? Let history answer this question.

Let us, then, with courage and confidence pursue our own federal and republican principles, our attachment to our union and representative government. Kindly separated by nature and a wide ocean from the exterminating havoc of one quarter of the globe; too high-minded to endure the degradations of the others; possessing a chosen country, with room enough for our descendants to the hundredth and thousandth generation; entertaining a due sense of our equal right to the use of our own faculties, to the acquisitions of our industry, to honor and confidence from our fellow citizens, resulting not from birth but from our actions and their sense of them; enlightened by a benign religion, professed, indeed, and practiced in various forms, yet all of them including honesty, truth, temperance, gratitude, and the love of man; acknowledging and adoring an overruling Providence, which by all its dispensations proves that it delights in the happiness of man here and his greater happiness hereafter; with all these blessings, what more is necessary to make us a happy and prosperous people? Still one thing more, fellow citizens—a wise and frugal government, which shall restrain men from injuring one another, which shall leave them otherwise free to regulate their own pursuits of industry and improvement, and shall not take from the mouth of labor the bread it has earned. This is the sum of good government, and this is necessary to close the circle of our felicities.

About to enter, fellow citizens, on the exercise of duties which comprehend everything dear and valuable to you, it is proper that you should understand what I deem the essential principles of our government, and consequently those which ought to shape its administration. I will compress them within the narrowest Compass they will bear, stating the general principle, but not all its limitations. Equal and exact justice to all men, of whatever state or persuasion, religious or political; peace, commerce, and honest friendship, with all nations—entangling alliances with none; the support of the state governments in all their rights, as the most competent administrations for our domestic concerns and the surest bulwarks against anti-republican tendencies; the preservation of the general government in its whole constitutional vigor, as the sheet anchor of our peace at home and safety abroad; a jealous care of the right of election by the people—a mild and safe corrective of abuses which are lopped by the sword of the revolution where peaceable remedies are unprovided; absolute acquiescence in the decisions of the majority—the vital principle of republics, from which there is no appeal but to force the vital principle and immediate parent of despotism; a well-disciplined militia—our best reliance in peace and for the first moments of war, till regulars may relieve them; the supremacy of the civil over the military authority; economy in the public expense, that labor may be lightly burdened; the honest payment of our debts and sacred preservation of the public faith; encouragement of agriculture, and of commerce as its handmaid; the diffusion of information and the arraignment of all abuses at the bar of public reason; freedom of religion; freedom of the press; freedom of person under the protection of the *habeas corpus;* and trial by juries impartially selected—these principles form the bright constellation which has gone before us, and guided our steps through an age of revolution and reformation. The wisdom of our sages and the blood of our heroes have been devoted to their attainment. They should be the creed of our political faith—the text of civil instruction—the touchstone by which to try the services of those we trust; and should we wander from them in moments of error or alarm, let us hasten to retrace our steps and to regain the road which alone leads to peace, liberty, and safety. . . .

Relying, then, on the patronage of your good will, I advance with obedience to the work, ready to retire from it whenever you become sensible how much better choice it is in your power to make. And may that Infinite Power which rules the destinies of the universe, lead our councils to what is best, and give them a favorable issue for your peace and prosperity.

3. CONTROVERSIES OF THE JEFFERSONIAN ERA

What measures were necessary to implement Republican ideals? In his inaugural Jefferson had asserted that everyone agreed on basic principles, but this could scarcely be construed as general agreement on a legislative program. Indeed, the *National Intelligencer,* on March 9, 1801, made it clear that "the voice of a majority of the people had declared itself in

launching the new government

favour, not only of particular men, but of particular measures. The contest, which has just passed, was a contest of principle."

During the decade following Jefferson's inaugural, issues arose over the federal judiciary, over economic policy and diplomacy, and, indeed, as with the Federalists, over the interpretation of the Constitution itself. The primary question to ask and to answer, when examining these controversies, is: Did the Republicans, in reality, carry out their declared objective to change the course of the new government, to set the ship of state, as Jefferson had phrased it, on a "Republican tack"? If so, how much of a change was it? This is the question to be kept uppermost when reading the following pages, where a representative sample of some of the major issues are presented, for it is important to judge the influence of the Republican administration during these formative years upon the development and traditions of our nation.

The Republicans Attack the Judiciary

During the final years of Federalist control, the Republicans singled out the judiciary for their severest criticism. The Federalists, as if to throw fuel on the flames, passed a Judiciary Act on February 13, 1801, just as their grip on the legislative and executive branches of the government was loosening. This measure, which provided for a revamping of the judicial system and an increase in the number of judges, permitted President John Adams to appoint all Federalists to the bench just as his own term of office was expiring.

The Republicans vigorously condemned this last-ditch effort by the Federalists to assure control of the judiciary, and Jefferson moved swiftly to repeal the act after taking office. The debates which followed transcended the immediate issue and significantly mirrored the basic position of the two parties with respect to the relative balance of the three branches of government.

The first selection is taken from a powerful speech delivered on February 18, 1802 by William B. Giles of Virginia, a staunch Republican. The second selection is taken from a speech given on February 16, 1802 by Archibald Henderson of Kentucky, an equally ardent defender of Federalist principles.[9]

Giles

Mr. Giles said . . . it was natural that men should differ in the choice of means to produce a given end, and more natural that they should differ in the choice of political means than any other. . . . Hence what is called party in the United States, grew up from a division of opinion respecting these two great characteristic principles. Patronage, or the creation of partial

---

[9] *Annals of Congress*, 11:579–602, 523–30.

interest for the protection and support of Government, on the one side: On the other side, to effect the same end, a fair responsibility of all representatives to the people; an adherence to the general interests, and a reliance on the confidence of the people at large, resulting from a sense of their common interests. A variety of circumstances existed in the United States, at the commencement of the Government, and a great number of favorable incidents continued afterwards to arise, which gave the patronage system the preponderancy, during the first three Presidential terms of election. . . . The general disquietude which manifested itself in consequence of these enterprising measures, in the year 1800, induced the Federal party to apprehend that they had pushed their principles too far, and they began to entertain doubts of the result of the Presidential election, which was approaching. In this state of things, it was natural for them to look on for some department of the Government in which they could entrench themselves in the event of an unsuccessful issue in the election, and continue to support those favorite principles of irresponsibility which they could never consent to abandon.

The Judiciary department, of course, presented itself as best fitted for their object, not only because it was already filled with men who had manifested the most indecorous zeal in favor of their principles, but because they held their offices by indefinite tenures, and of course were further removed from any responsibility to the people, than either of the other departments. Accordingly, on the 11th of March 1800, a bill for the more convenient organization of the courts of the United States, was presented to the House of Representatives. This bill appears to have had for its objects, First, the gradual demolition of the State courts, by increasing the number and extending the jurisdiction of the Federal courts. Second, to afford additional protection to the principles of the then existing Administration by creating a new corps of judges of concurring political opinions. This bill, however, was not passed into a law during that session of Congress, perhaps from an apprehension that it would tend to increase the disquietudes which other measures had before excited, and therefore operate unfavorably to the approaching Presidential election. At the next session, after the result of the late election was ascertained, the bill, after having undergone some considerable alterations, was passed into the law now under discussion. This law, it is now said, is inviolable and irrepealable. It is said, the independence of the judge will be thereby immolated. Yes, sir, this law is now considered as the sanctuary of the principles of the last Administration, and the tenures of the judges as the horns of inviolability within that sanctuary. He [Giles] said, we are now called upon to rally round the Constitution as the ark of our political safety. Gentlemen, discarding all generalizing expressions, and the spirit of the instrument, tie down all construction to the strict letter of the Constitution. He said, it gave him great pleasure to meet gentlemen on this ground; and the more so because he had long been in the habit of hearing very different language from the same gentlemen. He had long been in the habit of hearing the same gentlemen speak of the expressions of "the common defence and the general welfare," as the only valuable part of the Constitution; that they were sufficient to obliterate all specifications and limitations of power. That the Constitution was a mere nose of wax, yielding to every impression it received. That every "opening wedge" which was driven into it, was highly beneficial in severing asunder the limitations and restrictions of power. That the republicanism it secured, meant anything or nothing. It gave him, therefore, great pleasure at this time to obey the injunctions of gentlemen in rallying round the Constitution as the ark of our political safety, and of interpreting it by the plain and obvious meaning and letter of the specified powers. But, he said, as if it was always the unfortunate destiny of these gentlemen to be upon extremes, they have now got round to the opposite extreme point of the political compass, and even beyond it. For, he said, they not only tied down all construction to the letter of the instrument, but they tell us that they see and call upon us also to see written therein, in large capital characters, "the independence of judges": which, to the extent they carry the meaning of the term, is neither to be found in the letter or spirit of that instrument, or in any other political establishment, he believed, under the sun. . . .

He said he would not proceed to examine whether the repeal of the Judiciary law of the last session of Congress would in any respect violate that salutary and practicable independence of the judges which was secured to them by the Constitution. He said the term *independence of Judges or of the Judiciary department* was not to be found in the Constitution. It was, therefore, a mere inference from some of the specified powers. . . . He should discard, in his interpretation, the terms "common defence and general welfare," which had been restorted to by some gentlemen. He considered these words as containing no grant of power whatever, but merely the expression of the ends or objects to be effected by the grants of specified powers. . . . He said he had read through the whole Constitution, to enable him to form his opinion upon this question, for fear there might be in some hidden corner of it some provision which might demonstrate the unconstitutionality of the present bill; and if so (although he should lament such a provision), he would instantly give up the bill. But his researches had terminated in a different result. He said he found, from the general character of the Constitution, that the general will was its basis, the general good its object, and the fundamental principle for effecting this object was the responsibility of all public agents, either mediately or immediately to the people. . . .

Here there arises an important difference of opinion between the different sides of this House. It is contended on one side that the Judiciary department is formed by the Constitution itself. It is contended on the other side, that the Constitution does no more than to declare that there shall be a Judiciary department, and directs that it shall be formed by the other two departments, under certain modifications. Article third, section first, the Constitution has these words: "The Judicial power of the United States shall be vested in one

Supreme Court and in such inferior courts as Congress shall from time to time ordain and establish." Here, then, the power to ordain and establish inferior courts is given to Congress in the most unqualified terms, and also to ordain and establish "one Supreme Court." The only limitation upon the power of Congress in this clause consists in the number of supreme courts to be established; the limitation is to the number of one, although that is an affirmative and not a negative expression. The number of judges, the assignation of duties, the fixing compensations, the fixing the times when, and places where, the courts shall exercise their functions, etc., are left to the entire discretion of Congress. The spirit, as well as the words of the Constitution are completely satisfied, provided one Supreme Court be established. Hence, when all these essential points in the organization and formation of courts is intrusted to the unlimited discretion of Congress, it cannot be said that the courts are formed by the Constitution. . . .

The Constitution has ordained, that Congress, or in other words, the Representatives of the people, shall be the tribunal. . . .

Mr. G. concluded by observing, that, upon the whole view of the subject, feeling the firmest conviction that there is no Constitutional impediment in the way of repealing the act in question, upon the most fair and candid interpretation of the Constitution:—believing that principles advanced in opposition, go directly to the destruction of the fundamental principle of the Constitution, the responsibility of all public agents to the people—that they go to the establishment of a permanent corporation of individuals invested with ultimate censorial and controlling power over all the departments of the Government, over legislation, execution, and decision, and irresponsible to the people; believing that these principles are in direct hostility to the great principle of Representative Government; believing that the courts formerly established, were fully competent to the business they had to perform, and that the present courts are useless, unnecessary, and expensive; believing that the Supreme Court has heretofore discharged all the duties assigned to it in less than one month in the year, and that its duties could be performed in half that time; considering the compensations of the judges to be among the highest given to any of the highest officers of the United States for the services of the whole year; considering the compensations of all the judges greatly exceeding the services assigned them, as well as considering all the circumstances attending the substitution of the new system for the old one, by increasing the number of judges and compensations, and lessening their duties by the distribution of the business into a great number of hands, etc., while acting under these impressions, he should vote against the motion now made for striking out the first section of the repealing bill.

Henderson

Having premised thus much, Mr. Chairman, I will proceed to an examination of the question under consideration. It has been usual to divide it into two parts: first, the expediency; and, secondly, the authority of Congress to pass the law on the table. This is a natural and correct division; but I shall invert the order of considering the question, and first examine our power to act, before we consider the expediency of acting. And if, after a calm and candid review of the Constitution, it should be found that we are prohibited from passing the bill, there will be no necessity for inquiring into the expediency of repealing the law passed at the last session of Congress for organizing our courts of justice. The relative merits of the old and new Judiciary system will be entirely out of view. For I am confident that there is not a member of this body who would wish to pass the bill on your table, if in doing it we must violate the sacred charter under which we are now assembled. . . .

It will be easily discovered from this cursory view of our Constitution, the caution and jealousy with which the people have conferred the power of making laws, of commanding what is right, and prohibiting what is wrong. But, sir, after this law was made, after its authoritative mandate was acknowledged by the nation, it became necessary to establish some tribunal to judge of the extent and obligation of this law. The people did not see proper to entrust this power of judging of the meaning of their laws, either to the Legislative or to the Executive, because they participated in the making of these laws; and experience had shown that it is essential for the preservation of liberty that the Judicial and Legislative authorities should be kept separate and distinct.

They therefore enacted a third department, called the Judicial, and said that "the Judicial power of the United States shall be vested in one Supreme Court, and in such inferior courts as Congress may from time to time ordain and establish. The judges both of the Supreme and inferior courts shall hold their offices during good behaviour, and shall at stated times receive for their services a compensation which shall not be diminished during their continuance in office."

It is admitted, I understand, by all parties, by every description of persons, that these words, "shall hold their offices during good behaviour," are intended as a limitation of power. The question is, what power is thus to be limited and checked? I answer, that all and every power, which would have had the authority of impairing the tenure by which the judges hold their offices (if these words were not inserted), is checked and limited by these words; whether that power should be found to reside in Congress, or in the Executive. These words are broad and extensive in their signification, and can only be satisfied by being construed to control the Legislative as well as the Executive power. But gentlemen contend that they must be confined to limiting the power of the President. I ask gentlemen, what is there in the Constitution to prove their signification to this end alone? When you erect a court and fill it with a judge, and tell him in plain, simple language, that he shall hold his office during good behaviour, or as long as he shall behave well; what, I beseech you, sir, will any man, whose mind is not bewildered in the mazes of modern metaphysics, infer from the declaration? Certainly that the office will not be taken from him until he misbehaves; nor that he will be taken from the office during his good behaviour. Under this impression he enters upon his duty, performing it with the most perfect satisfaction to all persons who have business before him; and the Legislature, without whispering a complaint, abolishes the office and thereby turns out the judge. The judge is told this is no violation of the compact; although you have behaved well, although we have promised that as long as you did behave well you should continue in office, yet, there is now no further necessity for your services, and you may retire. These words, "during good behaviour," are intended to prevent the President from dismissing you from office, and not the Legislature from destroying your office. Do you suppose, sir, that there is a man of common understanding in the nation, whose mind is not alive to the influence of party spirit, that would yield his assent to this reasoning? I hope and believe there is not. . . .

But it has been said that the powers of each Congress are equal, and that a subsequent Legislature can repeal the acts of a former; and as this law was passed by the last Congress, we have the same power to repeal it which they had to enact it. This objection is more plausible than solid. It is not contended by us that legislatures who are not limited in their powers have not the same authority. The question is not what omnipotent Assemblies can do, but what *we* can do under a Constitution defining and limiting with accuracy the extent and boundaries of our authority. The very section in the Constitution (art. third, sec. first) which I have read, is a proof against the power of every Congress to repeal the acts of their predecessors. . . .

Again, sir, the construction which gentlemen on the other side of the House contend for, tends to the concentration of Legislative and Executive powers in the same hands. If Congress, who have the power of making laws, can also displace their judges by repealing that which creates the offices they fill, the irresistible consequence is, that whatever law is passed the judges must carry into execution, or they will be turned out of office. It is of little importance to the people of this country whether Congress sit in judgment upon their laws themselves, or whether they sit in judgment upon those who are appointed for that purpose. It amounts to the same despotism; they in fact judge the extent and obligations of their own statutes by having those in their power who are placed on the sacred seat of justice. Whatever the Legislature declares to be law must be obeyed. The Constitutional check which the judges were to be on the Legislature is completely done away. . . . All the ramparts which the Constitution has erected around the liberties of the people, are prostrated at one blow by the passage of this law. The monstrous and unheard of doctrine which has been lately advanced, that the judges have not the right of declaring unconstitutional laws void, will be put into practice by the adoption of this measure. New offences may be created by law. Associations and combinations may be declared treason, and the affrighted and appalled citizen may in vain seek refuge in the independence of your courts. In vain may he hold out the Constitution and deny the authority of Congress to pass a law of such undefined signification, and call upon the judges to protect him; he will be told that the opinion of Congress now is, that we have no right to judge of their authority; this will be the consequence of concentrating Judicial and Legislative power in the same hands. It is the very definition of tyranny, and wherever you find it, the people are slaves, whether they call their Government a Monarchy, Republic, or Democracy.

Mr. Chairman, I see, or think I see, in this attempt, that spirit of innovation which has prostrated before it a great part of the old world —every institution which the wisdom and experience of ages had reared up for the benefit of man. A spirit which has rode in the whirlwind and directed the storm, to the destruction of the fairest portion of Europe; which has swept before it every vestige of law, religion, morality, and rational government; which has brought twenty millions of people at the feet of one, and compelled them to seek refuge from their complicated miseries in the calm of despotism. It is against the influence of this tremendous spirit that I wish to raise my voice, and exert my powers, weak and feeble as they are. I fear, sir, on the seventh of December, it made its appearance within these walls, clothed in a gigantic body, impatient for action. I fear it has already begun to exert its all-devouring energy. Have you a judiciary system extending over this immense country, matured by the wisdom of your ablest and best men? It must be destroyed. Have you taxes which have been laid since the commencement of the Government? And is the irritation consequent upon the laying of taxes worn off? Are they paid exclusively by the wealthy and the luxurious part of the community? And are they pledged for the payment of the public debt? They must be abolished. Have you a Mint establishment, which is not only essentially necessary to protect the country against the influx of base foreign metals, but is a splendid attribute of sovereignty? It must be abolished. Have you laws which require foreigners coming to your country to go through a probationary state, by which their habits, their morals, and propensities may be known, before they are admitted to all the rights of native Americans? They must be repealed, and our shores crowded with the outcasts of society, lest oppressed humanity then should find no asylum on this globe!

Mr. Chairman, if the doctrine contended for by gentlemen on the other side of the House should become the settled construction of the Constitution, and enlightened America acquiesce with that construction, I declare for myself, and for myself alone, I would not heave a sigh nor shed a tear over its total desolation. The wound you are about to give it will be mortal; it may languish out a miserable existence for a few years, but it will surely die. It will neither serve to protect its friends nor defend itself from the omnipotent energies of its enemies. Better at once to bury it with all our hopes.

A Change of Economic Policy?

The Republicans had been so thoroughly antagonized by the Hamiltonian spirit in the economic policies of the Federalists that they injected the issue into debates, pamphlets, editorials, and letters at every opportunity. In his draft of the Kentucky Resolutions, for example, Jefferson included a denunciation of Hamilton's plan to fund the national debt, although these resolutions were primarily directed at the Alien and Sedition acts as usurpations of power by the national government.

In this light, Republican ideas on economic policy take on a deeper meaning. Did the party desire to destroy the economic edifice erected by the Federalists, or did it merely intend to remodel the exterior according to "Republican principles"? And of course, what was the reaction of the Federalists?

Jefferson's first message to Congress, dated December 8, 1801, contains the most complete Republican answer, although it is heavily fortified by the recommendations of Albert Gallatin, Secretary of the Treasury, on elimination of the national debt, the reduction of taxation, and the curtailment of expenditures. The first selection is taken from this message.[10] The second selection is taken from a lengthy series of articles written in the *New York Post* by no less an authority than Hamilton. These excerpts are dated December 21, 24, and 26, 1801.[11]

Jefferson

It is a circumstance of sincere gratification to me that on meeting the great council of our nation, I am able to announce to them, on the grounds of reasonable certainty, that the wars and troubles which have for so many years afflicted our sister nations have at length come to an end, and that the communications of peace and commerce are once more opening among them. While we devoutly return thanks to the beneficent Being who has been pleased to breathe into them the spirit of conciliation and forgiveness, we are bound with peculiar gratitude to be thankful to him that our own peace has been preserved through so perilous a season, and ourselves permitted quietly to cultivate the earth and to practice and improve those arts which tend to increase our comforts. . . .

Other circumstances, combined with the increase of numbers, have produced an augmentation of revenue arising from consumption, in a ratio far beyond that of population alone, and though the changes of foreign relations now taking place so desirably for the world, may for a season affect this branch of revenue, yet, weighing all probabilities of ex-

---

[10] *The Writings of Jefferson*, 3:327–40.

[11] Henry Cabot Lodge, ed., *The Works of Alexander Hamilton*, 9 vols. (New York, 1885–86), 7:206–23.

pense, as well as of income, there is reasonable ground of confidence that we may now safely dispense with all the internal taxes, comprehending excises, stamps, auctions, licenses, carriages, and refined sugars, to which the postage on newspapers may be added, to facilitate the progress of information, and that the remaining sources of revenue will be sufficient to provide for the support of government, to pay the interest on the public debts, and to discharge the principals in shorter periods than the laws or the general expectations had contemplated. War, indeed, and untoward events, may change this prospect of things, and call for expenses which the imposts could not meet; but sound principles will not justify our taxing the industry of our fellow citizens to accumulate treasure for wars to happen we know not when, and which might not perhaps happen but from the temptations offered by that treasure.

These views, however, of reducing our burdens, are formed on the expectation that a sensible, and at the same time a salutary reduction, may take place in our habitual expenditures. For this purpose those of the civil government, the army, and navy, will need revisal.

When we consider that this government is charged with the external and mutual relations only of these states; that the states themselves have principal care of our persons, our property, and our reputation, constituting the great field of human concerns, we may well doubt whether our organization is not too complicated, too expensive; whether offices and officers have not been multiplied unnecessarily, and sometimes injuriously to the service they were meant to promote. I will cause to be laid before you an essay toward a statement of those who, under public employment of various kinds, draw money from the treasury or from our citizens. Time has not permitted a perfect enumeration, the ramifications of office being too multiplied and remote to be completely traced in a first trial. Among those who are dependent on executive discretion, I have begun the reduction of what was deemed necessary. The expenses of diplomatic agency have been considerably diminished. The inspectors of internal revenue who were found to obstruct the accountability of the institution, have been discontinued. Several agencies created by executive authority, on salaries fixed by that also, have been suppressed, and should suggest the expediency of regulating that power by law, so as to subject its exercises to legislative inspection and sanction. Other reformations of the same kind will be pursued with that caution which is requisite in removing useless things, not to injure what is retained. But the great mass of public offices is established by law, and, therefore, by law alone can be abolished. Should the legislature think it expedient to pass this roll in review, and try all its parts by the test of public utility, they may be assured of every aid and light which executive information can yield. Considering the general tendency to multiply offices and dependencies, and to increase expense to the ultimate term of burden which the citizen can bear, it behooves us to avail ourselves of every occasion which presents itself for taking off the surcharge; that it never may be seen here that, after leaving to labor the smallest portion of its earnings on which it can subsist, government shall itself consume the residue of what it was instituted to guard.

In our care, too, of the public contributions intrusted to our direction, it would be prudent to multiply barriers against their dissipation, by appropriating specific sums to every specific purpose susceptible of definition; by disallowing all applications of money varying from the appropriation in object, or transcending it in amount; by reducing the undefined field of contingencies, and thereby circumscribing discretionary powers over money; and by bringing back to a single department all accountabilities for money where the examination may be prompt, efficacious, and uniform.

An account of the receipts and expenditures of the last year, as prepared by the secretary of the treasury, will as usual be laid before you. The success which has attended the late sales of the public lands shows that with attention they may be made an important source of receipt. Among the payments, those made in discharge of the principal and interest of the national debt, will show that the public faith has been exactly maintained. To these will be added an estimate of appropriations necessary for the ensuing year. This last will of course be effected by such modifications of the systems of expense, as you shall think proper to adopt. . . .

Agriculture, manufactures, commerce, and navigation, the four pillars of our prosperity, are the most thriving when left most free to individual enterprise. Protection from casual embarrassments, however, may sometimes be seasonably interposed. If in the course of your observations or inquiries they should appear to need any aid within the limits of our constitutional powers, your sense of their importance is a sufficient assurance they will occupy your attention. We cannot, indeed, but all feel an anxious solicitude for the difficulties under which our carrying trade will soon be placed. How far it can be relieved, otherwise than by time, is a subject of important consideration. . . .

These, fellow citizens, are the matters respecting the state of the nation, which I have thought of importance to be submitted to your consideration at this time. Some others of less moment, or not yet ready for communication, will be the subject of separate messages. I am happy in this opportunity of committing the arduous affairs of our government to the collected wisdom of the Union. Nothing shall be wanting on my part to inform, as far as in my power, the legislative judgment, nor to carry that judgment into faithful execution. The prudence and temperance of your discussion will promote, within your own walls, that conciliation which so much befriends rational conclusion; and by its example will encourage among our constituents that progress of opinion which is tending to unite them in object and in will. That all should be satisfied with any one order of things is not to be expected, but I indulge the pleasing persuasion that the great body of our citizens will cordially concur in honest and disinterested efforts, which have for their object to preserve the general and State governments in their constitutional form and equilibrium; to maintain peace abroad, and order and obedience to the laws at home; to establish principles and practices of administration favorable to the security of liberty and property, and to reduce expenses to what is necessary for the useful purposes of government.

Hamilton

The next most prominent feature in the message is the proposal to abandon at once all the internal revenue of the country. The motives avowed for this astonishing scheme are, that

there is *reasonable ground of confidence* that this part of the revenue may not be safely dispensed with; that the remaining sources will be sufficient to provide for the support of government, *to pay the interest* of the public debt, and to *discharge the principal* in shorter periods than the *laws* or the *general expectation* had contemplated; and that though wars and untoward events might change this prospect of things, and call for expenses which the *impost* could not meet, yet that sound principles would not justify our taxing the industry of our fellow-citizens to *accumulate treasure* for wars to happen we know not when, and which might not perhaps happen but from the *temptations offered* by that treasure.

If we allow these to be more than ostensible motives, we shall be driven to ascribe this conduct to a deficiency of intellect, and to an ignorance of our financial arrangements, greater than could have been suspected; if but ostensible, it is then impossible to trace the suggestion to any other source than the culpable desire of gaining or securing popularity at an immediate expense of public utility, equivalent, on a pecuniary scale, to a million of dollars annually, and at the greater expense of a very serious invasion of our system of public credit.

That these at least are the certain consequences of the measure shall be demonstrated by arguments which are believed to be unanswerable . . .

The first inducement offered for relinquishing the internal revenue is a *reasonable ground of confidence* that it may safely be dispensed with.

When it is considered that we are in the very crisis of an important change of situation; passing from a state in which neutrality had procured to our commerce, and to the revenues depending on it, a great artificial increase—with good reason to look for a diminution, and without satisfactory *data* to enable us to fix the extent of this diminution—can any thing be more rash. . . .

But how can they be unnecessary? . . . Is it not desirable that government should have it in its power to discharge the debt faster than may have been contemplated? Is not this a felicity in our situation which ought to be improved; a precious item in the public fortune which ought not rashly to be squandered? . . .

How is this reconcilable with the wanton and unjust clamors heretofore vented against those who projected and established our present system of public credit; charging them with a design to perpetuate the debt, under the pretext that *a public debt was a public blessing?* It is not to be forgotten, that in these clamors Mr. Jefferson liberally participated! Now, it seems, the tone is entirely changed. The past administrations, who had so long been calumniated by the imputation of that pernicious design, are of a sudden discovered to have done too much for the speedy discharge of the debt, and its duration is to be prolonged, by throwing away a part of the fund destined for its prompt redemption. Wonderful union of consistency and wisdom! . . .

In addition to objects of national security, there are many purposes of great public utility to which the revenues in question might be applied. The improvement of the communications between the different parts of our country is an object well worthy of the national purse, and one which would abundantly repay *to labor* the portion of its *earnings,* which may have been borrowed for the purpose. To provide roads and bridges is within the direct purview of the Constitution. In many parts of the country, especially in the Western Territory, a matter in which the Atlantic States are equally interested, aqueducts and canals would also be fit subjects of pecuniary aid, from the general government. In France, England, and other parts of Europe, institutions exist supported by public contributions, which eminently promote agriculture and the arts. Such institutions merit imitation by our government; they are of the number of those which directly and sensibly recompense *labor* for what it lends to their agency.

To suggestions of the last kind, the adepts of the new school have a ready answer: *Industry will succeed and prosper in proportion as it is left to the exertions of individual enterprise.* This favorite dogma, when taken as a general rule, is true; but as an exclusive one, it is false, and leads to error in the administration of public affairs. In matters of industry, human enterprise ought, doubtless, to be left free in the main; not fettered by too much regulation; but practical politicians know that it may be beneficially stimulated by prudent aids and encouragements on the part of the government. This is proved by numerous examples too tedious to be cited; examples which will be neglected only by indolent and temporizing rulers, who love to loll in the lap of epicurean ease, and seem to imagine that to govern well, is to amuse the wondering multitude with sagacious aphorisms and oracular sayings. . . .

What, then, are we to think of the ostentatious assurance in the Inaugural speech as to the preservation of PUBLIC FAITH? Was it given merely to amuse with agreeable but deceptive sounds? Is it possible that it could have been intended to conceal the insidious design of aiming a deadly blow at a system which was opposed in its origin, and has been calumniated in every state of its progress?

Alas! how deplorable will it be, should it ever become proverbial, that a President of the United States, like the *Weird Sisters* in Macbeth, *"Keeps his word of promise to our ear, but breaks it to our hope!"*

The Embargo Issue

Although the tension between the United States and France had been eased with the acquisition of Louisiana, the friction between the United States and Great Britain tended to increase. After all, the territory of Britain was adjacent to that of the United States, and this resulted in disputes ove borders, fur trade, and Indian hostility. The United States was, moreover, a predominantly agrarian-commercial nation which depended on the Atlantic as a gigantic artery of trade. With the Napoleonic Wars raging in Europe and with His Majesty's fleet in control of the seas, the United States ran into troublesome quarrels over neutral rights and the impressment of American seamen.

The *Chesapeake-Leopard* Affair in 1807 moved the accent from quarrel to crisis. Jefferson's answer to the British action was economic coercion. Our commerce was so vital to Europe, he reasoned, that the economy of any country would be badly hurt if we withheld our trade. The legislation implementing this idea was the Embargo Act, which was passed on December 22, 1807.

The embargo met the strongest resistance from New England partly because the measure proved disastrous for much of the commercial community, and partly because that section harbored the most vigorous remnant of Federalist opposition. For some years the extreme Federalists in New England had been talking privately about secession as a recourse against the "usurpation of power" by the national government under the control of the Republicans. At this time their discontent became more vocal. An extremist like Dr. Timothy Dwight, President of Yale, preached a sermon with important political overtones on the text, "Come out therefore from among them, and be ye separate, saith the Lord, and touch not the unclean thing."

The selections that follow reflect the opposing points of view. The first selection, written by Albert Gallatin, Secretary of the Treasury, to Jefferson on July 29, 1808, gives an indication of the lengths to which some administration leaders were willing to go to enforce the Embargo.[12] The second selection comes from a letter of January 8, 1809, by Timothy Pickering to a fellow Federalist; it represents concisely the view of the potential secessionists.[13] In reading these selections it is enlightening to recall that the Republicans had been traditionally the party of limited executive power and strict construction, while the opposite view had been traditionally upheld by the Federalists.

Gallatin

I sent yesterday to the Secretary of the Navy, and he will transmit to you, a letter from General Dearborn, and another from General Lincoln, showing the violations of the embargo. As these are now effected by vessels which go off without clearances, with intention either of putting their loads on board of vessels at sea, chiefly British, or of sailing over to Nova Scotia or the West Indies, the danger is much greater from New York northwardly, principally from Massachusetts, than from either the Delaware, Chesapeake, or North Carolina. This arises from the proximity of the Northern seaports to the sea, which enables them to be at sea in two

[12] Henry Adams, ed., *The Writings of Albert Gallatin*, 3 vols. (Philadelphia, 1879), 1:396–99.

[13] Henry Adams, ed., *Documents Relating to New England Federalism* (Boston, 1877), 376–78.

hours from the time they leave the wharf, from the vicinity of Nova Scotia, and from the number of British vessels hovering for that purpose between that colony and Massachusetts. There are some, also, in Long Island Sound, and amongst the islands between Nantucket and Rhode Island. . . .

With those difficulties we must struggle as well as we can this summer; but I am perfectly satisfied that if the embargo must be persisted in any longer, two principles must necessarily be adopted in order to make it sufficient: 1st, that not a single vessel shall be permitted to move without the special permission of the Executive; 2d, that the collectors be invested with the general power of seizing property anywhere, and taking the rudders or otherwise effectually preventing the departure of any vessel in harbor, though ostensibly intended to remain there; and that without being liable to personal suits. I am sensible that such arbitrary powers are equally dangerous and odious. But a restrictive measure of the nature of the embargo applied to a nation under such circumstances as the United States cannot be enforced without the assistance of means as strong as the measure itself. To that legal authority to prevent, seize, and detain must be added a sufficient physical force to carry it into effect; and although I believe that in our seaports little difficulty would be encountered, we must have a little army along the Lakes and British lines generally. With that result we should not perhaps be much astonished. For the Federalists, having at least prevented the embargo from becoming a measure generally popular, and the people being distracted by the complexity of the subject, orders of council, decrees, embargoes, and wanting a single object which might rouse their patriotism and unite their passions and affections, selfishness has assumed the reins in several quarters, and the people are now there altogether against the law.

In such quarters the same thing happens which has taken place everywhere else, and even under the strongest governments under similar circumstances. The navy of Great Britain is hardly sufficient to prevent smuggling; and you recollect, doubtless, the army of *employés* and the sanguinary code of France—hardly adequate to guard their land frontiers.

That in the present situation of the world every effort should be attempted to preserve the peace of this nation cannot be doubted. But if the criminal party-rage of Federalists and Tories shall have so far succeeded as to defeat our endeavors to obtain that object by the only measure that could possibly have effected it, we must submit and prepare for war. I am so much overwhelmed even here with business and interruptions, that I have not time to write correctly or even with sufficient perspicuity; but you will guess at my meaning where it is not sufficiently clear. I mean generally to express an opinion founded on the experience of this summer, that Congress must either invest the Executive with the most arbitrary powers and sufficient force to carry the embargo into effect, or give it up altogether. And in this last case I must confess that, unless a change takes place in the measures of the European powers, I see no alternative but war. But with whom? This is a tremendous question if tested only by policy; and so extraordinary is our situation that it is equally difficult to decide it on the ground of justice, the only one by which I wish the United States to be governed. At all events, I think it the duty of the Executive to contemplate that result as probable, and to be prepared accordingly.

Pickering

... It is scarcely conceivable that Mr. Jefferson should so obstinately persevere in the odious measure of the embargo, which he cannot but see has impaired his popularity and hazards its destruction, if he were not under secret engagements to the French emperor; unless you can suppose that he would run that hazard and the ruin of his country, rather than that a measure which he explicitly recommended should be pronounced unwise. As the embargo, with all its mischievous improvements, is agreeable to Bonaparte; and as his outrageous captures and confiscations of American property have outraged even Armstrong, so that he has boldly recommended what would readily have occurred to an American ruler who possessed common sense and common honesty, and one grain of magnanimity; or, if not, who would readily adopt the measure recommended—I am warranted in supposing that Armstrong is not privy to the whole of Mr. Jefferson's French negotiations. The President who could basely employ, as his confidential messenger, so execrable a villain and so devoted a partisan of France as Haley, must be bad enough; and, when we advert to the real character of Mr. Jefferson, there is no nefarious act of which we may not suppose him capable. *He would rather the United States should sink than change the present system of measures.* This is not opinion, but history. I repeat it confidentially to you, until I obtain permission to vouch it on evidence, which I trust I can obtain.

Yesterday, Mr. Giles's bill for enforcing the embargo was taken up in the Senate, and all the amendments made in the House concurred in. The President's approbation of his own measure need not be waited for. I recollect but one feature in the bill which is softened by these amendments. Gilman of N.H., and Reed of Maryland, joined us in voting against this final passage of the bill. Other Democratic members writhed under the dire necessity imposed on them by the force of party to vote for the bill. Henceforward I shall be disposed to consider Gilman and Reed to have quitted the President's ranks.

New England must be united in whatever great measure shall be adopted. During the approaching session of our legislature, there may be such farther advances in mischief as may distinctly point out the course proper to be adopted. A convention of delegates from those States, including Vermont, seems obviously proper and necessary. Massachusetts and Connecticut can appoint their delegates with regular authority. In the other States they might be appointed by county conventions. A strong and solemn address, stating as concisely as will consist with perspicuity the evil conduct of our administration as manifested in their measures, ought to be prepared to be laid before our legislature when they meet, to be sent forth by their authority to the people. But the fast, which I have repeatedly heard mentioned here, I hope will be postponed till the very crisis of our affairs, if such a crisis should be suffered to arise: to proclaim a fast sooner would, I fear, have more the appearance of management than of religion.

I wish you to show this letter to Mr. Cabot, as I have not time to write to him. Pray look into the Constitution, and particularly to the 10th article of the amendments. How are the powers reserved to the States respectively, or to the people, to be maintained, *but by the respective States judging for themselves and putting their negative on the usurpations of the general government?*

The unceasing cry of war among the President's pack is a gross artifice, so gross that I wonder men of understanding here are alarmed by it. Its sole object is to make them and the people at large acquiesce in the embargo; for the administration believe that the alternative of war is not terrible to mothers only, but to the men of the United States. . . .

CONCLUSION

What does the record show the course of the nation to be in these formative years, 1789–1809? Did a change take place in 1800 with the election of Jefferson? Contemporaries certainly disagreed when answering these questions. Jefferson conceived the "revolution of 1800" to be as real and as significant in "the principles of our government as that of 1776 was in its form," but Hamilton protested vigorously against any such assertion. Some contemporaries changed their minds. John Taylor of Virginia, a strong initial supporter of Jefferson and often quoted as the political theorist of the Republicans, at one time remarked that Jefferson bore a "distinct character from that of his predecessor." Yet when Taylor assessed the Republican record near the close of Jefferson's administration, he declared that many persons found Jefferson's policy to be a compromise with Hamilton's: "Federalism, indeed having been defeated, has gained a new footing, by being taken into partnership with republicanism."

Historians who have studied the period tend to reflect the varied views of contemporaries. One recent student of the American mind, Vernon L. Parrington, has based a distinguished three-volume work on the liberal Republican spirit as typified by Jefferson, and another writer, Claude G. Bowers, saw the Federalist decade as a struggle between democratic and anti-democratic forces with the Republican years signifying the "triumph of democracy." On the other hand, Henry Adams, great-grandson of President John Adams and the historical master of the Republican era, quoted with approval the comment of John Randolph: "Never has there been any administration which went out of office and left the nation in a state so deplorable and calamitous." Indeed, Adams found the Republican principles as represented by Jefferson deflected by the political realities of the time. Jefferson, said Henry Adams

> had undertaken to create a government which should interfere in no way with private action, and he had created one which interfered directly in the concerns of every private citizen in the land. He had come into power as the champion of states rights, and had driven states to the verge of armed resistance. He had begun by claiming credit for stern economy, and ended by exceeding the expenditure of his predecessors. He had invented a policy of peace, and his invention resulted in the necessity of fighting at once the two greatest Powers in the world.

If contemporaries disagree and historians disagree, surely each reader is entitled to form his own conclusions. Perhaps three important questions would give some direction and added meaning to the problem. Was it fortunate, as is often stated, that the Federalists, with their determination to launch the new government successfully and their enthusiasm in making it function, were the first party to hold office? Was it fortunate that the Republicans, with their reaffirmation of the individual rights and their reemphasis on the electorate as the basis of good government, came into power after the Federalists had proved that the new government was practicable? Was a successful government permeated with the spirit of liberty necessary as a solid foundation on which actual democratic government could be erected during the "Age of Jackson"?

Certainly many of the issues which arose in this formative period emerged in various forms during the years following. And the ideas so forcefully expressed by the leading Federalists and Republicans have been referred to time and again by spokesmen for later eras. All of this emphasizes two facts—that the early years made a lasting imprint upon the development of the United States, and that the problem of government never ceases.

6 RICHARD N. CURRENT

foundations of foreign policy: beginning the great debate, 1776-1826

"One World" is a recent idea. It occurred to few Americans during the first half-century of their national independence. Most of them believed in the existence of Two Worlds, the Old and the New, which were distinct and different. The Old World was monarchical and often tyrannical; it was corrupt, degenerate, distracted by ancient hatreds and torn by frequent wars. The New World was republican, free, vigorous, and full of promise for previously undreamed-of prosperity and peace. It had a future all its own. The immediate objective of diplomacy, Americans generally thought, should be to secure the safety of the young republic; but it should aim at something far more important—the realization of the grand possibilities of a new and unique civilization. In other words, the objective was to make the American dream come true.

Though Americans agreed pretty well upon this attractive goal, they often disagreed about ways of reaching it. So they began a great debate on foreign policy, even before declaring their independence, a debate which they continued for more than fifty years. For the most part, they accepted certain propositions as true and beyond dispute. Among the widely held axioms were these: The United States ought to keep apart from European politics, remain neutral during European wars, uphold the freedom of the seas, promote commerce and shipping, and advance the cause of liberty throughout the world. But the nation's leaders, in trying to carry out these principles, found that the principles sometimes conflicted with one another, and sometimes conflicted with the facts of international politics. Whether clearly recognized or not, the central problem was always to find a workable compromise between the ideal and the practical, between the desirable and the possible.

During the fifty years here under review, at least half a dozen broad questions of foreign policy arose, each demanding an answer in terms of American ideals or practical necessity or a little of both. At the time of the Revolution, and for a generation thereafter, the overriding issue was whether the United States should rely for its safety on an alliance with France, or alliance with England, or whether the new nation should strike out boldly to assert and maintain a policy of diplomatic independence. At the time of the War of 1812 the question was whether a desirable goal—the freedom of the seas—justified involvement in one of Europe's wars. When the Latin Americans were on the point of winning their national independence, the desirable and the possible and the necessary again had to be carefully weighed. For the United States it was a question of the obligations of neutrality and the threat of a combined Europe, as against the duty of the United States to assume leadership of the New World and promote liberty and trade within it. Then, with a free Latin America seemingly menaced by a reactionary Europe, the American government had to consider a statement, or a restatement, of its basic policy, and had to decide whether to make this statement alone or in company with a disaffected European power, Great Britain. Even after a policy was announced in the Monroe Doctrine, the debate was by no means closed, for there arose controversies about the meaning of the Doctrine and the requirements of American tradition and interest. How far should the United States go in aiding the cause of Greek freedom against the forces of reaction, as represented by the Turks and the Holy Alliance? In America, how far should the United States go in cooperating with the other republics of this hemisphere?

The purpose of the selections that follow is to illustrate how these questions were formulated and what kinds of answers were given to them in the years from 1776 to 1826. The object is not to present a full and detailed account of American diplomacy during the period, valuable though such a study would be, but to introduce the reader to the great debate on American foreign policy as it developed in the beginning, in the hope that he will then be a little better prepared to take intelligent part in the great debate as it goes on today.

1. ALLIANCE—OR DIPLOMATIC INDEPENDENCE?

The first generation of American statesmen repeatedly and almost unanimously espoused the idea of the two spheres, one for Europe, another for America. Thomas Paine, in his widely read pamphlet *Com-*

mon Sense, had argued that the colonists must break away from England in order to free themselves from England's wars in Europe. In the postwar decade John Adams, Thomas Jefferson, Richard Henry Lee, and other leaders continued to insist that the United States should have as little as possible to do with European politics. Alexander Hamilton, in one of the *Federalist Papers* urging a new Constitution, exclaimed: "Let the Thirteen States . . . concur in erecting one great American system, superior to the control of all transatlantic force or influence, and able to dictate the terms of the connection between the Old and the New World." George Washington gave the classic expression to the idea in his famous Farewell Address, written with the collaboration of Hamilton.

The ideal was to keep the two worlds apart politically—though not commercially or otherwise. But it proved difficult, if not impossible, in actual practice. To win their independence, Americans allied themselves with a European power, France, and took part in what eventually amounted to a world war. Once the Revolution was over, they still could not avoid dangerous political contacts with the powers of Europe, for two of them, England and Spain, were near and threatening neighbors, with territorial possessions and claims on the North American continent. Then, in 1793, France and England began a war which would not end until Napoleon was defeated at Waterloo in 1815. To maintain friendly relations with both belligerents, and to enjoy the profits of a neutral trade with both, proved to be a difficult assignment for American policy makers. They did not quite succeed, for the United States became involved in an undeclared naval war with France in 1798. Even after the Franco-American alliance (of 1778) was mutually terminated in 1800, the United States was not quite safe from European entanglements. When France, by obtaining Louisiana, replaced Spain on the North American continent, even such a staunch friend of France and friend of peace as Thomas Jefferson began to talk of a possible alliance between the United States and Great Britain.

The French Alliance

When hostilities broke out between American colonists and British regulars, few Americans wanted either independence from England or entanglements with Europe. The colonists were fighting for a redress of grievances within the Empire. But they soon found that they could not win even such a limited war without foreign help, and they naturally turned to England's historic enemy, France. They could not get all-out aid from France unless they made independence their war aim, since the French would help them only in order to weaken England by disrupting her Empire. And to be sure of the fullest cooperation, they had to accept France as an ally. In 1778 two treaties were signed, one

foundations of foreign policy: beginning the great debate

commercial, the other defensive. The alliance, by implication, was to be a permanent one, for it bound each signatory to guarantee the other's American possessions "forever." The agreement was to go into effect as soon as England and France went to war.

The English government tried to head off this Franco-American rapprochement by what nowadays would be called a "peace offensive." A special peace commission sailed from England for America in an unsuccessful attempt to end the fighting and prevent ratification of the treaties with France. At that time one of the American diplomats abroad, John Adams, undertook to answer two questions: First, whether England and France, though they had not yet declared war, were actually at war with one another, and the Franco-American alliance therefore was in force; and second, whether the English peace offer should be considered, or the French alliance adhered to. John Adams expressed his opinions in a letter dated at Passy, France, July 28, 1778, and addressed to his cousin Samuel Adams, a prominent member of the Continental Congress.[1]

The sovereign of Britain and his council have determined to instruct their commissioners to offer you independence, provided you will disconnect yourselves from France.

The question arises, how came the king and council by authority to offer this? It is certain that they have it not.

In the next place, is the treaty of alliance between us and France now binding upon us? I think there is not room to doubt it; for declarations and manifestoes do not make the state of war—they are only publications of the reasons of war. Yet the message of the King of Great Britain to both houses of Parliament, and their answers to that message, were as full a declaration of war as ever was made, and accordingly hostilities have been frequent ever since. This proposal, then, is a modest invitation to a gross act of infidelity and breach of faith. It is an observation that I have often heard you make, that "France is the natural ally of the United States." This observation is, in my opinion, both just and important. The reasons are plain. As long as Great Britain shall have Canada, Nova Scotia, and the Floridas, or any of them, so long will Great Britain be the enemy of the United States, let her disguise it as much as she will.

It is not much to the honor of human nature, but the fact is certain that neighboring nations are never friends in reality. In the times of the most perfect peace between them their hearts and their passions are hostile, and this will certainly be the case forever between the thirteen United States and the English colonies. France and England, as neighbors and rivals, never have been and never will be friends. The hatred and jealousy between the nations are eternal and irradicable. As we therefore, on the one hand, have the surest ground to expect the jealousy and hatred of Great

---

[1] Francis Wharton, ed., *The Revolutionary Diplomatic Correspondence of the United States*, 6 vols. (Washington, 1889), 2:667–68.

Britain, so on the other we have the strongest reasons to depend upon the friendship and alliance of France, and no one reason in the world to expect her enmity or her jealousy, as she has given up every pretension to any spot of ground on the continent. The United States, therefore, will be for ages the natural bulwark of France against the hostile designs of England against her, and France is the natural defense of the United States against the rapacious spirit of Great Britain against them. France is a nation so vastly eminent, having been for so many centuries what they call the dominant power of Europe, being incomparably the most powerful at land, that united in a close alliance with our states, and enjoying the benefit of our trade, there is not the smallest reason to doubt but both will be a sufficient curb upon the naval power of Great Britain.

This connection, therefore will forever secure a respect for our States in Spain, Portugal, and Holland, too, who will always choose to be upon friendly terms with powers who have numerous cruisers at sea, and indeed in all the rest of Europe. I presume, therefore, that sound policy as well as good faith will induce us never to renounce our alliance with France, even although it should continue us for some time in war. The French are as sensible of the benefits of this alliance to them as we are, and they are determined as much as we to cultivate it.

A Declaration of Diplomatic Independence

When the French Revolutionary War began in 1793, the commitment to France made in 1778 became something of an embarrassment to the United States. France was now fighting England; the United States was France's ally. Was the United States obligated to go to war against England? In 1793 President Washington issued a proclamation of neutrality, and the next year Congress passed a neutrality law designed to prevent American citizens from aiding either belligerent. Thus the United States asserted a policy of keeping aloof from European quarrels.

To carry out the policy was not easy. First, the overenthusiastic young minister from revolutionary France, Citizen Edmond Genêt, flouted American neutrality by trying to use the United States as a base of French operations against England. Then the English seized American ships trading in the West Indies and stirred up the Indians against the American frontiersmen from posts on American soil still held in violation of the treaty of 1783. War with England threatened. To avert it, the Washington administration sent Chief Justice John Jay on an extraordinary mission to London in 1794. Jay's Treaty adjusted the worst of the disputes between the two countries and, in effect, aligned the United States on the side of England in her war against France.

To Jeffersonian critics of the Washington administration, and to the leaders of the French Republic, Jay's Treaty seemed incompatible with the Franco-

foundations of foreign policy: beginning the great debate

American treaties of 1778. With the cooperation of Washington's Secretary of State, Edmund Randolph, and the American Minister in Paris, James Monroe, the French undertook to prevent its ratification. Failing in that, they determined to defeat the Federalist party in the presidential election of 1796. They assumed that, once the Jeffersonians were in power, the United States would adopt a foreign policy conformable to the interests of France, though the French Minister in Philadelphia wrote home: "Mr. Jefferson likes us because he detests England. . . . Jefferson, I say, is an American, and as such, he cannot sincerely be our friend. An American is the born enemy of all the peoples of Europe." In their effort to influence the election, the French subsidized newspapers in America, broke off diplomatic relations, announced a new program of ship seizures, and threatened war.

This foreign interference in domestic politics and the apparent influence of a foreign government over two high American officials—the Secretary of State and the Minister to France—provided the background for Washington's remarks on foreign affairs in his Farewell Address, the classic statement of the policy afterwards called, somewhat inaccurately, isolationism. The Farewell Address was not a speech but a communication, dated September 17, 1796, published in a Philadelphia newspaper.[2]

Observe good faith and justice toward all nations. Cultivate peace and harmony with all. Religion and morality enjoin this conduct. And can it be that good policy does not equally enjoin it? It will be worthy of a free, enlightened, and at no distant period a great nation to give to mankind the magnanimous and too novel example of a people always guided by an exalted justice and benevolence. Who can doubt that in the course of time and things the fruits of such a plan would richly repay any temporary advantages which might be lost by a steady adherence to it? Can it be that Providence has not connected the permanent felicity of a nation with its virtue? The experiment, at least, is recommended by every sentiment which ennobles human nature. Alas! is it rendered impossible by its vices?

In the execution of such a plan nothing is more essential than that permanent, inveterate antipathies against particular nations and passionate attachments for others should be excluded, and that in place of them just and amicable feelings toward all should be cultivated. The nation which indulges toward another an habitual hatred or an habitual fondness is in some degree a slave. It is a slave to its animosity or to its affection, either of which is sufficient to lead it astray from its duty and its interest. Antipathy in one nation against another disposes each more readily to offer insult and injury, to lay hold of slight causes of umbrage, and to be haughty and intractable when accidental or trifling occasions of dispute occur.

---

[2] James D. Richardson, *A Compilation of the Messages and Papers of the Presidents*, 11 vols. (Washington, 1896–99), 1:221–24.

Hence frequent collisions, obstinate, envenomed, and bloody contests. The nation prompted by ill will and resentment sometimes impels to war the government contrary to the best calculations of policy. The government sometimes participates in the national propensity, and adopts through passion what reason would reject. At other times it makes the animosity of the nation subservient to projects of hostility, instigated by pride, ambition, and other sinister and pernicious motives. The peace often, sometimes perhaps the liberty, of nations has been the victim.

So, likewise, a passionate attachment of one nation for another produces a variety of evils. Sympathy for the favorite nation, facilitating the illusion of an imaginary common interest in cases where no real common interest exists, and infusing into one the enmities of the other, betrays the former into a participation in the quarrels and wars of the latter without adequate inducement or justification. It leads also to concessions to the favorite nation of privileges denied to others, which is apt doubly to injure the nation making the concessions by unnecessarily parting with what ought to have been retained, and by exciting jealousy, ill will, and a disposition to retaliate in the parties from whom equal privileges are withheld; and it gives to ambitious, corrupted, or deluded citizens (who devote themselves to the favorite nation) facility to betray or sacrifice the interests of their own country without odium, sometimes even with popularity, gilding with the appearance of a virtuous sense of obligation, a commendable deference for public opinion, or a laudable zeal for public good the base or foolish compliances of ambition, corruption, or infatuation.

As avenues to foreign influence in innumerable ways, such attachments are particularly alarming to the truly enlightened and independent patriot. How many opportunities do they afford to tamper with domestic factions, to practice the arts of seduction, to mislead public opinion, to influence or awe the public councils! Such an attachment of a small or weak toward a great and powerful nation dooms the former to be the satellite of the latter. Against the insidious wiles of foreign influence (I conjure you to believe me, fellow-citizens) the jealousy of a free people ought to be *constantly* awake, since history and experience prove that foreign influence is one of the most baneful foes of republican government. But that jealousy, to be useful, must be impartial, else it becomes the instrument of the very influence to be avoided, instead of a defense against it. Excessive partiality for one foreign nation and excessive dislike of another cause those whom they actuate to see danger only on one side and serve to veil and even second the arts of influence on the other. Real patriots who may resist the intrigues of the favorite are liable to become suspected and odious, while its tools and dupes usurp the applause and confidence of the people to surrender their interests.

The great rule of conduct for us in regard to foreign nations is, in extending our commercial relations to have with them as little *political* connection as possible. So far as we have already formed engagements, let them be fulfilled with perfect good faith. Here let us stop.

Europe has a set of primary interests which to us have none or a very remote relation. Hence she must be engaged in frequent controversies, the causes of which are essentially foreign to our concerns. Hence, therefore, it must be unwise in us to implicate ourselves by artificial ties in the ordinary vicissitudes of her politics or the ordinary combinations and collisions of her friendships or enmities.

Our detached and distant situation invites and enables us to pursue a different course. If we remain one people, under an efficient government, the period is not far off when we may defy material injury from external annoyance; when we may take such an attitude as will cause the neutrality we may at any time resolve upon to be scrupulously respected; when belligerent nations, under the impossibility of making acquisitions upon us, will not lightly hazard the giving us provocation; when we may choose peace or war, as our interest, guided by justice, shall counsel.

Why forego the advantages of so peculiar a situation? Why quit our own to stand upon foreign ground? Why, by interweaving our destiny with that of any part of Europe, entangle our peace and prosperity in the toils of European ambition, rivalship, interest, humor, or caprice?

It is our true policy to steer clear of permanent alliances with any portion of the foreign world, so far, I mean, as we are now at liberty to do it; for let me not be understood as capable of patronizing infidelity to existing engagements. I hold the maxim no less applicable to public than to private affairs that honesty is always the best policy. I repeat, therefore, let those engagements be observed in their genuine sense. But in my opinion it is unnecessary and would be unwise to extend them.

Taking care always to keep ourselves by suitable establishments on a respectable defensive posture, we may safely trust to temporary alliances for extraordinary emergencies.

Jefferson Considers an Alliance with Britain

Franco-American relations went from bad to worse. The X Y Z Affair, in which the French government demanded a loan and either an apology or a bribe as the price of re-establishing diplomatic relations with the United States, was followed by an undeclared naval war between the two countries (1798–1800). Meanwhile the United States moved to closer cooperation with England. Neutrality and nonentanglement, the ideals so well expressed by Washington, appeared to be dead, until 1800, when the United States made a peace which ended the old French alliance. New trouble soon appeared, however, when the rumor spread that France had got Louisiana back from Spain (as in fact France had, in a secret agreement signed on the very day after the settlement between France and the United States). The rumors gained strength from the news, in 1802, that the Spanish in New Orleans had withdrawn the right of Americans to deposit goods there for transfer from river boats to ocean ships. This meant that Americans could not fully use the Mississippi, and they suspected that France was back of the Spanish action.

Jefferson, whom the French had schemed to put in power four years earlier, was now President. His handling of the situation confirmed the prediction then made by the French Minister to the United States. The new President's diplomatic strategy is seen in the letter of April 18, 1802, which he sent by special messenger to the American Minister in France, Robert R. Livingston.[3]

The cession of Louisiana and the Floridas by Spain to France works most sorely on the U.S. On this subject the Secretary of State has written to you fully. Yet I cannot forbear recurring to it personally, so deep is the impression it makes in my mind. It compleatly reverses all the political relations of the U.S., and will form a new epoch in our political course. Of all nations of any consideration France is the one which hitherto has offered the fewest points on which we could have any conflict of right, and the most points of a communion of interests. From these causes we have ever looked to her as our *natural friend,* as one with which we never could have an occasion of difference. Her growth, therefore, we viewed as our own, her misfortunes ours. There is on the globe one single spot, the possessor of which is our natural and habitual enemy. It is New Orleans, through which the produce of three-eighths of our territory must pass to market, and from its fertility it will ere long yield more than half of our whole produce and contain more than half our inhabitants. France placing herself in that door assumes to us the attitude of defiance. Spain might have retained it quietly for years. Her pacific dispositions, her feeble state would induce her to increase our facilities there, so that her possession of the place would be hardly felt by us, and it would not perhaps be very long before some circumstance might arise which might make the cession of it to us the price of something of more worth to her. Not so can it ever be in the hands of France. The impetuosity of her temper, the energy and restlessness of her character, placed in a point of eternal friction with us, and our character, which though quiet, and loving peace and the pursuit of wealth, is high-minded, despising wealth in competition with insult or injury, enterprising and energetic as any nation on earth, thse circumstances render it impossible that France and the U.S. can continue long friends when they meet in so irritable a position. They as well as we must be blind if they do not see this; and we must be very improvident if we do not begin to make arrangements on that hypothesis. The day that France takes possession of N. Orleans fixes the sentence which is to restrain her forever within her low water mark. It seals the union of two nations who in conjunction can maintain exclusive possession of the ocean. From that moment we must marry ourselves to the British fleet and nation. We must turn all our attentions to a maritime force, for which our resources place us on very high

---

[3] Paul L. Ford, ed., *The Writings of Thomas Jefferson*, 10 vols. (New York, 1892–99), 3:143–47.

grounds: and having formed and cemented together a power which may render reinforcement of her settlements here impossible to France, make the first cannon, which shall be fired in Europe the signal for tearing up any settlement she may have made, and for holding the two continents of America in sequestration for the common purposes of the united British and American nations. This is not a state of things we seek or desire. It is one which this measure, if adopted by France, forces on us, as necessarily as any other cause, by the laws of nature, brings on its necessary effect. It is not from a fear of France that we deprecate this measure proposed by her. For however greater her force is than ours compared in the abstract, it is nothing in comparison of ours when to be exerted on our soil. But it is from a sincere love of peace, and a firm persuasion that bound to France by the interests and the strong sympathies still existing in the minds of our citizens, and holding relative positions which ensure their continuance we are secure of a long course of peace. Whereas the change of friends, which will be rendered necessary if France changes that position, embarks us necessarily as a belligerent power in the first war of Europe. . . .

If France considers Louisiana, however, as indispensable for her views, she might perhaps be willing to look about for arrangements which might reconcile it to our interests. If anything could do this it would be the ceding to us the island of New Orleans and the Floridas. This would certainly in a great degree remove the causes of jarring and irritation between us, and perhaps for such a length of time as might produce other means of making the measure permanently conciliatory to our interests and friendships. It would at any rate relieve us from the necessity of taking immediate measures for countervailing such an operation by arrangements in another quarter.

2. WAR FOR NEUTRAL RIGHTS?

A complete diplomatic reversal seemed to be in the making. In 1778 John Adams had recommended that the French alliance be cherished permanently; in 1796 George Washington had advised against permanent alliances (except for the one to which we were already committed); and now, in 1802, Thomas Jefferson was talking of an alliance with England! A close study of their statements, however, will show that actually the three men differed less than might seem; they held certain basic assumptions in common. In any case, Jefferson was not called upon to demonstrate whether he was merely trying to bluff the French. Napoleon suddenly decided to sell all Louisiana, and by accepting his offer the United States escaped the necessity of a new entanglement.

American neutrality, meantime, badly strained by Jay's Treaty, had broken down almost completely in 1798 with the undeclared war against France and the close cooperation with England. After the renewal of the European war in 1803 (following a truce of less than two years), American neutrality was again to be badly strained. Eventually, in 1812, the United States was to rejoin the war, this time against England, though without any ties to Napoleon's France.

With France supreme on the European continent and with Britain ruling the sea, the United States found itself in a dilemma. Napoleon, with his Continental System, tried to force the English into submission by closing Europe to their trade. The English countered by attempting to force English goods, and neutral goods by way of England, into continental ports. American shippers were caught in the crossfire of Napoleonic decrees and British orders-in-council. If a Yankee headed his ship directly for Europe, he was liable to have it seized by the British. If he sailed first to an English port, he would have to pay a fee before getting permission to proceed; and if he then went on to the continent, he ran the risk of losing everything to the French.

In an effort to compel respect from both belligerents, the administrations of Jefferson and Madison used various forms of what in a later generation might have been called "economic sanctions": First, an embargo on all foreign trade; second, a prohibition on trade with only England and France; and, finally, a reopening of trade with both accompanied by a threat that, if one of them ended its violation of neutral rights, then an embargo would be re-imposed against the other. Pretending to lift his obnoxious decrees so far as they affected American shipping, Napoleon tricked Madison into prohibiting commercial intercourse with Great Britain. The War of 1812 soon followed.

But there were other causes of trouble between England and the United States besides the offensive orders-in-council. One was impressment, which was the Royal Navy's practice of taking British subjects, or alleged British subjects, from among crewmen on American merchant ships (and, in the case of the *Chesapeake* in 1807, even off an American warship!). Another cause of ill feelings was border friction in the Northwest: Americans accused the British of stirring up the Indians against the frontier, and Canadians feared that the United States, urged on by its aggrieved frontiersmen, might seek to conquer Canada.

The question, as some contemporary American statesmen saw it, was, did the circumstances justify a war against England? In other words, did the defense of neutral rights require a temporary abandonment of neutrality?

Virtual Allies of Bonaparte

John Randolph of Roanoke, Congressman from Virginia, began public life as a Jeffersonian, then accused Jefferson of violating his own principles, and finally became practically a party to himself. A tall, skinny man with a squeaky voice, Randolph would appear in Congress with boots, spurs, and riding whip, to harangue his colleagues for hours, while his hunting dogs curled themselves up at his feet and his slave brought him refreshing drafts of ale. But his colleagues had to take him seriously, for they admired his flashes of brilliant phraseology and feared his accusing finger and his sharp wit. He was usually "agin'" things, and he was against war with England in 1812. In a letter of May 30, 1812, to his "fellow-citizens," the "Freeholders of Charlotte, Prince Edward, Buckingham, and Cumberland" counties, he explained his stand to his constituents.[4]

Having learned from various sources that a declaration of war would be attempted on Monday next, *with closed doors,* I deemed it my duty to endeavor, by an exercise of my constitutional functions, to arrest this heaviest of all calamities, and avert it from our happy country.... My design is simply to submit to you the views which have induced me to consider a war with England, under existing circumstances, as comporting neither with the *interest* nor the *honor* of the American people; but as an idolatrous sacrifice of both, on the altar of *French rapacity, perfidy, and ambition.*

France has for years past offered us terms of undefined commercial arrangement, as the price of a war with England, which hitherto we have not wanted firmness and virtue to reject. That price is now to be paid. We are tired of holding out; and, following the example of continental Europe, entangled in the artifices, or awed by the power of the destroyer of mankind, we are prepared to become instrumental to his projects of universal dominion. *Before these pages meet your eye, the last republic of the earth will have enlisted under the banners of the tyrant and become a party to his cause.* The blood of the American freeman must flow to cement his power, to aid in stifling the last struggles of afflicted and persecuted man, to deliver up into his hands the patriots of Spain and Portugal, to establish his empire over the ocean and over the land that gave our fathers birth—to forge our own chains! And yet, my friends, we are told, as we were told in the days of Mr. Adams, *"the finger of heaven points to war."* Yes, the finger of heaven *does* point to war! It points to war, as it points to the mansions of eternal misery and torture—as a flaming beacon warning us of that vortex which we may not approach but with certain destruction. It points to desolated Europe, and warns us of the chastisement of those nations who have offended against the justice, and almost beyond the mercy, of heaven. It announces the wrath to come upon those who, ungrateful for the bounty of Providence, not satisfied with the peace, liberty, security, and plenty at home, fly, as it were, into the face of the Most High, and tempt his forebearance.

To you, *in this place,* I can speak with freedom; and it becomes me to do so; nor shall I be deterred by the cavils and the sneers of those who hold as "foolishness" all that savors not of wordly wisdom, from express-

---

[4] Hugh A. Garland, *The Life of John Randolph of Roanoke,* 2 vols. (New York, 1850), 1:299–303.

ing fully and freely those sentiments which it has pleased God, in his mercy, to engrave on my heart.

These are not ordinary times; the state of the world is unexampled; the war of the present day is not like that of our revolution, or any which preceded it, at least in modern times. It is a war against the liberties and the happiness of mankind; it is a war in which the whole human race are the victims, to gratify the pride and lust of power of a single individual. I beseech you, put it to your own bosoms, how far it becomes you as freemen, as Christians, to give your aid and sanction to this impious and bloody war against your brethren of the human family. To such among you, if any such there be, who are insensible to motives not more dignified and manly than they are intrinsically wise, I would make a different appeal. I adjure you by the regard you have for your own safety and property, for the liberty and inheritance of your children—by all that you hold dear and sacred—to interpose your constitutional powers to save your country, and yourselves from the calamity, the issue of which it is not given to human foresight to divine.

Ask yourselves if you are willing to become the virtual allies of Bonaparte? Are you willing for the sake of annexing Canada to the Northern States, to submit to that overgrowing system of taxation which sends the European laborer supperless to bed, to maintain, by the sweat of your brow, armies at whose hands you are to receive a future master? Suppose Canada ours; is there any one among you who would ever be, in any respect, the better for it?—the richer, the freer, the happier, the more secure? And is it for a boon like this that you would join in the warfare against the liberties of man in the other hemisphere, and put your own in jeopardy? Or is it for the *nominal* privilege of a licensed trade with France that you would abandon your lucrative commerce with Great Britain, Spain, and Portugal, and their Asiatic, African, and American dependencies; in a word, with every region of those vast continents?—that commerce which gives vent to your tobacco, grain, flour, cotton; in short, to all your native products, which are denied a market in France? There are not wanting men so weak as to suppose that their approbation of warlike measures is a proof of personal gallantry, and that opposition to them indicates a want of that spirit which becomes a friend of his country; as if it required more courage and patriotism to join in the acclamation of the day, than steadily to oppose one's self to the mad infatuation to which every people and all governments have, at some time or other, given way. . . .

My friends, do you expect to find those who are now loudest in the clamor for war, foremost in the ranks of battle? Or, is the honor of this nation indissolubly connected with the political reputation of a few individuals, who tell you *they* have gone too far to recede, and that you must pay, with *your ruin,* the price of their *consistency?*

My friends, I have discharged my duty towards you, lamely and inadequately, I know, but to the best of my poor ability. The destiny of the American people is in their own hands. The net is spread for their destruction. You are enveloped in the toils of French duplicity, and if—which may Heaven in its mercy forbid—you and your posterity are to become hewers of wood and drawers of water to the modern Pharaoh, it shall not be for the want of my best exertions to rescue you from the cruel and abject bondage. This sin, at least, shall not rest upon my soul.

Free Trade and Seamen's Rights

The man most responsible for the declaration of war in 1812 was Henry Clay, the youthful Speaker of the House, who had come from Kentucky to assume leadership of the "War Hawks" in Congress. His predictions of an easy march into Canada were not borne out. When the early Canadian campaign failed, criticism of the war increased, and enlistments lagged. Clay attempted to justify the hostilities by his statement of war causes and war aims, given in the course of a speech in the House, January 8, 1813, in which he urged a bill to increase the Army.[5]

Sir, gentlemen appear to me to forget that they stand on American soil; that they are not in the British house of commons, but in the chamber of the house of representatives of the United States; that we have nothing to do with the affairs of Europe, the partition of territory and sovereignty there, except so far as these things affect the interests of our own country. Gentlemen transform themselves into the Burkes, Chathams, and Pitts, of another country, and forgetting, from honest zeal, the interests of America, engage with European sensibility in the discussion of European interests. If gentlemen ask me, whether I do not view with regret and horror the concentration of such vast power in the hands of Bonaparte, I reply, that I do. I regret to see the emperor of China holding such immense sway over the fortunes of millions of our species. I regret to see Great Britain possessing so uncontrolled a command over all the waters of our globe. If I had the ability to distribute among the nations of Europe their several portions of power and of sovereignty, I would say, that Holland should be resuscitated, and given the weight she enjoyed in the days of her De Witts. I would confine France within her natural boundaries, the Alps, Pyrenees, and the Rhine, and make her a secondary naval power only. I would abridge the British maritime power, raise Prussia and Austria to their original condition, and preserve the integrity of the empire of Russia. But these are speculations. I look at the political transactions of Europe, with the single exception of their possible bearing upon us, as I do at the history of other countries, or other times. I do not survey them with half the interest that I do the movements in South America. Our

---

[5] Calvin Colton, *The Life and Times of Henry Clay,* 2nd ed., 2 vols. (New York, 1846), 1:173–81.

political relation with them is much less important than it is supposed to be. I have no fears of French or English subjugation. If we are united, we are too powerful for the mightiest nation in Europe, or all Europe combined. If we are separated and torn asunder, we shall become an easy prey to the weakest of them. In the latter dreadful contingency, our country will not be worth preserving. . . .

The war was declared, because Great Britain arrogated to herself the pretension of regulating our foreign trade, under the delusive name of retaliatory orders in council—a pretension by which she undertook to proclaim to American enterprise, "thus far shalt thou go, and no further"—orders which she refused to revoke, after the alleged cause of their enactment had ceased; because she persisted in the practice of impressing American seamen; because she had instigated the Indians to commit hostilities against us; and because she refused indemnity for her past injuries upon our commerce. I throw out of the question other wrongs. The war in fact was announced, on our part, to meet the war which she was waging on her part. So undeniable were the causes of the war, so powerfully did they address themselves to the feelings of the whole American people, that when the bill was pending before this house, gentlemen in the opposition, although provoked to debate, would not, or could not, utter one syllable against it. It is true, they wrapped themselves up in sullen silence, pretending they did not choose to debate such a question in secret session. While speaking of the proceedings on that occasion, I beg to be admitted to advert to another fact which transpired—an important fact, material for the nation to know, and which I have often regretted had not been spread upon our journals. My honorable colleague [Mr. McKee] moved, in committee of the whole, to comprehend France in the war; and when the question was taken upon the proposition, there appeared but ten votes in support of it, of whom seven belonged to this side of the house, and three only to the other! It is said, that we were inveigled into the war by the perfidy of France; and that, had she furnished the document in time, which was first published in England, in May last, it would have been prevented. I will concede to gentlemen everything they ask about the injustice of France toward this country. I wish to God that our ability was equal to our disposition, to make her feel the sense that we entertain of that injustice. . . .

It is not to the British principle [of allegiance], objectionable as it is, that we are alone to look; it is to her practice, no matter what guise she puts on. It is in vain to assert the inviolability of the obligation of allegiance. It is in vain to set up the plea of necessity, and to allege that she can not exist, without the impressment of HER seamen. The naked truth is, she comes, by her press-gangs, on board of our vessels, seizes OUR native as well as naturalized seamen, and drags them into her service. It is the case, then, of the assertion of an erroneous principle, and of a practice not conformable to the asserted principle—a principle, which, if it were theoretically right, must be for ever practically wrong—a practice which can obtain countenance from no principle whatever, and to submit to which, on our part, would betray the most abject degradation. We are told, by gentlemen in the opposition, that [the] government has not done all that was incumbent on it to do, to avoid just cause of complaint on the part of Great Britain; that in particular the certificates of protection, authorized by the act of 1796, are fraudulently used. Sir, government has done too much in granting those paper protections. I can never think of them without being shocked. They resemble the passes which the master grants to his negro slave—"Let the bearer, Mungo, pass and repass without molestation." What do they imply? That Great Britain has a right to seize all who are not provided with them. From their very nature, they must be liable to abuse on both sides. If Great Britain desires a mark, by which she can know her own subjects, let her give them an ear-mark. The colors that float from the mast-head should be the credentials of our seamen. There is no safety to us, and the gentlemen have shown it, but in the rule, that all who sail under the flag (not being enemies) are protected by the flag. It is impossible that this country should ever abandon the gallant tars, who have won for us such splendid trophies. . . .

An honorable peace is attainable only by an efficient war. My plan would be, to call out the ample resources of the country, give them a judicious direction, prosecute the war with the utmost vigor, strike wherever we can reach the enemy, at sea or on land, and negotiate the terms of a peace at Quebec or at Halifax. We are told, that England is a proud and lofty nation, which, disdaining to wait for danger, meets it half way. Haughty as she is, we once triumphed over her, and, if we do not listen to the counsels of timidity and despair, we shall again prevail. In such a cause, with the aid of Providence, we must come out crowned with success; but if we fail, let us fail like men, lash ourselves to our gallant tars, and expire together in one common struggle, fighting for FREE TRADE AND SEAMEN'S RIGHTS.

The Voice of the Commercial Interests

Criticism of the war continued, particularly in New England. There, the shipping interests, represented by the Federalist party, preferred peace and trade, even at the risk of seizure, to war and the commercial restrictions that accompanied it. Daniel Webster, a young Congressman from New Hampshire, spoke for the dominant interests of his section in a speech of January 14, 1814, opposing a bill to encourage Army enlistments.[6]

Whoever, sir, would discover the causes which have produced the present state of things, must look for them, not in the efforts of opposition, but in the nature of the war, in which we are engaged, and in the manner in which its professed objects have been attempted to be ob-

---

[6] *The Writings and Speeches of Daniel Webster*, National Edition, 18 vols. (Boston, 1903), 14:18–34.

tained. Quite too small a portion of public opinion was in favor of the war, to justify it, originally. A much smaller portion is in favor of the mode in which it has been conducted. This is the radical infirmity. Public opinion, strong and united, is not with you, in your Canada project. Whether it ought to be or ought not to be, the fact that it is not, should, by this time, be evident to all; and it is the business of practical statesmen, to act upon the state of things as it is, and not to be always attempting to prove what it ought to be. The acquisition of that country is not an object, generally desired by the people. Some gentlemen, indeed, say it is not *their ultimate* object; and that they wish it only as the means of effecting other purposes. But, sir, a large portion of the people believe that a desire for the conquest and final retention of Canada is the mainspring of public measures. Nor is the opinion without ground. It has been distinctly avowed, by public men, in a public manner. And if this be not the object, it is not easy to see the connection between your means and ends. At least, that portion of the people, that is not in the habit of refining far, cannot see it. You are, you say, at war for maritime rights, and free trade. But they see you lock up your commerce and abandon the ocean. They see you invade an interior province of the enemy. They see you involve yourselves in a bloody war with the native savages; and they ask you, if you have, in truth, a maritime controversy with the western Indians, and are really contending for sailors' rights with the tribes of the Prophet? In my judgment, the popular sentiment, in this case, corresponds with the soundest political discretion. In my humble opinion, you are not able to travel in the road you have taken, but if you were, it would not conduct you to your object. . . .

Let me suppose, sir, that when the Convention of one of the commercial States, Massachusetts for example, was deliberating on the adoption of this Constitution, some person, to whose opening vision the future had been disclosed, had appeared among them. He would have seen there the Patriots who rocked the cradle of liberty in America. He would have seen there statesmen and warriors, who had borne no dishonorable parts in the councils of their country, and on her fields of battle. He would have found these men recommending the adoption of this Instrument to a people, full of the feeling of independence, and naturally jealous of all governments but their own. And he would have found that the leading, the principal, and the finally prevalent argument, was the *protection and extension of commerce*.

Now suppose, sir, that this person, having the knowledge of future times, had told them, "This Instrument, to which you now commit your fates, shall for a time not deceive your hopes. Administered and practised, as you now understand it, it shall enable you to carry your favorite pursuits to an unprecedented extent. The increase of your numbers, of your wealth, and of your general prosperity shall exceed your expectations. But other times shall arrive. Other counsels shall prevail. In the midst of this extension and growth of commerce and prosperity, an Embargo, severe and universal, shall be laid upon you, for eighteen months. This shall be succeeded by non-importations, restrictions, and embarrassments, of every description. War, with the most powerful maritime nation on earth, shall follow. This war shall be declared professedly for *your* benefit, and the protection of *your* interest. It shall be declared nevertheless *against* your urgent remonstrance. Your voice shall be heard, but it shall be heard only to be disregarded. It shall be a war for sailors' rights, against the sentiments of those to whom eight-tenths of the seamen of the country belong. It shall be a war for maritime rights, forced upon those who are alone interested in such concerns. It shall be brought upon you by those to whom seamen and commerce shall be alike unknown; who shall never have heard the surges of the sea; and into whose minds the idea of a ship shall never have entered, through the eye, till they shall come, from beyond the western hills, to take the protection of your maritime rights, and the guardianship of your commercial interests into their skilful and experienced hands. Bringing the enemy to the blockade of your ports, they shall leave your coasts to be undefended, or defended by yourselves. Mindful of what may yet remain of your commerce, they shall visit you with another Embargo. They shall cut off your intercourse of every description with foreign nations. This not only; they shall cut off your intercourse of every description by water, with your sister States. This not only; they shall cut off your intercourse of every description by water, between the ports of your own States. They shall seize your accustomed commerce, in every limb, nerve, and fibre, and hold it, as in the jaws of death."

I now put it to you, sir, whether, if this practical administration of the Constitution had been laid before them, they would have ratified it. . . .

A naval force, competent to defend your coast against considerable armaments, to convoy your trade, and perhaps raise the blockade of your rivers, is not a chimera. It may be realized. If, then, the war must continue, go to the ocean. If you are seriously contending for maritime rights, go to the theatre where alone those rights can be defended. Thither every indication of your fortunes points you. There the united wishes and exertions of the nation will go with you. Even our party divisions, acrimonious as they are, cease at the water's edge. They are lost in attachment to national character, on the element where that character is made respectable. In protecting naval interests by naval means, you will arm yourselves with the whole power of national sentiment, and may command the whole abundance of the national resources. In time you may enable yourselves to redress injuries, in the place where they may be offered, and if need be, to accompany your own flag throughout the world, with the protection of your own cannon.

3. EUROPEAN LEAGUE—OR AMERICAN BALANCE?

In 1814 American and British commissioners negotiated the Treaty of Ghent, which terminated the Anglo-American fighting and provided for a return to the *status quo*. Next year the Napoleonic Wars ended at

Waterloo. For more than two decades, war in Europe had complicated the job of American policy makers. But the outbreak of peace brought new problems. In Europe the victorious and the defeated powers joined in combinations to keep the peace by preventing change either within or between countries. In Central and South America the rebellious colonies of Portugal and Spain asserted their independence. Here was a challenge to the postwar program of the European allies. And here, equally, was a challenge to the United States.

The Holy Alliance

A possible alternative for the United States was to align itself with the powers of Europe. The guiding spirit of the European united nations, Czar Alexander I of Russia, was eager to welcome the Americans. The decision was largely up to Secretary of State John Quincy Adams, who had had wide diplomatic experience, including that of American Minister to St. Petersburg. In his instructions of July 5, 1820, to Henry Middleton, then Minister to Russia, Adams expressed his views of the proper American policy with respect to the Czar's program.[7]

The present political system of Europe is founded upon the overthrow of that which had grown out of the French Revolution, and has assumed its shape from the body of treaties concluded at Vienna in 1814 and '15, at Paris, towards the close of the same year 1815, and at Aix la Chapelle in the autumn of 1818. Its general character is that of a compact between the five principal European powers, Austria, France, Great Britain, Prussia, and Russia, for the preservation of universal peace. These powers having then just emerged victorious from a long, portentous, and sanguinary struggle against the oppressive predominancy of one of them, under revolutionary sway, appear to have bent all their faculties to the substitution of a system which should preserve them from that evil: the preponderancy of one power by the subjugation, virtual if not nominal, of the rest . . .

The League of Peace, so far as it was a covenant of organized governments, has proved effectual to its purposes by an experience of five years. Its only interruption has been in this hemisphere, though between nations strictly European, by the invasion of the Portuguese on the territory claimed by Spain, but already lost to her, on the eastern shore of the Rio de la Plata. This aggression too the European alliance have undertaken to control, and in connection with it they have formed projects, hitherto abortive, of interposing in the revolutionary struggle

---

[7] Worthington C. Ford, ed., *The Writings of John Quincy Adams,* 7 vols. (New York, 1913–17), 7:46–51.

between Spain and her South American colonies. . . .

. . . The political system of the United States is . . . essentially extra-European. To stand in firm and cautious independence of all entanglement in the European system, has been a cardinal point of their policy under every administration of their government from the peace of 1783 to this day. If at the original adoption of their system there could have been any doubt of its justice or its wisdom, there can be none at this time. Every year's experience rivets it more deeply in the principles and opinions of the nation. Yet in proportion as the importance of the United States as one of the members of the general society of civilized nations increases in the eyes of the others, the difficulties of maintaining this system, and the temptations to depart from it increase and multiply with it. The Russian government has not only manifested an inclination that the United States should concur in the general principles of the European league, but a direct though inofficial application has been made by the present Russian minister here, that the United States should become formal parties to the Holy Alliance. It has been suggested as inducement to obtain their compliance, that this compact bound the parties to no specific engagement of any thing; that it was a pledge of mere principles; that its real as well as its professed purpose was merely the general preservation of peace, and it was intimated that if any question should arise between the United States and other governments of Europe, the Emperor Alexander, desirous of using his influence in their favor, would have a substantial motive and justification for interposing, if he could regard them as *his allies,* which as parties to the Holy Alliance they would be.

. . . It might perhaps be sufficient to answer that the organization of our government is such as not to admit of our acceding formally to that compact. But it may be added that the President, approving the general principles, and thoroughly convinced of the benevolent and virtuous motives which led to the conception and presided at the formation of this system by the Emperor Alexander, believes that the United States will more effectually contribute to the great and sublime objects for which it was concluded, by abstaining from a formal participation in it, than they could as stipulated members of it. As a general declaration of principles, disclaiming the impulses of vulgar ambition and unprincipled aggrandizement, and openly proclaiming the peculiarly christian maxims of mutual benevolence and brotherly love, to be binding upon the intercourse between nations no less than upon those of individuals, the United States, not only give their hearty assent to the articles of the Holy Alliance, but will be among the most earnest and conscientious in observing them. But independent of the prejudices which have been excited against this instrument in the public opinion, which time and an experience of its good effects will gradually wear away, it may be observed that for the repose of Europe as well as of America, the European and American political systems should be kept as separate and distinct from each other as possible. . . .

A New World "Counterpoise"

In the United States the leading champion of the Latin American cause was Henry Clay. He advocated not only prompt recognition of the rebellious colonies but also close relations with them to form an "American System" under the leadership of the United States—or what later was to be known as Pan-Americanism. In Congress Clay repeatedly made stirring orations in favor of establishing immediate relations with the United Provinces of Rio de la Plata and with other newly proclaimed republics to the south. The following two selections consist of parts of his speeches of March 24, 1818 and May 10, 1820.[8]

March 24, 1818

In the establishment of the independence of Spanish America, the United States have the deepest interest. I have no hesitation in asserting my firm belief, that there is no question in the foreign policy of this country which has ever arisen, or which I can conceive as ever occurring, in the decision of which we have had or can have so much at stake. This interest concerns our politics, our commerce, our navigation. There can not be a doubt that Spanish America, once independent, whatever may be the form of the governments established in its several parts, these governments will be animated by an American feeling, and guided by an American policy. They will obey the laws of the system of the New World, of which they will compose a part, in contradistinction to that of Europe. Without the influence of that vortex in Europe, the balance of power between its several parts, the preservation of which has so often drenched Europe in blood, America is sufficiently remote to comtemplate the new wars which are to afflict that quarter of the globe, as a calm, if not a cold and indifferent spectator. In relation to those wars the several parts of America will generally stand neutral. And as, during the period when they rage, it will be important that a liberal system of neutrality should be adopted and observed, all America will be interested in maintaining and enforcing such a system. The independence of Spanish America, then, is an interest of primary consideration. . . .

We are the natural head of the American family. I would not intermeddle in the affairs of Europe. We wisely keep aloof from their broils. . . .

May 10, 1820

It is in our power to create a system of which we shall be the center and in which all South America will act with us. In respect to commerce, we shall be most benefited; this

---

[8] Calvin Colton, ed., *Works of Henry Clay*, 7 vols. (New York, 1897), 5:145–55, 242–43.

country would become the place of deposit of the commerce of the world. Our citizens engaged in foreign trade at present are disheartened by the condition of that trade; they must take new channels for it, and none so advantageous could be found, as those which the trade with South America would afford. Let us take a prospective view of the growth of wealth, and increase of population of this country and South America. That country has now a population of upward of eighteen millions. The same activity in the principle of population will exist in that country as here. Twenty-five years hence it might be estimated at thirty-six millions; fifty years hence, at seventy-two millions. We now have a population of ten millions. From the character of our population, we must always take the lead in the prosecution of commerce and manufactures. Imagine the vast power of the two countries, and the value of the intercourse between them, when we shall have a population of forty millions, and they of seventy millions! In relation to South America, the people of the United States will occupy the same position as the people of New England do to the rest of the United States. Our enterprise, industry, and habits of economy, will give us the advantage in any competition which South America may sustain with us, and so forth.

But, however important our early recognition of the independence of the South might be to us, as respects our commercial and manufacturing interests, is there not another view of the subject, infinitely more gratifying? We shall become the center of a system which can constitute the rallying-point of human freedom against all the despotism of the old world. Does any man doubt the feelings of the South toward us? In spite of our coldness toward them, of the rigor of our laws, and the conduct of our officers, their hearts still turn toward us, as to their brethren, and I have no earthly doubt, if our government would take the lead and recognize them, they would become yet more anxious to imitate our institutions, and to secure to themselves and to their posterity the same freedom which we enjoy. . . .

4. AN ANGLO-AMERICAN DOCTRINE?

Continuing to urge immediate recognition, Clay in 1821 advocated a grand American combination to oppose the allied powers of Europe. He declared that "a sort of counterpoise of the Holy Alliance should be formed in the two Americas, in favor of national independence and liberty, to operate by the force of example and by moral influence, that here a rallying point and an asylum should exist for freemen and for freedmen." But Adams was no more eager to align the United States with the other American nations than with the Holy Alliance. He feared that Clay's policy might lead to war, and he believed that if this country were to enlist "under other banners than her own, were they even the banners of foreign independence," the eventual result would be a curtailment of freedom at home. As for recognizing Latin American independence, he desired to wait until that independence had been established beyond a shadow of a doubt. Not till 1822 did the United States begin to recognize the new nations to the south. At that, this country was the first to grant them recognition.

The powers of Europe, far from doing likewise, seemed on the verge of a combined movement to destroy the newly won independence of the Latin Americans. In the spring of 1823 the Holy Alliance (as the European concert usually was called), which already had acted to crush other national revolts, authorized the French to put down an uprising in Spain. After that, according to rumor, the Holy Alliance was going to send a French and Spanish army to deal with the Latin American revolutionists. Great Britain did not approve these plans. Though she had not yet recognized the new nations, she opposed the reestablishment of the old Spanish colonial system. To this extent, Great Britain and the United States appeared to have a common interest. Should the two countries, then, issue a joint statement of policy?

The Case of Cuba

Though Great Britain and the United States had common interests, they also had conflicting ones. Examples of the latter were to be found in regard to Cuba and, less importantly, Puerto Rico. These conflicts of interest the Secretary of State, John Quincy Adams, explained in a letter of April 28, 1823, to Hugh Nelson, the American Minister to Spain.[9]

Whatever may be the issue of this war, as between those two European powers [Spain and France], it may be taken for granted that the dominion of Spain upon the American continents, North and South, is irrecoverably gone. But the islands of Cuba and of Porto Rico still remain nominally and so far really dependent upon her, that she yet possesses the power of transferring her own dominion over them, together with the possession of them, to others. These islands, from their local position, are natural appendages to the North American continent; and one of them, Cuba, almost in sight of our shores, from a multitude of considerations has become an object of transcendent importance to the political and commercial interests of our Union. Its commanding position with reference to the Gulf of Mexico and the West India seas; the character of its population; its situation midway between our southern coast and the island of San Domingo; its safe and capacious harbor of the Havana, fronting a long line of our shores destitute of the same advantage; the nature of

---

[9] Ford, *The Writings of John Quincy Adams*, 7:372–79.

its productions and of its wants, furnishing the supplies and needing the returns of a commerce immensely profitable and mutually beneficial; give it an importance in the sum of our national interests, with which that of no other foreign territory can be compared, and little inferior to that which binds the different members of this Union together.

Such indeed are, between the interests of that island and of this country, the geographical, commercial, moral, and political relations, formed by nature, gathering in the process of time, and even now verging to maturity, that in looking forward to the probable course of events for the short period of half a century, it is scarcely possible to resist the conviction that the annexation of Cuba to our federal republic will be indispensable to the continuance and integrity of the Union itself. It is obvious, however, that for this event we are not yet prepared. Numerous and formidable objections to the extension of our territorial dominions beyond the sea present themselves to the first contemplation of the subject. Obstacles to the system of policy by which it alone can be compassed and maintained are to be foreseen and surmounted, both from at home and abroad. But there are laws of political as well as of physical gravitation; and if an apple severed by the tempest from its native tree cannot choose but fall to the ground, Cuba, forcibly disjoined from its own unnatural connection with Spain, and incapable of self-support, can gravitate only towards the North American Union, which by the same law of nature cannot cast her off from its bosom. . . .

Hitherto the wishes of this government have been that the connection between Cuba and Spain should continue as it has existed for several years. These wishes are known to the principal inhabitants of the island, and instructions, copies of which are now furnished you, were some months since transmitted to Mr. Forsyth, authorizing him in a suitable manner to communicate them to the Spanish government. These wishes still continue, so far as they can be indulged with a rational foresight of events beyond our control, but for which it is our duty to be prepared. If a government is to be imposed by foreign violence upon the Spanish nation, and the liberties which they have assisted by their constitution are to be crushed, it is neither to be expected nor desired that the people of Cuba, far from the reach of the oppressors of Spain, should submit to be governed by them. Should the cause of Spain herself issue more propitiously than from its present prospects can be anticipated, it is obvious that the trial through which she must pass at home, and the final loss of *all* her dominions on the American continents, will leave her unable to extend to the island of Cuba that protection necessary for its internal security and its outward defence.

Great Britain has formally withdrawn from the councils of the European Alliance in regard to Spain. She disapproves the war which they have sanctioned, and which is undertaken by France: and she avows her determination to defend Portugal against the application of the principles upon which the invasion of Spain raises its only pretence of right. To the war as it commences, she has declared her intention of remaining neutral; but the spirit of the British nation is so strongly and with so much unanimity pronounced against France, their interests are so deeply involved in the issue, their national resentments and jealousies will be so forcibly stimulated by the progress of the war, whatever it may be, that unless the conflict should be as short and the issue as decisive as that of which Italy was recently the scene, it is scarcely possible that the neutrality of Great Britain should be long maintained. The prospect is that she will be soon engaged on the side of Spain; but in making common cause with her, it is not to be supposed that she will yield her assistance upon principles altogether disinterested and gratuitous. As the price of her alliance the two remaining islands of Spain in the West Indies present objects no longer of much possible value or benefit to Spain, but of such importance to Great Britain, that is is impossible to suppose her indifferent to the acquisition of them.

The motives of Great Britain for desiring the possession of Cuba are so obvious, especially since the independence of Mexico, and the annexation of the Floridas to our Union; the internal condition of the island since the recent Spanish revolution, and the possibility of its continued dependence upon Spain, have been so precarious; the want of protection there; the power of affording it possessed by Great Britain, and the necessities of Spain to secure, by some equivalent, the support of Great Britain for herself; have formed a remarkable concurrence of predispositions to the transfer of Cuba; and during the last two years rumors have been multiplied, that it was already consummated. . . .

The transfer of Cuba to Great Britain would be an event unpropitious to the interests of this Union. This opinion is so generally entertained, that even the groundless rumors that it was about to be accomplished, which have spread abroad and are still teeming, may be traced to the deep and almost universal feeling of aversion to it, and to the alarm which the mere probability of its occurrence has stimulated. The question both of our right and our power to prevent it, if necessary, by force, already obtrudes itself upon our councils, and the administration is called upon, in the performance of its duties to the nation, at least to use all the means within its competency to guard against and forefend it.

England's Overture

In August 1823, the British Foreign Secretary, George Canning, proposed to the American Minister in London, Richard Rush, that their two governments act together to warn the Holy Alliance against intervention in Latin America, while agreeing not to take any Latin American territory for themselves. Earlier the United States repeatedly had taken the initiative in suggesting a joint policy in Latin American affairs. At the moment, however, Minister Rush lacked authorization to enter into an understanding with the Foreign Secretary. He would have gone ahead, anyhow, except for one thing: Canning's refusal to commit his government to immediate recognition of Latin American independence. As it was, Rush sent home for instructions, and President Monroe referred his communications to former presidents Jefferson and Madison for their advice. Monroe's letter of October 17, 1823, and Jefferson's reply of October 24 follow.[10]

Monroe

I transmit to you two despatches, which were receiv'd from Mr. Rush, while I was lately in Washington, which involve interests of the highest importance. They contain two letters from Mr. Canning, suggesting designs of the holy alliance against the Independence of So[uth] America, and proposing a co-operation between G. Britain and the U. States in support of it, against the members of that alliance. The project aims in the first instance at a mere expression of opinion, somewhat in the abstract, but which it is expected by Mr. Canning will have a great political effect, by defeating the combination. By Mr. Rush's answers, which are also inclosed, you will see the light in which he views the subject, and the extent to which he may have gone. Many important considerations are involved in this proposition. 1st Shall we entangle ourselves, at all, in European politicks and wars on the side of any power, against others, presuming that a concert by agreement, of the kind proposed, may lead to that result? 2d If a case can exist in which a sound maxim may and ought to be departed from, is not the present instance precisely that case? 3d Has not the epoch arriv'd when G. Britain must take her stand either on the side of the monarchs of Europe or the U. States, and in consequence either in favor of Despotism or of liberty, and may it not be presum'd that, aware of necessity, her government has seiz'd on the present occurrence as that which it deems the most suitable to announce and mark the commenc'ment of that career.

My own impression is that we ought to meet the proposal of the British govt., and to make it known that we would view an interference on the part of the European powers, and especially an attack on the Colonies by them, as an attack on ourselves, presuming that if they succeeded with them, they would extend it to us. I am sensible however of the extent and difficulty of the question, and shall be happy to have yours and Mr. Madison's opinions on it. I do not wish to trouble either of you with small objects, but the present one is vital, involving the high interests for which we have so long and so faithfully and harmoniously, contended together. Be so kind as to inclose to him the despatches, with an intimation of the motive.

Jefferson

The question presented by the letters you have sent me, is the most momentous which has ever been

---

[10] *American Historical Review* (1901–2), 7:684–85; T. J. Randolph, *Memoir, Correspondence, and Miscellanies from the Papers of Thomas Jefferson*, 4 vols. (Charlottesville, Va., 1829), 4:381–83.

offered to my contemplation since that of Independence. That made us a nation, this sets our compass and points the course which we are to steer through the ocean of time opening on us. And never could we embark on it under circumstances more auspicious. Our first and fundamental maxim should be, never to entangle ourselves in the broils of Europe. Our second, never to suffer Europe to intermeddle with cis-Atlantic affairs. America, North and South, has a set of interests distinct from those of Europe, and peculiarly her own. She should therefore have a system of her own, separate and apart from that of Europe. While the last is laboring to become the domicile of despotism, our endeavor should surely be to make our hemisphere that of freedom. One nation, most of all, could disturb us in this pursuit; she now offers to lead, aid, and accompany us in it. By acceding to her proposition, we detach her from the band of despots, bring her mighty weight into the scale of free government, and emancipate a continent at one stroke, which might otherwise linger in doubt and difficulty. Great Britain is the nation which can do us the most harm of any one, or all on earth; and with her on our side we need not fear the whole world. With her, then, we should most sedulously cherish a cordial friendship; and nothing would tend more to knit our affections than to be fighting once more, side by side, in the same cause. Not that I would purchase even her amity at the price of taking part in her wars. But the war in which the present proposition might engage us, should that be its consequence, is not her war, but ours. Its object is to introduce and establish the American system, of keeping out of our land all foreign powers, of never permitting those of Europe to intermeddle with the affairs of our nations. It is to maintain our own principle, not to depart from it. And if, to facilitate this, we can effect a division in the body of the European powers, and draw over to our side its most powerful member, surely we should do it. But I am clearly of Mr. Canning's opinion, that it will prevent instead of provoking war. With Great Britain withdrawn from their scale and shifted into that of our two continents, all Europe combined would not undertake such a war. For how would they propose to get at either enemy without superior fleets? Nor is the occasion to be slighted, which this proposition offers, of declaring our protest against the atrocious violations of the rights of nations, by the interference of any one in the internal affairs of another, so flagitiously begun by Buonaparte, and now continued by the equally lawless Alliance, calling itself Holy.

But we have first to ask ourselves a question. Do we wish to acquire to our own confederacy any one or more of the Spanish provinces? I candidly confess, that I have ever looked on Cuba as the most interesting addition which could ever be made to our system of States. The control which, with Florida Point, this island would give us over the Gulf of Mexico, and the countries and isthmus bordering on it, as well as all those whose waters flow into it, would fill up the measure of our political wellbeing. Yet, as I am sensible that this can never be obtained, even with her own consent, but by war; and its independence, which is our second interest, (and especially its independence of England), can be secured without it, I have no hesitation in abandoning my first wish to future chances, and accepting its independence, with peace and the friendship of England, rather than its association, at the expense of war and her enmity.

No Cock-boat

Madison agreed with Jefferson as to the advisability of accepting Canning's offer. Most of Monroe's cabinet members acquiesced. One of them strongly dissented, as Secretary of State Adams recorded in his diary on November 7, 1823.[11]

Cabinet meeting at the President's from half-past one till four. Mr. Calhoun, Secretary of War, and Mr. Southard, Secretary of the Navy, present. The subject for consideration was, the confidential proposals of the British Secretary of State, George Canning, to R. Rush, and the correspondence between them relating to the projects of the Holy Alliance upon South America. There was much conversation, without coming to any definite point. The object of Canning appears to have been to obtain some public pledge from the Government of the United States, ostensibly against the forcible interference of the Holy Alliance between Spain and South America; but really or especially against the acquisition to the United States themselves of any part of the Spanish-American possessions.

Mr. Calhoun inclined to giving a discretionary power to Mr. Rush to join in a declaration against the interference of the Holy Allies, if necessary, even if it should pledge us not to take Cuba or the province of Texas; because the power of Great Britain being greater than ours to *seize* upon them, we should get the advantage of obtaining from her the same declaration we should make ourselves.

I thought the cases not parallel. We have no intention of seizing either Texas or Cuba. But the inhabitants of either or both may exercise their primitive rights, and solicit a union with us. They will certainly do no such thing to Great Britain. By joining with her, therefore, in her proposed declaration, we give her a substantial and perhaps inconvenient pledge against ourselves, and really obtain nothing in return. Without entering now into the enquiry of the expediency of our annexing Texas or Cuba to our Union, we should at least keep ourselves free to act as emergencies may arise, and not tie ourselves down to any principle which might immediately afterwards be brought to bear against ourselves.

---

[11] C. F. Adams, ed., *Memoirs of John Quincy Adams*, 12 vols. (Philadelphia, 1874–77), 6:177–79.

... It would be more candid, as well as more dignified, to avow our principles explicitly to Russia and France, than to come in as a cockboat in the wake of the British man-of-war.

Monroe's Message

Canning's overture to Rush led eventually to Monroe's famous pronouncement on foreign policy in his message to Congress on December 2, 1823. It was a unilateral statement, but it did not necessarily preclude a later joint statement with England (though actually no such combined declaration did follow). The immediate background was the apparent threat of the Holy Alliance to recover for Spain her lost American colonies. But there were also other considerations in the background. One of these, as has been seen, was interest in Cuba; another was a regard for the Northwest, where Russian and British imperial ambitions seemed to menace the future expansion of the United States; and still another was the concern of many Americans for the cause of the Greeks, who were fighting for their independence against the Turks. Following are several passages on these and other topics of foreign affairs taken from Monroe's message (some but not all of which comprise what was afterwards to be known as the Monroe Doctrine).[12]

At the proposal of the Russian Imperial Government, made through the minister of the Emperor residing here, a full power and instructions have been transmitted to the minister of the United States at St. Petersburg to arrange by amicable negotiation the respective rights and interests of the two nations on the northwest coast of this continent. A similar proposal had been made by His Imperial Majesty to the Government of Great Britain, which has likewise been acceded to. The Government of the United States has been desirous by this friendly proceeding of manifesting the great value which they have invariably attached to the friendship of the Emperor and their solicitude to cultivate the best understanding with his Government. In the discussions to which this interest has given rise and in the arrangements by which they may terminate the occasion has been judged proper for asserting, as a principle in which the rights and interests of the United States are involved, that the American continents, by the free and independent condition which they have assumed and maintain, are henceforth not to be considered as subjects for future colonization by any European powers. . . .

A strong hope has been long entertained, founded on the heroic struggle of the Greeks, that they would succeed in their contest and resume their equal station among the nations of the earth. It is believed that the whole civilized world take a deep interest in their welfare.

---

[12] *Messages and Papers of the Presidents*, 2:207–10, 217–19.

Although no power has declared in their favor, yet none, according to our information, has taken part against them. Their cause and their name have protected them from dangers which might ere this have overwhelmed any other people. The ordinary calculations of interest and of acquisition with a view to aggrandizement, which mingles so much in the transactions of nations, seem to have had no effect in regard to them. From the facts which have come to our knowledge there is good cause to believe that their enemy has lost forever all dominion over them; that Greece will become again an independent nation. That she may obtain that rank is the object of our most ardent wishes.

. . . In the wars of the European powers in matters relating to themselves we have never taken any part, nor does it comport with our policy so to do. It is only when our rights are invaded or seriously menaced that we resent injuries or make preparation for our defense. With the movements in this hemisphere we are of necessity more immediately connected, and by causes which must be obvious to all enlightened and impartial observers. The political system of the allied powers is essentially different in this respect from that of America. This difference proceeds from that which exists in their respective Governments; and to the defense of our own, which has been achieved by the loss of so much blood and treasure, and matured by the wisdom of their most enlightened citizens, and under which we have enjoyed unexampled felicity, this whole nation is devoted. We owe it, therefore, to candor and to the amicable relations existing between the United States and those powers to declare that we should consider any attempt on their part to extend their system to any portion of this hemisphere as dangerous to our peace and safety. With the existing colonies or dependencies of any European power we have not interfered and shall not interfere. But with the Governments who have declared their independence and maintained it, and whose independence we have, on great consideration and on just principles, acknowledged, we could not view any interposition for the purpose of oppressing them, or controlling in any other manner their destiny, by any European power in any other light than as the manifestation of an unfriendly disposition toward the United States. In the war between those new Governments and Spain we declared our neutrality at the time of their recognition, and to this we have adhered, and shall continue to adhere, provided no change shall occur which, in the judgment of the competent authorities of this Government, shall make a corresponding change on the part of the United States indispensable to their security.

The late events in Spain and Portugal shew that Europe is still unsettled. Of this important fact no stronger proof can be adduced than that the allied powers should have thought it proper, on any principle satisfactory to themselves, to have interposed by force in the internal concerns of Spain. To what extent such interposition may be carried, on the same principle, is a question in which all independent powers whose governments differ from theirs are interested, even those most remote, and surely none more so than the United States. Our policy in regard to Europe, which was adopted at an early stage of the wars which have so long agitated that quarter of the globe, nevertheless remains the same, which is, not to interfere in the internal concerns of any of its powers; to consider the government *de facto* as the legitimate government for us; to cultivate friendly relations with it, and to preserve those relations by a frank, firm, and manly policy, meeting in all instances the just claims of every power, submitting to injuries from none. But in regard to these continents circumstances are eminently and conspicuously different. It is impossible that the allied powers should extend their political system to any portion of either continent without endangering our peace and happiness; nor can anyone believe that our southern brethren, if left to themselves, would adopt it of their own accord. It is equally impossible, therefore, that we should behold such interposition in any form with indifference. If we look to the comparative strength and resources of Spain and those new Governments, and their distance from each other, it must be obvious that she can never subdue them. It is still the true policy of the United States to leave the parties to themselves, in the hope that other powers will pursue the same course.

5. CRUSADE FOR FREEDOM?

A "Greek fever" infected many Americans after the start of the Greek war for independence in 1821, and the fever reached its peak late in 1823, at the time of Monroe's famous message to Congress. Atrocity stories (the Turks, it was said, gathered human ears by the bushel) stimulated the sympathies of Americans, who proceeded to aid the Hellenic cause with sermons, poems, bazaars, mass meetings, fund drives, and petitions to Congress, where several bills and resolutions on the subject were introduced. While Monroe was preparing his message, various friends of Greece, including Madison, urged him to include a statement looking toward American intervention on behalf of the Greeks. Adams opposed this, and Monroe finally included only a relatively mild expression of sympathy, as quoted in the preceding selection. This passage in the presidential message touched off a long and heated Congressional debate. Nothing came of it. But if the Greek question as such was relatively unimportant, the issues and arguments which it uncovered were of basic and enduring significance. More than a century later, parts of some of the speeches were still to sound surprisingly up-to-date.

American Interest in the Greek Cause

In the United States the leading advocate of Greek independence was Edward Everett, the Massachusetts scholar, orator, and politician. Everett interested his friend Daniel Webster, now a Congressman from Massachusetts, but

Webster had to be a little cautious in what he said, since some of the merchants among his constituents feared that to antagonize the Turkish Empire might cost them their Smyrna trade. Nevertheless, about a week after Monroe's message, Webster did introduce in the House the following resolution: "That provision ought to be made by law, for defraying the expense incident to the appointment of an Agent or Commissioner to Greece, whenever the President shall deem it expedient to make such appointment." Here was a proposal for the House to use its power of appropriation as a means of influencing the administration in its conduct of foreign affairs. On January 19, 1824, Webster rose in the House to make a speech in support of his resolution. He began, in his artfully eloquent way, by pointing to the Greek columns in the House chamber as evidence of the influence of Greek civilization to be seen on every hand. Then, coming to the resolution itself, he proceeded on the assumption that the Holy Alliance was about to assist the Turks in suppressing the Greek rebellion.[13]

It may be easy to call this resolution *Quixotic*, the emanation of a crusading or propagandist spirit. All this, and more, may be readily said; but all this, and more, will not be allowed to fix a character upon this proceeding, until that is proved which it takes for granted. Let it first be shown that in this question there is nothing which can affect the interest, the character, or the duty of this country. Let it be proved that we are not called upon, by either of these considerations, to express an opinion on the subject to which the resolution relates. Let this be proved, and then it will indeed be made out that neither ought this resolution to pass, nor ought the subject of it to have been mentioned in the communication of the President to us. But, in my opinion, this cannot be shown. . . .

It may be required of me to show what interest *we* have in resisting this new system. What is it to *us*, it may be asked, upon what principles, or what pretences, the European governments assert a right of interfering in the affairs of their neighbors? The thunder, it may be said, rolls at a distance. The wide Atlantic is between us and danger; and, however others may suffer, *we* shall remain safe.

I think it is a sufficient answer to this to say that we are one of the nations of the earth; that we have an interest, therefore, in the preservation of that system of national law and national intercourse which has heretofore subsisted, so beneficially for all. Our system of government, it should be remembered, is throughout, founded on principles utterly hostile to the new code; and if we remain undisturbed by its operation, we shall owe our security either to our situation or our spirit. The enterprising character of the age, our own active, commercial spirit, the great increase which has taken place in the intercourse among civilized and commerical states, have necessarily connected us with other nations, and given us a high concern in the preservation of those salutary

---

[13] *Writings and Speeches of Webster*, 5:62, 75–80.

principles upon which that intercourse is founded. We have as clear an interest in international laws as individuals have in the laws of society.

But apart from the soundness of the policy, on the ground of direct interest, we have, Sir, a duty connected with this subject, which I trust we are willing to perform. What do *we* not owe to the cause of civil and religious liberty? to the principle of lawful resistance? to the principle that society has a right to partake in its own government? As the leading republic of the world, living and breathing in these principles, and advanced, by their operation, with unequalled rapidity in our career, shall we give *our* consent to bring them into disrepute and disgrace? It is neither ostentation nor boasting to say that there lies before this country, in immediate prospect, a great extent and height of power. We are borne along towards this, without effort, and not always with a full knowledge of the rapidity of our own motion. Circumstances which never combined before have cooperated in our favor, and a mighty current is setting us forward which we could not resist even if we would, and which, while we would stop to make an observation, and take the sun, has set us, at the end of the operation, far in advance of the place where we commenced it. Does it not become us, then, is it not a duty imposed on us, to give our weight to the side of liberty and justice, to let mankind know that we are not tired of our own institutions, and to protest against the asserted power of altering at pleasure the law of the civilized world?

But whatever we do in this respect, it becomes us to do upon clear and consistent principles. There is an important topic in the [President's] message to which I have yet hardly alluded. I mean the rumored combination of the European Continental sovereigns against the newly established free states of South America. Whatever position this government may take on that subject, I trust it will be one which can be defended on known and acknowledged grounds of right. The near approach or the remote distance of the danger may affect policy, but cannot change principle. The same reason that would authorize us to protest against unwarrantable combinations to interfere between Spain and her former colonies, would authorize us equally to protest if the same combination were directed against the smallest state in Europe, although our duty to ourselves, our policy, and wisdom, might indicate very different courses as fit to be pursued by us in the two cases. We shall not, I trust, act upon the notion of dividing the world with the Holy Alliance, and complain of nothing done by them in their hemisphere if they will not interfere with ours. At least this would not be such a course of policy as I could recommend or support. We have not offended, and I hope we do not intend to offend, in regard to South America, against any principle of national independence or of public law. We have done nothing, we shall do nothing, that we need to hush up or to compromise by forbearing to express our sympathy for the cause of the Greeks, or our opinion of the course which other governments have adopted in regard to them.

It may, in the next place, be

foundations of foreign policy: beginning the great debate

asked, perhaps, Supposing all this to be true, what can *we* do? Are we to go to war? Are we to interfere in the Greek cause, or any other European cause? Are we to endanger our pacific relations? No, certainly not. What, then, the question recurs, remains for us? If we will not endanger our own peace, if we will neither furnish armies nor navies to the cause which we think the just one, what is there within our power?

Sir, this reasoning mistakes the age. The time has been, indeed, when fleets, and armies, and subsidies, were the principal reliances even in the best cause. But, happily for mankind, a great change has taken place in this respect. Moral causes come into consideration, in proportion as the progress of knowledge is advanced; and the public opinion of the civilized world is rapidly gaining an ascendency over mere brutal force. It is already able to oppose the most formidable obstruction to the progress of injustice and oppression; and as it grows more intelligent and more intense, it will be more and more formidable. It may be silenced by military power, but it cannot be conquered. . . .

Conquest and subjugation, as known among European states, are inadequate modes of expression by which to denote the dominion of the Turks. A conquest in the civilized world is generally no more than an acquisition of a new dominion to the conquering country. It does not imply a never-ending bondage imposed upon the conquered, a perpetual mark—an opprobrious distinction between them and their masters; a bitter and unending persecution of their religion; an habitual violation of their rights of person and property, and the unrestrained indulgence towards them of every passion which belongs to the character of a barbarous soldiery. Yet such is the state of Greece. The Ottoman power over them, obtained originally by the sword, is constantly preserved by the same means. Wherever it exists, it is a mere military power. The religious and civil code of the state being both fixed in the Koran, and equally the object of an ignorant and furious faith, have been found equally incapable of change. "The Turk," it has been said, "has been *encamped* in Europe for four centuries." He has hardly any more participation in European manners, knowledge, and arts, than when he crossed the Bosphorus. . . . In short, the Christian subjects of the Sublime Porte feel daily all the miseries which flow from despotism, from anarchy, from slavery, and from religious persecution. . . . In the whole world, Sir, there is no such oppression felt as by the Christian Greeks. . . . The world has no such misery to show; there is no case in which Christian communities can be called upon with such emphasis of appeal.

Meddle Not with Greece

Secretary of State Adams believed that Webster's real aim was a political one—to embarrass the administration. Adams consulted with Representative Joel R. Poinsett, of South Carolina, and primed him for a reply to Webster. On

January 20, 1824 Poinsett offered, as a substitute for Webster's resolution, the following: "That this House view with deep interest the heroic struggle of the Greeks to elevate themselves to the rank of a free and independent nation; and unite with the President in the sentiments he has expressed in their favor: in sympathy for their sufferings, in interest in their welfare, and in ardent wishes for their success." Four days later John Randolph of Virginia denounced both Webster's and Poinsett's resolutions. On January 26, Alexander Smyth, also of Virginia, spoke up to deprecate the Hellenic enthusiasm in the United States by saying, among other things, that the present inhabitants of the Morea were savages quite unlike the classical Greeks and that the Turks were actually more civilized. In the end Congress passed no resolution on Greece. Parts of the remarks of Poinsett, Randolph, and Smyth follow.[14]

Poinsett

Our first and most important duty is to maintain peace, whenever that can be done consistently with the honor and safety of the nation; and we ought to be slow to adopt any measure which might involve us in a war, except where those great interests are concerned. The gentleman [Webster] disclaims any such intention. He does not believe that we run the slightest risk, by adopting the resolution on your table. He considers it as a pacific measure, and relies entirely upon the discretion of the President, to accept or reject our recommendation, as the interests of the country may require. The object of passing such a resolution can only be to give an impulse to the Executive and to induce him, by an expression of the opinion of this House, to send a commission to Greece. I have as great a reliance upon the discretion of the Executive as the gentleman from Massachusetts. I believe that he would resist the suggestion of this House in favor of any measure, if he thought the public interest required him to do so. But, unless we wish and expect him to act upon our recommendation, we ought not to throw upon him, alone, the responsibility of resisting the strong public feeling which has been excited on this subject. The question for us to consider appears to me to be whether, if the power rested with us, we would exercise it to this extent. I think we could not do so without incurring some risk of involving the country in a war foreign to its interests. Let us suppose that these commissioners were to fall into the hands of the Turks; an event by no means impossible, in the present state of Greece —what would be their fate? The Porte has not been remarkable for its strict observance of the laws of nations, in its intercourse with the Powers of Europe; and it is not probable that such a Court would be very scrupulous in its conduct towards a nation whose flag it has never acknowledged. Or let us imagine, what is much more probable, that on the rumor of our having taken any measure in favor of Greece, the barbarous and infuri-

---

[14] *Annals of Congress*, 18th Cong., 1st Sess., Columns 1105–7, 1182–88, 1207–12.

ated Janissaries at Smyrna were to assassinate our Consul and fellow-citizens residing there; might not a war grow out of such acts? . . .

It appears to me that in the consideration of this [Greek] question we have been misled by comparing this revolution with that of Spanish America. And I have heard it argued that, as we sent commissioners to Buenos Ayres without rousing the jealousy of any nation, and recognized the independence of those Governments without exciting the hostility of Spain, we may do the same in relation to Greece without offending any nation in Europe.

Independently of the different attitude it becomes us to assume towards America, there is no similarity in the two cases. When we adopted the first measure, Buenos Ayres had been independent *de facto* for more than eight years, and Spain had not, during the whole of that period, made the slightest effort to recover possession of that country. When we recognised the independence of the American Governments south of us, they were all free, from the Sabine to the La Plata. The tide could not be rolled back; but, in whatever light Spain may have regarded our conduct on those occasions, the situation of the internal concerns of that country prevented any manifestation of its resentment. No, sir; it is to Europe that we must look for a case parallel to that of Greece. Let us suppose that the Italian states had made an attempt to shake off the iron yoke of Austria, would there be any doubt as to the course of policy this country ought to pursue in that case? Or if Poland were again to make a desperate effort to recover its liberties, and to re-establish its political existence, that gallant nation would have a claim to our sympathies. Yet I apprehend we should hesitate before we took any step which might offend the Emperor of Russia. Is there a country on earth in whose fate we feel a deeper interest than that of Ireland? A braver or more generous nation does not exist. Her exiled patriots have taken refuge here, and are among our most useful and distinguished citizens. They are identified with us, and the land which gave them birth must always inspire us with the warmest interest. But, if the Irish were to make a general effort to separate themselves from England, we should pause before we adopted a measure which might be interpreted by Great Britain as an interference with her domestic policy. And yet the Turks are more regardless of the laws of nations, more violent in character, and more reckless of consequences, than any Power in Europe.

Randolph

It is with serious concern and alarm . . . that I have heard doctrines broached in this debate, fraught with consequences more disastrous to the best interest of this people, than any that I ever heard advanced during the five and twenty years since I have been honored with a seat on this floor. They imply, to my apprehension, a total and fundamental change of the policy pursued by this Government *ab urbe condita* —from the foundation of the Republic to the present day. Are we, sir, to go on a crusade, in another hemisphere, for the propagation of two objects as dear and delightful to my heart as to that of any gentleman in this or in any other assembly—Liberty and Religion—and in the name of those holy words—by this powerful spell, is this nation to be conjured and beguiled out of the highway of Heaven—out of its present comparatively happy state, into all the disastrous conflicts arising from the policy of European Powers, with all the consequences which flow from them? Liberty and Religion, sir! Things that are yet dear, in spite of all the mischief that has been perpetrated in their name. . . .

Sir, I am afraid that, along with some most excellent attributes and qualities—the love of liberty, jury trial, the writ of habeas corpus, and all the blessings of free government, that we have derived from our Anglo-Saxon ancestors, we have got not a little of their John Bull or rather John Bull Dog Spirit—their readiness to fight for anybody, and on any occasion. Sir, England has been for centuries the game cock of Europe. It is impossible to specify the wars in which she has been engaged for contrary purposes; and she will, with great pleasure, see us take off her shoulders the labor of preserving the balance of power. We find her fighting, now, for the Queen of Hungary—then, for her inveterate foe, the King of Prussia—now at war for the restoration of the Bourbons—and now on the eve of war with them for the liberties of Spain. These lines on the subject were never more applicable than they have now become—

"Now Europe's balanced—neither
    side prevails;
For nothing's left in either of the
    scales."

If we pursue the same policy, we must travel the same road, and endure the same burdens, under which England now groans. . . .

Let us adhere to the policy laid down by the second as well as the first founder of our Republic—by him who was the Camillus, as well as the Romulus, of the infant state;—to the policy of peace, commerce, and honest friendship with all nations, entangling alliances with none: for to entangling alliances we must come, if you once embark in projects such as this.

Smyth

We say to the Allies that any attempt on their part to extend their system to any portion of this hemisphere, we shall consider as dangerous to our peace and safety. And is not the extension of our system to their hemisphere equally dangerous to their peace and safety? We say that with the existing colonies or dependencies of any European Power we have not interfered and shall not interfere. How can we then interfere with the Morea, a province of Turkey, without a violation of our solemn declaration? Sir, by this proceeding, you will make the declaration of the President, as to the future course of policy to be observed by this Government, a falsehood. . . .

You profess to interfere on behalf of the Greeks for liberty and religion. What have you to do with the liberty of any people, except the people you govern, unless the subjection of a neighboring foreign people endangers your safety? You have nothing to do with religion, even here, and why should you meddle with it elsewhere? In a treaty made with one of those Turkish nations, during the Administration of Mr. Adams, it was explicitly and truly declared that the Government of the United States is in no respect founded on religion. The Turk may become a citizen of the United States, and have his mosque in our country, as well as the Jew his synagogue. . . .

Sir, the present is a time of imminent danger and, therefore, a time for caution. Remember the words of WASHINGTON: "Why quit your own, to stand on foreign ground?" Meddle not with Greece. . . .

The cause of freedom, the hope of mankind, depends on the ultimate success of the hitherto successful experiment in the science of government, making in the United States. When we consider the importance of the interests confided to us, it must appear unpardonable wantonly to hazard the success of that experiment. If there be a mode of destroying civil liberty, it is by leading this Government into unnecessary wars.

CONCLUSION

The words of Washington were quoted against interfering on behalf of Greece; they were also against close cooperation with Latin America. In 1825 John Quincy Adams, then President, appointed two delegates to attend a conference of all the American nations at Panama. His Jacksonian opponents in Congress objected on the grounds that the conference might lead to an entangling alliance. American participation in such a conference, said Representative James Buchanan, of Pennsylvania, would mean disregarding "the farewell address of the man who was first in war, first in peace, and first in the hearts of his countrymen." Finally the two American delegates prepared to leave for Panama, but the long debate had delayed their departure. One died before he could get there, and the other arrived after the conference was over. Though the United States thus had nothing to do with this first effort at Pan-American cooperation, the time eventually came when Pan-Americanism was generally regarded as a corollary of the Monroe Doctrine. Since the 1880s, when Secretary of State James G. Blaine initiated a still-continuing series of Pan-American conferences, the United States has taken the lead in promoting the solidarity of the Western Hemisphere.

The idea of noninterference in the internal concerns of Europe (originally a part of the Monroe Doctrine) afterwards was viewed as a separate policy, the policy of "isolation." There were ample reasons for the comparative isolation of the United States during the century between the Napoleonic wars and the First World War. Americans were preoccupied with their own problems—the westward movement, the sectional controversy, the growth of industry—and they could concentrate upon these problems with little fear of foreign danger because of the general peace and the balance of power which prevailed throughout the world. With the rise of Germany, Japan, and later Soviet Russia and Red China, Americans faced in a more urgent form than ever the question of participating in alliances and strengthening the forces of freedom in other lands.

In the twentieth century, as in the nineteenth, every great discussion of American foreign policy had to take into account the old ideal of a United States detached politically from the rest of the world and free to work out its own special destiny. Of course, the actual policies were not made solely on the basis of abstract principles. Policy making was influenced by the pressures of interest groups, the maneuverings of political parties, the ambitions of individual men, and the necessities of military and naval strategy. Yet the terms in which foreign policy could be discussed had been firmly fixed by the end of the first fifty years of independence. Thereafter the proponents of any course of diplomacy felt called upon to show not only that their program would meet the immediate needs of the nation but also that it conformed to the principles laid down by Washington and Monroe—as if the Farewell Address and the Monroe Doctrine formed a kind of Constitution for Foreign Affairs, every step inconsistent therewith being, so to speak, "unconstitutional." Only in recent years, since the Second World War, have the American people shown a strong disposition to abandon the traditional approach to foreign policy. Even so, the words of Washington are still quoted, and quotable.

7 *CHARLES G. SELLERS, JR.*

jacksonian democracy

The personality of Andrew Jackson, swashbuckling frontiersman, Indian fighter, military hero, and President, is one which Americans have never been able to view with calm detachment. Idolized or hated, praised or excoriated, he has been a figure of compelling interest from his day to our own. But Jackson was more than a fascinating personality. The political movement he led and the political philosophy he symbolized have profoundly influenced our national development. Yet the experts still disagree about the nature and significance of what is called Jacksonian Democracy.

The surging demand for thoroughgoing popular control of state and national governments that swept over the country in the 1820s and 1830s is often chosen as the dominating feature of Jacksonian Democracy. The term can also mean the philosophy of popular virtue and sovereignty that developed simultaneously, with related manifestations in the areas of literature, religion, education, and humanitarian reform. It can mean the social and political instrumentalities—labor unions, national parties, political conventions, partisan newspapers, the spoils system—that arose to implement the democratic impulse. Finally Jacksonian Democracy can mean Jackson's own Democratic party and its program of public policy.

The following selections focus on these closely interrelated phenomena from several points of view. The first section looks at the movement for democracy, its social basis, the philosophy that undergirded it, and the arguments of its supporters and critics. The second section seeks to discover what kind of government and society the Jacksonians wanted and how they proposed to achieve it, by examining the most important segment of their program—monetary and banking policy. Finally the reader will have a chance to weigh the conflicting views recently advanced by historians on the nature and meaning of Jacksonian Democracy.

1. POLITICAL DEMOCRACY

Though the early republic was democratic in theory, in practice the will of the great body of the people was rarely registered in the actions of government. Most of the original states required some property qualification for voting and holding office, while the legislatures were usually arranged so that the older and wealthier sections had disproportionate strength. More important was the fact that the people tacitly left public affairs to the educated and well-to-do. Local governments were commonly in the hands of small groups of prominent citizens, and these county or town rings determined who went to the legislatures. The ambitious politician first curried favor with the established local leaders rather than with the voters, and then sought national promotion by faithful service to the "Virginia Dynasty," which chose the Presidents at quadrennial Congressional caucuses. All this was natural enough when the influence of government was little felt by the people generally. Widespread interest in state or national issues was rare, and elections ordinarily served merely to ratify the decisions of the entrenched politicians, or occasionally to decide between rival factions of the dominant group.

The revolutionary transformation that overtook this comfortable political system in the 1820s and 1830s was rooted in certain long-term tendencies in the social character and attitudes of the American people. More immediately, however, the political ferment arose from economic distress. The Panic of 1819 had ushered in the country's first severe nationwide depression and fostered an abrupt reaction against the mood of generous nationalism that had followed the War of 1812. As sections and interest groups competed bitterly for relief at the hands of government in the early 1820s, the states began to experience a surging demand for thoroughgoing political democracy.

Popular agitation at the national level was directed against "King Caucus." In the Presidential campaign of 1824, Andrew Jackson—a national hero by virtue of his victory over the British at New Orleans—made himself the symbol of this democratic ferment by astutely identifying his candidacy with the fight against the caucus. Receiving the largest vote in a field of four candidates, he became a martyr to democracy when the House of Representatives chose John Quincy Adams. Though Adams' inauguration seemed to spell complete victory for the nationalistic tendencies that had come to dominate Jefferson's Republican party, the nationalists were doomed to disappointment. The campaign for 1828 began immediately, as a four-year struggle to vindicate popular rule, and the Adams administration was subjected to an implacable opposition that did not rest until it had ousted Adams from the Presidency and put Andrew Jackson in his place.

The Ballot Demanded

One of the bitterest struggles between the old order and the new occurred in the Virginia constitutional convention of 1829. The reformers directed their fire against the provisions of the old constitution regulating qualifications for voting and the apportionment of representation. Only freeholders, or landowners, were allowed to vote, which according to Thomas Jefferson disfranchised a majority of the adult white males. An even greater grievance was the fact that each county had the same number of representatives in the legislature. The small counties of the wealthy, slaveholding eastern section had only grudgingly allowed the creation of new counties for the small farmers of the west, with the result that a white population of 362,000 east of the Blue Ridge had 130 representatives, while 319,000 white persons west of the mountains had only 68. And the western population would soon outstrip the eastern.

The widespread exasperation with the suffrage requirement was forcefully expressed in a memorial to the convention on October 13, 1829, from the nonfreeholders of Richmond.[1]

Your memorialists, as their designation imports, belong to that class of citizens, who, not having the good fortune to possess a certain portion of land, are, for that cause only, debarred from the enjoyment of the right of suffrage. . . . Comprising a very large part, probably a majority of the male citizens of mature age, they have been passed by, like aliens or slaves, as if destitute of interest, or unworthy of a voice, in measures involving their future political destiny: whilst the freeholders, sole possessors, under the existing Constitution, of the elective franchise, have, upon the strength of that possession alone, asserted and maintained in themselves, the exclusive power of new-modelling the fundamental laws of the State: in other words, have seized upon the sovereign authority. . . .

The object, it is presumed, meant to be attained, was, so far as practicable, to admit the meritorious, and reject the unworthy. And had this object really been attained, what-

---

[1] *Proceedings and Debates of the Virginia State Convention of 1829–30* (Richmond, 1830), 25–28.

ever opinions might prevail as to the mere right, not a murmur probably would have been heard. Surely it were much to be desired that every citizen should be qualified for the proper exercise of all his rights, and the due performance of all his duties. But the same qualifications that entitle him to assume the management of his private affairs, and to claim all other privileges of citizenship, equally entitle him, in the judgment of your memorialists, to be entrusted with this, the dearest of all his privileges, the most important of all his concerns. But if otherwise, still they cannot discern in the possession of land any evidence of peculiar merit, or superior title. To ascribe to a landed possession, moral or intellectual endowments, would truly be regarded as ludicrous, were it not for the gravity with which the proposition is maintained, and still more for the grave consequences flowing from it. Such possession no more proves him who has it, wiser or better, than it proves him taller or stronger, than him who has it not. That cannot be a fit criterion for the exercise of any right, the possession of which does not indicate the existence, or the want of it the absence, of any essential qualification. . . .

But, it is said, yield them this right, and they will abuse it: property, that is, landed property, will be rendered insecure, or at least overburdened, by those who possess it not. The freeholders, on the contrary, can pass no law to the injury of any other class, which will not more injuriously affect themselves. The alarm is sounded too, of danger from large manufacturing institutions, where one corrupt individual may sway the corrupt votes of thousands. It were a vain task to attempt to meet all the flimsy pretexts urged, to allay all the apprehensions felt or feigned by the enemies of a just and liberal policy. . . . No community can exist, no representative body be formed, in which some one division of persons or section of country, or some two or more combined, may not preponderate and oppress the rest. The east may be more powerful than the west, the lowlanders than the highlanders, the agricultural than the commercial or manufacturing classes. To give all power, or an undue share, to one, is obviously not to remedy but to ensure the evil. Its safest check, the best corrective, is found in a general admission of all upon a footing of equality. So intimately are the interests of each class in society blended and interwoven, so indispensable is justice to all, that oppression in that case becomes less probable from any one, however powerful. . . .

Property over Numbers

The Virginia reformers registered a small gain when the suffrage was broadened to include heads of families who paid taxes. But on the more hotly contested question of representation, they were able to secure only a nominal reform permanently apportioning fifty-six representatives to the growing western counties and seventy-eight to the declining eastern plantation section.

The fears that caused some slaveholding easterners to oppose even this compromise were revealed with startling frankness and clarity by Benjamin

Watkins Leigh in the following speech to the convention on November 3–4, 1829.[2]

Mr. Leigh of Chesterfield, said . . . he believed, if George Washington were to rise from the dead, and to propose such a compromise as that offered by the venerable gentleman, so partial as in his conception it was, so ruinous, so destructive, so so damnatory, to the dearest interests of the people who had sent him here, he should . . . be apt to utter a shriek of alarm and terror, that would strike the dullest ear and the dullest understanding, though not perhaps the hearts of such reformers as were willing to make the experiment on the body politic, how large a dose of French rights of man it can bear, without fever, frenzy, madness, and death. . . .

Sir, the resolution reported by the Legislative Committee, in effect, proposes to divorce power from property—to base representation on numbers alone, though numbers do not quadrate with property—though mountains rise between them—to transfer in the course of a very few years, the weight of power over taxation and property to the west, though it be admitted, on all hands, that the far greater mass of property is now, and must still be held in the east. Power and property may be separated for a time, by force or fraud—but divorced, never. For, so soon as the pang of separation is felt—if there be truth in history, if there be any certainty in the experience of ages, if all pretensions to knowledge of the human heart be not vanity and folly—property will purchase power, or power will take property. And either way, there must be an end of free Government. If property buy power, the very process is corruption. If power ravish property, the sword must be drawn —so essential is property to the very being of civilized society, and so certain that civilized man will never consent to return to a savage state. Corruption and violence alike terminate in despotism. All the Republics in the world have died this death. In the pursuit of a wild impracticable liberty, the people have first become disgusted with all regular Government, then violated the security of property which regular Government alone can defend, and been glad at last to find a master. License, is not liberty, but the bane of liberty. . . .

The resolution of the Legislative Committee, proposes to give to those who have comparatively little property, power over those who have a great deal—to give to those who contribute the least, the power of taxation over those who contribute the most, to the public treasury— and (what seems most strange and incongruous) to give the power over property to numbers alone, in that branch of the legislature which should be the especial guardian of property—in the revenue-giving branch. To my mind, Sir, the scheme is irreconcilable with the fundamental principle of representative Government, and militates against its peculiar mode of operation, in producing liberty at first, and then nurturing, fostering, de-

---

[2] *Proceedings and Debates of the Virginia State Convention of 1829–30,* 151, 156–58, 173.

fending and preserving it, for a thousand years. . . . Give me liberty in the English sense—liberty founded on law, and protected by law—no liberty held at the will of demagogue or tyrant (for I have no choice between them)—no liberty for me to prey on others—no liberty for others to prey on me. . . . Sir, the true, the peculiar advantage of the principle of representative Government, is, that it holds Government absolutely dependent on individual property—that it gives the owner of property an interest to watch the Government—that it puts the pursestrings in the hands of its owners. Leave those who are to contribute money, to determine the measure and the object of contribution, and none will ever knowingly give their money to destroy their own liberty. Give to those who are not to contribute the power to determine the measure and object of the contribution of others, and they may give it to destroy those from whom it is thus unjustly taken. . . .

Sir, the venerable gentleman from Loudoun [ex-President James Monroe, a member of the convention] has told us of the awful and horrid scenes he was an eye-witness of, in France, during the reign of democracy, or rather of anarchy, there. I wish he had told us (as he told the House of Delegates in 1810, when he opposed the call of a Convention, and recounted those same horrors) that "he had seen liberty expiring from excess"—those were his words. France was then arranged into equal departments with equal representation, and general suffrage —in short, enjoying the unalloyed blessing of the natural rights of man! Have I lost my senses! Is the phantom that fills my heart with horror—*the liberty of Virginia expiring with excess*—a creature of the imagination that can never be realized! The venerable gentleman has described those horrors in France— has painted them to us in all the freshness of reality—and then told us, in the same breath, that he is prepared to vote for the same system here. The same causes uniformly produce the same effects.—I mean to speak with freedom, yet not without the respect due to the venerable gentleman, and which I should render as a willing tribute: I cannot forbear to express my astonishment that he should be willing to adopt, for his own country, the principles that led to those horrors he has so feelingly described. . . .

Liberty is only a *mean:* the *end* is *happiness.* It is, indeed, the wine of life; but like other wines, it must be used with temperance, in order to be used with advantage: taken to excess, it first intoxicates, then maddens, and at last destroys.

Romantic Democracy

Until 1850, when further reforms were made, Virginia continued to be a conservative stronghold, while South Carolina remained essentially aristocratic until the Civil War. Reform triumphed in almost all the other states, however, and the country was converted into a thoroughgoing democracy. Underlying this revolution in political behavior and institutions was a shift in attitudes that deserves special attention.

The advance of representative government in the eighteenth century had been aided by a set of ideas that intellectual historians call Rationalism. Following the English philosopher, John Locke, the Rationalists held that all human knowledge is derived from sense perceptions of the external world and that every man possesses the faculty of Reason, which enables him to order this sense-derived knowledge so as to arrive at Truth. This faith in every man's essential rationality was an important factor in the eighteenth century's steady movement toward democracy. Other aspects of Rationalist thought, however, created a curiously negative attitude toward democratic government. Society was regarded as a field on which free individuals pursued their separate ends; and a beneficent Creator had regulated the game so wisely that only a little government was needed to deal with the occasional players who disregarded the rules (or natural laws) and endangered their fellows. Liberty was the highest social value, and government (even democratic government) was a necessary evil, which should be held to the smallest scope possible. The eighteenth century's faith in democracy was further limited by the conviction that Reason was better developed in some men than in others. Even Thomas Jefferson, the patron saint of American democracy, viewed all government with deep suspicion and relied on an "aristocracy of talent" to govern.

In conservative Virginia the debate over democracy in 1829 was conducted mainly within the framework of eighteenth-century ideas, even the reformers contending only that the nonfreeholders had the requisite intellectual qualifications to vote and that the interests of all were best protected by suffrage extension. Elsewhere, however, Rationalism was being supplanted by a new set of ideas, usually called Romanticism, which yielded more positive attitudes toward democracy. Truth was not derived from sense perceptions, ran the key Romantic notion, but from an intuitive faculty in the soul of every man, educated or uneducated, that enabled him to connect with ultimate reality, variously described as Truth, God, or the Over-Soul.

The implications of the Romantic doctrine for democratic politics were most forcefully expressed by George Bancroft, Democratic party leader of Massachusetts in the 1830s, Secretary of the Navy under Polk, and author of the nineteenth century's most influential history of the United States. The following selection is taken from Bancroft's oration on "The Office of the People in Art, Government, and Religion," delivered before an undergraduate literary society at Williams College in August 1835.[3]

There is a *spirit in man:* not in the privileged few; not in those of us only who by the favor of Providence have been nursed in public schools: IT IS IN MAN: it is the attribute of the race. The spirit, which is the guide to truth, is the gracious gift to each member of the human family.

Reason exists within every breast. I mean not that faculty which de-

---

[3] George Bancroft, *Literary and Historical Miscellanies* (New York, 1855), 409–10, 415–16, 421–22, 424–25.

duces inferences from the experience of the senses, but that higher faculty, which from the infinite treasures of its own consciousness, originates truth, and assents to it by the force of intuitive evidence; that faculty which raises us beyond the control of time and space, and gives us faith in things eternal and invisible. There is not the difference between one mind and another, which the pride of philosophers might conceive. To them no faculty is conceded, which does not belong to the meanest of their countrymen. In them there can not spring up a truth, which does not equally have its germ in every mind. They have not the power of creation; they can but reveal what God has implanted in every breast. . . .

If reason is a universal faculty, the universal decision is the nearest criterion of truth. The common mind winnows opinions; it is the sieve which separates error from certainty. The exercise by many of the same faculty on the same subject would naturally lead to the same conclusions. . . . Thus there can be no continuing universal judgment but a right one. Men cannot agree in an absurdity; neither can they agree in a falsehood. . . .

In like manner the best government rests on the people and not on the few, on persons and not on property, on the free development of public opinion and not on authority; because the munificent Author of our being has conferred the gifts of mind upon every member of the human race without distinction of outward circumstances. . . . A government of equal rights must, therefore, rest upon mind; not wealth, not brute force, [but] the sum of the moral intelligence of the community should rule the State. . . .

. . . There may be those who scoff at the suggestion that the decision of the whole is to be preferred to the judgment of the enlightened few. They say in their hearts that the masses are ignorant; that farmers know nothing of legislation; that mechanics should not quit their workshops to join in forming public opinion. But true political science does indeed venerate the masses. It maintains, not as has been perversely asserted, that "the people can make right," but that the people can DISCERN right. Individuals are but shadows, too often engrossed by the pursuit of shadows; the race is immortal: individuals are of limited sagacity; the common mind is infinite in its experience: individuals are languid and blind; the many are ever wakeful: individuals are corrupt; the race has been redeemed: individuals are time-serving; the masses are fearless: individuals may be false; the masses are ingenuous and sincere: individuals claim the divine sanction of truth for the deceitful conceptions of their own fancies; the Spirit of God breathes through the combined intelligence of the people. Truth is not to be ascertained by the impulses of an individual; it emerges from the contradictions of personal opinions; it raises itself in majestic serenity above the strifes of parties and the conflict of sects; it acknowledges neither the solitary mind, nor the separate faction as its oracle; but owns as its only faithful interpreter the dictates of pure reason itself, proclaimed by the general voice of mankind. The decrees of the universal conscience are the nearest approach to the presence of God in the soul of man. . . .

Equality

The democratic impulse was closely related to the development in the United States of a social structure and a social character that were unique in the history of Western civilization. Beginning far back in the colonial period, this development reached its culmination in the early nineteenth century. Its principal features were an absence of extremes in wealth or status, a large degree of social mobility, and a widespread feeling that one man was as good as another.

These features were most characteristic of the Western states, but foreign observers found them conspicuous in all sections. Britons had particular "difficulty in . . . accommodating themselves to the manners of the Americans," as the Scotsman, James Stuart, reported, because they "consider it so great a hardship to be obliged to eat or associate with those whom they consider to be their inferiors, in point of station." For whatever reason, the horde of British travelers who crossed the Atlantic in the 1820s and 1830s shared Stuart's preoccupation with one striking difference between the two countries: "In the United States the slightest assumption of superiority over a person conceived to be merely lower in point of station or wealth, is not tolerated." The following selections from the writings of British travelers afford many insights into this distinctive quality of American society.[4]

James Flint

Here are multitudes of persons who have no accurate notions of decorous behaviour. This, no doubt, may arise partly from their ideas of the equality of men, without making due allowances for morals, manners, intellect, and education. Accustomed to mix with a diversity of company at taverns, elections, and other places of public resort, they do not well brook to be excluded from private conversation. On such occasions, they exclaim, *"This is a free country"* or a *"land of liberty,"* adding a profane oath. . . . This extension of liberty and equality is injurious, inasmuch as it prevents the virtuous part of society from separating from the vicious; and so far as it removes [from] the unprincipled and untutored part, the salutary incitement to rest character on good behaviour and intelligence, instead of citizenship, or an allusion to the *land of liberty,* or the favourite maxim that one man is as good as another.

---

[4] James Flint, *Letters from America* (Edinburgh, 1882), 142–143; Richard Flower, *Letters from Lexington and the Illinois* (London, 1819), 10; Charles A. Murray, *Travels in North America during the Years 1834, 1835, & 1836,* 2 vols. (New York, 1839), 1:92; Isaac Holmes, *An Account of the United States of America* (London, 1823), 343–44; Frances Trollope, *Domestic Manners of the Americans* (New York, 1832), 93–95, 108–9.

Richard Flower

The American notion of liberty and equality is highly gratifying to me. The master or employer is kept within the bounds of reason and decency towards his labourer. No curses or oaths towards their servants, or HELPS as they choose to call themselves; (for every one who takes money or wages, is, after all, a servant;) he obeys all reasonable orders for his remuneration; and when this obedience ceases, the contract of service is at an end. I have often been surprised at the highmindedness of American labourers, who are offended at the name of *servant*.

Sir Charles Augustus Murray

There is nothing more amusing among Americans than the jealous care and assiduity with which they assert and maintain the republican doctrine of equality; while, on the other hand, they observe distinctions and interchange titles which would appear ridiculous in England. For instance the very first evening that I passed under the roof of my worthy host, not only he, but his farm assistants and labourers, called me *"Charlie";* which Christian appellation would doubtless appear very *familiar* to an English ear in the mouth of a person whose acquaintance is just made: the curious observer of character, who wishes to see the *per contra* side of the picture may find in the first village to which he comes, the small tavern where he lodges kept by a general, the broken wheel of his waggon mended by a colonel, and the day-labourers and mechanics speaking of one another as "this gentleman," and "that gentleman."

Isaac Holmes

If a stranger arrives at an inn or tavern in the country, and several persons are in the room, they will just give a vacant sort of stare or gaze, but they will soon settle into their wonted indifference. If a person should be travelling in some of the back settlements, perhaps, on his first arrival, he may be greeted in a different manner. But if the company should think, by the stranger's dress, appearance, or behaviour, that he fancied himself superior to them, it is very probable that some one would rise, and look at him in a very impudent manner, and perhaps address him in a taunting mode, to excite his notice; and unless he pacified the party by treating them with whiskey, it is likely he would be abused.

Frances Trollope

The extraordinary familiarity of our poor neighbours startled us at first, and we hardly knew how to receive their uncouth advances, or what was expected of us in return; however, it sometimes produced very laughable scenes. . . .

My general appellation among my neighbours was "the English old woman," but in mentioning each other they constantly employed the term "lady"; and they evidently had a pleasure in using it, for I repeatedly observed, that in speaking of a neighbour, instead of saying Mrs. Such-a-one, they described her as "the lady over the way what takes in washing," or as "that there lady, out by the gully, what is making dip-candles." Mr. Trollope was as constantly called "the old man," while draymen, butchers' boys, and the labourers on the canal were invariably denominated "them gentlemen"; nay, we once saw one of the most gentlemanlike men in Cincinnati introduce a fellow in dirty shirtsleeves, and all sorts of detestable et cetera, to one of his friends, with this formula, "D*****, let me introduce this gentleman to you." . . .

There was one man whose progress in wealth I watched with much interest and pleasure. When I first became his neighbour, himself, his wife, and four children were living in one room, with plenty of beef-steaks and onions for breakfast, dinner, and supper, but with very few other comforts. He was one of the finest men I ever saw, full of natural intelligence and activity of mind and body, but he could neither read nor write. He drank but little whiskey, and but rarely chewed tobacco, and was therefore more free from that plague-spot of spitting which rendered male colloquy so difficult to endure. He worked for us frequently, and often used to walk into the drawing-room and seat himself on the sofa, and tell me all his plans. . . . He hopes to make his son a lawyer, and I have little doubt that he will live to see him sit in Congress; when his time arrives, the wood-cutter's son will rank with any other member of Congress, not of courtesy, but of right, and the idea that his origin is a disadvantage, will never occur to the imagination of the most exalted of his fellow-citizens.

This is the only feature in American society that I recognize as indicative of the equality they profess. Any man's son may become the equal of any other man's son, and the consciousness of this is certainly a spur to exertion; on the other hand, it is also a spur to that coarse familiarity, untempered by any shadow of respect, which is assumed by the grossest and the lowest in their intercourse with the highest and most refined. This is a positive evil, and, I think, more than balances its advantages.

And here again it may be observed, that the theory of equality may be very daintily discussed by English gentlemen in a London dining-room, when the servant, having placed a fresh bottle of cool wine on the table, respectfully shuts the door, and leaves them to their walnuts and their wisdom; but it will be found less palatable when it presents itself in the shape of a hard, greasy paw, and is claimed in accents that breathe less of freedom than of onions and whiskey. Strong, indeed, must be the love of equality in an English breast if it can survive a tour through the Union.

The Conservative Democrat

Many Americans, of course, bewailed the leveling spirit of the Jacksonian period as stridently as the British travelers. "Had I the power," exclaimed a Tennessee judge in 1825, "no exertion of which I was capable should be wanting to arrest the progress of that wild & furious democracy which has long threatened to overwhelm our Country at no distant day in the Vortex of Anarchy." But the judge and his kind were disheartened by the futility of protest, and only an occasional Benjamin Watkins Leigh had the courage to argue openly against the democratic dogma.

Thus the single extended American critique of Jacksonian society was left to come from a friend of democracy, James Fenimore Cooper. The first American novelist to win wide European acclaim, Cooper defended majority rule, supported Jackson, and opposed the business leaders. Yet by the late 1830s he was appalled at some of the apparently inevitable by-products of democratic institutions, especially the dogma of equality and the tyranny of public opinion. The following selections from *The American Democrat,* published in 1838, deal first with equality and then with the tyranny of public opinion. They represent Cooper's most telling criticisms of American democracy, for on the whole his book is a defense of representative government as opposed to monarchy or aristocracy.[5]

The celebrated proposition contained in the declaration of independence is not to be understood literally. All men are not "created equal," in a physical sense, or even in a moral sense, unless we limit the signification to one of political rights. . . .

As a principle, one man is as good as another in rights. Such is the extent of the most liberal institutions of this country, and this provision is not general. The slave is not as good as his owner, even in rights. But in those states where slavery does not exist, all men have essentially the same right, an equality, which, so far from establishing that "one man is as good as another," in a social sense, is the very means of producing the inequality of condition that actually exists. By possessing the same rights to exercise their respective faculties, the active and frugal become more wealthy than the idle and dissolute; the wise and gifted more trusted than the silly and ignorant; the polished and refined more respected and sought, than the rude and vulgar. . . . Idle declamation on these points, does not impair the force of things, and life is a series of facts. These inequalities of condition, of manners, of mental cultivation must exist, unless it be intended to reduce all to a common level of ignorance and vulgarity, which would be virtually to return to a condition of barbarism. . . .

There are numerous instances in which the social inequality of Americans may do violence to our notions of abstract justice, but the compromise of interests under which all civilized society must exist renders this unavoidable. . . . If we would have civilization and the exertion indispensable to its success, we must have property; if we have property, we must have its rights; if we have the rights of property, we

---

[5] J. Fenimore Cooper, *The American Democrat* (Cooperstown, N.Y., 1838); passages are here quoted in revised order, from pp. 47–48, 70–71, 78–80, 82, 85, 93, 96, 147, 182–84.

must take those consequences of the rights of property which are inseparable from the rights themselves. . . .

They who have reasoned ignorantly, or who have aimed at effecting their personal ends by flattering the popular feeling, have boldly affirmed that "one man is as good as another"; a maxim that is true in neither nature, revealed morals, nor political theory. . . .

The tendency of democracies is, in all things, to mediocrity, since the tastes, knowledge, and principles of the majority form the tribune of appeal. This circumstance, while it certainly serves to elevate the average qualities of a nation, renders the introduction of a high standard difficult. Thus do we find in literature, the arts, architecture, and in all acquired knowledge, a tendency in America to gravitate towards the common center in this, as in other things; lending a value and estimation to mediocrity that are not elsewhere given. . . .

The danger to the institutions of denying to men of education their proper place in society, is derived from the certainty that no political system can long continue in which this violence is done to the natural rights of a class so powerful. It is as unjust to require that men of refinement and training should defer in their habits and associations to the notions of those who are their inferiors in these particulars, as it is to insist that political power should be the accompaniment of birth. All, who are in the least cultivated, know how irksome and oppressive is the close communion with ignorance and vulgarity, and the attempt to push into the ordinary associations, the principles of equality that do and ought to govern states in their political characters, is, virtually, an effort to subvert a just general maxim, by attaching to it impracticable consequences. . . .

All that democracy means, is as equal a participation in rights as is practicable; and to pretend that social equality is a condition of popular institutions, is to assume that the latter are destructive of civilization, for, as nothing is more self-evident than the impossibility of raising all men to the highest standard of tastes and refinement, the alternative would be to reduce the entire community to the lowest. . . .

In Democracies there is a besetting disposition to make publick opinion stronger than the law. This is the particular form in which tyranny exhibits itself in a popular government; for wherever there is power, there will be found a disposition to abuse it. Whoever opposes the interests, or wishes, of the publick, however right in principle, or justifiable by circumstances, finds little sympathy; for, in a democracy, resisting the wishes of the many, is resisting the sovereign in his caprices. . . .

In this country, in which political authority is the possession of the body that wields opinion, influences that elsewhere counteract each other, there is a strong and dangerous disposition to defer to the publick, in opposition to truth and justice. This is a penalty that is paid for liberty, and it depends on the very natural principle of flattering power. . . . The man who resists the tyranny of a monarch, is often sustained by the voices of those around him; but he who opposes the innovations of the publick in a democracy, not only finds himself struggling with power, but with his own neighbors. It follows that the oppression of the publick is of the worst description. . . .

Individuality is the aim of political liberty. By leaving to the citizen as much freedom of action and of being, as comports with order and the rights of others, the institutions render him truly a freeman. He is left to pursue his means of happiness in his own manner. . . .

The habit of seeing the publick rule, is gradually accustoming the American mind to an interference with private rights that is slowly undermining the individuality of the national character. There is getting to be so much publick right, that private right is overshadowed and lost. A danger exists that the ends of liberty will be forgotten altogether in the means.

All greatness of character is dependent on individuality. The man who has no other existence than that which he partakes in common with all around him, will never have any other than an existence of mediocrity. In time, such a state of things would annihilate invention and paralyze genius. A nation would become a nation of common place labourers. . . .

Of all Christian countries, individuality, as connected with habits, is perhaps the most encouraged in England; and of all Christian countries this [the United States] is the one, perhaps, in which there is the least individuality of the same nature. . . . This feature of the American character, therefore, is to be ascribed, in part, . . . to the natural tendency in democracies to mistake and augment the authority of the publick.

2. THE JACKSONIAN PROGRAM: BANKING

What the democratic upsurge meant in terms of national policy was far from clear at first. The accidental collection of groups that elected Jackson in 1828 was united only by a common sense of grievance against the prevailing order and by specific dissatisfactions with different phases of the nationalistic American System of Adams and Clay. This system the Jacksonians were bound to attack in part, but only gradually did they develop a rounded public philosophy of their own. In the slow process by which various factions were either forced out of the Democratic party or compelled to conform to the policies that embodied its emerging philosophy of government, Andrew Jackson himself played a major role.

A thoroughgoing respecter of the popular will (which he was inclined to read as agreeing with him), Old Hickory invariably saw things in black and white. What he thought wrong, he seldom hesitated to attack; and he was constantly urging his followers to "carry the war into affrica." Jackson's personality, therefore, had much to do with the assault on the American System. His Maysville Veto of 1830 sharply checked internal improvements by the federal government. On the tariff question he was embarrassed by a protectionist faction in his own party, but the issue was settled for a decade by the Compromise of 1833, and meanwhile the Democrats moved steadily toward an anti-tariff position. A defender of states' rights in theory, Jackson also showed himself an ardent defender of the federal Union in the nullification controversy. By the end of his two terms, moreover, Jackson had elaborated in his public papers a philosophy of government that justified his policies.

Historians are not all convinced, however, that Jackson's own public philosophy expressed very well the diverse motivations and ideals of those who supported his policies. In order to come closer to the objectives and ambiguities of Jacksonian Democracy in this broader sense, it is necessary to examine some of the Jacksonian policies, who supported them, how they were adopted, and what their results were. The hardest battles of the 1830s were fought over the money and banking question, and it is here we must search for an answer to our questions about the real nature and meaning of Jacksonian Democracy.

In the early days of the republic, the only legal tender, or money, that a creditor had to accept in payment of debts, was gold and silver coin. But a new kind of currency was introduced when state legislatures began issuing limited-liability charters to banking corporations. These banks, like their modern counterparts, made profits by lending money; but unlike modern banks they lent money in the form of their own bank notes. Thus it was to their interest to keep as many of their notes in circulation as possible. These bank notes were simply certificates bearing a promise by the issuing bank to pay on demand a designated amount in gold or silver, and they generally supplanted coin as the circulating medium in the vicinity of the bank. So long as people had confidence in a bank's ability to redeem its notes in coin ("specie" was the more common term), they were seldom returned for redemption. This fact enabled the banks to multiply their profits by multiplying their loans and thus their note issues many times beyond their actual specie reserves.

The Jeffersonians had been hostile to these institutions from the beginning. John Taylor of Caroline had inveighed against the "paper system" as a fraud whereby wealth was transferred from labor to a privileged few; and Jefferson himself had declared that "the *Bank mania* is . . . raising up a money aristocracy in our country which has already set the government at defiance." The boom years of 1815–1818 had brought an extravagant expansion of banks and bank issues. When panic struck in 1819, the banks had to suspend specie payments, and the depreciation of their notes caused widespread suffering. The rapid growth of anti-bank sentiment was a major factor in the democratic ferment of the 1820s.

The Monster of Chestnut Street

Some Jacksonians, including Jackson himself, were neo-Jeffersonian "hard-money" men, who opposed all paper-money banks and insisted on a return to a gold and silver currency. A larger group of Jackson's supporters, however, were for a variety of reasons primarily hostile to the powerful National Bank that stood at the head of the whole banking system. Both groups could agree that the Second Bank of the United States had to be dealt with before there could be any general banking reform.

The First National Bank had been established on Alexander Hamilton's recommendation in 1791, but Congress had refused to renew its charter in 1811. In 1816 a new and larger institution had been chartered for twenty years. The Second Bank was irresponsibly administered at first, saving itself in the Panic of 1819 only by sacrificing its debtors and the state banks. But after Nicholas Biddle's election as its president in 1823, the Bank pursued a course profitable to its stockholders and beneficial to the country. It had an almost life-and-death power over the state banks, because it received large quantities of their notes in federal deposits and in the ordinary course of business. By promptly returning their notes for redemption in specie, it could force them to keep ample specie reserves on hand. By extending or restricting its own issues, it could encourage the state banks to follow suit. Thus it could serve as a balance wheel for the entire financial structure, restraining the state banks in times of inflationary pressure and succoring them in periods of stringency.

A modern scholar sympathetic to the Jacksonians, Arthur M. Schlesinger, Jr., explains in *The Age of Jackson* why they opposed the Bank despite its obvious benefits.[6]

In 1836 the charter of the Second Bank of the United States was to expire. This institution was not in the later sense a national bank. It was a banking corporation, located in Philadelphia, privately controlled, but possessing unique and profitable relations with the government. To the capital of thirty-five million dollars, the government had subscribed one fifth. It served as repository of the public funds, which it could use for its own banking purposes without payment of interest. It could issue bank notes up to the physical ability of the president and cashier to sign them; after 1827 it evaded this limitation by the invention of "branch drafts," which looked and circulated like notes but were actually bills of exchange. The Bank was not to be taxed by the states, and no similar institution was to be chartered by Congress. In return for these privileges the Bank

---

[6] Arthur M. Schlesinger, Jr., *The Age of Jackson* (Boston: Little, Brown & Co., 1945), 74–79. Reprinted by permission of the author.

paid a bonus of one and a half million dollars, transferred public funds and made public payments without charge, and allowed the government to appoint five out of the twenty-five directors. The Secretary of the Treasury could remove the government deposits provided he laid the reasons before Congress.

Even advocates of the Bank conceded that this charter bestowed too much power. . . . Nathan Appleton, who had tried vainly to modify the charter in 1832, wrote carefully but emphatically in 1841:

A great central power, independent of the general or state governments, is an anomaly in our system. Such a power over the currency is the most tremendous which can be established. Without the assurance that it will be managed by men, free from the common imperfections of human nature, we are safer without it.

There could be no question about the reality of the Bank's power. It enjoyed a virtual monopoly of the currency and practically complete control over credit and the price level. Biddle's own testimony disclosed its extent:—

Q.3. Has the bank at any time oppressed any of the State banks?
A. Never. There are very few banks which might not have been destroyed by an exertion of the powers of the bank. None have ever been injured.

To radical Democrats like Taney, Biddle's tone implied that he thought himself entitled to credit for his forbearance. "It is this power concentrated in the hands of a few individuals," Taney declared, "—exercised in secret and unseen although constantly felt—irresponsible and above the control of the people or the Government for the 20 years of its charter, that is sufficient to awaken any man in the country if the danger is brought distinctly to his view."

There could be no question either about the Bank's pretensions to complete independence of popular control. . . . In Biddle's eyes the Bank was thus an independent corporation, on a level with the state, and not responsible to it except as the narrowest interpretation of the charter compelled. Biddle tried to strengthen this position by flourishing a theory that the Bank was beyond political good or evil, but Alexander Hamilton had written with far more candor that "such a bank is not a mere matter of private property, but a political machine of the greatest importance to the State." The Second Bank of the United States was, in fact, as Hamilton had intended such a bank should be, the keystone in the alliance between the government and the business community.

Though conservative Jeffersonians, led by Madison and Gallatin, had come to accept Hamilton's Bank as necessary, John Taylor's dialectics and Randolph's invective kept anti-Bank feeling alive, and men in the old radical tradition remained profoundly convinced of the evil of paper money. Jackson's hard-money views prompted his opposition to the Tennessee relief system in 1820. "Every one that knows me," he told Polk in 1833, "does know, that I have been always opposed to the U. States Bank, nay all Banks." Benton, from talks with Macon and Randolph and his observation of the collapse of the paper system in 1819, similarly concluded that the only safeguard against future disaster lay in restricting the system; and that, to this end, the government should deal only in gold and silver, thus withdrawing support from the issues of privately owned banks. Van Buren, Cambreleng, Taney, and Polk more or less shared these views.

The ordinary follower of Jackson in the West also regarded the Bank with strong latent antagonism, but for very different reasons. Its policy in 1819 of recalling specie and checking the note issue of state banks had gained it few friends in any class, and, in Kentucky especially, the Relief War kept resentments alive. But this anti-Bank feeling owed little to reasoned distrust of paper money or to a Jeffersonian desire for specie. As a debtor section the West naturally preferred cheap money; and Kentucky, for example, which most vociferously opposed the United States Bank, also resorted most ardently to wildcat banking of its own. The crux of the Kentucky fight against the Bank was not the paper system, but outside control; the Bank's sin lay not in circulating paper money itself, but in restraining its circulation by Kentucky banks. Almost nowhere, apart from doctrinaires like Jackson and Benton, did Westerners object to state banks under local control. . . .

Similar objections to control from Philadelphia ranged many Easterners against the Bank. State institutions hoped, by falling heir to the government deposits, to enlarge their banking capital, at no expense to themselves. Special grievances multiplied the motives. The state banks of New York, for example, envied the United States Bank because its loan operations were not restricted by Van Buren's safety-fund system. New York City had long resented the choice of Philadelphia as the nation's financial capital. Thus in a fight against the Bank Jackson could expect the backing of a decent minority of the local banking interests.

But there was still another and more reliable source of support. In March, 1829, after the grim depression winter, a group of Philadelphia workingmen, under the very shadow of the Bank, called a meeting "opposed to the chartering of any more new banks." The hard times were blamed upon the "too great extension of paper credit," and the gathering concluded by appointing a committee, "without confining ourselves to the working classes," to draw up a report on the banking system. . . . A week later the committee pronounced its verdict on the paper system:—". . . If the present system of banking and paper money be extended and perpetuated, the great body of the working people must give over all hopes of ever acquiring any property."

This view was spreading rapidly through the Middle and Northern states of the East in the later eighteen-twenties. The working class was no more affected by an instinctive antipathy toward banking than the backwoodsmen beyond the Alleghenies; but they never enjoyed the Western opportunity of having banks under their own control. Their opposition, instead of remaining fitful and capricious, began slowly to harden into formal anti-banking principle. Their bitter collective experience with paper money brought them to the same doctrines which Jackson and Benton gained from the Jeffersonian inheritance.

The Bank Veto

Though Biddle hoped for several years to secure Jackson's assent to a renewal of the Bank's charter with slight modifications, the President's ultimate course was never really in doubt. Finally, on the eve of the presidential election of 1832, the Bank forces tried to force his hand by pushing a recharter bill through Congress. The bill reached the White House on Independence Day, and on July 10 Jackson returned it with a ringing veto containing an eloquent summary of his political philosophy. The most important parts of this veto follow.[7]

The present corporate body, denominated the president, directors, and company of the Bank of the United States, will have existed at the time this act is intended to take effect twenty years. It enjoys an exclusive privilege of banking under the authority of the General Government, a monopoly of its favor and support, and, as a necessary consequence, almost a monopoly of the foreign and domestic exchange. The powers, privileges, and favors bestowed upon it in the original charter, by increasing the value of the stock far above its par value, operated as a gratuity of many millions to the stockholders. . . . The act before me proposes another gratuity to the holders of the same stock, and in many cases to the same men, of at least seven millions more. . . . It appears that more than a fourth part of the stock is held by foreigners and the residue is held by a few hundred of our own citizens, chiefly of the richest class. For their benefit does this act exclude the whole American people from competition in the purchase of this monopoly and dispose of it for many millions less than it is worth. . . .

. . . As little stock is held in the West, it is obvious that the debt of the people in that section to the bank is principally a debt to the Eastern and foreign stockholders; that the interest they pay upon it is carried into the Eastern States and into Europe, and that it is a burden upon their industry and a drain of their currency, which no country can bear without inconvenience and occasional distress. To meet this burden and equalize the exchange operations of the bank, the amount of specie drawn from those States through its branches within the last two years, as shown by its official reports, was about $6,000,000. More than half a million of this amount does not stop in the Eastern States, but passes on to Europe to pay the dividends of the foreign stockholders. . . .

Is there no danger to our liberty and independence in a bank that in its nature has so little to bind it to our country? The president of the bank has told us that most of the State banks exist by its forbearance.

---

[7] *Register of Debates*, 22nd Cong., 1st Sess., Appendix, 73–75, 79.

Should its influence become concentrated, as it may under the operation of such an act as this, in the hands of a self-elected directory whose interests are identical with those of the foreign stockholders, will there not be cause to tremble for the purity of our elections in peace and for the independence of our country in war? Their power would be great whenever they might choose to exert it; but if this monopoly were regularly renewed every fifteen or twenty years on terms proposed by themselves, they might seldom in peace put forth their strength to influence elections or control the affairs of the nation. But if any private citizen or public functionary should interpose to curtail its powers or prevent a renewal of its privileges, it can not be doubted that he would be made to feel its influence. . . .

It is to be regretted that the rich and powerful too often bend the acts of government to their own selfish purposes. Distinctions in society will always exist under every just government. Equality of talents, of education, or of wealth can not be produced by human institutions. In the full enjoyment of the gifts of Heaven and the fruits of superior industry, economy, and virtue, every man is equally entitled to protection by law; but when the laws undertake to add to these natural and just advantages artificial distinctions, to grant titles, gratuities, and exclusive privileges, to make the rich richer and the potent more powerful, the humble members of society—the farmers, mechanics, and laborers—who have neither the time nor the means of securing like favors to themselves, have a right to complain of the injustice of their Government.

There are no necessary evils in government. Its evils exist only in its abuses. If it would confine itself to equal protection, and, as heaven does its rains, shower its favors alike on the high and the low, the rich and the poor, it would be an unqualified blessing. In the act before me there seems to be a wide and unnecessary departure from these just principles. Nor is our Government to be maintained or our Union preserved by invasions of the rights and powers of the several States. In thus attempting to make our General Government strong we make it weak. Its true strength consists in leaving individuals and States as much as possible to themselves—in making itself felt, not in its power, but in its beneficence; not in its control, but in its protection; not in binding the States more closely to the center, but leaving each to move unobstructed in its own proper orbit.

Experience should teach us wisdom. Most of the difficulties our Government now encounters and most of the dangers which impend over our Union have sprung from an abandonment of the legitimate objects of Government by our national legislation, and the adoption of such principles as are embodied in this act. Many of our rich men have not been content with equal protection and equal benefits, but have besought us to make them richer by act of Congress. By attempting to gratify their desires we have in the results of our legislation arrayed section against section, interest against interest, and man against man, in a fearful commotion which threatens to shake the foundations of our Union. If we can not at once, in justice to interests vested under improvident legislation, make our Government what it ought to be, we can at least take a stand against all new grants of monopoly and exclusive privileges, against any prostration of our Government to the advancement of the few at the expense of the many, and in favor of compromise and gradual reform in our code of laws and system of political economy.

The Bank Defended

Appearing in the middle of an angry Presidential campaign, the Bank veto became at once the main issue. Conservative orators denounced its appeals to class feeling and to prejudice against foreigners as demagogic. Biddle thought its absurdities so evident that he used Bank funds to distribute the veto message itself by the thousands. But the election returns showed that Old Hickory's reasoning had carried conviction with the voters. Jackson was re-elected by an overwhelming majority.

On September 26, 1832, the conservative *Boston Daily Advertiser & Patriot* carried the following vigorous criticism of the veto.[8]

We shall not undertake to say which of the various impolitic, illegal, and unconstitutional proceedings of the present administration will prove, in the end, most injurious to the country; but the one which will be attended with the greatest amount of immediate and therefore certain and irremediable evil, is probably the *destruction of the bank*. . . .

The national bank, though not properly a *political* institution, is one of the most important and valuable instruments that are used in the practical administration of the government. . . . As the fiscal agent of the executive, it has exhibited a remarkable intelligence, efficiency, energy, and above all, INDEPENDENCE. This—as we shall presently see—has been its real crime. As the regulator of the currency, it has furnished the country with a safe, convenient, and copious circulating medium, and prevented the mischiefs that would otherwise result from the insecurity of the local banks. As a mere institution for loaning money, it has been, as it were, the Providence of the less wealthy sections of the Union. It has distributed with unsparing hand almost the whole of its vast capital throughout the western states, where capital, at any moderate rate of interest, would be otherwise almost inaccessible. The extent of the benefit conferred in this way, not on the west only, but on the whole country, will never be fully appreciated except, should that unfortunately happen, by its loss. Through its dealings in exchange at home and abroad, the bank has materially facilitated the operations of our foreign and domestic trade. The important advantages which have thus been de-

[8] "The Conduct of the Administration: The Bank," *Boston Daily Advertiser & Patriot*, September 26, 1832.

rived from this institution have been unattended by any countervailing evil. As its term advanced, and its officers acquired additional experience, it has been constantly gaining on the public favor. There has been no suspicion of abuse; not a lisp of complaint has been heard on any account throughout the country. . . .

The bill for rechartering the bank passed triumphantly through both houses. The President returned it with his celebrated Veto message.

This document—when Jackson shall have been, as we trust he will be within a very few months, remanded to the Hermitage:—when the people shall have long since recovered from the temporary delusion that placed him in office:—when most of the messages and other papers to which his name has been affixed, shall have been sunk by their leaden dullness in the gulf of oblivion:—this document—the Veto message—will probably be kept in memory, and often appealed to as a curious example of the extent to which, at the commencement of the nineteenth century, the elected chief magistrate of a free civilized and enlightened people dared to insult the common sense and moral feeling of his constituents. The indignant outcry of the people has already passed judgment upon this unworthy paper and its author, so that it is nearly as superfluous as it would be, within the limits of the present essay, impossible to examine its contents in detail. We shall confine ourselves to a few remarks upon those parts in which the subject is treated under an economical point of view.

On this head, the doctrine of the President, has at least the merit of novelty. . . . Gen. Jackson is evidently of opinion that to put money in a man's pocket, is to subject him to great and grievous embarrassment. Now the bank has, it seems, been guilty of the high crime and misdemeanor of placing sundry millions of foreign capital in the pockets of the people of the United States, and also sundry millions of capital belonging to the Atlantic cities, in the pockets of the west. This is not all. . . . "The debt due to the bank by the West," says the Veto message, "is principally a debt to the eastern and foreign stockholders; the *interest* they pay upon it (mark the villainy!) is carried into the eastern states and to England, and is a burden upon their industry (poor souls!) and a drain of currency which no country can bear without inconvenience and occasional distress." It seems then from the President's shewing that these poor people of the west are not allowed, as honest men should be, to appropriate the earnings of others to their own use, without fee or reward, as the SPOILS OF VICTORY, but are actually subjected to the enormous imposition of paying upon all the money they borrow, the charge of six per cent. annual interest. This, to be sure, is "flat burglary." The bank permits itself to be made the instrument of this work of iniquity and oppression, and is of course fairly obnoxious to the execration of all the friends of justice and humanity. But how is the mischief to be remedied?—If the President is admirable in discovering the nature of the disease, he is no less admirable in applying the cure. These western states, who are thus *oppressed* with a loan of thirty millions of dollars, and who are subjected to the intolerable hardship and burden of paying six per cent. interest upon it are to be *relieved*—how, gentle reader? —by being suddenly called upon to pay to these eastern and foreign stockholders, instead of the intolerable six per cent. interest, the whole hundred per cent. capital within two or three years.

Is not this excellent?—Is not this creditable to the government and country?—Is not this a fine piece of work to go out to Europe as a specimen of the perfection to which the science of political economy has been carried by the freest and most enlightened nation on the globe?— It is an act of oppression to furnish a man with capital to carry on his business; the way to relieve him is to compel him to pay it back again at all sacrifices and at a moment's notice. These are discoveries of which Alexander Hamilton and Albert Gallatin never dreamed. Smith, Say, and Ricardo might have pored over their books for centuries, without ever stumbling upon them. The document which contains them will doubtless be valued, when the Wealth of Nations and the Report on Manufacturers are forgotten. Did it never occur to the worthies of the *Kitchen Cabinet,* in the course of their learned speculations on capital and credit, to ask themselves the question: Who compels the western people to borrow this money, if they do not want it? . . .

The spirit that breathes through all these denunciations of the bank is, if possible, still worse than the reasoning contained in them. For the first time, perhaps, in the history of civilized communities, the chief magistrate of a great nation—the natural and chosen guardian of order and the public peace—is found appealing to the worst passions of the uninformed part of the people, and endeavoring to stir up the poor against the rich. If the bank should be rechartered, "the humble members of society, the farmers, mechanics, and laborers, who have neither the time nor the means of securing like favors to themselves, have a right," says the veto message, "to complain of the injustice of the government." The party journals are constantly harping on the same string. The bank is denounced as a *monied aristocracy,* subsisting in bloated arrogance upon the plunder of the poor. . . . They think, or hope, that by boldly misrepresenting facts, and perpetually stimulating the vicious propensities of the mass of the people, they shall be able to obtain the number of votes necessary to continue them in office, and secure for another term the possession of the SPOILS OF VICTORY. Such is the object; and, in the Jackson code of morality, the end sanctifies the means: ALL'S FAIR IN POLITICS. . . .

Such have been the proceedings in regard to the Bank, and such the manner in which they have been defended. What would be the effect of its destruction? It would unsettle the currency and carry desolation and bankruptcy through the whole Western country. The debt of thirty millions due from that section to the Bank CANNOT BE PAID. The attempt to enforce it would ruin thousands of our most industrious and valuable citizens, and arrest for years the prosperity of the whole West. Will the people consent to this for the mere purpose of securing to the military chieftain and his partizans the SPOILS OF VICTORY for another term! THEY WILL NOT.

Reforming the State Banks

The veto did not kill the Bank. Its charter still had four years to run, and Biddle lost no time in marshaling its great economic and political power to win the two-thirds Congressional majority needed to pass the recharter bill over the President's veto. Newspapers were subsidized, large sums were loaned to congressmen, and local businessmen were enlisted to put pressure on their representatives. By the summer of 1833 Jackson was convinced that he must cripple his antagonist before it crippled him. When the President ordered the federal deposits transferred from the National Bank to a selected group of state-chartered banks, Biddle deliberately provoked a depression, hoping that a frightened Congress would order restoration of the deposits as a prelude to recharter. But the Democrats managed to hold on to their slim majority in the House of Representatives at the "panic session" of 1833–34, and the Bank had to begin winding up its affairs.

All of this happened unfortunately at the beginning of another inflationary upswing of the business cycle, and the state banks got out of hand almost immediately. Fortified by the federal deposits, they launched the economy on a speculative boom more extravagant than the country had ever experienced. The hard-money Democrats were dismayed, but their scruples against federal intervention in the economy or the affairs of the states inhibited any direct efforts to regulate the currency.

In this crisis Jackson's advisers conceived a plan for using the government deposits to reform the state bank currency indirectly. Secretary of the Treasury Roger B. Taney drafted a deposit bill requiring state banks that received federal deposits to cease issuing notes under five dollars or dealing in such notes issued by other banks; in a few years the prohibition was to be extended to notes under ten dollars and later to those under twenty. Small notes would be driven from circulation and replaced by gold and silver, while the steady demand for specie thus created would force the banks to curtail their issues so as to keep a larger store of the precious metals on hand. Banks would continue to exist but would serve only their legitimate functions of providing sound credit and commercial facilities.

The painful ambiguity of the Jacksonian position in the debate over Taney's deposit bill was expressed most clearly by Representative Churchill C. Cambreleng, who spoke for the free-trade commercial interests and the workingmen's "Loco Foco" Democracy of New York City in Congress. On February 11, 1835, Cambreleng addressed the House as follows.[9]

---

[9] *Register of Debates*, 23rd Cong., 2nd Sess., 1306, 1310–12, 1315.

... The strongest motive which induces me at this time to advocate the system [of depositing the federal funds in state banks] is, that by continuing to collect our revenue through these agents, we can make them instrumental in the great work which has been so successfully commenced, of reform in our currency, by aiding in excluding our small note circulation. ...

But, sir, the reform must not stop with an inquiry into the corruptions and abuses of federal legislation. Our State Governments, some at least, if not all, have outstripped even this Government in a rapid career of vicious and corrupt legislation. We have spread over the country thousands of corporations in every branch of trade, and erected Government companies to disturb and rival the ancient and natural establishments of frugality and enterprise. We have introduced a spirit of gambling into every branch of trade, by giving these companies credit not founded upon capital, but law, and have granted our chartered adventurers the privilege of bankruptcy without holding their property responsible to their honest, and, in some instances, ruined creditors. ... We have travelled through the whole circle of industry, and have given a political power to corporations, which, if this spirit be not arrested, will control every State Government, introduce gambling into every branch of trade, and pauperism into every county in the Union. ...

But, Mr. Speaker, the greatest and most alarming abuse now existing in this country is the incorporation of near 600 banks of circulation, with an aggregate capital of more than two hundred millions of dollars. ... When we see these institutions spread over the land, founded upon a basis so speculative and absurd, forcing by every possible means their notes into circulation, promising impossibilities, can we be surprised at panics, and commercial alarms, and embarrassments? ... It is worthy of the inquiry of every State legislature in the Union, whether the evils resulting from a bank note circulation do not greatly overbalance all its convenience as a currency. But if, sir, this currency is to be perpetuated in defiance of our constitution—if we mean to persist in a course of legislation as vicious as it is unjust—we owe it to the country, at least, to protect trade and labor from the effects of this abominable legislative abuse. If we will have Government banks, we ought certainly to require that they should never abandon the prudent rules of trade. We must either limit their dividends, or reduce their circulation to one fourth, or at least one third the amount of their capital. Without these restrictions, no matter what examinations, what guards, or what proportion of specie may be required, trade is destined for ever to suffer from panics and alarms of legislative origin; and a suffering community will contribute an annuity of millions to those who are authorized to abuse the credit of the State—to the very authors of their embarrassments. ...

Sir, if these abuses be persisted in, if corporations are to be multiplied throughout the land; if the credit of the State is to be abused for banking purposes, and the dignity of the Government degraded by partnerships in trade; if a perpetual annuity of millions is to be thus indirectly collected for the benefit of banks established under the authority of Government—then may we anticipate, before many generations shall have passed away, the thorough corruption and revolution of every Government in the Union. Perpetuate these legislative abuses, and the time is not distant when your Representatives will volunteer their services to your thousands of powerful corporations, and when avarice will control every Legislature in the land. Whatever controls your laws governs your country. You will be ruled by avarice—that "domineering, paramount evil," to which "there is a natural allegiance and fealty due from all the vassal vices, which acknowledge its superiority and readily militate under its banners." Your Hamiltonian plan of legislation will thus exhibit its revolting results: your Government will be founded upon wealth, your people ruled by legislative corruption and despotism.

Dénouement

Despite everything the hard-money men could do, the inflationary boom roared out of control and on to its inevitable result. In May 1837, only two months after Jackson left office, the immense structure of speculative credit came toppling down, and the country was plunged into the most severe and prolonged depression of its history.

Jackson's hand-picked successor, Martin Van Buren, promptly abandoned the state banks, proposing that the federal government deal only in specie and keep its funds in its own independent treasury offices. After three years of bitter debate, the independent treasury system was finally adopted and, except for a brief Whig interregnum in the 1840s, continued in use until the twentieth century. Though the system exercised a moderate restraint on inflation, the federal government had for the most part washed its hands of the currency problem.

In the light of this result, how are the Jacksonian monetary policies to be evaluated? An economic historian renders a critical judgment.[10]

Hard money was a cardinal tenet of the left wing of the Democratic party. It belonged with an idealism in which America was still a land of refuge and freedom rather than a place to make money. Its aim was to clip the wings of commerce and finance by restricting the credit that paper money enabled them to obtain. . . .

---

[10] Bray Hammond, "Jackson, Biddle, and the Bank of the United States," *Journal of Economic History*, 7 (May 1947), 6–10. Reprinted with permission of the *Journal of Economic History*.

There was also a pro-bank, "paper money wing," which harbored the Democratic party's less spiritual virtues. Its strength lay with free enterprise, that is, with the new generation of businessmen, promoters, and speculators, who found the old Hamiltonian order of the Federalists too stodgy and confining. . . .

The private banks and their friends had helped to kill the first Bank of the United States twenty years before, but the strength they could muster against the second was much greater. . . . These banks were associated to a marked extent with the Democratic party, especially New York. . . . Without them, it is doubtful if the Jacksonians could have destroyed the B.U.S.

The Jacksonian effort to realize the hard-money ideals was admirable, viewed as Quixotism. For however much good one may find in these ideals, nothing could have been more unsuited than they were to the American setting. In an austere land or among a contemplative and self-denying people they might have survived but not in one so amply endowed as the United States and so much dominated by an energetic and acquisitive European stock. Nowhere on earth was the spirit of enterprise to be more fierce, the urge for exploitation more restless, or the demand for credit more importunate. The rise of these reprobated forces spurred the agrarians, and as business itself grew they came to seek nothing less than complete prohibition of banking. Yet they chose to destroy first the institution which was curbing the ills they disapproved of, and to that end they leagued with the perpetrators of those ills. Jackson made himself, as de Tocqueville observed, the instrument of the private banks. He took the government's funds out of the central bank, where they were less liable to speculative use and put them in the private banks, where they were fuel to the fire. He pressed the retirement of the public debt, and he acquiesced in distribution of the federal surplus. These things fomented the very evils he deplored and made the Jacksonian inflation one of the worst in American history. . . .

But this was the inevitable result of the agrarian effort to ride two horses bound in opposite directions: one being monetary policy and the other states' rights. Monetary policy must be national, as the Constitution doubly provides. The agrarians wanted the policy to be national, but they eschewed the practicable way of making it that, and, instead of strengthening the national authority over the monetary system, they destroyed it.

. . . As it was, they helped an acquisitive democracy take over the conservative system of bank credit introduced by Hamilton and by the merchants of Philadelphia and New York and limber it up to suit the popular wish to get rich quick. Wringing their hands, they let bank credit become the convenient key to wealth—the means of making capital accessible in abundance to millions of go-getting Americans who otherwise could not have exploited their natural resources with such whirlwind energy.

3. THE MEANING OF JACKSONIAN DEMOCRACY

Throughout the latter half of the nineteenth century, a narrowly political "Whig interpretation" of Jacksonian Democracy prevailed. As late as 1922, a distinguished historian, Arthur M. Schlesinger of Harvard University, complained that most people thought of Jacksonian Democracy as "a violent change in American government and politics effected during the years from 1829 to 1837 by an irresponsible and erratic military chieftain at the head of the newly enfranchised and untutored masses." Professor Schlesinger wanted a more sympathetic treatment of democratic forces—and, in fact, a "democratic interpretation" of American history was already replacing the "Whig interpretation"—but he also urged a broader perspective. Jacksonian Democracy, he insisted, was not just a movement in national politics, but a pervasive democratic ferment that affected such varied areas of American culture as literature, corporate development, religion, labor organization, and humanitarian reform. Only in this broader context could even the political developments be properly understood.

Professor Schlesinger's call for a more inclusive interpretation met no substantial response, however, until 1945, when Arthur M. Schlesinger, Jr., published *The Age of Jackson*. Brilliantly fulfilling the specifications laid down by his father twenty-three years before, the younger Schlesinger opened up a fruitful debate among historians on the broad meaning of Jacksonian Democracy, as seen mainly through its monetary policies.

The selections that follow present the conclusions of three historians with differing points of view. All of them would agree, however, that the crucial questions are: "What kind of America were the Jacksonians trying to bring about?" "What were the actual consequences of their efforts?" and "What is the heritage of Jacksonian Democracy and its meaning for our own day?"

To Restrain the Power of the Business Community

In *The Age of Jackson*, published in 1945, Arthur M. Schlesinger, Jr., sees in Jacksonian Democracy many significant parallels with Franklin D. Roosevelt's New Deal. A selection from the book follows.[11]

---

[11] Arthur Schlesinger, Jr., *The Age of Jackson* (Boston: Little, Brown & Co., 1945), pp. 125, 128–29, 218, 306–7, 307–10, 312, 505. Reprinted with permission of the author.

The Jacksonians believed that there was a deep-rooted conflict in society between the "producing" and "nonproducing" classes—the farmers and laborers, on the one hand, and the business community on the other. The business community was considered to hold high cards in this conflict through its network of banks and corporations, its control of education and the press, above all, its power over the state; it was therefore able to strip the working classes of the fruits of their labor. "Those who produce all wealth," said Amos Kendall, "are themselves left poor. They see principalities extending and palaces built around them, without being aware that the entire expense is a tax upon themselves."

If they wished to preserve their liberty, the producing classes would have to unite against the movement "to make the rich richer and the potent more powerful." ... The specific problem was to control the power of the capitalistic groups, mainly Eastern, for the benefit of the noncapitalist groups, farmers and laboring men, East, West and South. The basic Jacksonian ideas came naturally enough from the East, which best understood the nature of business power and reacted most sharply against it. The legend that Jacksonian democracy was the explosion of the frontier, lifting into the government some violent men filled with rustic prejudices against big business, does not explain the facts, which were somewhat more complex. Jacksonian democracy was rather the second phase of that enduring struggle between the business community and the rest of society which is the guarantee of freedom in a liberal capitalist state. ...

The paper banking system was considered to play a leading role in this everlasting struggle. Men living by the issue and circulation of paper money produced nothing; they added nothing to the national income; yet, they flourished and grew wealthy. Their prosperity, it was argued, must be stolen from the proceeds of productive labor—in other words, from the honest but defenseless "humble members of society." ...

The hard-money policy attacked both the techniques of plunder and the general strategy of warfare. By doing away with paper money, it proposed to restrict the steady transfer of wealth from the farmer and laborer to the business community. By limiting banks to commercial credit and denying them control over the currency, it proposed to lessen their influence and power. By reducing the proportion of paper money, it proposed to moderate the business cycle, and order the economy to the advantage of the worker rather than the speculator. It was a coherent policy, based on the best economic thought of the day, and formulated on a higher intellectual level than the alternatives of the opposition. ...

But the administration's campaign came too late. The wise counsels of the hard-money advocates were drowned out by the roar of the nation's greatest boom in years. The bank of the United States alone enlarged its loans an average of two and a half million dollars a month and its paper circulation by a total of ten million dollars between December, 1834, and July, 1835.

Smaller banks rushed to follow, increasing the amount of paper money from eighty-two million dollars on January 1, 1835, to one hundred and eight million, a year later, and one hundred and twenty million by December 1, 1836. . . .

In destroying the Bank, Jackson had removed a valuable brake on credit expansion; and in sponsoring the system of deposit in state banks, he had accelerated the tendencies toward inflation. Yet the hard-money Democrats at least understood the danger and tried vainly, by the example of the federal government and by pressure within the states, to halt the dizzy pyramiding of paper credits. The business community, however, fascinated by the illusion of quick returns, fought the hard-money program all along the line. . . .

Like any social philosophy, Jacksonian democracy drew on several intellectual traditions. . . . The inspiration of Jeffersonianism was so all-pervading and fundamental for its every aspect that Jacksonian democracy can be properly regarded as a somewhat more hard-headed and determined version of Jeffersonian democracy. But it is easy to understate the differences. . . .

The central Jefferson hope had been a nation of small freeholders, each acquiring thereby so much moral probity, economic security, and political independence as to render unnecessary any invasion of the rights or liberties of others. The basis of such a society, as Jefferson clearly recognized, was agriculture and handicraft. What was the status of the Jeffersonian hope now that it was clear that, at best, agriculture must share the future with industry and finance? . . .

The new industrialism had to be accepted: banks, mills, factories, industrial capital, industrial labor. These were all distasteful realities for orthodox Jeffersonians, and, not least, the propertyless workers. "The mobs of great cities," Jefferson had said, "add just so much to the support of pure government, as sores do to the strength of the human body." . . . Yet the plain political necessity of winning the labor vote obliged a change of mood. Slowly, with some embarrassment, the Jeffersonian preferences for the common man were enlarged to take in the city workers. . . .

In several respects, then, the Jacksonians revised the Jeffersonian faith for America. They moderated that side of Jeffersonianism which talked of agricultural virtue, independent proprietors, "natural" property, abolition of industrialism, and expanded immensely that side which talked of economic equality, the laboring classes, human rights, and the control of industrialism. This readjustment enabled the Jacksonians to attack economic problems which had baffled and defeated the Jeffersonians. It made for a greater realism, and was accompanied by a general toughening of the basic Jeffersonian conceptions. . . .

The tradition of Jefferson and Jackson might recede, but it could never disappear. It was bound to endure in America as long as liberal capitalist society endured, for it was the creation of the internal necessities of such a society. American democracy has come to accept the struggle among competing groups for the control of the state as a positive virtue—indeed, as the only foundation for liberty. The business community has been ordinarily the most powerful of these groups, and liberalism in America has been ordinarily the movement on the part of the other sections of society to restrain the power of the business community. This was the tradition of Jefferson and Jackson, and it has been the basic meaning of American liberalism.

To Liberate Business

Bray Hammond's economic analysis of the Bank controversy may have already suggested to the reader that Jacksonian Democracy, far from being antibusiness, was actually the political phase of an emerging "liberal capitalism." This view is expressed forcefully by Richard Hofstadter of Columbia University. The following extract is taken from a chapter entitled "Andrew Jackson and the Rise of Liberal Capitalism," which appeared in a volume published in 1948.[12]

For those who have lived through the era of Franklin D. Roosevelt it is natural to see in Jacksonian democracy an earlier version of the New Deal, for the two periods have many superficial points in common. The Jacksonian movement and the New Deal were both struggles of large sections of the community against a business elite and its allies. There is a suggestive analogy between Nicholas Biddle's political associates and the "economic royalists" of the Liberty League, and, on the other side, between the two dynamic landed aristocrats who led the popular parties. Roosevelt himself did not fail to see the resemblance and exploit it.

But the two movements differed in a critical respect: the New Deal was frankly based upon the premise that economic expansion had come to an end and economic opportunities were disappearing; it attempted to cope with the situation by establishing governmental ascendancy over the affairs of business. The Jacksonian movement grew out of expanding opportunities and a common desire to enlarge these opportunities still further by removing restrictions and privileges that had their origin in acts of government; thus with some qualifications, it was essentially a movement of laissez-faire, an attempt to divorce government and business. It is commonly recognized in American historical folklore that the Jackson movement was a phase in the expansion of democracy, but it is too little appreciated that it was also a phase in the expansion of liberated capitalism. While in the New Deal the democratic reformers were driven to challenge many assumptions of traditional American capitalism, in the Jacksonian period the democratic upsurge was closely linked to the ambitions of the small capitalist.

To understand Jacksonian democracy it is necessary to recreate the social complexion of the United States in the 1830's. Although industrialism had begun to take root, this was still a nation of farms and small

---

[12] Reprinted from Richard B. Hofstadter, *The American Political Tradition and the Men Who Made It*, pp. 54–56, 58, 60–61, 65–66, by permission of Alfred A. Knopf, Inc. Copyright 1948 by Alfred A. Knopf, Inc.

towns, which in 1830 found only one of every fifteen citizens living in cities of over 8,000. Outside the South, a sweeping majority of the people were independent property-owners. Factories had been growing in some areas, but industry was not yet concentrated in the factory system; much production was carried out in little units in which the employer was like a master craftsman supervising his apprentices. The development of transportation made it possible to extend trade over large areas, which resulted in a delay in collections and increased the dependence of business upon banks for credit facilities. The merchant capitalist found it easier to get the necessary credits than humbler masters and minor entrepreneurs, but the hope of growing more prosperous remained intensely alive in the breast of the small manufacturer and the skilled craftsman. . . . The typical American was an expectant capitalist, a hardworking ambitious person for whom enterprise was a kind of religion, and everywhere he found conditions that encouraged him to extend himself. . . .

More than one type of American, caught up in this surge of ambition, had reason to be dissatisfied with the United States Bank. Some farmers were more interested in the speculative values of their lands than in their agricultural yield. Operators of wildcat banks in the South and West and speculators who depended upon wildcat loans shared the farmers' dislike of Biddle's bank for restraining credit inflation. In the East some of the heads of the strong, sound state banks were jealous of the privileged position of the national bank —particularly the bankers of New York City, who resented the financial supremacy that the bank brought to Philadelphia. In Eastern cities the bank was also widely disliked by workers, craftsmen, shopkeepers, and small business people. Labor was hard hit by the rising cost of living, and in many cases the workmen's agitation was directed not so much against their immediate employers as against the credit and currency system. Small business and working men felt that banks restricted competition and prevented new men from entering upon the avenues of enterprise. . . .

Jackson himself was by no means unfamiliar with the entrepreneurial impulse that gave Jacksonian democracy so much of its freshness and vitality. An enterpriser of middling success, he could spontaneously see things from the standpoint of the typical American who was eager for advancement in the democratic game of competition—the master mechanic who aspired to open his own shop, the planter or farmer who speculated in land, the lawyer who hoped to be a judge, the local politician who wanted to go to Congress, the grocer who would be a merchant. . . .

Certainly [Jackson's Bank veto] is not the philosophy of a radical leveling movement that proposes to uproot property or to reconstruct society along drastically different lines. It proceeds upon no Utopian premises—full equality is impossible, "distinctions will always exist," and reward should rightly go to "superior industry, economy, and virtue." What is demanded is only the classic bourgeois ideal, equality before the law, the restriction of government to equal protection of its citizens. This is the philosophy of a rising middle class; its aim is not to throttle but to liberate business, to open every possible pathway for the creative enterprise of the people. Although the Jacksonian leaders were more aggressive than the Jeffersonians in their crusades against monopoly and "the paper system," it is evident that the core of their philosophy was the same: both aimed to take the grip of government-granted privileges off the natural economic order. . . .

With Old Hickory's election a fluid economic and social system broke the bonds of a fixed and stratified political order. Originally a fight against political privilege, the Jacksonian movement had broadened into a fight against economic privilege, rallying to its support a host of "rural capitalists and village entrepreneurs." When Jackson left office he was the hero of the lower and middling elements of American society who believed in expanding opportunity through equal rights. . . . "This," exulted Calvin Colton, "is a country of self-made men, than which there can be no better in any state of society."

To Restore the Ways of the Plain Republican Order

The wide disagreement about the meaning of Jacksonian Democracy impelled still another historian, Marvin Meyers of the University of Chicago, to examine Jackson's own public papers in an attempt to discover "the sort of values offered to and preferred by the Jacksonian public." Meyers finds "a revealing and somewhat unexpected commentary upon the character of Jacksonian Democracy," which seems to contradict the conclusions of both Schlesinger and Hofstadter. The following selection is from an article published in 1953.[13]

On the side of virtue, in Jackson's world, one finds the plain republican—direct descendant of Jefferson's yeoman hero—along with Poor Richard and such other, lesser friends. The presence of the sturdy, independent citizen-toiler has been no secret to historians—yet some interesting possibilities have been missed. In creating the character and role of the plain republican Jackson has provided, I think, an important clue for the interpretation of Jacksonian values. . . .

When Jackson speaks of the people—the real people—he regularly specifies: planters and farmers, mechanics and laborers, "the bone and sinew of the country." . . . Jackson's real people are essentially those four specified occupational groups, whose "success depends upon their own industry and economy," who know "that they must not expect to become suddenly rich by the fruits of their toil." The lines are fixed by the moral aspects of occupation. . . .

---

[13] "The Jacksonian Persuasion," *American Quarterly*, 5 (Spring 1953), 5, 8–15, Reprinted with permission of the *American Quarterly*.

The positive definition of the real people significantly excludes pursuits which are primarily promotional, financial, or commercial. . . . The point seems to be that virtue naturally attaches to, and in fact takes much of its definition from, callings which involve some immediate engagement in the production of goods. Vice enters most readily through the excluded pursuits, though it may infect all classes and "withdraw their attention from the sober pursuits of honest industry." As indicated before, vice is to be understood largely in terms of certain occupational ways, the morals, habits, and character imputed to the trades which seek wealth without labor, employing the strategems of speculative maneuver, privilege-grabbing, and monetary manipulation.

Like the Jeffersonians, Jackson regularly identifies the class enemy as the money power, the moneyed aristocracy, etc. . . . More important, however, is the meaning given to phrases like "money power"—and note that Jackson typically uses this expression and not "the rich." The term occurs invariably in discussions of corporations and, particularly, of banking corporations; it signifies the *paper* money power, the *corporate* money power—i.e., concentration of wealth arising suddenly from financial manipulation and special privilege, ill-gotten gains. If the suggestion persists in Jackson's public statements that such is the common road to wealth—and certainly the only quick way—then it is still the mode and tempo of acquisition and not the fact of possession which is made to damn the rich before Jackson's public. . . .

Thus, Jackson's representation of the real people in the plain republican order supplies at least tentative ground for an interpretation of Jacksonian Democracy as, in vital respects, an appeal to an idealized ancestral way. Beneath the gross polemical image of people *vs.* aristocracy, though not at all in conflict with it, one finds the steady note of praise for simplicity and stability, self-reliance and independence, economy and useful toil, honest and plain dealing. These ways are in themselves good, and take on the highest value when they breed a hardy race of free citizens, the plain republicans of America.

As a national political phenomenon, Jacksonian Democracy drew heavily upon the Bank War for its strength and its distinctive character. . . . The Bank of the United States, veritable incarnation of evil in Jackson's argument, assumes the shape of "the monster," which is to say, the unnatural creature of greed for wealth and power. Its managers, supporters, and beneficiaries form the first rank of the aristocracy, i.e., the artificial product of legislative prestidigitation. The monster thrives in a medium of paper money, the mere spectre of palpable value. The bank system suspends the real world of solid goods, honestly exchanged, upon a mysterious, swaying web of speculative credit. The natural distributive mechanism, which proportions rewards to "industry, economy, and virtue," is fixed to pay off the insider and the gambler.

To knock down this institution then, and with it a false, rotten, insubstantial world, becomes the compelling object of Jackson's case. He removed the deposits, so he said, "to preserve the morals of the people, the freedom of the press, and the purity of the elective franchise." Final victory over the Bank and its paper spawn "will form an era in the history of our country which will be dwelt upon with delight by every true friend of its liberty and independence," not least because the dismantling operation will "do more to revive and perpetuate those habits of economy and simplicity which are so congenial to the character of republicans than all the legislation which has yet been attempted."

The Jacksonian appeal for a dismantling operation and the restoration of old republican ways flows easily into the course of the hard coin argument. Hard coin, I have already suggested, stands for palpable value against the spectral issue of the printing press. . . . Above all it is banks and their paper system which "engender a spirit of speculation injurious to the habits and character of the people," which inspire "this eager desire to amass wealth without labor," which turn even good men from "the sober pursuits of honest industry." To restore hard coin is to restore the ways of the plain republican order. Dismantling of the unnatural and unjust bank and paper system is the necessary first step. . . .

And so the circuit of Jackson's public appeal may be closed. Plain, honest men; simple, stable economy; wise and frugal government. It reads less as the herald of modern times and a grand project for reform than as a reaction against the spirit and body of the changing world. Jacksonian Democracy, viewed through Jackson's public statements, wants to undo far more than it wishes to do; and not for the purpose of a fresh creation, but for the restoration of an old republican idyl. The tremendous popularity of Andrew Jackson and his undoubted public influence suggest that this theme can be ignored only at great peril in any general interpretation of Jacksonian Democracy. We must prepare for a paradox: the movement which in many ways cleared the path for the triumph of laissez-faire capitalism and its culture in America, and the public which in its daily life acted out that victory, held nevertheless in their conscience an image of a chaste republican order, resisting the seductions of risk and novelty, greed and extravagance, rapid motion and complex dealings.

CONCLUSION

The foregoing readings provide material for reflection on one of the major issues in American history. Most people would probably agree that "democracy" has been the most distinctive feature of American culture, but this same "democracy" has been so much an unarguable dogma that many Americans would have a hard time saying precisely what is it, or under what conditions it can flourish.

The current interest in the Jacksonian period is closely related to our troubled generation's renewed concern for democracy. It was in the Jacksonian period that democratic tendencies crystallized into the characteristic attitudes and political institutions that have continued to pervade our culture. It was in the Jacksonian period that we had our last real debate over the merits of democracy. And it was in the Jacksonian period, some historians would argue, that political democracy was most fully practiced. Thus Jacksonian Democracy raises a series of extremely crucial questions about American democracy in general. What have been the chief characteristics of our democracy? What beliefs and what environmental circumstances were associated with the full flowering of democracy in the Jacksonian period? What kind of society were these Jacksonians trying to create? And finally, what changes has American democracy undergone between Jackson's day and our own—in character, in the beliefs and social environment on which it rests, and in the kind of society it tries to achieve.

Most Americans suppose they know what democracy is, yet precise definition proves difficult. What, for example, do we mean when we say that one man is as good as another? Both Mrs. Trollope and Fenimore Cooper identified two different definitions of "equality." Which would Benjamin Watkins Leigh, the nonfreeholders of Richmond, Bancroft, and Jackson himself approve? Which has been more characteristic of Americans—in the Jacksonian period, and later?

Most Americans suppose, likewise, that democracy is a near-perfect form of government and society, yet we are apt to find some of the critics of Jacksonian Democracy strangely persuasive. Compare the criticisms by Leigh, the British travelers, and Cooper. Which of their criticisms seem valid, or relevant to the twentieth century? On the other hand, do the arguments for democracy made by George Bancroft and the nonfreeholders of Richmond really carry conviction to twentieth-century readers? Has the theoretical basis for democracy weakened or changed since the Jacksonian period? And what of the environmental basis for democracy, as described by Richard Hofstadter? How have the revolutionary changes in our social environment affected democracy?

Of course, we cannot understand Jacksonian Democracy very well until we turn from what the Jacksonians said to what they did, the policies they supported. The controversy over banking throws a flood of light on the several kinds of "democratic" forces present in Jacksonian America, and its outcome provides a clue as to which of these forces were strongest and most characteristic of American culture.

The disagreement among the historians, Schlesinger, Hammond, Hofstadter, and Meyers, may make the problem of evaluating Jacksonian Democracy seem more complex than it actually is. The disagreement really exists on two levels. It is sharpest on the less important question of judging the specific monetary policies of the Jacksonians. Here a historian who is concerned mainly with the political effects of economic policies and institutions might well differ from a historian who is concerned mainly with their economic effects.

On the second and more significant level, the disagreement among our experts may turn out to be more apparent than real. Here they are trying to define the essential character of democracy in the Jacksonian period, and they seem to have found at least three different versions of democracy. Meyers discovers, especially in Jackson's own thought, the neo-Jeffersonian ideal of "the plain republican order"; Hammond and Hofstadter emphasize "the entrepreneurial democracy," the drive "to liberate business"; while Schlesinger finds the essence of democracy in the efforts of disadvantaged groups "to restrain the power of the business community," so that political power and economic benefits can be widely and equitably distributed.

Actually, all three versions of democracy may have been present, not only in Jacksonian society, but throughout American history, with Schlesinger's version forming the basis for modern "welfare state" democracy. If this is true, then our historians differ only in the relative weight they attach to each in the Jacksonian period; and on this point the reader should now have enough information to reach some sound conclusions of his own. But even more important is the way this kind of analysis can clarify the nature and meaning of democracy throughout our history, and so help us to cope with the challenges and problems that beset our democratic society in the twentieth century.

8 DOUGLASS C. NORTH

acceleration in economic growth

The history of the United States has been characterized not only by a uniquely successful experiment in political democracy but also by the most rapid sustained economic growth that man has ever known. The average American enjoys a standard of living unequalled elsewhere in the world. Presently, we have become acutely self-conscious of this extraordinary living standard in comparison with that of underdeveloped areas in the world. What accounts for this unparalleled prosperity of the United States and to a lesser degree that of the modern Western world as a whole? Why did the rate of American economic development begin to spurt late in the first half of the nineteenth century? Our search for answers has not been altogether satisfactory. We have only clues, but we have come a long way toward understanding many aspects of the problem.

It is important to understand exactly what is meant by economic growth. Throughout American history population grew immensely both because of a very high birth rate in the early years and because of sustained and very high immigration during a long period. But, if the output in American society had grown no more rapidly than the number of people, then we would be no better off than we were at the beginning; or, to use a more precise term, income per capita would have remained constant throughout the period. Therefore, what we really are focusing on when we examine economic growth is what happens to output per head and its corollary income per head. We shall see that the peopling of the United States, and the growth of a large population and of large markets, had something to do with this increasing income per head, but the main focus of our attention will be on factors determining increasing production and efficiency.

Most economic historians, in looking at the growth of the Western world, emphasize technological change, particularly the revolutionary techniques first introduced in the British industrial revolution between the middle of the eighteenth century and the first third of the nineteenth century. No one can doubt that the advent of the steam engine and the development of cotton textile machinery, iron, and other machinery and tools underlay the successful expansion of England and, ultimately, that of the United States and other countries. Moreover, we cannot help but be impressed by the continuation of the technological revolution which has radically changed the character of our society. A man living in 1750 would have been more at home in the Rome of Julius Caesar than in the United States of the 1960s. A moment's reflection should convince us that technology alone is not responsible for economic growth. After all, technology is freely available to anyone or any nation in the world. What prevents other nations from using technology to achieve high living standards and high rates of growth? We do not know all the answers, but we do have some clues. Surprisingly enough, some of them first appeared in the writings of our forefathers as they searched for economic growth. Indeed, many of their controversies over proper economic policy are controversies that have modern counterparts in the United States today as well as in other parts of the world.

1. THE UNDERLYING INFLUENCES

America was settled by a vigorous, pioneering, adventuresome people. Whether they came over to escape religious persecution or to carry forth a business venture, they were already motivated to improve their standard of life. The character of the people was obviously important in determining the economic life of the New World.

The Leveling Influence of Democracy

When Alexis de Tocqueville came to America in the 1830s, he was struck by the bustle and energy of the people. His description of his travels in America was not always flattering. He believed that democracy sacrificed the artistic and the ornamental for the useful. Nevertheless, his acute observations caught the flavor of the ubiquitous drive of the Americans for material success, a drive which was such an important element in the attitudes that made for economic growth.[1]

---

[1] Alexis de Tocqueville, *Democracy in America* (London and New York, 1900), 2:50–52.

It would be to waste the time of my readers and my own, if I strove to demonstrate how the general mediocrity of fortunes, the absence of superfluous wealth, the universal desire of comfort, and the constant efforts by which every one attempts to procure it, make the taste for the useful predominate over the love of the beautiful in the heart of man. Democratic nations, amongst whom all these things exist, will therefore cultivate the arts which serve to render life easy, in preference to those whose object is to adorn it. They will habitually prefer the useful to the beautiful, and they will require that the beautiful should be useful.

It commonly happens that, in the ages of privilege, the practice of almost all the arts becomes a privilege; and that every profession is a separate walk, upon which it is not allowable for every one to enter. Even when productive industry is free, the fixed character which belongs to aristocratic nations gradually segregates all the persons who practise the same art, till they form a distinct class, always composed of the same families, whose members are all known to each other, and amongst whom a public opinion of their own, and a species of corporate pride, soon spring up. In a class or guild of this kind, each artisan has not only his fortune to make, but his reputation to preserve. He is not exclusively swayed by his own interest, or even by that of his customer, but by that of the body to which he belongs; and the interest of that body is, that each artisan should produce the best possible workmanship. In aristocratic ages, the object of the arts is therefore to manufacture as well as possible—not with the greatest despatch, or at the lowest rate.

When, on the contrary, every profession is open to all—when a multitude of persons are constantly embracing and abandoning it—and when its several members are strangers, indifferent to, and from their numbers hardly seen by, each other—the social tie is destroyed, and each workman, standing alone, endeavors simply to gain the most money at the least cost. The will of the customer is then his only limit. But at the same time, a corresponding change takes place in the customer also. In countries in which riches, as well as power, are concentrated and retained in the hands of a few, the use of the greater part of this world's goods belongs to a small number of individuals, who are always the same. Necessity, public opinion, or moderate desires, exclude all others from the enjoyment of them. As this aristocratic class remains fixed at the pinnacle of greatness on which it stands, without diminution or increase, it is always acted upon by the same wants, and affected by them in the same manner. The men of whom it is composed naturally derive from their superior and hereditary position a taste for what is extremely well made and lasting. This affects the general way of thinking of the nation in relation to the arts. It often occurs, among such a people, that even the peasant will rather go without the objects he covets, than procure them in a state of imperfection. In aristocracies, then, the handicraftsmen work for only a limited number of fastidious customers: the profit they hope to make depends principally on the perfection of their workmanship.

Such is no longer the case when, all privileges being abolished, ranks are intermingled, and men are forever rising or sinking upon the social scale. Amongst a democratic people, a number of citizens always exist whose patrimony is divided and decreasing. They have contracted, under more prosperous circumstances, certain wants, which remain after the means of satisfying such wants are gone; and they are anxiously looking out for some surreptitious method of providing for them. On the other hand, there are always in democracies a large number of men whose fortune is upon the increase, but whose desires grow much faster than their fortunes: and who gloat upon the gifts of wealth in anticipation, long before they have means to command them. Such men are eager to find some short cut to these gratifications, already almost within their reach. From the combination of these two causes the result is, that in democracies there is always a multitude of persons whose wants are above their means, and who are very willing to take up with imperfect satisfaction, rather than abandon the object of their desires.

The artisan readily understands these passions, for he himself partakes in them: in an aristocracy, he would seek to sell his workmanship at a high price to the few; he now conceives that the more expeditious way of getting rich is to sell them at a low price to all. But there are only two ways of lowering the price of commodities. The first is to discover some better, shorter, and more ingenious method of producing them: the second is to manufacture a larger quantity of goods, nearly similar, but of less value. Amongst a democratic population, all the intellectual faculties of the workman are directed to these two objects: he strives to invent methods which may enable him not only to work better, but quicker and cheaper. . . .

The Matrix

The interplay of a pioneering people with the vast and rich lands to be settled in America under conditions of individual freedom has been a recurring theme in American history; one whose importance for economic growth was mentioned by many observers of the expanding American economy. No one has caught the feeling of this complex interplay between man and his environment better than Stanley Lebergott, a modern author, writing on the subject.[2]

A New Society

Passing through the Kentucky wilderness in 1832, a traveler came upon the camp of "a petit bon homme and his wife," who had just arrived from France. Life in the rugged land that Boone had only recently left was surely strange, unsettling. Yet it was certain that even the newest nation required a cafe and restaurant. And so "there they were on the banks of the Mississippi,

[2] From *Manpower in Economic Growth: The American Record Since 1800* by Stanley Lebergott. Copyright © 1964 by McGraw-Hill, Inc. Used by permission of McGraw-Hill Book Company.

standing guard over their little pile of trunks full of napkins, liqueur glasses, coffee cups, curacao, anisette, and parfait amour, with looks of infinite *sang froid* and gaiety; and long ere this they have doubtless found their nest." This quick note of arrant confidence leads to the great theme of American history, that of the open society. It is impossible to understand our changing patterns of manpower use and reward without seeing how they sprang from the broader patterns of national belief and action—which they in turn deflected. We consider three elements in this broader system: hope, ignorance, and space.

Hope. And the greatest of these is hope. Hope springs from many an obscure source, and the motives of those men who became America's entrepreneurs and laborers have been described with many a differing insight. Dipping his eighteenth-century pen in acid, the Reverend James MacSporran wrote that "Great numbers have chose this province [Rhode Island] for their habitation not to avoid any violence to their persons or principles (as is more commonly than truly alledged, in New England especially) but to improve their fortunes in those parts." A century later an observer of the new West wondered: "Will laborers be wanting" to develop these territories? and concluded that "where food is abundant and cheap, there cannot long be a deficiency of laborers. What brought our ancestors (with the exception of the few who fled from persecution) from the other side of the Atlantic, but the greater abundance of the means of subsistence on this side? What other cause has so strongly operated in bringing to our valley [of the Mississippi] the 10 or 11 million who now inhabit it? The cause continuing, will the effect cease?" Of course, differences in wages offer a perfectly straightforward explanation of labor mobility. But hope of improvement is not to be equated with rational calculation. Some who arrived came with skills almost classically unsuited to American needs. Our earliest official report on immigrant entrances (for 1821) reports a falconer, a dancing master, a hairdresser, even a rope dancer. In the following year two rope dancers arrived, plus an elephant keeper. And so they came from every country on earth. Unequal in wealth, station, or the talents required in a new nation, they were equal in the intensity of their expectations. And it was this intensity that caught the attention of almost every European who came to observe this new land and its people. They found a settled belief that "there is not an avenue to wealth or distinction which is closed—not a post unattainable." In America "there existed no prerogative rights. . . . There was a completely open field; neither the immunities of an ancient hereditary nobility, nor the privileges of a reigning church, nor the difference of colour as in South America, presented obstacles to a new organization; for at that time [1776] the whites constituted alone the citizens of the state. . . ." Looking to the "fertile country . . . in and around the Illinois Valley" where lay the bounty lands due the soldiers of the Revolution, one dreamer wrote in 1819: "We deem it not romantic nor visionary to predict that the man who shall live twenty years to come may anticipate with confidence the voyages of steam boats from the Gulf of Mexico . . . to the falls of Niagara. . . . What a prospect of commercial advancement! What motives to the industrious and skilful cultivation of the soil does the contemplation of this stupendous enterprise open to the views of the people of the west!"

From hope came energy. As late as 1850 a French visitor marveled at the obvious: The Puritans "have remained the dominant element in the American society. . . . They have carried everywhere their spirit of initiative and their indomitable energy." Cobbett, in lauding "the great quantity of work performed by the American laborer," declared his wages high but his day's work unscanted: "The sun, who seldom hides his face, tells him when to begin in the morning and when to leave off at night." All things, of course, have deteriorated since that happy day, including the weather. But the contrast between high-money wages and low-efficiency wages still appears to be sharper in the United States than in many parts of the world.

Ignorance. Next only to hope as a constructive factor in our economic development has been that of ignorance—and the recognition of ignorance. "What a blessing to mankind it is," Justice Holmes once wrote, "that men begin life ignorant. . . . Everyone knows that it often happens that, from historical causes, analogous cases are governed by dissimilar rules, and that forms which have lost their significane by lapse of time remain as technicalities." The elder Holmes, for once, put the matter better than his son: "To think of trying to waterproof the American mind against the questions that Heaven rains down upon it shows a misapprehension of our new condition. . . . What the Declaration means is the right to question everything."

In Europe the answers were all known. Entrepreneurs and workmen alike had discovered the best methods of production; the centuries had taught them. American attempts to reproduce English and continental patterns of production did not work. The resource pattern was so different, costs of land so much lower, costs of labor so much greater, that new solutions offered fantastic promise. Mere technological invention was not the key: The ingenuity of Oliver Evans was great, but that of James Watt was fully as great. The most dismal years of the reign of Justinian, Suleiman, or the Ming emperors saw vital technical advances discerned. Every added inquiry into the past finds still more technical innovation, precursors, "mute inglorious Miltons" in the most unlikely nations and periods. Inventions occur everywhere; innovations do not. Nor are innovations adopted with impartial and equal frequency. For it is not the man but the nation that is the significant innovator—in Schumpeter's sense—adopting new technologies, new ways of doing business, new systems of action.

The most brilliant innovation in economic growth may well be the willingness to consider innovation itself as a permanent regimen. What was strikingly new about America was such willingness. Here was no established production system in which the classical entrepreneur made one marginal change in a factor input after another, improving an established process. Here was the very choice of the process itself, in every industry and region. Perry Miller's description of the ceaseless adaptability of our Puritan forebears is no less precise a description of the eighteenth- and nineteenth-century labor force. "Men who started as millers, being paid in grain, were compelled to find buyers and so grew to be traders, perceiving therein the guiding hand of providence; men who started as artisans settled down in workshops, took apprentices, and shortly were made capitalists."

Travelers accustomed to the guild traditions of Europe were amazed at the reckless adaptiveness of the American labor force. From an English migrant in 1818: Besides the "great quantity of work performed by the American laborer his skill and the versatility of his talent is a great thing. Every man can use an axe, a saw, and a hammer. Scarcely one who cannot do any job of rough carpentering, and mind a plough or a wagon." From a Frenchman in 1836: The American workman may be inferior in particular skills to the British workman but he has a "more general aptitude." From a British *vade mecum* for immigrants to the United States: "Most mechanics of the 'Old Country' are wedded as it were to the old order of things, but in each particular profession the workmen should be prepared at least to meet with new and peculiar, if not improved, modes and ideas. . . . Most of the variations he may meet with in the manner of his work have had their origin in something either of necessity or use." From a Swiss visitor in 1848: Everything in America is in a "transitory state." Here, a wine merchant who had been a railway director, a watch merchant who now sold shoes; there a farmer selling butter but formerly the proprietor of a factory for making calicoes; and a postman who became a flour merchant! No one seemed to remain in his proper occupation: "The Yankees believe themselves suited to anything, there is no status to which they do not feel themselves predestined, not a situation which they do not feel they understand to its depths. . . . Everything here speaks in dollars, everything is measured in dollars, everything is done for dollars."

He who has tasted only the staid pleasures of the quadrille can hardly anticipate the delights of the waltz; they are too far from his ken. And in a country where for twenty centuries seasonal workers have been hired for the harvest, a farmer's vision of his productive alternatives is bleakly narrowed to such questions as precisely when to hire such workers. Such traditional wisdom may divest him of the ability to consider one dizzying possibility: dispensing altogether with a summer harvest force, and its high wage rates. But given a new country, where a multitude of alternative work opportunities present themselves, a mechanical reaper to cut 12 acres of wheat a day (compared to 2 acres by hand) is not only conceived of, but put into production. In a new country, with so varied a mixture of migrants that the technological or guild tradition of no single European nation could be adopted, vastly different production methods and factor combinations could be and were attempted. The result was revolutionary change —revolutionary not in the hackneyed tradition of invoking elderly theories where they do not apply, but in the sense of adopting new solutions suited to new conditions. We may summarize in the words of a Danish observer in 1820:

History is unable to produce a more evident proof . . . that in order to develop the energies of a nation quickly and from all sides, the removing of every obstacle and the full enjoyment of independence and property, are alone requisite.

Space. Third of the major sections of that matrix within which our labor force developed was the land. In 1800, nearly 900,000 square miles; after the Louisiana Purchase, nearly double that area. Land of boundless fertility, it was available to those with strength to settle it. How few the Indians, how many the acres, the pioneers observed. In 1789 (according to Secretary of War Knox) there were only 76,000 Indians in the East. By 1817 a mere 100,000 Pani, Chackshahs, Soukies, Foxes roamed the plains beyond the Appalachians —fewer than the number of some major Indian tribes of our own day.

Against this enormous background of possibility a mere handful of Americans were at work, leaving almost infinite room for the hopeful migrant. In 1812 the hunting and trading parties up the Missouri and Mississippi totaled perhaps 300 persons—to tap one of the greatest supplies of furs in the world. By 1831 the number did not reach above 500. In 1819 the total number working the lead mines of Missouri, long destined to be the greatest in the nation, totaled slightly over 1,100. In 1800 the entire codfishing industry of the nation, after a century of colonial development, occupied— part year—fewer than 4,000 people. Above all, the number of farmers was decisive—perhaps 900,000 in 1810, or about one farmer for 2 square miles. What an incredible ratio to those who lived in European countries where densities a hundred times as great prevailed.

And the land, in addition to being sparsely settled, was rich. So rich, William Dunbar wrote rhapsodically (about his explorations for President Jefferson), that "a couple of acres of Indian corn" suffices to stock the pioneers' "magazine with bread for the year; the forest supplies venison, bear, turkey. . . . In a year or two he arrives at a state of independence; he purchases horses, cows and other domestic animals, perhaps a slave also who shares with him the labours and productions of his fields and the adjoining forests. How happy the contrast, when we compare the fortune of the new settler in the United States with the misery of the half-starving, oppressed, and degraded peasant of Europe!"

With space and opportunity came growth—ebullient, swift, irresistible. Did not Charles Carroll, who had signed the Declaration of Independence, live to see Baltimore (a "village of only seven houses within his memory") become a city of 70,000? And did not Griffith Yeatman, who had built one of the first huts on the banks of the Ohio, see Cincinnati grow from a handful of people to more than 200,000 before he died?

The growth was dominated by successive waves of migration. For three centuries, from 1602 to 1922, men migrated freely to the United States—those who sought Dunbar's Greek democracy, the Mike Fink types in search of mere open land for hunting, and the solid citizens who desired a landed heritage to pass on to their descendants. All were welcomed in a flood of immigration without parallel in modern history. For the rest of the world's nations, whether or not close to the point of diminishing returns from land, have usually limited the type and quantity of migrants during their periods of substantial economic growth. Of America alone in the modern world can it be said: This nation was built by immigrants and by the children of immigrants.

While American history has been marked by conflicting attitudes toward particular components of the labor supply, there was for long a widespread agreement on the desirability of retaining and increasing the supply. On the one hand a Northern promanufacturing group could wish that "if it please heaven to redeem the thousands and tens of thousands, that groan in the land of bondage [i.e., Europe], and open them a passage through the waves, as to the Israelites of old, this shall be their land of promise. . . . They may shape their course to any part of a territory as expansive as the ocean they have traversed, find a thousand ways to bestow their industry to their advantage, with land, free and unoccupied, on which to settle." With equal vigor and identical reference, one who addressed the Virginia State Agricultural Society in 1852 urged letting slavery "fulfill its mission until the same Power that opened the water of the Red Sea . . . [should] make dry the waters of the great deep for the passage of the African to his native shores." The promanufacturing group wished to increase its labor supply. The proslavery group wished to retain its labor supply— the best that could be done when the slave trade was forbidden. The fact that the point of reference for both was the exodus through the Red Sea is a happy demonstration that some North-South differences involved no basic theological but only economic aspects.

Whether American economic growth could have been what it was failing these three elements—hope, ignorance, space—there is no way of knowing. But they appeared throughout our growth and, as Thoreau remarked about finding trout in the milk can, there is some circumstantial evidence that can be awfully convincing. The mere prospect of available lands would not per se have brought the dynamic growth of the American economy. (Indeed, some could rationalize a contrary argument.)

The broad acres of rich soil, the exuberant rivers, and the dimly concealed mineral wealth of America attracted migrants and helped create a new economy because with the land went a new social order open to all talents. After all, what did the European immigrant need to do? Little enough. As the Prince Royal of the Two Sicilies mused near Tallahassee in 1833: "Let him harden himself against privations by a passing effort. If he destine himself to trade let him establish a market where none are in existence. . . . If he be a physician, let him establish his reputation where he will have nobody, not even the dead, to contradict him; if he would be an agriculturalist let him grub about in new soils alone, without a neighbor, depending upon himself; he will be very liberally recompensed." Possibly the Prince was too sanguine;

royalty was not always properly informed about this new nation. But the endless extravagant stories—some false, but many true—when told to those who found no places for them at nature's table in the Old World reported the differential advantage that spurred immigration and the development of a new nation.

2. THE SOURCES OF ECONOMIC GROWTH

The year 1776 not only marks the Declaration of Independence and the beginning of the New Nation, but it also marks the beginning of modern economics. Adam Smith's *The Wealth of Nations* was published in that year, and it remains the landmark in the organization of economics as an analytical discipline. Adam Smith was writing a book about economic growth in which he first set down the fundamental principles that determined the wealth of a nation. Beyond that he was concerned to show how the reigning system of political economy—what he called mercantilism—was bound to have adverse and injurious effects upon the wealth of nations.

The Mainspring of Growth

Adam Smith's analysis of the importance of specialization and division of labor for economic growth and in turn their dependence on the size of the market remains a classic and one that is hardly likely to be controversial.[3]

The greatest improvement in the productive powers of labour, and the greater part of the skill, dexterity, and judgment with which it is any where directed, or applied, seem to have been the effects of the division of labour. . . . The division of labour, however, so far as it can be introduced, occasions, in every art, a proportionable increase of the productive powers of labour. The separation of different trades and employments from one another, seems to have taken place, in consequence of this advantage. This separation too is generally carried furthest in those countries which enjoy the highest degree of industry and improvement; what is the work of one man in a rude state of society, being generally that of several in an improved one. In every improved society, the farmer is generally nothing but a farmer; the manufacturer, nothing but a manufacturer. The labour too which is necessary to produce any one complete manufacture, is almost always divided among a great number of hands. How many

---

[3] Adam Smith, *The Wealth of Nations* (New York, 1901), 1:43, 45–46, 48, 60.

different trades are employed in each branch of the linen and woollen manufactures, from the growers of the flax and the wool, to the bleacher and smoothers of the linen, or to the dyers and dressers of the cloth! . . . This great increase of the quantity of work, which, in consequence of the division of labour, the same number of people are capable of performing, is owing to three different circumstances; first, to the increase of dexterity in every particular workman; secondly, to the saving of the time which is commonly lost in passing from one species of work to another; and lastly, to the invention of a great number of machines which facilitate and abridge labour, and enable one man to do the work of many. . . . As it is the power of exchanging that gives occasion to the division of labour, so the extent of this division must always be limited by the extent of that power, or, in other words, by the extent of the market. When the market is very small, no person can have any encouragement to dedicate himself entirely to one employment, for want of the power to exchange all that surplus part of the produce of his own labour, which is over and above his own consumption, for such parts of the produce of other men's labour as he has occasion for.

Attack on Mercantilism

Adam Smith's attack upon the mercantilism, with its implications for the neutral role of government in economic life, was not only controversial at the time he wrote it, but remains so today when expressed by his modern counterparts.[4]

Consumption is the sole end and purpose of all production; and the interest of the producer ought to be attended to, only so far as it may be necessary for promoting that of the consumer. The maxim is so perfectly self-evident, that it would be absurd to attempt to prove it. But in the mercantile system, the interest of the consumer is almost constantly sacrificed to that of the producer; and it seems to consider production, and not consumption, as the ultimate end and object of all industry and commerce.

In the restraints upon the importation of all foreign commodities which can come into competition with those of our own growth, or manufacture, the interest of the home consumer is evidently sacrificed to that of the producer. It is altogether for the benefit of the latter, that the former is obliged to pay that enhancement of price which this monopoly almost always occasions.

It is altogether for the benefit of the producer that bounties are granted upon the exportation of some of his productions. The home-consumer is obliged to pay, first, the tax which is necessary for paying the bounty, and, secondly, the still greater tax which necessarily arises from the enhancement of the price

[4] *Ibid.*, 2:442–44.

of the commodity in the home market.

By the famous treaty of commerce with Portugal, the consumer is prevented by high duties from purchasing of a neighbouring country, a commodity which our own climate does not produce, but is obliged to purchase it of a distant country, though it is acknowledged, that the commodity of the distant country is of a worse quality than that of the near one. The home-consumer is obliged to submit to this inconveniency, in order that the producer may import into the distant country some of his productions upon more advantageous terms than he would otherwise have been allowed to do. The consumer, too, is obliged to pay, whatever enhancement in the price of those very productions, this forced exportation may occasion in the home market.

But in the system of laws which has been established for the management of our American and West Indian colonies, the interest of the home-consumer has been sacrificed to that of the producer with a more extravagant profusion than in all our other commercial regulations. A great empire has been established for the sole purpose of raising up a nation of customers who should be obliged to buy from the shops of our different producers, all the goods with which these could supply them. For the sake of that little enhancement of price which this monopoly might afford our producers, the home-consumers have been burdened with the whole expense of maintaining and defending that empire. For this purpose, and for this purpose only, in the two last wars, more than two hundred millions have been spent, and a new debt of more than a hundred and seventy millions has been contracted over and above all that had been expended for the same purpose in former wars. The interest of this debt alone is not only greater than the whole extraordinary profit, which, it ever could be pretended, was made by the monopoly of the colony trade, but than the whole value of that trade, or than the whole value of the goods, which at an average have been annually exported to the colonies.

It cannot be very difficult to determine who have been the contrivers of this whole mercantile system; not the consumers, we may believe, whose interest has been entirely neglected; but the producers, whose interest has been so carefully attended to; and among this latter class our merchants and manufacturers have been by far the principal architects. In the mercantile regulations, which have been taken notice of in this chapter, the interest of our manufacturers has been most peculiarly attended to; and the interest, not so much of the consumers, as that of some other sets of producers, has been sacrificed to it.

In Defense of Goverment Intervention

Alexander Hamilton had read Adam Smith, and indeed he had, in general, been impressed by his study. But, like many contemporary Americans, Hamilton was convinced that the growth of the United States basically depended upon its ability to become a manufacturing nation, and he did not believe that manufacturing would develop automatically, without the aid of the government. Accordingly, in his celebrated *Report on Manufactures,* he not only described the benefits that would accrue from manufacturing, but he went on to recommend a set of policies aimed at promoting the development of these manufactures. These policies involved exactly the kind of subsidies and bounties which Adam Smith had attacked in his polemic against mercantilism.[5]

If the system of perfect liberty to industry and commerce were the prevailing system of nations, the arguments which dissuade a country, in the predicament of the United States, from the zealous pursuit of manufactures, would doubtless have great force. It will not be affirmed that they might not be permitted, with few exceptions, to serve as a rule of national conduct. In such a state of things, each country would have the full benefit of its peculiar advantages to compensate for its deficiencies or disadvantages. If one nation were in a condition to supply manufactured articles, on better terms than another, that other might find an abundant indemnification in a superior capacity to furnish the produce of the soil. And a free exchange, mutually beneficial, of the commodities which each was able to supply on the best terms might be carried on between them, supporting in full vigor the industry of each. And though the circumstances which have been mentioned, and others which will be unfolded hereafter, render it probable that nations, merely agricultural, would not enjoy the same degree of opulence, in proportion to their numbers, as those which unite manufactures with agriculture; yet the progressive improvement of the lands of the former might, in the end, atone for an inferior degree of opulence in the meantime; and in a case in which opposite considerations are pretty equally balanced, the option ought, perhaps, always to be in favor of leaving industry to its own direction.

But the system which has been mentioned is far from characterizing the general policy of nations. The prevalent one has been regulated by an opposite spirit. The consequence of it is that the United States are, to a certain extent, in the situation of a country precluded from foreign commerce. They can, indeed, without difficulty, obtain from abroad the manufactured supplies of which they are in want; but they experience numerous and very injurious impediments to the emission and vent of their own commodities. Nor is this the case in reference to a single foreign nation only. The regulations of several countries, with which we have the most extensive intercourse, throw serious obstructions in the way of the principal staples of the United States.

In such a position of things, the United States cannot exchange with Europe on equal terms; and the want of reciprocity would render them the victim of a system which would induce them to confine their views to agriculture, and refrain from manufactures. A constant and

---

[5] Alexander Hamilton, *Report on the Subject of Manfacturers* (Philadelphia: William Brown, 1827), 26–30.

increasing necessity, on their part, for the commodites of Europe, and only a partial and occasional demand for their own, in return, could not but expose them to a state of impoverishment, compared with the opulence to which their political and natural advantages authorize them to aspire.

Remarks of this kind are not made in the spirit of complaint. It is for the nations whose regulations are alluded to to judge for themselves, whether, by aiming at too much, they do not lose more than they gain. It is for the United States to consider by what means they can render themselves least dependent on the combinations, right or wrong, of foreign policy.

It is no small consolation, that, already, the measures which have embarrassed our trade, have accelerated internal improvements, which, upon the whole, have bettered our affairs. To diversify and extend these improvements is the surest and safest method of indemnifying ourselves for any inconveniences which those or similar measures have a tendency to beget. If Europe will not take from us the products of our soil, upon terms consistent with our interest, the natural remedy is to contract, as fast as possible, our wants of her.

The conversion of their waste into cultivated lands is certainly a point of great moment, in the political calculations of the United States. But the degree in which this may possibly be retarded, by the encouragement of manufactories, does not appear to countervail the powerful inducements to afford that encouragement.

An observation made in another place is of a nature to have great relevance upon this question. If it cannot be denied that the interests, even of agriculture, may be advanced more by having each of the lands of a State as are occupied, under good cultivation, than by having a greater quantity occupied under a much inferior cultivation; and if manufactories, for the reasons assigned, must be admitted to have a tendency to promote a more steady and vigorous cultivation of the lands occupied, than would happen without them, it will follow that they are capable of indemnifying a country for a diminution of the progress of new settlements; and may serve to increase both the capital value, and the income of its lands, even though they should abridge the number of acres under tillage.

But it does by no means follow that the progress of new settlements would be retarded by the extension of manufactures. The desire of being an independent proprietor of land is founded on such strong principles in the human breast, that, where the opportunity of becoming so is as great as it is in the United States, the proportion will be small of those whose situations would otherwise lead to it, who would be diverted from it toward manufactures. And it is highly probable, as already intimated, that the accessions of foreigners, who, originally drawn over by manufacturing views, would afterward abandon them for agricultural [pursuits], would be more than an equivalent for those of our own citizens who might happen to be detached from them.

The remaining objections to a particular encouragement of manufactures in the United States now require to be examined.

One of these turns on the proposition that industry, if left to itself, will naturally find its way to the most useful and profitable employment. Whence it is inferred, that manufactures, without the aid of government, will grow up as soon and as fast as the natural state of things and the interest of the community may require.

Against the solidity of this hypothesis, in the full latitude of the terms, very cogent reasons may be offered. These have relation to the strong influence of habit and the spirit of imitation; the fear of want of success in untried enterprises; the intrinsic difficulties incident to first essays toward a competition with those who have previously attained to perfection in the business to be attempted; the bounties, premiums, and other artificial encouragements, with which foreign nations second the exertions of their own citizens, in the branches in which they are to be rivalled.

Experience teaches that men are often so much governed by what they are accustomed to see and practice, that the simplest and most obvious improvements, in the most ordinary occupations, are adopted with hesitation, reluctance, and by slow gradations. The spontaneous transition to new pursuits, in a community long habituated to different ones, may be expected to be attended with proportionately greater difficulty. When former occupations ceased to yield a profit adequate to the subsistence of their followers; or when there was an absolute deficiency of employment in them, owing to the superabundance of hands, changes would ensue; but these changes would be likely to be more tardy than might consist with the interest either of individuals or of the society. In many cases they would not happen, while a bare support could be ensured by an adherence to ancient courses, though a resort to a more profitable employment might be practicable. To produce the desirable changes as early as may be expedient may, therefore, require the incitement and patronage of government.

The apprehension of failing in new attempts is, perhaps, a more serious impediment. There are dispositions apt to be attracted by the mere novelty of an undertaking; but these are not always those best calculated to give it success. To this, it is of importance that the confidence of cautious, sagacious capitalists, both citizens and foreigners, should be excited. And to inspire this description of persons with confidence, it is essential that they should be made to see in any project which is new—and for that reason alone, if for no other—precarious, the prospect of such a degree of countenance and support from government, as may be capable of overcoming the obstacles inseparable from first experiments.

The superiority antecedently enjoyed by nations who have preoccupied and perfected a branch of industry constitutes a more formidable obstacle than either of those which have been mentioned, to the introduction of the same branch into a country in which it did not before exist. To maintain, between the recent establishments of one country, and the long matured establishments of another country, a competition upon equal terms, both as to quality and price, is, in most cases, impracticable. The disparity, in the one, or in the other, or in both, must necessarily be so considerable, as to forbid a successful rivalship, without the extraordinary aid and protection of government.

But the greatest obstacle of all to

the successful prosecution of a new branch of industry in a country in which it was before unknown, consists, as far as the instances apply, in the bounties, premiums, and other aids, which are granted in a variety of cases, by the nations in which the establishments to be imitated are previously introduced. It is well known (and particular examples, in the course of this report, will be cited) that certain nations grant bounties on the exportation of particular commodities, to enable their own workmen to undersell and supplant all competitors, in the countries to which those commodities are sent. Hence the undertakers of a new manufacture have to contend, not only with the natural disadvantages of a new undertaking, but with the gratuities and remunerations which other governments bestow. To be enabled to contend with success, it is evident that the interference and aid of their own governments are indispensable.

Combinations by those engaged in a particular branch of business in one country, to frustrate the first efforts to introduce it into another, by temporary sacrifices, recompensed, perhaps, by extraordinary indemnifications of the government of such country, are believed to have existed, and are not to be regarded as destitute of probability. The existence or assurance of aid from the government of the country in which the business is to be introduced, may be essential to fortify adventurers against the dread of such combinations; to defeat their efforts, if formed; and to prevent their being formed, by demonstrating that they must in the end prove fruitless.

Whatever room there may be for an expectation, that the industry of a people, under the direction of private interest, will, upon equal terms, find out the most beneficial employment for itself, there is none for a reliance, that it will struggle against the force of unequal terms, or will, of itself, surmount all the adventitious barriers to a successful competition, which may have been erected, either by the advantages naturally acquired from practice, and previous possession of the ground, or by those which may have sprung from positive regulations and an artificial policy. This general reflection might alone suffice as an answer to the objection under examination, exclusively of the weighty considerations which have been particularly urged.

The objections to the pursuit of manufactures in the United States, which next present themselves to discussion, represent an impracticability of success, arising from three causes: scarcity of hands, dearness of labor, want of capital.

The two first circumstances are, to a certain extent, real; and, within due limits, ought to be admitted as obstacles to the success of manufacturing enterprise in the United States. But there are various considerations which lessen their force, and tend to afford an assurance that they are not sufficient to prevent the advantageous prosecution of many very useful and extensive manufactories.

With regard to scarcity of hands, the fact itself must be applied with no small qualification to certain parts of the United States. There are large districts which may be considered as pretty fully peopled; and which, notwithstanding a continual drain for distant settlement, are thickly interspersed with flourishing and increasing towns. If these districts have not already reached the point at which the complaint of scarcity of hands ceases, they are not remote from it, and are approaching fast towards it; and having, perhaps, fewer attractions to agriculture than some other parts of the Union, they exhibit a proportionably stronger tendency towards other kinds of industry. In these districts may be discerned no inconsiderable maturity for manufacturing establishments.

3. OBSTACLES TO EXPANSION

Following the achievement of independence in the 1780s, Americans debated the proper course for the future. The major part of the debate revolved around the course to follow to prosperity for the New Nation. It was not self-evident at this time that the American future was bright. Indeed, Lord Sheffield's *Observations on the American States*, predicting a gloomy future for the newly independent states, appeared on the face of it to make good sense. The Confederation period was a time of recession and then gradual recovery. But there was no booming expansion, and it is doubtful that the average per capita income was as high in the 1780s as it had been during late colonial times.

The Need for a Strong Central Government

One clearly evident difficulty was the lack of a well-organized central government able to provide the public confidence so essential for economic growth. This deficiency is vividly described by Alexander Hamilton in *Federalist Paper No. 15*.[6]

We may indeed with propriety be said to have reached almost the last stage of national humiliation. There is scarcely any thing that can wound the pride or degrade the character of an independent nation which we do not experience. Are there engagements to the performance of which we are held by every tie respectable among men? These are the subjects of constant and unblushing violation. Do we owe debts to foreigners and to our own citizens contracted in time of imminent peril for the preservation of our political existence? These remain without any proper or satisfactory provision for their discharge. Have we valuable territories and important posts in the possession of a foreign power which, by express stipulations, ought long since to have been surrendered? These are still retained, to the prejudice of our interests, not less than of our rights. Are we in a condition to resent or to repel the aggression? We have neither troops, nor treasury, nor government. Are we even in a condition to remon-

---

[6] *The Federalist* (Hallowell: Masters, Smith & Co., 1857), 15:66–67.

strate with dignity? The just imputations on our own faith, in respect to the same treaty, ought first to be removed. Are we entitled by nature and compact to a free participation in the navigation of the Mississippi? Spain excludes us from it. Is public credit an indispensable resource in time of public danger? We seem to have abandoned its cause as desperate and irretrievable. Is commerce of importance to national wealth? Ours is at the lowest point of declension. Is respectability in the eyes of foreign powers a safeguard against foreign encroachments? The imbecility of our government even forbids them to treat with us. Our ambassadors abroad are the mere pageants of mimic sovereignty. Is a violent and unnatural decrease in the value of land a symptom of national distress? The price of improved land in most parts of the country is much lower than can be accounted for by the quantity of waste land at market, and can only be fully explained by that want of private and public confidence, which are so alarmingly prevalent among all ranks, and which have a direct tendency to depreciate property of every kind. Is private credit the friend and patron of industry? That most useful kind which relates to borrowing and lending is reduced within the narrowest limits, and this still more from an opinion of insecurity than from the scarcity of money. To shorten an enumeration of particulars which can afford neither pleasure nor instruction, it may in general be demanded, what indication is there of national disorder, poverty, and insignificance that could befall a community so peculiarly blessed with natural advantages as we are, which does not form a part of the dark catalogue of our public misfortunes.

Foreign Discrimination

Even after adoption of the Constitution, American prosperity was far from assured. In 1790 the United States had less than four million people scattered over a vast area, no cities of even 50,000, and only five per cent of its population living in urban areas over 2,500. The domestic market was so small and scattered that it could not encourage the development of any large-scale enterprise. As in colonial days, Americans still relied upon foreign markets for their future for rapid expansion. Before 1776 Americans had depended upon shipping and the export of tobacco, rice, indigo, and other commodities for their then relatively high living standards. But Americans free and independent found themselves facing all the mercantilist restrictions imposed by other nations. Americans were foreigners outside the British imperial system. Thomas Jefferson described some of the discriminatory foreign policies which hamstrung American efforts to find markets overseas.[7]

---

[7] Thomas Jefferson, "Report of Secretary of State on the Privileges and Restrictions on the Commerce of the United States in Foreign Countries." Report to the 3rd Cong., 1st Sess., Dec. 16, 1793, printed in *American State Papers, 1789–1794* (Boston: T. B. Wait and Sons, 1817), 1:431–32, 428.

First. In Europe—

Our bread stuff is at most times under prohibitory duties in England, and considerably dutied on re-exportation from Spain to her colonies.

Our tobaccos are heavily dutied in England, Sweden, France, and prohibited in Spain and Portugal.

Our rice is heavily dutied in England and Sweden, and prohibited in Portugal.

Our fish and salted provisions are prohibited in England, and under prohibitory duties in France.

Our whale oils are prohibited in England and Portugal. And our vessels are denied naturalization in England, and of late, in France.

Second. In the West Indies—

All intercourse is prohibited with the possession of Spain and Portugal.

Our salted provisions and fish are prohibited by England.

Our salted pork and bread stuff (except maize) are received under temporary laws only in the dominions of France, and our salted fish pays there a weighty duty.

Third. In the article of navigation—

Our own carriage of our own tobacco is heavily dutied in Sweden, and lately in France.

We can carry no article, not of our own production, to the British ports in Europe. Nor even our own produce to her American possessions.

. . . Our ships, though purchased and navigated by their own subjects, are not permitted to be used, even in their trade with us.

While the vessels of other nations are secured by standing laws, which cannot be altered but by the concurrent will of the three branches of the British legislature, in carrying thither any produce or manufacture of the country to which they belong, which may be lawfully carried in any vessels, ours, with the same prohibition of what is foreign, are further prohibited by a standing law (12 Car. 2, 18. sect. 3.) from carrying thither all and any of our own domestic productions and manufactures. A subsequent act, indeed, has authorized their executive to permit the carriage of our own productions in our own bottoms at its sole discretion; and the permission has been given from year to year by proclamation, but subject every moment to be withdrawn on that single will, in which event, our vessels, having any thing on board, stand interdicted from the entry of all British ports. The disadvantage of a tenure which may be so suddenly discontinued was experienced by our merchants on a late occasion (April 12, 1792) when an official notification that this law would be strictly enforced, gave them just apprehensions for the fate of their vessels and cargoes despatched or destined to the ports of Great Britain. The minister of that court, indeed, frankly expressed his personal conviction, that the words of the order went farther than was intended, and so he afterwards officially informed us; but the embarrassments of the moment were real and great, and the possibility of their renewal lays our commerce to that country under the same species of discouragement as to other countries, where it is regulated by a single legislator; and the distinction is too remarkable not to be noticed, that our navigation is excluded from the security of fixed laws, while that security is given to the navigation of others.

Our vessels pay in their ports one shilling and nine pence, sterling, per ton, light and trinity dues, more than is paid by British ships, except in the port of London, where they pay the same as British.

The greater part of what they receive from us is re-exported to other countries, under the useless charges of an intermediate deposite, and double voyage.

4. THE LACK OF CAPITAL AND HIGH PRICE OF LABOR

War in Europe in 1793 began a period of very substantial American prosperity based upon exports and re-exports to all belligerents. It was a boom period in American history, and the seaports of New York, Philadelphia, Baltimore, and Boston grew rapidly. But this prosperity came to an end when Jefferson imposed an embargo on American shipping and exports. The result was to turn the resources of America toward producing manufactured goods rather than importing them, and, while the prosperity did not equal that enjoyed before 1807, it nevertheless led to cautious optimism on the part of some American observers with respect to the future. Secretary of the Treasury Albert Gallatin describes these in his report of 1810.[8]

From that imperfect sketch of American manufactures, it may, with certainty, be inferred that their annual product exceeds one hundred and twenty millions of dollars. And it is not improbable that the raw materials used, and the provisions and other articles consumed, by the manufacturers, create a home market for agricultural products not very inferior to that which arises from foreign demand. A result more favorable than might have been expected from a view of the natural causes which impede the introduction, and retard the progress of manufactures in the United States.

The most prominent of those causes are the abundance of land compared with the population, the high price of labor, and the want of a sufficient capital. The superior attractions of agricultural pursuits, the great extension of American commerce during the late European wars, and the continuance of habits after the causes which produced them have ceased to exist, may also be numerated. Several of those obstacles have, however, been removed or lessened. The cheapness of provisions had always, to a certain extent, counterbalanced the high price of manual labor; and this is now, in many important branches, nearly superseded by the introduction of machinery; a great American capital has been acquired during the last twenty years; and the injurious violations of the neutral commerce

---

[8] Albert Gallatin, *American State Papers, Finance* (Washington: Gales and Seaton, 1832–61), 2:430–31.

of the United States, by forcing industry and capital into other channels, have broken inveterate habits, and given a general impulse, to which must be ascribed the great increase of manufactures during the two last years.

The revenue of the United States, being principally derived from duties on the importation of foreign merchandise, these have also operated as a premium in favor of American manufactures, whilst, on the other hand, the continuance of peace, and the frugality of Government, have rendered unnecessary any oppressive taxes, tending materially to enhance the price of labor, or impeding any species of industry.

No cause, indeed, has, perhaps, more promoted, in every respect, the general prosperity of the United States than the absence of those systems of internal restrictions and monopoly which continue to disfigure the state of society in other countries. No law exists here, directly or indirectly, confining man to a particular occupation or place, or excluding any citizen from any branch, he may, at any time, think proper to pursue. Industry is, in every respect, perfectly free and unfettered; every species of trade, commerce, art, profession, and manufacture, being equally opened to all, without requiring any previous regular apprenticeship, admission, or licence. Hence the progress of America has not been confined to the improvement of her agriculture, and to the rapid formation of new settlements and States in the wilderness; but her citizens have extended their commerce through every part of the globe, and carry on with complete success, even those branches for which a monopoly had heretofore been considered essentially necessary.

The same principle has also accelerated the introduction and progress of manufactures, and must ultimately give in that branch, as in all others, a decided superiority to the citizens of the United States over the inhabitants of countries oppressed by taxes, restrictions, and monopolies. It is believed that, even at this time, the only powerful obstacle against which American manufactures have to struggle, arises from the vastly superior capital of the first manufacturing nation of Europe, which enables her merchants to give very long credits, to sell on small profits, and to make occasional sacrifices.

The information which has been obtained is not sufficient to submit, in conformity with the resolution of the House, the plan best calculated to protect and promote American manufactures. The most obvious means are bounties, increased duties on importation, and loans by Government.

Occasional premiums might be beneficial; but a general system of bounties is more applicable to articles exported than to those manufactured for home consumption.

The present system of duties may, in some respects, be equalized and improved, so as to protect some species of manufactures without affecting the revenue. But prohibitory duties are liable to the treble objection of destroying competition, of taxing the consumer, and of diverting capital and industry into channels generally less profitable to the nation than those which would have naturally been pursued by individual interest left to itself. A moderate increase will be less dangerous, and, if adopted, should be continued during a certain period; for the repeal of a duty once laid, materially injures those who have relied on its permanency, as has been exemplified in the salt manufacture.

Since, however, the comparative want of capital, is the principal obstacle to the introduction and advancement of manufactures in America, it seems that the most efficient, and most obvious remedy would consist in supplying that capital. For, although the extension of banks may give some assistance in that respect, their operation is limited to a few places, nor does it comport with the nature of those institutions to lend for periods as long as are requisite for the establishment of manufactures. The United States might create a circulating stock, bearing a low rate of interest, and lend it at par to manufacturers, on principles somewhat similar to that formerly adopted by the States of New York and Pennsylvania, in their *loan offices*. It is believed that a plan might be devised by which five millions of dollars a year, but not exceeding, in the whole, twenty millions, might be thus lent, without any material risk of ultimate loss, and without taxing or injuring any other part of the community.

5. ACCELERATION IN ECONOMIC GROWTH

Americans have always enjoyed a living standard which was high relative to European countries with rich natural resources. Even the farmer and pioneer on the frontier seldom lacked for food or the wherewithal to build shelter and make his own clothes. The United States was a rich country. Nevertheless, growth of efficiency, which made possible economic growth and increasing prosperity, probably occurred slowly. This rate of growth accelerated at some time between 1815 and 1860. We have figures for the rate of growth from 1839 onward. If we project these backwards, we find that it leads to a level so low by the end of the eighteenth and early nineteenth centuries as to be simply inconsistent with our knowledge about the standard of living at that time. Thus it is clear that at some time before 1840 there was a substantial increase in the rate of efficiency. But developments of the previous era had been important. The expansion that occurred during the Napoleonic wars stimulated the growth of larger cities, efficiency in shipping, and investments in roads, turnpikes, and improved facilities for docks, warehouses, and the like, all of which were important for the subsequent era. We should also note another development that took place in the earlier period: the invention of the cotton gin and the spread of cotton culture throughout the South. By 1815 cotton was pre-eminent in the Southern economy, and cotton had become the major export commodity, so much so indeed that over the rest of the period, until 1860, cotton accounted for more than half of total exports. But as the South became committed to cotton, the West, particularly after the advent of the steamboat in 1816, became a rapidly expanding area producing wheat, corn, and livestock products for markets at home and abroad. The Northeast continued to be predominantly devoted to shipping, commerce, and agriculture, but manufacturing gradually took hold during this period. This was not accomplished without painful readjustment. The early manufacturing which Gallatin had believed would be sustained as a result of separation of trade with England in the period from 1807 to 1814 mostly went bankrupt in the face of the competition of more efficient English manufacturers after the return of peace. But some of the mills survived and other mills gradually developed in New England, and manufacturing continued a steady expansion thereafter.

Internal and Interregional Trade

The growth of three separate and distinct regions specializing in different kinds of economic activity made possible the specialization and division of labor on an international and interregional trade, which was consistent with Adam Smith's argument. The result was a pattern of trade and commerce which characterized the American economy during the ante-bellum period and was an important cause of growth, as the following comments by an economic historian reveal.[9]

It was cotton which was the most important influence in the growth in the market size and the consequent expansion of the economy: the slow development of the 1820's, the accelerated growth in the 1830's. In this period of rapid growth, it was cotton that initiated the concomitant expansion in income, in the size of domestic markets, and creation of the social overhead investment (in the course of its role in the marketing of cotton) in the Northeast which were to facilitate the subsequent rapid growth of manufactures. Cotton also accounted for the accelerated pace of westward migration as well as for the movement of people out of self-sufficiency into the market economy.

Cotton was not the only expansive influence in the economy during this period. Clearly there were others, and they will be considered. Had there been no cotton gin, it is certain that the resources directly and indirectly devoted to the cotton trade would have been at least partially absorbed in other types of economic activity. Given the social structure, attitudes and motivation of American society, and the rich quantity and quality of resources which made even the self-sufficient

[9] Douglass C. North, *The Economic Growth of the United States, 1790–1860,* 68–74. Copyright © 1961. Reprinted by permission of Prentice-Hall, Inc.

farmer well off as compared with his European counterpart, the United States economy would not have stagnated. But cotton was the commodity for which foreign demand was significantly increasing, it accounted for over half the value of exports, and the income directly or indirectly from cotton was the major independent influence on the evolving pattern of interregional trade. Without cotton the development in the size of the market would have been a much more lengthy process, since there was no alternative way to expand the domestic market rapidly without recourse to external demand. In short, cotton was the most important proximate cause of expansion, and by tracing out the resulting interrelationships light may be shed on the pace and character of the economy's development, particularly in the years up to 1843.

... A great deal of economic activity is a passive rather than an active source of economic expansion. It grows up either dependent upon an "active" industry or in response to the growth of income initially generated by the carriers of economic change. In the examination of economic change it is important to distinguish between an independent variable initiating the change and the expansion of dependent economic activity which is induced by the "carrier" industry. This distinction is undoubtedly more difficult to make today than it was before 1860, when transport barriers and distinct patterns of regional specialization and internal trade all pointed to the strategic role of cotton. Direct income from the cotton trade was probably no more than six per cent of any plausible estimate of national income which we might employ, but when income from cotton exports, including shipments to textile mills in our own Northeast, grew from $25 million in 1831 to $70 million in 1836, it set in motion the whole process of accelerated expansion which culminated in 1839. Certainly the views of contemporaries, Northern observers as well as Southerners, support the position that in this period cotton was indeed king.

The cotton trade remained an important influence upon the economy until 1860, but its role declined in relative importance after the boom and depression that followed 1938. It is not that income from cotton did not grow. On the contrary, the 1850's represented another prosperous era, though not as wildly speculative as former ones, in which the value of the cotton trade exceeded any former period. However, a major consequence of the expansive period of the 1830's was the creation of conditions that made possible industrialization in the Northeast. Transport facilities developed to connect the East and West more efficiently; a new market for western staples developed in the rapidly urbanizing East and, sporadically, in Europe. The dependence of both the Northeast and the West on the South waned.* The discovery of gold in California in 1848 created a third source of expansion outside the South. The Far West was

---

* The most striking evidence of the changing role of cotton is provided by its role in cyclical turning points. While cotton set the pace in the booms and depressions of 1815–1823 and 1823–1843, it lagged a full two years behind the recovery that began in 1843 and was clearly not a major influence in the cyclical downturn of 1857. In fact, the South was relatively unaffected by that depression.

not only a major market for the goods and services of the Northeast, but its one export, gold, played a vital role in the whole expansion of the 1850's.

It should not be forgotten that the United States expansion was taking place within the larger context of the Atlantic economy. While the demand for cotton in England and to a lesser extent in France played perhaps the most prominent part, the terms of trade, relative price levels here and abroad, the movement of productive factors, and the flow of ideas, particularly technological information, were all a part of the interrelated pattern of development.

Throughout the whole period the secular movement of the terms of trade became increasingly favorable. In the expansive surges of 1815–1818 and 1832–1839 they became very favorable, reflecting a rapid rise in the price of American exports. In these two periods, it was cotton that accounted for the rise and appeared to initiate the subsequent flow of capital in response to the increased profitability of opening up and developing new sources of supply of the export staple and western foodstuffs. The consequent divergence of domestic and foreign price levels, and the increase in imports and specie movements, determined the timing of cyclical movements. Attractive employment opportunities during these surges of expansion were the pull which brought immigrants to American shores in increasing numbers.

Expansion in the 1850's, unlike that of the two previous booms, was not preceded by favorable movements of the terms of trade—instead it was the domestic price level which began to rise before the export price index. Cotton played a part in the boom, but it was industrialization in the Northeast and the opening up of the West and Far West which were primarily responsible for the growth of the 1840's and 1850's. The influence of the international economy was felt less in the flow of capital than in the flow of people, with the first big wave of immigration coming in this period.

The foregoing summary has emphasized surges in growth followed by periods of depression, then gradual expansion preceding still another boom. The explanation of these long swings is that these movements are initiated by the movement of prices in the key "carrier" industries. Shifts in supply and demand result in a shift of resources into these areas in periods of rising prices. There is concomitant expansion in the wide variety of subsidiary, complementary, and residentiary activities whose fortunes are tied to the growth of the "carrier" industries and to the rise in income that is initiated by these surges of expansion. The process is a lengthy and cumulative one, ultimately overlaid with speculative excesses; the tremendous expansion in supply results in a painful period of declining prices and readjustment. In the first two expansive periods analyzed here, 1815 to 1818 and 1832 to 1839, cotton was the key industry in both the boom and the subsequent collapse and readjustment. In the last period the sources of expansion are more diffuse, but grain in the West played the most important role.

. . . While there had been little incentive to buy and clear new land for cotton during the period of low prices, rising prices triggered a land boom in the new South. Millions of acres of virgin land were sold; planters and their slaves migrated in large numbers to open up and exploit the rich land in the Southwest —Alabama, Louisiana, Mississippi, and Arkansas were the major states. A lengthy period intervened between the initial impetus from rising prices and substantial output increases for putting this land into production. While imperfections in the capital market and land speculation partially explain this delay, the more important reasons were the time it took to obtain slaves from the old South, clear the land, and plant a crop or two of corn to prepare the soil. . . . There was a lag of approximately four years between the peak in land sales and a large increase in cotton production. The consequence was a vast shift to the right in the supply curve of cotton and the beginning of a new period of depressed prices. Cotton output actually fell as some of this land was diverted into corn with the low cotton prices that prevailed after 1839.

In the West, the same general pattern prevailed with respect to wheat and corn. Land sales in the western states paralleled the prices of those staples, with one important difference. Little transportation or other social overhead investment was necessary to increase the supply of cotton in the South. In the West, transportation was the major limiting factor in increasing supply. The accessible lands close to water transportation were taken up first. Initially, the rise in prices brought into cultivation land further and further from cheap transportation. As a result, the supply curve of wheat and corn land was probably less inelastic than cotton as it began to slope upward. However, it also encouraged a boom in land sales and at the same time a growing agitation for large-scale investment in new transportation facilities. Canal and railroad building was a lengthy process, but a completed canal or railroad opened up large amounts of new land. The canal construction era of the 1830's and the railroad construction period of the 1850's each served to make possible, along with the land sales and influx of settlers that accompanied them, a large shift to the right in wheat and corn supplies, with much the same results as cotton.

Protection and Manufacturing

Growth of a home market and regional specialization helped Northeastern manufacturers to compete with those from abroad, particularly England. Inevitably, there was continuing controversy over tariff protection. Was it necessary for the industrial expansion which was clearly an integral part of the growing part of the American economy? In a celebrated speech in 1824, Daniel Webster opposed such protection. However, by 1828 the economy of New England and particularly of his constituents had so changed that Webster, in spite of doubts and misgivings, supported increasing tariffs on manufactured goods. Webster's arguments as well as some of his doubts are well expressed in his speech of 1828.[10]

New England, sir, has not been a leader in this policy. On the contrary, she held back herself and tried to hold others back from it, from the adoption of the Constitution to 1824. Up to 1824, she was accused of sinister and selfish designs, because she discountenanced the progress of this policy. It was laid to her charge then, that, having established her manufactures herself, she wished that others should not have the power of rivalling her, and for that reason opposed all legislative encouragement. Under this angry denunciation against her, the act of 1824 passed. Now, the imputation is precisely of an opposite character. The present measure is pronounced to be exclusively for the benefit of New England; to be brought forward by her agency, and designed to gratify the cupidity of the proprietors of her wealthy establishments.

Both charges, sir, are equally without the slightest foundation. The opinion of New England up to 1824 was founded in the conviction that, on the whole, it was wisest and best, both for herself and others, that manufactures should make haste slowly. She felt a reluctance to trust great interests on the foundation of government patronage; for who could tell how long such patronage would last, or with what steadiness, skill, or perseverance it would continue to be granted? It is now nearly fifteen years since, among the first things which I ever ventured to say here, I expressed a serious doubt whether this government was fitted, by its construction, to administer aid and protection to particular pursuits; whether, having called such pursuits into being by indications of its favor, it would not afterwards desert them, should troubles come upon them, and leave them to their fate. Whether this prediction, the result, certainly, of chance, and not of sagacity, is about to be fulfilled, remains to be seen.

At the same time it is true, that, from the very first commencement of the government, those who have administered its concerns have held a tone of encouragement and invitation towards those who should embark in manufactures. All the Presidents, I believe without exception, have concurred in this general sentiment; and the very first act of Congress laying duties on imports adopted the then unusual expedient of a preamble, apparently for little other purpose than that of declaring that the duties which it imposed were laid for the encouragement and protection of manufactures. When, at the commencement of the late war, duties were doubled, we were told that we should find a mitigation of the weight of taxation in the new aid and succor which would be thus afforded to our own manufacturing labor. Like arguments were urged, and prevailed, but not by the aid of New England votes,

---

[10] Guy Stevens Callender, ed., *Selections from the Economic History of the United States, 1765–1860* (Boston: Ginn and Company, 1909), 510–13.

when the tariff was afterwards arranged, at the close of the war in 1816. Finally, after a whole winter's deliberation, the act of 1824 received the sanction of both houses of Congress, and settled the policy of the country. What, then, was New England to do? She was fitted for manufacturing operations, by the amount and character of her population, by her capital, by the vigor and energy of her free labor, by the skill, economy, enterprise, and perseverance of her people. I repeat, what was she under these circumstances to do? A great and prosperous rival in her near neighborhood, threatening to draw from her a part, perhaps a great part, of her foreign commerce; was she to use, or to neglect, those other means of seeking her own prosperity which belonged to her character and her condition? Was she to hold out forever against the course of the government, and see herself losing on the one side, and yet make no effort to sustain herself on the other? No, sir. Nothing was left to New England, after the act of 1924, but to conform herself to the will of others. Nothing was left to her, but to consider that the government had fixed and determined its own policy; and that policy was protection.

New England, poor in some respects, in others is as wealthy as her neighbors. Her soil would be held in low estimation by those who are acquainted with the valley of the Mississippi and the fertile plains of the South. But in industry, in habits of labor, skill, and in accumulated capital, the fruit of two centuries of industry, she may be said to be rich. After this final declaration, this solemn promulgation of the policy of the government, I again ask, What was she to do? Was she to deny herself the use of her advantages, natural and acquired? Was she to content herself with useless regrets? Was she longer to resist what she could no longer prevent? Or was she, rather, to adapt her acts to her condition; and, seeing that policy of the government thus settled and fixed, to accommodate to it as well as she could her own pursuits and her own industry? Every man will see that she had no option. Every man will confess that there remained for her but one course. She not only saw this herself, but had all along foreseen, that, if the system of protecting manufactures should be adopted, she must go largely into them. I believe, sir, almost every man from New England who voted against the law of 1824 declared that, if, notwithstanding his opposition to that law, it should still pass, there would be no alternative but to consider the course and policy of the government as then settled and fixed, and to act accordingly. The law did pass; and a vast increase of investment in manufacturing establishments was the consequence. Those who made such investments probably entertained not the slightest doubt that as much as was promised would be effectually granted; and that if, owing to any unforeseen occurrence or untoward event, the benefit designed by the law to any branch of manufactures should not be realized, it would furnish a fair case for the consideration of government. Certainly they could not expect, after what had passed, that interests of great magnitude would be left at the mercy of the very first change of circumstances which might occur.

Human Capital and Manufacturing

The success of American manufacturing came in spite of formidable obstacles. Some of these obstacles have been described earlier. Wages were higher in America than Europe, as were interest rates. These were two important elements in manufacturing costs and, on the face of it, made it difficult for the New Nation to compete with England's large-scale factories. Yet, compete Americans did. A large part of the success of this growing competition came from the ubiquitous character of American skills. The ability of craftsmen, mechanics, and carpenters to take, adapt, and modify existing technology so as to conserve scarce labor and utilize abundant resources must play a big part in any analysis.

In his account of the development of the Saco-Lowell shops, the first important American manufacturers of machinery, G. S. Gibb describes these characteristics:[11]

The fact that Samuel Slater, in 1790, and Francis Lowell, in 1813, could find skilled native workmen to assist them is attributable to the training of many generations of farmer-mechanics in the workshops of colonial New England. The manufacturing enterprises which existed in the heart of America's eighteenth-century mercantile-agricultural economy were numerous and diversified, and the many skills of American craftsmen were full of portent for future industrial development. Varied and dextrous mechanical abilities were all but universal, and it is a fact of great significance that large segments of the population had long been accustomed to working with their hands. In organization the factories of the early nineteenth century were a distinct departure from the colonial workshops, but the Industrial Revolution in its infancy produced surprisingly few basic technical skills not already familiar to American mechanics. In the experimental decade which followed 1800 there was little of the precision and there were few of the power tools which later were to come. Superb skill was displayed in the use of hand tools, but machine tolerances of $\frac{1}{32}$ of an inch were the best that toolmakers strove for. By 1813, workers in iron were being called mechanics as well as blacksmiths, but few mechanics and even fewer blacksmiths could aspire to the title of machinist. There were few mechanical engineers and no industrial scientists, for the union of scientific theory with workbench skills was too new to have borne fruit. The competent mechanic at that time was the man who could hang a water wheel and rig the shafting with the precise balance of forces which transferred clumsy wood and iron into harnessed power, and who

---

[11] George Sweet Gibb, *The Saco-Lowell Shops* (Cambridge: Harvard University Press, 1950), 10–11. Reprinted by permission.

could work a true plane surface with tools which he had made himself. The mechanic of 1813 was at once a carpenter, a millwright, and a toolmaker. Yet America, in 1813, had machine tools of a kind, and men who could use them to build intricate machines. Even if, as a Massachusetts manufacturer of the time said, these machines were slightly constructed and had to be nursed with all the attention required by rickety children, the very existence of these machines was prophetic. If the gulf which separated English and American achievements in machine-building was wide, America needed only the stimulus of men like Slater and Lowell to give fresh motion and new direction to the tremendous forces of existing native genius.

Slater had required assistance to put his machines together. George S. White, his biographer, says, "it appears, that at the commencement of the business, Mr. Slater was under the necessity of hiring mechanics, or workmen, in iron and wood, of the then common trades of the country, and teaching them the trade of building machinery." Thirteen years later Francis Cabot Lowell, however, had a double advantage. He had at his disposal mechanics who possessed not only their basic skills in the "then common trades" but also a practical knowledge of textile machinery as it then existed. Paul Moody was such a mechanic, and even though he was Lowell's second choice, he immediately proved to be as powerful and significant a figure in the Boston Manufacturing Company as Francis Lowell himself.

A British Appraisal

American manufacturing development was so impressive in the 1830s and 1840s that it was attracting world-wide attention by 1850, and several British commissions came to the United States to investigate the character and sources of American success. The most notable of these was headed by Joseph Whitworth and George Wallis and was composed of specialists in manufacturing techniques who were in a position to appraise the success of the manufacturing in the American nation. The following is a summary of their analysis. It stresses some of the points described earlier, particularly the size of the market, the importance of education, the ability to adapt and modify techniques, and the driving energy of the American populace.[12]

The industry of the United States has to be estimated by the peculiar circumstances of the country to which it has been devoted. In the States the labor market is higher than with ourselves, especially as respects skilled labor. It has, therefore, been a principal aim as much as possible to apply machinery for the

---

12 Sir Joseph Whitworth and George Wallis, *The Industry of the United States in Machinery, Manufacturers, and Useful and Ornamental Arts* (London: George Routledge & Co., 1854), 482–86.

purpose of supplying this want, and, as the consequence, it will be seen that some of the principal achievements of American inventors have been acquired in this department. To this very want of human skill, and the absolute necessity for supplying it, may be attributed the extraordinary ingenuity displayed in many of their labor-saving machines, where automatic action so completely supplies the place of the more abundant hand labor of older manufacturing countries.

Of this we have an illustration in the machine for the manufacture of the seamless grain bags, the loom for which is described as a perfect self-actor or automaton, commencing the bag, and continuing the process until the work is turned out complete.

For another curious illustration of this automatic action we have the manufacture of ladies' hair-pins at Waterbury. A quantity of wire is coiled upon a drum or cylinder, and turns round upon its axis, as suspended from the ceiling of the workshop. The point of the wire being inserted into the machine, and the power applied, the wire is cut off to the requisite length, carried forward and bent to the proper angle, and then pointed with the necessary blunt points, and finally dropped into a receiver, quite finished, all but the lacquering or japanning. These pins are made at the rate of 180 per minute.

The reader is referred also to the automaton machine for shanking buttons. The blanks being cut in thin brass, are put into a curved feeding-pipe, in which they descend to the level of the machine, by which a hole is stamped in the center of each. Then the shank is formed by another portion of the machine, from a continuous wire carried along horizontally, the wire being shaped into the shank, and pushed up into its proper place. These operations are completed at the rate of 200 a minute, the only attendance required being that of one person to feed this automaton with the blanks and the wires, which he is so well able to work up to the satisfaction of his masters.

There is, of course, nothing to boast of on the ground of superiority on account of these inventions; but it is much to the credit of the American inventor, that he is able so to meet the necessities of his case, and supply the want of fingers, which are at present so scarce.

Another peculiarity observable in American industry, is the want of that division of labor which is one of the great causes of excellence in the productions of our own and other of the older countries in which art is carried to a high point of perfection. With us, trades and manufactures branch out into a variety of subdivisions, from which, besides the perfection noticed, we have a great economy of time, and, consequently, of expense. The citizen of the United States knows that matters are different with him, and seems really to pride himself in not remaining over long at any particular occupation, and being able to turn his hand to some dozen different pursuits in the course of his life.

This knowledge of two or three departments of one trade, or even the pursuit of several trades, by one individual, does not interfere so much with the systematic division of labor as may be supposed. In most instances the change of employment is made at convenient periods, or as a relief to the workman from the monotony of always doing the same thing. This change and variety of occupation is, in many respects, favorable to the man, as distinguished from the operative or the artist. In many cases our economic laws enhance the work or the value of time, when they degrade the workmen, between whom and the perfection of their works a singular contrast exists. While our American operative is a man and a citizen, he is often found wanting in that perfect skill of hand and marvelous accuracy which distinguish the workmen of this country. So much is there to check the national tendencies of self-congratulation and boasting on either side of the Atlantic, and to promote respect and good feeling among us all.

The machinery of a country will naturally correspond with its wants, and with the history and state of its people. Testing the machinery of the United States by this rule of adaptation, the mechanical appliances in use must call forth much admiration. A large proportion of the mechanical power of the United States has, from its earliest application, been from the circumstances of the country, directed to wood, this being the material on which it has been requisite to operate for so many purposes, and which is presented in the greatest abundance. Stone, for a similar reason, has been subdued to man's use by the application of machinery, of which we have an instance in the fact that one man is able to perform as much work by machinery in stone-dressing as twenty persons by hand. In common with our own and other great manufacturing countries, the Union presents remarkable illustrations of the amazingly productive power of machinery, as compared with mere manual operations. Into the details of these triumphs of machinery it is unnecessary here to enter. It may suffice to refer to the improvements effected in spinning machinery, by which one man can attend to a mule containing 1,088 spindles, each spinning three hanks, or 3,264 hanks a day; so that, as compared with the operations of the most expert spinner in Hindustan, the American operative can perform the work of 3,000 men.

The Law of Limited Liability, which is now engaging public attention, is an important source of the prosperity which attends the industry of the United States. This law affords the most ample facilities for the investment of capital, and has led to a much greater development of the industrial resources and skill of that country than could have resulted under other circumstances for many years to come. In the United States, the agent or secretary, manager, treasurer, and directors being also shareholders, are held by the law responsible to the extent of their means for the results of the management intrusted to them. The limited responsibility is confined to the non-managing shareholders only. It will be seen from the several illustrations given in the following pages, that this law works well in America; and these facts will strengthen the case of those who advocate its application to our country.

The comparative density of the old and the new countries, differing as they do, will account for the very different feelings with which the increase of machinery has been regarded in many parts of this country and the United States, where the workmen hail with satisfaction all mechanical improvements, the importance and value of which, as releasing them from the drudgery of unskilled labor, they are enabled by education to understand and appreciate. This statement is not intended to disparage the operatives of our own country, who in many respects are placed in a position different from that of their class in the United States, where the principles that ought to regulate the relations between the employer and the employed are thoroughly understood, and where the law of limited liability, to which we have just referred, affords the most ample facilities for the investment of capital in business, and where the skilled laborer is in many respects furnished with many opportunities of advancement which he has not among us. Particularly it should be noticed that no taxation of any kind is suffered to interfere with the free development of the press, and that the humblest laborer can indulge in the luxury of his daily paper, so that everybody reads, and intelligence penetrates through the lowest grades of society.

The compulsory educational clauses adopted in the laws of most of the States, and especially those of New England, by which some three months of every year must be spent at school by the young factory operative under 14 or 15 years of age, secure every child from the cupidity of the parent, or the neglect of the manufacturer; since to profit by the child's labor during *threefourths* of the year, he or she must be regularly in attendance in some public or private school conducted by some authorized teacher during the other fourth.

This lays the foundation for that widespread intelligence which prevails amongst the factory operatives of the United States; and though at first sight the manufacturer may appear to be restricted in the free use of the labor offered to him, the system reacts to the permanent advantage of both the employer and employed.

The skill of hands which comes of experience is, notwithstanding present defects, rapidly following the perceptive power so keenly awakened by early intellectual training. Quickly learning from the skillful European artisans thrown amongst them by emigration, or imported as instructors, with minds, as already stated, prepared by sound practical education, the Americans have laid the foundation of a widespread system of manufacturing operations, the influence of which cannot be calculated upon, and are daily improving upon the lessons obtained from their older and more experienced compeers of Europe.

Commercially, advantages of no ordinary kind are presented to the manufacturing States of the American Union. The immense development of its resources in the west, the demands of a population increasing daily by emigration from Europe, as also by the results of a healthy natural process of inter-emigration, which tends to spread over an enlarged surface the population of the Atlantic States; the facilities of communication by lakes, rivers, and railways; and the cultivation of European tastes, and consequently of European wants; all tend to the encouragement of those arts and manufactures which it is the interest of the citizens of the older states to cultivate, and in which they have so far succeeded that their markets may be said to be secured to them as much as manufacturers, as they have hitherto been, and will doubtless continue to be, as merchants. For whether the supply is derived from the home or foreign manufacturer, the demand cannot fail to be greater than the industry of both can supply. This once fairly recognised, those jealousies which have ever tended to retard the progress of nations in the peaceful arts, will be no longer suffered to interfere, by taking the form of restrictions on commerce and the free intercourse of peoples.

The extent to which the people of the United States have as yet succeeded in manufactures may be attributed to indomitable energy and an educated intelligence, as also to the ready welcome accorded to the skilled workmen of Europe, rather than to any peculiar native advantages; since these latter have only developed themselves as manufacturing skill and industry have progressed. Only one obstacle of any importance stands in the way of constant advance towards greater perfection, and that is the conviction that perfection is already attained. This opinion, which prevails to a large extent, is unworthy of that intelligence which has overcome so many difficulties, and which can only be prevented from achieving all it aspires to, by a vain-glorious conviction that it has nothing more to do.

CONCLUSION

The acceleration in the economic growth of the United States in the first half of the nineteenth century was a striking phenomenon. At the same time that industrialization was occurring in the Northeast there was expansion and improving efficiency in the agriculture of the West and even in the slave-plantation cotton economy of the South. What accounts for the surging expansion and growing efficiency which has continued to characterize the economy ever since? Were the underlying attitudes of the American people the dominant factor? Or was it the growing specialization by regions and the resultant expansion of interregional trade that made possible improving efficiency not only in manufacturing but also in agriculture? Was it primarily the expansion of industry in the Northeast, a factor which has been such a conspicuous explanation for success for most countries in the world? Even if we give a large share of the credit for the sustained growth to increasing industrial productivity, what accounts for the success of America's manufacturing? How much should we ascribe to the high levels of education that characterized the American worker, or to the skilled talent of both the workers and the immigrant who adapted and modified British technology to make it suitable for American needs? Finally, how much importance should we ascribe to the size of the American market?

We could solve the problems of poverty in the underdeveloped areas in the world today if we had simple answers to these questions. But the tentative and sketchy conclusions we can draw from material, such as that presented above, mirror the state of our knowledge about the sources of economic growth in the world as a whole. We still are experimenting, hopeful that our guesses are correct.

9 ARTHUR BESTOR

the ferment of reform

"In the history of the world," wrote Ralph Waldo Emerson in 1841, "the doctrine of Reform had never such scope as at the present hour."[1] In 1815 there began, for the United States and Europe alike, an unprecedented period of peace. On both sides of the Atlantic reformers took up again the unfinished business that had been postponed during long years of crisis and war. And they began to tackle the new problems that the nineteenth century was creating—problems arising from the increased speed of communication, from the growth of factories and cities, from the stirring of new ideas in masses of men hitherto little touched by the currents of change.

That the ferment of reform was indeed international was shown by the numerous parallels between developments in different countries. In the United States, for example, the inauguration of Andrew Jackson as President in 1829 symbolized the assumption of political power by social classes whose influence in times past had been strictly limited. In Great Britain the passage of the Reform Bill of 1832 produced a shift of power comparable in direction although far from identical in character. On the Continent the revolutions of 1830 brought forward similar demands.

In 1848 virtually the whole of Europe erupted in revolution, while the United States, attempting to deal with the territorial acquisitions that followed the Mexican War, found itself face to face with the gravest internal crisis of its history—a crisis involving slavery, and eventually

---

[1] Ralph Waldo Emerson, "Man the Reformer," *The Dial*, 1 (April 1841), 523.

producing the Civil War of 1861–65. These same years saw Europe torn by conflicts that resulted in the unification of Italy (1859–61) and of Germany (1864–71), the reorganization of the Austro-Hungarian Empire (1867), the emergence of the Third French Republic (1870), and such internal changes as the freeing of the serfs in Russia (1861) and the Second Reform Bill in Britain (1867).

These were not ordinary political changes. They furnished evidence that profound forces were at work beneath the surface, remaking the whole character of Western civilization. Economic factors were especially obvious, for what came to be called an "Industrial Revolution" was under way, made possible by a corresponding revolution in transportation. Agriculture was drastically affected, and thereby the ancient balance between rural and urban ways of living. The situation of the new factory worker was markedly different from that of either the craftsman or the peasant of older days, and the problems of labor accordingly became, for the nineteenth century, the subject of acute and heated debate.

To some historians economic change has seemed a sufficient explanation for the great upheavals of the nineteenth century. Without denying the significance of economic factors, however, most historians insist that changes in men's outlook on the world must also be taken into account in explaining the tremendous power of such ideas as nationalism, democracy, and humanitarianism. Even doctrines like socialism—and its opposite, *laissez faire*—ostensibly concerned with economic matters, were shaped by the prevailing climate of opinion—that is, by the complex of scientific, religious, philosophical, and political theories that the age took for granted and made the basis of its thought and action.

Because change was so marked a feature of the nineteenth century, particular interest attaches to the men and women who actively sought change—the reformers. The fields in which they labored, the ends they sought, and the methods they used were of the most varied character. Mere political change was of interest to only part of the number. A larger group were seeking economic reforms of one kind or another, but even these concerns did not engross the whole attention of reformers. The extension of education, the propagation of religion, the reorganization of prisons, the abatement of drunkenness, the alleviation of suffering—these were examples of reforms that had little or no connection with politics or economics, but which received ardent support from numerous citizens.

Although stirrings of reform affected both Europe and America, there were marked differences in the situation on the two sides of the Atlantic. In certain respects the United States was more advanced than Europe. The doctrine that "all men are created equal" had been proclaimed as far back as 1776, and American political institutions had a more democratic character than those of the Old World. In particular, the common man in the United States could employ the ballot to bring about certain of the reforms he desired, while in Europe the extension of the franchise was one of the reforms still to be achieved. On the other hand, Great Britain and parts of the Continent had undergone a greater degree of industrialization and were thus wrestling with the problems confronting the laboring classes in the new factories and cities, a full generation or more before they became pressing on the western side of the Atlantic. American reformers were thus able to draw upon a substantial fund of European ideas and experience, at the same time that the example of the United States in other matters was serving as an inspiration to reformers abroad.

In one respect the United States lagged far behind the other nations that considered themselves civilized. "Under which of the old tyrannical governments of Europe," asked a British reviewer in 1820, "is every sixth man a Slave, whom his fellow-creatures may buy and sell and torture?"[2] Taunts like these seared the consciences of American reformers. Slavery gradually became the supreme evil in their eyes, and by the 1850s antislavery was engrossing most of the energies of the reform movement. As this happened, the South assumed a more and more defiant attitude, and its leaders frequently extended their hatred from abolitionists to reformers in general.

The reform movement was profoundly affected by religious developments in the nineteenth century. Changes were taking place in two contrary directions. A series of revival movements within the various Protestant denominations restored to orthodox religion the strength it had largely lost during the heyday of the eighteenth-century Enlightenment. At the same time, the rationalistic ideas of the Enlightenment itself penetrated many of the churches, producing a liberal theology of which Unitarianism was the most striking example. Opposite though these two tendencies were, they shared in common a disposition to make social reform a prominent feature of religious activity. Besides supporting societies for home and foreign missions and for circulating Bibles and tracts, the churches were frequently active in organizing temperance societies and in supporting the anti-slavery movement.

Conflicts between religious and secular attitudes did, on occasion, arise. The separation of church and state had been carried out in most of the states at the time of the American Revolution; it was completed in the rest by the 1830s; and it was embodied as a principle in the federal constitution from the beginning. Since education had previously been closely associated with religion, friction frequently accompanied the growth of educational agencies. Leaders of the common-school revival often felt called upon to resist what they conceived to be the threat of clerical domination of the public-school system. And the founders of church-supported colleges sometimes attacked the alleged "godlessness" of nondenominational state universities. The leaders of certain other

---

[2] Rev. Sydney Smith, "America," *Edinburgh Review*, 33 (January 1820), 80.

reform movements, dismayed at what they considered the hesitant and lukewarm support received from the churches, became critical of organized religion as such. A free-thought movement thus constituted a separate bubble in the ferment of reform.

Few whole-hearted reformers were content to limit their interest to a single cause. One philanthropic activity reinforced and led to another. Thus the contribution that women were making to various crusades induced them to demand changes in the legal and political status of their own sex; the women's rights agitation thus began. Occasionally a flourishing movement might be split apart by the intrusion of some other question of reform, on which some members took one side and others the opposite. The slavery issue was peculiarly divisive, especially in organizations that tried to maintain membership both north and south of the Mason-Dixon line.

On its positive side, this interpenetration of different reforms induced in the minds of some philanthropists the dream of a total and complete reformation of all abuses. This all-embracing perfectionism was a notable feature of early nineteenth-century humanitarianism. The wholesale reconstruction of society has, of course, figured in the propaganda of numerous revolutionaries. In America during this era, however, the idea assumed a wholly peaceable guise. Confident that men would follow the right if only the right were placed before them in tangible form, reformers who believed in a total reconstruction of social institutions pinned their faith upon model communities. A small society, they argued, might put into effect voluntarily among its members all the practices that reformers extolled. These perfected institutions, once successfully demonstrated, would be imitated far and wide until at length—and at perhaps no great length—society as a whole would be peacefully transformed. This belief accounted for the numerous communitarian colonies that dotted the American countryside during the period, including Robert Owen's experiment at New Harmony and the community at Brook Farm, which figures significantly in literary as well as social history.

The reform movements of the early nineteenth century were too numerous and too varied in kind to be treated individually in the present problem. Nor would such a collection of separate annals be particularly illuminating or valuable. The crucial matter, for the general student of American history, is the impact of the reform movement as a whole upon the life and thought of the nation. To illustrate the scope and range of reform activity, as many different movements as possible have been drawn upon for the following selections.

Some half-dozen questions are raised in the following sections of the present problem: What was the essential spirit that animated the reformer? From what varied sources did he derive his inspiration? What themes did he play upon in his propaganda, and how do these strike the modern ear? What methods did he propose to use, and what were the advantages and drawbacks of each? How did defenders of the status quo answer him or parry his attacks? What ultimate accomplishments can be credited to his efforts, and how long did it take for them to become effective?

The answers are for the reader to discover. The compiler has allowed reformers and their critics to speak in the words they addressed to their own contemporaries. The strength of their arguments is a matter for the reader to judge for himself, not only in terms of how they sound today, but also in terms of how they must have sounded in their historical context.

1. REFORM AND REFORMERS: A CONTEMPORARY INTERPRETATION

No one grasped more perceptively than Ralph Waldo Emerson (1803–1882) the spirit that underlay the era of reform. A remarkable balance of mind permitted him to be both a participant in reform movements and also a reserved, even aloof, observer of them. Though he had been educated as a Unitarian clergyman, he was caught up by a liberal theological current that carried him out of the ministry and made him the principal spokesman of a form of philosophic idealism that is usually called Transcendentalism. In his essays and speeches Emerson emphasized the supreme importance of the individual soul, as opposed to institutions and forms. He insisted that men should rely upon their own intuitions of truth and righteousness rather than upon tradition, no matter how sacred or revered the latter might be. Such an attitude was an encouragement to reform, and partisans of almost every conceivable cause sought and received a sympathetic hearing from Emerson. Individualism, however, was an essential part of his creed, and he refused to submerge himself in organized movements even when he approved of their goals. During the late 1830s and the 1840s, in particular, Emerson pondered deeply the character of the reform movement, praising the nobility of its motives yet looking critically at its shortcomings.

Emerson on the Reform Movement

In December 1841 Emerson began a series of "Lectures on the Times." The following passages are from the introductory address.[3]

---

[3] Ralph Waldo Emerson, "Lectures on the Times," *The Dial*, 3 (July 1842), 6–8, 10–13.

The present age will be marked by its harvest of projects, for the reform of domestic, civil, literary, and ecclesiastical institutions. The leaders of the crusades against War, Negro slavery, Intemperance, Government based on force, usages of trade, Court and Custom-house Oaths, and so on to the agitators on the system of Education and the laws of Property, are the right successors of Luther, Knox, Robinson, Fox, Penn, Wesley, and Whitfield. They have the same virtues and vices; the same noble impulse, and the same bigotry. These movements are on all accounts important; they not only check the special abuses to which they address themselves, but they educate the conscience and the intellect of the people. How can such a question as the Slave trade be agitated for forty years by all the Christian nations, without throwing great light on ethics into the general mind? The fury, with which the slave-trader defends every inch of his bloody deck, and his howling auction-platform, is a trumpet to alarm the ear of mankind, to wake the dull, and drive all neutrals to take sides, and listen to the argument and the verdict which justice shall finally pronounce. The Temperance-question, which rides the conversation of ten thousand circles, and is tacitly recalled at every public and at every private table, drawing with it all the curious ethics of the Pledge, of the Wine-question, of the equity of the manufacture and the trade, is a gymnastic training to the casuistry and conscience of the time. . . . The political questions touching the Banks; the Tariff; the limits of the executive power; the right of the constituent to instruct the representative; the treatment of the Indians; the Boundary wars; the Congress of nations; are all pregnant with ethical conclusions. . . .

The history of reform is always identical; it is the comparison of the idea with the fact. Our modes of living are not agreeable to our imagination. We suspect they are unworthy. We arraign our daily employments. They appear to us unfit, unworthy of the faculties we spend on them. . . . It is the testimony of the soul in man to a fairer possibility of life and manners, which agitates society every day with the offer of some new amendment. . . . For the origin of all reform is in that mysterious fountain of the moral sentiment in man. . . .

These Reforms are our contemporaries; they are ourselves; our own light, and sight, and conscience; they only name the relation which subsists between us and the vicious institutions which they go to rectify. They are the simplest statements of man in these matters; the plain right and wrong. I cannot choose but allow and honor them.

So much for the Reforms; but we cannot say as much for the Reformers. Beautiful is the impulse and the theory; the practice is less beautiful. . . .

The Reforms have their high origin in an ideal justice, but they do not retain the purity of an idea. They are quickly organized in some low, inadequate form, and present no more poetic image to the mind, than the evil tradition which they reprobated. They mix the fire of the moral sentiment with personal and party heats, with measureless exaggerations, and the blindness that prefers some darling measure to justice and truth. Those, who are urging with most ardor what are called the greatest benefits of mankind, are narrow, self-pleasing, conceited men, and affect us as the insane do. They bite us, and we run mad also. I think the work of the reformer as innocent as other work that is done around him; but when I have seen it near, I do not like it better. It is done in the same way, it is done profanely, not piously; by management, by tactics, and clamor. It is a buzz in the ear. . . . To the youth diffident of his ability, and full of compunction at his unprofitable existence, the temptation is always great to lend himself to public movements, and as one of a party accomplish what he cannot hope to effect alone. But he must resist the degradation of a man to a measure. . . .

This then is our criticism on the reforming movement; that it is in its origin divine; in its management and details timid and profane. These benefactors hope to raise man by improving his circumstances: by combination of that which is dead, they hope to make something alive. In vain. By new infusions alone of the spirit by which he is made and directed, can he be remade and reinforced.

2. ROOTS OF THE REFORM MOVEMENT

The reform movement spread its branches over wide areas of American life. Like a tree, moreover, it thrust out its roots in various directions, drawing nourishment from many different veins of idealism. For some reformers religion furnished the highest inspiration; for others, the principles of democracy. All were, in a measure, impelled by a fervent belief in progress. Though these ideals were inextricably intertwined in most actual movements, it is nevertheless possible to recognize the different strands. Each of the following extracts emphasizes a different motive to reform, a distinctive source of inspiration from which philanthropists drew.

The Religious Inspiration of Reform

Religion played a more important role in the thinking of early nineteenth-century Americans than it had played at the time of the Revolution or than it plays today. Reformers made effective use of religious arguments, and religious leaders frequently pointed to successful reform movements as evidence of the vitality of the churches. The connection between religion and reform was given special emphasis by many religious revivalists. One of the most influential of these was the Reverend Charles G. Finney (1792–1875), from whose volume of *Lectures on Revivals of Religion,* published in 1835, the following extract is taken.[4]

---

[4] Charles G. Finney, *Lectures on Revivals of Religion* (Boston, 1835), 270, 274–75, 278–81.

I proceed to mention some things *which ought to be done,* to continue this great and glorious revival of religion, which has been in progress for the last ten years. . . .

4. *The church must take right ground in regard to politics.* Do not suppose, now, that I am going to preach a political sermon, or that I wish to have you join and get up a *Christian party* in politics. No, I do not believe in that. But the time has come that Christians must vote for honest men, and take consistent ground in politics, or the Lord will curse them. . . . They must let the world see that the church will uphold no man in office, who is known to be a knave, or an adulterer, or a Sabbath-breaker, or a gambler. . . . Politics are a part of religion in such a country as this, and Christians must do their duty to the country as a part of their duty to God. . . .

5. *The churches must take right ground on the subject of slavery.* . . . Christians can no more take neutral ground on this subject, since it has come up for discussion, than they can take neutral ground on the subject of the sanctification of the Sabbath. It is a great national sin. . . . The fact is that slavery is, pre-eminently, the *sin of the church*. It is the very fact that ministers and professors of religion of different denominations hold slaves, which sanctifies the whole abomination, in the eyes of ungodly men. Who does not know that on the subject of temperance, every drunkard in the land, will skulk behind some rum-selling deacon, or wine-drinking minister? . . . It is *this* that creates the imperious necessity for excluding traffickers in ardent spirit, and rum-drinkers from the communion. Let the churches of all denominations speak out on the subject of temperance, let them close their doors against all who have any thing to do with the death-dealing abomination, and the cause of temperance is triumphant. A few years would annihilate the traffic. Just so with slavery.

It is the church that mainly supports this sin. Her united testimony upon this subject would settle the question. Let Christians of all denominations meekly but firmly come forth, and pronounce their verdict, let them clear their communions, and wash their hands of this thing, let them give forth and write on the head and front of this great abomination, SIN! and in three years, a public sentiment would be formed that would carry all before it, and there would not be a shackled slave, nor a bristling, cruel slave-driver in this land. . . .

7. The church must take right ground on the subject of Temperance, and Moral Reform, and all the subjects of practical morality which come up for decision from time to time.

There are those in the churches who are standing aloof from the subject of Moral Reform, and who are as much afraid to have any thing said in the pulpit against lewdness, as if a thousand devils had got up into the pulpit. On this subject, the church need not expect to be permitted to take neutral ground. In the providence of God, it is up for discussion. The evils have been exhibited, the call has been made for reform. And what is to reform mankind but the truth? And who shall present the truth if not the church and the ministry? Away with the idea, that Christians can remain neutral and keep still, and yet enjoy the approbation and blessing of God.

Humanitarianism

The sheer repugnance to cruelty, the desire to lessen the quantity of pain and suffering in the world, provided another motive to philanthropy and reform. The title "humane society" began to be used in the later eighteenth century by organizations devoted to the rescue of drowning persons. Before long the term came to embrace efforts to prevent cruelty of all kinds to men and to animals. In the 1840s the word "humanitarian" came into use to describe benevolent and reform movements motivated primarily by the wish to alleviate the misery of living beings.

Humanitarian feelings were invoked by the anti-slavery movement, as a subsequent selection will show. Humanitarianism also inspired a movement against war. The following passages are from a pamphlet of 1842 which contributed importantly to the advancement of the practice of international arbitration.[5] Its author, Judge William Jay (1789–1858; son of the Revolutionary statesman and jurist John Jay) was a leader in both the anti-slavery and the peace movements.

We would appeal . . . to christians, to philanthropists, and to patriots, and ask them, if there is not an evil under which humanity is groaning, as great, as universal, and yet as surmountable as the slave trade, or intemperance? WAR still extends his bloody sceptre over the nations of the earth, and is still dooming countless multitudes to wretchedness and slaughter. And shall we not rise in resistance to this remorseless tyrant, and may we not hope at least to curb his power, if we do not overthrow his throne? . . . Let us recollect the anti-slavery societies of Great Britain, and the temperance societies of America, and believe that the blessing of Heaven may also descend upon the humble labors of PEACE SOCIETIES. . . .

The supposed necessity of war is founded on the idea that however much we may deprecate it, it nevertheless prevents a greater evil than itself. But alas! few have any just conception of the calamities inflicted by war, and fewer still have ever inquired whether the evils it is intended to prevent cannot be averted by other means. . . . The horrors of the battlefield, the confused noise of the warrior, the garments rolled in blood, the shrieks of the wounded and the dying, the groans and tears of widows and of orphans, the conflagration of cities and the devastation of kingdoms may indeed be portrayed with such pathos and eloquence as to cause a thrill to vibrate through every nerve. . . .

Let us then take a sober and unimpassioned view of war, not as it existed in remote antiquity, when whole nations contended in arms, and the soil was literally drenched with human gore—when no quarter

---

[5] William Jay, *War and Peace: The Evils of the First, and a Plan for Preserving the Last* (New York, 1842), 8–9, 11–12, 15, 19–20, 41.

was given in the field—when kings and princes were chained to the triumphal car of the victor, and their surviving subjects doomed to hopeless slavery; but of war as it exists in our own days, and as waged by enlightened and Christian nations. . . .

He is a superficial inquirer who, in investigating the evils of war, confines his observation to the scenes and consequences of actual hostility. War is a demon whose malignant influence is felt at all times and in all places. Paradoxical as it may seem in the very midst of peace and security, it is blighting the labor of man, adding weight to his burdens, and laying snares for his virtue. . . . Were the millions yearly lavished by our country in military preparation devoted to the cause of science and religion, to the facilities of intercourse, and the promotion of social and individual comfort, an amount of happiness would be diffused through our land that would cast in the shade all our past prosperity, unexampled as it has been. . . .

But what imagination can conceive, what pen portray that mass of wretchedness, desolation and woe, which mankind are capable of accumulating, when all their malevolent passions are in full activity, and are aided by the resources of art and science, by the wealth and the physical strength of nations! It is moreover an appalling reflection that all this wretchedness, and desolation and woe, is the serious and avowed object of war, a means to an end, and not an incidental and lamented consequence. They who wage war desire and intend to slay their enemies. It is for this express purpose men are hired and armed, and navies equipped and sent to sea. The greater the havoc made of human life and happiness, the more glorious the victory, and the more successful the war. . . .

Let the mind dwell for a few moments on the invasion of Russia by Napoleon, and reflect on the griefs, the anxieties, the pangs of separation endured by the innumerable families from which were gathered the vast host composing the contending armies; let it watch the progress of the war—the toilsome marches—the carnage of battle—the conflagrations of Smolensko and Moscow—the desolation of whole provinces—the famine and cold, and agonizing deaths which overwhelmed the retreating army; let it imagine the wailings of multitudes for their slaughtered relatives, and let it contemplate the fearful account to which hundreds of thousands of immortal souls were untimely summoned, and it will form some idea of the nature and extent of that awful retribution with which war is visited by the Governor of the universe. And let it be remembered that this retribution . . . is not confined to the defeated party. Russia was victorious over her invaders, but being the seat of war, the amount of suffering that fell to her share was immensely more than that endured by her enemy.

Reform as a Corollary of Democratic Principles

The Declaration of Independence had proclaimed that "all men are created equal." This phrase furnished one of the most potent arguments that reformers could use. The advocates of women's rights employed it in the most explicit way possible, by offering their views in the form of a direct paraphrase of the great Declaration. The first Women's Rights Convention was held at Seneca Falls, New York, in 1848. In the following passage Elizabeth Cady Stanton (1815–1902), one of the participants, describes in amusing fashion the process by which she and her three feminine colleagues drafted the "Declaration of Sentiments" which the Convention adopted.[6]

On the first attempt to frame a resolution; to crowd a complete thought, clearly and concisely, into three lines; they felt as helpless and hopeless as if they had been suddenly asked to construct a steam engine. And the humiliating fact may as well now be recorded that before taking the initiative step, those ladies resigned themselves to a faithful perusal of various masculine productions. The reports of Peace, Temperance, and Anti-Slavery conventions were examined, but all alike seemed too tame and pacific for the inauguration of a rebellion such as the world had never before seen. . . .

After much delay, one of the circle took up the Declaration [of Independence] of 1776, and read it aloud with much spirit and emphasis, and it was at once decided to adopt the historic document, with some slight changes such as substituting "all men" for "King George." Knowing that women must have more to complain of than men under any circumstances possibly could, and seeing the Fathers had eighteen grievances, a protracted search was made through statute books, church usages, and the customs of society to find that exact number. . . . One youthful lord remarked, "Your grievances must be grievous indeed, when you are obliged to go to books in order to find them out." . . .

Declaration of Sentiments

When, in the course of human events, it becomes necessary for one portion of the family of man to assume among the people of the earth a position different from that which they have hitherto occupied, but one to which the laws of nature and of nature's God entitle them, a decent respect to the opinions of mankind requires that they should declare the causes that impel them to such a course.

We hold these truths to be self-evident: that all men and women are created equal; that they are endowed by their Creator with certain inalienable rights; that among these are life, liberty, and the pursuit of happiness; that to secure these rights governments are instituted, deriving their just powers from the consent of the governed. Whenever any form of government becomes destructive of these ends, it is the right of those who suffer from it to refuse allegiance to it, and to insist upon the institution of a new government, laying its foundation on such principles, and organizing its powers in such form, as to them shall seem most likely to effect their safety and happiness. . . .

---

[6] Elizabeth Cady Stanton, Susan B. Anthony, and Matilda Joslyn Gage, eds., *History of Woman Suffrage* (New York, 1881), 1:68–71.

The history of mankind is a history of repeated injuries and usurpations on the part of man toward woman, having in direct object the establishment of an absolute tyranny over her. To prove this, let facts be submitted to a candid world.

He has never permitted her to exercise her inalienable right to the elective franchise.

He has compelled her to submit to laws, in the formation of which she had no voice. . . .

He has taken from her all right in property, even to the wages she earns. . . .

He has denied her the facilities for obtaining a thorough education, all colleges being closed against her. . . .

He has created a false public sentiment by giving to the world a different code of morals for men and women, by which moral delinquencies which exclude women from society, are not only tolerated, but deemed of little account in man. . . .

Now, in view of this entire disfranchisement of one-half the people of this country, their social and religious degradation—in view of the unjust laws above mentioned, and because women do feel themselves aggrieved, oppressed, and fraudulently deprived of their most sacred rights, we insist that they have immediate admission to all the rights and privileges which belong to them as citizens of the United States.

The Doctrine of Progress

Confirming all the hopes of reformers was a conviction that progress was an inevitable thing. This idea was well expressed by Horace Greeley (1811–1872), founder, in 1841, of *The New York Tribune*. In the columns of his newspaper, and in public speeches, Greeley made himself the champion of a multitude of humanitarian causes, ranging from the sublime to (as his critics thought) the ridiculous. In 1850 he gathered a number of his utterances together in a volume entitled *Hints Toward Reforms,* from which this selection is taken.[7]

Let us take courage from the evidences of Progress all around us. It is not half a century since the Slave-Trade was in its glory, and men eminent in Church and State made fortunes by engaging in it without reproach or scruple. We have yet Doctors of Divinity who justify laws which authorize the buying and selling of mothers from their children; but this is evidently dying out; and, in a few years, Sermons proving Slavery a Bible institution will be advertised as antique curiosities. So of Privateering, War, and the traffic in Intoxicating Liquors. To our impatient spirits, the march of improvement often seems mournfully slow; but when we consider where the world is and where it has been

---

[7] Horace Greeley, *Hints Toward Reforms, in Lectures, Addresses, and Other Writings* (New York, 1850), 48–50.

... we ought to be assured that the age which has given us Railroads and Locomotives, Steam Presses and Electric Telegraphs, will not pass away without having effected or witnessed a vast change for the better, alike in the moral and the physical condition of mankind.

For that change let us faithfully labor and undoubtingly hope. Whether its consummation shall take the precise form which you or I now anticipate or prefer, who shall say? Nay, who need seriously care? Enough that we know well that all things are wisely ordered by One whose observation no sparrow's fall can escape: in whose providence no generous effort can fail of its reward. ... We could not retard the great forward movement of Humanity if we would; but each of us may decide for himself whether to share in the glory of promoting it or incur the shame of having looked coldly and indifferently on, preferring present ease and pleasure to the stern calls of Duty. ...

Each age summons its own heroes; ours demands those who will labor and if need be suffer reproach in behalf of a Social Order based on Universal Justice, not the dominion of Power over Need; on the spirit of Christianity, not the supremacy of Mammon. The struggle may be long, but the issue can not be doubtful. Fortunate shall they be esteemed by future generations who are privileged to stand in Earth's noblest Thermopylæ and battle for the rights, for the hopes, for the enduring good, of Humanity in all time to come. It is a distinction to which the loftiest might well aspire, but which proffers opportunity alike to the humblest. Who would slumber through life ingloriously when such crowns are to be won?

Appeals from Disadvantaged Groups Themselves

As the foregoing passages have revealed, the reform movement of the early nineteenth century in America was not primarily an effort on the part of victims of injustice to right their wrongs. It was not the slaves who were abolitionists, but free white men in the Northern states. And though reformed drunkards might organize temperance societies, the typical temperance leader was out to reform someone else than himself. Altruism—a word invented in this period by Auguste Comte to denote the principle of acting for the welfare of others—was characteristic of this age of reform. Occasionally, however, the disadvantaged classes in society raised their own voices in their own behalf. The following extract is from an address to the public by the working people of Manayunk, an industrial suburb of Philadelphia containing several cotton mills. It was adopted by the Manayunk Working People's Committee on August 23, 1833.[8]

Fellow Citizens—Deeply impressed with a sense of our inability to combat single-handed the evils that now threaten us, and being fully convinced, that the future happiness of ourselves and families depend on our present exertions, we

---

[8] Philadelphia *Pennsylvanian,* August 28, 1833, p. 2, col. 6.

are, with reluctance, obliged to lay our grievances and petition before you, well knowing that we are appealing to an enlightened and generous public. . . .

We are obliged by our employers to labor at this season of the year, from 5 o'clock in the morning until sunset, being fourteen hours and a half, with an intermission of half an hour for breakfast, and an hour for dinner, leaving thirteen hours of hard labor, at an unhealthy employment, where we never feel a refreshing breeze to cool us. . . .

Often do we feel ourselves so weak as to be scarcely able to perform our weak [sic], on account of the overstrained time we are obliged to labour through the long and sultry days of summer, in the impure and unwholesome air of the factories, and the little rest we receive during the night not being sufficient to recruit our exhausted physical energies, we return to our labor in the morning, as weary as when we left it; but nevertheless work we must, worn down and debilitated as we are, or our families would soon be in a starving condition, for our wages are barely sufficient to supply us with the necessaries of life. We cannot provide against sickness or difficulties of any kind, by laying by a single dollar, for our present wants consume the little we receive, and when we are confined to a bed of sickness any length of time, we are plunded [sic] into the deepest distress, which often terminates in total ruin, poverty and pauperism. . . .

"The laborer is worthy of his hire," is a maxim acknowledged to be true in theory by all, and yet how different is the practice. Are we not worthy of our hire? Most certainly we are, and yet our employers would wish to reduce our present wages twenty per cent! and tell us their reason for so doing is, that cotton has risen in value, but is it not a necessary consequence of the rise of cotton that cotton goods will rise also; and what matters it to us what the price of cotton is, our wants are as great when cotton is dear as they are when it is cheap; if our employers make more profit on their goods at any one time than they do at others, they do not give us better wages, and is it justice that we should bear all the burthen and submit to a reduction of our wages? No, we could not consistently with our duty to ourselves and to each other, submit to it, and rivet our chains still closer! We have long suffered the evils of being divided in our sentiments, but the universal oppressions that we now all feel, have roused us to a sense of our oppressed condition, and we are now determined to be oppressed no longer! We know full well that the attempted reduction in our wages is but the forerunner of greater evils, and greater oppressions, which would terminate, if not resisted, in absolute slavery.

3. VARIETIES OF PROPAGANDA

Not only did reformers draw inspiration from many different sources—religious, democratic, and the rest—but they also phrased their appeals in many different ways. Factual reports alternated with sentimental appeals, vitriolic denunciations with calmly reasoned arguments. These differences in tone and approach are illustrated in the four examples of reform propaganda that make up this section.

Factual Indictment

One of the most powerful weapons that a reformer can employ is the unadorned statement of fact. The anti-slavery leaders knew how to use this with telling effect. Obviously they were not presenting a full and balanced picture of slavery, but only a picture of its darker aspects. This they were ready to admit, but they argued that a system which permitted any such cruelties as they described was an evil system, regardless of any better side it might possess. One of the most effective pieces of abolitionist propaganda was the booklet, *American Slavery As It Is: Testimony of a Thousand Witnesses,* compiled largely by Theodore Dwight Weld (1803-1895) and published by the American Anti-Slavery Society in 1839. The following extracts include the preface, in which the factual nature of the material is emphasized, a few of the items from Southern newspapers that were presented as evidence out of the slaveholders' own mouths, and one of the concluding replies to pro-slavery arguments.[9]

Advertisement to the Reader

A majority of the facts and testimony contained in this work rests upon the authority of SLAVEHOLDERS, whose names and residences are given to the public. . . .

Their testimoney is taken, mainly, from recent newspapers, published in the slave states. Most of those papers will be deposited at the office of the American Anti-Slavery Society, 143 Nassau street, New-York City. Those who think the atrocities, which they describe, incredible, are invited to call and read for themselves. . . .

---

[9] *American Slavery As It Is: Testimony of a Thousand Witnesses* (New York, 1839), iii, 77-79, 132. In the original the names of witnesses were printed in one column, with their testimony alongside in a second, wider column.

Brandings, Maimings, Gun-Shot Wounds, &c.

The slaves are often branded with hot irons, pursued with fire arms and *shot,* hunted with dogs and torn by them, shockingly maimed with knives, dirks, etc.; have their ears cut off, their eyes knocked out, their bones dislocated and broken with bludgeons, their fingers and toes cut off, their faces and other parts of their persons disfigured with scars and gashes, *besides* those made with the lash.

We shall adopt, under this head, the same course as that pursued under previous ones,—first give the testimony of the slaveholders themselves, to the mutilations, &c. by copying their own graphic descriptions of them, in advertisements published under their own names, and in newspapers published in the slave states, and, generally, in their own immediate vicinity. . . .

Witness: Mr. Micajah Ricks, Nash County, North Carolina, in the Raleigh "Standard," July 18, 1838. *Testimony:* "Ranaway, a negro woman and two children; a few days before she went off, *I burnt her with a hot iron,* on the left side of her face, *I tried to make the letter M.*" . . .

Witness: Mrs. Sarah Walsh, Mobile, Ala. in the "Georgia Journal," March 27, 1837. *Testimony:* "Twenty-five dollars reward for my man Isaac, he has a scar on his forehead caused by a *blow,* and one on his back made by *a shot from a pistol."*

Witness: Mr. J. P. Ashford, Adams Co. Mi., in the "Natchez Courier," August 24, 1838. *Testimony:* "Ranaway a negro girl called Mary, has a small scar over her eye, a *good many teeth missing,* the letter A. *is branded on her cheek and forehead."* . . .

Witness: J. L. Jolley, Sheriff of Clinton, Co. Mi., in the "Clinton Gazette," July 23, 1836. *Testimony:* "Was committed to jail a negro man, says his name is Josiah, his back very much scarred by the whip, and *branded on the thigh and hips, in three or four places,* thus (J.M.) the *rim of his right ear has been bit or cut off."* . . .

Witness: Mr. Robert Beasley, Macon, Georgia, in the "Georgia Messenger," July 27, 1837. *Testimony:* "Ranaway, my man Fountain —has *holes in his ears,* a *scar* on the right side of his forehead—has been *shot in the hind parts of his legs*—is marked on the back with the whip." . . .

Objections Considered— . . ."It is for the Interest of the Masters to Treat Their Slaves Well."

. . . If the objector means that it for the *pecuniary* interests of masters to treat their slaves well, and thence infers their good treatment, we reply, that though the love of money is strong, yet appetite and lust, pride, anger and revenge, the love of power and honor, are each an overmatch for it. . . . Besides, a master can inflict upon his slave horrible cruelties without perceptibly injuring his health, or taking time from his labor, or lessening his value as property. Blows with a small stick give more acute pain, than with a large one. A club bruises, and benumbs the nerves, while a *switch,* neither breaking nor bruising the flesh, instead of blunting the sense of feeling, wakes up and stings to torture all the susceptibilities of pain. By this kind of infliction, more actual cruelty can be perpetrated in the giving of pain at the instant, than by the most horrible bruisings and lacerations; and that, too, with little comparative hazard to the slave's health, or to his value as property, and without loss of time from labor. Even giving to the objection all the force claimed for it, what protection is it to the slave? It *professes* to shield the slave from such treatment alone, as would either lay him aside from labor, or injure his health, and thus lessen his value as a working animal, making him a *damaged article* in the market. Now, is nothing *bad treatment* of a human being except that which produces these effects? Does the fact that a man's constitution is not actually shattered, and his life shortened by his treatment, prove that he is treated well?

Tearful Sentimentality

If facts could be harnessed to the cause of reform, so too could emotions. Even the unbearable sentimentality that marked much of the popular literature of mid-nineteenth century America was turned to account, especially in the temperance movement. The following stanzas are from a poem entitled "The Watcher," written by Mrs. Emeline S. Smith and published in *The Sons of Temperance Offering*,[10] one of the ornately bound gift annuals that were produced for the Christmas trade. This particular volume was edited by Timothy S. Arthur (1809–1885), author of *Ten Nights in a Bar-Room*, most famous of all the novels attacking the Demon Rum.

She sits alone—her infant calmly sleepeth,
   And dreams sweet dreams within its cradle-bed,
And smiles, unconscious that its mother weepeth
   The bitterest tears that mortal eyes can shed.
. . .
"This cannot last;—his heart, once proudly leaping
   To every lofty thought and noble aim,
Will break the fatal spells that now are keeping
   The light of honor from his once-fair name."
. . .
Alas, she knows not, in her guileless dreaming,
   Half the wild witchery of the maddening bowl;
Nor thinks how soon its flame may quench the beaming
   Of virtue's purer radiance in the soul.
. . .
He comes at last—but, oh! so much degraded
   By the wild orgies of the vanished night,
That every lofty lineament hath faded,
   And reason's ray withholds its heavenly light.

The fatal wine cup, rousing him to madness,
   Hath lured him on to do a deed of shame,—
And now, farewell to every hope of gladness,
   For lasting darkness settles on his name.

No love, no tears, no prayers can now defend him
   From the sad evils that must surely come;
Remorse and deep regret shall now attend him,
   And the dark prison-cell will be his home.

---

[10] T. S. Arthur, ed., *The Sons of Temperance Offering: for 1850* (New York, 1849), 202–4.

Then weep, fond wife, thy lease of joy is ended—
  Weep for thyself, thy child, but most for him
Whose every thought in life will now be blended
  With memories that shall make the day-star dim.

Yes, weep, but also pray—thou'rt not forsaken,
  Though darkness rests upon thy home and heart;
There is a Friend on High who yet shall waken
  The light that bids all earthly gloom depart.

Outspoken Denunciation

Emotional fervor could take other forms besides the sentimental teardrop. It could, for example, be distilled as pure vitriol. William Lloyd Garrison (1805–1879) launched his anti-slavery periodical, *The Liberator*, in 1831 with the announcement: "I *will be* as harsh as truth, and as uncompromising as justice. On this subject, I do not wish to think, or speak, or write with moderation." For thirty-five years his wish was granted. The following extract from a collection of his writings published in 1852 contains one of his numerous defenses of the blistering language he felt called upon to use.[11]

I am accused of using hard language. I admit the charge. I have not been able to find a soft word to describe villainy, or to identify the perpetrator of it. The man who makes a chattel of his brother—what is he? The man who keeps back the hire of his laborers by fraud—what is he? They who prohibit the circulation of the Bible—what are they? They who compel three millions of men and women to herd together, like brute beasts—what are they? They who sell mothers by the pound, and children in lots to suit purchasers—what are they? I care not what terms are applied to them, provided they do apply. If they are not thieves, if they are not tyrants, if they are not men-stealers, I should like to know what is their true character, and by what names they may be called. It is as mild an epithet to say that a thief is a thief, as it is to say that a spade is a spade. . . . The whole scope of the English language is inadequate to describe the horrors and impieties of slavery, and the transcendent wickedness of those who sustain this bloody system. . . .

Still, the popular cry against me is, that I have spoken of slavery, and slaveholders, and the apologists of slavery, in harsh, denunciatory language, so as greatly to injure the cause I profess to love. . . . That my language has been rough, vehement, denunciatory, is true: but why? Because the exigency of the times demanded it; because any other language would have been inappropriate and ineffectual; because my theme was not a gentle one, about buds, and blossoms, and flowers, and gentle zephyrs, and starry skies; but about a nation of boasting republi-

---

[11] *Selections from the Writings and Speeches of William Lloyd Garrison* (Boston, 1852), 121–22, 126–27, 133.

cans and Christians, ruthlessly consigning to chains and slavery every sixth person born in the land, . . . about one vast system of crime and blood, and all imaginable lewdness and villainy—about the robbers of God's poor, those who keep back the hire of their laborers by fraud, those who sin against the clearest light, and in the most awful manner. Now, what words shall I use to express the convictions of an honest soul, in view of such atrocious impiety, and such unequalled meanness and baseness? Shall they be gentle, and carefully selected, and cautiously expressed? Away with such counsel; it is treason against the throne of God! . . .

I am ready to make a truce with the South: if she will give up her stolen property, I will no longer brand her as a thief; if she will desist from driving woman into the field, like a beast, under the lash of a brutal overseer,—from stealing infants, from trafficking in human flesh, from keeping back the hire of the laborer by fraud—I will agree not to call her a monster; if she will honor the marriage institution, and sacredly respect the relations of life, and no longer license incest, pollution and adultery, I will not represent her as Sodomitish in spirit and practice; if she will no longer prevent the unobstructed circulation of the Scriptures, and the intellectual and religious education of her benighted population, I will not stigmatize her as practically atheistical. In short, if she will abolish her cruel slave-system, root and branch, at once and for ever, we will instantly disband all our anti-slavery societies, and no longer agitate the land. But, until she thus acts, we shall increase, instead of relaxing our efforts—multiply, instead of diminishing our associations—and make our rebukes more terrible than ever!

Reasoned Argument

Emotion was a powerful instrument of propaganda. But the main force of the reform movement necessarily lay in reasoned argument, without which it could hardly have prospered long. The substantial achievements made in such fields as public education depended on the thoughtful way in which reformers marshalled their arguments. None did so more effectively than Horace Mann (1796–1859), secretary of the Massachusetts Board of Education from 1837 to 1848. The following extract is taken from the twelfth and final annual report which he made in that capacity.[12]

I proceed . . . to show how the true business of the schoolroom connects itself, and becomes identical, with the great interests of society. . . . As "the child is father to the man," so may the training of the schoolroom expand into the institutions and fortunes of the State. . . .

---

[12] Massachusetts Board of Education, *Twelfth Annual Report* (Boston, 1849), 42–43, 55, 57, 59–60, 67–68, 76–79.

According to the European theory, men are divided into classes,—some to toil and earn, others to seize and enjoy. According to the Massachusetts theory, all are to have an equal chance for earning, and equal security in the enjoyment of what they earn. The latter tends to equality of condition; the former to the grossest inequalities. Tried by any Christian standard of morals, or even by any of the better sort of heathen standards, can any one hesitate, for a moment, in declaring which of the two will produce the greater amount of human welfare; and which, therefore, is the more conformable to the Divine will? . . .

But, is it not true, that Massachusetts, in some respects, instead of adhering more and more closely to her own theory, is becoming emulous of the baneful examples of Europe? The distance between the two extremes of society is lengthening, instead of being abridged. With every generation, fortunes increase, on the one hand, and some new privation is added to poverty, on the other. We are verging towards those extremes of opulence and of penury, each of which unhumanizes the human mind. . . .

Now, surely, nothing but Universal Education can counterwork this tendency to the domination of capital and the servility of labor. If one class possesses all the wealth and the education, while the residue of society is ignorant and poor, it matters not by what name the relation between them may be called; the latter, in fact and in truth, will be the servile dependants and subjects of the former. But if education be equably diffused, it will draw property after it, by the strongest of all attractions; for such a thing never did happen, and never can happen, as that an intelligent and practical body of men should be permanently poor. Property and labor, in different classes, are essentially antagonistic; but property and labor, in the same class, are essentially fraternal. . . .

Education, then, beyond all other devices of human origin, is the great equalizer of the conditions of men—the balance-wheel of the social machinery. . . . It gives each man the independence and the means, by which he can resist the selfishness of other men. It does better than to disarm the poor of their hostility towards the rich; it prevents being poor. . . .

The necessity of general intelligence,—that is, of education, . . . —under a republican form of government, like most other very important truths, has become a very trite one. . . . That the affairs of a great nation or state are exceedingly complicated and momentous, no one will dispute. Nor will it be questioned that the degree of intelligence that superintends, should be proportioned to the magnitude of the interests superintended. . . . And hence it is, that the establishment of a republican government, without well-appointed and efficient means for the universal education of the people, is the most rash and foolhardy experiment ever tried by man. . . . It may be an easy thing to make a Republic; but it is a very laborious thing to make Republicans; and woe to the Republic that rests upon no better foundations than ignorance, selfishness, and passion. Such a republic may grow in numbers and in wealth. . . . But if such a Republic be devoid of intelligence, it will only the more closely resemble an obscene giant who has waxed strong in his youth, and grown wanton in his strength; whose brain has been developed only in the region of the appetites and passions, and not in the organs of reason and conscience; and who, therefore, is boastful of his bulk alone, and glories in the weight of his heel and in the destruction of his arm. Such a republic, with all its noble capacities for beneficence, will rush with the speed of a whirlwind to an ignominious end; and all good men of after-times would be fain to weep over its downfall, did not their scorn and contempt at its folly and its wickedness, repress all sorrow for its fate.

4. PROPOSED ROADS TO REFORM

The methods that reformers proposed to use were as varied as the sources of inspiration upon which they drew or the kinds of propaganda they employed. Today we are apt to assume that men interested in change or reform will seek it either through action by the government or through the revolutionary overthrow of the existing order. Though these two approaches to reform can be illustrated from early nineteenth-century American writings, they were actually the least typical of all the procedures which reformers of that day advocated. The present section explores the several roads that idealists expected to follow into the promised land. Some of the alternatives are unfamiliar to us; others have lost for us their reformist connotations; but all were alive and full of promise to the men and women of this era of reform.

Individualism

Individualism is commonly thought of today as a conservative doctrine. In the late eighteenth century, however, it figured rather as an attack upon than a defense of the established order in government, economics, and even religion. Constitutional thinking emphasized the defense of individual rights. Economists advocated *laissez faire* as a means of ridding economic life of a burden of archaic restrictions and regulations. The reformist implications of individualism were still obvious in the first half of the nineteenth century. Jacksonian Democracy, for example, stressed individual opportunity in opposition to chartered monopoly as represented by the Bank of the United States. A notable statement of individualism as a doctrine of reform—even a doctrine of peaceable revolution—was that made by Henry David Thoreau (1817–1862) in "Resistance to Civil Government," an address delivered in 1847. It was occasioned by the

Mexican War, which Thoreau saw as a plot for the extension of slavery. But its argument transcended the particular historical situation that called it forth, and the essay has influenced many men of later generations living far beyond the boundaries of the United States.[13]

I heartily accept the motto,—"That government is best which governs least"; and I should like to see it acted up to more rapidly and systematically. Carried out, it finally amounts to this, which also I believe,—"That government is best which governs not at all"; and when men are prepared for it, that will be the kind of government which they will have. Government is at best but an expedient; but most governments are usually, and all governments are sometimes, inexpedient. The objections which have been brought against a standing army, and they are many and weighty, and deserve to prevail, may also at last be brought against a standing government. . . .

This American government,—what is it but a tradition, though a recent one, endeavoring to transmit itself unimpaired to posterity, but each instant losing some of its integrity? It has not the vitality and force of a single living man; for a single man can bend it to his will. . . . It is excellent, we must all allow; yet this government never of itself furthered any enterprise, but by the alacrity with which it got out of its way. *It* does not keep the country free. *It* does not settle the West. *It* does not educate. The character inherent in the American people has done all that has been accomplished; and it would have done somewhat more, if the government had not sometimes got in its way. . . .

After all, the practical reason why, when the power is once in the hands of the people, a majority are permitted, and for a long period continue, to rule, is not because they are most likely to be in the right, nor because this seems fairest to the minority, but because they are physically the strongest. But a government in which the majority rule in all cases cannot be based on justice, even as far as men understand it. . . . Must the citizen ever for a moment, or in the least degree, resign his conscience to the legislator? Why has every man a conscience, then? . . .

How does it become a man to behave toward this American government to-day? I answer that he cannot without disgrace be associated with it. I cannot for an instant recognize that political organization as *my* government which is the *slave's* government also. . . .

Those who, while they disapprove of the character and measures of a government, yield to it their allegiance and support, are undoubtedly its most conscientious supporters, and so frequently the most serious obstacles to reform. Some are petitioning the State to dissolve the Union, to disregard the requisitions

---

[13] Elizabeth P. Peabody, ed., *Aesthetic Papers* (Boston, 1849), 189–90, 192, 199–200, 211. The essay, under the later and more familiar title of "Civil Disobedience," it to be found in Thoreau's *Writings*, Riverside Edition (Boston, 1893), 10:131–70.

of the President. Why do they not dissolve it themselves,—the union between themselves and the State,—and refuse to pay their quota into its treasury? Do not they stand in the same relation to the State, that the State does to the Union? . . .

I do not hesitate to say, that those who call themselves abolitionists should at once effectually withdraw their support, both in person and property, from the government of Massachusetts, and not wait till they constitute a majority of one, before they suffer the right to prevail through them. I think that it is enough if they have God on their side, without waiting for that other one. Moreover, any man more right than his neighbors, constitutes a majority of one already. . . .

Under a government which imprisons any unjustly, the true place for a just man is also a prison. The proper place to-day, the only place which Massachusetts has provided for her freer and less desponding spirits, is in her prisons, to be put out and locked out of the State by her own act, as they have already put themselves out by their principles. It is there that the fugitive slave, and the Mexican prisoner on parole, and the Indian come to plead the wrongs of his race, should find them; on that separate, but more free and honorable ground, where the State places those who are not *with* her but *against* her,—the only house in a slave-state in which a free man can abide with honor. . . . If the alternative is to keep all just men in prison, or give up war and slavery, the State will not hesitate which to choose. If a thousand men were not to pay their tax-bills this year, that would not be a violent and bloody measure, as it would be to pay them, and enable the State to commit violence and shed innocent blood. This is, in fact, the definition of a peaceable revolution, if any such is possible. . . .

The progress from an absolute to a limited monarchy, from a limited monarchy to a democracy, is a progress toward a true respect for the individual. . . . There will never be a really free and enlightened State, until the State comes to recognize the individual as a higher and independent power, from which all its own power and authority are derived, and treats him accordingly.

Organized Movements

Despite the appeal of individualism as a doctrine of reform, there were many who doubted its sufficiency. Concerted effort, they felt—denying the arguments of Thoreau and Emerson—could be more effective than individual action in removing many kinds of abuses. A network of benevolent and reform societies sprang up in America in the second quarter of the nineteenth century, constituting the most important institutional innovation of the era of reform. These societies were perfectly adapted to conditions in the United States, with its separation of church and state, its multiplicity of religious denominations, its tradition of political decentralization combined with federal action for limited purposes, and its high level of literacy. The typical benevolent or reform association had its local societies scattered throughout the nation, it held an annual convention to which most of these sent representatives, it maintained a small central organization to coordinate but not necessarily to direct the work, it employed traveling agents and lecturers, it collected funds by voluntary subscription, and it published a weekly or monthly or quarterly journal as well as occasional pamphlets and regular annual reports.

The prevalence of such societies attracted the attention of foreign travelers, such as the French observer Alexis de Tocqueville (1805–1859), who commented on the matter in the following passage from the second part of his influential book, Democracy in America, first published in 1840 and translated the same year.[14]

The political associations which exist in the United States are only a single feature in the midst of the immense assemblage of associations in that country. Americans of all ages, all conditions, and all dispositions constantly form associations. They have not only commercial and manufacturing companies, in which all take part, but associations of a thousand other kinds—religious, moral, serious, futile, extensive or restricted, enormous or diminutive. The Americans make associations to give entertainments, to found establishments for education, to build inns, to construct churches, to diffuse books, to send missionaries to the antipodes; and in this manner they found hospitals, prisons, and schools. If it be proposed to advance some truth, or to foster some feeling by the encouragement of a great example, they form a society . . .

Thus the most democratic country on the face of the earth is that in which men have in our time carried to the highest perfection the art of pursuing in common the object of their common desires, and have applied this new science to the greatest number of purposes. Is this the result of accident? or is there in reality any necessary connexion between the principle of association and that of equality?

Aristocratic communities always contain, among a multitude of persons who by themselves are powerless, a small number of powerful and wealthy citizens, each of whom can achieve great undertakings single-handed. In aristocratic societies men do not need to combine in order to act, because they are strongly held together. . . .

Among democratic nations, on the contrary, all the citizens are independent and feeble; they can do hardly anything by themselves, and none of them can oblige his fellow-men to lend him their assistance. They all, therefore, fall into a state of incapacity, if they do not learn voluntarily to help each other. . . . A people among which individuals should lose the power of achieving great things single-handed, without acquiring the means of producing

---

[14] Alexis de Tocqueville, *Democracy in America*, Henry Reeve, trans., 4th ed. (New York, 1841), 2:114–20.

them by united exertions, would soon relapse into barbarism. . . .

As soon as several of the inhabitants of the United States have taken up an opinion or a feeling which they wish to promote in the world, they look out for mutual assistance; and as soon as they have found each other out, they combine. From that moment they are no longer isolated men, but a power seen from afar, whose actions serve for an example, and whose language is listened to. The first time I heard in the United States that a hundred thousand men had bound themselves publicly to abstain from spirituous liquors, it appeared to me more like a joke than a serious engagement; and I did not at once perceive why these temperate citizens could not content themselves with drinking water by their own firesides. I at last undersood that these hundred thousand Americans, alarmed by the progress of drunkenness around them, had made up their minds to patronise temperance. They acted just in the same way as a man of high rank who should dress very plainly, in order to inspire the humbler orders with a contempt of luxury. . . .

It frequently happens . . . in democratic countries, that a great number of men who wish or who want to combine cannot accomplish it, because as they are very insignificant and lost amid the crowd, they cannot see, and know not where to find, one another. A newspaper then takes up the notion or the feeling which had occurred simultaneously, but singly, to each of them. All are then immediately guided toward this beacon; and these wandering minds, which had long sought each other in darkness, at length meet and unite. . . .

There is consequently a necessary connexion between public associations and newspapers: newspapers make associations, and associations make newspapers; and if it has been correctly advanced that associations will increase in number as the conditions of men become more equal, it is not less certain that the number of newspapers increases in proportion to that of associations.

Legislative Action

By the middle of the nineteenth century the evils of the factory system, already familiar in Great Britain, had begun to appear in New England, where cotton manufacturing was established on a large scale. An insistent demand for laws regulating the hours of labor met with some response in state legislatures. Massachusetts refused to pass such a law in 1850, but a *minority* of the special committee appointed by the House of Representatives brought in the following report.[15]

---

[15] Massachusetts House of Representatives, *House Document No. 153*, 1850; reprinted by permission of the publishers, The Arthur H. Clark Company, from John R. Commons and others, eds., *A Documentary History of American Industrial Society* (Cleveland, 1909–11), 8:155, 157–58, 176–78, 180–81, 186.

In relation to the hours of labor, the undersigned agree . . . that a necessity exists for legislative interference to restrict them, and deem it proper to present to the Legislature their reasons for this conclusion.

They fully believe, and think that nearly all intelligent persons, who have thought upon the subject, will admit, that the present hours of labor in the manufactories of this State, are too many, for the moral welfare and physical health of the operatives, and that this system of labor is a great evil, which, not only immediately affects the laborers themselves, but is diffused into society, and will entail serious effects upon posterity. . . .

By this table [of hours of labor in the Lowell factories], it appears, that the daily average time of labor throughout the year, is less than two minutes short of twelve hours. . . .

If any reliance can be placed upon the teachings of physiological science, and the opinions of eminent physiologists, the human constitution was never intended, or framed by the Creator, for such long continued and exclusive devotion to labor of any kind. . . .

It is the opinion of the undersigned, that it is a sound general principle, that government should not interfere with the industrial pursuits of the people any further, than is necessary for the preservation of order and the rights of individuals. . . . But in relation to the great business of manufacturing in this State, the Legislature, with the intention of promoting the manufacturing interest, has by its action, interfered with, and destroyed the natural relations ordinarily existing between the class of employers and the class of employees. . . . The Legislature, . . . has by its acts of incorporation, created, as it were, immense artificial persons, with far larger powers than are possessed by individuals. . . . They are thus enabled to fix inexorably, without consultation with the laboring class, all the terms and conditions of labor. . . . From this decision of these powerful employers, large masses of the laboring people have practically no escape. Circumstances, practically compel them to submit to the offered terms. . . .

If the two classes—the employers and the employed, stood upon the general platform of our institutions, with the powers alone of natural and ordinary persons, the necessity now urged, might not exist, and they might probably, be safely left to arrange all matters, including the hours of labor, by mutual agreement. But the natural state of equality having been destroyed, as regards this large class of persons who work for the large manufacturing corporations, a manifestly different state of things is presented for consideration. If their hours of labor be excessive, or if they be subjected, by the nature and condition of their employment, to other evils and abuses, they have in themselves, no power of remedy. If they suffer wrongs and evils which they ought not to suffer, they can look only to the Legislature for redress. If the Legislature has, on the one hand, exercised its power to strengthen the capitalist for the more successful prosecution of useful enterprises, it should, on the other hand, when occasion requires, uphold and protect the interest and welfare of the laborer against the crushing effects of that augmented power. . . .

The excessive hours of labor in

manufacturing establishments is not a new subject of legislation. It has attracted the attention of legislators in various parts of the United States as well as those of other countries. . . . In England, the accumulating evils concomitant with the progress of manufactures, made it necessary, as long ago as 1802, to interpose an act of Parliament for the "preservation of the health and morals" of those employed in cotton and other factories. . . . In the year 1847, an act of Parliament was passed, further limiting the time of work to ten hours a day, and not exceeding fifty-eight hours in any one week. . . . It appears from this, that the operatives in the factories of Massachusetts, work, on an average throughout the year, fourteen hours a week more than the factory operatives of England do. . . .

In England, the restriction of the hours of labor has worked successfully, and is now acknowledged by some of the most distinguished manufacturers there, to have resulted advantageously to proprietors as well as laborers. . . . The undersigned believe similar beneficial results to proprietors, laborers, and to the community generally, will ensue in Massachusetts, from a reduction of the hours of labor in the manufacturing establishments. They therefore respectfully recommend the passage of the . . . Bill.

Reform Through Model Communities

One distinctive program of reform of the period was that offered by certain forerunners of modern socialism, who can best be described as communitarian socialists. Unlike most of their successors, they repudiated the idea of class struggle and refused to look to government for leadership and aid. At the same time they proposed a reorganization of society more thoroughgoing than most reformers contemplated. Communitarian socialists solved the paradox of drastic yet peaceable change by urging the establishment of small communities within which far-reaching reforms might be tried out without disturbing society as a whole.

The germs of communitarianism were to be found among various religious sects in colonial America. The first fully developed program of communitarian reform under nonreligious auspices was that offered by Robert Owen (1771–1858), who founded the New Harmony Community in Indiana. A second wave of communitarian enthusiasm occurred in the 1840s, resulting in the establishment of scores of communities, the best known of which was Brook Farm in Massachusetts. Particularly influential in the latter period were the ideas of the French socialist Charles Fourier (1772–1837). His leading disciple in America was Albert Brisbane (1809–1890), who published in Horace Greeley's *New York Tribune* a column in which he expounded Fourierism. As the movement gathered momentum, he gathered some of his articles together in a widely circulated pamphlet, from which the following excerpt comes.[16]

---

[16] Albert Brisbane, *A Concise Exposition of the Doctrine of Association, or Plan for a Re-Organization of Society* (New York, 1843), 73–74.

The idea of effecting a reform in the present organization of Society and of establishing a new Social Order in its place, appears at first sight so vast and stupendous an undertaking, that it is deemed impracticable, and beyond the means and power of Man. An examination of the subject, however, will satisfy the most incredulous and prejudiced minds that it is neither wild nor impracticable, but, on the contrary, that it is feasible and easy, and that Association offers us the means of effecting peaceably and in the interest of all classes, a complete transformation in the social condition of the world.

The whole question of effecting a Social Reform may be reduced to the establishment of one Association, which will serve as a model for, and induce the rapid establishment of others. If one Association be established, and *it is of little consequence where,* which will prove practically to the world the immense advantages of the system, its vast economies, its safe and profitable investment of Capital, and the prosperity, health and happiness which it will secure to mankind, it will spread with a rapidity which the most sanguine cannot anticipate.

It will be with Association as with all those great practical improvements, which are adopted at once and by general consent and approbation, when the immense benefits which they confer are demonstrated by experiment. The Steamboat offers among a thousand others a striking illustration of this. It was only necessary for Fulton to build one steamboat, and to prove to the world by one practical experiment the great advantages of steam navigation, and soon the rivers, the lakes and even the oceans of the world began to be covered with them. It will only be necessary to establish one Association, and demonstrate by one successful experiment the immense advantages which the system offers, and the same results will follow, except that Association will spread with infinitely more rapidity than the steamboat, because it affects directly all the interests and the happiness of mankind.

An Association of eighteen hundred persons is the primary and simplest element of the social Organization which we advocate, and is to the Combined Order what the Township is to the present Social Order.

What is a Township? It is the smallest element, germ or political compact of the State. . . . Now if we can, with a knowledge of true architectural principles, build one house rightly, conveniently and elegantly, we can, by taking it for a model and building others like it, make a perfect and beautiful city: in the same manner, if we can, with a knowledge of true social principles, organize one township rightly, we can, by organizing others like it, and by spreading and rendering them universal, establish a true Social and Political Order in the place of the old and false one. . . .

An Association such as we propose, is nothing more nor less than a rightly organized township; it will require a tract of land about three miles square, on which about eighteen hundred persons or three hundred families will reside; and instead of living separately in isolated dwellings, they will live unitedly in one noble edifice; there will be economy and order, there will be unity of interests, concert of action, a judicious application of labor, capital and skill, and general ease, intelligence and affluence. If we can substitute peaceably and gradually Associations, or *rightly organized townships,* in the place of the present *falsely and defectively organized townships,* we can effect quietly and easily, without commotion or violence, and to the advantage of all classes, a social transformation and a mighty reform.

Social Revolution

Scarcely a hint of the revolutionary spirit with which Continental Europe was seething can be found in the writings of American reformers. Many of the latter, in fact, urged the adoption of their proposals as a means of preventing such a spirit from ever arising. The slavery issue, however, generated tensions that in the end erupted into violence and war. Even so, leaders of both sides carefully avoided describing their positions as revolutionary, even when in fact they were ready to overturn existing institutions and to resort to violence. In his first inaugural Lincoln conceded that there existed a "revolutionary right to dismember or overthrow" the Union while denying that there was a constitutional right to secede, but Southern leaders declined to justify secession on revolutionary grounds, instead insisting upon the strict constitutionality of what they were doing. Only a few radical abolitionists were prepared to call a spade a spade and to speak frankly of social revolution.

One of these was John Brown, whose most famous exploit was a raid on Harper's Ferry, October 16–18, 1859, in which he captured the United States arsenal and sought to inaugurate a great slave revolt under the aegis of an insurrectionary government. The speech excerpted below was delivered by Brown at Chatham, in Upper Canada, on May 8, 1858, at a secret convention which adopted a Provisional Constitution for the insurrectionary state which Brown planned to create. His remarks were not recorded at the time, but were summarized from recollection by one of his hearers, Richard Realf, in testimony given before the so-called Mason Committee of the Senate on January 21, 1860.[17]

John Brown, on rising, stated that for twenty or thirty years the idea had possessed him like a passion of giving liberty to the slaves. He stated immediately thereafter, that . . . in 1851 . . . he made a tour upon the European continent, inspecting all fortifications, and especially all earth-work forts which he could find, with a view, as he stated, of applying the knowledge thus gained, with modifications and inventions of his own, to such a

---

[17] 36th Congress, 1st Session, *Senate Report No. 278*, 96–98.

mountain warfare as he thereafter spoke upon in the United States. John Brown . . . stated that he had read all the books upon insurrectionary warfare which he could lay his hands upon—the Roman warfare; the successful opposition of the Spanish chieftains during the period when Spain was a Roman province; how with ten thousand men divided and subdivided into small companies, acting simultaneously, yet separately, they withstood the whole consolidated power of the Roman empire through a number of years. In addition to this, he said . . . he had become thoroughly acquainted with the wars in Hayti and the islands round about; and from all these things he had drawn the conclusion . . . that upon the first intimation of a plan formed for the liberation of the slaves, they would immediately rise all over the Southern States. He supposed that they would come into the mountains to join him, where he purposed to work, and that by flocking to his standard they would enable him (by making the line of mountains which cuts diagonally through Maryland and Virginia down through the Southern States into Tennessee and Alabama, the base of his operations) to act upon the plantations on the plains lying on each side of that range of mountains, and that we should be able to establish ourselves in the fastnesses, and if any hostile action (as would be) were taken against us, either by the militia of the separate States, or by the armies of the United States, we purposed to defeat first the militia, and next, if it were possible, the troops of the United States, and then organize the freed blacks under this provisional constitution, which would carve out for the locality of its jurisdiction all that mountainous region in which the blacks were to be established, and in which they were to be taught the useful and mechanical arts, and to be instructed in all the business of life. . . .

The negroes were to constitute the soldiers. John Brown expected that all the free negroes in the Northern States would immediately flock to his standard. He expected that all the slaves in the Southern States would do the same. . . .

The slaveholders were to be taken as hostages, if they refused to let their slaves go. It is a mistake to suppose that they were to be killed; they were not to be. They were to be held as hostages for the safe treatment of any prisoners of John Brown's who might fall into the hands of hostile parties. . . .

All the non-slaveholders were to be protected. Those who would not join the organization of John Brown, but who would not oppose it, were to be protected; but those who did oppose it, were to be treated as the slaveholders themselves. . . .

Thus, John Brown said that he believed, a successful incursion could be made; that it could be successfully maintained; that the several slave States could be forced (from the position in which they found themselves) to recognize the freedom of those who had been slaves within the respective limits of those States; that immediately such recognitions were made, then the places of all the officers elected under this provisional constitution became vacant, and new elections were to be made. Moreover, no salaries were to be paid to the officeholders under this constitution. It was purely out of that which we supposed to be philanthropy—love for the slave.

5. THE REFORM MOVEMENT AS VIEWED BY ITS OPPONENTS

By its very nature, any reform movement pushes against a tremendous weight of opposition. Part consists of the sheer inertia which any established order of things possesses, and which hardly needs to find expression in words. But reform also provokes opposition, and the arguments used by defenders of the status quo need to be attended to if the reform movement itself is to be fully understood and correctly assessed. Reformers, after all, present a one-sided view of a given problem, rarely calling attention to values that might be destroyed by too drastic an uprooting of established institutions. To be sure, their opponents are likely to draw an equally one-sided picture, in which the crooked is made straight, and the rough places plain. The historian is bound to cut through the distortions of both sides to get at the truth of the situation. And he is obliged also to recognize that the existence of opposing arguments (however valid or invalid they may be) is an inescapable historical fact, which determines the speed with which proposed reforms win support and move toward final adoption.

Three types of criticism directed by contemporaries against the aims or the methods of reformers are represented in the selections that follow.

Laissez Faire

The most potent weapon used against reformers who sought to alter existing economic arrangements was the dogma of *laissez faire*. The economic world, according to this view, was governed by inexorable laws, any interference with which would, in the long run, make the evils worse. When, as often happened, economic laws were thought of as emanating from the Creator Himself, disregard of them was not merely imprudent, it was a violation of the moral law. Such a fusion of economics and ethics was made by the Reverend Francis Wayland (1790–1865), president of Brown University, in a textbook published in 1837, which dominated college instruction in America for a generation or more. The following quotation is from that work, *The Elements of Political Economy*.[18]

---

[18] Francis Wayland, *The Elements of Political Economy* (New York, 1837), 111, 124–27.

Although God has designed men to labor, yet he has not designed them to labor without reward. . . . As it is unnatural to labor without receiving benefit from it, men will not labor continuously nor productively, unless they receive such benefit. And, hence, the greater this benefit, the more active and spontaneous will be their exertion.

In order that every man may enjoy, in the greatest degree, the advantages of his labor, it is necessary, provided always he do not violate the rights of his neighbor, 1st. *That, he be allowed to gain all that he can;* and, 2d. *That having gained all that he can, he be allowed to use it as he will.* . . .

A man may possess himself, either dishonestly or by begging, of the property for which he has not labored. The dishonest acquisition of property, as by cheating, stealing, or robbery, will be prevented by the strict and impartial administration of just and equitable laws. Hence, we see that the benefit of such laws is two fold. They encourage industry, first, by securing to the industrious the righteous reward of their labor; and secondly, by inflicting upon the indolent the just punishment of their idleness. . . .

But secondly: Men may be relieved from the necessity of labor, by charity. . . . I do not here refer to the sick, the infirm, the aged, the helpless, the widow, the fatherless, and the orphan. When God has seen fit to take away the power to labor, he then calls upon us to bestow liberally. . . . With this mode of charity I have now nothing to do. I speak only of provisions for the support of the poor, simply because he is poor; and of provision to supply his wants, without requiring the previous exertion of his labor. Of this kind are poor laws, as they are established in England, and in some parts of our own country; and permanent endowments left to particular corporations for the maintenance of the simply indigent. Now, such provisions we suppose to be injurious, for several reasons.

1. They are at variance with the fundamental law of government, that he who is able to labor, shall enjoy only that for which he has labored. . . . If labor be a curse, it is unjust that one part, and that, the industrious part, should suffer it all. If, as is the fact, it be a blessing, there is no reason why all should not equally enjoy its advantages.

2. They remove from men the fear of want, one of the most natural and universal stimulants to labor. Hence, in just so far as this stimulus is removed, there will be in a given community less labor done; that is, less production created.

3. By teaching a man to depend upon others, rather than upon himself, they destroy the healthful feeling of independence. . . . It is in evidence, before the committee of the British House of Commons, that, after a family has once applied for assistance from the parish, it rarely ceases to apply regularly, and, most frequently, in progress of time, for a larger and larger measure of assistance.

4. Hence, such a system must tend greatly to increase the number of paupers. It is a discouragement to industry, and a bounty upon indolence. . . .

5. They are, in principle, destructive to the right of property, because they must proceed upon the

concession, that the rich are under obligation to support the poor. . . .

6. Hence, they tend to insubordination. For, if the rich are under obligation to support the poor, why not to support them better; nay, why not to support them as well as themselves. Hence, the more provision there is of this kind, the greater will be the liability of collision between the two classes.

If this be so, we see, that in order to accomplish the designs of our Creator in this respect, and thus present the strongest inducement to industry,

1. Property should be universally appropriated, so that nothing is left in common.
2. The right of property should be perfectly protected, both against individual and social spoliation.
3. There should be no common funds for the support of those who are not willing to labor.
4. That if a man be reduced, by indolence or prodigality, to such extreme penury that he is in danger of perishing, he be relieved, through the medium of labor; that is, that he be furnished with work, and be remunerated with the proceeds.
5. That those who are enabled only in part to earn their subsistences, be provided for, to the amount of that deficiency, only.

And hence, that all our provisions for the relief of the poor, be so devised as not to interfere with this law of our nature. By so directing our benevolent energies, the poor are better provided for; they are happier themselves; and a great and constantly increasing burden is removed from the community.

The Fanaticism and Irreligion of the Reform Movement

Attack is often the best defense. Conservatives often addressed themselves not to a defense of the status-quo but to the shortcomings of those who attacked it. Reformers were pictured as reckless fanatics, hostile to true religion and morality, and purveying remedies far worse than the disease. The following excerpt from the October 1838 issue of the *Princeton Review,* a Presbyterian quarterly published in Philadelphia and Princeton, was frequently reprinted, especially in the South.[19]

The mass of the pious and thinking people in this country are neither abolitionists nor the advocates of slavery. They stand where they ever have stood on the broad scriptural foundation; maintaining the obligation of all men in their several places and relations, to act on the law of love, and to promote the spiritual and temporal welfare of others by every means in their power. They stand aloof from the abolitionists for various reasons. In the first place, they disapprove of their principles. The leading characteristic doctrine of this sect is that slave-holding is in all cases a sin,

---

[19] *Biblical Repertory and Princeton Review,* 10 (October 1838), 603–6.

and should therefore, under all circumstances, be immediately abandoned. As nothing can be plainer than that slaveholders were admitted to the Christian church by the inspired apostles; the advocates of this doctrine are brought into direct collision with the scriptures. This leads to one of the most dangerous evils connected with the whole system, viz. a disregard of the authority of the word of God, a setting up a different and higher standard of truth and duty, and a proud and confident wresting of scripture to suit their own purposes. The history of interpretation furnishes no examples of more wilful and violent perversions of the sacred text than are to be found in the writings of the abolitionists. They seem to consider themselves above the scriptures, and when they put themselves above the law of God, it is not wonderful that they should disregard the laws of men.

Significant manifestations of the result of this disposition to consider their own light a surer guide than the word of God, are visible in the anarchical opinions about human governments, civil and ecclesiastical, and on the rights of women, which have found appropriate advocates in the abolition publications. Let these principles be carried out, and there is an end to all social subordination, to all security for life or property, to all guarantee for public or domestic virtue. If our women are to be emancipated from subjection to the law which God has imposed upon them, if they are to quit the retirement of domestic life where they preside in stillness over the character and destiny of society; if they are to come forth in the liberty of men, to be our agents, our public lecturers, our committeemen, our rulers; if, in studied insult to the authority of God, we are to renounce, in the marriage contract, all claim to obedience, we shall soon have a country . . . from which all order and all virtue would speedily be banished. There is no form of human excellence before which we bow with profounder deference than that which appears in a delicate woman adorned with the inward graces, and devoted to the peculiar duties of her sex; and there is no deformity of human character from which we turn with deeper loathing than from a woman forgetful of her nature, and clamorous for the vocations and rights of men. It would not be fair to object to the abolitionists the disgusting and disorganizing opinions of even some of their leading advocates and publications, did they not continue to patronize these publications and were not these opinions the legitimate consequences of their own principles. . . .

In the second place, the majority of good men object to the spirit of the abolitionists. . . . It is a spirit of exaggeration, misrepresentation, and of calumny. We hardly know how to account for the fact that men and women, in other respects correct and amiable, should be transformed into violent and reckless detractors when the subject of slavery has engrossed their feelings. Yet there is abundant evidence that such is the fact in a multitude of cases. Had this cause fallen into the hands of men in whose judgment and spirit the Christian community had confidence, it would have had far greater success and been far less dangerous. As it is, every man of correct feeling turns with disgust from the vulgar tirades of the Liberator, or the cool, sardonic jeers of the Emancipator, with the conviction that nothing holy can be promoted by such instrumentality.

The Tyranny of Organized Mass Opinion

Rational discussion is the only possible basis for democratic and peaceable solutions to social problems, so moderate-minded men insisted. Their ideal was the free exchange of ideas, eventuating, through tolerance and compromise, in programs acceptable to all. Such harmonious adjustment was endangered, they felt, by the intransigence of extremists—by the blind obstinacy of conservatives and the reckless temper of reformers. Moderates were particularly concerned lest public opinion be deliberately inflamed to such a degree as to make impossible the kind of reasoned discussion out of which acceptable solutions might be expected to come. William Ellery Channing (1780–1842), a liberal clergyman and a founder of Unitarianism in America, published in 1829 the following thoughtful discussion of the benefits and dangers inherent in organized mass propaganda for particular reforms, however desirable.[20]

In truth, one of the most remarkable circumstances or features of our age, is the energy with which the principle of combination, or of action by joint forces, by associated numbers, is manifesting itself. It may be said, without much exaggeration, that everything is done now by Societies. . . . So extensive have coalitions become, through the facilities now described, and so various and rapid are the means of communication, that when a few leaders have agreed on an object, an impulse may be given in a month to the whole country. Whole States may be deluged with tracts and other publications, and a voice like that of many waters, be called forth from immense and widely separated multitudes. Here is a new power brought to bear on society, and it is a great moral question, how it ought to be viewed, and what duties it imposes.

That this mode of action has advantages and recommendations, is very obvious. The principal arguments in its favor may be stated in a few words. Men, it is justly said, can do jointly, what they cannot do singly. The union of minds and hands, works wonders. Men grow efficient by concentrating their powers. . . .

Nor is this all. Men not only accumulate power by union, but gain warmth, and earnestness. . . . Union not only brings to a point forces which before existed, and which were ineffectual through separation, but, by the feeling and interest which it rouses, it becomes a creative principle, calls forth new forces, and gives the mind a con-

---

[20] *Christian Examiner,* 7 (September 1829), 105–7, 112, 121–23.

sciousness of powers, which would otherwise have been unknown. . . .

Still we apprehend, that on this subject there is a want of accurate views and just discrimination. . . . The truth is, and we need to feel it most deeply, that our connexion with society, as it is our greatest aid, so it is our greatest peril. . . . Our great and most difficult duty as social beings, is, to derive constant aid from society without taking its yoke; to open our minds to the thoughts, reasonings, and persuasions of others, and yet to hold fast the sacred right of private judgment. . . .

Associations often injure free action by a very plain and obvious operation. They accumulate power in a few hands, and this takes place just in proportion to the surface over which they spread. . . . Through such an Association, widely spread, yet closely connected by party feeling, a few leaders can send their voices and spirit far and wide, and, where great funds are accumulated, can league a host of instruments, and by menace and appeals to interest, can silence opposition. . . . Public opinion may be so combined, and inflamed, and brought to bear on odious individuals or opinions, that it will be as perilous to think and speak with manly freedom, as if an Inquisition were open before us. It is now discovered that the way to rule in this country, is by an array of numbers, which a prudent man will not like to face. Of consequence, all Associations aiming or tending to establish sway by numbers, ought to be opposed. They create tyrants as effectually as standing armies. Let them be withstood from the beginning. No matter whether the opinions which they intend to put down be true or false. Let no opinion be put down by such means. Let not error be suppressed by an instrument, which will be equally powerful against truth, and which must subvert that freedom of thought on which all truth depends. . . .

In this country, few things are more to be dreaded, than organizations or institutions by which public opinion may be brought to bear tyrannically against individuals or sects. From the nature of things, public opinion is often unjust; but when it is not embodied and fixed by pledged Societies, it easily relents, it may receive new impulses, it is open to influences from the injured. On the contrary, when shackled and stimulated by vast Associations, it is in danger of becoming a steady, unrelenting tyrant, browbeating the timid, proscribing the resolute, silencing free speech, and virtually denying the dearest religious and civil rights.

6. THE ULTIMATE ACCOMPLISHMENT: A FEW LANDMARKS

Reform is a slow business, with many tedious interruptions and heartbreaking reversals. In the long run, however, most of the reform movements that we have been examining made a decisive impact upon American life and American institutions. Though actual practices often lag far behind written laws, one measure of the influence of a movement of reform is the degree to which its central principles, once regarded with skepticism if not contempt, are eventually written into the law of the land. Sometimes a constitutional amendment embodies the results of a successful effort at reform. Sometimes the preamble of a statute enshrines the ideas for which reformers have striven. Sometimes a court decision transforms a hitherto unrealized ideal into a binding legal precedent. All three processes are illustrated by the formal documents excerpted below.

Constitutional Amendments

Each of the twenty-six amendments added to the Constitution since its adoption (up to and including the year 1971) has been the outcome of a determined struggle on someone's part. The six amendments quoted here[21] had their real inception in the early nineteenth-century agitations with which this problem has dealt. The three amendments dealing with slavery and racial discrimination (the 13th, 14th, and 15th) were added to the Constitution within five years of the end of the Civil War, but determined, vigorous enforcement can hardly be said to have begun until the middle of the twentieth century. By contrast, the women's suffrage amendment (the 19th) lagged until 1920, but once ratified it was almost automatically effective. Still different was the history of the prohibition amendment (the 18th), which enjoyed less than a decade and a half of life before repeal (by the 21st amendment).

Thirteenth Amendment (1865). Section 1. Neither slavery nor involuntary servitude, except as a punishment for crime whereof the party shall have been duly convicted, shall exist within the United States, or any place subject to their jurisdiction.
. . .
Fourteenth Amendment (1868). Section 1. All persons born or naturalized in the United States and subject to the jurisdiction thereof, are citizens of the United States and of the State wherein they reside. No State shall make or enforce any law which shall abridge the privileges or immunities of citizens of the United States; no shall any State deprive any person of life, liberty, or property, without due process of law; nor deny to any person within its jurisdiction the equal protection of the laws.
. . .
Fifteenth Amendment (1870). Section 1. The right of citizens of the United States to vote shall not be denied or abridged by the United States or by any State on account of

---

[21] Library of Congress, *The Constitution of the United States of America: Analysis and Interpretation* (Washington, 1964), 62–72.

race, color, or previous condition of servitude.

. . .

Eighteenth Amendment (1919). After one year from the ratification of this article the manufacture, sale, or transportation of intoxicating liquors within, the importation thereof into, or the exportation thereof from the United States and all territory subject to the jurisdiction thereof for beverage purposes is hereby prohibited.

. . .

Nineteenth Amendment (1920). The right of citizens of the United States to vote shall not be denied or abridged by the United States or by any State on account of sex.

. . .

Twenty-First Amendment (1933). Section 1. The eighteenth article of amendment to the Constitution of the United States is hereby repealed.

Section 2. The transportation or importation into any State, Territory or possession of the United States for delivery or use therein of intoxicating liquors, in violation of the laws thereof, is hereby prohibited.

. . .

Legislative Action

Complex social problems obviously cannot be solved by a single stroke of the pen, even so conspicuous a stroke as a constitutional amendment. To bring a problem effectively under control, it must be analyzed into its components, and an appropriate remedy devised for each particular factor. As a consequence social legislation ordinarily consists of a mass of detailed provisions, intricate, tedious, and difficult to grasp as a whole. Occasionally, however, these opaque details are illuminated by a well-drafted preamble or statement of policy. The effectiveness of the measure will still depend on the adequacy of its specific provisions, but the statement of policy serves to make clear the principles which the legislators have been prevailed upon to accept—initially at the prompting of those whom we think of as reformers.

An excellent example is afforded by the Norris-LaGuardia Anti-Injunction Act of 1932. A century earlier, when trade unions first came into being, they were looked upon askance by public opinion and were prosecuted as criminal conspiracies by the state. Labor leaders and liberal reformers took up the task of arguing for the legitimacy of labor unions and the desirability of orderly collective bargaining. Finally in the twentieth century public opinion swung round, and Congress enacted a series of crucial statutes outlawing in detail the various practices that had been used to thwart unionization and impede collective bargaining. Quoted below is an explanatory section from one of these measures.[22] It signalizes the fact that ideas championed by reformers have at last become avowed public policy.

---

[22] An Act to amend the Judicial Code and to define and limit the jurisdiction of courts sitting in equity (Norris-LaGuardia Act), March 23, 1932. 47 U.S. Statutes at Large 70.

Be it enacted by the Senate and House of Representatives of the United States of America in Congress assembled, That no court of the United States, as herein defined, shall have jurisdiction to issue any restraining order or temporary or permanent injunction in a case involving or growing out of a labor dispute, except in a strict conformity with the provisions of this Act; nor shall any such restraining order or temporary or permanent injunction be issued contrary to the public policy declared in this Act.

SEC. 2. In the interpretation of this Act and in determining the jurisdiction and authority of the courts of the United States, . . . the public policy of the United States is hereby declared as follows:

Whereas under prevailing economic conditions, developed with the aid of governmental authority for owners of property to organize in the corporate and other forms of ownership association, the individual unorganized worker is commonly helpless to exercise actual liberty of contract and to protect his freedom of labor, and thereby to obtain acceptable terms and conditions of employment, wherefore, though he should be free to decline to associate with his fellows, it is necessary that he have full freedom of association, self-organization, and designation of representatives of his own choosing, to negotiate the terms and conditions of his employment, and that he shall be free from the interference, restraint, or coercion of employers of labor, or their agents, in the designation of such representatives or in self-organization or in other concerted activities for the purpose of collective bargaining or other mutual aid or protection. . . .

Judicial Decision

Because of the power of the courts of the United States to review the constitutionality of legislative acts, decisions of the Supreme Court often furnish the most eloquent as well as the most authoritative proof that ideas once championed by a mere handful of reformers have finally won a place among the fundamentals of American democratic thought. The Court is obliged, after all, to give specific meaning to such broad phrases of the Constitution as "general Welfare," "Privileges and Immunities of Citizens," "a Republican Form of Government," laws "in Pursuance" of the Constitution, "due process of law," and "equal protection of the laws." In doing so the Court has, in many periods of its history, read into the Constitution a meaning derived from the most conservative of the philosophies prevalent at the time. In particular the Court has frequently been accused of trying to enact into constitutional law the doctrine of *laissez faire,* pretty much as expounded in President Francis Wayland's treatise of 1837, excerpted above. When therefore the Supreme Court repudiates—as it does in the opinion quoted below—a whole series of *laissez-faire* precedents, and accepts as legitimate the concept of wide-ranging governmental responsibility for social welfare, the reversal furnishes striking evidence of the inherent power of reformist ideas.

The decision in question, handed down on March 29, 1937, in the midst of the controversy over President Franklin D. Roosevelt's "court-packing" proposal, upheld a Washington State minimum-wage law for women. The opinion of the court, quoted here, was written by Chief Justice Charles Evans Hughes, but for the time being it represented the views of no more than a bare majority of the nine-man Court.[23] Four conservatives, still unconvinced, filed a dissenting opinion.

What can be closer to the public interest than the health of women and their protection from unscrupulous and overreaching employers? And if the protection of women is a legitimate end of the exercise of state power, how can it be said that the requirement of the payment of a minimum wage fairly fixed in order to meet the very necessities of existence is not an admissible means to that end? The legislature of the State was clearly entitled to consider the situation of women in employment, the fact that they are in the class receiving the least pay, that their bargaining power is relatively weak, and that they are the ready victims of those who would take advantage of their necessitous circumstances. The legislature was entitled to adopt measures to reduce the evils of the "sweating system," the exploiting of workers at wages so low as to be insufficient to meet the bare cost of living, thus making their very helplessness the occasion of a most injurious competition. The legislature had the right to consider that its minimum wage requirements would be an important aid in carrying out its policy of protection. The adoption of similar requirements by many States evidences a deepseated conviction both as to the presence of the evil and as to the means adapted to check it. Legislative response to that conviction cannot be regarded as arbitrary or capricious, and that is all we have to decide. Even if the wisdom of the policy be regarded as debatable and its effects uncertain, still the legislature is entitled to its judgment.

There is an additional and compelling consideration which recent economic experience has brought into a strong light. The exploitation of a class of workers who are in an unequal position with respect to bargaining power and are thus relatively defenceless against the denial of a living wage is not only detrimental to their health and well being but casts a direct burden for their support upon the community. What these workers lose in wages the taxpayers are called upon to pay. The bare cost of living must be met. We may take judicial notice of the unparalleled demands for relief which arose during the recent period of depression and still continue to an alarming extent despite the degree of economic recovery which has been achieved. . . . The community is not bound to provide what is in effect a subsidy for unconscionable employers. The community may direct its law-making power to correct the abuse which springs from their selfish disregard of the public interest.

---

[23] West Coast Hotel Co. *v.* Parrish, 300 U.S. 379, at 398–400.

CONCLUSION

Though enthusiasm for reform has its ups and down, and the pace of reform sometimes quickens and sometimes slackens, no society can ever be without movements for reform unless it has reached the final stage of ossification and death. When one period of reform gives place to a succeeding one, old problems take on new guises (as when the curse of slavery is transformed into the curse of racial discrimination). Entirely new problems appear (as problems of ecology are now arising). Moods change from optimism to pessimism (as today they seem to have changed), and perhaps change back again. Old forms of propaganda become ludicrously ineffective, and new ones (often devised for their shock value) enjoy their own brief power of arresting attention. Particular imperfections are eliminated from human institutions, but perfection itself remains a goal, not an achievement. And thus the yeast of reform must work to produce its ferment in every age. That it is doing so today, few would think of denying.

To say that history *teaches* no lessons is true enough. But this is not the same thing as saying that nothing can be *learned* from history. To a closed mind the past is irrelevant. There is nothing surprising in this, for to the possessor of a closed mind no fact or idea outside the zealously fortified enclosure of his skull is ever relevant or even interesting. To an inquiring mind, however—to a mind anxious to understand how things came to be what they are and how they can be made better than they are—the past is inescapably relevant. How a given approach has worked in the past, what unforeseen side-effects have resulted from a particular course of action, what the gestation period of a new idea has usually turned out to be—these are things that a man or woman needs to know if he or she is to push or pry the massive but not altogether immovable world into a somewhat more acceptable posture. To gain partial answers to vital questions like these is one reason for combing the records of past movements devoted to the reform of human institutions and the betterment of the quality of men's lives.

10 EUGENE D. GENOVESE

the civilization of the slaveowning south

The slaveholding states that comprised the South in late ante-bellum times exhibited something generally called Southern civilization, the existence of which remains both beyond doubt and beyond adequate definition. It is clear that slavery shaped the South's social, political, economic, and moral life, but it is also clear that slavery, considered either as a social system or as an institution, differed radically from one part of the South to another and that its impact in Maryland cannot be equated with its impact in Louisiana. If it is proper to speak of a Southern civilization, it is nonetheless necessary to avoid homogenizing it; its variations are fully as striking as its unity.

The problem of variation, even of antagonistic variation, concerns more than differences between upper South and lower South or between older and newer regions; concerns more than differences between lowlands and up country within a given state. The very nature of the constituent social classes and races must be examined, for South Carolina's low-country aristocracy did not simply expand into the nearby Piedmont and certainly did not simply reappear in the Mississippi black belt; similarly, the Gullah-speaking blacks of the Georgia-South Carolina rice coast should not be confused with the black slaves of the interior. For these and other reasons such brief selections as those which follow must be understood as comprising a more or less arbitrary way of plunging into only one or two major features of a many-sided problem. Taken together they introduce the master class of the South—the men and women who had the primary role in shaping its politics and culture—and at least glance at those on whose labor they depended and at those whose political support they needed. Although we shall be concerned with the last thirty years of the regime, we shall be able to trace some features of the metamorphosis of the master class and perhaps in so doing be able to illuminate the central problem in the definition and characterization of the civilization of the Old South.

1. THE ARISTOCRATIC LOW COUNTRY

The claims of the Old South to an aristocratic civilization rest primarily on the history and traditions of Tidewater Virginia and the rice coast of South Carolina and Georgia. By late ante-bellum times the economy of Virginia had declined, and, as a result, many of the great families had disappeared, moved south, or were supporting their life in Virginia with the income of absentee plantations elsewhere. The great families of the South Carolina-Georgia coast, despite growing difficulties, looked much more formidable in the 1850s. In this first section, therefore, we shall consider the testimony of the families themselves and, in so doing, try to get some idea of the slave plantation as it looked from the vantage point of the Big House.

The Rice Coast

This opening selection is excerpted from the narrative provided by Herbert Ravenel Sass for a book of thirty paintings in water-color by Alice R. Huger Smith.[1] In addition to sensitive paintings of the South Carolina plantation world, the book contains chapters from an unpublished memoir of D. E. Huger Smith. In these three different ways it provides a view of that antebellum world by a significant contemporary figure and the heirs of the low-country tradition.

The Rice Coast: Its Story and Its Meaning

1. "The Gentlemen seated in the Country are very courteous, live very nobly in their Houses, and give very genteel Entertainment to Strangers and others that come to visit them." Thus wrote in the year 1709 John Lawson, a traveler in Carolina when the Province was in its infancy. It is one of the first clear glimpses that we have of the plantations of Carolina and it shows that even then, when most of America was an untamed wilderness, the civilization already developing in the rich lowlands near Charles Town had

[1] Herbert Ravenal Sass, Narrative for *A Carolina Rice Plantation of the Fifties: Thirty Paintings in Water-Colour* by Alice R. Huger Smith (New York: William Morrow and Co., 1936), 3–5, 13–25.

taken on the character which was to distinguish it through all its days. A century and a half later another traveler in the ante-bellum South, Frederick Law Olmsted of New York, came to a fork in the road he had been following.

"Here," he wrote, "the road divided, running each way at right angles; on one side to barns and a landing on the river, on the other toward the mansion of the proprietor. A negro boy opened the gate of the latter, and I entered.

"On either side, at fifty feet distant, were rows of old live-oak trees, their branches and twigs slightly hung with a delicate fringe of gray moss, and their dark, shining green foliage meeting and intermingling naturally but densely overhead. The sunlight streamed through and played aslant the lustrous leaves, and fluttering, pendulous moss; the arch was low and broad; the trunks were huge and gnarled, and there was a heavy groining of strong, rough, knotty branches. I stopped my horse and held my breath; for I have hardly in all my life seen anything so impressively grand and beautiful. I thought of old Kit North's rhapsody on trees; and it was no rhapsody—it was all here and real: 'Light, shade, shelter, coolness, freshness, music, dew, and dreams dropping through their umbrageous twilight—dropping direct, soft, sweet, soothing, and restorative from heaven.'"

Olmsted was no Southern enthusiast. In his "fault-finding book," as he himself described it, published in 1856, he was an outspoken critic of the Southern life and scene. On this occasion he had happened upon one of the stately live-oak avenues through which, on many of the Carolina rice plantations, the "Great House" was approached. The beauty of it took his breath; and yet perhaps he missed the deeper meaning.

These long cathedral naves of massive-trunked, wide-spreading, evergreen oaks, extending perhaps a quarter of a mile or more and forming a covered way to the plantation house at the avenue's end, still speak eloquently—for many of them survive—of the spirit which animated the founders of the Carolinian civilization. They were building not for the day or for the morrow but for their children's children. Thus the oak avenues, which only the long years could bring to perfection, are an expression of a steadfast faith as admirable as it was in one sense tragic; and in their simple and reticent dignity they are symbolical of that to which they led the wayfarer —the human life of the plantations, the generations of men and women who dwelt there. The great oaks which held Frederick Olmsted spellbound may have been planted in John Lawson's day. It was in the 1850's that Olmsted saw them, in the fullness of that strength and beauty which those who planted them could only foresee. So, too, the life of the Carolina rice plantations, which began even before Lawson's time, came in the 1850's to its fullest flowering; and certain aspects of that life in its strong and fine maturity this book attempts to picture and in some sort interpret.

That it was strong and fine can not be doubted by those of us who had the good fortune to know personally some of the men and women it produced. That there was beauty in it is demonstrated by much that it created and left behind it as its tangible memorial. Under this beauty, we believe, was something else of lasting importance—something the true nature of which has often been obscured and the continuing value of which has not been grasped.

The South is being urged by many to forget its past, and the Southern artist or writer who ventures to look back at the South's past—unless, indeed, he look through the spectacles of the satirist or the muck-raker—runs the risk of being catalogued as a mere sentimentalist animated by nothing more virile than a "nostalgic yearning for the vanished glories of the plantation era." Though this criticism has a certain justification, it can be carried too far. There is a completely valid motive for looking back at the Carolinian civilization which reached its zenith in the 1850's.

Of all the widely different Souths of which the Old South was composed the South of the great Carolina plantations must be most interesting to the student of the deep and broad main-currents of our national life. In its culminating and most distinctive and most significant period (from about 1820 to 1861) the Old South's thought and action were shaped mainly by South Carolina, and to this leadership the rice plantation region, of which Charleston was the capital, contributed a vital part. Hence the "Rice Coast" was much more than a tract of territory; nor does the now familiar phrase, "a way of living," express it adequately. It was also a way of thinking; and whatever has happened to its physical body, the invisible essential part of it may, in some new adaptation to the new times that are upon us, assume a new vitality. Long regarded as having been in its great days the last stronghold of an obsolete Romanticism, the Rice Coast may, in the changed perspective of these new times, take on a totally different significance. It was in essence an attempt to re-create in America the classic Greek ideal of democracy, the ideal which produced the great civilizations of ancient Greece and Rome; and this attempt may come at last to be recognized as a memorable effort in behalf of Realism in social and political thought—an effort perhaps destined to become once more, through a revival of its essential philosophy, an important animating force in American life.

This surely is reason enough why nothing about it should be forgotten, why all that it was should be kept clear in record and in understanding; and this, no less than the beauty that was here, is why Alice Smith's paintings have a value perhaps transcending even their exquisite art. She has pictured, as no one else could, the physical aspect, and in a true sense the soul, of a region, a period, of extraordinary interest to the student of the past and perhaps also of significance to the future. It is my task to help tell in words the story that she has beautifully told in pictures—pictures which her father's memoirs, so admirably simple and straightforward, render all the more vivid—and to suggest the reasons why the story has seemed worth telling. . . .

III. The "rice rivers" were eleven in number. From north to south they were the Waccamaw, the Pee Dee, the Black, the Sampit, the Santee, the Cooper, the Ashley, the Edisto, the Ashepoo, the Combahee, the

Savannah. On the tidewater of these rivers most of the rice planters were "seated," and the river was their friend and sometimes their foe so that the planter knew his river and most of the time loved it as he knew and loved the ancient oaks shading the plantation yard. From the river his fields drew their life; from it, in time of freshet or storm, devastation and ruin might come. Hence he had to know all its whims and caprices; its capacity for good, its power for harm.

"Sailing up one of those fruitful rivers," wrote Governor R. F. W. Allston, himself a great rice planter, in 1854, "the traveler may now behold many miles of serpentine embankment (continuous save where a water thoroughfare occurs) enclosing thousands of acres, checked into fields, which bear in waving luxuriance crops of this translucent grain." He might have beheld, too,—if the stage of the crop was one which required their presence—hundreds of black men and women working in those fields, working cheerfully and not too strenuously at tasks which would be completed by early afternoon (from one to four o'clock), leaving them the rest of the day for their own concerns.

From end to end of the rice plantation country, roughly a rectangle about one hundred and fifty miles long by forty or fifty miles wide, the picture varied only in details of its setting of rice fields, forest and river. In these details, however, it varied endlessly, so that in spite of the flatness of the landscape there was no monotony. An essential, in fact the central, feature of it was always the plantation house, placed usually upon some slight rise of the ground —for the Low Country is not utterly flat and along the rivers there are some fairly bold bluffs—whence a wide prospect of water and rice fields might be viewed.

The house stood as a rule among trees, some of them probably the original forest growth, others planted around the house-site in the colony's early days. Live-oaks and magnolias were the favorites, two of the noblest American species, which here attain magnificent proportions; the "burly-barked, man-bodied" live-oaks, as Sidney Lanier called them, stretching their massive limbs, as large as the trunks of ordinary trees, perhaps fifty feet from the enormous gnarled trunk; the magnolias towering straight upward, clothed at all seasons in their large, lustrous, dark-green leaves and especially beautiful in late spring and early summer with their superb ivory-white blooms.

Besides these trees around the house and in the plantation yard, there was often, though not invariably, the avenue, lined with live-oaks, usually of great size, through which the carriages of visitors approached the house from the main-road beyond the gate. The avenue, generally formed by single rows of oaks on each side, occasionally by double rows, was likely to be the most impressive feature of the place, and it was hard to say which was more beautiful—the view of river and rice fields from the piazza fronting the river, or the view from the landward piazza whence one looked straight down the long wide aisle of the avenue, a shadowy, colonnaded, high-ceilinged vista, festooned and tapestried with Spanish moss.

The approach was not always so stately; the house-groves, the plantation yards, the gardens differed in scale and effect and arrangement; most of the rice plantation places were pleasing to the eye, many were beautiful, a lesser number could claim a certain grandeur. This was true also of the houses themselves.

Some, like Newington and Drayton Hall on the Ashley, were large and imposing mansions modelled in some cases, it is said, after ancestral manors in England; others, perhaps not less spacious and often handsomely panelled, like Harrietta and Hampton on Santee and Dean Hall on the Cooper, were of cypress or heart-pine upon high brick foundations or basements; still others, including most of the very oldest built when the Low Country was a wilderness, were houses of small or moderate size, with no pretension to elegance or luxury. Large or small, simple or elaborate, they were nearly always houses of excellent workmanship and genuine dignity; and here, too, monotony was escaped, for the homes of the rice planters were of widely varying designs, the classic type with its columns being not nearly so general as is commonly supposed.

Similarly, there were degrees of elaborateness in the interior furnishings which ranged from comfortable simplicity to something approaching or achieving sumptuousness.

In the larger houses there was much fine furniture, a great deal of handsome silverware, in many cases an impressive array of family portraits on the panelled walls. There were excellent libraries too—as might be expected in houses many of whose young men had been educated in Europe, while others had attended the best American institutions of learning, and whose women were, as Olmsted himself frankly declared, "unexcelled for every quality which commands respect, admiration and love." In short, varying widely as they did in accord with the wealth and personal tastes of master and mistress, the homes of the rice planters were as a group the homes of a prosperous, happy and liberal people, who, as Thomas R. Waring has expressed it in his admirable essay on Charleston, respected scholarship, patronized the arts and cultivated manners and who drew upon literature, music and painting for a way of life—"perhaps . . . the greatest of the arts, as it is the only one whose prime objective is human happiness."

A fairly typical "mansion"—neither so large as "stately Newington," which is said to have had a hundred windows on its front, nor so simple as ancient Medway where Landgrave Thomas Smith lies buried—was Cedar Grove on the Ashley River, built probably between 1740 and 1750. Of the "seated rivers" the Ashley, because it was short and often salt, was least useful as a rice river, but this disadvantage was partly offset by easy accessibility from Charleston so that many planters established seats on the Ashley's banks. In 1857 Richard Yeadon, a Charleston litterateur and journalist, wrote a long and detailed if somewhat flowery account of Cedar Grove house and grounds. This was printed at the time in the Charleston Courier and is worth preserving in condensed form.

"The fine old residence," the writer begins, "worthy of our Colonial nobility or aristocracy, at which I am temporarily tabernacling, is a noble and capacious brick mansion of two stories, on a high basement, with an attic besides, its walls wainscoted and paintings let into the wainscoting." The house, we learn, had two fronts and its four corners denoted the cardinal points of the compass. The southwestern front, with a spacious piazza entered by a flight of iron-railed stone steps, faced the river which flowed at a distance of some two hundred yards; the eastern front faced a fine avenue leading to the Charleston-Dorchester public road about three quarters of a mile distant.

On the first floor, facing the avenue, "the great hall," with a chimney place "as wide as a church door," and "as deep as a well," ensconced almost in the western corner, occupied a central position. The high mantelpiece was composed of various and variegated marbles; over it was set in the wainscoting a pictorial representation of an old Roman arch and other ancient ruins, with monks reading or at their devotions. This picture was enclosed in richly carved frame-work, florally decorated and capped in the centre with a female bust, "handsomely draped and bejewelled with necklace and broach or breast ornament of some kind."

On the opposite side of the room was a handsome mirror attached centrally, also in richly carved frame wood-work of wreath and flowers, supported at the base by a floral urn and crowned with a floral basket. The hall was lighted by means of a double-barred and partly-sashed door at the front entrance and a large window on each side; also by arched sash-lights over the back door and a false door alongside the real door.

On the northwestern side of the hall, a door in the northern corner opened into a small apartment, with a fireplace, used as a library, and occasionally as a bedroom when the house overflowed with excessive hospitality. On the other side was a large chamber, also with fireplace, and with dressing room and wardrobe, having a door opening from the apartment and another opening into the dining room.

From the "noble hall" a wide passage-way led to the southwestern piazza, fronting the river. On the right of this passage-way, was a room, with fireplace, used as a pantry, but suitable for any other domestic use, and further on, a door opened on a stairway, leading down into the offices and kitchen below— an unusual arrangement, the kitchen occupying on most plantations a separate building. On the left another door opened into the dining room which was well lighted by means of four large windows. The dining room had, of course, a comfortable fireplace, with gray marble mantelpiece, over which was let into the wainscoting a scene of shepherd or country life in the midst of romantic mountain and river landscape with a pillared Greek or Roman temple in the background. Fronting the chimney place, in the centre of the southwestern wall, a handsome bouffet or cupboard, with a two-leafed door in the form of an arch, was let into the wainscoting.

On the second floor, up an easy flight of "mahogany-railed and bannistered stairs, were four spacious, well lighted and airy bed-chambers, two on each side, separated by an unusually wide passage-way, all with fireplaces and each furnished with a dressing room, large enough for a child's dormitory."

The grounds about Cedar Grove

house are described as very beautiful, though at an earlier period, when the place was a seat of the prominent Izard family, they had been even finer.

"A noble campus or greensward," Yeadon wrote, "stretched out in front of the mansion toward the avenue, and yet does so, and a beautiful flower garden and bower of floral and ornamental trees bloomed at the sides and on the river front; and in the southern border of the grounds there is yet a beautiful mall or walk between a double row of the noblest live-oaks, with occasional magnolias, uniting their kingly and queenly coronals, and at its extremity an artificial mound, now crowned with several well grown forest trees, as well as with woodbine and other jewels of the forest flora, from which is enjoyed a fine and extensive view of river and forest scenery, including that of the river plantations in the vicinity. Handsome hexagonal stone posts, with connecting iron chains or loops, enclosed portions of the campus and lined a part of the carriage way to the house, and also the garden walks; and leaden statuary, representing Venus and other mythological divinities, were dispersed about the garden and grounds."

Equally or even more elaborate were the grounds of Crowfield Plantation near Goose Creek, a tributary of the Cooper River. In a letter to a friend in England, written about 1744 and reproduced in Mrs. St. Julien Ravenel's biography of Eliza Lucas, the latter relates that she had been taken on "a most agreeable tour to Goose Creek, St. John's, . . . in which are several very handsome Gentleman's seats, at all of which we were entertained with the most friendly politeness. The first we arrived at was Mr. William Middleton's 'Crowfield' where we spent a most agreeable week.

"The house stands a mile from, but in sight of the road, and makes a very handsome appearance; as you draw near it new beauties discover themselves; first the fruitful vine mantleing the wall, loaded with delicious clusters. Next a spacious Basin in the midst of a large Green presents itself as you enter the gate that leads to the House which is neatly finished, the rooms well contrived and Elegantly furnished.

"From the back door is a spacious walk a thousand feet long; each side of which nearest the house is a grass plot ornamented in a Serpentine manner with Flowers; next to that on the right hand is what immediately struck my rural taste, a thicket of young, tall live-oaks where a variety of airey Chorristers pour forth their melody, and my darling the mocking bird joyn'd in the artless Concert and inchanted me with his harmony. Opposite on the left hand is a large square boling green, sunk a little below the level of the rest of the garden, with a walk quite round composed of a double row of fine large flowering Laurel (magnolia) and Catalpas which afford both shade and beauty.

"My letter will be of an unreasonable length if I don't pass over the Mounts, wilderness, etc., and come to the bottom of this charming spot where is a large fish pond with a mount rising out of the middle the top of which is level with the dwelling House, and upon it is a roman temple, on each side of this are other large fish ponds properly disposed which form a fine Prospect of water from the house. Beyond this are the smiling fields dressed in vivid green; here Ceres and Pomona joyn hand in hand to crown the hospitable board . . . I am quite tired of writing as I sopose you are of reading and can't say a word of the other seats I saw in this ramble except the Counts large double row of Oaks, on each side of the Avenue which leads to the House, and seems designed by Nature for pious meditation and friendly converse."

"A passion for flowers has of late astonishingly increased," observed the historian Ramsay in 1809. "Many families in the capital (Charleston) and several in the country for some years past have been uncommonly attentive to flower gardens." By the 1850's the "several in the country" had in their turn greatly increased.

"One who was still under fifteen when South Carolina seceded from the Union," Alice Smith wrote in an article on plantation gardens, "has vivid recollections of the plantations of relatives and friends which he visited before that date. All of them had gardens of one sort or another and most of these were well laid out and well kept. The general type was rather that of a shrubbery than an open garden, though generally at some point there were beds of roses, bulbs and annuals. The shrubbery portions were traversed by wide walks or allees, through the trees, many of them flowering: japonicas, lilacs, Cape jessamine, spirea, wild orange, holly, sweet olive, strawberry shrub, fringe trees, oppoponax, oaks, cedars, magnolias, sweet bay and many others, some indigenous and some imported. The boundary of the garden would frequently be marked with running roses such as Lady Banksia and the Cherokee rose or with hedges of China briar, jessamine, cassena, or Spanish bayonet. Memory brings back an occasional garden broken up with formal hedges of box or cassena or privet, kept carefully trimmed. One such remains in mind as an humble imitation of the famous maze at Hampton Court."

Thus the men and women of the plantations drew not only upon the arts for the "way of life" which they had created and found good; they drew also upon the natural beauty around them and improved the opportunity afforded by a long growing season to enhance the attractions of the places where they lived.

In general the gardens were pretty rather than magnificent, but in other cases, such as the Hermitage on the Savannah, Dean Hall on the Cooper, Belle Isle, Prospect Hill and Brookgreen in the Georgetown regions, a master or mistress's love of beauty made use of the plantation's large resources of labour to achieve notable results. Ramsay mentions among others of his day the Draytons of Ashley River whose garden, he says, "is arranged with exquisite taste and contains an extensive collection of trees, shrubs and flowers which are natives of the country," besides many valuable exotics, the whole making "an elegant and concentrated display of the native botanic riches of Carolina." The Williamson garden in St. Paul's district, he continues, "contains twenty-six acres, six of which are in sheets of water . . . ten acres in pleasure grounds, walks and banks . . . The pleasure grounds are planted with every species of flowering trees, shrubs and flowers that this and the neighboring states can furnish."

The Drayton place to which Ramsay refers was evidently Drayton Hall. "We stopped to dine with Dr. Drayton, at Drayton-Hall," wrote the Duke de la Rochefoucault-Liancourt describing his visit to Carolina in 1796. "The house is an ancient building but convenient and good; and the garden is better laid out, better cultivated and stocked with good trees, than any I have hitherto seen." The house, one of the finest in the Low Country, still stands, the sole survivor of the many fine houses which formerly lined the Ashley's banks and all except three of which were burned by the invading forces in the last days of the Confederate War. Farther up the river was another Drayton plantation, Magnolia, where was developed, chiefly by the Rev. John Grimke Drayton to whom it descended in 1825, a garden still so magnificent today that John Galsworthy, a man not given to exaggeration, declared it "the most beautiful spot in the world." The old house has gone, but the garden, of unbelievable splendor when its masses of azaleas and camellias are in bloom, is famous and is visited by thousands every year.

Most vividly of all Middleton Place, also an Ashley River rice plantation, conveys to present generations a conception of what life was at its best in the great days of the plantation country. The house, with the exception of one detached wing which has now been restored, was destroyed by the Federal forces in 1865; but one can still trace the foundations of the large three-storied brick mansion which stood between the two wings looking out over a series of beautifully proportioned terraces descending to the river which curves outward at the foot of the lawn to form a long straight vista; and there still stands the imposing mausoleum in the old plantation graveyard, now encircled by the garden, where, among others of the name, Arthur Middleton, a signer of the Declaration of Independence, and his son, Henry Middleton, Governor, Senator, and Minister to Russia, lie buried.

One can still see, too, the identical camellias, the first of the kind to be planted in America, presented to Governor Middleton about 1785 by André Michaux, the famous French botanist, who was a frequent visitor to Middleton Place; and after Henry Middleton's death in 1846, his son Williams Middleton further developed the already beautiful grounds, crowning the terraces above the ornamental lakes with lines and masses of gorgeous blooms. Today this plantation garden, formed on a larger and nobler plan than any other in the Low Country, formal in design, yet, with its superb live-oaks and other forest trees, rich in natural beauty, is still owned by a descendant of the original grantee and is still an indescribable fairyland through which one wanders down aisles walled in and in many places roofed over by azalea and camellia bushes some of them twenty feet in height and often so completely covered with flowers as almost to obscure the foliage.

Magnolia is an enchanted garden, undoubtedly one of the loveliest on earth. Over Middleton Place, with its unobtrusive yet significant memorials of the past, the atmosphere of the plantation era in its brightest noontide glow still hovers. To the student of that past, Middleton Place is more informative than any historical document; soon or late it must be visited and studied by every one who wishes to know what the Carolinian civilization really was in its golden days and at its handsome best. If he will stand on the stone steps of the ruined house looking down over the terraces at the long sweep of the river and will consider what all this stately beauty, so nobly planned and so perfectly created, tells us of the people who made it—of their tastes and desires, of what seemed to them fine and beautiful and what they wished to have around them and before them as they lived and worked—he will find at least a part of the answer to his question at Middleton Place.

IV. House, grounds and garden, whether simple as many of them were or elaborate as some of them became with increasing prosperity, were only part, though an important part, of the plantation. The plantation was a complex and delicately adjusted organism of which the Great House or Big House was both the heart and brain—an organism which was very much alive. There was often much beauty about it but it did not exist primarily for beauty. Every rice plantation was a going concern, as practical, as much under compulsion to make receipts exceed expenses, as any great industrial plant of today.

Whether this was accomplished depended primarily upon the planter. Hence within easy distance of the residence where the planter and his family lived were the buildings concerned exclusively with the actual working of the plantation, its operation as a business enterprise, and with the housing of those who helped to operate it. On a rice plantation these buildings were many.

The kitchen was generally a separate structure and in many cases the planter's office was in a small building of its own. The dairy and smokehouse were usually at no great distance from the residence, but the position of the stables, barns, wagon sheds, smithy, winnowing house and threshing floors depended upon the lie of the land and of the river or creek.

On comparatively small plantations the negro settlement, where the field hands were quartered, was generally situated close to the plantation house, but on the larger places, where there might be three or four of these settlements, each constituting a little village of cabins, they were generally placed at a considerable distance. So too the position of other units, such as the overseer's house, the hospital or "sick-house" and the plantation church, was governed not only by the topography of the place but also to some extent by the plantation's size.

The rice mill (or mills, for there might be both a pounding mill and a threshing mill or the two might be housed in one building) was an important unit the location of which was dictated by convenience. Prior to the Revolution the grain was milled or dressed partly by hand and partly by animal power—a slow and laborious process. One of the great forward steps taken by the rice industry was the invention by Jonathan Lucas of the pounding mill. The first pounding mill, run by water from a reserve, was followed by others operated by the tides or by steam, which last often furnished the power also for the threshing mills, a much later development, the threshing having been done up to that time by hand with flails.

With the perfecting of the threshing mills, pounding on the plantations began gradually to be abandoned, the rough rice being sent in schooners to Charleston to be pounded by toll mills there. The flail, however, continued to be employed for the threshing of rice to be used for seed, because grain threshed in a mill seldom gave a good stand. An even better method of obtaining good seed rice was by the whipping off of the grain against a barrel, plank or log.

Passing now from the "Big House," the mill and the other plantation buildings to the fields, it will be well to consider how a rice plantation was made and how the crop was grown.

In the early days of rice planting and indeed throughout most of the pre-Revolutionary period the culture of the grain was confined to the "inland swamps"—that is, the forested swamps not necessarily immediately adjacent to the rivers. An abundant supply of water being needed not only for the growth of the rice but also for the elimination of grass and weeds in the rice fields, this was obtained by damming a swamp or lead situated at a slightly higher level than the fields, thus forming a lake known as a "reserve" or "backwater." From this reserve the water was drawn at need for use on the planted land.

This method was limited in its possibilities. The inland swamp fields were widely scattered and frequently rather small, their soils were often shallow, there might occur in time of drought a fatal deficiency of water in the reserve. A tremendous expansion of rice culture was made possible when experiments, beginning about the middle of the eighteenth century, began to demonstrate that the great level areas of marsh and swamp-land lying directly along the fresh-water rivers, and until then considered of little or no value because subject to periodical overflow, could be made to produce rice crops by utilizing for their irrigation and drainage the rise and fall of the river tides. In all the rivers which became important in the culture of rice the influence of the tides extends inland well beyond the point where the water ceases to be salt; and it was through the ingenious harnessing of these tides, making them operate the plantation as a huge hydraulic machine, that rice culture reached a development and a degree of perfection in the Carolina lowlands which had not been attained in any other rice-growing country in two thousand years.

The achievement involved not only enormous labor but also, and primarily, engineering skill of a high order. It is probably well within the mark to say that nowhere else in America at that time were there engineering works demonstrating such vision and practical ability as were manifested in the making of the great Carolina rice plantations. In a paper published in the South Carolina Historical and Genealogical Magazine for April, 1913, the late Judge Henry A. M. Smith, a careful and accurate student, thus describes the reclamation of certain extensive swamplands of Hobcaw Barony on the Waccamaw.

"Originally, from the contemporaneous descriptions, this swamp was covered with a thick forest growth of cypress and gum, intermixed with other swamp growths. It was also subject to the flux and reflux of the tides. Twice in every twenty-four hours the land was submerged by the tidal flow and no work could be performed on it until the water receded. In periods of excessive rain, and the freshets thereby caused, the swollen waters from the river might remain on the land for days or weeks, the fall of the tide on such occasions being insufficient to lay bare the land. To reclaim the soil under such circumstances it had first to be dyked or banked in and then the forest growth had to be removed, and then the land had to be again canalled, ditched and banked into smaller subdivisions, so as to permit the tilth of the soil and its proper drainage and irrigation. Nothing but an ocular inspection of the area can give an adequate idea of the skilful engineering and patient, intelligent supervision that went to the successful result. The only labor at the disposal of the settlers who accomplished the feat was of the most unskilled character, African savages fresh from the Guinea coast. It was an achievement no less skilful than that which excites our wonder in viewing the works of the ancient Egyptians. The task of reclaiming a swamp delta such as that between the Waccamaw and Peedee Rivers involved an engineering skill no less than the construction of a pyramid, yet no one knows how many decades went to the last, and the first was performed in comparatively a few years . . .

"The Southern planter who accomplished this result was a man who worked with his brains on an extended scale; but he gave to his task no less assiduous, continuous and patient industry than the Northern farmer who worked with his hands in the field on a small scale."

The clearing and banking in of the land so that it was no longer subject to unregulated overflow from the river was the first step in the construction of the complicated hydraulic machine which every rice plantation was.

The next step was to divide the whole area by cross embankments and ditches into fields of varying sizes, according to the lie of the land, taking care that each field should be as nearly as possible of uniform level so that an even depth of water could be maintained over the whole field. In each field a large and deep "face-ditch" was dug, leaving a margin of from ten to twenty feet between it and the enclosing embankment or dam. The field was then subdivided into sections, usually long parallelograms, by "quarter-drains," small ditches running parallel with one another and opening at each end into the face-ditches.

In order to grow rice successfully, the fields thus banked and ditched had to be low enough to permit their being flooded with water from the river when the tide was high, and high enough to permit this water to be drained off whenever necessary into the river when the tide there was low. Many factors entered into the problem so that the nicest calculation was required in the selection of the fields. There was necessary also a means of controlling the ingress and egress of water, keeping it on the land as long as needed and getting rid of it completely at other stages of the crop.

This was accomplished by means of rectangular wooden culverts from twenty to thirty feet long, known as "trunks," placed in the main bank along the river, extending, of course, clear through the bank and equipped with a hanging door at each end.

To flood the field, the door at the outer end of the trunk was lifted by hand while tide was flooding in the river, the water poured in and, pushing open the door at the inner end of the trunk, passed on into the canals and ditches, finally covering the field itself to the desired depth. It was kept there as long as needed by the automatic closing of the inner door of the trunk as soon as ebb tide in the river set up a return current in the canal. When it was desired to remove the impounded water from the field, the inner door of the trunk was raised while tide was ebbing in the river, the pressure of the outgoing water forced open the outer door and the water was discharged into the river. This outward flow continued until the tide ceased to ebb in the river and began to flood, when the pressure from without would immediately close the outer door of the trunk so that no water could flow through it into the field.

Fields lying directly along the river were flowed and drained by means of trunks placed in the main river-bank—the dyke or levee as it would be called elsewhere. On many plantations, where the area planted extended a considerable distance from the river, especially large canals were dug, with floodgates on the river, and through these canals the water was carried to and from the "back fields." Each back field was connected with the canal by one or more trunks, so that each could be flowed or drained independently of others in the group.

These large canals served also another useful purpose—they were so linked up that a flat or lighter could be poled within a short distance of any point in the rice fields. Hence the large canals were also water thoroughfares, performing an important function of transportation. The flats which navigated these canals were used for many purposes, such as carrying earth and other materials for the mending of breaks in the banks, lumber for the replacement of trunks, and especially the transportation of loads of rice-in-the-sheaf to the threshing mill on the river, whence the grain was taken in schooners or other flats to a pounding mill on the same or another plantation or else to one of the toll-mills in Charleston.

Thus a rice plantation was a delicately adjusted and extensive "apparatus of levels, floodgates, trunks, canals, banks and ditches . . . requiring skill and unity of purpose to keep in order." When it was kept in order, as it necessarily was on successful plantations, it functioned admirably, but to that end constant care and attention were essential.

In sharp contrast with the rather widespread conception of the rice planter as a gentleman of elegant leisure, the fact is that the management of his fields, aside from the even more imperative duty of taking care of his perhaps several hundred people, imposed upon him a heavy burden which could be lightened only to a certain extent by the assistance of a competent overseer and of selected individuals, especially the head-driver and the trunk-minder, among the negroes themselves. The mere routine was exacting enough and when this was interrupted by one of the many hazards of the tideflow system, such as a freshet in the river or a hurricane from the ocean threatening to overtop and break the banks and flood the fields with salt water to the ruin of the crop, the planter's life became one not only of desperate anxiety but also of exhausting effort.

Rose Hill Plantation

The Heywards were at the very top of the scale in plantation wealth and slaveownership. Here we have a descendant's description of the Big House and of the plantation and the quarters as seen from the Big House.[2]

From early manhood, Charles Heyward considered Rose Hill plantation his home and lived there until the Civil War. Rose Hill adjoined the Bluff, and the residences of Charles and his father were only a short distance from each other. A canal, along which grew a line of cedar trees, separated the two plantations. The canal and the cedars are there yet, but of the two houses, nothing remains. At Rose Hill, only a walkway of flagstones, which led from the front steps of the residence, indicates the exact spot where it stood.

On August 1, 1835, Charles Heyward in his diary drew a picture of his home in Charleston, located in one of the uppermost wards, then known as Wraggborough. In fact, it was so far from the center of the city that he refers to it as being located on "Charleston Neck." The picture shows a two-story white house built on a high, arched, brick foundation, with a piazza running the entire length of the first story and a high flight of steps leading up to the front door. On the second story, above the front door, is a triple-arched window. The roof of the house and of the front piazza are painted, as are also the shutters; and the lot in which the house stands appears to be quite an extensive one. A picket fence separates the front and back yards.

On the death of his father in 1851, Charles Heyward fell heir to the home in Charleston, but he makes no reference to this, simply heading the pages of his diary, "241 East Bay," and then he comments on the coldness of the weather. In this house he lived approximately ten years.

Although Charles Heyward was nearly fifty years old before his father died, he had by no means lost his love for boats, for on October 23, 1850, he cut the following notice from the *Charleston Courier,* and

---

[2] Duncan Clinch Heyward, *Seed from Madagascar* (Chapel Hill: University of North Carolina Press, 1937), 99–104. Reprinted by permission of the publisher.

pasted it in his diary, "Launch—A fine new schooner, built by Messers Addison & McIntosh for Nathaniel Heyward, Esq., intended for the coasting trade, and commanded by Capt. J. B. Morgan, will be launched, full rigged, from their Ship Yard this morning at 9 o'clock."

This schooner was named the "Acorn" and later became the property of Charles Heyward, carrying his rice to Charleston for eleven years. His diary shows that he sold the "Acorn" on March 15, 1862, for he could use her no longer after the Civil War began.

Although I cannot state it positively, I am sure that Captain Morgan of the "Acorn" was the first and only white captain in charge of any of the schooners owned by either Nathaniel or Charles Heyward. All of the other captains of their schooners were their own slaves. Morgan, however, did not remain captain on the "Acorn" very long, for Charles Heyward's records show that one of his slaves, Richard, succeeded him, and remained in charge of the vessel until it was sold.

Viewed from the adjacent highland, the rice field at Rose Hill plantation, lying in a bend of the Combahee River, stretched away almost as far as the eye could see. The river bank, protecting the field, could be dimly traced by a few trees and a growth of cane. In the marsh just outside the bank there stood, at intervals, great cypress trees, their long limbs drooping gracefully, where many birds congregated during the day and some roosted at night.

Perched on the very top of the tallest of these trees, bald eagles could often be seen, calmly surveying the surrounding country, while they rested their wings before returning to soar among the clouds. For many years the oldest trees had grown on the river's edge, and generations of eagles had rested on their tops. From the size of some of these cypresses, one could well imagine that if the ships of Velasquez de Ayllon had, more than three centuries before, pressed farther up the Combahee, or the Jordan, as Velasquez named the river, when for the first time a white man set foot upon the soil of Carolina, the eagles of that day, from their eyries in these trees, must have looked down with wonderment upon the quaint ships of the Spaniards, while the cool shade of the trees protected the bold mariners from the summer sun, as they fraternized with the Indians.

At Rose Hill plantation, on the highest part of the highland, quite near the river and overlooking the rice fields, there stood before the Civil War an old dwelling house, painted white with green blinds. Not a great pretentious mansion designed by an architect following a style of long ago, but just a plain simple country home, like many others of its kind to be found on rice plantations in the Low Country.

In front of the dwelling on Rose Hill plantation a lawn, green with rye in winter, sloped to the river's edge, and there a few live oaks, their leaves green throughout the year, spread their wide extending limbs, from which hung long streams of gray moss swaying gently in the wind. On the left, at the edge of the lawn, bordering the river, lay the barnyard, where stood the threshing mill with its tall square chimney. The schooner "Acorn," succeeding the old "Elizabeth," which had carried many a crop from Rose Hill to Charleston, could often be seen moored to the wharf, while the crew, consisting of the captain and four sailors, all of them slaves, were busy lifting from her hatches large boxes of woolen cloth and shoes imported from England through Charleston. Soon she would be loading the first cargo of rice to be threshed from the great ricks, which stood side by side in the barnyard with their narrow, peaked tops and broadening sides, thatched with sheaves like a roof.

To the left of the house was the coach house with a gabled roof, the stables, and the barn. Several servant houses were back of the "big house," facing the same way, and within and before their doors Negro children could be seen at play. In the more distant background, across the road and cornfields, were the two settlements. These consisted of rather small whitewashed houses in two rows, facing each other, with the street between them thoroughly swept and as clean as a city boulevard. At the head of each street was the house of the driver, a little larger and somewhat better than the rest. Not very far from each settlement was the nursery. Lizette, one of the most intelligent and trustworthy Negroes on the plantation, was in charge of one child house, and for many years the other, at Pleasant Hill, had been under the supervision of old Mary, equally reliable. For these nurseries, two special cooks were provided.

Some little distance back of one of the nurseries was the hospital, or sick house, as the Negroes called it, a building of good size with several rooms, neat and clean and containing beds and bedding. Here Clarissa, the plantation nurse, could always be found. And here also were the headquarters of Hannah, the plantation midwife. Beyond the settlement was another cornfield, which reached back to the blue pines, where began the great primeval forest.

Throughout the forest many cattle grazed the entire year upon native grasses and the short cane which kept green during the winter months. Droves of hogs also ranged in the woods. Stepney, the hogminder, who years later worked for me, followed them closely and several times each year penned and counted them. Both cattle and hogs were far outnumbered by the red deer, for these lands were once the favorite hunting grounds of the Indians, and on them many deer were killed and their hides sold to traders and exported. But many deer still remained; their tracks could be seen everywhere, and also the paths they made leading to the fields where at night during autumn they often fed on the peas growing in the corn.

A broad piazza extended the entire length of the Rose Hill house, and from this piazza could be seen plainly the rice fields and the barnyard and a part of the highlands. From its western end, both of the settlements were in sight; and thus the owner of Rose Hill could always know what was taking place on the plantation. He could not only see the hands at work in every part of his rice fields, but in the squares nearest the house could note the progress they were making. The driver, as he walked through the fields inspecting the tasks, might readily be distinguished from the others by his blue suit and his hat, for all the field hands in those days dressed in light-colored clothes, and the men wore caps. When the Negroes worked in these near-by squares, they always thought "Maussuh" was watching them. "Maussuh, him hab 'e eye puntop ona [you] all de time," they would say, but what they pretended to fear most of all was a certain pair of spyglasses. "W'en Maussuh trow 'e eye tru dem ting 'e fetch 'eself nigh for we. Dem glasses 'e pint out ebry spec' of grass de hoe lef'. De grass 'e git by March [the driver] but 'e ain't git by Maussuh."

Random Notes from a Great Southern Lady

Mary Boykin Chesnut, in every way a "Southern Lady," was a brilliant and critical woman whose diary is a major source for ante-bellum social history and a penetrating commentary on Confederate politics. The wife of an important politician and herself a passionate secessionist, she never blinded herself to the grimmer sides of the world she defended. These three comments from a long and full diary—brief as they are—illuminate their respective subjects and give some indication of her intellectual quality.[3]

I wonder if it be a sin to think slavery a curse to any land. Men and women are punished when their masters and mistresses are brutes, not when they do wrong. Under slavery, we live surrounded by prostitutes, yet an abandoned woman is sent out of any decent house. Who thinks any worse of a Negro or mulatto woman for being a thing we can't name? God forgive us, but ours is a monstrous system, a wrong and an iniquity! Like the patriarchs of old, our men live all in one house with their wives and their concubines; and the mulattoes one sees in every family partly resemble the white children. Any lady is ready to tell you who is the father of all the mulatto children in everybody's household but her own. Those, she seems to think, drop from the clouds. My disgust sometimes is boiling over. Thank God for my country women, but alas for the men! They are probably no worse than men everywhere, but the lower their mistresses, the more degraded they must be.

I think this journal will be disadvantageous for me, for I spend my time now like a spider spinning my own entrails, instead of reading as my habit was in all spare moments. . . .

Not by one word or look can we detect any change in the demeanor of these Negro servants. Lawrence sits at our door, as sleepy and as respectful and as profoundly indifferent. So are they all. They carry it too far. You could not tell that they even hear the awful noise that is going on in the bay, though it is dinning in their ears night and day. And people talk before them as if they were chairs and tables, and they make no sign. Are they stolidly stupid, or wiser than we are, silent and strong, biding their time. . . .

Wilmot DeSaussure telegraphs

---

[3] Mary Boykin Chesnut, *A Diary from Dixie*, edited by Ben Ames Williams (Boston, 1949), 21–22, 38, 237–38. Reprinted by permission of Houghton Mifflin Co.

for sandbags, cannon-powder and flatboats. Powder sent, the other things not ready. Those rude Yankees; they will not wait until we are properly prepared to receive them. We take it easy, we love the *dolce far niente*. We are the nine Lotus Eaters. We cannot get accustomed to being hurried about things.

This race have brains enough, but they are not active minded. Those old revolutionary characters —Middletons, Lowndeses, Rutledges, Marions, Sumters—they came direct from active-minded forefathers, or they would not have been here. But two or three generations of gentlemen planters and how changed the blood became! Of late, all of the active-minded men who sprang to the front in our government were the immediate descendants of Scotch or Scotch-Irish; Calhoun, McDuffie, Cheves, Petigru —who Huguenotted his name, but could not tie up his Irish. Our planters are nice fellows, but slow to move; impulsive but hard to keep moving. They are wonderful for a spurt, but that lets out all their strength, and then they like to rest. . . .

2. THE CHIVALRY AND ITS LADIES

The planters of the late ante-bellum South increasingly and proudly referred to themselves as "The Chivalry." To what extent their pretensions to aristocracy should be taken seriously is a question that has provoked heated debate and that may remain with us indefinitely. What is beyond dispute is that the big slaveholders who claimed the title of gentlemen in Mississippi and Alabama, as well as in Virginia and South Carolina, were by no means a single social type—by no means men who adhered to a single, well-defined social philosophy or who exhibited a common sensibility.

We begin with a self-image; proceed to a critical look by an outsider; take a historian's testimony on the place of the ladies in society; turn back to a witty contemporary's discussion of the fate of the Virginia gentleman in the Southwest of the 1830s; and end with a black historian's evaluation of the planter class as a whole in the 1850s. The range of behavior and personality is suggested by the juxtaposition of these selections, but so, with careful reading, are the elements of unity.

A Southern Planter

Susan Dabney Smedes' recollections of her father and of the old regime contain much useful data on life in the Big House and on the painful adjustment of an old planter to poverty and disillusionment after the war. Here she gives her impressions of the kind of man her father was and, in so doing, suggests something of the plight of a gentleman from the aristocratic Southeast in the rougher plantation world of the Southwest.[4]

Perhaps no life was more independent than that of a Southern planter before the late war. One of the Mississippi neighbors said that he would rather be Colonel Dabney on his plantation than the President of the United States.

Managing a plantation was something like managing a kingdom. The ruler had need of a great store, not only of wisdom, but of tact and patience as well.

When there was trouble in the house the real kindness and sympathy of the servants came out. They seemed to anticipate every wish. In a thousand touching little ways they showed their desire to give all the comfort and help that lay in their power. They seemed to claim a right to share in the sorrow that was their master's, and to make it their own. It was small wonder that the master and mistress were forbearing and patient when the same servants who sorrowed with them in their affliction should, at times, be perverse in their days of prosperity. Many persons said that the Burleigh servants were treated with overindulgence. It is true that at times some of them acted liked spoiled children, seeming not to know what they would have. Nothing went quite to their taste at these times. The white family would say among themselves, "What is the matter now? Why these martyr-like looks?" Mammy Maria usually threw light on these occasions. She was disgusted with her race for posing as martyrs when there was no grievance. A striking illustration of this difficulty in making things run smoothly occurred one summer, when the family was preparing to go to the Pass. The mistress made out her list of the servants whom she wished to accompany her. She let them know that they were to be allowed extra time to get their houses and clothes in order for the three months' absence from home. Some of them answered with tears. It would be cruel to be torn from home and friends, perhaps husband and children, and not to see them for all that time. Sophia regretfully made out a new list, leaving out the most clamorous ones. There were no tears shed nor mournful looks given by the newly elected, for dear to the colored heart was the thought of change and travel. It was a secret imparted by Mammy Maria to her mistress that great was the disappointment of those who had overacted their part, thereby cutting themselves off from a much-coveted pleasure.

Thomas was never an early riser. He maintained that it did not so much matter when a man got up as what he did after he was up. He woke up in the morning as gay as a boy, and when Sophia, fully dressed, informed him that it was time to get up, received the announcement with one of his liveliest tunes. That was the only answer usually to the first summons or two. She could not help laughing; no one could who heard

---

[4] Susan Dabney Smedes, *A Southern Planter* (London: John Murray, 1889), 74–79.

him. When she remonstrated he sang only the more gayly.

Every one knew when he was awake by the merry sounds proceeding from his chamber. He did not go in to breakfast till he had danced the Fisher's Hornpipe for the baby, singing along with the steps and drawing an imaginary bow across imaginary strings. All the nursery flocked about him at the signal, one or two of the little tots joining in the capering. This habit he kept up to the end of his life, and his grown children would smile as they heard the cherry notes sounding through the house on his awaking. Then he walked with his quick, half-military step, the laugh still on his face, into the dining-room, where breakfast was already in progress. It was not a ceremonious meal he maintained. Dinner was a ceremonious meal in his house. Every one was expected to be ready, and sitting with the family in the hall or drawing-room or dining-room not less than five minutes before the last bell was rung. If there was a lady guest, the master of the house handed her in to dinner. If the guest was a gentleman, he was expected to hand in one of the ladies, as Thomas showed by offering his arm to one.

He was the life of the company, as he sat at the foot of his own table. Many of his most amusing anecdotes and stories, as well as those of deeper meaning, are associated with the dinner-table. No one could fill his place when he was absent.

He was often absent, being called from home by matters of business or duty or pleasure. In addition to spending some time every other summer with his mother in Virginia, and going occasionally to New York, and two weeks every fall on the deer-hunt, he made frequent visits to New Orleans, Vicksburg, and Jackson, and occasional visits to other places. He rarely spent a week without passing a day with Augustine.

In travelling on steamboats, if alone, he always selected for himself the state-room just over the boiler. If the boat were to blow up, he said he should prefer being killed outright to running a risk of being only half killed, or of being maimed for life. It need hardly be added that he found no difficulty in securing his chosen state-room.

His interest in public affairs sometimes called him off to distant cities.

January always found him in New Orleans for a three weeks' visit. After attending to his business with his commission merchants and buying the plantation supplies, he enjoyed the pleasures of this brilliant city. He was a member of the Boston Club, and he there met the most interesting and distinguished citizens of New Orleans. One of the chief attractions of this place was the game of whist to be had there. He was considered authority on whist. A game that he once played at the Greenbrier White Sulphur Springs, in Virginia, was considered remarkable. His old friend, Mr. John Tabb, of Whitemarsh, Gloucester County, had invited him to a game of whist in his cottage at the Springs. Three whist-players of known skill were invited to play with him, and a company invited to witness the game. During the evening a singular incident took place. Twelve cards had been played out of each hand, leaving each gentleman with his thirteenth card only. At this point

Thomas Dabney said to them that he wished to call their attention to a singular coincidence in the fact that every man present held in his hand a nine. When the cards were laid on the table this was seen to be true, to the surprise of all. One gentleman said he could show a more remarkable thing than that, it was the man who knew it.

He was never but once a candidate for any office in Mississippi; that was for the State Legislature. He was defeated by one vote. The contest was strictly a party one, and all the candidates on the Whig ticket were defeated by their Democratic opponents.

Thomas Dabney was enthusiastic in his admiration of Henry Clay, and followed his career with the deepest interest. He seemed almost to know Mr. Clay's speeches by heart, and delighted in talking of him and quoting his brilliant sayings. "I had rather be right than President" was a great utterance, he said. He contracted a warm personal friendship for him, and was anxious to accept Mr. Clay's invitation to visit him at Ashland. But my mother objected. She knew that the great statesman had his failings as well as his virtues. She had a very gentle way of objecting, but her gentle way was a law to him. He yielded, and did not go. He greatly admired S. S. Prentiss, and enjoyed having a visit from him at the Pass Christian house.

The *National Intelligencer* was the most ably conducted paper in the United States, in his opinion. He kept it on file. In sending on his subscription his custom was to send twenty-five dollars at a time.

His lively interest in public affairs made him write a good deal for the public press. Unfortunately, the many papers stowed away with his articles in them have been destroyed.

Tutors were employed to teach in the family until the boys were old enough to be sent off to college. In order to make the boys study with more interest, the children of the neighbors were received into the school. When the three sons were sent off to college, a governess was employed to teach the daughters. The teachers at Burleigh were treated like guests and friends. Thomas said that he did not wish any but ladies to have the charge of his daughters, and they should be treated as ladies. Miss Dyott, the beloved governess, who lived in the house five years, loved the family like dear relatives. When Mrs. Moncure's daughter was taken as a pupil along with his daughters, he handed to Miss Dyott, in addition to her salary, the money paid for this child's tuition. She objected, and said that another pupil or two would really make her school duties more interesting to his daughters and to herself; but he was firm, and she had to receive the money.

During her stay at Burleigh, when there was company to dinner, the master of the house took her in on his arm. At her death, many years later, the Burleigh family stood around her grave with her family as mourners.

It may be said that all honest men who had business transactions with Thomas Dabney became his personal friends. It was evident that he did not wish to get the advantage of any one. Several of his overseers soon became able to buy farms of their own, and grew to be rich men. He was so liberal in his dealings with them, that it was said they made as much in fattening and selling their riding-horses as their salaries amounted to. He was often cheated and imposed upon. Instead of worrying over it, he said he was very glad that he had found the scoundrels out. . . .

What Manner of Men?

Fanny Kemble, toast of the English stage, did not surrender her liberal abolitionist sentiments when she married a wealthy absentee slaveholder and decided to spend some time on his plantations. Years later, in 1863, after a painful divorce, she published her journal, which caused a sensation and played no small part in hardening the antislavery views of people in the North and in Europe.

Mrs. Kemble (as she called herself in later years) appended to her book a letter to the London *Times* in which she characterized the planters. An excerpt from that letter follows.[5]

The South Carolinian gentry have been fond of styling themselves the chivalry of the South, and perhaps might not badly represent, in their relations with their dependents, the nobility of France before the purifying hurricane of the Revolution swept the rights of the suzerain and the wrongs of the serf together into one bloody abyss. The planters of the interior of the Southern and Southwestern states, with their furious feuds and slaughterous combats, their stabbings and pistolings, their gross sensuality, brutal ignorance, and despotic cruelty, resemble the chivalry of France before the horrors of the *Jacquerie* admonished them that there was a limit even to the endurance of slaves. With such men as these, human life, even when it can be bought or sold in the market for so many dollars, is but little protected by considerations of interest from the effects of any violent passion. There is yet, however, another aspect of the question, which is, that it is sometimes clearly *not* the interest of the owner to prolong the life of his slaves; as in the case of inferior or superannuated laborers, or the very notorious instance in which some of the owners of sugar plantations stated that they found it better worth their while to *work off* (i.e., kill with labor) a certain proportion of their force, and replace them by new hands every seven years, than work them less severely and maintain them in diminished efficiency for an indefinite length of time. Here you will observe a precise estimate of the planter's material interest lead to a result which you argue passion itself can never be so blind as to adopt. This was a deliberate economical

[5] Frances Anne Kemble, *Journal of Residence on a Georgian Plantation in 1838–1839*, 351–54. Copyright © 1961 by Alfred A. Knopf, Inc.

calculation, openly avowed some years ago by a number of sugar planters in Louisiana. If, instead of accusing Mrs. Stowe of exaggeration, you had brought the same charge against the author of the *White Slave,* I should not have been surprised;* for his book presents some of the most revolting instances of atrocity and crime that the miserable abuse of irresponsible power is capable of producing, and it is by no means written in the spirit of universal humanity which pervades Mrs. Stowe's volumes; but it is not liable to the charge of exaggeration any more than her less disgusting delineation. The scenes described in the *White Slave do* occur in the slave states of North America; and in two of the most appalling incidents of the book—the burning alive of the captured runaway, and the hanging without trial of the Vicksburg gamblers—the author of the *White Slave* has very simply related positive facts of notorious occurrence. To which he might have added, had he seen fit to do so, the instance of a slave who perished in the sea swamps, where he was left bound and naked, a prey to the torture inflicted upon him by the venomous mosquito swarms. My purpose, however, in addressing you was not to enter into a disquisition on either of these publications; but I am not sorry to take this opportunity of bearing witness to the truth of Mrs. Stowe's admirable book, and I have seen what few Englishmen can see—the working of the system in the midst of it.

In reply to your "Dispassionate Observer," who went to the South professedly with the purpose of seeing and judging of the state of things for himself, let me tell you that, little as he may be disposed to believe it, his testimony is worth less than nothing; for it is morally impossible for any Englishman going into the Southern states, except as a *resident,* to know anything whatever of the real condition of the slave population. This was the case some years ago, as I experienced, and it is now likely to be more the case than ever; for the institution is not *yet* approved divine to the perceptions of Englishmen, and the Southerners are as anxious to hide its uglier features from any note-making observer from this side of the water as to present to his admiration and approval such as can by any possibility be made to wear the most distant approach to comeliness.

The gentry of the Southern states are pre-eminent in their own country for that species of manner which, contrasted with the breeding of the Northerners, would be emphatically pronounced "good" by Englishmen. Born to inhabit landed property, they are not inevitably made clerks and countinghouse men of, but inherit with their estates some of the invariable characteristics of an aristocracy. The shop is not their element; and the eager spirit of speculation and the sordid spirit of gain do not infect their whole existence, even to their very demeanor and appearance, as they too manifestly do those of a large proportion of the inhabitants of the Northern states. Good manners have an undue value for Englishmen, generally

---

* Richard Hildreth's *The Slave: or Memoirs of Archy Moore* (New York: 1836), enjoyed great popularity on both sides of the Atlantic as the first antislavery novel. It was published in London under the title *The White Slave, or Memoirs of a Fugitive.*

speaking; and whatever departs from their peculiar standard of breeding is apt to prejudice them, as whatever approaches it prepossesses them, far more than is reasonable. The Southerners are infinitely better bred men, according to English notions, than the men of the Northern states. The habit of command gives them a certain self-possession, and the enjoyment of leisure a certain ease. Their temperament is impulsive and enthusiastic, and their manners have the grace and spirit which seldom belong to the deportment of a Northern people; but, upon more familiar acquaintance, the vices of the social system to which they belong will be found to have infected them with their own peculiar taint; and haughty, overbearing irritability, effeminate indolence, reckless extravagance, and a union of profligacy and cruelty, which is the immediate result of their irresponsible power over their dependents, are some of the less pleasing traits which acquaintance develops in a Southern character. In spite of all this, there is no manner of doubt that the "candid English observer" will, for the season of his sojourning among them, greatly prefer their intercourse to that of their Northern brethren. Moreover, without in the least suspecting it, he will be bribed insidiously and incessantly by the extreme desire and endeavor to please and prepossess him which the whole white population of the slave states will exhibit—as long as he goes only as a "candid observer," with a mind not *yet* made up upon the subject of slavery, and open to conviction as to its virtues. Every conciliating demonstration of courtesy and hospitable kindness will be extended to him, and, as I said before, if his observation is permitted (and it may even appear to be courted), it will be to a fairly bound, purified edition of the black book of slavery, in which, though the inherent viciousness of the whole story cannot be suppressed, the coarser and more offensive passages will be carefully expunged. . . .

The Ladies

Around the Southern Lady centered much of the slaveholders' mythology. Between the myth and the reality, however, fell a long shadow. Professor Anne Firor Scott has explored myth and reality with depth and insight. The following is the first part of a chapter in her book entitled "Discontent."[6]

Open complaint about their lot was not the custom among southern ladies; yet their contented acceptance of the home as the "sphere to which God had appointed them" was sometimes more apparent than real. Most southern women would not have tried, or known how, to free themselves from the system which was supposed to be divinely ordained, but there is considerable

---

[6] Anne Firor Scott, *The Southern Lady: From Pedestal to Politics, 1830–1930*, pp. 46–51. Copyright © 1970 by The University of Chicago Press.

evidence that many of them found the "sphere" very confining.

Women's expressions of unhappiness centered in two principal areas of life. One was their relationship to slaves. This complex web encompassed marriage, family life, and sexual mores as these were defined by the patriarchal doctrine. The second area of constant concern was education. Many women felt deeply deprived because their opportunities for learning were so limited.

For women, as for men, slaves were a troublesome property. It was not only that the administration of a large establishment was complex and demanding, or even that the mistress was expected to be a combination of supervisor, teacher, doctor, and minister to a large family of slaves. The greatest burden was psychological, of being day in and day out the arbiter of so many relationships, the person upon whom so many human beings depended. There was no privacy. "These women," Mrs. Chesnut wrote, ". . . have less chance to live their own lives than if they were African missionaries. They have a swarm of blacks about them like children under their care . . . and they hate slavery worse than Mrs. Stowe does."

Such conditions were bound to breed antagonism toward slaves. The expressions of it were common in diaries and letters, right through the Civil War. "I wish I could for once see a hearty negro woman who admitted herself to be over 40, one who was not 'poorly, Thank God.!' To be 'poorly', is their aim and object, as it ends in the house and spinning." "I cannot, nor will not, spend all these precious days of my life following after and watching Negroes. It is a terrible life!" "We contemplate removing to a free state. There we hope to be relieved of many unpleasant things, but particularly of the evils of slavery, for slaves are a continual source of trouble. . . . They are a source of more trouble to housewives than all other things, vexing them and causing much sin." "I sometimes think I would not care if they all did go, they are so much trouble to me." "When we change our residence, I cast my vote for a free state. . . . Negroes are nothing but a tax and annoyance to their owners." "The negroes are a weight continually pulling us down! Will the time *ever* come for us to be free of them?" "Mr. Dunbar's Joe left Monday. He was a consummate hypocrite, in fact they all are."

Antagonism was only one part of the picture. There was also affection. It is possible to jettison nine-tenths of the sentiment about Negro mammies and still have substantial evidence of what was not, after all, a surprising phenomenon. Women who lived and worked together often formed bonds of friendship and mutual dependency across the color bar. "An affectionate friendship that was to last for more than sixty years," one man wrote of his mother and a slave. "She was a member of the family," wrote a Mississippi woman, and another, "She loved me devotedly and I was much attached to her." A visiting Englishman commented upon the close relationship between the Calhoun ladies and their slaves.

In the end antagonism and love led to the same conclusion: slavery was an evil. Most southern women who expressed themselves on the peculiar institution opposed slavery and were glad when it was ended.

Mrs. Chesnut quoted her friend and confidante Isabella Martin as saying she never saw a true woman who was not an abolitionist, and Mrs. Chesnut herself claimed to have been one from the age of nineteen. The motives for antislavery feelings were mixed. Susan Dabney Smedes, describing her grandmother's abolitionism, was unable to say whether those sentiments were based on "sympathy with the colored race or with their owners." Whatever the motive, expressions of antislavery feelings ran through many personal documents.

"I must say that my mother never did like slavery and did not hesitate to say so. Her father once sent her a present of ten slaves which she sent back." "In some mysterious way I had drunk in with my mother's milk . . . a detestation of the curse of slavery laid upon our beautiful southern land." "Had slavery lasted a few years longer, I have heard my mother say, it would have killed Julia, my head-woman, and me. Our burden of work and responsibility was simply staggering. . . . I was glad and thankful—on my own account when slavery ended, and I ceased to belong body and soul to my negroes. As my mother said, so said other southern mistresses." "I often said to my husband that the freedom of the Negroes was a freedom to me." "I do not see how I can live my life amid these people! . . . To be always among people whom I do not understand and whom I must guide, and teach and lead on like children. It frightens me." "I wish we could get rid of all [slaves] at their value and leave this wretched country. I am more and more convinced that it is no place to rear a family of children." "[I could not see] how the men I most honored and admired, my husband among the rest [,] could constantly justify it, and not only that but say that it was a blessing to the slave." Years later a Louisiana woman wrote that she had been "subject at all times to the exactions and dictations of the black people who belonged to me, which now seems too extraordinary and incredible to relate." "All my family on both sides . . . were slave owners . . . but I do not hesitate to say that slavery was a curse to the South." "I was born and raised in the South . . . as were all my relations before me. . . . Yet . . . my first recollection is of pity for the Negroes and desire to help them. . . . Always I felt the moral guilt of it, felt how impossible it must be for an owner of slaves to win his way into Heaven." "Southern women are all, I believe, abolitionists."

In the spring of 1855 Charles Eliot Norton visited friends in Charleston. Writing to James Russell Lowell on Good Friday of that year he reflected:

> It is a very strange thing to hear men of character and cultivation . . . expressing their belief in open fallacies and monstrous principles [e.g., the defense of slavery]. . . . It seems to me sometimes as if only the women here read the New Testament, and as if the men regarded Christianity rather as a gentlemanly accomplishment than as anything more serious. It is very different with the women . . . but they are bewildered often, and their efforts are limited by weakness, inexperience, and opposition. Their eyes fill with tears when you talk with them about it.

A number of women saw a parallel between their own situation and that of slaves, a comparison made too often to be counted simply as rhetoric. "There is no slave, after all, like a wife," Mary Chesnut wrote in a bitter moment. Or, "You know how women sell themselves and are sold in marriage, from queens downward. . . . Poor women, poor slaves." And yet again, "All married women, all children and girls who live in their father's houses are slaves." "It was a saying that the mistress of a plantation was the most complete slave on it."

Perhaps it was understanding growing from this identification with slaves which led so many southern women to be private abolitionists, and even a few to be public ones. Of the latter Sarah and Angelina Grimké were the most striking. Sarah was from childhood rebellious against the lot of southern women and fought throughout her adult life for the emancipation of women and slaves. Angelina also worked to free the slaves, married a leading abolitionist, and in her *Appeal to the Christian Women of the South* addressed herself to the parallels between the experiences of women and of slaves.

Mary Berkeley Minor Blackford was another southern woman who took her discontent with slavery to the world. A Virginian of bluest blood and a busy housewife with six children, she spent her spare time and money, as well as all the money she could charm from her friends, buying slaves to be sent to freedom in Liberia. Although the colonization movement was regarded by radical abolitionists as a refuge for people unwilling to face the true dimensions of the slavery question, Mrs. Blackford's diagnosis of the ills of slavery was radical enough.

Think what it is to be a Slave!!! To be treated not as a man but as a personal chattel, a thing that may be *bought* and *sold,* to have *no right* to the fruits of your own labour, *no right* to your own wife and children, liable at any moment to be seperated [*sic*] at the arbitrary will of another from all that is dearest to you on earth, & whom it is your duty to love & cherish. Deprived by the law of learning to read the Bible, compelled to know that the purity of your wife and daughters is exposed without protection of law to the assault of a brutal white man! Think of this, and all the nameless horrors that are concentrated in that one word *Slavery.*

The evils of slavery tended to merge with the grievances, even the repressed grievances, of southern women. The slave was deprived of a secure family life, had to obey his master, and in some states was denied by law the right to learn. For women, family life had its quota of pain, much of it related to slavery, and they, too, were supposed to take orders from men and to learn only so much as would not unfit them for their appropriate role in the patriarchy.

Few southern women appreciated the argument of a South Carolina gentleman who thought the availability of slave women avoided the horrors of prostitution. He pointed out that men could satisfy their sexual needs while increasing their slave property. The bitterness of southern women on this subject came out again and again. One spoke of "violations of the moral law that made mulattoes as common as blackberries," and suggested that the four years of bloody war was a fit penance for so many sins. "I saw slavery in its bearing on my sex," wrote another. "I saw that it teemed with injustice and shame to all womankind and I hated it."

There was an undercurrent of concern about venereal disease. The fiction women wrote and read was full of mysteriously disillusioned brides and dissolute men. A North Carolina student in the 1840s could remark without comment that the university was "never free from clap." Conversely, the exaggerated praise heaped upon "pure" men reflected something more than admiration of good character. It was an index to the anxiety of women endangered by their husbands. Primitive medical knowledge offered little protection to the wives of men whose visits to the slave quarters left them diseased.

Miscegenation was only one grievance. Women felt deeply aggrieved by the prevailing double standard. The conventions of nineteenth-century discourse make precise evidence difficult to come by, but veiled comments suggest that many women found the social standards governing sexual life hard to accept. The accepted belief was that only men and depraved women were sexual creatures and that pure women were incapable of erotic feeling. The inadequacy of this description is made apparent in fiction, biography, personal documents, and court records.

The syrupy descriptions of romantic love nearly always carried erotic overtones, and the constant emphasis upon woman's "magic spell," indicated something about the unconscious preoccupations of the society. A Methodist minister thought it self-evident that puberty was the period when "the female, pressed by a new want . . . should renounce that inexperience in love which was becoming in tranquil youth," should, in other words, begin to think of marriage. "The villain . . . had at length found the unguarded moment in which a woman can deny nothing to the man she loves," said one of Beverly Tucker's characters. A college boy expressing horror at the rumor of Daniel Webster's marital infidelities also noted (possibly from his own observation but more likely from student gossip) that "women of late have become unfaithful to their husbands. Some women I don't believe can be satisfied." Mrs. Chesnut recorded premarital as well as extramarital sex among her friends and acquaintances and the historian of antebellum North Carolina found many respected citizens asking the legislature to legitimize their bastard children. Angelina Grimké, whose ideas on the subject began to be formed in Charleston, in a letter to her fiancé threw light on the sexual scene:

I have been tempted to think marriage was *sinful,* because of what appeared to me almost invariably to prompt and lead to it. Instead of the higher, nobler sentiments being first aroused, and leading on the lower passions *captive* to their will, the *latter* seemed to be *lords* over the former. Well I am convinced that men in general, the vast majority, believe most seriously that women were made to gratify their animal appetites.

The evidence does not bear out the notion that all the good women, all the respectable wives, totally suppressed their sexuality, though the values of their society certainly encouraged them to do so. It suggests instead a bitterness against the freedom which men arrogated to themselves and the restrictions they laid upon women. Mrs. Chesnut quoted one Charleston matron:

Now I assert that the theory upon which modern society is based is all wrong. A man is supposed to confide his honor to his wife. If she misbehaves herself, his honor is tarnished. But how can a man be disgraced by another person's doing what, if he did it himself . . . he would not be hurt at all in public estimation?

A Georgia woman commented upon a friend who had left her husband when she discovered him to be supporting a mistress and a second family. She approved the woman's courage, adding, "I do think she would have been doing an injustice to herself to remain with him—yet how often this is done—How often let Martyr women testify!" She went on to discuss another case in which a married woman had run away with another man, saying that the husband would be considered quite justified if he refused to take her back, while the other man's wife would of course be expected to receive her wayward spouse without comment. "Custom does indeed sanction many a wrong. But I mount my hobby horse when I converse on the subject of woman and her wrongs."

Some discreet Charleston ladies appeared to manage their affairs without disgrace, but the theory was that one misstep ruined a woman forever. The diary of a well-educated and intelligent New Orleans concubine made it clear that while she was seeking counsel from a minister and hoping for God's forgiveness, she accepted without question the fact that the local community would not forgive her. In a popular novel a beautiful and capable "good" girl put herself beyond the pale in one half-hour, in her own eyes as well as those of a would-be suitor.

There were still other reasons, besides miscegenation and the double standard, for a good deal of well-concealed misery in marriage. Oscar Handlin has suggested that the increase in life expectancy in the nineteenth century, preceding as it did the widespread understanding of contraception, increased the strain on domestic tranquility.* Earlier, in the eighteenth century, the high mortality rate made it possible for some persons to marry three or four times. If one marriage was unsuccessful, the next might be better. By the 1830s, however, when the glorification of family life and domestic joy was at its peak, declining death rates increased the likelihood of having to live a whole lifetime with the same mate.

Even in happy marriages, patriarchal assumptions could cause some

---

* *Race and Nationality in American Life* (Boston: Little, Brown, 1957), 148. The whole chapter "The Horrors" is relevant here. Of course, measuring happiness, much less comparing it from one person or period to another, is something no historian has yet found a way to do. Hence the comparative statements sometimes made about the greater degree of happiness in marriage at one period or another are entirely intuitive. It seems likely that the supposedly "disintegrating" family of the twentieth century may represent, on balance, a larger number of comfortable relationships than did the "stable" family of the early nineteenth century, though expectations regarding marriage may have differed from present-day ones. The only thing that can be said with a degree of certainty is that when women had few alternatives to marriage a great deal of discontent was suppressed.

chafing. Mary Chesnut admired her husband and enjoyed his company, yet her comments on men in general and James Chesnut in particular were frequently acerb: "What a blessed humbug domestic felicity is, eh? . . . But he is master of the house. To hear is to obey. . . . all the comfort of my life depends upon his being in a good humor. . . . Does a man ever speak to his wife and children except to find fault. . . . It is only in books that people fall in love with their wives." Many diaries and letters speak openly of bitter unhappiness, and one woman prayed to be able to control her "roving fancy."

Such evidence of domestic discontent is reinforced by the observations of southern ministers. A North Carolina Quaker named Thomas Arnett, for example, published a biting critique of family life as it had come under his view. Parents, he said, were capricious in their discipline and preoccupied with false values. John Bayley, a Virginia Methodist, devoted a whole book to the varieties of marital unhappiness he saw around him, and urged both men and women to become more reflective about this vital institution. The practical advice he offered suggests what he had observed: Wives should be neat and clean. ("A minister who travels extensively sees how many wives become disgracefully negligent in a short time. When I have visited some places, and have looked at the wife and children I have soon understood why the husband was seldom at home in his leisure hours.") It was very important to take care of health. ("Every third woman with whom we meet is an invalid.") Husbands should honor their wives, tend the flame of affection, and defeat the whole idea of the "rights of women" by keeping their wives happy.

Augustus Baldwin Longstreet was also a minister—but only incidentally. He was successively president of three colleges, a lawyer of some repute, and best known to posterity as the author of *Georgia Scenes,* which he offered to the public in 1835 as a reasonably accurate description of life in middle Georgia. One of his stories, "A Charming Creature," offers much the same criticism of marriage, albeit in fictional form. The "charming creature" was a beautiful girl, daughter of a successful businessman in a Georgia town, who had been sent to school in Philadelphia to polish her feminine arts. So successful was she in this endeavor that, when she came home, a hardworking, intelligent young lawyer was completely taken in by her flirtatious ways. After amusing herself for a while, as cat with mouse, she lured him to the altar. Naturally her coquettish habits, so well cultivated, did not disappear after marriage, and her total lack of domestic training led to miserable housekeeping and unbearable extravagance. Her disillusioned husband was driven to drink and an early death. Longstreet's young woman had been raised to believe that the most important thing in her life was her "magic spell"—the ability to entice a man into marriage—but there her education ended. The consequences were disastrous.

If, as the evidence suggests, marriages so eagerly sought were not always satisfactory afterward; if family life for all its potential joys was shadowed by the deaths of children and constant pregnancy; if the lord and master, in close daily encounter, turned out not to be the superior being of the myth; if his sexual freedom was in marked contrast to the perfect chastity of thought and deed demanded of his wife, it was no wonder that some women wondered why life had to be so one-sided. One young woman lamented in her diary: "Oh! the disadvantages we labor under, in not possessing the agreeable independence with the men; tis shameful that all the superiority, authority and freedom in all things should by partial Nature be thrown into their scale." Another, very happily married, occasionally expressed a sense of injustice: ". . . what a drag it is sometimes on a woman to 'lug about' the ladder upon which man plants his foot and ascends to the intellectual heaven of peace in ignorance of the machinery which feeds his daily life." The wife of a distinguished Louisiana judge who would invent a wholly new pattern of life for herself after the war, found housewifely chores a bore and longed for an opportunity to develop her literary and political interests. Guilt-ridden, she looked for religious consolation and made stern resolutions to do better. "I . . . am determined to be more contented . . . in the future."

An anonymous author, probably female, writing in the *Southern Ladies Companion* in 1849 cried out against the paradox of demanding perfection from an inferior being.

Much is always expected of her, in all the spheres of life where she is found. And particularly as a matron, where the functions of wife, mother and mistress are all blended, she is expected to perform duties so complicated and important in character, and so far-reaching in their ultimate consequences, as would require all the tact of the diplomatist, the wisdom of the sage, and the graces of the perfect Christian. In a word, she is expected to be a living encyclopedia of human endowments and perfections. . . .

And yet these very sticklers for perfection . . . on woman's part, are not infrequently found to hold surprising opinions as to her natural inferiority to the other sex. . . . A singular phenomenon this, for which a satisfactory explanation would be thankfully received.

There followed an impassioned statement of the injustice of the one-sided emphasis upon education for men, the denial to women of any right to mental cultivation or even of preparation for what all agreed were womanly responsibilities. "The wonder is," said the author caustically, "that women generally make out as well as they do in after life.". The article was signed at Charleston. . . .

The Virginians in the Southwest

Long before W. J. Cash's *Mind of the South*, Joseph G. Baldwin, a transplanted Virginian, said his piece on the outcome of the Virginia tradition in the Southwest. He was writing of the "flush times," of course, and one could argue that life settled down a good deal by the 1850s; but his account remains unsurpassed as a sketch of Alabama and Mississippi during the thirties.[7]

Virginians in a New Country. The Rise, Decline, and Fall of the Rag Empire

The disposition to be proud and vain of one's country, and to boast of it, is a natural feeling, indulged or not in respect to the pride, vanity, and boasting, according to the character of the native: but, with a Virginian, it is a passion. It inheres in him even as the flavor of a York river oyster in that bivalve, and no distance of deportation, and no trimmings of a gracious prosperity, and no pickling in the sharp acids of adversity, can destroy it. It is a part of the Virginia character—just as the flavor is a distinctive part of the oyster—"which cannot, save by annihilating, die." It is no use talking about it—the thing may be right, or wrong:—like Falstaff's victims at Gadshill, it is past praying for: it is a sort of cocoa grass that has got into the soil, and has so matted over it, and so *fibred* through it, as to have become a part of it; at least, there is no telling which is the grass and which is the soil; and certainly it is useless labor to try to root it out. You may destroy the soil, but you can't root out the grass.

Patriotism with a Virginian is a noun personal. It is the Virginian himself and something over. He loves Virginia *per se* and *propter se:* he loves her for herself and for himself—because *she is* Virginia and—everything else beside. He loves to talk about her: out of the abundance of the heart the mouth speaketh. It makes no odds where he goes, he carries Virginia with him; not in the entirety always—but the little spot he came from is Virginia —as Swedenborg says the smallest part of the brain is an abridgment of all of it. "*Cœlum non animum mutant qui trans mare currunt,*" was made for a Virginian. He never gets acclimated elsewhere; he never loses citizenship to the old Home. The right of expatriation is a pure abstraction to him. He may breathe in Alabama, but he lives in Virginia. His treasure is there, and his heart also. If he looks at the Delta of the Mississippi, it reminds him of James River "low grounds;" if he sees the vast prairies of Texas, it is a memorial of the meadows of the Valley. Richmond is the centre of attraction, the "*depot* of all that is grand, great, good and glorious. . . .

Eminently social and hospitable, kind, humane and generous is a Virginian, at home or abroad. They are so by nature and habit. These qualities and their exercise develop and strengthen other virtues. By reason of these social traits, they necessarily become well mannered, honorable, spirited, and careful of reputation, desirous of pleasing, and skilled in the accomplishments which please. Their insular position and sparse population, most rural, and easy but not affluent fortunes kept them from the artificial refinements and

---

[7] Joseph G. Baldwin, *The Flush Times of Alabama and Mississippi* (New York: Sagamore Press, 1957), 52–53, 57–61, 66–72. First published in 1853.

the strong temptations which corrupt so much of the society of the old world and some portions of the new. There was no character more attractive than that of a young Virginian, fifteen years ago, of intelligence, of good family, education and breeding.

It was of the instinct of a Virginian to seek society: he belongs to the gregarious, not to the solitary division of animals; and society can only be kept up by grub and gab—something to eat, and, if not something to talk about, talk. Accordingly they came accomplished already in the knowledge and the talent for these important duties.

A Virginian could always get up a good dinner. He could also do his share—a full hand's work—in disposing of one after it was got up. The qualifications for hostmanship were signal—the old Udaller himself, assisted by Claud Halrco, could not do up the thing in better style, or with a heartier relish, or a more cordial hospitality. In *petite* manners—the little attentions of the table, the filling up of the chinks of the conversation with small fugitive observations, the supplying the hooks and eyes that *kept* the discourse together, the genial good humor, which, like that of the family of the good Vicar, made up in laughter what was wanting in wit—in these, and in the science of getting up and in getting through a picnic or chowder party, or fish fry, the Virginian, like Eclipse, was first, and there was no second. Great was he too at mixing an apple toddy, or mint julep, where ice could be got for love or money; and not deficient, by any means, when it came to his turn to do honor to his own fabrics. It was in this department, that he not only shone but *out*shone, not merely all others but himself. Here he was at home indeed. His elocution, his matter, his learning, his education, were of the first order. He could discourse of every thing around him with an accuracy and a fulness which would have put Coleridge's or Mrs. Ellis's table talk to the blush. Every dish was a text, horticulture, hunting, poultry, fishing—(Isaac Walton or Daniel Webster would have been charmed and instructed to hear him discourse piscatory-wise,)—a slight divergence in favor of foxchasing and a detour towards a horse-race now and then, and continual parentheses of recommendation of particular dishes or glasses—Oh! I tell you if ever there was an interesting man it was he. Others might be agreeable, but he was fascinating, irresistible, not-to-be-done-without.

In the fulness of time the new era had set in—the era of the second great experiment of independence: the experiment, namely, of credit without capital, and enterprise without honesty. The Age of Brass had succeeded the Arcadian period when men got rich by saving a part of their earnings, and lived at their own cost and in ignorance of the new plan of making fortunes on the profits of what they owed. A new theory, not found in the works on political economy, was broached. It was found out that the prejudice in favor of the metals (brass excluded) was an absurd superstition; and that, in reality, any thing else, which the parties interested in giving it currency chose, might serve as a representative of value and medium for exchange of property; and as gold and silver had served for a great number of years as representatives, the republican doctrine of rotation in office required they should give way. Accordingly it was decided that Rags, a very familiar character, and very popular and easy of access, should take their place. Rags belonged to the school of progress. He was representative of the then Young America. His administration was not tame. It was *very* spirited. It was based on the Bonapartist idea of keeping the imagination of the people excited. The leading fiscal idea of his system was to *democratize* capital, and to make, for all purposes of trade, credit and enjoyment of weath, the man that had *no* money a little richer, if anything, than the man that had a million. The principle of success and basis of operation, though inexplicable in the hurry of the time, is plain enough now: it was faith. Let the public believe that a smutted rag is money, it is money: in other words, it was a sort of financial biology, which made, at night, the thing conjured for, the thing that was seen, so far as the patient was concerned, while the fit was on him—except that now a man does not do his trading when under the mesmeric influence: in the flush times he did.

This country was just settling up. Marvellous accounts had gone forth of the fertility of its virgin lands; and the productions of the soil were commanding a price remunerating to slave labor as it had never been remunerated before. Emigrants came flocking in from all quarters of the Union, especially from the slave-holding States. The new country seemed to be a reservoir, and every road leading to it a vagrant stream of enterprise and adventure. Money, or what passed for money, was the only cheap thing to be had. Every crossroad and every avocation presented an opening,—through which a fortune was seen by the adventurer in near perspective. Credit was a thing of course. To refuse it—if the thing was ever done—were an insult for which a bowie-knife were not a too summary or exemplary a means of redress. The State banks were issuing their bills by the sheet, like a patent steam printing-press *its* issues; and no other showing was asked of the applicant for the loan than an authentication of his great distress for money. Finance, even in its most exclusive quarter, had thus already got, in this wonderful revolution, to work upon the principles of the charity hospital. If an overseer grew tired of supervising a plantation and felt a call to the mercantile life, even if he omitted the compendious method of buying out a merchant wholesale, stock, house and good will, and laying down, at once, his bull-whip for the yard-stick —all he had to do was to go on to New-York, and present himself in Pearl-street with a letter avouching his citizenship, and a clean shirt, and he was regularly given a through ticket to speedy bankruptcy.

Under this stimulating process prices rose like smoke. Lots in obscure villages were held at city prices; lands, bought at the minimum cost of government, were sold at from thirty to forty dollars per acre, and considered dirt cheap at that. In short, the country had got to be a full ante-type of California, in all except the gold. Society was wholly unorganized: there was no restraining public opinion: the law was well-nigh powerless—and religion scarcely was heard of except as furnishing the oaths and *technics* of profanity. The world saw a fair experiment of what it would have been, if the fiat had never been pronounced which decreed subsistence as the price of labor.

Money, got without work, by those unaccustomed to it, turned the heads of its possessors, and they spent it with a recklessness like that with which they gained it. The pursuits of industry neglected, riot and coarse debauchery filled up the vacant hours. . . .

The old rules of business and the calculations of prudence were alike disregarded, and profligacy, in all the departments of the *crimen falsi*, held riotous carnival. Larceny grew not only respectable, but genteel, and ruffled it in all the pomp of purple and fine linen. Swindling was raised to the dignity of the fine arts. . . .

Such is a charcoal sketch of the interesting region—now inferior to none in resources, and the character of its population—during the FLUSH TIMES; a period constituting an episode in the commercial history of the world—the reign of humbug, and wholesale insanity, just overthrown in time to save the whole country from ruin. But while it lasted, many of our countrymen came into the South-West in time to get "a benefit." The *auri sacra fames* is a catching disease. Many Virginians had lived too fast for their fortunes, and naturally desired to recuperate: many others, with a competency, longed for wealth; and others again, with wealth, yearned—the common frailty—for still more. Perhaps some friend or relative, who had come out, wrote back flattering accounts of the El Dorado, and fired with dissatisfaction those who were doing well enough at home, by the report of his real or imagined success; for who that ever moved off, was not "doing well" in the new country, himself or friends being chroniclers?

Superior to many of the settlers in elegance of manners and general intelligence, it was the weakness of the Virginian to imagine he was superior too in the essential art of being able to hold his hand and make his way in a new country, and especially *such* a country, and at *such* a time. What a mistake that was! The times were out of joint. It was hard to say whether it were more dangerous to stand still or to move. If the emigrant stood still, he was consumed, by no slow degrees, by expenses: if he moved, ten to one he went off in a galloping consumption, by a ruinous investment. Expenses then—necessary articles about three times as high, and extra articles still more extra-priced—were a different thing in the new country from what they were in the old. In the old country, a jolly Virginian, starting the business of free living on a capital of a plantation, and fifty or sixty negroes, might reasonably calculate, if no ill luck befell him, by the aid of a usurer, and the occasional sale of a negro or two, to hold out without declared insolvency, until a green old age. His estate melted like an estate in chancery, under the gradual thaw of expenses; but in this fast country, it went by the sheer cost of living—some *poker* losses included—like the fortune of the confectioner in California, who failed for one hundred thousand dollars in the six months keeping of a candy-shop. But all the habits of his life, his taste, his associations, his education—every thing—the trustingness of his disposition—his want of business qualifications—

his sanguine temper—all that was Virginian in him, made him the prey, if not of imposture, at least of unfortunate speculations. Where the keenest jockey often was bit, what chance had *he*? About the same that the verdant Moses had with the venerable old gentleman, his father's friend, at the fair, when he traded the Vicar's pony for the green spectacles. But how could he believe it? how *could* he believe that that stuttering, grammarless Georgian, who had never heard of the resolutions of '98, could beat him in a land trade? "Have no money dealings with my father," said the friendly Martha to Lord Nigel, "for, idiot though he seems, he will make an ass of thee." What a pity some monitor, equally wise and equally successful with old Trapbois' daughter, had not been at the elbow of every Virginian! "Twad frae monie a blunder free'd him—an' foolish notion."

If he made a bad bargain, how could he expect to get rid of it? *He knew nothing of the elaborate machinery of ingenious chicane,*—such as feigning bankruptcy—fraudulent conveyances—making over to his wife—running property—and had never heard of such tricks of trade as sending out coffins to the graveyard, with negroes inside, carried off by sudden spells of imaginary disease, to be "resurrected," in due time, grinning, on the banks of the Brazos.

The new philosophy, too, had commended itself to his speculative temper. He readily caught at the idea of a new spirit of the age having set in, which rejected the saws of Poor Richard as being as much out of date as his almanacs. He was already, by the great rise of property, compared to his condition under the old-time prices, rich; and what were a few thousands of debt, which two or three crops would pay off, compared to the value of his estate? (He never thought that the value of property might come down, while the debt was a fixed fact.) He lived freely, for it was a liberal time, and liberal fashions were in vogue, and it was not for a Virginian to be behind others in hospitality and liberality. He required credit and security, and, of course, had to stand security in return. When the crash came, and no "accommodations" could be had, except in a few instances, and in those on the most ruinous terms, he fell an easy victim. They broke by neighborhoods. They usually endorsed for each other, and when one fell—like the child's play of putting bricks on end at equal distances, and dropping the first in the line against the second, which fell against the third, and so on to the last—all fell; each got broke as security, and yet few or none were able to pay their own debts! So powerless of protection were they in those times, that the witty H. G. used to say they reminded him of an oyster, both shells torn off, lying on the beach, with the sea-gulls screaming over them; the only question being, *which* should "gobble them up."

There was one consolation—if the Virginian involved himself like a fool, he suffered himself to be sold out like a gentleman. When his card house of visionary projects came tumbling about his ears, the next question was, the one Webster plagiarised—"Where am I to go?" Those who had fathers, uncles, aunts, or other like dernier resorts, in Virginia, limped back with feathers moulted and crestfallen, to the old stamping ground, carrying the returned Californian's fortune of ten thousand dollars—six bits in money, and the balance in experience. Those who were in the condition of the prodigal, (barring the father, the calf—the fatted one I mean—and the fiddle,) had to turn their accomplishments to account; and many of them, having lost all by eating and drinking, sought the retributive justice from meat and drink, which might, at least, support them in poverty. Accordingly, they kept tavern, and made a barter of hospitality, a business, the only disagreeable part of which was receiving the money, and the only one I know of for which a man can eat and drink himself into qualification. And while I confess I never knew a Virginian, out of the State, to keep a bad tavern, I never knew one to draw a solvent breath from the time he opened house, until death or the sheriff closed it.

Others again got to be, not exactly overseers, but some nameless thing, the duties of which were nearly analogous, for some more fortunate Virginian, who had escaped the wreck, and who had got his former boon companion to live with him on board, or other wages, in some such relation that the friend was not often found at table at the dinings given to the neighbors, and had got to be called Mr. Flournoy instead of Bob, and slept in an outhouse in the yard, and only read the *Enquirer* of nights and Sundays.

Some of the younger scions that had been transplanted early, and stripped of their foliage at a tender age, had been turned into birches for the corrective discipline of youth. Yes; many, who had received academical or collegiate educations, disregarding the allurements of the highway—turning from the gala-day exercise of ditching—scorning the effeminate relaxation of splitting rails—heroically led the Forlorn Hope of the battle of life, the corps of pedagogues of country schools— *academies,* I beg pardon for *not* saying; for, under the Virginia economy, every cross-road log-cabin, where boys were flogged from B-a-k-e-r to Constantinople, grew into the dignity of a sort of runt college; and the teacher vainly endeavored to hide the meanness of the calling beneath the sonorous *sobriquet* of Professor. "Were there no wars?" Had *all* the oysters been opened? Where was the regular army? Could not interest procure service as a deckhand on a steamboat? Did no stage-driver, with a contract for running at night, through the prairies in midwinter, want help, at board wages, and sweet lying in the loft, when off duty, thrown in? What right had the Dutch Jews to monopolize *all* the peddling? "To such vile uses may we come at last, Horatio." The subject grows melancholy. . . .

One thing I will say for the Virginians—I never knew one of them, under any pressure, extemporize a profession. The sentiment of reverence for the mysteries of medicine and law was too large for a deliberate quackery; as to the pulpit, a man might as well do his starving without the hypocrisy.

But others were not so nice. I have known them to rush, when the wolf was after them, from the counting-house or the plantation, into a doctor's shop or a law office, as if those places were the sanctuaries from the avenger; some pretending to be doctors that did not know a liver from a gizzard, administering medicine by the guess, without knowing enough of pharmacy to tell whether the stuff exhibited in the big-bellied blue, red and green bottles at the show-windows of the apothecaries' shops, was given by the drop or the half-pint.

Divers others left, but what became of them, I never knew any more than they know what becomes of the sora after frost.

Many were the instances of suffering; of pitiable misfortune, involving and crushing whole families; of pride abased; of honorable sensibilities wounded; of the provision for old age destroyed; of the hopes of manhood overcast: of independence dissipated, and the poor victim without help, or hope, or sympathy, forced to petty shifts for a bare subsistence, and a ground-scuffle, for what in happier days, he threw away. But there were too many examples of this sort for the expenditure of a useless compassion; just as the surgeon after a battle, grows casehardened, from an excess of objects of pity....

Gentlemen and Parvenus

In this selection a brilliant black historian and sociologist assesses the planters with a combination of that scrupulous detachment and firm commitment to his own social views which marked his great career. Perhaps the most impressive part of *Black Reconstruction* was its analyses of the several classes and races in Southern life; here, he speaks of the planters.[8]

... What the planters wanted was income large enough to maintain the level of living which was their ideal. Naturally, only a few of them had enough for this, and the rest, striving toward it, were perpetually in debt and querulously seeking a reason for this indebtedness outside themselves. Since it was beneath the dignity of a "gentleman" to encumber himself with the details of his finances, this lordly excuse enabled the planter to place between himself and the black slave a series of intermediaries through whom bitter pressure and exploitation could be exercised and large crops raised. For the very reason that the planters did not give attention to details, there was wide tendency to commercialize their growing business of supplying raw materials for an expanding modern industry. They were the last to comprehend the revolution through which that industry was passing and their efforts to increase income succeeded only at the cost of raping the land and degrading the laborers.

Theoretically there were many ways of increasing the income of the planter; practically there was but one. The planter might sell his crops at higher prices; he might increase his crop by intensive farming, or he might reduce the cost of handling and transporting his crops; he might

---

[8] W. E. B. DuBois, *Black Reconstruction in America, 1860–1880* (Copyright, 1935, New York: Russell & Russell, 1956), 36–37, 43, 52–54.

increase his crops by making his laborers work harder and giving them smaller wages. In practice, the planter, so far as prices were concerned, was at the mercy of the market. Merchants and manufacturers by intelligence and close combination set the current prices of raw material. Their power thus exercised over agriculture was not unlimited but it was so large, so continuous and so steadily and intelligently exerted that it gradually reduced agriculture to a subsidiary industry whose returns scarcely supported the farmer and his labor.

The Southern planter in the fifties was in a key position to attempt to break and arrest the growth of this domination of all industry by trade and manufacture. But he was too lazy and self-indulgent to do this and he would not apply his intelligence to the problem. His capitalistic rivals of the North were hard-working, simple-living zealots devoting their whole energy and intelligence to building up an industrial system. They quickly monopolized transport and mines and factories and they were more than willing to include the big plantations. But the planter wanted results without effort. He wanted large income without corresponding investment and he insisted furiously upon a system of production which excluded intelligent labor, machinery, and modern methods. He toyed with the idea of local manufactures and ships and railroads. But this entailed too much work and sacrifice. . . .

. . . The theory was clear and lofty; slaves were a part of the family—"my people," George Washington called them. Under ordinary circumstances they were never to be alienated, but supported during good behavior and bad, punished and corrected for crime and misdemeanor, rewarded for good conduct. It was the patriarchal clan translated into modern life, with social, religious, economic and even blood ties.

This was the theory; but as a matter of fact, the cotton planters were supplied with laborers by the Border States. A laboring stock was deliberately bred for legal sale. A large number of persons followed the profession of promoting this sale of slaves. There were markets and quotations, and the stream of black labor, moving continuously into the South, reached yearly into the thousands.

Notwithstanding these perfectly clear and authenticated facts, the planter persistently denied them. He denied that there was any considerable interstate sale of slaves; he denied that families were broken up; he insisted that slave auctions were due to death or mischance, and particularly did he insist that the slave traders were the least of human beings and most despised.

This deliberate contradiction of plain facts constitutes itself a major charge against slavery and shows how the system often so affronted the moral sense of the planters themselves that they tried to hide from it. They could not face the fact of Negro women as brood mares and of black children as puppies.

Indeed, while we speak of the planters as one essentially unvarying group, there is evidence that the necessities of their economic organization were continually changing and deteriorating their morale and pushing forward ruder, noisier, less cultivated elements than characterized the Southern gentleman of earlier days. Certainly, the cursing, brawling, whoring gamblers who largely represented the South in the late fifties, evidenced the inevitable deterioration that overtakes men when their desire for income and extravagance overwhelms their respect for human beings. Thus the interstate slave trade grew and flourished and the demand for the African slave trade was rapidly becoming irresistible in the late fifties. . . .

The ethical problem here presented was less important than the political and far less than the economic. The Southerners were as little conscious of the hurt they were inflicting on human beings as the Northerners were of their treatment of the insane. It is easy for men to discount and misunderstand the suffering or harm done others. Once accustomed to poverty, to the sight of toil and degradation, it easily seems normal and natural; once it is hidden beneath a different color of skin, a different stature or a different habit of action and speech, and all consciousness of inflicting ill disappears.

The Southern planter suffered, not simply for his economic mistakes—the psychological effect of slavery upon him was fatal. The mere fact that a man could be under the law, the actual master of the mind and body of human beings had to have disastrous effects. It tended to inflate the ego of most planters beyond all reason; they became arrogant, strutting, quarrelsome kinglets; they issued commands; they made laws; they shouted their orders; they expected deference and self-abasement; they were choleric and easily insulted. Their "honor" became a vast and awful thing, requiring wide and insistent deference. Such of them as were inherently weak and inefficient were all the more easily angered, jealous and resentful; while the few who were superior, physically or mentally, conceived no bounds to their power and personal prestige. As the world had long learned, nothing is so calculated to ruin human nature as absolute power over human beings.

On the other hand, the possession of such power did not and could not lead to its continued tyrannical exercise. The tyrant could be kind and congenial. He could care for his chattels like a father; he could grant indulgence and largess; he could play with power and find tremendous satisfaction in its benevolent use.

Thus, economically and morally, the situation of the planter became intolerable. What was needed was the force of great public opinion to make him see his economic mistakes and the moral debauchery that threatened him. But here again in the planter class no room was made for the reformer, the recalcitrant. The men who dared such thought and act were driven out or suppressed with a virulent tyranny reminiscent of the Inquisition and the Reformation. For these there was the same peculiar way of escape that lay before the slave. The planter who could not stand slavery followed the poor whites who could not stand Negroes, they followed the Negro who also could not stand slavery, into the North; and there, removed from immediate contact with the evils of slavery, the planter often became the "copperhead," and theoretical champion of a system which he could not himself endure.

Frederick Douglass thus summed

up the objects of the white planter:

"I understand this policy to comprehend five cardinal objects. They are these: 1st, The complete suppression of all anti-slavery discussion. 2d, The expatriation of the entire free people of color from the United States. 3d, The unending perpetuation of slavery in this republic. 4th, The nationalization of slavery to the extent of making slavery respected in every state of the Union. 5th, The extension of slavery over Mexico and the entire South American states."

This whole system and plan of development failed, and failed of its own weakness. Unending effort has gone into painting the claims of the Old South, its idyllic beauty and social charm. But the truth is inexorable. With all its fine men and sacrificing women, its hospitable homes and graceful manners, the South turned the most beautiful section of the nation into a center of poverty and suffering, of drinking, gambling and brawling; an abode of ignorance among black and white more abysmal than in any modern land; and a system of industry so humanly unjust and economically inefficient that if it had not committed suicide in civil war, it would have disintegrated of its own weight.

With the Civil War, the planters died as a class. We still talk as though the dominant social class in the South persisted after the war. But it did not. It disappeared. Just how quickly and in what manner the transformation was made, we do not know. No scientific study of the submergence of the remainder of the planter class into the ranks of the poor whites, and the corresponding rise of a portion of the poor whites into the dominant portion of landholders and capitalists, has been made. Of the names of prominent Southern families in Congress in 1860, only two appear in 1870, five in 1880. Of 90 prominent names in 1870, only four survived in 1880. Men talk today as though the upper class in the white South is descended from the slaveholders; yet we know by plain mathematics that the ancestors of most of the present Southerners never owned a slave nor had any real economic part in slavery. The disaster of war decimated the planters, the bitter disappointment and frustration led to a tremendous mortality after the war, and from 1870 on the planter class merged their blood so completely with the rising poor whites that they disappeared as a separate aristocracy. It is this that explains so many characteristics of the post-war South: its lynching and mob law, its murders and cruelty, its insensibility to the finer things of civilization. . . .

3. INSIDE VIEWS FROM THE OUTSIDE

The lower-class whites and blacks had their own views of Southern civilization, of the Big House, of "The Chivalry," but we have yet to compile an adequate record of those views. We can here only hint at the complex and contradictory nature of the scattered evidence. The yeomen and poor whites, especially, have not been studied, and their testimony has not been accumulated. For the slaves we at least have the ex-slave narratives, compiled in the 1930s and, of course, the accounts of the successful runaways. We also have the evidence from black culture, which Du Bois analyzed impressively in *Souls of Black Folk* and elsewhere and which is now receiving the attention it deserves. We are further behind in assessing the culture of the middle- and lower-class whites, although Frank Owsley's *Plain Folk of the Old South* and Roger Shugg's *Origin of Class Struggles in Louisiana,* in quite different ways, were promising beginnings.

Aware, then, of the dangers of looking at partial and arbitrarily selected fragments, let us take our chances on a brief look at the views of an antislavery Southern white and several ex-slaves.

Bitter Words from a Non-Slaveholder

Hinton Helper's *Impending Crisis of the South* may well qualify as the harshest and most important call to class war ever published in the United States. A product of North Carolina, Helper called for the expropriation of the master class, but he did so in the name of white liberation and had no sympathy for the black man.[9]

As a striking illustration of the selfish and debasing influences which slavery exercises over the hearts and minds of slaveholders themselves, we will here state the fact that, when we, the non-slaveholders, remonstrate against the continuance of such a manifest wrong and inhumanity—a system of usurpation and outrage so obviously detrimental to *our* interests—they fly into a terrible passion, exclaiming, among all sorts of horrible threats, which are not unfrequently executed, "It's none of your business!"—meaning to say thereby that their slaves do not annoy us, that slavery affects no one except the masters and their chattels personal, and that *we* should give ourselves no concern about it, whatever! To every man of common sense and honesty of purpose the preposterousness of this assumption is so evident, that any studied attempt to refute it would be a positive insult. Would it be none of our business, if they were to bring the small-pox into the neighborhood, and, with premeditated design, let "foul contagion spread?" Or, if they were to throw a pound of strychnine into a public spring, would that be none of our business? Were they to turn a pack of mad dogs loose on the community, would we be performing the part of good citizens by closing ourselves within doors for the space of nine days, saying nothing to anybody? Small-pox is a nuisance;

---

[9] Hinton R. Helper, *The Impending Crisis of the South: How to Meet It,* edited by George M. Frederickson (Cambridge: The Belknap Press of Harvard University Press, 1968), 139–41, 380–82. First published in 1857.

strychnine is a nuisance; mad dogs are a nuisance; slavery is a nuisance; slaveholders are a nuisance, and so are slave-breeders; it is our business, nay, it is our imperative duty, to abate nuisances; we propose, therefore, with the exception of strychnine, which is the least of all these nuisances, to exterminate this catalogue from beginning to end.

We mean precisely what our words express, when we say we believe thieves are, as a general rule, less amenable to the moral law than slaveholders; and here is the basis of our opinion: Ordinarily, thieves wait until we acquire a considerable amount of property, and then they steal a dispensable part of it; but they deprive no one of physical liberty, nor do they fetter the mind; slaveholders, on the contrary, by clinging to the most barbarous relic of the most barbarous age, bring disgrace on themselves, their neighbors, and their country, depreciate the value of their own and others' lands, degrade labor, discourage energy and progress, prevent non-slaveholders from accumulating wealth, curtail their natural rights and privileges, doom their children to ignorance, and all its attendant evils, rob the negroes of their freedom, throw a damper on every species of manual and intellectual enterprise, that is not projected under their own roofs and for their own advantage, and, by other means equally at variance with the principles of justice, though but an insignificant fractional part of the population, they constitute themselves the sole arbiters and legislators for the entire South. Not merely so; the thief rarely steals from more than one man out of an hundred; the slaveholder defrauds ninety and nine, and the hundredth does not escape him. Again, thieves steal trifles from rich men; slaveholders oppress poor men, and enact laws for the perpetuation of their poverty. Thieves practice deceit on the wise; slaveholders take advantage of the ignorant.

We contend, moreover, that slaveholders are more criminal than common murderers. We know all slaveholders would not wilfully imbue their hands in the blood of their fellow-men; but it is a fact, nevertheless, that all slaveholders are under the shield of a perpetual license to murder. This license they have issued to themselves. According to their own infamous statutes, if the slave raises his hand to ward off an unmerited blow, they are permitted to take his life with impunity. We are personally acquainted with three ruffians who have become actual murderers under circumstances of this nature. One of them killed two negroes on one occasion; the other two have murdered but one each. Neither of them has ever been subjected to even the preliminaries of a trial; not one of them has ever been arrested; their own private explanations of the homicides exculpated them from all manner of blame in the premises. They had done nothing wrong in the eyes of the community. The negroes made an effort to shield themselves from the tortures of a merciless flagellation, and were shot dead on the spot. Their murderers still live, and are treated as honorable members of society! No matter how many slaves or free negroes may witness the perpetration of these atrocious homicides, not one of them is ever allowed to lift up his voice in behalf of his murdered brother. In the

South, negroes, whether bond or free, are never, under any circumstances, permitted to utter a syllable under oath, except for or against persons of their own color; their testimony against white persons is of no more consequence than the idle zephyr of the summer. . . .

Black slave labor, though far less valuable, is almost invariably better paid than free white labor. The reason is this: The fiat of the oligarchy has made it *fashionable* to "have negroes around," and there are, we are grieved to say, many non-slaveholding whites, (lickspittles), who, in order to retain on their premises a hired slave whom they falsely imagine secures to them not only the appearance of wealth, but also a position of high social standing in the community, keep themselves in a perpetual strait.

Last Spring we made it our special business to ascertain the ruling rates of wages paid for labor, free and slave, in North Carolina. We found sober, energetic white men, between twenty and forty years of age, engaged in agricultural pursuits at a salary of $84 per annum—including board only; negro men, slaves, who performed little more than half the amount of labor, and who were exceedingly sluggish, awkward, and careless in all their movements, were hired out on adjoining farms at an average of about $115 per annum, including board, clothing, and medical attendance. Free white men and slaves were in the employ of the North Carolina Railroad Company; the former, whose services, in our opinion, were at least twice as valuable as the services of the latter, received only $12 per month each; the masters of the latter received $16 per month for every slave so employed. Industrious, tidy white girls, from sixteen to twenty years of age, had much difficulty in hiring themselves out as domestics in private families for $40 per annum—board only included; negro wenches, slaves, of corresponding ages, so ungraceful, stupid and filthy that no decent man would ever permit one of them to cross the threshold of his dwelling, were in brisk demand at from $65 to $70 per annum, including victuals, clothes, and medical attendance. These are facts, and in considering them, the students of political and social economy will not fail to arrive at conclusions of their own.

Notwithstanding the greater density of population in the free States, labor of every kind is, on an average, about one hundred per cent. higher there than it is in the slave States. This is another important fact, and one that every non-slaveholding white should keep registered in his mind.

Poverty, ignorance, and superstition, are the three leading characteristics of the non-slaveholding whites of the South. Many of them grow up to the age of maturity, and pass through life without ever owning as much as five dollars at any one time. Thousands of them die at an advanced age, as ignorant of the common alphabet as if it had never been invented. All are more or less impressed with a belief in witches, ghosts, and supernatural signs. Few are exempt from habits of sensuality and intemperance. None have anything like adequate ideas of the duties which they owe either to their God, to themselves, or to their fellow-men. Pitiable, indeed, in the fullest sense of the term, is their condition.

It is the almost utter lack of an education that has reduced them to their present unenviable situation. In the whole South there is scarcely a publication of any kind devoted to their interests. They are now completely under the domination of the oligarchy, and it is madness to suppose that they will ever be able to rise to a position of true manhood, until after the slave power shall have been utterly overthrown.

An Ex-Slave Surveys the Plantation

Of all the narratives by escaped slaves that of Frederick Douglass is the most famous. Having fled Maryland, he went on to a distinguished career as an abolitionist leader and national political figure. His survey of the plantation is preceded here by the biting and ironical paragraph with which he opened the book.[10]

In Talbot County, Eastern Shore, State of Maryland, near Easton, the county town, there is a small district of country, thinly populated, and remarkable for nothing that I know of more than for the worn-out, sandy, desertlike appearance of its soil, the general dilapidation of its farms and fences, the indigent and spiritless character of its inhabitants, and the prevalence of ague and fever. It was in this dull, flat, and unthrifty district or neighborhood, bordered by the Choptank River, among the laziest and muddiest of streams, surrounded by a white population of the lowest order, indolent and drunken to a proverb, and among slaves who, in point of ignorance and indolence, were fully in accord with their surroundings, that I, without any fault of my own, was born, and spent the first years of my childhood. . . .

It was generally supposed that slavery in the State of Maryland existed in its mildest form, and that it was totally divested of those harsh and terrible peculiarities which characterized the slave system in the southern and southwestern states of the American Union. The ground of this opinion was the contiguity of the free states, and the influence of their moral, religious, and humane sentiments. Public opinion was, indeed, a measurable restraint upon the cruelty and barbarity of masters, overseers, and slave-drivers, whenever and wherever it could reach them; but there were certain secluded and out-of-the-way places, even in the State of Maryland, fifty years ago, seldom visited by a single ray of healthy public sentiment, where slavery, wrapt in its own congenial darkness, could and did develop all its malign and shocking characteristics, where it could be indecent without shame, cruel without shuddering, and murderous without apprehension or fear of exposure or punishment. Just such a secluded, dark, and out-of-the-way place was the home plantation of Colonel Edward Lloyd, in Talbot County,

---

[10] Frederick Douglass, *Life and Times of Frederick Douglass, Written by Himself* (New York: Collier Books, 1962), 27, 37–44.

Eastern Shore of Maryland. It was far away from all the great thoroughfares of travel and commerce, and proximate to no town or village. There was neither schoolhouse nor townhouse in its neighborhood. The schoolhouse was unnecessary, for there were no children to go to school. The children and grandchildren of Col. Lloyd were taught in the house by a private tutor (a Mr. Page from Greenfield, Massachusetts, a tall, gaunt sapling of a man, remarkably dignified, thoughtful, and reticent, and who did not speak a dozen words to a slave in a whole year). The overseer's children went off somewhere in the state to school, and therefore could bring no foreign or dangerous influence from abroad to embarrass the natural operation of the slave system of the place. Here, not even the commonest mechanics, from whom there might have been an occasional outburst of honest and telling indignation at cruelty and wrong on other plantations, were white men. Its whole public was made up of and divided into three classes, slaveholders, slaves, and overseers. Its blacksmiths, wheelwrights, shoemakers, weavers, and coopers, were slaves.

Not even commerce, selfish and indifferent to moral considerations as it usually is, was permitted within its secluded precincts. Whether with a view of guarding against the escape of its secrets, I know not, but it is a fact, that every leaf and grain of the products of this plantation and those of the neighboring farms belonging to Col. Lloyd were transported to Baltimore in his own vessels, every man and boy on board of which, except the captain, were owned by him as his property. In return, everything brought to the plantation came through the same channel. To make this isolation more apparent, it may be stated that the estates adjoining Col. Lloyd's were owned and occupied by friends of his, who were as deeply interested as himself in maintaining the slave system in all its rigor. These were the Tilgmans, the Goldboroughs, the Lockermans, the Pacas, the Skinners, Gibsons, and others of lesser affluence and standing.

Public opinion in such a quarter, the reader must see, was not likely to be very efficient in protecting the slave from cruelty. To be a restraint upon abuses of this nature, opinion must emanate from humane and virtuous communities, and to no such opinion or influence was Col. Lloyd's plantation exposed. It was a little nation by itself, having its own language, its own rules, regulations, and customs. The troubles and controversies arising here were not settled by the civil power of the State. The overseer was the important dignitary. He was generally accuser, judge, jury, advocate, and executioner. The criminal was always dumb, and no slave was allowed to testify other than against his brother slave.

There were, of course, no conflicting rights of property, for all the people were the property of one man, and they could themselves own no property. Religion and politics were largely excluded. One class of the population was too high to be reached by the common preacher, and the other class was too low in condition and ignorance to be much cared for by religious teachers, and yet some religious ideas did enter this dark corner.

This, however, is not the only view which the place presented.

Though civilization was, in many respects, shut out, nature could not be. Though separated from the rest of the world, though public opinion, as I have said, could seldom penetrate its dark domain, though the whole place was stamped with its own peculiar iron-like individuality, and though crimes, high-handed and atrocious, could be committed there with strange and shocking impunity, it was, to outward seeming, a most strikingly interesting place, full of life, activity, and spirit, and presented a very favorable contrast to the indolent monotony and languor of Tuckahoe. It resembled, in some respects, descriptions I have since read of the old baronial domains of Europe. Keen as was my regret and great as was my sorrow at leaving my old home, I was not long in adapting myself to this my new one. A man's troubles are always half disposed of when he finds endurance the only alternative. I found myself here, there was no getting away, and naught remained for me but to make the best of it. Here was plenty of children to play with and plenty of pleasant resorts for boys of my age and older. The little tendrils of affection, so rudely broken from the darling objects in and around my grandmother's home, gradually began to extend and twine themselves around the new surroundings. Here, for the first time, I saw a large windmill, with its wide-sweeping white wings, a commanding object to a child's eye. This was situated on what was called Long Point—a tract of land dividing Miles River from the Wye. I spent many hours here watching the wings of this wondrous mill. In the river, or what was called the "Swash," at a short distance from the shore, quietly lying at anchor, with her small rowboat dancing at her stern, was a large sloop, the *Sally Lloyd,* called by that name in honor of the favorite daughter of the Colonel. These two objects, the sloop and mill, awakened, as I remember, thoughts, ideas, and wondering. Then here were a great many houses, human habitations full of the mysteries of life at every stage of it. There was the little red house up the road, occupied by Mr. Seveir, the overseer. A little nearer to my old master's stood a long, low, rough building literally alive with slaves of all ages, sexes, conditions, sizes, and colors. This was called the long quarter. Perched upon a hill east of our house, was a tall, dilapidated old brick building, the architectural dimensions of which proclaimed its creation for a different purpose, now occupied by slaves, in a similar manner to the long quarters. Besides these, there were numerous other slave houses and huts scattered around in the neighborhood, every nook and corner of which were completely occupied.

Old master's house, a long brick building, plain but substantial, was centrally located, and was an independent establishment. Besides these houses there were barns, stables, storehouses, tobacco-houses, blacksmith shops, wheelwright shops, cooper shops; but above all there stood the grandest building my young eyes had ever beheld, called by every one on the plantation the *great* house. This was occupied by Col. Lloyd and his family. It was surrounded by numerous and variously shaped outbuildings. There were kitchens, washhouses, dairies, summerhouses, greenhouses, henhouses, turkey-houses, pigeon-houses and arbors of many sizes and devices, all neatly painted or whitewashed, interspersed with grand old trees, ornamental and primitive, which afforded delightful shade in summer and imparted to the scene a high degree of stately beauty. The *great* house itself was a large white wooden building with wings on three sides of it. In front, extending the entire length of the building and supported by a long range of columns, was a broad portico, which gave to the Colonel's home an air of great dignity and grandeur. It was a treat to my young and gradually opening mind to behold this elaborate exhibition of wealth, power, and beauty.

The carriage entrance to the house was by a large gate, more than a quarter of a mile distant. The intermediate space was a beautiful lawn, very neatly kept and tended. It was dotted thickly over with trees and flowers. The road or lane from the gate to the great house was richly paved with white pebbles from the beach and in its course formed a complete circle around the lawn. Outside this select enclosure were parks, as about the residences of the English nobility, where rabbits, deer, and other wild game might be seen peering and playing about, with "none to molest them or make them afraid." The tops of the stately poplars were often covered with redwinged blackbirds, making all nature vocal with the joyous life and beauty of their wild, warbling notes. These all belonged to me as well as to Col. Edward Lloyd, and, whether they did or not, I greatly enjoyed them.

Not far from the great house were the stately mansions of the dead Lloyds—a place of somber aspect. Vast tombs, embowered beneath the weeping willow and the fir tree, told of the generations of the family, as well as of their wealth. Superstition was rife among the slaves about this family burying-ground. Strange sights had been seen there by some of the older slaves, and I was often compelled to hear stories of shrouded ghosts, riding on great black horses, and of balls of fire which had been seen to fly there at midnight, and of startling and dreadful sounds that had been repeatedly heard. Slaves knew enough of the orthodox theology of the time to consign all bad slaveholders to hell, and they often fancied such persons wishing themselves back again to wield the lash. Tales of sights and sounds strange and terrible, connected with the huge black tombs, were a great security to the grounds about them, for few of the slaves had the courage to approach them during the daytime. It was a dark, gloomy, and forbidding place, and it was difficult to feel that the spirits of the sleeping dust there deposited reigned with the blest in the realms of eternal peace.

At Lloyd's was transacted the business of twenty or thirty different farms, which, with the slaves upon them, numbering, in all, not less than a thousand, all belonged to Col. Lloyd. Each farm was under the management of an overseer, whose word was law.

Mr. Lloyd was, at this time, very rich. His slaves alone, numbering as I have said not less than a thousand, were an immense fortune, and though scarcely a month passed without the sale to the Georgia traders of one or more lots, there was no apparent diminution in the number of his human stock. The selling of any to the State of Georgia was a sore and mournful event to those left behind, as well as to the victims themselves.

The reader has already been informed of the handicrafts carried on here by the slaves. "Uncle" Toney was the blacksmith, "Uncle" Harry the cartwright, and "Uncle" Abel was the shoemaker, and these had assistants in their several departments. These mechanics were called "Uncles" by all the younger slaves, not because they really sustained that relationship to any, but according to plantation etiquette, as a mark of respect, due from the younger to the older slaves. Strange and even ridiculous as it may seem, among a people so uncultivated and with so many stern trials to look in the face, there is not to be found among any people a more rigid enforcement of the law of respect to elders than is maintained among them. I set this down as partly constitutional with the colored race and partly conventional. There is no better material in the world for making a gentleman than is furnished in the African.

Among other slave notabilities, I found here one called by everybody, white and colored, "Uncle" Isaac Copper. It was seldom that a slave, however venerable, was honored with a surname in Maryland, and so completely has the South shaped the manners of the North in this respect that their right to such honor is tardily admitted even now. It goes sadly against the grain to address and treat a Negro as one would address and treat a white man. But once in a while, even in a slave state, a Negro had a surname fastened to him by common consent. This was the case with "Uncle" Isaac Copper.

When the "Uncle" was dropped, he was called Doctor Copper. He was both our Doctor of Medicine and our Doctor of Divinity. Where he took his degree I am unable to say, but he was too well established in his profession to permit question as to his native skill or attainments. One qualification he certainly had. He was a confirmed cripple, wholly unable to work, and was worth nothing for sale in the market. Though lame, he was no sluggard. He made his crutches do him good service, and was always on the alert looking up the sick, and such as were supposed to need his aid and counsel. His remedial prescriptions embraced four articles. For diseases of the body, epsom salts and castor oil; for those of the soul, the "Lord's prayer," and a few stout hickory switches.

I was, with twenty or thirty other children, early sent to Doctor Isaac Copper, to learn the Lord's Prayer. The old man was seated on a huge three-legged oaken stool, armed with several large hickory switches, and from the point where he sat, lame as he was, he could reach every boy in the room. After our standing a while to learn what was expected of us, he commanded us to kneel down. This done, he told us to say everything he said. "Our Father"—this we repeated after him with promptness and uniformity—"who art in Heaven," was less promptly and uniformly repeated, and the old gentleman paused in the prayer to give us a short lecture, and to use his switches on our backs.

Everybody in the South seemed to want the privilege of whipping somebody else. Uncle Isaac, though a good old man, shared the common passion of his time and country. I cannot say I was much edified by attendance upon his ministry. There was in my mind, even at that time, something a little inconsistent and laughable in the blending of prayer with punishment.

I was not long in my new home before I found that the dread I had conceived of Captain Anthony was in a measure groundless. Instead of leaping out from some hiding-place and destroying me, he hardly seemed to notice my presence. He probably thought as little of my arrival there as of an additional pig to his stock. He was the chief agent of his employer. The overseers of all the farms composing the Lloyd estate were in some sort under him. The Colonel himself seldom addressed an overseer, or allowed himself to be addressed by one. To Captain Anthony, therefore, was committed the headship of all the farms. He carried the keys of all the storehouses; weighed and measured the allowances of each slave at the end of each month; superintended the storing of all goods brought to the storehouse; dealt out the raw material to the different handicraftsmen; shipped the grain, tobacco, and all other salable produce of the numerous farms to Baltimore, and had a general oversight of all the workshops of the place. In addition to all this he was frequently called abroad to Easton and elsewhere in the discharge of his numerous duties as chief agent of the estate.

The family of Captain Anthony consisted of two sons—Andrew and Richard—and his daughter Lucretia and her newly-married husband, Captain Thomas Auld. In the kitchen were Aunt Katy, Aunt Esther, and ten or a dozen children, most of them older than myself. Captain Anthony was not considered a rich slaveholder, though he was pretty well off in the world. He owned about thirty slaves and three farms in the Tuckahoe district. The more valuable part of his property was in slaves, of whom he sold one every year, which brought him in seven or eight hundred dollars, besides his yearly salary and other revenue from his lands.

I have been often asked, during the earlier part of my free life at the North, how I happened to have so little of the slave accent in my speech. The mystery is in some measure explained by my association with Daniel Lloyd, the youngest son of Col. Edward Lloyd. The law of compensation holds here as well as elsewhere. While this lad could not associate with ignorance without sharing its shade, he could not give his black playmates his company without giving them his superior intelligence as well. Without knowing this, or caring about it at the time, I, for some cause or other, was attracted to him, and was much his companion.

I had little to do with the older brothers of Daniel—Edward and Murray. They were grown up and were fine-looking men. Edward was especially esteemed by the slave children, and by me among the rest—not that he ever said anything to us or for us which could be called particularly kind. It was enough for us that he never looked or acted scornfully toward us. The idea of rank and station was rigidly maintained on this estate. The family of Captain Anthony never visited the great house, and the Lloyds never came to our house. Equal non-intercourse was observed between Captain Anthony's family and the family of Mr. Seveir, the overseer.

Such, kind readers, was the community and such the place in which my earliest and most lasting impressions of the workings of slavery were received, of which impressions you will learn more in the after coming chapters of this book.

Two Recollections

We end with the recollections of two simple ex-slaves who were interviewed by the WPA Federal Writers Project in the 1930s. They tell different stories and show different attitudes. They thereby give some idea of the richness and range of the narrative collection as a whole. Yet, in some ways they are not so different as they might seem on first reading.[11]

Andrew Goodman

Interviewed at Dallas, Texas. Interviewer not identified. Age when interviewed: 97. I was born in slavery and I think them days was better for the niggers than the days we see now. One thing was, I never was cold and hungry when my old master lived, and I has been plenty hungry and cold a lot of times since he is gone. But sometimes I think Marse Goodman was the bestest man God made in a long time.

My mother, Martha Goodman, belonged to Marse Bob Goodman when she was born, but my paw come from Tennessee and Marse Bob heired* him. . . . They must have been fine folks all-a-way round, 'cause my paw said them that raised him was good to they niggers. Old Marse never 'lowed none of his nigger families separated. He 'lowed he thought it right and fittin' that folks stay together, though I heard tell of some that didn't think so.

My missus was just as good as Marse Bob. My maw was a puny little woman that wasn't able to do work in the fields, and she puttered round the house for the Missus, doin' little odd jobs. I played round with little Miss Sallie and little Mr. Bob, and I ate with them and slept with them. I used to sweep off the steps and do things, and she'd brag on me. Many is the time I'd get to noddin' and go to sleep, and she'd pick me up and put me in bed with her chillen.

Marse Bob didn't put his little niggers in the fields till they's big 'nough to work, and the mammies was give time off from the fields to come back to the nursin' home to suck the babies. He didn't never put the niggers out in bad weather. He give us somethin' to do, in out of the weather, like shellin' corn, and the women could spin and knit. They made us plenty of good clothes. In summer we wore long shirts, split up

---

[11] From *Life Under the "Peculiar Institution"*: Selections from the Slave Narrative Collection by Norman R. Yetman, pp. 140–43, 310–15. Copyright © 1970 by Holt, Rinehart and Winston, Inc. Reprinted by permission of Holt, Rinehart and Winston, Inc.

* Inherited.

the sides, made out of lowerings—that's same as cotton sacks was made out of. In winter we had good jeans and knitted sweaters and knitted socks.

My paw was a shoemaker. He'd take a calfhide and make shoes with the hairy sides turned in, and they was warm and kept your feet dry. My maw spent a lot of time cardin' and spinnin' wool, and I always had plenty things.

Life was purty fine with Marse Bob. He was a man of plenty. He had a lot of land and he built him a log house when he come to Texas. He had several hundred head of cattle and more than that many hogs. We raised cotton and grain and chickens and vegetables and most anything anybody could ask for.

Some places the masters give out a peck of meal and so many pounds of meat to a family for them a week's rations, and if they et it up that was all they got. But Marse Bob always give out plenty and said, "If you need more, you can have it, 'cause ain't any going to suffer on my place."

He built us a church, and a old man, Kenneth Lyons, who was a slave of the Lyons family nearby, used to get a pass every Sunday mornin' and come preach to us. He was a man of good learnin' and the best preacher I ever heard. He baptized in a little old mudhole down back of our place. Nearly all the boys and gals gets converted when they's about twelve or fifteen year old. Then on Sunday afternoon, Marse Bob learned us to read and write. He told us we oughta get all the learnin' we could.

Once a week the slaves could have any night they want for a dance or frolic. Mance McQueen was a slave belonging on the Dewberry place what could play a fiddle, and his master give him a pass to come play for us. Marse Bob give us chickens or kilt a fresh beef or let us make 'lasses candy. We could choose any night, 'cept in the fall of the year. Then we worked awful hard and didn't have the time. We had a gin run by horsepower and after sundown, when we left the fields, we used to gin a bale of cotton every night. Marse always give us from Christmas Eve through New Year's Day off, to make up for the hard work in the fall.

Christmas time everybody got a present and Marse Bob give a big hog to every four families. We had money to buy whiskey with. In spare time we'd make corn-shuck horse collars and all kinds of baskets, and Marse bought them off us. What he couldn't use, he sold for us. We'd take post oak and split it thin with drawin' knives and let it get tough in the sun, and then weave it into cotton baskets and fish baskets and little fancy baskets. The men spent they money on whiskey, 'cause everything else was furnished. We raised our own tobacco and hung it in the barn to season, and anybody could go get it when they wanted it. We always got Saturday afternoons off to fish and hunt. We used to have fish fries and plenty of game in dem days.

Course, we used to hear about other places where they had nigger drivers and beat the slaves. But I never did see or hear tell of one master's slaves gettin' a beatin'. We had a overseer, but didn't know what a nigger driver was. Marse Bob had some nigger dogs like other places and used to train them for fun. He'd get some of the boys to run for a hour or so and then put the dogs on the trail. He'd say, "If you hear them gettin' near, take to a tree." But Marse Bob never had no niggers to run off.

Old man Briscoll, who had a place next to ours, was vicious cruel. He was mean to his own blood, beatin' his chillen. His slaves was a-feared all the time and hated him. Old Charlie, a good old man who belonged to him, run away and stayed six months in the woods before Briscoll cotched him. The niggers used to help feed him, but one day a nigger 'trayed him and Briscoll put the dogs on him and cotched him. He made to Charlie like he wasn't goin' to hurt him none and got him to come peaceful. When he took him home, he tied him and beat him for a terrible long time. Then he took a big, pine torch and let burnin' pitch drop in spots all over him. Old Charlie was sick about four months and then he died.

Marse Bob knowed me better'n most the slaves, 'cause I was round the house more. One day he called all the slaves to the yard. He only had sixty-six then, 'cause he 'vided with his son and daughter when they married. He made a little speech. He said, "I'm going to a war, but I don't think I'll be gone long, and I'm turning the overseer off and leaving Andrew in charge of the place, and I wants everything to go on, just like I was here. Now, you all mind what Andrew says, 'cause if you don't, I'll make it rough on you when I come back home." He was joking, though, 'cause he wouldn't have done nothing to them.

Then he said to me, "Andrew, you is old 'nough to be a man and look after things. Take care of Missus and see that none the niggers wants, and try to keep the place going."

We didn't know what the War was about, but Master was gone four years. When Old Missus heard from him, she'd call all the slaves and tell us the news and read us his letters. Little parts of it she wouldn't read. We never heard of him getting hurt none, but if he had, Old Missus wouldn't tell us, 'cause the niggers used to cry and pray over him all the time. We never heard tell what the War was about.

When Marse Bob come home, he sent for all the slaves. He was sitting in a yard chair, all tuckered out, and shook hands all round, and said he's glad to see us. Then he said, "I got something to tell you. You is just as free as I is. You don't belong to nobody but yourselves. We went to the War and fought, but the Yankees done whip us, and they say the niggers is free. You can go where you wants to go, or you can stay here, just as you likes." He couldn't help but cry.

The niggers cry and don't know much what Marse Bob means. They is sorry about the freedom, 'cause they don't know where to go, and they's always 'pend on Old Marse to look after them. Three families went to get farms for theyselves, but the rest just stay on for hands on the old place.

The Federals has been coming by, even before Old Marse come home. They all come by, carrying they little budgets and if they was walking they'd look in the stables for a horse or mule, and they just took what they wanted of corn or livestock. They done the same after Marse Bob come home. He just said,

"Let them go they way, 'cause that's what they're going to do, anyway." We was scareder of them than we was of the devil. But they spoke right kindly of us colored folks. They said, "If you got a good master and want to stay, well, you can do that, but now you can go where you want to, 'cause ain't nobody going to stop you."

The niggers can't hardly get used to the idea. When they wants to leave the place, they still go up to the Big House for a pass. They just can't understand about the freedom. Old Marse or Missus say, "You don't need no pass. All you got to do is just take your foot in your hand and go."

It seem like the War just plumb broke Old Marse up. It wasn't long till he moved into Tyler and left my paw running the farm on a halfacre with him and the nigger workers. He didn't live long, but I forgets just how long. But when Mr. Bob heired the old place, he 'lowed we'd just go 'long the way his paw has made the trade with my paw.

Young Mr. Bob apparently done the first rascality I ever heard of a Goodman doing. The first year we worked for him we raised lots of grain and other things and fifty-seven bales of cotton. Cotton was fifty-two cents a pound, and he shipped it all away, but all he ever gave us was a box of candy and a sack of store tobacco and a sack of sugar. He said the 'signment done got lost. Paw said to let it go, 'cause we had always lived by what the Goodmans had said.

I got married and lived on the old place till I was in my late fifties. I had seven chillen, but if I got any livin' now, I don't know where they is. My paw and maw got to own a little piece of land not far from the old place, and paw lived to be 102 and maw 106. I'm the last one of any of my folks.

Mingo White

Interviewed at Burleson, Alabama. Interviewed by Levi D. Shelby, Jr. Age when interviewed: 85–90. I was born in Chester, South Carolina, but I was mostly raised in Alabama. When I was about four or five years old, I was loaded in a wagon with a lot more people in it. Where I was bound I don't know. Whatever become of my mammy and pappy I don't know for a long time. I was told there was a lot of slave speculators in Chester to buy some slaves for some folks in Alabama. I 'members dat I was took up on a stand and a lot of people come round and felt my arms and legs and chest, and ask me a lot of questions. Before we slaves was took to de tradin' post Old Marsa Crawford told us to tell everybody what asked us if we'd ever been sick dat us'd never been sick in our life. Us had to tell 'em all sorts of lies for our marsa or else take a beatin'.

I was just a li'l thing, tooked away from my mammy and pappy, just when I needed 'em most. The only carin' that I had or ever knowed anything about was give to me by a friend of my pappy. His name was John White. My pappy told him to take care of me for him. John was a fiddler and many a night I woke up to find myself 'sleep 'twixt his legs whilst he was playin' for a dance for de white folks. My pappy and mammy was sold from each other, too, de same time as I was sold. I used to wonder if I had any brothers or sisters, as I had always wanted some. A few years later I found out I didn't have none.

I'll never forget de trip from Chester to Burleson. I wouldn't 'member so well, I don't guess, 'ceptin' I had a big old sheep dog named Trailer. He followed right in back of de wagon dat I was in. Us had to cross a wide stream what I took to be a river. When we started cross, old Trailer never stopped followin'. I was watchin' him close so if he gived out I was goin' to try to get him. He didn't give out; he didn't even have to swim. He just walked along and lapped de water like a dog will.

John took me and kept me in de cabin with him. De cabin didn't have no furniture in it like we has nowadays. De bed was one-legged. It was made in de corner of de room, with de leg settin' out in de middle of de floor. A plank was runned 'twixt de logs of de cabin and nailed to de post on de front of de bed. Across de foot another plank was runned into de logs and nailed to de legs. Den some straw or corn shucks was piled on for a mattress. Us used anything what we could get for cover. De table had two legs, de legs set out to de front whilst de back part was nailed to de wall. Us didn't have no stove. There was a great big fireplace where de cookin' was done. Us didn't have to cook, though, lessen us got hungry after supper been served at de house.

I weren't nothin' but a child endurin' slavery, but I had to work de same as any man. I went to de field and hoed cotton, pulled fodder and picked cotton with de rest of de hands. I kept up, too, to keep from gettin' any lashes dat night when us got home. In de winter I went to de woods with de menfolks to help get wood or to get sap from de trees to make turpentine and tar. Iffen us didn't do dat we made charcoal to run de blacksmith shop with.

De white folks was hard on us. Dey would whip us about de least li'l thing. It wouldn'ta been so bad iffen us had a had comforts, but to live like us did was 'nough to make anybody soon as be dead. De white folks told us dat us born to work for 'em and dat us was doin' fine at dat.

De next time dat I saw my mammy I was a great big boy. Dere was a woman on de place what everybody called "Mammy"—Selina White. One day Mammy called me and said, "Mingo, you mammy is comin'." I said, "I thought dat you was my mammy." She said, "No, I ain't your mammy. Your mammy is away from here." I couldn't believe dat I had another mammy and I never thought about it anymore.

One day I was sittin' down at de barn when a wagon come up de lane. I stood round like a child will. When de wagon got to de house, my mammy got out and broke and run to me and throwed her arms round my neck and hug and kiss me. I never been put my arms round her or nothin' of de sort. I just stood dere lookin' at her. She said, "Son, ain't you glad to see your mammy?" I looked at her and walked off. Mammy Selina call me and told me dat I had hurt my mammy's feelins', and dat dis woman was my mammy.

I went off and studied and I begins to 'member things. I went to Selina and asked her how long it been since I seen my mammy. She told me dat I had been away from her since I was just a li'l chile. I went to my mammy and told her dat

I was sorry I done what I did and dat I would like for her to forget and forgive me for de way I act when I first saw her. After I had talked with my real mammy, she told me of how de family had been broke up and dat she hadn't seed my pappy since he was sold.

My mammy never would of seen me no more if de Lord hadn'ta been in de plan. Tom White's daughter married one of Mr. Crawford's sons. Dey lived in Virginia. Back den it was de custom for women to come home whenever dey husbands died or quit 'em. Mr. Crawford's son died and dat forced her to come home. My mammy had been her maid, so when she got ready to come home she brung my mammy with her.

It was hard back in dem days. Every mornin' before daybreak you had to be up and ready to get to de field. It was de same every day in de year 'cept on Sunday, and den we was gettin' up earlier dan de folks do now on Monday. De drivers was hard, too. Dey could say whatever dey wanted to and you couldn't say nothin' for yourself. Somehow or other us had a instinct dat we was goin' to be free.

In de event when de day's work was done de slaves would be found locked in deir cabins prayin' for de Lord to free dem like he did de chillen of Israel. Iffen dey didn't lock up, de marsa or de driver would of heard 'em and whipped 'em. De slaves had a way of puttin' a wash pot in de door of de cabin to keep de sound in de house.

I 'members once old Ned White was caught prayin'. De drivers took him de next day and carried him to de pegs, what was four stakes drove in de ground. Ned was made to pull off everything but his pants and lay on his stomach between de pegs whilst somebody strapped his legs and arms to de pegs. Den dey whipped him till de blood run from him like he was a hog. Dey made all of de hands come and see it, and dey said us'd get de same thing if us was cotched. Dey don't allow a man to whip a horse like dey whipped us in dem days.

After my mammy come where I was I helped her with her work. Her task was too hard for any one person. She had to serve as maid to Mr. White's daughter, cook for all of de hands, spin and card four cuts of thread a day, and den wash. Dere was one hundred and forty-four threads to be cut. If she didn't get all of dis done she got fifty lashes dat night. Many de night me and her would spin and card so she could get her task de next day. No matter what she had to do de next day she would save to get dem cuts of thread, even on wash day.

Wash day was on Wednesday. My mammy would have to take de clothes about three-quarters of a mile to de branch where de washin' was to be done. She didn't have no washboard like dey have nowadays. She had a paddle what she beat de clothes with. Everybody knowed when wash day was 'cause dey could hear de paddle for about three or four miles. "Pow-pow-pow," dats how it sound. She had to iron de clothes de same day dat she washed and den get dem four cuts of thread.

Lots of times she failed to get 'em and got de fifty lashes. One day when Tom White was whippin' her she said, "Lay it on, Marsa White, 'cause I'm goin' to tell de Yankees when dey come." When Mammy got through spinnin' de cloth she had to dye it. She used sumac berries, indigo, bark from some trees, and dere was some kind of rock what she got red dye from. De clothes wouldn't fade, neither.

De white folks didn't learn us to do nothin' but work. Dey said dat us weren't supposed to know how to read and write. Dere was one feller name E. C. White what learned to read and write endurin' slavery. He had to carry de chillen's books to school for 'em and go back after dem. His young marsa taught him to read and write unbeknownst to his father and de rest of de slaves.

Us didn't have nowhere to go 'cept church and we didn't get no pleasure outen it 'cause we weren't allowed to talk from de time we left home till us got back. If us went to church de drivers went with us. Us didn't have no church 'cept de white folks church.

After old Ned got such a terrible beatin' for prayin' for freedom he slipped off and went to de North to join de Union Army. After he go in de army he wrote to Marsa Tom. In his letter he had dese words: "I am layin' down, Marsa, and gettin' up, Marsa," meaning dat he went to bed when he felt like it and got up when he pleased to. He told Tom White dat iffen he wanted him he was in the army and dat they could come after him.

After old Ned had got to de North, de other hands begin to watch for a chance to slip off. Many a one was cotched and brung back. Dey knowed de penalty what dey would have to pay, and dis cause some of 'em to get desperate. Druther dan to take a beatin' dey would choose to fight it out till dey was able to get away or die before dey would take de beatin'.

Lots of times when de patterrollers would get after de slaves dey would have de worse fight and sometimes de patterrollers would get killed. After de War I saw Ned, and he told me de night he left the patterrollers runned him for four days. He say de way he hid to keep dem from catchin' him was he went by de woods. De patterrollers come in de woods lookin' for him, so he just got a tree on 'em and den followed. Dey figured dat he was headin' for de free states, so dey headed day way too, and Ned just followed dem far as dey could go. Den he clumb a tree and hid whilst dey turned round and come back. Ned went on without any trouble much. De patterrollers used to be bad. Dey would run de folks iffen dey was caught out after eight o'clock in de night, iffen dey didn't have no pass from de marsa.

After de day's work was done there weren't anything for de slaves to do but go to bed. Wednesday night they went to prayer meetin'. We had to be in de bed by nine o'clock. Every night de drivers come round to make sure dat we was in de bed. I heerd tell of folks goin' to bed and den gettin' up and goin' to another plantation.

On Saturday de hands worked till noon. Dey had de rest of de time to work dey gardens. Every family had a garden of deir own. On Saturday nights the slaves could frolic for a while. Dey would have parties sometimes and whiskey and home-brew for de servants. On Sundays we didn't do anything but lay round and sleep, 'cause we didn't like to go to church. On Christmas we didn't have to do no work, no more'n feed the stock and do de li'l work round de house. When we got through with dat we had de rest of de day to run round wherever we wanted to go. 'Course, we had to get permission from de marsa.

De owners of slaves used to give corn shuckin' parties, and invite slaves from other plantations. Dey would have plenty of whiskey and other stuff to eat. De slaves would shuck corn and eat and drink. Dey used to give cotton pickin's de same way. All of dis went on at night. Dey had jacklights in de cotton patch for us to see by. De lights was made on a forked stick and moved from place to place whilst we picked. De corn shuckin' was done at de barn, and dey didn't have to have lights so dey could move dem from place to place.

I was pretty big boy when de War broke out. I 'member seein' de Yankees cross Big Bear Creek bridge one day. All of de soldiers crossed de bridge but one. He stayed on de other side till all de rest had got across, den he got down offen his horse and took a bottle of somethin' and strewed it all over de bridge. Den he lighted a match to it and followed de rest. In a few minutes de Rebel soldiers come to de bridge to cross but it was on fire and dey had to swim across to de other side. I went home and told my mammy dat de Rebels was chasin' de Union soldiers, and dat one of de Unions has poured some water on de bridge and set it afire. She laugh and say: "Son, don't you know dat water don't make a fire? Dat musta been turpentine or oil."

I 'member one day Mr. Tom was havin' a big barbecue for de Rebel soldiers in our yard. Come a big roarin 'down de military road, and three men in blue coats rode up to de gate and come on in. Just as soon as de Rebels saw 'em dey all run to de woods. In about five minutes de yard was full of blue coats. Dey et up all de grub what de Rebels had been eatin'. Tom White had to run away to keep de Yankess from gettin' him. Before de Yankees come, de white folks took all dey clothes and hung 'em in de cabins. Dey told de colored folks to tell de Yankees dat de clothes was deir'n. Dey told us to tell 'em how good dey been to us and dat we liked to live with 'em.

De day dat we got news dat we was free, Mr. White called us niggers to the house. He said: "You are all free, just as free as I am. Now go and get yourself somewhere to stick your heads."

Just as soon as he say dat, my mammy hollered out: "Dat's 'nough for a yearlin'." She struck out across de field to Mr. Lee Osborn's to get a place for me and her to stay. He paid us seventy-five cents a day, fifty cents to her and two bits for me. He gave us our dinner along with de wages. After de crop was gathered for that year, me and my mammy cut and hauled wood for Mr. Osborn. Us left Mr. Osborn dat fall and went to Mr. John Rawlins. Us made a sharecrop with him. Us'd pick two rows of cotton and he'd pick two rows. Us'd pull two rows of corn and he'd pull two rows of corn. He furnished us with rations and a place to stay. Us'd sell our cotton and open corn and pay Mr. John Rawlins for feedin' us. Den we moved with Mr. Hugh Nelson and made a sharecrop with him. We kept movin' and makin' sharecrops till us saved up 'nough money to rent us a place and make a crop for ourselves.

Us did right well at dis until de Ku Klux got so bad, us had to move back with Mr. Nelson for protection. De mens that took us in was Union men. Dey lived here in the South but dey taken us part in de slave business. De Ku Klux threat to whip Mr. Nelson, 'cause he took up for de niggers. Heap of nights we would hear of de Ku Klux comin' and leave home. Sometimes us was scared not to go and scared to go away from home.

One day I borrowed a gun from Ed Davis to go squirrel huntin'. When I taken de gun back I didn't unload it like I always been doin'. Dat night de Ku Klux called on Ed to whip him. When dey told him to open de door, he heard one of 'em say, "Shoot him time he gets de door open." "Well," he says to 'em, "Wait till I can light de lamp." Den he got de gun what I had left loaded, got down on his knees and stuck it through a log and pull de trigger. He hit Newt Dobbs in de stomach and kilt him.

He couldn't stay round Burleson any more, so he come to Mr. Nelson and got 'nough money to get to Pine Bluff, Arkansas. The Ku Klux got bad sure 'nough den and went to killin' niggers and white folks, too.

I married Kizi Drumgoole. Reverend W. C. Northcross perform de ceremony. Dere weren't nobody dere but de witness and me and Kizi. I had three sons, but all of 'em is dead 'ceptin' one and dat's Hugh. He got seven chillens.

CONCLUSION

A society such as that of the Old South, bound together by slaveholding but divided by geography, economy, race, class, and a variety of circumstances, appeared differently to different contemporaries and appears differently to different historians in each generation. It was to be expected that so complex a reality would inspire contrary interpretations and emphases: the complexity itself is about all that everyone can agree on.

Yet, a certain unity imposes itself even upon the most resistant and skeptical historians. The South had interests enough and cultural distinctiveness enough for at least a portion of its social, economic, and political leaders to be willing to risk war with the North. In themselves, these interests, this distinctiveness, this political impulse, hardly constitute a different and separate civilization, however that elusive word may be defined. But they do suggest the reason that so many, then and now, have thought so. And they do, in themselves, add up to the fascinating story of a way of life.

The most intrusive fact about the Old South remains slavery. Everywhere one turns and everything one touches has borne its marks. The proud and powerful old families derived their income from slave labor and lived in intimate relationship to their black slaves. The yeomen and poor whites, however far removed from the center of the system, could not escape the influences, for good or ill, of slaveholders or slaves or the exigencies of the slave system.

The South, in any case, went to war in the famous words of the Vice-President of the Confederacy, as the cornerstone of its constitution. However closely one judges the myth of the Old South to have corresponded to the reality, the defeat of the Confederacy guaranteed that the myth, if anything, would be embellished and would grow stronger. At the core of that myth stood the planters, their ladies, their slaves, and their poorer neighbors—stood, that is, the plantation world. And the debate over what manner of men the plantation produced is likely to remain with us.

11 KENNETH M. STAMPP

what caused the civil war?

As early as the summer of 1787, when the Constitutional Convention was meeting in Philadelphia, James Madison observed signs of disagreement between the slaveholding planters of the South and the commercial capitalists of the North. On several occasions questions such as slavery, the slave trade, the counting of slaves in apportioning representation in the lower house of Congress, and the regulation of commerce were subjects of animated debate. However, these sectional controversies were then only minor irritants and did not seriously divide the Convention. Few delegates seemed to be much concerned about whether the Union could "endure permanently half slave and half free." Instead, most Northern and Southern conservatives united to secure the ratification of the new Constitution over the opposition that existed in both sections. In the years that followed, there were other occasions when some of the men of property, North and South, perceived their common interests and acted in unison.

But eventually their conflicting interests, first seen by Madison, reached such dimensions as to overshadow all else. During the 1790s Southern agrarians became Jeffersonian Republicans in order to fight Hamilton's policies, which appeared to enrich only the Northern merchants, manufacturers, bondholders, and speculators. Even then petitions from Northern anti-slavery societies provoked angry protests from congressmen representing South Carolina and Georgia. At no time thereafter did the North lack a party, or at least an organized political faction, pledged to a legislative program that suited its economic needs—tariffs to protect manufacturers, navigation acts to encourage merchants and shipowners, subsidies to aid New England fishermen, and appropriations to finance internal improvements. Hardly a session of Congress passed without the slavery issue being raised in some form. Given the population trends—the rapid growth of the North in comparison with the slow progress of the South—it seemed to be only a matter of time until Northerners would have complete control of the federal government.

Southerners, seeing their power declining, their interests in jeopardy, and their institutions under attack, soon began to behave in the manner of a "conscious minority." They were convinced that something had to be done to keep the two great sections in political balance. Perhaps a "strict" construction of the Constitution would limit the danger by keeping federal power at a minimum. Perhaps a vigorous defense of "state rights" against "federal encroachments," even to the extreme of nullification, would save the South. If nothing else worked, perhaps secession and the formation of two confederacies would be the final solution.

These sectional differences carried the country through a series of paroxysmal crises. Missouri's petition for admission as a slave state first made slavery expansion a major issue, and it continued as such for the next forty years. South Carolina's attempt to nullify the Tariff of 1832 signified the persistence of economic antagonisms between North and South. During the 1830s, abolitionism, one of many reform movements that swept the North, became a permanently significant political force. The moral indictment of slavery, the fear of slave rebellions, and the desire for internal unity drove Southern leaders to a defense of slavery as a "positive good" and to violent action against all critics. In effect, they created an "intellectual blockade," a hostility to nineteenth-century liberal thought that matched the "unprogressive" nature of their agricultural economy.

To be sure, there were moderates in both sections who deplored "sectional agitation," who feared disunion and civil war, and who labored hard for compromise. With much difficulty they arranged sectional adjustments in 1820, in 1833, and again in 1850. But after each "settlement" a new crisis, more severe than the last, soon emerged. The final crisis began in 1854 with the introduction of the Kansas-Nebraska bill; it was climaxed by the election of Abraham Lincoln and the secession of the Deep South. This time the opponents of compromise controlled both sections, and in April, 1861, war finally came.

What caused the Civil War? Or, as some historians prefer to put it, how did the American people happen to get themselves into a war in 1861? Was this an "irrepressible conflict"? Why did compromise fail to save the Union and prevent war? Though historians have debated these questions for many years, they still are not in agreement.

what caused the civil war?

Six possible causes of the Civil War are presented here, together with extracts from documents that explain or illustrate each of them. Perhaps out of the confusion may come some light.

1. WAS IT THE AGGRESSIONS OF THE SLAVE POWER?

During the years of bitter sectional conflict that preceded the Civil War, Northern abolitionists, editors, and politicians repeatedly charged that the South—in fact, the entire country—was ruled by a ruthless "Slave Power." This Slave Power, well-organized and conspiratorial in its methods, consisted of the Southern slaveholding planters and political leaders who were determined to convert the whole United States into a nation of masters and slaves. Advancing from one conquest to another, they imperiled the rights and liberties of every freeman. They shaped national policy to serve exclusively their own selfish ends. When, at last, the free states rebelled and elected Abraham Lincoln to the presidency, the Slave Power, unwilling to submit peacefully, attempted to destroy the Union and to establish a pro-slavery confederacy of its own. It was this, said Northern partisans, that caused the Civil War.

The Record of the Slave Power

After the Civil War the first generation of Northern historians generally agreed that the conflict resulted from the aggressions of the Slave Power. Among these historians was Henry Wilson of Massachusetts. Wilson, a "radical" Republican, was an active participant in the politics of that era, serving for many years as a United States Senator and as Vice-President in Grant's second administration until his death in 1875. The following extracts from his massive history of the period, written in the 1870s, will illustrate the severe indictment of the Slave Power which was typical of these sectional historians.[1]

God's Holy Word declares that man was doomed to eat his bread in the sweat of his face. History and tradition teach that the indolent, the crafty, and the strong, unmindful of human rights, have ever sought to evade this Divine decree by filching their bread from the constrained and unpaid toil of others. From inborn indolence, conjoined with avarice, pride, and lust of power, has sprung slavery in all its Protean forms. . . . Thus have

[1] Henry Wilson, *History of the Rise and Fall of the Slave Power in America*. (Boston: 1872–1877), 1:1–2, 165–66, 567; 2:174–75, 188, 406, 462–64, 534–35, 655–56, 666, 673–74, 703–4; 3:1–2.

grown and flourished caste and privilege, those deadly foes of the rights and well-being of mankind, which can exist only by despoiling the many for the benefit of the few.

American slavery reduced man, created in the Divine image, to property.... It made him a beast of burden in the field of toil, an outcast in social life, a cipher in the courts of law, and a pariah in the house of God. To claim himself, or to use himself for his own benefit or the benefit of wife or child, was deemed a crime. His master could dispose of his person at will, and of everything acquired by his enforced and unrequited toil.

This complete subversion of the natural rights of millions ... constituted a system antagonistic to the doctrines of reason and the monitions of conscience, and developed and gratified the most intense spirit of personal pride, a love of class distinctions, and the lust of dominion. Hence arose a commanding power, ever sensitive, jealous, proscriptive, dominating, and aggressive, which was recognized and fitly characterized as the Slave Power.

This slavery and this Slave Power, in their economical, social, moral, ecclesiastical, and political relations to the people and to the government, demoralizing the one and distracting the councils of the other, made up the vital issues of that "irrepressible conflict" which finally culminated in a civil war....

In the Missouri struggle freedom and slavery grappled for the mastery. Freedom lost, and slavery won. Freedom became timid, hesitating, yielding; slavery became bolder, more aggressive, and more dominating. Freedom retreated from one lost position to another; slavery advanced from conquest to conquest. Several years of unresisted despotism of the Slave Power followed this consummation of the Missouri compromise. The dark spirit of slavery swayed the policy of the republic.... Institutions of learning, benevolence, and religion, political organizations, and public men bent in unresisting submission before this all-conquering despotism, whose aggressive advances became more resistless, as its successive victories became more complete. But amid this general defection and complete surrender there were a few who kept the faith of the fathers, and firmly and bravely adhered to the doctrines of human rights....

[Then] the startling issues growing out of the Texas plot, the increasing aggressions of the Slave Power, brought the various questions pertaining to slavery to the hearts and homes of hundreds of thousands who had heretofore given little heed to abolition movements. They broadened and deepened the public interest, so that the conflicts of opinion and the adoption of policies passed, in a large degree, from the arena and control of antislavery societies to the wider domain of general debate and political combinations.... And thus the subject which had been discussed only by the few became the theme of the many, and that which had been confined to scattered circles overspread the land....

The years intervening between the opening of negotiations for the annexation of Texas in 1843 and the close of the Presidential election in 1852 have no parallel for the intensity, variety, and disastrous results of the slavery struggle. During those years the successful attempt was made to annex the foreign nation of Texas to the United States; the war with Mexico was fought; vast accessions of territory were secured, and the effort to devote them to freedom was made and failed; the Fugitive Slave Law was enacted and mercilessly executed; the misnamed compromise measures proposed by the slave-masters were adopted and accepted as a "finality" by the conventions of the great national parties; while the crowning act of those years of disaster and infamy was the indorsement by the people of this whole series of aggressions by the triumphant election of Franklin Pierce, whose whole public and partisan career had ever been fully and even ostentatiously committed to the purposes and plans of the Slave Power. . . .

These persistent efforts of the propagandists in behalf of slavery could not but fix attention upon it as the cause of all these constant and disturbing movements, while it challenged investigation anew into the merits of a system for which such efforts were made and such sacrifices called for. Especially did this result from the relinquishment by its defenders of the former arguments that slavery was an entailed evil, for which the present generations were not responsible—a temporary evil, that carried within itself the seeds of its own destruction, and which must soon pass away in the presence and by the workings of free institutions. The new dogmas that slavery was a good, and not an evil; that it was not temporary, but to be permanent; that it was not sectional, but national; and that the Constitution carried it wherever it went, presented the whole subject in a new light. Many felt that it must be reexamined, and that the arguments and considerations that formerly reconciled could satisfy them no longer. . . .

The determined purpose of the Slave Power to make slavery the predominating national interest was never more clearly revealed than by the proposed repeal of the Missouri compromise. This was a deliberate and direct assault upon freedom. Many, indeed, under the pleas of fraternity and loyalty to the Union, palliated and apologized for this breach of faith; but the numbers were increasing every hour, as the struggle progressed, who could no longer be deceived by these hollow pretences. They could not close their eyes to the dangers of the country, and they were compelled to disavow what was so manifestly wrong, and to disconnect themselves from men and parties who were making so little concealment of their nefarious purposes and of their utter profligacy of principle. . . .

The Kansas-Nebraska Act was no mere abstraction. Though its most prominent and persistent advocates, in their noisy clamor and claim in its behalf, pleaded chiefly its vindication of the principle of local self-government, it soon became apparent that its ultimate purpose occupied a far higher place in their regard. Slavery, and not popular sovereignty, was the object aimed at. . . . Calculating that this action of Congress and the close contiguity of slaveholding Missouri, with such co-operation as the known sympathy of the other slaveholding States would afford, could easily throw into Kansas a sufficient population to give to slavery the necessary preponderance, the slave propagandists regarded their victory in the halls of legislation as tantamount to the final success of their deep-laid schemes. . . . When, therefore, Congress had been dragooned into the adoption of the Kansas-Nebraska Act, with its newly invented and much vaunted doctrine of popular sovereignty, it was supposed . . . that it was only a question of time when Kansas should become a slave State. . . . But they miscalculated. They did not fully comprehend the forces which freedom had at command, nor the purposes of Providence concerning the nation. . . .

The purpose to make Kansas a free State and the systematized efforts to carry that purpose into effect mark an important era in the progress of the slavery struggle. It was a deliberate and successful stand made by the friends of freedom against the aggressions of the Slave Power. . . . But it was a purpose that foretokened a fearful contest, fierce encounters, and bloody strifes. . . .

When the prohibition of slavery embodied in the Missouri compromise was repealed, it was declared to be the intent to leave the people of Kansas and Nebraska "perfectly free to form and regulate their domestic institutions in their own way, subject only to the Constitution of the United States." But this was a pretext, a device, a trick. The slavemasters who believed that the Constitution carried slavery into the Territories used this artifice as a temporary expedient to secure the overthrow of the principle of its prohibition, and to open a vast Territory to its polluting touch. . . . The Dred Scott decision and the Lecompton constitution . . . revealed the real character of the "sovereignty" involved, or, rather, it made apparent the utter insincerity of all pretensions of regard for the popular will, and the shameless duplicity that characterized the course of those who conceived and engineered that astounding fraud. . . .

During the closing days of the rule of the Slave Power in America madness seemed to rule in the counsels of the Southern leaders. . . . As if assured that they had but to speak to be heeded, had but to command to be obeyed, they seemed to regard the results already achieved as but stepping-stones to a higher position and more complete control, the advances already made as only affording a new base of operations. . . . Not satisfied with past concessions, the obliteration of the landmarks of freedom and the refusal of all discrimination in behalf of human rights, they seemed resolved that slavery should become emphatically national, that no part of the Republic should be beyond the reach of its encroachments, . . . and that the flag of the Union should wave only over the land of the slave. . . .

The proscription, lawlessness, and barbarism of slavery were the necessary conditions of its existence. Its essential injustice and inevitable cruelties, its malign and controlling influences upon society and the state, its violence of word and conduct, its unfriendliness to freedom of thought and its repression of free speech . . . , its stern and bloody defiance of all who questioned its action or resisted its behests, were specially manifest during the closing years of its terrible reign. Statutes, however severe, and courts, however servile, were not enough. The mob was sovereign. Vigilance committees took the law into their own hands, prompting and executing the verdicts and decisions of self-constituted judges and self-selected juries. Merchants on lawful business, travellers for pleasure, teachers and day-laborers, all felt alike the proscriptive ban. A merciless vindictiveness prevailed, and held its stern and pitiless control over the whole South. The privileges and immunities of citizenship were worthless, and the law afforded no protection. Southern papers were filled with accounts of the atrocities perpetrated, and volumes alone could contain descriptions of all that transpired during their reign of terror. . . .

The Democratic national convention of 1860 was memorable . . . because it marked an epoch in the history of the Slave Power. It was the culmination of the irrepressible conflict, the turning-point in the tide of oppression which had flooded the land for so many years, and which from that hour began to subside. . . . The Slave Power went into that convention master of the situation, with the prestige of almost uninterrupted victories on its banners, in possession of every department of the government . . . ; and yet it recklessly abandoned its vantage-ground, threw away the sceptre it had so long and so remorselessly wielded, and with suicidal hands began the work of its own destruction.

The . . . question that distracted and at length divided the convention, was that of nominating Mr. Douglas as the Democratic candidate in the pending canvass. His acknowledged ability, his prominence in the party, his leadership in the Kansas-Nebraska struggle, his long and loudly proclaimed Southern proclivities, all pointed to him as the Democratic standard-bearer in the coming strife. But with all his devotion to Southern interests, his record was not sufficiently clean to satisfy their exacting demands. He had faltered, and for once had failed to come up to their full measure of fealty upon the Lecompton issue; and it became an unpardonable sin, not to be forgotten or forgiven. Though consistency, the instinct of self-preservation, and a wise regard for the preservation of his party's ascendency in the Northern States demanded this course, Mr. Douglas was made the victim of the most unrelenting opposition, and that from the very men for whom he had made the greatest sacrifices. . . . That they were unwisely violent, that their vaulting ambition o'erleaped itself, and that they themselves inflicted fatal wounds upon their own cause, which no opposition then organized could have done, are matters of general belief, if not of historic record. . . .

The canvass . . . closed on the 6th of November by the election of Abraham Lincoln. . . . The slavemasters . . . fully comprehended the real significance of the result. They saw how much freedom had gained and how much slavery had lost. For more than two generations they had dictated principles, shaped policies, made Presidents and cabinets, judges of the Supreme Court, Senators, and Representatives. Now, for the first time, they had been beaten, the charm of invincibility was broken, the prestige of success was gone. Their cherished policy of slavery-expansion had been arrested, and their new dogma of slavery-protection had been forever defeated. . . . And slavery in the States, hedged in, surrounded, and pressed upon by the growing numbers and increasing vigor of free institutions and by the combined forces of advancing civilization and the manifest providences of God, must inevitably be put in process of ultimate, though it might be gradual extinction.

... [Hence southern leaders,] appealing to local interests, pandering to prejudices, painting in glowing colors the advantages of separation, ... pleading the State-rights theory that it was one of their reserved powers to withdraw at will from the Union, ... did not find it difficult to persuade the class of large slaveholders to make the rash experiment, and enter upon the perilous venture of revolution. Small slaveholders, too, and non-slaveholders even, confused by the blinding counsels and dominating influence of leaders they had been accustomed to follow, could not withstand the current, and were rapidly drifting into rebellion.

The Defensive South

Chauncey S. Boucher insists that there was no Slave Power Conspiracy, because the South was never united behind a political program. Most of the time, according to Boucher, Southerners were on the defensive against the aggressive action of the abolitionists.[2]

From most of the historical works covering the ante-bellum period one gains the impression that the dominant factor, controlling the course of events, is found in a powerful, united, well-organized, aggressive slavocracy. ... It is the purpose of this monograph to examine the picture in detail and see whether it is true to facts. Was the South united throughout the ante-bellum period in its position on big questions of policy and action? Was it normally aggressive, or was it on the defensive?

Those historians who see in the ante-bellum south only an aggressive slavocracy admit that a primary requisite for that section to have been on the aggressive would seem to have been unity of purpose and action. ... One does not read very far in newspaper files or correspondence collections of the ante-bellum period in the south before one encounters frequent complaints and laments, registered in all seriousness, that such a situation—unity of purpose and action politically—did not exist. Party divisions were not mere surface affairs; party ties did not hang loosely, and party allegiance was not renounced lightly. Indeed, the true state of affairs seems to have been that party divisions cut deeply through the body politic; party ties were strong, and party allegiance was renounced only under most abnormal and forceful circumstances. Personal political feuds between individuals and groups were as

[2] Chauncey S. Boucher, "*In Re* That Aggressive Slavocracy," *Mississippi Valley Historical Review*, 8 (1921), 13–79. Reprinted by permission of the *Mississippi Valley Historical Review*.

bitter and persistent as in any other section of the union. . . . Even in congress the south did not present a united front which might have enabled it to make demands with assurance of having them met; however, there was a nearer approach to unity of purpose and action among southern men in congress than among their constituents at home, the section over. It was difficult enough to get the people of a single state to agree upon and take a definite stand, as is witnessed by the history of South Carolina from 1828 to 1861; and as for getting several states to agree even upon an interpretation of the situation at any given time, to say nothing of concerted action, it seemed to be utterly hopeless. . . .

The ante-bellum period was characterized, in South Carolina and in the south generally, by waves of excitement. An examination of any one of these will reveal the same general story: much talk about necessity of action—of united action; but it never materializes. Always there are bitter party feuds, distrust of leaders, complaints of lack of proper leadership, et cetera, *ad infinitum.*

The story of the whig party in the south is a forceful proof of the lack of unity. When the "peculiar institution" was assailed from the north, of course the state-rights whigs came to its defense. As it was early seen that the northern whigs tended to be more actively hostile to slavery than were the northern democrats, the southern whigs were reminded of the fact and taunted with being traitors to their own interests. Quite naturally, perhaps, then, as long as the alliance between the southern and the northern wings of the party was continued, the southern whigs were more moderate in their defense of slavery than were the southern democrats. Throughout the struggle in congress over the gag resolutions the compact front of the south was broken again and again quite perceptibly by whig votes. The same was true of the votes in the house on the election of a speaker and in the senate on the ratification of appointments made by the president, when objection was raised that the man under consideration was an antislavery man. Indeed, through the eighteen-forties many southern whigs denounced the democrats for eternally dragging forth the slavery question to cover up the real issue, whatever it might be, and to stir up agitation. When the national whig party became irreparably split over the slavery question, it did not mean that from that time on there was a united south with a single purpose and a single policy. Though southern whigs agreed to disagree with their northern party brethren they could not agree among themselves nor with the southern democrats on a position to be held against the common foe; and, though the national democratic party continued its existence down to 1860, there was marked disagreement in the southern ranks of that party as to policy. . . .

It was the irony of fate that the southern statesman who saw, perhaps more clearly than any other, the necessity of southern unity for defense through the maintenance of the "true Republican principles," and who strove earnestly to promote such unity of action in support of basic principles, was the very one who perhaps caused more division and bitterness of strife within the section than any other man. No man ever had followers more devoted and enemies more bitter among the "people at home" than John C. Calhoun.

Instead of a united, aggressive slavocracy, one finds evidence at almost every turn that the true picture is quite the reverse, and that keen students of public affairs realized full well that cross-purposes and disorganization prevailed. Again and again, throughout the period from 1835 to 1860, complaint was registered that, vainly putting its trust in national parties, without unanimity of opinion either as to the dangers that menaced or the remedies to be applied, with no distinct issue, no certain aim, no wise plan of statesmanship, no well-defined ideas of what it might have to fear, to hope, or to do, the south was dragged along, ingloriously enough, by the fatal delusions of national partyism, a source of profit to its southern betrayers and a spoil and a mockery to its northern enemies. Though the opinion was frequently offered that if united the south would be invincible, at least in the protection of its rights, it was almost as frequently admitted that it seemed impossible to get the section to unite even for self-defense, let alone for a positive or an aggressive program, within the union. Hence it was that toward the end of the period some sincere believers in the preservation of the "Constitutional Union" as the best policy for both sections began to hope for secession by a single state as the only development that could bring about southern unity; and many of these men admitted at the same time that they feared that such unity would last but a short time beyond the formation of a southern confederacy, and that disorganization and disintegration would soon follow.

When the historian finds that some southerners boasted of how they might control the nation if they could but secure unity among southern statesmen and politicians, and that individuals or groups urged this item or that one for a southern program and boasted of the wonders it would work, is the historian to interpret them literally? In most of such instances were they not in the mood of a small boy going down a dark alley, whistling as loud as he can to keep up his courage? Just as the boy's whistling is so forced and strained that he hits many false notes, so the boasting of southerners gives one the impression that it was forced, unnatural, not sincere, and hence false notes were struck.

When the south struggled for power in national councils, was it for political strength to be used aggressively? Did the south have a positive program to be put through in its own interest to the exclusion of, or the positive injury of, the other sections? Did not the south want political strength mainly or simply to block and stop the aggressions of its opponents? Did it ask anything more than to be let alone and not to be made to bear the burden of legislation injurious to itself alone? . . .

. . . From [the time of the Mexican War] . . . until 1861 the charge of aggression was hurled with ever increasing vigor against the south by the abolitionists, and the writer believes that the persistence of the charge from the end of the war to the present in historical works is due to the fact that most of these works have been based on sources which, in the final analysis, are really of abolitionist origin. The writer believes that the south, instead of being the aggressor, was on the defensive throughout almost the entire ante-bellum period; and that so far from having the unity which was a primary necessity for an offensive campaign, the south could not often, nor for long, agree upon even a defensive program, down to the very eve of the civil war. Individuals at times took a stand which may perhaps best be termed "aggressively defensive." The well-known individualism of the southerner, however, militated against united action to the extent that there was no organized, unified aggression.

2. WAS IT THE ISSUE OF STATE SOVEREIGNTY VS. NATIONALISM?

Was the Union older than the states? Or was it the other way around? Did the framers of the Constitution create a perpetual Union, a truly national government with substantial powers? Or did they create a mere voluntary federation of sovereign states? These questions were almost continuously debated from the birth of the republic to the end of the Civil War. There were impressive and persuasive arguments on both sides. The state-rights argument was developed by Jefferson and Madison in their famous Kentucky and Virginia Resolutions, by Calhoun to support his doctrine of Nullification, and by Southern-rights men to justify secession. The nationalist argument was used at various times to prove the constitutionality of such measures as a national banking act, a protective tariff, federal aid for internal improvements, and federal exclusive of slavery from the Territories. In effect, the Civil War settled the issue of state sovereignty vs. nationalism by military force.

The Constitutional Interpretation

Post-Civil War Southern historians rarely admitted that slavery was a fundamental cause of the Civil War. Instead, they found the real cause in conflicting interpretations of the Constitution. One of the most ardent defenders of the "Lost Cause" was Alexander H. Stephens of Georgia, who had served as Vice President of the Confederacy. As he saw it, the South seceded to prevent the subversion of the rights of the states, not to save slavery. A few passages from the Introduction of 1868 to his history of the Civil War neatly summarize his point of view.[3]

---

[3] *A Constitutional View of the Late War between the States* (Philadelphia, 1868–70), 1: Introduction, 9–12.

It is a postulate, with many writers of this day, that the late War was the result of two opposing ideas, or principles, upon the subject of African Slavery. Between these, according to their theory, sprung the "irrepressible conflict," in principle, which ended in the terrible conflict of arms. Those who assume this postulate, and so theorize upon it, are but superficial observers.

That the War had its origin in *opposing principles,* which, in their action upon the *conduct of men,* produced the ultimate collision of arms, may be assumed as an unquestionable fact. But the opposing principles which produced these results in physical action were of a very different character from those assumed in the postulate. They lay in the organic Structure of the Government of the States. The conflict in principle arose from different and opposing ideas as to the nature of what is known as the General Government. The contest was between those who held it to be strictly Federal in its character, and those who maintained that it was thoroughly National. It was a strife between the principles of Federation, on the one side, and Centralism, or Consolidation, on the other.

Slavery, so called, was but *the question* on which these antagonistic principles, which had been in conflict, from the beginning, on diverse *other questions,* were finally brought into actual and active collision with each other on the field of battle.

Some of the strongest Anti-slavery men who ever lived were on the side of those who opposed the Centralizing principles which led to the War. Mr. Jefferson was a striking illustration of this, and a prominent example of a large class of both sections of the country, who were, most unfortunately, brought into hostile array against each other. No more earnest or ardent devotee to the emancipation of the Black race, upon humane, rational and Constitutional principles, ever lived than he was. . . . And yet Mr. Jefferson . . . is well known to have been utterly opposed to the Centralizing principle, when *first* presented, on *this question,* in the attempt to impose conditions and restrictions on the State of Missouri, when she applied for admission into the Union, under the Constitution. He looked upon the movement as a political manoeuvre to bring this delicate subject . . . into the Federal Councils, with a view, by its agitation in a forum where it did not properly belong, to strengthen the Centralists in their efforts to revive their doctrines, which had been so signally defeated on so many other questions. The first sound of their movements on this question fell upon his ear as a "fire bell at night." . . .

It is the fashion of many writers of the day to class all who opposed the Consolidationists in *this,* their *first* step, as well as all who opposed them in all their subsequent steps, on *this question,* with what they style the Pro-Slavery Party. No greater injustice could be done any public men, and no greater violence be done to the truth of History, than such a classification. Their opposition to that measure, or kindred subsequent ones, sprung from no attachment to Slavery; but . . . from their strong convictions that the Federal Government had no rightful or Constitutional control or jurisdiction over such questions; and that no such action, as that proposed upon them, could be taken by Congress without destroying the elementary and vital principles upon which the Government was founded.

By their acts, they did not identify themselves with the Pro-Slavery Party (for, in truth, no such Party had, at that time, or at any time in the History of the Country, any organized existence). They only identified themselves, or took position, with those who maintained the Federative character of the General Government.

In 1850, for instance, what greater injustice could be done any one, or what greater violence could be done the truth of History, than to charge Cass, Douglas, Clay, Webster, and Fillmore, to say nothing of others, with being advocates of Slavery, or following in the lead of the Pro-Slavery Party, because of their support of what were called the adjustment measures of that year?

Or later still, out of the million and a half, and more, of the votes cast, in the Northern States, in 1860, against Mr. Lincoln, how many, could it, with truth, be said, were in favor of Slavery, or even that legal subordination of the Black race to the White, which existed in the Southern States?

Perhaps, not one in ten thousand! It was a subject, with which, they were thoroughly convinced, they had nothing to do, and could have nothing to do, under the terms of the Union, by which the States were Confederated, except to carry out, and faithfully perform, all the obligations of the Constitutional Compact, in regard to it.

They simply arrayed themselves against that Party which had virtually hoisted the banner of Consolidation. The contest, so commenced, which ended in the War, was, indeed, a contest between opposing principles; but not such as bore upon the policy or impolicy of African Subordination. They were principles deeply underlying all considerations of that sort. They involved the very nature and organic Structure of the Government itself. The conflict, on *this question* of Slavery, in the Federal Councils, from the beginning, was not a contest between the advocates or opponents of that peculiar Institution, but a contest, as stated before, between the supporters of a strictly Federative Government, on the one side, and a thoroughly National one, on the other.

The State Sovereignty Argument

After unanimously adopting an Ordinance of Secession on December 20, 1860, the South Carolina convention issued a "Declaration of the Causes of Secession." The following extracts from that document present both the argument which "proved" the sovereignty of the states and evidence that the Northern states had violated the federal "compact," that is, the Constitution.[4]

---

[4] Frank Moore, ed., *The Rebellion Record* (New York, 1861–68), 1:3–4.

In the year 1765, that portion of the British Empire embracing Great Britain undertook to make laws for the Government of that portion composed of the thirteen American Colonies. A struggle for the right of self-government ensued, which resulted, on the 4th of July, 1776, in a Declaration, by the Colonies, "that they are, and of right ought to be, FREE AND INDEPENDENT STATES . . ."

In pursuance of this Declaration of Independence, each of the thirteen States proceeded to exercise its separate sovereignty; adopted for itself a Constitution, and appointed officers for the administration of government in all its departments—Legislative, Executive and Judicial. For purposes of defence they united their arms and their counsels; and, in 1778, they entered into a League known as the Articles of Confederation, whereby they agreed to intrust the administration of their external relations to a common agent, known as the Congress of the United States, expressly declaring, in the first article, "that each State retains its sovereignty, freedom, and independence, and every power, jurisdiction, and right which is not, by this Confederation, expressly delegated to the United States in Congress assembled." . . .

In 1787, Deputies were appointed by the States to revise the Articles of Confederation; and on the 17th September, 1787, these Deputies recommended, for the adoption of the States, the Articles of Union, known as the Constitution of the United States.

The parties to whom this Constitution was submitted were the several sovereign States; they were to agree or disagree, and when nine of them agreed, the compact was to take effect among those concurring; and the General Government as the common agent, was then to be invested with their authority. . . .

By this Constitution, certain duties were imposed upon the several States, and the exercise of certain of their powers was restrained. . . . But . . . an amendment was added, which declared that the powers not delegated to the United States by the Constitution, nor prohibited by it to the States, are reserved to the States respectively, or to the people. On the 23d May, 1788, South Carolina, by a Convention of her people, passed an ordinance assenting to this Constitution, and afterwards altered her own Constitution to conform herself to the obligations she had undertaken.

Thus was established, by compact between the States, a Government with defined objects and powers, limited to the express words of the grant. This limitation left the whole remaining mass of power subject to the clause reserving it to the States or the people, and rendered unnecessary any specification of reserved rights. We hold that the Government thus established is subject to the two great principles asserted in the Declaration of Independence; and we hold further, that the mode of its formation subjects it to a third fundamental principle, namely, the law of compact. We maintain that in every compact between two or more parties, the obligation is mutual; that the failure of one of the contracting parties to perform a material part of the agreement, entirely releases the obligation of the other; and that, where no arbiter is provided, each party is remitted to his own judgment to determine the fact of failure, with all its consequences.

In the present case, that fact is

established with certainty. We assert that fourteen of the States have deliberately refused for years past to fulfill their constitutional obligations. . . . Thus the constitutional compact has been deliberately broken and disregarded by the non-slaveholding States; and the consequence follows that South Carolina is released from her obligation. . . .

We affirm that . . . [the] ends for which this Government was instituted have been defeated, and the Government itself has been destructive of them by the action of the non-slaveholding States. Those States have assumed the right of deciding upon the propriety of our domestic institutions; and have denied the rights of property established in fifteen of the States and recognized by the Constitution; they have denounced as sinful the institution of Slavery; they have permitted the open establishment among them of societies, whose avowed object is to disturb the peace of and eloin the property of the citizens of other States. They have encouraged and assisted thousands of our slaves to leave their homes; and those who remain, have been incited by emissaries, books, and pictures, to servile insurrection. . . .

On the 4th of March next . . . [a sectional] party will take possession of the Government. It has announced that the South shall be excluded from the common territory, that the Judicial tribunal shall be made sectional, and that a war must be waged against Slavery until it shall cease throughout the United States.

The guarantees of the Constitution will then no longer exist; the equal rights of the States will be lost. The Slaveholding States will no longer have the power of self-government, or self-protection, and the Federal Government will have become their enemy. . . .

We, therefore, the people of South Carolina, by our delegates in Convention assembled, appealing to the Supreme Judge of the world for the rectitude of our intentions, have solemnly declared that the Union heretofore existing between this State and the other States of North America is dissolved, and that the State of South Carolina has resumed her position among the nations of the world, as a separate and independent State, with full power to levy war, conclude peace, contract alliances, establish commerce, and to do all other acts and things which independent States may of right do.

The Nationalist Argument

In his first inaugural address, March 4, 1861, Abraham Lincoln denied that the rights of the Southern states had been or would be violated and warned secessionists that it would be his duty to "enforce the laws" throughout the Union. He also presented the nationalist argument that the Union was perpetual and that secession was rebellion. These extracts from his address relate specifically to this subject.[5]

---

[5] James D. Richardson, ed., *A Compilation of the Messages and Papers of the Presidents* (Washington, 1897), 6:5–12.

Apprehension seems to exist among the people of the Southern States that by the accession of a Republican Administration their property and their peace and personal security are to be endangered. There has never been any reasonable cause for such apprehension. Indeed, the most ample evidence to the contrary has all the while existed and been open to their inspection. It is found in nearly all the published speeches of him who now addresses you. . . .

I now reiterate these sentiments, and in doing so I only press upon the public attention the most conclusive evidence of which the case is susceptible that the property, peace, and security of no section are to be in any wise endangered by the now incoming Administration. I add, too, that all the protection which, consistently with the Constitution and the laws, can be given will be cheerfully given to all the States when lawfully demanded, for whatever cause—as cheerfully to one section as to another. . . .

It is seventy-two years since the first inauguration of a President under our National Constitution. During that period fifteen different and greatly distinguished citizens have in succession administered the executive branch of the Government. They have conducted it through many perils, and generally with great success. Yet, with all this scope of precedent, I now enter upon the same task for the brief constitutional term of four years under great and peculiar difficulty. A disruption of the Federal Union, heretofore only menaced, is now formidably attempted.

I hold that in contemplation of universal law and of the Constitution the Union of these States is perpetual. Perpetuity is implied, if not expressed, in the fundamental law of all national governments. It is safe to assert that no government proper ever had a provision in its organic law for its own termination. Continue to execute all the express provisions of our National Constitution, and the Union will endure forever, it being impossible to destroy it except by some action not provided for in the instrument itself.

Again: If the United States be not a government proper, but an association of States in the nature of contract merely, can it, as a contract, be peaceably unmade by less than all the parties who made it? One party to a contract may violate it—break it, so to speak—but does it not require all to lawfully rescind it?

Descending from these general principles, we find the proposition that in legal contemplation the Union is perpetual confirmed by the history of the Union itself. The Union is much older than the Constitution. It was formed, in fact, by the Articles of Association in 1774. It was matured and continued by the Declaration of Independence in 1776. It was further matured, and the faith of all the then thirteen States expressly plighted and engaged that it should be perpetual, by the Articles of Confederation in 1778. And finally, in 1787, one of the declared objects for ordaining and establishing the Constitution was *"to form a more perfect Union."*

But if destruction of the Union by one or by a part only of the States be lawfully possible, the Union is *less* perfect than before the Constitution, having lost the vital element of perpetuity.

It follows from these views that no State upon its own mere motion can lawfully get out of the Union, that *resolves* and *ordinances* to that effect are legally void, and that acts of violence within any State or States against the authority of the United States are insurrectionary or revolutionary, according to circumstances.

I therefore consider that in view of the Constitution and the laws, the Union is unbroken, and to the extent of my ability I shall take care, as the Constitution itself expressly enjoins upon me, that the laws of the Union be faithfully executed in all the States. Doing this I deem to be only a simple duty on my part, and I shall perform it so far as practicable unless my rightful masters, the American people, shall withhold the requisite means or in some authoritative manner direct the contrary. I trust this will not be regarded as a menace, but only as the declared purpose of the Union that it *will* constitutionally defend and maintain itself. . . .

Plainly the central idea of secession is the essence of anarchy. A majority held in restraint by constitutional checks and limitations, and always changing easily with deliberate changes of popular opinions and sentiments, is the only true sovereign of a free people. Whoever rejects it does of necessity fly to anarchy or to despotism. Unanimity is impossible. The rule of a minority, as a permanent arrangement, is wholly inadmissible; so that, rejecting the majority principle, anarchy or despotism in some form is all that is left. . . .

The Chief Magistrate derives all his authority from the people, and they have conferred none upon him to fix terms for the separation of the States. The people themselves can do this . . . if they choose, but the Executive as such has nothing to do with it. His duty is to administer the present Government as it came to his hands and to transmit it unimpaired by him to his successor. . . .

In *your* hands, my dissatisfied fellow-countrymen, and not in *mine*, is the momentous issue of civil war. The Government will not assail *you*. You can have no conflict without being yourselves the aggressors. *You* have no oath registered in heaven to destroy the Government, while *I* shall have the most solemn one to "preserve, protect, and defend it."

I am loath to close. We are not enemies, but friends. We must not be enemies. Though passion may have strained it must not break our bonds of affection. The mystic chords of memory, stretching from every battlefield and patriot grave to every living heart and hearthstone all over this broad land, will yet swell the chorus of the Union, when again touched, as surely they will be, by the better angels of our nature.

3. WAS IT ECONOMIC SECTIONALISM?

While it is true that man lives not by bread alone, it is also true that without bread man lives not at all. The considerable attention that individuals and societies give to material problems has caused many twentieth-century historians to place great emphasis upon economic forces in history. In seeking the causes of the Civil War one must consider the basic differences between the economies of the two great sections, the numerous practical issues upon which sectional leaders were divided. It was opposition to the protective tariff that drove South Carolina to the edge of rebellion in 1832; it was the fact that Southerners repeatedly blocked the passage of internal improvements (rivers and harbors) bills that caused many Northerners to denounce the Slave Power so violently; and it was the payment to various Northern interests of subsidies from the federal treasury that prompted many Southerners to "calculate the value of the Union." Slavery and slavery expansion were, after all, economic as well as moral problems. Sectional leaders, while expounding great moral and constitutional issues, were often simply disguising economic self-interest with a thin veneer of idealism.

The Irrepressible Conflict

The late Charles A. Beard has made the greatest single contribution to the economic interpretation of American history. When he applied his keen mind to an examination of the background of the Civil War, he came to the conclusion in 1927 that there had existed an "irrepressible conflict" between the static, agrarian, staple-producing South and the expanding, commercialized, industrializing North. The ultimate triumph of industry over agriculture—of North over South—he described as a "Second American Revolution." Here, in brief, is Beard's interpretation.[6]

Had the economic systems of the North and the South remained static or changed slowly without effecting immense dislocations in the social structure, the balance of power might have been maintained indefinitely by repeating the compensatory tactics of 1787, 1820, 1833, and 1850; keeping in this manner the inherent antagonisms within the bounds of diplomacy. But nothing was stable in the economy of the United States or in the moral sentiments associated with its diversities.

Within each section of the country, the necessities of the productive system were generating portentous results. The periphery of the industrial vortex of the Northeast was daily enlarging, agriculture in the Northwest was being steadily supplemented by manufacturing, and the area of virgin soil open to exploitation by planters was diminishing with rhythmic regularity—shifting with mechanical precision the weights which statesmen had to adjust in their efforts to maintain the equilibrium of peace. Within each of the three sections also occurred an increasing intensity of social concen-

---

[6] From Charles A. and Mary R. Beard, *The Rise of American Civilization* (New York, 1927), 2:3–10. Copyright 1933 by The Macmillan Company. Reprinted by permission of the publishers.

tration as railways, the telegraph, and the press made travel and communication cheap and almost instantaneous, facilitating the centripetal process that was drawing people of similar economic status and parallel opinions into cooperative activities....

As the years passed, the planting leaders of Jefferson's agricultural party insisted with mounting fervor that the opposition, first of the Whigs and then of the Republicans, was at bottom an association of interests formed for the purpose of plundering productive management and labor on the land. And with steadfast insistence they declared that in the insatiable greed of their political foes lay the source of the dissensions which were tearing the country asunder.

"There is not a pursuit in which man is engaged (agriculture excepted)," exclaimed Reuben Davis of Mississippi in 1860,

which is not demanding legislative aid to enable it to enlarge its profits and all at the expense of the primary pursuit of man–agriculture.... Those interests having a common purpose of plunder, have united and combined to use the government as the instrument of their operation and have thus virtually converted it into a consolidated empire. Now this combined host of interests stands arrayed against the agricultural states; and this is the reason of the conflict which like an earthquake is shaking our political fabric to its foundation....

With challenging directness, [Jefferson] Davis [of Mississippi] turned upon his opponents in the Senate and charged them with using slavery as a blind to delude the unwary:

What do you propose, gentlemen of the Free-Soil party? Do you propose to better the condition of the slave? Not at all. What then do you propose? You say you are opposed to the expansion of slavery.... Is the slave to be benefited by it? Not at all. It is not humanity that influences you in the position which you now occupy before the country.... It is that you may have an opportunity of cheating us that you want to limit slave territory within circumscribed bounds. It is that you may have a majority in the Congress of the United States and convert the Government into an engine of northern aggrandizement. It is that your section may grow in power and prosperity upon treasures unjustly taken from the South.... You desire to weaken the political power of the southern states; and why? Because you want, by an unjust system of legislation, to promote the industry of the New England states, at the expense of the people of South and their industry.

Such in the mind of Jefferson Davis, fated to be president of the Confederacy, was the real purpose of the party which sought to prohibit slavery in the territories; that party did not declare slavery to be a moral disease calling for the severe remedy of the surgeon; it merely sought to keep bondage out of the new states as they came into the Union—with one fundamental aim in view, namely, to gain political ascendancy in the government of the United States and fasten upon the country an economic policy that meant the exploitation of the South for the benefit of northern capitalism.

But the planters were after all fighting against the census returns, as the phrase of the day ran current. The amazing growth of northern industries, the rapid extension of railways, the swift expansion of foreign trade to the ends of the earth, the attachment of the farming regions of the West to the centers of manufacture and finance through transportation and credit, the destruction of state consciousness by migration, the alien invasion, the erection of new commonwealths in the Valley of Democracy, the nationalistic drive of interstate commerce, the increase of population in the North, and the southward pressure of the capitalistic glacier all conspired to assure the ultimate triumph of what the orators were fond of calling "the free labor system." This was a dynamic thrust far too powerful for planters operating in a limited territory with incompetent labor on soil of diminishing fertility. Those who swept forward with it, exulting in the approaching triumph of machine industry, warned the planters of their ultimate subjection.

To statesmen of the invincible forces recorded in the census returns, the planting opposition was a huge, compact, and self-conscious economic association bent upon political objects—the possession of the government of the United States, the protection of its interests against adverse legislation, dominion over the territories, and enforcement of the national fugitive slave law throughout the length and breadth of the land. No phrase was more often on the lips of northern statesmen than "the slave power." The pages of the Congressional Globe bristled with references to "the slave system" and its influence over the government of the country. But it was left for William H. Seward of New York to describe it with a fullness of familiar knowledge that made his characterization a classic.

Seward knew from experience that a political party was no mere platonic society engaged in discussing abstractions. "A party," he said,

is in one sense a joint stock association, in which those who contribute most direct the action and management of the concern. The slaveholders contributing in an overwhelming proportion to the capital strength of the Democratic party, they necessarily dictate and prescribe its policy. . . . The slaveholding class has become the governing power in each of the slaveholding states and it practically chooses thirty of the sixty-two members of the Senate, ninety of the two hundred and thirty-three members of the House of Representatives, and one hundred and five of the two hundred and ninety-five electors of the President and Vice-President of the United States.

Becoming still more concrete, Seward accused the President [James Buchanan] of being "a confessed apologist of the slave-property class." Examining the composition of the Senate, he found the slave-owning group in possession of all the important committees. Peering into the House of Representatives he discovered no impregnable bulwark of freedom there. Nor did respect for judicial ermine compel him to spare the Supreme Court. . . .

Seward then analyzed the civil service of the national government and could descry not a single person among the thousands employed in the post office, the treasury, and other great departments who was "false to the slaveholding interest." Under the spoils system, the dominion of the slavocracy extended into all branches of the federal administration. "The customs-houses and the public lands pour forth two golden streams—one into the elections to procure votes for the slaveholding class; and the other into the treasury to be enjoyed by those whom it shall see fit to reward with places in the public service." . . .

Having described the gigantic operating structure of the slavocracy, Seward drew with equal power a picture of the opposing system founded on "free labor." He surveyed the course of economy in the North—the growth of industry, the spread of railways, the swelling tide of European immigration, and the westward roll of free farmers—rounding out the country, knitting it together, bringing "these antagonistic systems" continually into closer contact. Then he uttered those fateful words which startled conservative citizens from Maine to California—words of prophecy which proved to be brutally true—"the irrepressible conflict."

This inexorable clash, he said, was not "accidental, unnecessary, the work of interested or fanatical agitators and therefore ephemeral." No. "It is an irrepressible conflict between opposing and enduring forces." The hopes of those who sought peace by appealing to slave owners to reform themselves were as chaff in a storm.

How long and with what success have you waited already for that reformation? Did any property class ever so reform itself? Did the patricians in old Rome, the noblesse or clergy in France? The landholders in Ireland? The landed aristocracy in England? Does the slave-holding class even seek to beguile you with such a hope? Has it not become rapacious, arrogant, defiant?

All attempts at compromise were "vain and ephemeral." There was accordingly but one supreme task before the people of the United States—the task of confounding and overthrowing "by one decisive blow the betrayers of the Constitution and freedom forever." . . .

Given an irrepressible conflict which could be symbolized in such unmistakable patterns by competent interpreters of opposing factions, a transfer of the issues from the forum to the field, from the conciliation of diplomacy to the decision of arms was bound to come. Each side obdurately bent upon its designs and convinced of its rectitude, by the fulfillment of its wishes precipitated events and effected distributions of power that culminated finally in the tragedy foretold by Seward.

Southern Grievances

Many Southerners were convinced that the North was growing rich through the economic exploitation of their section. As they saw it, this process was aided by the policies of the federal government. Sectional legislation, such as subsidies to merchants and manufacturers, took money from the pockets of the planters and farmers and transferred it to the pockets of Northern capitalists. In November 1860, Senator Robert Toombs of Georgia described the process in a speech before the legislature of his state.[7]

---

[7] Frank Moore, ed., *The Rebellion Record,* Supplement (New York: Van Nostrand, 1866), 1:362–68.

The instant the Government was organized, at the very first Congress, the Northern States evinced a general desire and purpose to use it for their own benefit, and to pervert its powers for sectional advantage, and they have steadily pursued that policy to this day. They demanded a monopoly of the business of ship-building, and got a prohibition against the sale of foreign ships to citizens of the United States, which exists to this day.

They demanded a monopoly of the coasting trade, in order to get higher freights than they could get in open competition with the carriers of the world. Congress gave it to them, and they yet hold this monopoly. And now, to-day, if a foreign vessel in Savannah offer to take your rice, cotton, grain, or lumber to New York, or any other American port, for nothing, your laws prohibit it, in order that Northern ship-owners may get enhanced prices for doing your carrying. This same shipping interest, with cormorant rapacity, have steadily burrowed their way through your legislative halls, until they have saddled the agricultural classes with a large portion of the legitimate expenses of their own business. We pay a million of dollars per annum for the lights which guide them into and out of your ports. We built and kept up, at the cost of at least another million a year, hospitals for their sick and disabled seamen, when they wear them out and cast them ashore. We pay half a million per annum to support and bring home those they cast away in foreign lands. They demand, and have received, millions of the public money to increase the safety of harbors, and lessen the danger of navigating our rivers. All of which expenses legitimately fall upon their business, and should come out of their own pockets, instead of a common treasury.

Even the fishermen of Massachusetts and New-England demand and receive from the public treasury about half a million of dollars per annum as a pure bounty on their business of catching cod-fish. The North, at the very first Congress, demanded and received bounties under the name of protection, for every trade, craft, and calling which they pursue, and there is not an artisan in brass, or iron, or wood, or weaver, or spinner in wool or cotton, or a calico maker, or iron-master, or a coal owner, in all the Northern or Middle States, who has not received what he calls the protection of his government on his industry to the extent of from fifteen to two hundred per cent from the year 1791 to this day. They will not strike a blow, or stretch a muscle, without bounties from the government. No wonder they cry aloud for the glorious Union. . . . By it they got their wealth; by it they levy tribute on honest labor. It is true . . . that the present tariff was sustained by an almost unanimous vote of the South; but it was a reduction—a reduction necessary from the plethora of the revenue; but the policy of the North soon made it inadequate to meet the public expenditure, by an enormous and profligate increase of the public expenditure; and at the last session of Congress they brought in and passed through the House the most atrocious tariff bill that ever was enacted, raising the present duties from twenty to two hundred and fifty per cent above the existing rates of duty. That bill now lies on the table of the Senate. It was a master stroke of abolition policy; it united cupidity to fanaticism, and thereby made a combination which has swept the country. There were thousands of protectionists in Pennsylvania, New Jersey, New York, and in New-England, who were not abolitionists. There were thousands of abolitionists who were free traders. The mongers brought them together upon a mutual surrender of their principles. The free-trade abolitionists became protectionists; the non-abolition protectionists became abolitionists. The result of this coalition was the infamous Morrill bill—the robber and the incendiary struck hands, and united in joint raid against the South.

Thus stands the account between the North and the South. Under its ordinary and most favorable action, bounties and protection to every interest and every pursuit in the North, to the extent of at least fifty millions per annum, besides the expenditure of at least sixty millions out of every seventy of the public expenditure among them, thus making the treasury a perpetual fertilizing stream to them and their industry, and a suction-pump to drain away our substance and parch up our lands.

Northern Grievances

Northerners did not agree. If their spokesmen are to be believed, every other economic group was sacrificed to the slaveholders of the South. A solid bloc of Southern votes defeated measure after measure introduced in Congress to advance the "free-labor" interests of the North. It was to increase this power of obstruction that Southerners sought to create additional slave states. Thus Northern leaders saw that there was a connection between the expansion of slavery and the curtailment of the economic prosperity of their section. Representative Joshua R. Giddings of Ohio, in a speech in the House, May 21, 1844, used this as an argument against the annexation of Texas. On July 14, 1846, after Texas had been annexed, he reminded his colleagues of his prediction. Extracts from these two speeches appear below.[8]

It is well known, Mr. Chairman, that, since the formation of this confederacy, there has been a supposed conflict between the interests of free labor and of slave labor, between the southern and the northern States. . . . This has given rise to a difference of policy in our national councils. I refer to the tariff in particular, as being a favorite measure of the North, while free trade is advocated more generally by the South. I refer also to our harbor improvements, and the improvement of our river navigation, as other measures in which the Northwest and West have felt great inter-

[8] Joshua R. Giddings, *Speeches in Congress* (Boston, 1853), 104–5, 254–57.

est, and to which the South have been constantly opposed. But so equally balanced has been the political power between these opposing interests, that for five years past our lake commerce has been entirely abandoned; and such were the defects of the tariff, that for many years our revenues were unequal to the support of government

By the fixed order of nature's law, our population at the North has increased so much faster than it has in the slave States, that under the late census the North and West hold the balance of political power; and at the present session, we have passed through this body a bill for the protection of our lake and river commerce, which awaits the action of the Senate to become a law. But let us admit Texas, and we shall place the balance of power in the hands of the Texans. They, with the southern States, will control the policy and the destiny of this nation; our tariff will then be held at the will of the Texan advocates of free trade. Are our friends of the North prepared to deliver over this policy to the people of Texas? Are the liberty-loving democrats of Pennsylvania ready to give up the tariff? To strike off all protection from the articles of iron and coal and other productions of that State, in order to purchase a slave-market for their neighbors . . . ?

I do not argue to the policy of protecting our American manufactures. I only say, that at this time, New England and the free States generally are in favor of it, while the slave States are equally opposed to it. And I ask, are the mechanics and manufactures of the North prepared to abandon their employments, in order that slave-markets may be established in Texas, and a brisk traffic in the bodies, the flesh and blood of our southern population may be maintained? Are the farmers of the West, of Ohio, Indiana, and Illinois, prepared to give up the sale of their beef, pork, and flour, in order to increase the profits of those who raise children for sale, and deal in the bodies of women? Are the free States prepared to suspend their harbor and river improvements for the purpose of establishing this slave-trade with Texas, and to perpetuate slavery therein?

. . . .

While on the subject of vindicating myself, I will refer to another important event which lately occurred in this hall. I refer to the repeal of the tariff of 1842. While speaking upon the annexation of Texas, on the 21st May, 1844, . . . I had endeavored to caution our friends against this disastrous result at a time when the vote of Pennsylvania might have saved the tariff of 1842, protected her interest in iron and coal, and saved many of her people from that distress and ruin which now awaits them.

It is now more than two years since I declared to this House and the country, that if Texas were admitted, "our tariff would be held at the will of Texan advocates of free trade." . . . The . . . bill to repeal the tariff of 1842 . . . was carried through the Senate by a majority of only one vote, while both Senators from Texas voted for it. Thus was my prediction most amply fulfilled. As I have already remarked, I then felt that the annexation of Texas was to determine the fate of northern industry. I regarded that as the time for the friends of free labor to rally in behalf of northern interests. But, Sir, opposition to that measure proved unavailing. The resolutions annexing Texas were passed. Her representatives took their seats on this floor; and the first important vote given by them was to strike down the most vital interests of Pennsylvania, of New Jersey, New York, and New England, as well as of the northwestern States; for I regarded the interest of those States as much involved as I do those of New England. I do not, in these remarks, charge southern men with inconsistency. I have no doubt that the cotton-growing interest, separately considered, may be benefited by free trade. It is opposed to all the other great interests of the country. In order to strike down the industry of the North, they must have the numerical force. To obtain this, they must extend the slave-holding territory. . . . Sir, their political power was extended, and we now see the consequences. The people of the free States will soon feel its weight, and will realize the loss they have sustained by their inactivity.

I would not impugn the motives or the judgment of northern whigs, who hold out to their constituents the hope that they may by their political efforts regain the ascendency, and restore the lost rights of the free States. I may, however, be permitted to say, that when they shall have watched the operations of the slave power as long and as carefully as I have; when they shall have made themselves as familiar with its influences, its designs, and the agencies used to effect its ulterior objects, they will change their views. . . . I should fail to express the solemn convictions of my heart if I were not to say, in the most emphatic terms, that the rights and the interests of the free States have been sacrificed; and will not be regained until the North shall be awakened to its interests, its honor, and to its political duties. . . .

4. WAS IT THE WORK OF IRRESPONSIBLE AGITATORS?

Partisan propaganda is not noted for its accuracy, and the propaganda disseminated by sectional leaders before the Civil War was no exception. Northern abolitionists probably exaggerated the physical cruelties inflicted by Southern masters upon their slaves. Southern "fire-eaters" doubtless distorted the true character of Northern "Yankees." Politicians in both sections kept the country in constant turmoil and whipped up popular emotions for the selfish purpose of winning elections. Irresponsible agitators generated hatreds and passions that made the rational settlement of sectional differences almost impossible, and thus encouraged an appeal to arms. Was it this that caused the Civil War? Some conservatives of the 1860s thought so, and some present-day so-called "revisionist" historians think so, too.

A Blundering Generation

Every generation of statesmen makes decisions that seem stupid and irrational—blundering—to later generations. But the historian James G. Randall apparently believed that pre-Civil War political leaders were unusually incompetent, that their acts and decisions were grotesque and abnormal. Their exaggeration of sectional differences, their creation of fictitious issues (such as slavery expansion) created a crisis that was highly artificial and precipitated a needless war. The following extracts from Randall's essay, "A Blundering Generation," published in 1940, illustrate his position.[9]

In the present vogue of psychiatry, individual mental processes and behavior have been elaborately studied. Psychiatry for a nation, however, is still in embryo, though it is much the fashion to have discussions of mass behaviorism, public opinion, pressure groups, thought patterns, and propaganda. Writers in the field of history tend more and more to speak in terms of culture; this often is represented as a matter of cultural conflict, as of German against Slav, of Japanese against Chinese, and the like. Scholars are doing their age a disservice if these factors of culture are carried over, as they often are, whether by historians or others, into justifications or "explanations" of war. . . .

As for the Civil War the stretch and span of conscious economic motive was much smaller than the areas or classes of war involvement. Economic diversity offered as much motive for union, in order to have a well rounded nation, as for the kind of economic conflict suggested by secession. One fault of writers who associate war-making with economic advantage is false or defective economics; another is the historical fault. It is surprising how seldom the economic explanation of war has made its case historically—i.e., in terms of adequate historical evidence bearing upon those points and those minds where actually the plunge into war, or the drive toward war, occurred. . . .

War causation tends to be "explained" in terms of great forces. Something elemental is supposed to be at work, be it nationalism, race conflict, or quest for economic advantage. With these forces predicated, the move toward war is alleged to be understandable, to be "explained," and therefore to be in some sense reasonable. Thought runs in biological channels and nations are conceived as organisms. Such thought is not confined to philosophers; it is the commonest of mental patterns. A cartoonist habitually draws a nation as a person. In this manner of thinking Germany does so and so, John Bull takes this

---

[9] Reprinted by permission of Dodd, Mead & Company, Inc. from *Lincoln, the Liberal Statesman* by James G. Randall. Copyright 1947 by Dodd, Mead & Company, Inc. First printed in the *Mississippi Valley Historical Review*.

or that course, and so on. When thought takes so homely a form, it is hardly called a philosophical concept; on the level of solemn learning the very same thing would appear under a Greek derivative or Freudian label. However labeled, it may be questioned whether the concept is any better than a poor figure of speech, a defective metaphor which is misleading because it has a degree of truth. . . .

War-making is too much dignified if it is told in terms of broad national urges, of great German motives, or of compelling Italian ambitions. When nations stumble into war, or when peoples rub their eyes and find they have been dragged into war, there is at some point a psychopathic case. Omit the element of abnormality, of bogus leadership, or inordinate ambition for conquest, and diagnosis fails. . . .

There is no intention here to draw a comparison of the American Civil War with recent wars. The point is that sweeping generalizations as to "war causation" are often faulty and distorted, and that when such distortion is assisted by taking the Civil War as an alleged example, a word by the historian is appropriate. . . . The "explaining" of war is one of the most tricky of subjects. If the explanation is made to rest on the cultural or economic basis, it is not unlikely that the American war in the eighteen-sixties will be offered as a supposedly convincing example. The writer, however, doubts seriously whether a consensus of scholars who have competently studied that war would accept either the cultural or the economic motive as the effective cause. . . .

Clear thinking would require a distinction between causing the war and getting into it. Discussion which overlooks this becomes foggy indeed. It was small minorities that caused the war; then the regions and sections were drawn in. No one seems to have thought of letting the minorities or the original trouble makers fight it out. Yet writers who descant upon the "causation" of the war write grandly of vast sections, as if the fact of a section being dragged into the slaughter was the same as the interests of that section being consciously operative in its causation. Here lies one of the chief fallacies of them all. . . .

In writing of human nature in politics Graham Wallas has shown the potent effect of irrational attitudes. He might have found many a Civil War example. Traditional "explanations" of the war fail to make sense when fully analyzed. The war has been "explained" by the choice of a Republican president, by grievances, by sectional economics, by the cultural wish for Southern independence, by slavery, or by events at Sumter. But these explanations crack when carefully examined. The election of Lincoln fell so far short of swinging Southern sentiment against the Union that secessionists were still unwilling to trust their case to an all-Southern convention or to cooperation among Southern states. . . . Alexander H. Stephens stated that secessionists did not desire redress of grievances and would obstruct such redress. Prophets of sectional economics left many a Southerner unconvinced. . . . The tariff was a potential future annoyance rather than an acute grievance in 1860. What existed then was largely a Southern tariff law. Practically all tariffs are one-sided. Sectional tariffs in other periods have existed without producing war. Such a thing as a Southern drive for independence on cultural lines is probably more of a modern thesis than a contemporary motive of sufficient force to have carried the South out of the Union on any broadly representative or all-Southern basis. . . .

It was hard for Southerners to accept the victory of a sectional party in 1860, but it was no part of the Republican program to smash slavery in the South, nor did the territorial aspect of slavery mean much politically beyond agitation. Southerners cared little about taking slaves into the territories; Republicans cared so little in the opposite sense that they avoided prohibiting slavery in territorial laws passed in February and March of 1861. . . .

Let one take all the factors traditionally presented—the Sumter maneuver, the election of Lincoln, abolitionism, slavery in Kansas, prewar objections to the Union, cultural and economic differences, etc.—and it will be seen that only by a kind of false display could any of these issues, or all of them together, be said to have caused the war if one omits the elements of emotional unreason and overbold leadership. If one word or phrase were selected to account for the war, that word would not be slavery, or economic grievance, or state rights, or diverse civilizations. It would have to be such a word as fanaticism (on both sides), misunderstanding, misrepresentation, or perhaps politics. . . .

As to wars, the ones that have not happened are perhaps best to study. Much could be said about such wars. There has been as much "cause" for wars that did not happen as for wars that did. Cultural and economic difficulties *in wars that have not occurred* are highly significant. The notion that you must have war when you have cultural variation, or economic competition, or sectional difference is an unhistorical misconception which it is stupid to promote. Yet some of the misinterpretations of the Civil War have tended to promote it.

This subject—war scares, or vociferous prowar drives which happily fizzled out—is a theme for a book in itself. There was the slogan "Fifty-four Forty or Fight" in 1844. If it meant anything, it meant that, in the international territorial difficulty as to the far Northwest, the United States should demand all the area in dispute with England, should refuse diplomatic adjustment, and should fight England if the full demand was not met. The United States did not get Fifty-four Forty—i.e., an enormous area of Canada—but it did not fight. The matter was easily adjusted by treaty in 1846. In retrospect, the settlement made the earlier slogan, and war drive, seem no better than sheer jingoism.

That was in the roaring forties. In the sixties the arguments with England, despite war cries, were adjusted by diplomacy; after the war they became the subject of successful arbitration. In the nineties the Venezuelan trouble with England caused a good deal of talk of coming war, while at the same time there was patriotic advocacy of peaceful adjustment. In the result, the Monroe Doctrine was peaceably vindicated. If that war over Venezuela had happened, one cannot doubt that writers would impressively have shown, by history, economics, etc., that it was "inevitable." Previous troubles with England would have been reviewed with exaggerated emphasis on a hostile background and with neglect of friendly factors. . . .

It would be instructive to examine such episodes and to show how easily the country accepted peaceful adjustment, or how life simply went on with continued peace; then, after the frenzy of war agitation had passed, reasonable men everywhere either forgot the agitation altogether or recognized how artificially and how mistakenly the "issues" had been misrepresented by those who gave out the impression of "inevitable" war. All the familiar arguments, replete with social and economic explanations, could be mustered up for "wars" that were avoided or prospectively imagined. The whole subject of war "causation" needs far more searching inquiry than it has received.

A Needless War

Believing that slavery was blocked from further expansion by geographical conditions, "revisionists" insist that the prewar agitators had raised and exploited a fictitious issue. Moreover, they maintain, by 1860 slavery had passed its peak and would soon have died of natural causes if the Civil War had not destroyed it by force. This point of view is developed in Charles W. Ramsdell, "The Natural Limits of Slavery Expansion."[10]

In the forefront of that group of issues which, for more than a decade before the secession of the cotton states, kept the northern and southern sections of the United States in irritating controversy and a growing sense of enmity, was the question whether the federal government should permit and protect the expansion of slavery into the western territories. . . . It was upon this particular issue that a new and powerful sectional party appeared in 1854, that the majority of the Secessionists of the cotton states predicated their action in 1860 and 1861, and it was upon this also that President-elect Lincoln forced the defeat of the compromise measures in the winter of 1860–61. It seems safe to say that had this question been eliminated or settled amicably, there would have been no secession and no Civil War. . . .

Disregarding the stock arguments —constitutional, economic, social, and what not—advanced by either group, let us examine afresh the real problem involved. Would slavery, if legally permitted to do so, have taken possession of the territories or of any considerable portion of them? . . .

The causes of the expansion of slavery westward from the South Atlantic Coast are now well understood. The industrial revolution and the opening of world markets had continually increased the consump-

---

[10] Charles W. Ramsdell, "The Natural Limits of Slavery," *Mississippi Valley Historical Review*, 16 (1929), 151–71. Originally published in the *Mississippi Valley Historical Review*.

tion and demand for raw cotton, while the abundance of fertile and cheap cotton lands in the Gulf States had steadily lured cotton farmers and planters westward. Where large-scale production was possible, the enormous demand for a steady supply of labor had made the use of slaves inevitable, for a sufficient supply of free labor was unprocurable on the frontier. . . . The most powerful factor in the westward movement of slavery was cotton, for the land available for other staples—sugar, hemp, tobacco—was limited, while slave labor was not usually profitable in growing grain. This expansion of the institution was in response to economic stimuli; it had been inspired by no political program nor by any ulterior political purpose. . . . The movement would go on as far as suitable cotton lands were to be found or as long as there was a reasonable expectation of profit from slave labor, provided, of course, that no political barrier was encountered.

The astonishing rapidity of the advance of the southern frontier prior to 1840 had alarmed the opponents of slavery, who feared that the institution would extend indefinitely into the West. But by 1849–50, when the contest over the principle of the Wilmot Proviso was at its height, the western limits of the cotton growing region were already approximated; and by the time the new Republican party was formed to check the further expansion of slavery, the westward march of the cotton plantation was evidently slowing down. The northern frontier of cotton production west of the Mississippi had already been established at about the northern line of Arkansas. Only a negligible amount of the staple was being grown in Missouri. West of Arkansas a little cotton was cultivated by the slaveholding, civilized Indians; but until the Indian territory should be opened generally to white settlement—a development of which there was no immediate prospect—it could not become a slaveholding region of any importance. The only possibility of a further westward extension of the cotton belt was in Texas. In that state alone was the frontier line of cotton and slavery still advancing. . . .

By the provisions of the Compromise of 1850, New Mexico, Utah, and the other territories acquired from Mexico were legally open to slavery. In view of well-known facts, it may hardly seem worth while to discuss the question whether slavery would ever have taken possession of that vast region; but perhaps some of those facts should be set down. The real western frontier of the cotton belt is still in Texas; for though cotton is grown in small quantities in New Mexico, Arizona, and California, in none of these states is the entire yield equal to that of certain single counties in Texas. In none is negro labor used to any appreciable extent, if at all. In New Mexico and Arizona, Mexican labor is cheaper than negro labor, as has been the case ever since the acquisition of the region from Mexico. It was well understood by sensible men, North and South, in 1850 that soil, climate, and native labor would form a perpetual bar to slavery in the vast territory then called New Mexico. Possibly southern California could have sustained slavery, but California had already decided that question for itself, and there was no remote probability that the decision would ever be reversed. As to New Mexico, the census of 1860, ten years after the territory had been thrown open to slavery, showed not a single slave; and this was true also of Colorado and Nevada. Utah, alone of all these territories, was credited with any slaves at all. Surely these results for the ten years when, it is alleged, the slave power was doing its utmost to extend its system into the West, ought to have confuted those who had called down frenzied curses upon the head of Daniel Webster for his Seventh-of-March speech.

At the very time when slavery was reaching its natural and impassable frontiers in Texas, there arose the fateful excitement over the Kansas-Nebraska Bill, or rather over the clause which abrogated the Missouri Compromise and left the determination of the status of slavery in the two territories to their own settlers. . . . But, in all candor, . . . [can] anyone who examines the matter objectively today say that there was any probability that slavery as an institution would ever have taken possession of either Kansas or Nebraska? Certainly cotton could not have been grown in either, for it was not grown in the adjacent part of Missouri. Hemp, and possibly tobacco, might have been grown in a limited portion of eastern Kansas along the Missouri and the lower Kansas rivers; and if no obstacle had been present, undoubtedly a few negroes would have been taken into eastern Kansas. But the infiltration of slaves would have been a slow process.

Apparently there was no expectation, even on the part of the pro-slavery men, that slavery would go into Nebraska. Only a small fraction of the territory was suited to any crops that could be grown with profit by slave labor, and by far the greater portion of Kansas—even of the eastern half that was available for immediate settlement—would have been occupied in a short time, as it was in fact, by a predominantly non-slaveholding and free-soil population. To say that the individual slaveowner would disregard his own economic interest and carry valuable property where it would entail loss merely for the sake of a doubtful political advantage seems a palpable absurdity. . . . The census of 1860 showed two slaves in Kansas and fifteen in Nebraska. In short, there is good reason to believe that had Douglas' bill passed Congress without protest, and had it been sustained by the people of the free states, slavery could not have taken permanent root in Kansas if the decision were left to the people of the territory itself.

The fierce contest which accompanied and followed the passage of Douglas' Kansas-Nebraska Bill is one of the sad ironies of history. Northern and southern politicians and agitators, backed by excited constituents, threw fuel to the flames of sectional antagonism until the country blazed into a civil war that was the greatest tragedy of the nation. There is no need here to analyze the arguments, constitutional or otherwise, that were employed. Each party to the controversy seemed obsessed by the fear that its own preservation was at stake. The northern anti-slavery men held that a legal sanction of slavery in the territories would result in the extension of the institution and the domination of the free

North by the slave power; prospective immigrants in particular feared that they would never be able to get homes in this new West. Their fears were groundless; but in their excited state of mind they could neither see the facts clearly nor consider them calmly. The slaveholding Southerners, along with other thousands of Southerners who never owned slaves, believed that a victory in Kansas for the anti-slavery forces would not only weaken southern defenses—for they well knew that the South was on the defensive—but would encourage further attacks until the economic life of the South and "white civilization" were destroyed. Though many of them doubted whether slavery would ever take permanent root in Kansas, they feared to yield a legal precedent which could later be used against them. And so they demanded a right which they could not actively use—the legal right to carry slaves where few would or could be taken. The one side fought rancorously for what it was bound to get without fighting; the other, with equal rancor, contended for what in the nature of things it could never use. . . .

If the conclusions that have been set forth are sound, by 1860 the institution of slavery had virtually reached its natural frontiers in the West. Beyond Texas and Missouri the way was closed. There was no reasonable ground for expectation that new lands could be acquired south of the United States into which slaves might be taken. There was, in brief, no further place for it to go. In the cold facts of the situation, there was no longer any basis for excited sectional controversy over slavery extension; but the public mind had so long been concerned with the debate that it could not see that the issue had ceased to have validity. In the existing state of the popular mind, therefore, there was still abundant opportunity for the politician to work to his own ends, to play upon prejudice and passion and fear. Blind leaders of the blind! Sowers of the wind, not seeing how near was the approaching harvest of the whirlwind!

Perhaps this paper should end at this point; but it may be useful to push the inquiry a little farther. If slavery could gain no more political territory, would it be able to hold what it had? Were there not clear indications that its area would soon begin to contract? Were there not even some evidences that a new set of conditions were arising within the South itself which would disintegrate the institution? Here, it must be confessed, one enters the field of speculation, which is always dangerous ground for the historian. But there were certain factors in the situation which can be clearly discerned, and it may serve some purpose to indicate them. . . .

As long as there was an abundance of cheap and fertile cotton lands, as there was in Texas, and the prices of cotton remained good, there would be a heavy demand for labor on the new plantations. As far as fresh lands were concerned, this condition would last for some time, for the supply of lands in Texas alone was enormous. But at the end of the decade, there were unmistakable signs that a sharp decline in cotton prices and planting profits was close at hand. The production of cotton had increased slowly, with some fluctuation, from 1848 to 1857, and the price varied from about ten cents to over thirteen cents a pound on the New York market. But a rapid increase in production began in 1858 and the price declined. The crop of 1860 was twice that of 1850. ... There was every indication of increased production and lower price levels for the future, even if large allowance be made for poor-crop years. There was small chance of reducing the acreage, for the cotton planter could not easily change to another crop. Had not the war intervened, there is every reason to believe that there would have been a continuous overproduction and very low prices throughout the sixties and seventies.

What would have happened then when the new lands of the Southwest had come into full production and the price of cotton had sunk to the point at which it could not be grown with profit on the millions of acres of poorer soils in the older sections? The replenishment of the soil would not have solved the problem for it would only have resulted in the production of more cotton. Even on the better lands the margin of profit would have declined. Prices of slaves must have dropped then, even in the Southwest; importation from the border states would have fallen off; thousands of slaves would have become not only unprofitable but a heavy burden, the market for them gone. Those who are familiar with the history of cotton farming, cotton prices, and the depletion of the cotton lands since the Civil War will agree that this is no fanciful picture.

What would have been the effect of this upon the slaveowner's attitude toward emancipation? No preachments about the sacredness of the institution and of constitutional guarantees would have compensated him for the dwindling values of his lands and slaves and the increasing burden of his debts. ... With prosperity gone and slaves an increasingly unprofitable burden, year after year, can there be any doubt that thousands of slaveowners would have sought for some means of relief? How they might have solved the problem of getting out from under the burden without entire loss of the capital invested in their working force, it is hard to say; but that they would have changed their attitude toward the institution seems inevitable. ...

In summary and conclusion: it seems evident that slavery had about reached its zenith by 1860 and must shortly have begun to decline, for the economic forces which had carried it into the region west of the Mississippi had about reached their maximum effectiveness. It could not go forward in any direction and it was losing ground along its northern border. A cumbersome and expensive system, it could show profits only as long as it could find plenty of rich land to cultivate and the world would take the product of its crude labor at a good price. It had reached its limits in both profits and lands. The free farmers in the North who dreaded its further spread had nothing to fear. Even those who wished it destroyed had only to wait a little while—perhaps a generation, probably less. It was summarily destroyed at a frightful cost to the whole country and one third of the nation was impoverished for forty years. One is tempted at this point to reflections on what has long passed for statesmanship on both sides of that long dead issue. But I have not the heart to indulge them.

5. WAS IT THE "MORAL URGENCY" OF THE SLAVERY ISSUE?

Moderate statesmen, such as Douglas, had no strong feelings of moral indignation about the existence of Negro slavery in America. Douglas did not care whether it was "voted up or down." But many Americans, even some Southerners, of the pre-Civil War generation looked upon slavery as a national disgrace and as a moral evil of major proportions. Our moral standards change as the society in which we live changes—the Northeastern states once permitted slavery, too. Nevertheless, there was as much idealism in the anti-slavery crusade and in the defense of the North's "free-labor" system as there has ever been in any great movement for social reform. In 1861, countless Northerners accepted war as an effective means of removing the curse of slavery and of creating a better and purer nation. Given such high moral purposes, they concluded that the war was both inevitable and justifiable.

Slavery the "Single Cause"

James Ford Rhodes, like other Northern historians of the post-Civil War generation, believed that slavery was the fundamental cause of the Civil War. His interpretation is summarized in the following passages from *Lectures on the American Civil War*.[11]

There is a risk in referring any historic event to a single cause. . . . [But] of the American Civil War it may safely be asserted that there was a single cause, slavery. In 1862 John Stuart Mill in *Fraser's Magazine*, and Professor Cairnes in a pamphlet on the Slave Power, presented this view to the English public with force, but it is always difficult to get to the bottom of a foreign dispute, and it is not surprising that many failed to comprehend the real nature of the conflict. When in July, 1862, William E. Forster said in the House of Commons that he believed it was generally acknowledged that slavery was the cause of the war, he was answered with cries, "No, no!" and "The tariff!" Because the South was for free grade and the North for a protective tariff, this was a natural retort, though proceeding from a misconception, as a reference to the most acute tariff crisis in our history will show.

In 1832, South Carolina, by act of her Convention legally called, declared that the tariff acts passed by

---

[11] James Ford Rhodes, *Lectures on the American Civil War* (New York: The Macmillan Company, 1913), 2–16, 76–77.

Congress in 1828 and 1832 were "null, void, no law," and that no duties enjoined by those acts should be paid or permitted to be paid in the State of South Carolina. It is a significant fact that she failed to induce any of her sister Southern States to act with her. By the firmness of President Jackson and a conciliatory disposition on the part of the high tariff party the act of nullification was never put in force; but the whole course of the incident and the yielding of South Carolina demonstrated that the American Union could not be broken up by a tariff dispute. . . .

Some of our younger writers, impressed with the principle of nationality that prevailed in Europe during the last half of the nineteenth century, have read into our conflict European conditions and asserted that the South stood for disunion in her doctrine of States' rights and that the war came because the North took up the gage of battle to make of the United States a nation. I shall have occasion to show the potency of the Union sentiment as an aid to the destruction of slavery, but when events are reduced to their last elements, it plainly appears that the doctrine of States' rights and secession was invoked by the South to save slavery, and by a natural antagonism, the North upheld the Union because the fight for its preservation was the first step toward the abolition of negro servitude. The question may be isolated by the incontrovertible statement that if the negro had never been brought to America, our Civil War could not have occurred. . . .

As slavery was out of tune with the nineteenth century, the States that held fast to it played a losing game. This was evident from the greater increase of population at the North. . . . The South repelled immigrants for the reason that freemen would not work with slaves. In the House of Representatives, chosen on the basis of numerical population, the North at each decennial census and apportionment, gained largely on the South, whose stronghold was the Senate. Each State, irrespective of population, had two senators, and since the formation of the Constitution, States had been admitted in pairs by a tacit agreement, each free State being counterbalanced by a slave State. The admission of California [as a free State] which would disturb this equilibrium was resisted by the South with a spirit of determination made bitter by disappointment over California's spontaneous act. The Mexican War had been for the most part a Southern war; the South, as Lowell made Hosea Biglow say, was "after bigger pens to cram with slaves," and now she saw the magnificent domain of California escaping her clutches. She had other grievances which, from the point of view of a man of 1850 reverencing the letter of the Constitution, were undoubtedly well founded, but the whole dispute really hinged on the belief of the South that slavery was right and the belief of the majority of Northerners that it was wrong.

At the time of the formation of the Constitution the two sections were not greatly at variance. A large number of Southern men, among them their ablest and best leaders, thought slavery was a moral and political evil to be got rid of gradually. In due time, the foreign slave trade was prohibited, but the

Yankee invention of the cotton-gin made slavery apparently profitable in the culture of cotton on the virgin soil of the new States in the South; and Southern opinion changed. From being regarded as an evil, slavery began to be looked upon as the only possible condition of the existence of the two races side by side and by 1850 the feeling had grown to be that slavery was "no evil, no scourge, but a great religious, social and moral blessing." As modern society required hewers of woods and drawers of water, the slave system of the South, so the argument ran, was superior to the industrial system of England, France and the North.

In 1831, William Lloyd Garrison began his crusade against slavery. In a weekly journal, the *Liberator*, published in Boston, he preached with fearless emphasis that slavery was wrong and, though his immediate followers were never many, he set people to thinking about the question, so that six years later Daniel Webster . . . said, the subject of slavery "has not only attracted attention as a question of politics, but it has struck a far deeper-toned chord. It has arrested the religious feeling of the country; it has taken strong hold on the consciences of men." . . . [The] opinion constantly gained ground at the North that slavery was an evil and that its existence was a blot on the national honor.

In 1850, there were at the South 347,000 slaveholders out of a white population of six millions, but the head and center of the oligarchy was to be found amongst the large planters, possessors of fifty or more slaves, whose elegance, luxury and hospitality are recited in tales of travellers, over whose estates and lives the light of romance and poetry has been profusely shed; of these, there were less than eight thousand. . . . The men composing this oligarchy were high-spirited gentlemen, with a keen sense of honor showing itself in hatred of political corruption, resentment of personal attack by speech or by pen, to the length of the fatal duel. . . . It is obvious that men of this stamp could not be otherwise than irritated when Northern speeches, books and newspapers were full of the charge that they were living in the daily practice of evil, that negro chattel slavery was cruel, unjust and barbaric. This irritation expressed itself in recrimination and insolent demands at the same time that it helped to bring them to the belief that property in negroes was as right and sacred as the ownership of horses and mules. . . .

The Civil War in England, wrote Gardiner, "was rendered inevitable" because "a reconciliation between opposing moral and social forces" could not be effected. Here is an exact statement of our own case in 1861. The Civil War might have been averted had the North yielded to the South and in the words of Lincoln ceased references to "slavery as in any way wrong" and regarded it "as one of the common matters of property" speaking "of negroes as we do of our horses and cattle." In other words, the North must repress its own enlightened sentiment regarding slavery. . . . Or, on the other hand, the war might have been prevented had the Southerners had a change of heart, reverted to the sentiment of the founders of the republic that slavery was an evil and agreed to limit its extension. The logical result would have been gradual abolition and the North stood ready to bear her share in compensating the owners of slaves. But anybody who should have promulgated such a doctrine in the South in 1861 would have been laughed at, hooted and mobbed.

"The Travail of Slavery"

Charles G. Sellers, Jr., in "The Travail of Slavery," believes that the "conflict of values" between slavery and the American liberal tradition produced tensions in Southerners that drove them to aggressive action. This psychological explanation of the Civil War is based on the assumption that slavery was the fundamental issue of the sectional conflict. The following extracts are reprinted with the permission of the University of North Carolina Press.[12]

The American experience knows no greater tragedy than the Old South's twistings and turnings on the rack of slavery. . . . Like no other Americans before or since, the white men of the ante-bellum South drove toward catastrophe by doing conscious violence to their truest selves. No picture of the Old South as a section confident and united in its dedication to a neo-feudal social order, and no explanation of the Civil War as a conflict between "two civilizations," can encompass the complexity and pathos of the antebellum reality. No analysis that misses the inner turmoil of the antebellum Southerner can do justice to the central tragedy of the southern experience.

The key to the tragedy of southern history is the paradox of the slaveholding South's devotion to "liberty." Whenever and wherever Southerners sought to invoke their highest social values—in schoolboy declamations, histories, Fourth of July orations, toasts, or newspaper editorials—"liberty" was the incantation that sprang most frequently and most fervently from their lips and pens. . . .

The Revolutionary struggle made this implicit colonial liberalism explicit and tied it to patriotic pride in the new American Union. From this time on, for Southerners as for other Americans, liberty was the end for which the Union existed, while the Union was the instrument by which liberty was to be extended to all mankind. Thus the Fourth of July, the birthday of both liberty and Union, became the occasion for renewing the liberal idealism and the patriotic nationalism which united Americans of all sections at the highest levels of political conviction. . . .

Although a massive reaction against liberalism is supposed to have seized the southern mind in the following decades, the Nullifiers of

[12] Charles G. Sellers, Jr., *The Southerner as American* (Chapel Hill: University of North Carolina Press, 1960), 40–71. Reprinted by permission of the publisher.

the thirties and the radical southern sectionalists of the forties and fifties did not ignore or reject the Revolutionary tradition of liberty so much as they transformed it, substituting for the old emphasis on the natural rights of all men a new emphasis on the rights and autonomy of communities. It was ironic that these slaveholding defenders of liberty against the tyranny of northern domination had to place themselves in the tradition of '76 at all, and the irony was heightened by their failure to escape altogether its universalist implications. . . .

What are we to make of these slaveholding champions of liberty? Was the ante-bellum Southerner history's most hypocritical casuist? Or were these passionate apostrophes to the liberty of distant peoples a disguised protest against, or perhaps an escape from, the South's daily betrayal of its liberal self? Southerners were at least subconsciously aware of the "detestable paradox" of "our every-day sentiments of liberty" while holding human beings in slavery, and many Southerners had made it painfully explicit in the early days of the republic. . . .

It is well known that the South's great statesmen of the Revolutionary generation almost unanimously condemned slavery as incompatible with the nation's liberal principles. Though these elder statesmen proved incapable of solving the problem, Thomas Jefferson consoled himself with the thought that it could safely be left to the "young men, grown up and growing up," who "have sucked in the principles of liberty, as it were, with their mother's milk." Such young men did indeed grow up, and they kept most Southerners openly apologetic about slavery for fifty years following the Declaration of Independence. . . .

Though open anti-slavery utterances grew infrequent after the 1830's, the generation which was to dominate southern life in the forties and fifties had already come to maturity with values absorbed from the afterglow of Revolutionary liberalism. . . .

A whole generation cannot transform its most fundamental values by a mere effort of will. Though Southerners tended during the latter part of the ante-bellum period to restrict their publicly voiced libertarian hopes to "oppressed distant lands," the old liberal misgivings about slavery did not die. Instead they burrowed beneath the surface of the southern mind, where they kept gnawing away the shaky foundations on which Southerners sought to rebuild their morale and self-confidence as a slaveholding people. . . .

If the Southerner had been embarrassed by his devotion to liberty and Union alone, he would have had less trouble easing his mind on the subject of slavery. But as a Virginia legislator exclaimed in 1832, "This, sir, is a Christian community." . . . During those early decades of the nineteenth century, when the South was confessing the evils of slavery, it had been swept by a wave of evangelical orthodoxy. Though the wave crested about the time some Southerners, including some clergymen, began speaking of slavery as a positive good, it does not follow that the evangelical reaction against the eighteenth century's religious ideas contributed significantly to the reaction against the eighteenth century's liberalism with regard to slavery.

On the contrary, the evangelical

denominations had strong anti-slavery tendencies. Methodists, Quakers, and Baptists nurtured an extensive abolitionist movement in the upper South during the twenties, when the rest of the country was largely indifferent to the slavery question; and the Presbyterians were still denouncing slavery in Kentucky a decade later. It would be closer to the truth to suggest that as Southerners wrestled with their consciences over slavery, they may have gained a first-hand experience with the concepts of sin and evil that made them peculiarly susceptible to Christian orthodoxy. . . .

Even the irreligious found it hard to resist the claims of simple humanity or to deny that slaves, as one Southerner put it, "have hearts and feelings like other men." And those who were proof against the appeals to Revolutionary liberalism, Christianity, and humanity, still faced the arguments of Southerners in each succeeding generation that slavery was disastrous to the whites. Jefferson's famous lament that the slaveholder's child, "nursed, educated, and daily exercised in tyranny . . . must be a prodigy who can retain his manners and morals undepraved," was frequently echoed. . . .

It is essential to understand that the public declarations of Southerners never revealed the full impact of all these anti-slavery influences on the southern mind. Fear of provoking slave insurrections had restrained free discussion of slavery even in the Revolutionary South, and an uneasy society exerted steadily mounting pressure against anti-slavery utterances thereafter. Only when Nat Turner's bloody uprising of 1831 shocked Southerners into open debate over the peculiar institution did the curtain of restraint part sufficiently to reveal the intensity of their misgivings. . . .

[Yet,] . . . when Nat Turner frightened Southerners into facing squarely the tragic ambiguity of their society, they found the price for resolving it too high. The individual planter's economic stake in slavery was a stubborn and perhaps insurmountable obstacle to change; and even Jefferson's nerve had failed at the task of reconstituting the South's social system to assimilate a host of Negro freedmen.

The whole South sensed that a fateful choice had been made. Slowly and reluctantly Southerners faced the fact that, if slavery were to be retained, things could not go on as before. The slaves were restive, a powerful anti-slavery sentiment was sweeping the western world, and southern minds were not yet nerved for a severe struggle in defense of the peculiar institution to which they were now committed. The South could no longer ease its conscience with hopes for the eventual disappearance of slavery, or tolerate such hopes in any of its people. . . . So southern leaders of the Calhoun school began trying to convince themselves and others that slavery was a "positive good," while southern legislatures abridge freedom of speech and press, made manumission difficult or impossible, and imposed tighter restrictions on both slaves and free Negroes. The Great Reaction was under way.

Yet the Great Reaction, for all its formidable façade and terrible consequences, was a fraud. Slavery simply could not be blended with liberalism and Christianity, while liberalism and Christianity were too deeply rooted in the southern mind to be torn up overnight. Forced to smother and distort their most fundamental convictions by the decision to maintain slavery, and goaded by criticism based on these same convictions, Southerners of the generation before the Civil War suffered the most painful loss of social morale and identity that any large group of Americans has ever experienced. . . .

Nowhere . . . was the South's painful inner conflict over slavery more evident than in the elaborate body of theory by which it tried to prove (mainly to itself) the beneficence of its peculiar social system. . . .

Close examination of the superficially impressive pro-slavery philosophy reveals, as Louis Hartz has brilliantly demonstrated, a "mass of agonies and contradictions in the dream world of southern thought." The peculiar institution could be squared theoretically with either the slave's humanity or democratic liberalism for whites, but not with both. Thus the necessity for justifying slavery, coupled with the white South's inability to escape its inherited liberalism or to deny the common humanity it shared with its Negro slaves, inspired "a mixture of pain and wild hyperbole." . . .

It was this inner conflict which produced the South's belligerent dogmatism in the recurrent crises of the fifties. The whole massive pro-slavery polemic had the unreal ring of logic pushed far beyond conviction. . . . If the South's best minds resolutely quashed their doubts, it is small wonder that crisis-tossed editors and politicians took refuge in positive and extreme positions. . . .

How, then, did the fundamentally liberal, Christian, American South ever become an "aggressive slavocracy"? How did it bring itself to flaunt an aristocratic social philosophy? To break up the American Union? To wage war for the purpose of holding four million human beings in a bondage that violated their humanity? The answer is that Southerners did not and could not rationally and deliberately choose slavery and its fruits over the values it warred against. Rather it was the very conflict of values, rendered intolerable by constant criticism premised on values Southerners shared, which drove them to seek a violent resolution.

Social psychologists observe that such value conflicts—especially when they give rise to the kind of institutional instability revealed by the ambiguities of southern slavery —make a society "suggestible," or ready to follow the advocates of irrational and aggressive action. Thus it was fateful that the Old South developed an unusually able minority of fire-eating sectionalists, who labored zealously, from the 1830's on, to unite the South behind radical measures in defense of slavery. Though a majority of Southerners remained profoundly distrustful of these extremists throughout the ante-bellum period, their unceasing agitation steadily aggravated the South's tensions and heightened its underlying suggestibility. By egging the South on to ever more extreme demands, the Calhouns, Rhetts, and Yanceys provoked violent northern reactions, which could then be used to whip the South's passions still higher. At length, in 1860, capitalizing on intrigues for the Democratic presidential nomination, the fire-eaters managed to split the Democratic party, thus insuring the election of a Republican President and paving the way for secession.

Inflammatory agitation and revolutionary tactics succeeded only because Southerners had finally passed the point of rational self-control. The almost pathological violence of their reactions to northern criticism indicated that their misgivings about their moral position on slavery had become literally intolerable under the mounting abolitionist attack. . . .

Superimposed on this fundamental moral anxiety was another potent emotion, fear. John Brown's raid in October, 1859, created the most intense terror of slave insurrection that the South had ever experienced; and in this atmosphere of dread the final crisis of 1860–61 occurred. . . . Southerners believed their land to be overrun by abolitionist emissaries, who were "tampering with our slaves, and furnishing them with arms and poisons to accomplish their hellish designs." Lynch law was proclaimed, and vigilance committees sprang up to deal with anyone suspected of abolitionist sentiments. . . .

From the circumstances of the secession elections—the small turnouts, the revolutionary tactics of the fire-eaters, the disproportionate weighting of the results in favor of plantation areas, the coercive conditions under which the upper South voted, and the hysteria that prevailed everywhere—it can hardly be said that a majority of the South's white people deliberately chose to dissolve the Union in 1861. . . .

Yet it is idle to wonder whether secession represented the deliberate choice of a majority of white Southerners, or to speculate about the outcome of a hypothetical referendum, free from ambiguity, coercion, and hysteria. Decisions like the one that faced the South in 1860–61 are never reached in any such ideal way. And even had the South decided for the Union, its and the nation's problem would have remained unsolved, and a violent resolution would only have been postponed. Slavery was doomed by the march of history and by the nature of Southerners themselves, but so deeply had it involved them in its contradictions that they could neither deal with it rationally nor longer endure the tensions and anxieties it generated. Under these circumstances the Civil War or something very like it was unavoidable. It was also salutary, for only the transaction at Appomattox could have freed the South's people—both Negro and white—to move again toward the realization of their essential natures as Southerners, liberals, Christians, and Americans.

The Inevitability of Violence

Some historians have denounced the "revisionists" for failing to appreciate the moral urgency of the slavery issue and for treating anti-slavery leaders who did as mere trouble makers. Moreover, is one not being sentimental and unrealistic to think that a moral issue as complex as slavery could be solved by any means other than war? An article by Professor Arthur M. Schlesinger, Jr., of Harvard University, printed in October 1949, from which extracts are presented here, argues along these lines.[13]

The Civil War was our great national trauma. A savage fraternal conflict, it released deep sentiments of guilt and remorse—sentiments which have reverberated through our history and our literature ever since. Literature in the end came to terms with these sentiments by yielding to the South in fantasy the victory it had been denied in fact; . . . But history, a less malleable medium, was constricted by the intractable fact that war had taken place, and by the related assumption that it was, in William H. Seward's phrase, an "irrepressible conflict," and hence a justified one.

As short a time ago as 1937, for example, even Professor James G. Randall could describe himself as "unprepared to go to the point of denying that the great American tragedy could have been avoided." Yet in a few years . . . Professor Randall would emerge as the leader of a triumphant new school of self-styled "revisionists." [The writings of this school] . . . brought about a profound reversal of the professional historian's attitude toward the Civil War. Scholars now denied the traditional assumption of the inevitability of the war and boldly advanced the thesis that a "blundering generation" had transformed a "repressible conflict" into a "needless war." . . .

The revisionist case . . . has three main premises. First:

[1] that the Civil War was caused by the irresponsible emotionalization of politics far out of proportion to the real problems involved. . . .

If uncontrolled emotionalism and fanaticism caused the war, how did they get out of hand? Who whipped up the "whipped up crisis"? Thus the second revisionist thesis:

[2] that sectional friction was permitted to develop into needless war by the inexcusable failure of political leadership in the fifties. . . .

It is hard to tell which was under attack here—the performance of a particular generation or democratic politics in general. But, if the indictment "blundering generation" meant no more than a general complaint that democratic politics placed a premium on emotionalism, then the Civil War would have been no more nor less "needless" than any event in our blundering history. The phrase "blundering generation" must consequently imply that the generation in power in the fifties was *below* the human or historical or democratic average in its blundering. Hence the third revisionist thesis:

[3] that the slavery problem could have been solved without war. For, even if slavery were as unimportant as the revisionists have insisted, they would presumably admit that it constituted the real sticking-point in the relations between the sections.

---

[13] Arthur M. Schlesinger, Jr., "The Causes of the Civil War: A Note on Historical Sentimentalism," *Partisan Review*, 16:969–81. Copyright 1949 by *Partisan Review*. Reprinted by permission of Arthur M. Schlesinger, Jr., and the *Partisan Review*.

They must show therefore that there were policies with which a non-blundering generation could have resolved the slavery crisis and averted war; and that these policies were so obvious that the failure to adopt them indicated blundering and stupidity of a peculiarly irresponsible nature. If no such policies could be produced even by hindsight, then it would seem excessive to condemn the politicians of the fifties for failing to discover them at the time. . . .

. . . The problem [of slavery] in America was peculiarly recalcitrant. The schemes for gradual emancipation got nowhere. Neither internal reform nor economic exhaustion contained much promise for a peaceful solution. The hard fact, indeed, is that the revisionists have not tried seriously to describe the policies by which the slavery problem could have been peacefully resolved. They have restored instead to broad affirmations of faith: if only the conflict could have been staved off long enough, then somehow, somewhere, we could have worked something out. It is legitimate, I think, to ask how? where? what?—at least, if these affirmations of faith are to be used as the premise for castigating the unhappy men who had the practical responsibility for finding solutions and failed.

Where have the revisionists gone astray? . . . I cannot escape the feeling that the vogue of revisionism is connected with the modern tendency to seek in optimistic sentimentalism an escape from the severe demands of moral decision; that it is the offspring of our modern sentimentality which at once evades the essential moral problems in the name of a superficial objectivity and asserts their unimportance in the name of an invincible progress.

The revisionists first glided over the implications of the fact that the slavery system was producing a closed society in the South. Yet that society increasingly had justified itself by a political and philosophical repudiation of free society; southern thinkers swiftly developed the anti-libertarian potentialities in a social system whose cornerstone, in Alexander H. Stephens's proud phrase, was human bondage. In theory and in practice, the South organized itself with mounting rigor against ideas of human dignity and freedom, because such ideas inevitably threatened the basis of their own system. . . .

A society closed in the defense of evil institutions thus creates moral differences far too profound to be solved by compromise. Such a society forces upon every one, both those living at the time and those writing about it later, the necessity for a moral judgment; and the moral judgment in such cases becomes an indispensable factor in the historical understanding.

The revisionists were commendably anxious to avoid the vulgar errors of the post-Civil War historians who pronounced smug individual judgments on the persons involuntarily involved in the tragedy of the slave system. Consequently they tried hard to pronounce no moral judgment at all on slavery. . . .

Because the revisionists felt no moral urgency themselves, they deplored as fanatics those who did feel it, or brushed aside their feelings as the artificial product of emotion and propaganda. The revisionist hero was Stephen A. Douglas, who always thought that the great moral problems could be solved by slight-of-hand. . . .

By denying themselves insight into the moral dimension of the slavery crisis, in other words, the revisionists denied themselves a historical understanding of the intensities that caused the crisis. It was the moral issue of slavery, for example, that gave the struggles over slavery in the territories or over the enforcement of the fugitive slave laws their significance. These issues, as the revisionists have shown with cogency, were not in themselves basic. But they were the available issues; they were almost the only points within the existing constitutional framework where the moral conflict could be faced; as a consequence, they became charged with the moral and political dynamism of the central issue. . . .

Let us be clear what the relationship of moral judgment to history is. Every historian . . . imports his own set of moral judgments into the writing of history by the very process of interpretation; and the phrase "every historian" includes the category "revisionist." . . . The whole revisionist attitude toward abolitionists and radicals, repeatedly characterized by Randall as "unctious" and "intolerant," overflows with the moral feeling which is so virtuously excluded from discussions of slavery. . . .

. . . Professor Randall [was guilty of] . . . uncritical optimism . . . when he remarked, "To suppose that the Union could not have been continued or slavery outmoded without the war and without the corrupt concomitants of war is hardly an enlightened assumption." We have here a touching afterglow of the admirable nineteenth-century faith in the full rationality and perfectibility of man; the faith that the errors of the world would all in time be "outmoded" . . . by progress. Yet the experience of the twentieth century has made it clear that we gravely overrated man's capacity to solve the problems of existence within the terms of history.

This conclusion about man may disturb our complacencies about human nature. Yet it is certainly more in accord with history than Professor Randall's "enlightened" assumption that man can solve peaceably all the problems which overwhelm him. The unhappy fact is that man occasionally works himself into a log-jam; and that the log-jam must be burst by violence. We know that well enough from the experience of the last decade. . . .

We delude ourselves when we think that history teaches us that evil will be "outmoded" by progress and that politics consequently does not impose on us the necessity for decision and for struggle. If historians are to understand the fullness of the social dilemma they seek to reconstruct, they must understand that sometimes there is no escape from the implacabilities of moral decision. When social conflicts embody great moral issues, these conflicts cannot be assigned for solution to the invincible march of progress; nor can they be by-passed with "objective" neutrality. Not many problems perhaps force this decision upon the historian. But, if any problem does in our history, it is the Civil War.

To reject the moral actuality of the Civil War is to foreclose the possibility of an adequate account of its causes. More than that, it is to

what caused the civil war?

misconceive and grotesquely to sentimentalize the nature of history. For history is not a redeemer, promising to solve all human problems in time; nor is man capable of transcending the limitations of his being. Man generally is entangled in insoluble problems; history is consequently a tragedy in which we are all involved, whose keynote is anxiety and frustration, not progress and fulfillment. Nothing exists in history to assure us that the great moral dilemmas can be resolved without pain; we cannot therefore be relieved from the duty of moral judgment on issues so appalling and inescapable as those involved in human slavery; nor can we be consoled by sentimental theories about the needlessness of the Civil War into regarding our own struggles against evil as equally needless.

One must emphasize, however, that this duty of judgment applies to issues. Because we are all implicated in the same tragedy, we must judge the men of the past with the same forbearance and charity which we hope the future will apply toward us.

6. WAS IT THE FAILURE OF DEMOCRACY?

The many issues, real or imagined, and the contrasting social and cultural values that divided Northerners and Southerners produced the most serious internal crisis the United States has ever faced. Whether it was "inevitable"—an "irrepressible conflict"—the crisis did finally lead to war. This fact might well have some depressing implications for those who believe in democratic processes. If there are some kinds of controversies that simply cannot be settled peacefully at the ballot box, then democracy may fail us when we need it most.

The Civil War and the Democratic Process

In April 1950, Professor Avery Craven of the University of Chicago gave his explanation for the failure of democracy in 1861.[14]

The most significant thing about the American Civil War is that it represents a complete breakdown of the democratic process. After years of strain, men ceased to discuss their problems, dropped the effort to compromise their differences, refused to abide by the results of a national election, and resorted to the use of force. After four years of bloody civil strife, one side was beaten into submission, and the other had its way in

[14] "The 1840's and the Democratic Process," *Journal of Southern History*, 16:161–76. By permission of Avery Craven and the *Journal of Southern History*.

national affairs. The emergence of modern America was largely the product of that outcome.

If the breakdown of the democratic process is the significant thing about the coming of the Civil War, then the important question is not *what* the North and South were quarreling about half as much as it is *how* their differences got into such shape that they could not be handled by the process of rational discussion, compromise, or the tolerant acceptance of majority decision. The question is not "What caused the Civil War?" but rather "How did it come about?" The two questions are quite different, yet hopelessly tangled. The effort to distinguish between them, however, is important and needs to be stressed.

If one were to discuss the *causes* of the Civil War, he might begin with geography, move on to historical developments in time and place, trace the growth of economic and social rivalries, outline differences in moral values, and then show the way in which personalities and psychological factors operated. The part which slavery played would loom large. It might even become the symbol of all differences and of all conflicts. State rights, territorial expansion, tariffs, lands, internal improvements, and a host of other things, real and imagined, would enter the picture. There would be economic causes, constitutional causes, social causes, moral causes, political causes involving the breaking of old parties and the rise of sectional ones, and psychological causes which ultimately permitted emotion to take the place of reason. There would be remote or background causes, and immediate causes, and causes resting on other causes, until the most eager pedagogue would be thoroughly satisfied.

The matter of how issues got beyond the abilities of the democratic process is, on the other hand, a bit less complex and extended. It has to do with the way in which concrete issues were reduced to abstract principles and the conflicts between interests simplified to basic levels where men feel more than they reason, and where compromise or yielding is impossible because issues appear in the form of right and wrong and involve the fundamental structure of society. This is not saying, as some have charged, that great moral issues were not involved. They certainly were, and it is a matter of choice with historians as to whether or not they take sides, praise or condemn, become partisans in the departed quarrel, or use past events for present-day purposes.

As an approach to this second more modest problem, a correspondence which took place between Abraham Lincoln and Alexander H. Stephens between November 30 and December 22, 1860, is highly revealing. On November 14, Stephens had delivered one of the great speeches of his life before the legislature of Georgia. It was a Union speech. He had begged his fellow Southerners not to give up the ship, to wait for some violation of the Constitution before they attempted secession. Equality might yet be possible inside the Union. At least, the will of the whole people should be obtained before any action was taken.

Abraham Lincoln, still unconvinced that there was real danger, wrote Stephens, as an old friend, for a revised copy of his speech. Stephens complied, and he ended his letter with a warning about the great peril which threatened the country and a reminder of the heavy responsibility now resting on the president-elect's shoulders. Lincoln answered with assurance that he would not "*directly,* or *indirectly,* interfere with the slaves" or with the southern people about their slaves, and then closed with this significant statement:

I suppose, however, this does not meet the case. You think slavery is right and ought to be extended, while we think it is *wrong* and ought to be restricted. That I suppose is the rub. It certainly is the only substantial difference between us.

The reduction of "the only substantial difference" between North and South to a simple question of *right and wrong* is the important thing about Lincoln's statement. It revealed the extent to which the sectional controversy had, by 1860, been simplified and reduced to a conflict of principles in the minds of the northern people.

Stephens' answer to Lincoln's letter is equally revealing. He expressed "an earnest desire to preserve and maintain the Union of the States, if it can be done upon the principles and in furtherance of the objects for which it was formed." He insisted, however, that private opinion on the question of "African Slavery" was not a matter over which "the Government under the Constitution" had any control. "But now," he said, "this subject, which is confessedly on all sides outside of the Constitutional action of the Government so far as the States are concerned, is made the 'central idea' in the Platform of principles announced by the triumphant Party."

It was this total disregard of the Constitution and the rights guaranteed under it that lay back of southern fears. It was the introduction into party politics of issues which projected action by Congress outside its constitutional powers that had made all the trouble. Stephens used the word "Constitution" seven times in his letter.

The significant thing here is Stephens' reduction of sectional differences to the simple matter of southern rights under the Constitution. He too showed how completely the sectional controversy had been simplified into a conflict of principles. And he with Lincoln, speaking for North and South, emphasized the fact that after years of strife the complex issues between the sections had assumed the form of a conflict between *right* and *rights.*

To the scholar it must be perfectly clear that this drastic simplification of sectional differences did not mean that either Lincoln or Stephens thought that all the bitter economic, social, and political questions could be ignored. It simply meant that *right* and *rights* had become the symbols or carriers of all those interests and values. Yet it is equally clear that as symbols they carried an emotional force and moral power in themselves that was far greater than the sum total of all the material issues involved. They suggested things which cannot be compromised—things for which men willingly fight and die. Their use, in 1860, showed that an irrepressible conflict existed. . . .

The [sectional conflict] had certainly shown the weakness of the democratic process in dealing with issues cast as moral conflicts or having to do with the fundamental structure of society. It seemed to show, as Carl Becker has said, that government by discussion works best when there is nothing of profound importance to discuss, and when there is plenty of time to discuss it. The party system works best when the rival programs involve the superficial aspects rather than the fundamental structure of the social system, and majority rule works best when the minority can meet defeat at the polls in good temper because they need not regard the decision as either a permanent or a fatal surrender of their vital interests.

That, however, was only half of the difficulty. The [sectional conflict] had also shown that a democratic society cannot stand still. The conservative urge to hold fast to that which has been established may prove as fatal as the fanatic's prod to constant change. Those who profess a belief in democracy must ever remember that alongside the Constitution of the United States stands that other troublesome document, the Declaration of Independence, with its promise of greater freedom and equality. If politicians and parties do not sometimes give it heed, they may learn to their sorrow that the great document was written to justify revolt. That too may be a fatal weakness in the democratic process.

CONCLUSION

After examining these six different explanations of what caused the Civil War, or how it came about, it may be asked whether any one of them is sufficient in itself. Or is it a combination of all of them? History is extremely complex, and determining the causes of a major event such as the Civil War is the most exasperating of all historical problems. As Professor Craven observed, there are always "remote or background causes, and immediate causes, and causes resting on other causes."

Most historians have abandoned what Charles A. Beard once called the "devil theory" of history—the idea that a human tragedy like the Civil War can be attributed to the sinister maneuvers of a Stephen A. Douglas, or a John Brown, or a Jefferson Davis, or an Abraham Lincoln. Though there were plenty of aggressive pro-slavery men, recent research also has made it impossible to accept at face value the Slave Power conspiracy described by Henry Wilson. Others have effectively penetrated the weaknesses of Alexander H. Stephens' state-rights interpretation. At most the issue of state rights seems to have been one of those "causes resting on other causes."

But slavery and the other deep social and economic differences described by Beard and many other historians cannot be so easily dismissed. Though slavery was a moral and, therefore, an emotion-packed issue, fundamentally it represented to slave owners a profitable labor system and an enormous capital investment. This carries one into the field of economic sectionalism. Northerners tended more and more to look upon slavery as the foundation of a social system whose interests ran counter to their own, and whose political spokesmen repeatedly stood in the way of the "elightened" legislation they wanted Congress to pass. The tariff, internal improvements, the homestead law, and federal subsidies were all hopelessly interlaced with slavery, especially with the issue of slavery expansion. Joshua R. Giddings, a devoted political abolitionist, showed how difficult it was to separate these issues when he spoke in opposition to the admission of Texas as a slave state. Year after year Southerners saw the North growing stronger and their staple economy becoming increasingly menaced by abolitionists, free-soilers, manufacturers, merchants, and free farmers. If slavery were to be confined to its existing limits, then all the territories would soon become free states and the South would be overwhelmed. Most of the political leaders of the Deep South preferred secession to this.

And what of that "Blundering Generation"? It was there all right—in fact there was not one but several blundering generations. For the fatal blunders began back in Revolutionary War days when Southern leaders refused to see the deep implications of the Declaration of Independence and failed to provide for the systematic abolition of slavery. It was this blunder that paved the way for the abolitionist "agitators." Could slavery conceivably have existed in nineteenth-century America without its bitter critics? What would indeed have been abnormal would have been the *absence* of abolitionists in the kind of society that was emerging in the North. The basic blunder, then, was permitting slavery to survive until 1861, not the "reckless" anti-slavery "agitation." Even in 1861 it was hard to find any evidence that slavery was a "dying" institution.

The second blunder was the refusal of the political spokesmen for commercial and industrial capitalism to heed more fully the grievances of the agricultural South. They were the same kinds of grievances that later produced the Granger movement and the Populist revolt. The exploitation of the men who lived on the land by those who owned ships and factories gave validity to the bitter complaints of Senator Robert Toombs of Georgia.

The final blunder that culminated in the Civil War came in 1860 when Southerners refused to abide by the results of a democratic election. Southerners still would not submit to the control of a party that menaced slavery, not immediately perhaps but certainly in the long run.

These were the fatal errors of the prewar generations. The errors in handling such problems as Kansas were mere by-products. By 1861, after the three great blunders had been made, the situation got out of control and the "inevitable" war finally came.

But what should interest us today, perhaps as much as anything else about the causes of the Civil War, are the lessons for democracy suggested by Arthur Schlesinger, Jr., and Avery Craven. Must man inevitably work himself into these "log-jams" that can only be "burst by violence"? Surely this is being unduly pessimistic. Few of us still believe that man will ever be perfect or that he will ever be completely rational. But education in the humanities and social sciences has already increased the average man's capacity for rational thought and logical social analysis, and this capacity can be further increased. After all, in the history of the United States our democratic system has broken down completely only once, though it has tolerated abuses that have sometimes cried out for drastic remedies. It is the belief that democracy is working better than it once did, the conviction that it can be made to work still better, that is the foundation of our democratic faith. The task of democracy is not to let the "log-jams" develop.

Avoiding issues that deal with the "fundamental structure of society" is not the way to do this. Avoiding them, as our major political parties have too often done, is what creates the "log-jams." Statesmen of compromise, such as Clay and Douglas, did not settle the problems of their generation; they merely evaded or postponed them and thus let them accumulate and build up to a major national crisis. These statesmen of compromise tried the same old medicine again in 1861, but events revealed what quacks they had been. Who blundered more than they? It is the capacity of a democracy to deal with fundamental issues—the very kinds that generate emotions—directly, decisively, and in time, that provides the real measure of its success. This above all is the lesson of the Civil War.

12 THOMAS J. PRESSLY

why did the union win the civil war?

"We are resolved on Independence," wrote the South Carolina novelist, William Gilmore Simms, in August, 1861. "We are prepared for a long war—preparing for it. It will fully establish the independence of the South."[1] Almost three years later, a New York lawyer wrote in his diary that these were:

> fearfully critical anxious days. . . . The destinies of the continent for centuries depend in great measure on what is now being done and suffered a few hundred miles south of Twenty-first Street. The howl of a newsboy may at any moment rise on the midnight air, announcing an extra with news of national success or ruin. At this very minute, it may be practically settled, at or about Spotsylvania Court House, whether American development is to be controlled by the ideas of New England and New York, or by those of South Carolina and Mississippi—whether an Algerine slaveocracy is or is not destined to bear sway from the Lakes to the Gulf and from the Atlantic to the Pacific for generations to come.[2]

The Confederate supporter William Gilmore Simms and the Union supporter George Templeton Strong did not agree in their definition of what was at stake in the Civil War, but they shared the opinion that the

---

[1] Mary C. Simms Oliphant, Alfred Taylor Odell, and T. C. Duncan Eaves, colls. and eds., *The Letters of William Gilmore Simms*, 5 vols. (Columbia, S.C.: University of South Carolina Press, 1955), 4:373–74.

[2] Allan Nevins and Milton H. Thomas, eds., *The Diary of George Templeton Strong*, 4 vols. (New York: The Macmillan Co., 1952), 3:449–50 (May 20, 1864).

war's outcome would make a tremendous difference—would decide whether there would be an independent Confederate nation on the North American continent or a restored United States of America, "controlled by the ideas of New England and New York." Like Simms and Strong, many other contemporaries and many later observers have concluded that the directions in which the United States developed after 1865 were decisively influenced by the outcome of the Civil War. The importance of which side won the war makes important the attempt to understand how and why the winning side won and the losing side lost.

Trying to account for the victory of one side and the defeat of the other side in a war is analogous in some respects to explaining the outcome of athletic or other such contests. Thus, in a certain sense, anyone who has discussed why one athletic team defeated another has become acquainted with some of the issues involved in accounting for victory and defeat in war. Explaining the outcome of either an athletic contest or a war almost invariably involves some sort of comparison of the resources available to the rival contestants, and such is the case with the Civil War in the United States.

Comparing the resources of the Union and the Confederacy reveals the more populous, more economically diversified, and more economically self-sufficient Union opposed to the less populous, less economically diversified, and more economically dependent Confederacy. That disparity in resources has seemed to some individuals virtually to have determined that the Union would be victorious and the Confederacy would lose. Many other observers, however, have not accepted that deterministic position and have concluded, instead, that either side could have won, depending on how events developed in the months and years after the Blue and Gray hosts joined in battle. The differences between the "inevitablist" and the "evitablist" outlook have constituted the most fundamental divergence in explaining the outcome of the Civil War.

Many, perhaps most, of the generation of Unionists and Confederates who fought the war seem to have shared the "evitablist" perspective, but within that general perspective they disagreed widely after 1865 over what or who was responsible for Union victory and Confederate defeat. Some of the disagreements pitted former Confederates against former Confederates, while in other disputes former Confederates opposed former Unionists as in 1861. In one disagreement, some ex-Confederates maintained that the failure of their war effort was caused by mismanagement by their leaders, but other ex-Confederates disagreed. To some former Confederates, the war's outcome was the result of the Union's larger army, a contention which was disputed by the leader of the Union's armies, Ulysses S. Grant. Not larger numbers, but a superior society was the explanation of victory which appealed to many former

why did the union win the civil war?

Unionists, although it was denied by Jefferson Davis, the onetime President of the Confederate States of America.

The selections which follow present differing views focused on all four of the explanations of Union victory and Confederate defeat mentioned above: (1) Was the outcome of the war inevitable? (2) Was the outcome of the war caused by Confederate mismanagement? (3) Was the outcome of the war the result of the Union's larger army? (4) Was the outcome of the war the result of the superior characteristics of the Union as a society?

1. WAS THE OUTCOME OF THE WAR INEVITABLE?

Some of the material resources of Union and Confederacy which seem most relevant to success in war are summarized in the table below. Whether those resources signify inevitable victory for the Union and defeat for the Confederacy is then discussed by two present-day historians. It is common observation that explanations of the outcome of contests formulated after the event do not always share the perspective which was common while the contest was under way and the winner was still undecided. Prevalent attitudes toward the outcome of the Civil War while it was yet in progress are reflected in the writings of five individuals which are presented following the accounts by the two historians.

"Inevitablist" Outlook

The favorable balance of material resources for the Union, particularly economic resources, is cited by one historian of our own day, Richard N. Current, as evidence that the Confederacy "was all but beaten before the first shot was fired."[3]

If wars are won by riches, there can be no question why the North eventually prevailed. The only question will be: How did the South manage to stave off defeat so long? Or perhaps the question ought to be: Why did the South even risk a war in which she was all but beaten before the first shot was fired? . . .

It is hard to believe, and impossible to prove, that the Southerners did a worse job with economic affairs than Northerners would have done in the same circumstances. It is unimportant and unnecessary to try

---

[3] Richard N. Current, "God and the Strongest Battalions," in David Donald, ed., *Why the North Won the Civil War* (Baton Rouge: Louisiana State University Press, 1960), 3-4, 15, 19-22. Copyright 1960; reprinted by permission of the Louisiana State University Press.

Union and Confederate Resources, 1860[4]

	20 of the 22 Union States (All except Missouri and Kentucky)	The 11 Confederate States	Border Union States of Missouri and Kentucky (divided in support of Union and Confederacy)
Total White Population	20,275,000	5,500,000	1,983,000
Total Negroes and Mulattoes	435,000	3,654,000	
Total White Negro, and Mulatto	20,710,000	9,154,000	
Total White Males, age 15–30	2,582,678 (17 States and 1 Territory, Maine through Nebraska)	791,000	300,000
Manufacturing Establishments	110,000	18,000	
Number of Industrial Workers	1,300,000	110,000	
Locomotives Constructed in year ending June 1, 1860	451	19	
Value of Firearms Manufactured in 1860	$2,269,700	$73,000	
Number of Draft Animals (horses, asses, and mules)	4,600,000	2,566,000	
Total Railroad Mileage, 1860	21,973	9,283	

[4] Based on Allan Nevins, *The War for the Union*, 2 vols. (New York: Charles Scribner's Sons, 1959), 1:424–426. All figures in the table are approximate.

to prove this. The point is that the North had an economic strength several times greater to start with. In order to overcome this handicap and attain even so much as equality in economic power, the civilians of the South would have had to be *several times* as able, man for man, as those of the North. And this, obviously, is too much to have expected of any people, however willing and determined they might have been.

If the South could not meet the North on anything like an equal economic footing, she would have to be blessed with better luck or higher achievement in matters political, diplomatic, military, or psychological. A mere glance at these other considerations reveals at once that they cannot be appraised apart from one another, or the economic apart from any of them. . . .

The prime cause [of Confederate defeat] must have been economic. Given the vast superiority of the North in men and materials, in instruments of production, in communication facilities, in business organization and skill—and assuming for the sake of the argument no more than rough equality in statecraft and generalship—the final outcome seems all but inevitable. At least, it seems to have become inevitable once two dangers for the Union had been passed. One of these was the threat of interference from abroad. The other was the possibility of military disaster resulting from the enemy's superior skill or luck on the battlefield, from his abil-

why did the union win the civil war?

ity to make decisive use of his power-in-being before the strong potential of the Union could be fully developed and brought into play. Both dangers appear to have been over by midsummer, 1863, if not already by autumn, 1862. Thereafter, month by month, the resources of the North began increasingly to tell, in what became more and more a war of attrition. . . .

For the North to win, she had only to draw upon her resources as fully and as efficiently as the South drew upon hers; or, rather, the North had to make good use of only a fraction of her economic potential. Her material strength was so much greater that she could, as it were, almost lick the South with one hand tied behind her back. . . . At the start the North had possessed no significant advantage in a narrowly military sense—certainly no advantage comparable to that of her economic power and potential. This vast productive ability made the Union armies the best fed, the best clothed, the best cared for that the world ever had seen. This economic might made it possible for the North to field the stronger forces and, when the final test came, to place at every crucial point, as A. B. Hart has said, "more officers, more men, more camp followers, and more army mules."

Some Northerners used to cherish a simple—and, it would seem, an irrefutable—explanation of the Northern victory. God had willed that the Union be preserved. Surely, in view of the disparity of resources, it would have taken a miracle, a direct intervention of the lord on the other side, to enable the South to win. As usual, God was on the side of the heaviest battalions.

"Evitablist" Outlook

In contrast to Professor Current's conclusion that the outcome of the war "seemed all but inevitable," a second present-day historian, David M. Potter, has expressed doubt "that the overwhelming statistical advantages of the North predestined the Confederacy to defeat."[5]

In terms of economic logic, it can perhaps be demonstrated that the Confederacy, hopelessly overmatched by almost every measure of strength, was doomed to defeat. But history not only shows that in war the lighter antagonist sometimes defeats the heavier, it also shows that what seems logically certain often fails to happen. Thus, if we survey the course of the Civil War, do we not find that, in actuality, the Confederacy developed very formidable striking power—power impressive enough to make Lincoln doubt, even as late as 1864, that the Union would be saved? Do we not find the effective power of the opposing

---

[5] David M. Potter, "Jefferson Davis and the Political Factor in Confederate Defeat," in David Donald, ed., *Why the North Won the Civil War* (Baton Rouge: Louisiana State University Press, 1960), 92–94, 112. Copyright 1960; reprinted by permission of the Louisiana State University Press.

forces balanced so evenly that sometimes great results seemed to swing on the hinge of relatively trivial events? If a Confederate soldier had not shot Stonewall Jackson in the dusk at Chancellorsville, if Gouverneur Warren had not had a quick eye for Little Round Top, if a duplicate copy of Lee's plan of campaign in September, 1862, had not been used by someone on D. H. Hill's staff to wrap three cigars, might not a delicate balance have swung the other way in spite of all the statistics?

In weighing the question whether inescapable forces doomed the South in advance, it is well also to remember that the question is not what the South might have done during the last twenty-one months of the forty-eight-month war. For in fact, the result had been registered after Gettysburg and perhaps even after Sharpsburg, and all the South could hope for then was that the Northern people might fail to notice that they had won—as indeed the Northern Democrats did fail to notice in the election campaign of 1864. But for fourteen months before Lee came to high command, and for perhaps thirteen months after he did so, the result often appeared to be in real doubt, and it seems legitimate to question whether more effective political policies by the Confederates might at that time have made a crucial difference.

If the balance was, in fact, a delicate one, the analysis of forces must go far beyond the *a priori* arguments of economic determinism. While no one will deny that economic factors gave to the North an immense advantage, the precise question is whether other countervailing factors could possibly have offset it. For instance, could superior military and political skill on the Confederate side have done so? Reducing this question still further: Was there a differential in military performance in favor of the South which tended to offset, in part, the economic differential in favor of the North? The preponderance of historical opinion has agreed that the answer to this question is yes. For four long years, Lee's army did stave off defeat. But was the differential in political performance also in favor of the South? If it was, then one can say that Southern military and political prowess were hopelessly overmatched by the Union's sheer economic weight. But unless the effectiveness of the Confederate government equalled or surpassed that of the Union government, we cannot rest the evaluation of Confederate policy, as some historians have done, with the affirmation that Confederate leaders should not be blamed for their mistakes since the problems that they faced were insuperable. Instead, we shall have to say that economic and political factors, in conjunction, produced the final result, despite military factors which had a contrary tendency. Can we not go a step farther and ask whether the difference between Union and Confederate political performance was not as great as or greater than the economic disparities—whether in fact, the discrepancy in ability between Abraham Lincoln and Jefferson Davis was not as real and as significant as the inequality in mileage between Union and Confederate railroad systems? . . . In this sense, is it not justifiable to doubt that the overwhelming statistical advantages of the North predestined the Confederacy to defeat?

Outlook of Contemporaries

If we seek what individuals at the time thought about the outcome of the war while the fighting was still in progress, we find few statements suggesting that Union victory was inevitable. Most people seemed to have assumed until 1863 or later that victory could go to either side. Typical expressions of those assumptions, and of the ideas upon which they rested, are found in the excerpts presented below from the wartime writings of two Confederates, one Unionist, and two officials of the British government. The fact that individuals at the time seemed to have assumed that either Union or Confederacy could win the war does not, of course, conclusively answer the question of "inevitability," since the outcome may have been inevitable, or determined, no matter what contemporaries thought. But an understanding of the outlook of participants while the war was in progress should serve as a guard against the danger of "being wise after the event," of seeing the past through the "20–20 hindsight" of the "Monday-morning quarterback," and thereby assuming too easily that what happened had to happen in the way it did and could not have happened in some other fashion. Thus, before an answer to the question of inevitability is formulated, the views of contemporaries should be examined.

William Gilmore Simms (1806–1870) was probably the Confederacy's most prominent literary figure; he spent most of the war at his plantation Woodlands, in South Carolina, where most of his letters printed below were written.[6]

To James Lawson

Woodlands. 20 Aug. 1861.

... after all the mighty preparations of the North, they still tremble for the safety of Washington, & every step in Virginia has lost them blood & treasure. We do not exult in this. We wish for peace.... Every battle, thus far, has resulted in a Southern Victory—Sumter, Bethel, Bull Run, Manassas, Harpers Ferry & Missouri—all tell the same tale. Your Generals are cashiered. Your army demoralized. Your papers are at a loss where to cast the blame. They will be at no loss before long. They will see that their cause is bad. We have now 200,000 men in the field, with 250,000 in preparation for it. We can feed our armies from the fields, without buying any thing but guns & ammunition. We shall make 4,500,000 bales of Cotton. We will look at the piles & if need be, burn them. We do not need to sell a bag.... We are now manufacturing guns, cannon, rifles, powder,

---

[6] Mary C. Simms Oliphant, Alfred Taylor Odell, and T. C. Duncan Eaves, colls. and eds., *The Letters of William Gilmore Simms*, 5 vols. (Columbia, S.C.: University of South Carolina Press, 1955), 4:373, 374, 388. Copyright 1955; reprinted by permission of the University of South Carolina Press.

shot, oils, machinery, wool & cotton clothing, percussion caps, sewing machines—every thing. Three years of war will be the making of our people; and they are all beginning to perceive it. Not a bale of Cotton will be sent to the seaports. Hardly one off the plantations.

To James Henry Hammond

Monday Night, Decr. [1861]

... [Great Britain] cannot be undesirous of the dismemberment of the late Confederacy—cannot be desirous of the perpetuation of a Union which was in conflict with all her intersts—to her shipping, trade, manufactures, & institutions—of which she was jealous—which she at once feared & despised—cannot be indifferent to Cotton supply, or regardless of the free trade with 10 millions of people, who do not conflict with her in any way, but on the contrary, as purely Agricultural, are her natural allies. I should not be surprised to find her at war with the U.S. in less than 3 weeks.

Less Confident of Confederate success than Simms but nevertheless optimistic was Mrs. Mary Boykin Chesnut (1823–1886). Like Simms, Mrs. Chesnut was a native of South Carolina, and she spent a portion of the war years there at Mulberry, the Chesnut plantation. But she also lived during much of the war in Richmond, where her husband was an aide to President Jefferson Davis. The Davises and the Chesnuts were personal friends, and there are frequent references to the Confederate first family in Mrs. Chesnut's diary.[7]

June 29th [1862] Victory! Victory heads every telegram one reads now on the bulletin board. It is the anniversary of the battle of Fort Moultrie. The enemy went off so quickly; I wonder if it is not a trap laid for us, to lead us away from Richmond, to some place where they can manage to do us more harm. ...

July 10 [1862] Mr. Chesnut has come. He believes from what he heard in Richmond that we are to be recognized as a nation by the crowned heads across the waters. Mr. Davis was very kind. He asked my husband to stay at his house, which he did; and he went every day with General Lee and Mr. Davis to the battlefield, as a sort of amateur aid of the President. Likewise, they admitted him to the informal Cabinet meetings at the President's house. He is so hopeful now that it is pleasant to hear him.

---

[7] Mary Boykin Chesnut, *A Diary from Dixie*, Ben Ames Williams, ed. (Boston: Houghton Mifflin Co., 1949), 260, 265, 266. Copyright 1949; reprinted by permission of the Houghton Mifflin Company.

The military victories reported by Mrs. Chesnut and by Simms appear as defeats in the diary of Unionist George Templeton Strong, lawyer and prominent citizen of New York and their optimism and hope in 1861 and 1862 are matched by his dismay.[8]

April 17. [1861] . . . We are on the eve of a civil war that will be bitter and bloody, and probably indecisive. . . .

April 23. . . . Everyone's future has changed in these six months last past. This is to be a terrible, ruinous war, and a war in which the nation cannot succeed. It can never subjugate these savage millions of the South. It must make peace at last with the barbarous communities off its Southern frontier. . . .

May 3. . . . We generally agreed that it is to be a sharp struggle in which we must use all our energies, but that the South is paralyzed when its ports are blockaded and that it has not the resources to keep up an efficient military organization very long; that it will have to concentrate itself for one aggressive movement on the North—at Washington or some other point—and collapse utterly if it fail. I hope that time may verify our predictions. . . .

August 22. . . . We being to receive the rebound from England and France of the first news of the Bull Run battle. It is bitterly galling. The nation is disgraced, for a time at least, in the eyes of Christendom. Later reports from Southern newspapers showing that the rebels were absolutely beaten when the arrival of reinforcements turned the tide of battle in their favor, and that their loss exceeded ours on their own showing, may restore our credit a little. But this more accurate statement of the case may come too late to prevent France and England from recognizing the rebellious confederation of our Southern States, and introducing new and serious complications into our national trouble. . . .

August 27. It is almost time for another great disaster. It will occur in Western Virginia, probably. Can any disaster and disgrace arouse us fully? Perhaps we are destined to defeat and fit only for subjugation. Perhaps the oligarchs of the South are our born rulers. Northern communities may be too weak, corrupt, gelatinous, and unwarlike to resist Jefferson Davis and his confederates. It is possible that New York and New England and the Free West may be unable to cope with the South. If so, let the fact be ascertained and established as soon as possible, and let us begin to recognize our masters. But I should like a chance to peril my life in battle before that question is decided. . . .

December 31. Poor old 1861 just going. It has been a gloomy year of

---

[8] Reprinted with permission of The Macmillan Company from *The Diary of George Templeton Strong*, 4 vols., edited by Allan Nevins and Milton H. Thomas, 3:123, 133, 139, 176, 177, 198, 241, 253. Copyright 1952 by The Macmillan Company.

trouble and disaster. I should be glad of its departure, were it not that 1862 is likely to be no better. But we must take what is coming. Only through much tribulation can a young people attain healthy, vigorous national life. The results of many years spent in selfish devotion to prosperous, easy money-making must be purged out of our system before we are well, and a drastic dose of European war may be the prescription Providence is going to administer.

July 14. [*1862*] . . . We are in the depths just now, permeated by disgust, saturated with gloomy thinking. I find it hard to maintain my lively faith in the triumph of the nation and the law. . . .

September 7. . . . Rebellion is on its legs again, East and West, rampant and aggressive at every point. Our lines are either receding or turned, from the Atlantic to the Mississippi. The great event now prominently before us is that the South has crossed the Potomac in force above Washington and invaded Maryland and occupied Frederick, proclaimed a provisional governor, and seems advancing on the Pennsylvania line. No one knows the strength of the invading column. Some say 30,000, and others five times that. A very strong force, doubtless, has pushed up the Potomac to cut off the rebel communications. If it succeed, the rebellion will be ruined, but if it suffer a disorganizing defeat, the North will be at Jefferson Davis's mercy. I dare not let my mind dwell on the tremendous contingencies of the present hour.

Strong, Mrs. Chesnut, and Simms all mentioned the possibility of intervention in the Civil War by foreign nations, particularly England, and the hope and expectation of such intervention was one of the major supports for the confidence of Confederates that they could win their independence. The British government had issued a Proclamation of Neutrality (May 13, 1861), which recognized the belligerent status of the Confederacy, and had allowed two warships built in England, the *Florida* and the *Alabama*, to depart (March and July 1862), despite the protests of the Union government, and become the highly successful commerce destroyers of the Confederate navy. By September of 1862, the Confederate hopes and expectations of foreign intervention seemed near realization when Lord Palmerston, the British Prime Minister, and Lord John Russell, the Foreign Minister, exchanged the following letters.[9]

94 Piccadilly: September 14, 1862

My Dear Russell,

—The detailed accounts given in the *Observer* to-day of the battles of August 29 and 30 between the Confederates and the Federals show that the latter got a very complete smashing; and it seems not altogether unlikely that still greater disasters await them, and that even Washington or Baltimore may fall into the hands of the Confederates.

If this should happen, would it not be time for us to consider

---

[9] Spencer Walpole, *The Life of Lord John Russell*, 2 vols. (London: Longmans, Green, and Co., 1891), 2:360–62.

whether in such a state of things England and France might not address the contending parties and recommend an arrangement upon the basis of separation? . . .

Yours sincerely,
Palmerston

Gotha: September 17, 1862

My Dear Palmerston,

—Whether the Federal army is destroyed or not, it is clear that it is driven back to Washington, and has made no progress in subduing the insurgent States. Such being the case, I agree with you that the time is come for offering mediation to the United States Government, with a view to the recognition of the independence of the Confederates. I agree further, that, in case of failure, we ought ourselves to recognise the Southern States as an independent State. For the purpose of taking so important a step, I think we must have a meeting of the Cabinet. The 23rd or 30th would suit me for the meeting.

We ought then, if we agree on such a step, to propose it first to France, and then, on the part of England and France, to Russia and other powers, as a measure decided upon by us. . . .

Yours truly,
J. Russell

Broadlands: September 23, 1862

My Dear Russell,

—Your plan of proceedings about the mediation between the Federals and Confederates seems to be excellent. Of course, the offer would be made to both the contending parties at the same time; for, though the offer would be as sure to be accepted by the Southerns as was the proposal of the Prince of Wales by the Danish Princess, yet, in the one case as in the other, there are certain forms which it is decent and proper to go through.

A question would occur whether, if the two parties were to accept the mediation, the fact of our mediating would not of itself be tantamount to an acknowledgment of the Confederates as an independent State.

Might it not be well to ask Russia to join England and France in the offer of mediation? . . .

We should be better without her in the mediation, because she would be too favourable to the North; but, on the other hand, her participation in the offer might render the North the more willing to accept it.

The after communication to the other European powers would be quite right, although they would be too many for mediation.

As to the time of making the offer, if France and Russia agree—and France, we know, is quite ready, and only waiting for our concurrence—events may be taking place which might render it desirable that the offer should be made before the middle of October.

It is evident that a great conflict is taking place to the northwest of Washington, and its issue must have a great effect on the state of affairs. If the Federals sustain a great defeat, they may be at once ready for mediation, and the iron should be struck while it is hot. If, on the other hand, they should have the best of it, we may wait awhile and see what may follow. . . .

Yours sincerely,
Palmerston

Lee's invasion of Maryland was checked, England did not intervene in the conflict, and by 1864 George Templeton Strong and many other Unionists seem to have concluded that their side would ultimately triumph. But even as late as mid-August, 1864, there were days when Strong saw "no bright spot anywhere."[10]

August 19 [*1864*] . . . I see no bright spot anywhere. Rebeldom is beginning to bother Sherman's long line of communications. We may expect to hear any day that he is fighting his way back to Chattanooga and that Grant has bid Richmond good-bye. I fear the blood and treasure spent on this summer's campaign have done little for the country. . . .

By 1864, also, Mrs. Chesnut and many other Confederates manifested their waning hopes for victory, and yet in September of 1864 William Gilmore Simms wrote that "all can be saved" for the Confederacy. It is noteworthy, however, that Simms at the same time criticized actions by Confederate officials.[11]

To Paul Hamilton Hayne

Woodlands, 19 Sep. 1864.

. . . The fall of Atlanta is nothing *per se*. But it is much that our armies should be confided to Generals who, however meritorious as fighters, are capable of very little generalship. Hood has been miserably outgeneralled by Sherman. Unless Johns[t]on is sent back, or Lee or Beauregard takes command of the army in Georgia, the enemy will penetrate to Macon, Augusta, Andersonville, &c. . . . All can be saved, if the exempts, detailed men & skulks can be brought promptly into the field, & subjected to timely discipline. Otherwise, we shall die by inches like the tail of a snake. Imbecility in office, civil & military, is tolling on the young life of our country, our youth, to unproductive peril & sure destruction. We are made daily to sup on horrors. The war will probably be of continued duration till both parties are exhausted—unless God shall more emphatically interpose—how he may, or will do so—we may conjecture, but none can predict. Put your house in order. God be merciful to you.

---

[10] Allan Nevins and Milton H. Thomas, eds., *The Diary of George Templeton Strong*, 4 vols. (New York: The Macmillan Co., 1952), 3:474. Copyright 1952; reprinted by permission of The Macmillan Company.

[11] Mary C. Simms Oliphant, Alfred Taylor Odell, and T. C. Duncan Eaves, colls. and eds., *The Letters of William Gilmore Simms*, 5 vols. (Columbia, S.C.: University of South Carolina Press, 1955), 4:463–64. Copyright 1955; reprinted by permission of the University of South Carolina Press.

2. WAS THE OUTCOME OF THE WAR CAUSED BY CONFEDERATE MISMANAGEMENT?

The apparent assumption of most contemporaries while the war was in progress that its outcome was not inevitably determined seems to have continued after the close of the fighting. That assumption was reflected after Appomattox in explanations of the war's outcome in which the implication was that either side could have been victorious. The defeated in a war (as in an athletic contest) are usually under much greater psychological pressure than are the victors to find reasons or excuses for the outcome of the conflict, and thus many of the explicit explanations are found in the writings by former Confederates. When the surrender of the armies of Lee and the other commanders presented Confederates with the task of explaining to themselves and to the world why their hopes of victory had not materialized, mismanagement by Confederate leaders was a reason frequently advanced, particularly by wartime critics of the Davis Administration. That reason was not accepted as valid, however, by many former Confederates, and in the years after the war ended a "great debate" took place among former Confederates over what or who caused the Confederacy to lose the war.

The debate was sometimes conducted face to face, shout against shout, as described in Mrs. Chesnut's diary for May 1865; a different form of the debate can be seen by comparing the selection from the book published in 1874 by former Confederate General Joseph E. Johnston with the prompt rejoinder by two former Confederate Treasury officials. The final selection, by Robert G. H. Kean, formerly a bureau chief in the Confederate War Department, is one of the most comprehensive brief statements of the view that mismanagement by its leaders caused the Confederate defeat; along with mismanagement, Kean also points to weaknesses in the structure of Confederate society.

Mrs. Chesnut Describes Arguments over Responsibility for Confederate Defeat[12]

May 1st [1865] . . . A terrible fire-eater . . . came here today. He is six feet two, an athlete, a splendid specimen of the animal man; but he has never been under fire. His place in the service was a bombproof office. With a face red-hot in its rage, he denounced Jeff Davis and Hood.

---

[12] Mary Boykin Chesnut, *A Diary from Dixie*, Ben Ames Williams, ed. (Boston: Houghton Mifflin Co., 1949), 526, 533.

Now Teddy Barnwell is always ready for a shindy, and does not care very much who he attacks or defends. "Come now," said Edward the handsome, "the men who could fight and did not, they are the people who ruined us. If the men who are cursing Jeff Davis now had fought with Hood and fought as Hood fought we'd be all right now." The fire-eater departed. . . .

May 10th [1865] . . . I went out on the piazza, but from the windows came loud screams of vituperation and insult. "Jeff Davis's stupidity, Joe Johnston's magnanimity, Bragg's insanity." So I fled. Next day she [a friend] flew at me again, and raved until I was led out in hysterics, and then I was very ill. They thought I was dying, and I wish I had died. . . .

May 16th [1865] . . . Such a hue and cry, everybody blamed by somebody else. Only the dead heroes left stiff and stark on the battle field escape. I cry: "Blame every man who stayed at home and did not fight, but not one word against those who stood out until the bitter end, and stacked muskets at Appomattox."

Former Confederate Officials Dispute over Reasons for Confederate Defeat

General Joseph E. Johnston had been one of the Confederacy's highest ranking generals, and his feud with Jefferson Davis started almost as soon as the Confederate military forces were organized. The feud was continued, in a sense, by Johnston's ascribing, in a volume published in 1874, Confederate defeat and Union victory to the mismanagement of financial policies by the Davis Administration.[13]

. . . The cause of the subjugation of the Southern States was neither want of wealth and population, nor of devotion to their own cause on the part of the people of those States. That people was not guilty of the high crime of undertaking a war without the means of waging it successfully. They had ample means, which, unfortunately, were not applied to the object of equipping great armies, and bringing them into the field.

A full treasury was necessary to defray the expenses of a great war. The South had the means of making one, in its cotton alone. But its Government rejected those means, and limited its financial efforts to printing bank-notes, with which the country was soon flooded. The necessity of actual money in the treasury, and the mode of raising it, were generally understood in the country. It was that the Government should take the cotton from the owners and send it to Europe as fast as possible, to be sold there. This was easily practicable; for the owners were ready to accept any terms the Government might fix; and sending

---
[13] Joseph E. Johnston, *Narrative of Military Operations* (New York: D. Appleton and Company, 1874), 421–25.

to Europe was easy in all the first year of the Confederacy's existence. Its Government went into operation early in February. The blockade of the Southern ports was proclaimed in May, but not at all effective until the end of the following winter; so that there was a period of about twelve months for the operation of converting four or five million bales of cotton into money. The sum raised in that way would have enabled the War Department to procure at once arms enough for half a million of men, and after that expenditure the Confederate treasury would have been much richer than that of the United States. By applying the first money obtained in this way, to the purchase of arms and military accoutrements, or using for the purpose the credit which such an amount of property would have given, the War Department would have been able to equip troops as fast as they could be assembled and organized. And, as the Southern people were full of enthusiasm, five hundred thousand men could have been ready and in the field had such a course been pursued, at the time when the first battle was actually fought—the 21st of July, 1861. Such a force placed on the Northern borders of the Confederacy before the United States had brought a fourth of the number into the field, would probably have prevented the very idea of "coercion." Such a disposition of such an army, and the possession of financial means of carrying on war for years, would have secured the success of the Confederacy.

The timely adoption of such a financial system would have secured to us the means of success, even without an extraordinary importation of arms, and the immediate organization of large armies. It would have given the Confederacy a treasury richer than that of the United States. We should thus have had, to the end of the war, the means of paying our soldiers; and that would have enabled such of them as belonged to the laboring class to remain in the ranks. This class, in the Confederacy as in all other countries, formed the body of the army. In all the earlier part of the war, when the Confederate money was not much below that of the United States in value, our troops were paid with some regularity, and the soldiers of the laboring class who had families, fed and clothed them with their pay, as they had formerly done with the wages of their labor. And so long as that state of things continued, the strength of the Confederate armies was little impaired; and those armies were maintained on such a footing as to justify the hope, which was general in the South until the fall of 1864, that we were to win in the contest. But after the Confederate currency had become almost worthless—when a soldier's month's pay would scarcely buy one meal for his family—and that was the case in all the last period of ten or twelve months—those soldiers of the laboring class who had families were compelled to choose between their military service and the strongest obligations men know—their duties to wives and children. They obeyed the strongest of those obligations, left the army, and returned to their homes to support their families.

The wretched impressment laws deprived the army of many valuable men of a class less poor than that just referred to. Those laws required the impressment of all articles of military necessity that could not be purchased. The Government had the power of regulating the prices to be paid by it for all such commodities; and its commissioners appointed for the purpose fixed them much below the market values. No one would sell to the Government, of course, when he could get from his neighbors twice the government price for his horses or grain; consequently the officers of the Government could never purchase, but had always to procure supplies by impressment. No rules for their guidance were prescribed; none at least that were observed by them or known to the public, and they were subjected to no supervision. All the property of Confederate citizens applicable to military purposes was, therefore, under their absolute control. The bad and indifferent officers impressed what they were called upon to furnish, in the manner least inconvenient to themselves, usually on the nearest plantations or farms, or those where opposition was not to be apprehended. The farms of soldiers were generally under the management of women, and therefore were, not unusually, drawn upon for much more than their proportion. Hence it was not uncommon for a soldier to be written to by his wife, that so much of the food he had provided for herself and his children had been impressed, that it was necessary that he should return to save them from suffering or starvation. Such a summons, it may well be supposed, was never unheeded.

The sufferings of the soldiers themselves, produced by the want of proper clothing, drove many of the least hardy out of the ranks. Want of food also is said to have had the same effect, especially in the army before Richmond, in the last winter of the war.

It was by such causes, all due to an empty treasury, that our armies were so reduced in the last months of the war. . . .

Johnston's explanation of Confederate defeat was immediately challenged by two former Secretaries of the Treasury in the Confederate Government, C. G. Memminger and George A. Trenholm.[14]

To the Editor of The News and Courier,

Charleston March 27th 1874.

I observe by your paper of yesterday which extracts a passage from Gen. Johnston's book, that he follows the ancient example of our forefather Adam in casting the fault of a general calamity on some other person. He attributes the failure of the Southern Confederacy to the blunder of the Government, at its first institution, in not possessing itself of the cotton crop then in the hands of the planters. This cotton (according to the General) should have been shipped in anticipation of the blockade, and it would then have fur-

---

[14] Dunbar Rowland, ed., *Jefferson Davis, Constitutionalist*, 10 vols. (Jackson, Mississippi, 1923), 8:42–45, 49–51. Copyright 1923; reprinted by permission of Department of Archives and History, State of Mississippi.

nished a basis for future credit. As I was at that time in charge of the Treasury Department, the responsibility of this failure would rest chiefly on me; and you will, therefore, not consider it out of place that I should correct misapprehensions which seem to have misled yourself as well as Gen. Johnston.

The Confederate Government was organized in February, the blockade was instituted in May, thus leaving a period of three months in which the whole cotton crop on hand, say four millions of bales, ought, according to the military financier, to have been got into the hands of the Confederate Government, and to have been shipped abroad.

This would have required a fleet of four thousand ships, allowing one thousand bales to the ship. Where would these vessels have been procured, in the face of the notification of the blockade? and was not as much of the cotton shippped by private enterprise as could have been shipped by the Government? When so shipped, the proceeds of the sale were in most cases sold to the Government in the shape of bills of exchange. The superior advantage of that plan is evinced by the fact that, throughout the year, the Government exchanged its own notes for bills in England at par, with which it paid for all its arms and munitions of war.

Of course this vast amount of cotton could only have been procured in one of three ways—by seizure, by purchase, or by donation.

Certainly no one at the first inception of the Confederacy would have ventured to propose to seize upon the crop then in the hands of the planters, and which furnished their only means of subsistence.

Could it not, then, have been purchased?

At the commencement of the Government the treasury had not funds to pay for the table on which the secretary was writing; and the first purchases of the Government made abroad were made on the private draft of the secretary. There was not to be found, in the whole Confederacy, a sheet of bank note paper on which to print a note. Forecasting this need, the secretary had ordered, from England, a consignment of note paper and lithographing materials, the vessel containing which was captured on the high seas; and many of the friends of the late Col. Evans, of our city, will remember that he nearly lost his life in the attempt to bring across the lines a single parcel of note paper. It is within the memory of the printers of these notes, that months elapsed before bonds or notes could be engraved and printed; and these constituted our entire currency.

How, then, was the cotton to be paid for?

And when the mechanical difficulties were overcome, the financial presented an equal barrier. The scheme for raising money, adopted by Congress, was to issue Confederate notes, funding the redundant notes in interest-bearing bonds; and all payments at the treasury were made with these notes. The daily demands on the treasury exceeded greatly the means of supply. Now, if instead of applying the notes to the daily payments required at the treasury they had been used to purchase cotton, the treasury would have found itself filled with cotton, without any money to meet the wants of the government until that cotton could be shipped abroad and sold.

If, instead of payment in notes,

the bonds of the government had been used to purchase the cotton crop, those bonds would have been thrown in the market to meet the necessities of the planters and their value as a means of funding the surplus currency would have been destroyed. It is obvious to any one acquainted with finance, that this would have broken down the Confederate currency within the first year of its existence. Whereas the plan pursued sustained the credit of the Confederacy until broken down by calamities under which no credit could survive.

The only remaining mode in which the cotton could have been procured by the government was by donation from the planters. So far was this donation from being possible, that the treasury actually had to issue a circular in response to applications to the Government for aid to the planters in making loans to them, and not a bale of the crop of that year was contributed to the government. An effort was made to get pledges of the next year's crop in exchange for bonds of the government. To accomplish this it was deemed necessary to allow the planters to get their own price through their own factors, without allowing the government to fix its price, and the whole amount thus pledged did not reach fifty millions or about two months' expenses of the government of which perhaps one third was never received.

Every one conversant with the politics of the day knows that it was the current expectation that the blockade could not be continued for a year. The Confederate Congress were so informed when they adopted the international agreement as to privateers. The Government of the United States equally supposed that the war would be of short duration, as is apparent from President Lincoln's proclamation calling for troops for ninety days. There could, therefore, be no motive to induce the Confederate Government to store up cotton as a basis of credit. When it became apparent that the blockade and the war would continue, the government then made arrangements for using cotton as the basis of a loan; and the large foreign cotton loan negotiated in Europe by Messrs. Erlanger furnished abundant resources to the government for its supplies from abroad. But even to the last its power over the crop was restricted by the large quantities held in private hands which could not be purchased at all. At no time that I am aware of was it in the power of the Government to get possession of the cotton crop, unless it had seized the same by force, and by the same force compelled payment in a depreciated currency; a high-handed course which could never receive the sanction of the statesmen who administered our government. The only approximation to it was in the shape of a tax in kind when the currency failed to command supplies, and which was made as just and equal as any other tax.

The truth is, that if Gen. Johnston's recollections of history were as vivid as his knowledge of military tactics is great, instead of censuring the financial administration of the Confederate Government, he would have discovered no instance on record where a war of such dimensions, in a constantly decreasing territory, has been sustained for four years by mere financial expedients, without the aid usually derived from taxes—for in the whole Confederate war but one general war tax was levied, and a great portion of that was never collected.

C. G. Memminger

The Confederate Collapse

A critical examination of the Facts cited by Gen. Johnston, in support of his Views of the Cause of the Failure of the South. (The following was written by George A. Trenholm and embodied in above report of C. G. Memminger.)

To the Editor of The News & Courier,

The News & Courier, quoting from the forthcoming work of Gen. Johnston, gives us the views of the author as to the cause of our failure. . . .

Let us examine the facts upon which this theory rests, and without the support of which it must necessarily fall to the ground. The crop of cotton available for this scheme must necessarily have been that of 1860–61. It could not have been the crop of which the seed was not yet put in the ground when the government was formed at Montgomery.

What was then the crop of 1860–61?

Was it 4,000,000 to 5,000,000 bales, and was it accessible for immediate exportation?

The crop of 1860–61 was officially stated at .... 3,849,000 bales
Of this quantity the consumption of the Southern States took off, ...   193,000 bales
Leaving for exportation 3,656,000 bales

Let us now see what proportion of this quantity was available in the way described by Gen. Johnston.

Up to the 28th of February, the month that gave birth to the infant government, 3,000,000 bales had been received at the seaports, and the great bulk of it had been exported to Europe or been sold to the New England spinners. By the 1st of May 586,000 bales more had been received and sold.

England and the
  Continent took ...... 3,127,000 bales
The New England
  spinners took ......   654,000 bales

It will thus be seen that before the new government was fairly organized, the entire crop was already beyond its reach. Another crop followed, it is true, but no part of it was ready for market before the month of September ensuing. This all will agree in; and they will also agree that the exportation in any quantity was an absolute impossibility. There were no vessels in the ports of the Confederacy; the last had left before the expiration of the sixty days allowed to foreign tonnage under the blockade proclamation.

The only vessels that took out Cotton after that time were the foreign steamers that ran the blockade to procure cargoes of cotton for the owners. They came in small numbers, and one or two at a time. Had the government seized one of them for its own use, or prevented them from leaving with cotton, they would have ceased to come.

A Former Official of the Confederate War Department Explains Why the Confederacy Lost

Like former General Joseph Johnston, Robert G. H. Kean cited "a bankrupt treasury" as one of the most important instances of the mismanagement by Confederate officials which led to defeat. Kean also ascribed the defeat to weaknesses in the Confederacy as a society, a theme which was to receive much emphasis and elaboration in the writings of twentieth-century historians. During a large part of the war, Kean was head of one of the nine bureaus in the Confederate War Department. The following selection is taken from an entry in his diary, written shortly after the war ended.[15]

The Causes of the Failure of Southern Independence

July 7 [1865] . . .
1. A bankrupt treasury. This was the prolific source of other evils: (a) high prices of all supplies, and parties unwilling to furnish even for them; (b) discontent of people and army for want of payment of dues and worthlessness of it when obtained; hence *desertion,* impressment; (c) decay of railroad transportation due in part to this cause, the roads not having wherewith to keep themselves up. Causes [for bankrupt treasury:] (a) belief of leaders in a short war; (b) inability to deal with a very large subject; First Congress responsible as well as the President and Memminger.

2. Want of men; exhaustion of supply from which recruits of effective qualities to be drawn; severity of the conscription; desertion due to insufficient supply and worthlessness of money.

3. Shortness of subsistence, military operations fettered by; armies obliged to occupy certain fixed positions with reference to this as a main question. Due (a) to bad currency, (b) to want of efficiency of transportation, (c) to defective system. Behind all this the country not a food producing one.

4. Incompetency of military men. Of the West Pointers; small, not capable of high command; promoted rapidly from grade of subalterns to command of divisions, corps, and armies. Obstruction of way to command by men of capacity not bred to arms. Defective system of promotion fixed by law and President's construction of "valor and skill." Want of discernment in the selection of general officers; consequently want of discipline, especially in cavalry. Rapid destruction

---

[15] Edward Younger, ed., *Inside the Confederate Government: The Diary of Robert Garlick Hill Kean* (New York: Oxford University Press, 1957), 213–15. Copyright 1957; reprinted by permission of the Oxford University Press.

of best material in grade of regimental and company officers; difficult towards the last to find officers competent to command regiments and brigades. Bad selections made; losses resulting, e.g., Bragg, Pemberton, Holmes, Hindman, A. P. Hill, J. E. B. Stuart, Ewell, F. Lee, D. H. Hill. Bad system of cavalry and want of capacity to deal with the questions.

5. Want of horses for transports and artillery; country stripped by impressment of horses, which straightway perished for want of forage; this want due to defective transportation by railroad and wagon, and limited supply in any given area of country.

6. Difficulties of supply and recruiting aggravated by *faction*—Stephens, Toombs, J. E. Brown, Vance.

7. Slavery an inherent weakness when deeply invaded, from desertion to the enemy and joining their army as recruits.

To these may be added one cause which in a certain sense may be said to include them all—the absence of a Representative Man, a *leader* in the *council* as well as in the field who should comprehend and express the movement. We had no one who approached it. The country by instinct, seeking such a reliance, gave its faith to Lee in vain.

3. WAS THE OUTCOME OF THE WAR THE RESULT OF THE UNION'S LARGER ARMY?

Among the former Confederates who did not accept the mismanagement explanation of the outcome of the war, a number accounted for the Confederacy's defeat and the Union's victory by citing the Union's larger army. This explanation did not imply that the outcome of the struggle had been inevitable, for presumably the Confederacy might have won if it could have secured the decision before its own reserves of manpower were exhausted. It spared from criticism the officials and the institutions of the government to which Confederates had given their loyalty, and thus did not require a break with previous allegiance. And this explanation also salved wounded pride, since the more numerous the Union soldiers, the greater the achievement of the outnumbered Confederates for holding out as long as they did. Former Confederates who expressed this widely held explanation of the war's outcome included Robert E. Lee, Alexander H. Stephens, the former Vice-President of the Confederacy, and Charles Henry Smith, who as "Bill Arp" had been the Confederacy's best-known humorist.

But this account did not go unchallenged. If the size of the Union's army was pictured as the crucial factor in Union victory and Confederate defeat, it was possible to infer that Union generals have been inferior to their Confederate counterparts and have won battles only because of the numerical superiority of their forces. The most famous Union general, Ulysses S. Grant, maintained that the large numbers of Union troops did not offset "the advantage of position and intrenchment occupied by the enemy," and thus cast doubt on the contention that superior numbers had been responsible for victory.

Lee, Stephens, "Bill Arp," and the Size of the Union Army

On March 9, 1865, one month before Lee surrendered his army, he stated in a letter to the Confederate Secretary of War that, "while the military situation" was "not favorable," yet it was "not worse than the superior numbers and resources of the enemy justified us in expecting from the beginning." After the war ended, Lee, in November 1865, described to a British traveler the effects of the Union's larger armies. Lee is quoted by the traveler, Herbert C. Saunders, as using the word "inevitable" with respect to the surrender at Appomattox, but the reader can judge whether the meaning is that Confederate defeat had been "inevitable" from 1861, or whether, given the situation of April 1865, surrender of Lee's army was by that time unavoidable.[16]

General Lee [wrote Saunders] . . . with reference to the small result of their numerous victories, accounted for it in this way: the force which the Confederates brought to bear was so often inferior in numbers to that of the Yankees that the more they followed up the victory against one portion of the enemy's line the more did they lay themselves open to being surrounded by the remainder of the enemy. He likened the operation to a man breasting a wave of the sea, who, as rapidly as he clears a way before him, is enveloped by the very water he has displaced. He spoke of the final surrender as inevitable owing to the superiority in numbers of the enemy. His own army had, during the last few weeks, suffered materially from defection in its ranks, and, discouraged by failures and worn out by hardships, had at the time of the surrender only 7,892 men under arms, and this little army was almost surrounded by one of 100,000. They might, the General said with an air piteous to behold, have cut their way out as they had done before, but, looking upon the struggle as hopeless, I was not surprised to hear him say that he thought it cruel to prolong it. In two other battles he named (Sharpsburg and Chancellorsville, I think he said), the Confederates were to the Federals in point of numbers as

---

[16] Robert E. Lee, Jr., *Recollections and Letters of General Robert E. Lee* (Garden City, N.Y.: Doubleday, Page & Company, 1924), 232–33.

35,000 to 120,000 and as 45,000 to 155,000 respectively, so that the mere disparity of numbers was not sufficient to convince him of the necessity of surrender; but feeling that his own army was persuaded of the ultimate hopelessness of the contest as evidenced by their defection, he took the course of surrendering his army in lieu of reserving it for utter annihilation. . . .

When Alexander H. Stephens, the former Vice-President of the Confederacy, published his two-volume history of the war in 1868 and 1870, he placed emphasis upon the differences in size of the rival armies.[17]

One of the most striking features in . . . [the Civil War] was the great disparity between the number of the forces on the opposite sides. From its beginning to its end, near, if not quite, *two millions* more Federals were brought into the field than the entire force of the Confederates. The Federal records show that they had, from first to last, over 2,600,000 men in the service; while the Confederates, all told in like manner, could not have much, if any, exceeded 600,000! No People on earth ever maintained the great Right of Self-government, so long as the Confederates did in this contest, with such sacrifices of blood and treasure, against such odds!

The view that the Union won because of its larger army was expressed in a terse analogy by the ex-Confederate humorist "Bill Arp" (Charles Henry Smith). Writing to one of his counterparts in the Union, Artemus Ward, Arp used the dialect spelling which was characteristic of the humorous writing, Unionist or Confederate, in that day.[18]

Now, I suppose that, poetically speakin', "In Dixie's fall, We sinned all." But talkin' the way I see it, a big feller and a little feller, *so-called*, got into a fite, and they fout and fout a long time, and everybody all 'round kept hollerin', "hands off," but helpin' the big feller, until finally the little feller caved in and hollered enuf. He made a bully fite, I tell you.

---

[17] Alexander H. Stephens, *A Constitutional View of the Late War Between the States*, 2 vols. (Philadelphia, 1868–70), 2:629–30.

[18] Charles Henry Smith, *Bill Arp: From the Uncivil War to Date, 1861–1903* (Atlanta: The Byrd Printing Company, 1903), 88–89—letter dated September 1, 1865.

General Grant Discounts the Effect of Larger Union Armies

Almost from the moment of victory, Ulysses S. Grant had expressed doubt that the size of the Union army was in itself responsible for victory. In his report of July 22, 1865, to the Secretary of War, Grant questioned whether Union numbers and resources were not "more than balanced" by Confederate advantages.[19]

The resources of the enemy and his numerical strength were far inferior to ours; but as an offset to this, we had a vast territory, with a population hostile to the government, to garrison, and long lines of river and railroad communications to protect, to enable us to supply the operating armies.

The armies in the East and West acted independently and without concert, like a balky team, no two ever pulling together, enabling the enemy to use to great advantage his interior lines of communication for transporting troops from East to West, reinforcing the army most vigorously pressed, and to furlough large numbers, during seasons of inactivity on our part, to go to their homes and do the work of producing, for the support of their armies. It was a question whether our numerical strength and resources were not more than balanced by these disadvantages and the enemy's superior position.

The question raised by Grant in the final sentence of the selection above was replaced by positive assertions in his *Personal Memoirs*, completed just before his death and published in 1885.[20]

. . . There has always been a great conflict of opinion as to the number of troops engaged in every battle, or all important battles, fought between the sections, the South magnifying the number of Union troops engaged and belittling their own. Northern writers have fallen, in many instances, into the same error. I have often heard gentlemen, who were thoroughly loyal to the Union, speak of what a splendid fight the South had made and successfully continued for four years before yielding, with their twelve million of people against our twenty, and of the twelve, four being colored slaves, non combatants. I will add to their argument. We had many regiments of brave and loyal men who volunteered under great difficulty from

---

[19] Ulysses S. Grant, *Personal Memoirs of U. S. Grant*, 2 vols. (New York: 1885), 2:555–56.

[20] Ulysses S. Grant, *Personal Memoirs of U. S. Grant*, 2 vols. (New York, 1885), 2:500–5.

why did the union win the civil war?

the twelve million belonging to the South.

But the South had rebelled against the National government. It was not bound by any constitutional restrictions. The whole South was a military camp. The occupation of the colored people was to furnish supplies for the army. Conscription was resorted to early, and embraced every male from the age of eighteen to forty-five, excluding only those physically unfit to serve in the field, and the necessary number of civil officers of State and intended National government. The old and physically disabled furnished a good portion of these. The slaves, the noncombatants, one-third of the whole, were required to work in the field without regard to sex, and almost without regard to age. Children from the age of eight years could and did handle the hoe; they were not much older when they began to hold the plough. The four million of colored non-combatants were equal to more than three times their number in the North, age for age and sex for sex, in supplying food from the soil to support armies. Women did not work in the fields in the North, and children attended school.

The arts of peace were carried on in the North. Towns and cities grew during the war. Inventions were made in all kinds of machinery to increase the products of a day's labor in the shop, and in the field. In the South no opposition was allowed to the government which had been set up and which would have become real and respected if the rebellion had been successful. No rear had to be protected. All the troops in service could be brought to the front to contest every inch of ground threatened with invasion. The press of the South, like the people who remained at home, were loyal to the Southern cause.

In the North, the country, the towns, and the cities presented about the same appearance they do in time of peace. The furnace was in blast, the shops were filled with workmen, the fields were cultivated, not only to supply the population of the North and the troops invading the South, but to ship abroad to pay a part of the expense of the war. In the North the press was free up to the point of open treason. The citizen could entertain his views and express them. Troops were necessary in the Northern States to prevent prisoners from the Southern army being released by outside force, armed, and set at large to destroy by fire our Northern cities. Plans were formed by Northern and Southern citizens to burn our cities, to poison the water supplying them, to spread infection by importing clothing from infected regions, to blow up our river and lake steamers—regardless of the destruction of innocent lives. The copperhead disreputable portion of the press magnified rebel successes, and belittled those of the Union army. It was, with a large following, an auxiliary to the Confederate army. The North would have been much stronger with a hundred thousand of these men in the Confederate ranks and the rest of their kind thoroughly subdued, as the Union sentiment was in the South, than we were as the battle was fought. . . .

Under such circumstances it is hard to conceive how the North showed such a superiority of force in every battle fought. I know they did not.

During 1862 and '3, John H. Morgan, a partisan officer, of no military education, but possessed of courage and endurance, operated in the rear of the Army of the Ohio in Kentucky and Tennessee. He had no base of supplies to protect, but was at home wherever he went. The army operating against the South, on the contrary, had to protect its lines of communication with the North, from which all supplies had to come to the front. Every foot of road had to be guarded by troops stationed at convenient distances apart. These guards could not render assistance beyond the points where stationed. Morgan was footloose and could operate where his information—always correct—led him to believe he could do the greatest damage. During the time he was operating in this way he killed, wounded, and captured several times the number he ever had under his command at any one time. He destroyed many millions of property in addition. Places he did not attack had to be guarded as if threatened by him. Forrest, an abler soldier, operated farther west, and held from the National front quite as many men as could be spared for offensive operations. It is safe to say that more than half the National army was engaged in guarding lines of supplies, or were on leave, sick in hospital, or on detail which prevented their bearing arms. Then, again, large forces were employed where no Confederate army confronted them. I deem it safe to say that there were no large engagements where the National numbers compensated for the advantage of position and intrenchment occupied by the enemy. . . .

4. WAS THE OUTCOME OF THE WAR THE RESULT OF THE SUPERIOR CHARACTERISTICS OF THE UNION AS A SOCIETY?

If defeat led former Confederates to debates and disagreements after 1865 over the reasons for their failure in war, victory confirmed the former Unionists in the conviction that theirs had been the superior society which "deserved" to win. Whether the superiority resided in the ideology of the society, or in its technology, or in some other factor, was a comparatively minor point which need not cause conflict among the victorious Unionists. George Bancroft, considered by many of his contemporaries to be the nation's leading historian, found the Union's superior characteristics in its cause, "liberty" and "freedom itself," while Samuel S. Cox, longtime Congressman from Ohio, found the superiority in the inventive skill of Unionists. The ascription by Bancroft and Cox of Union victory to its superior characteristics as a society complements in some respects the description of Confederate weaknesses by the former Confederate, R. G. H. Kean, in the selection printed above. Unlike Kean, however, the former President of the Confederacy, Jefferson Davis, pictured no weaknesses in the Confederacy as a society. Davis vigorously rejected any claim of superior characteristics pertaining to the Union, asserting instead that events after 1865 had demonstrated that superiority lay with the principles which had animated the Confederacy.

Bancroft and Cox Extol the Union

The following remarks are taken from the memorial address on Lincoln which George Bancroft delivered before both Houses of Congress on February 12, 1866. Bancroft described the superiority of the Union cause in more mystical language than did most of his fellow Unionists, but many of them shared his fundamental assumptions of victory due to greater merit on the side of the Union.[21]

. . . When it came home to the consciousness of the Americans that the war which they were waging was a war for the liberty of all the nations of the world, for freedom itself, they thanked God for giving them strength to endure the severity of the trial to which He put their sincerity, and nerved themselves for their duty with an inexorable will. The President was led along by the greatness of their self-sacrificing example; and as a child, in a dark night, on a rugged way, catches hold of the hand of its father for guidance and support, he clung fast to the hand of the people, and moved calmly through the gloom. While the statesmanship of Europe was mocking at the hopeless vanity of their efforts, they put forth such miracles of energy as the history of the world had never known. . . .

There went into the field, for various terms of enlistment, about two million men, and in March last the men in the army exceeded a million: that is to say, nine of every twenty able-bodied men in the free Territories and States took some part in the war; and at one time every fifth of their able-bodied men was in service. . . . In the movements of troops science came in aid of patriotism, so that, to choose a single instance out of many, an army twenty-three thousand strong, with its artillery, trains, baggage, and animals, were moved by rail from the Potomac to the Tennessee, twelve hundred miles, in seven days. On the long marches, wonders of military construction bridged the rivers, and wherever an army halted, ample supplies awaited them at their ever-changing base.

. . . The country had for its allies the river Mississippi, which would not be divided, and the range of mountains which carried the stronghold of the free through Western Virginia and Kentucky and Tennessee to the highlands of Alabama. But it invoked the still higher power of immortal justice. In an-

---

21 George Bancroft, *Memorial Address on the Life and Character of Abraham Lincoln* (Washington, D.C.: U.S. Government Printing Office, 1866), 34–41, 50.

cient Greece, where servitude was the universal custom, it was held that if a child were to strike its parent, the slave would defend the parent, and by that act recover his freedom. After vain resistance, LINCOLN, who had tried to solve the question by gradual emancipation, by colonization, and by compensation, at last saw that slavery must be abolished, or the republic must die; and on the first day of January, 1863, he wrote liberty on the banners of the armies.

. . . . The proclamation accomplished its end, for, during the war, our armies came into military possession of every State in rebellion. Then, too, was called forth the new power that comes from the simultaneous diffusion of thought and feeling among the nations of mankind. The mysterious sympathy of the millions throughout the world was given spontaneously. The best writers of Europe waked the conscience of the thoughtful, till the intelligent moral sentiment of the Old World was drawn to the side of the unlettered statesman of the West.

. . . The war continued, with all the peoples of the world for anxious spectators. . . . the armies of the country, moving with one will, went as the arrow to its mark, and, without a feeling of revenge, struck a death-blow at rebellion. . . .

. . . the American people was the hero of the war.

Samuel S. Cox, in a volume published in 1885, contrasted the inventive genius found in the Union with the lack of skill and invention in the Confederacy, and described the Union inventive genius as the cause of Confederate defeat. Cox had been a member of Congress from the State of Ohio during the Civil War years and for a grand total of almost a quarter of a century.[22]

It does not detract from the chivalric courage of the Confederate soldier, however humble his station or high his rank, that he succumbed before the vast mechanical forces of the North. The South was not distinguished for inventive mechanical genius. It was only in a few localities that she had the facilities to construct what was indispensable to war. Her mechanical instrumentalities were few and far between, for the South was a country of planters. Her ways, one would have supposed, would have been the ways of pleasantness and all her paths—of peace. But there was a sentiment of chivalry about the nature of her sons which led them inconsiderately to dash, Quixotically, against the locomotive, which is the emblem and the proof of the chemical and mechanical forces of our time. If the South at last lost her cause, it was because she had never gained that skill in invention which has no parallel in the world, and which has had its home in the North, and principally in the New England States.

---

[22] Samuel S. Cox, *Union—Disunion—Reunion. Three Decades of Federal Legislation. 1855 to 1885* (Providence, R.I.: J. A. and R. A. Reid, 1885), 215.

Jefferson Davis Praises the Principles of the Confederacy

Jefferson Davis opposed the views of the victorious Unionists by suggesting that the Union had not won the battle of opposing principles. Conceding that the Union had won military victory, Davis insisted that "force decides no truth." He wrote in 1881 that the events of the Reconstruction era had demonstrated the validity of the struggle made by Confederates from 1861 to 1865 against the Union and for "constitutional liberty." The principles supported by the Confederacy would prevail, Davis predicted, "in God's appointed time and place," and thus he asked, "On which side was the victory?"[23]

... Although the Confederate armies may have left the field, although the citizen-soldiers may have retired to the pursuits of peaceful life, although the Confederate States may have renounced their new Union, they have proved their indestructibility by resuming their former places in the old one, where, by the organic law, they could only be admitted as republican, equal, and sovereign States of the Union. And, although the Confederacy as an organization may have ceased to exist as unquestionably as though it had never been formed, the fundamental principles, the eternal truths, uttered when our colonies in 1776 declared their independence, on which the Confederation of 1781 and the Union of 1788 were formed, and which animated and guided in the organization of the Confederacy of 1861, yet live, and will survive, however crushed they may be by despotic force, however deep they may be buried under the *débris* of crumbling States, however they may be disavowed by the time-serving and the faint-hearted; yet I believe they have the eternity of truth, and that in God's appointed time and place they will prevail.

The contest is not over, the strife is not ended. It has only entered on a new and enlarged arena. The champions of constitutional liberty must spring to the struggle, like the armed men from the seminated dragon's teeth, until the Government of the United States is brought back to its constitutional limits, and the tyrant's plea of "necessity" is bound in chains strong as adamant:

"For Freedom's battle once begun,
  Bequeathed by bleeding sire to son,
Though baffled oft, is ever won."

When the war closed, who were the victors? Perhaps it is too soon to answer that question. Nevertheless, every day, as time rolls on, we look with increasing pride upon the struggle our people made for constitutional liberty. The war was one in which fundamental principles were involved; and, as force decides no truth, hence the issue is still undetermined, as has been already

---

[23] Jefferson Davis, *The Rise and Fall of the Confederate Government*, 2 vols. (New York, 1881), 2:294-95.

shown. We have laid aside our swords; we have ceased our hostility; we have conceded the physical strength of the Northern States. But the question still lives, and all nations and peoples that adopt a confederated agent of government will become champions of our cause. While contemplating the Northern States—with their Federal Constitution gone, ruthlessly destroyed under the tyrant's plea of "necessity," their State sovereignty made a byword, and their people absorbed in an aggregated mass, no longer, as their fathers left them, protected by reserved rights against usurpation—the question naturally arises: On which side was the victory? Let the verdict of mankind decide.

CONCLUSION

Disparity in material resources, Confederate mismanagement, the Union's larger army, the superior characteristics of the Union as a society—all of these various explanations of the outcome of the Civil War should be assessed in light of the chronological development of the war as seen by contemporaries. Such individuals who lived at the time as George Templeton Strong, William Gilmore Simms, Mrs. Mary Chesnut, and Lords Palmerston and Russell seem clearly to have considered Confederate victory in the Civil War a real possibility as of the late summer or autumn of 1862. And up to that time, the several explanations of the war's outcome presented above do not seem to indicate insuperable difficulties within the Confederacy. Whether a decisive Confederate victory at Antietam in September of 1862 would have led to recognition as an independent nation by England and other countries; whether such recognition would have been accepted voluntarily by the Union; whether, if the Union had not voluntarily accepted the independence and separation of the Confederacy, England, France, and other countries would have used economic, diplomatic, or naval-military means of persuasion sufficient to compel Union acceptance of Confederate independence—the answers to these questions are obviously unknowable. But it is conceivable that the Confederacy did not win its independence by the winter of 1862–1863 largely because of the accidents and chances of war. In a "damn near thing," to use Wellington's description of the battle of Waterloo, any number of factors, major or minor, might turn the tide.

After the winter of 1862–1863, the effects of disparity in material resources, mismanagement by Confederates, the Union's larger army, the "inventive genius," and, perhaps, the ideology of the Union were increasingly in evidence. It may be that all those factors reflect the inherent limitations on the effectiveness in war of a less populous, less centralized, less economically diversified, and less economically independent society in comparison with its more modern rival. Some societies at war have transcended what seemed to be their inherent limitations, and for a time it appeared that the Confederacy might do so. Once the opportunities of the winter of 1862–1863 were lost, however, the Confederacy did not transcend its limitations, while the Union did successfully develop enough of its potentialities to insure victory.

13 JOHN HOPE FRANKLIN
reconstruction

Few periods in our history have witnessed such drastic alterations of the entire fabric of American life as the Civil War and the decade that followed it. There were numerous social and economic changes that stemmed from the emancipation of four million Negroes in the South, but these changes were so completely interwoven with other consequences of the war as to make them wholly inseparable. The South did not experience great industrial development during the war, but the North did; and the forces let loose by this industrial expansion were so powerful that they affected the entire course of Reconstruction. The political changes that began with the secession of the Southern states and continued until those states had resumed their places in the national picture created, of course, national problems. But the economic transformation brought on by numerous modifications in production and distribution demanded the attention of every practical-minded man in the United States.

It must be remembered that there is no way of understanding Reconstruction unless it is studied in its proper setting. It is not a history of "Negro rule," as many have incorrectly dubbed the period of Radical Reconstruction, nor is it Southern history, however much students have approached it from a regional point of view. It is an integral part of our national development. From 1865 to the end of the century the people of the United States were picking up the threads of their social, political, and economic life, so abruptly severed in 1861, and were attempting to tie them together in a new pattern. The political life of the former

Confederate states after 1865 was affected by more than the presence of Negroes in the state legislatures or in other positions of public trust. It was affected, as well, by the knotty and seemingly insoluble constitutional questions and by the dynamic changes of economic reconstruction.

During the war the President had exercised many powers that would not have been tolerated in peace, and even before the conflict's end Congress signified that it was anxious to restore the balance of the three branches of the government. The unexpected accession to the Presidency of Andrew Johnson merely complicated matters and made Congress more determined than ever to have a full share in governing the country. The fear of Republicans that they would lose political control, the pressure of new industrialists for favorable legislation, and the conflicting philosophies of Reconstruction are all considerations that cannot be overlooked in studying the politics of the period.

The political chaos that followed in the wake of war carried with it the almost inherent element of corruption. The extravagance of wartime spending encouraged corruption, and the beneficiaries of graft and bribery in the North and in the South had no intention of retiring from their pursuits at the end of the struggle. As the more able men went into industry and other economic activities, numerous incompetent people, the easy prey of cunning industrialists and unscrupulous politicians, infiltrated into high places in the management of government. After 1867 a considerable number of Negroes, many of whom had little understanding of the intricacies of the operations of government, were in positions of responsibility which they were hardly qualified to fill.

It is not possible, however, to dismiss the problem of American political intelligence after the Civil War merely by observing that there were four million Negroes who were without experience in public affairs. To these must be added the millions of whites in the South who had little or no political experience and who, long before the war, had surrendered responsibility to a very small group of leaders who constituted a veritable autocracy. One must include, also, the millions of Europeans who poured into the country and who muddied the political waters considerably. Many of them had not participated in any kind of government, and most of them had no understanding of the operation of representative institutions. All these groups, and more, were exposed to venal and corrupt politicians and frequently became unwitting accessories to the crimes of corrupt governments. It is obvious that they added to the political chaos of Reconstruction and made it vastly more difficult.

The immediate problems of Reconstruction were numerous. There was the task of rebuilding the war-torn South and restoring its economic life on the basis of free labor. At the end of the war there was no civil authority in the Carolinas, Georgia, Florida, Alabama, Mississippi, and Texas. Everywhere there was suffering from war devastation, starvation, and disease. Some despondent whites had abandoned their homes and fled to distant points, while thousands of Negroes, shelterless and without jobs, wandered from place to place. Perhaps as difficult as any task for Southern whites was the one of accepting the Negro as a free man and learning to deal with him on that basis. The white man's problem of reconciling himself to the new status of the Negro seemed to loom larger and larger before his vision, thereby blinding him to the objective consideration of other weighty matters.

The needs of the South were great, both in number and variety. There was the perplexing problem of finding a way for the states to resume their places in the Union; and out of the controversies of the victors regarding this issue some Southerners hoped that there would emerge a solution that would make it easy to take this humiliating step. Inseparably connected with the rebuilding of the South and bringing it back into the Union was the question of the Negro. There was no dispute over the fact that he was in dire need, but there was serious doubt regarding the capacity of the North to serve his needs. There was no question regarding his status as a freeman, but conflict arose over the possible distinctions that could be maintained between him and a white man. Even more serious was the problem of whether his status should be settled and his condition improved before the Southern states were permitted to return to the Union.

A formidable barrier to solving these pressing postwar riddles was the legacy of hate which both sections had inherited from a generation of bitter intersectional strife. Perhaps this animosity was the most grievous wound to heal, for it lay deep in the hearts of both Northerners and Southerners. Most people seemed helpless when confronted with it. There was little hope of solving any problem until a new spirit of conciliation and goodwill could be created. In this intangible and elusive area lay the key to intersectional peace.

While Reconstruction was essentially a national, not a sectional or racial matter, the problems to be discussed here will center mainly around the efforts to bring the Southern states back into the Union, to revive the economic strength of the region, and to stabilize the position of the Negro. One must bear in mind, however, the fact that all these problems had important implications for the entire nation and that in the slow, painful movement toward greater economic and political democracy, they loomed large in the period between 1865 and 1877.

As early as 1862 Lincoln saw the need for a policy of dealing with the Southern states as they capitulated to the Union army and of handling the large number of Negroes who came under the control of the United States even during the war. Insisting that the war was actually a rebellion of some Southern citizens rather than a revolt of the states, the President took steps, as soon as possible, to reorganize the states in the South. In December 1863, he outlined to Congress his comprehensive plan for

Reconstruction. He extended general amnesty to the people of the South, except certain high Confederate civilian and military officials, and called on them to swear allegiance to the United States. When a state could certify that as many as one tenth of its population as had cast votes in the election of 1860 had taken the oath, a government might be established that would recognized by the President. Neither this plan nor the similar one outlined by Lincoln's successor, Andrew Johnson, was acceptable to Congress. In his last public address, April 11, 1865, Lincoln discussed his plan of Reconstruction and urged Congress to accept the former Confederate states that had complied with its requirements.

1. CONFLICTING VIEWS REGARDING THE FUTURE OF THE SOUTH

Long before the end of the conflict others besides the President gave attention to the problem of Reconstruction, and especially to what should be done with the states that had seceded from the Union and with the economic and social order to which they were so deeply committed. Those who were war weary and anxious for peace were willing to accept much of the *status quo ante bellum* and to accept the South's minimal concessions regarding emancipation and the illegality of secession. Others wanted something more, perhaps greater guarantees regarding the maintenance of peace and the protection of the basic legal and political rights of the freedmen. A few, among whom was Thaddeus Stevens, were convinced that nothing short of a complete economic and social revolution in the South would make permanent the great objectives for which the war was fought. On September 6, 1865, Stevens, a powerful member of the House of Representatives from Pennsylvania, set forth his views in a memorable speech in Lancaster, Pennsylvania. A few days later, in two editorials the editor of the New York *Times* took sharp issue with Stevens's position. The portions of the Stevens speech and the *Times* editorials that follow indicate the remarkable polarization of ardent Unionists in the months following the close of the War.

Thaddeus Stevens at Lancaster, Pennsylvania, September 6, 1865[1]

The whole fabric of Southern society must be changed, and never can it be done if this opportunity is lost. Without this, this government can never be, as it never has been, a true republic. Heretofore it had more the features of aristocracy than of democracy. The Southern States have been despotisms, not governments of the people. It is impossible that any practical equality of rights can exist where a few thousand men

[1] *The New York Times*, September 10, 1865.

monopolize the whole landed property. The larger the number of small proprietors the more safe and stable the government. As the landed interest must govern, the more it is subdivided and held by independent owners, the better. . . . How can republican institutions, free schools, free churches, free social intercourse, exist in a mingled community of nabobs and serfs; of the owners of twenty thousand acre manors with lordly palaces, and the occupants of narrow huts inhabited by "low white trash?" If the South is ever to be made a safe republic, let her lands be cultivated by the toil of the owners, or the free labor of intelligent citizens. This must be done even though it drive her nobility into exile. If they go, all the better. . . .

When our ancestors found a "more perfect Union" necessary, they found it impossible to agree upon a constitution without tolerating, nay, guaranteeing, slavery. They were obliged to acquiesce, trusting to time to work a speedy cure, in which they were disappointed. They had some excuse, some justification. But we can have none if we do not thoroughly eradicate slavery and render it forever impossible in this republic. The slave power made war upon the nation. They declared the "more perfect Union" dissolved—solemnly declared themselves a foreign nation, alien to this republic; for four years were in fact what they claimed to be. We accepted the war which they tendered and treated them as a government capable of making war. We have conquered them, and as a conquered enemy we can give them laws; can abolish all their municipal institutions and form new ones. If we do not make those institutions fit to last through generations of freemen, a heavy curse will be on us. . . .

Editorial in *The New York Times*, September 15, 1865

Mr. S. insists that we must revolutionize by the vigorous exercise of the absolute powers we have acquired by conquest of the South, the whole structure of Southern society. . . . He claims *for Congress* the right of thus "giving law to the vanquished [sic]" and thus sets forth his view of the duty of that body, and his definition of the parties of the political future. . . .

We do not propose to enter upon any special criticism of the platform . . . laid down by Mr. Stevens. But we beg leave to doubt his right thus to prescribe new principles and a new policy for the Union party, and to brand as "Copperheads and rebels" all who refuse their adhesion to them. . . . We do not believe that the people have fought this war for the purpose of establishing at Washington the most relentless despotism the civilized world has ever seen. Nor are they at all likely to regard the extermination of the Southern people as the most likely means of restoring tranquility, promoting order and forming a "more perfect Union."

Editorial in *The New York Times*, September 15, 1865

There are a great many Southerners in this city trying to make arrangements for a resumption of business. As a general thing, their conduct is manly, frank, and sensible—calculated to win the confidence and respect of every generous and just community. Nine in every ten of them have been utterly ruined by the rebellion. . . . They have lost position, influence, property, children, friends—everything which makes life desirable. Under such circumstances, weak men sink down into abject despair, or drag out the rest of their lives in the safe obscurity of foreign lands. The defeated Southerners meet their calamity in a more manly style. They show in their defeat, as they did in their struggle—courage, desperate tenacity of purpose, and that high spirited readiness to meet all the responsibilities of their conduct, which never fails to command the respect of the world.

It may not seem wholly in keeping with their courageous temper, that quite a number of these persons, on reading the speech of Hon. Thad Stevens, have abandoned their business projects and gone home discouraged. They say they cannot face the desolation which his plans propose for the South. They cannot put their farms again in order, clear them of their incumbrances, rebuild their ruined dwellings, plant fresh crops and get a new start in life for their children and themselves, with the prospect at any moment, of seeing the whole swept away by a ruthless confiscation. . . .

We cannot blame them for this feeling, but the fear out of which it grows seems to us quite unwarranted. There is nothing in the past conduct or the present temper of the North to justify the belief that any such policy as recommended by Mr. Stevens will be adopted. . . . We trust the people of the South will prosecute, with continued energy and confidence, their efforts to renew the prosperity of the Southern States. . . . They have their fate in their own hands. If they will take hold promptly and properly of the task that awaits them, appreciate aright the new relations, political, industrial, and social, which the war has brought about, and act with wise reference to the necessities which those changed relations have created, they can easily disarm all distrust and command the hearty and effective sympathy of all the people in the Northern States.

2. DID THE SOUTH ACCEPT THE VERDICT OF THE WAR?

When the war came to a close, there were conflicting reports regarding the willingness of the South to accept the verdict of the battlefield. Everyone conceded that much of the South was laid waste by the victorious armies of Sherman, Sheridan, and other Union generals. There was agreement regarding the impoverishment of Southerners at every level. No one questioned the wretched plight of the millions of Negroes who, although free, had few resources with which to become responsible, self-sufficient citizens. But there seemed to be no agreement with respect to the attitudes of Southerners who, under the Reconstruction policies of

Lincoln and Johnson, would have the responsibility for rebuilding the section and leading it back into the Union. Former abolitionists saw in the first acts of the reconstructed legislatures the loss of everything for which the war had been fought, and they became convinced that the Southern leaders were incapable of participating in building the kind of civilization that the crusaders had envisioned. They were dismayed by the rumors that the whites were continuing to treat Negroes as though they were slaves and that cruelty and violence toward Negroes prevailed in many portions of the South. They viewed with inexpressible alarm the exclusion of even the literate, responsible Negroes from the franchise and the enactment of Black Codes that bore a striking resemblance to the slave codes of the ante-bellum period.

While the new laws would recognize the right of Negroes to seek protection in the courts, to have their marriages validated, and to enjoy certain other rights as freemen, they would also impose great limitations regarding the ownership of property, the right to seek employment, and the contractual relationships between white employers and Negro workers. For example, the Mississippi apprentice law gave former owners preference in the employment of Negro minors, and the Louisiana Code prohibited Negroes from renting or keeping houses in certain parishes. Mississippi forbade Negroes to ride in first-class passenger cars with whites, and the vagrancy law of South Carolina forced large numbers of Negroes against their will into a relationship with white employers. These initial steps taken by Southern leaders were sufficient to distress even the lukewarm former abolitionist.

Nor did all the unfavorable reports indict the white Southerners. There were ugly rumors of vindictiveness and violence on the part of the freedmen. One report circulated widely that the Negroes were planning a general uprising in which they would take vengeance on the whites and dispossess them of their property. Another was that Negro soldiers stationed in the South took pleasure in terrorizing the whites and used their advantageous position in numerous unsavory ways. There were numerous assertions that the freedmen would not work and that they expected the federal government to provide them with food, clothing, and housing. It was, indeed, difficult for an objective person to reach any conclusions regarding conditions in the South. Beginning in the fall of 1865 President Johnson, apparently hoping to secure reliable information on which to carry out his plans of Reconstruction, sent several emissaries into the Southern states to make observations and report to him. Among them were Harvey M. Watterson, Chief Justice Salmon P. Chase, General Ulysses S. Grant, Benjamin C. Truman, and Carl Schurz. They represented a wide variety of backgrounds, experiences, and points of view. Out of their reports it would seem to be possible to arrive at a fair conclusion regarding conditions in the South.

The Vindictive South

By 1865, after having been in the United States for only fifteen years, German-born Carl Schurz already had behind him many years of distinguished public service to his adopted country. As an anti-slavery leader in Wisconsin, he had helped to establish the Republican party in that state. Before the outbreak of the Civil War he was a figure of national importance and was in great demand as a writer and speaker. During the war his outstanding service won for him promotion to the rank of major-general. In July 1865, at the request of President Johnson, indeed, prompted by Schurz, he visited South Carolina, Georgia, Alabama, Mississippi, and Louisiana. Upon his return after publishing some of his report in a Boston newspaper, he called upon the President who, according to Schurz, received him with "great coldness," and asked him no questions about the results of his investigations and "seemed to desire not to have any conversation about them at all." Nevertheless, Schurz prepared his report and submitted it to the President. The latter made no acknowledgment of it and did not allow it to be published until Congress, perhaps on the suggestion of Schurz's friend, Charles Sumner, requested it. For its detailed analysis and clarity of statement, it is hardly surpassed by any report that was made during this period. The portions that are given below show clearly the conviction of Schurz that the South was not ready for the kind of lenient treatment that the President's policy allowed.[2]

It would be superfluous to enumerate instances of insult offered to our soldiers, and even to officers high in command; the existence and intensity of this aversion is too well known to those who have served or are now serving in the south to require proof, . . . This feeling of aversion and resentment with regard to our soldiers may, perhaps, be called natural. The animosities inflamed by a four years' war, and its distressing incidents, cannot be easily overcome. But they extend beyond the limits of the army, to the people of the north. I have read in southern papers bitter complaints about the unfriendly spirit exhibited by the northern people—complaints not unfrequently flavored with an admixture of vigorous vituperation. But, as far as my experience goes, the "unfriendly spirit" exhibited in the north is all mildness and affection compared with the popular temper which in the south vents itself in a variety of ways and on all possible occasions. . . .

It would have been a promising indication of returning loyalty if the old, consistent, uncompromising Unionists of the south, and those northern men who during the war settled down there to contribute to

---

[2] 39th Cong., 1st Sess., *Senate Executive Documents*, no. 2, 7–9, 12–13, 17–18, 20, 25–26, 38, 43–44.

the prosperity of the country with their capital and enterprise, had received that measure of consideration to which their identification with the new order of things entitled them. It would seem natural that the victory of the national cause should have given those who during the struggle had remained the firm friends of the Union, a higher standing in society and an enlarged political influence. This appears to have been the case during that "first period" of anxious uncertainty when known Unionists were looked up to as men whose protection and favor might be of high value. . . . But the close of that "first period" changed the aspect of things.

It struck me soon after my arrival in the south that the known Unionists—I mean those who during the war had been to a certain extent identified with the national cause—were not in communion with the leading social and political circles; and the further my observations extended the clearer it became to me that their existence in the south was of a rather precarious nature. . . . Mr. William King, a citizen of Georgia well-known in that State, stated to me in conversation: "There are a great many bad characters in the country, who would make it for some time unsafe for known Union people and northerners who may settle down here to live in this country without the protection of the military. . . ."

While I was in New Orleans an occurrence took place which may be quoted as an illustration of the sweep of what I might call the *reactionary movement*. When General Shepley was military governor of Louisiana, under General Butler's *regime*, a school board was appointed for the purpose of reorganizing the public schools of New Orleans. A corps of loyal teachers was appointed, and the education of the children was conducted with a view to make them loyal citizens. The national airs were frequently sung in the schools, and other exercises introduced, calculated to impregnate the youthful minds of the pupils with affection for their country. It appears that this feature of the public schools was distasteful to the class of people with whose feelings they did not accord.

Mr. H. Kennedy, acting mayor of New Orleans, early in September last, disbanded the school board which so far had conducted the educational affairs of the city, and appointed a new one. The composition of this new school board was such as to induce General Canby to suspend its functions until he could inquire into the loyalty of its members. The report of the officer intrusted with the investigation . . . shows that a large majority of the members had sympathized with the rebellion, and aided the confederate government in a variety of ways. But as no evidence was elicited proving the members legally incapable of holding office, General Canby considered himself obliged to remove the prohibition, and the new school board entered upon its functions. . . .

[The] real substance, stripped of all circumlocutions, [of an editorial taken from the New Orleans *Times,* of September 12, evidently written in defense of the measure] can be expressed in a few words: "The schools of New Orleans have been institutions so intensely and demonstratively loyal as to become unpopular with those of our fellow citizens to whom such demonstrations are distasteful, and they must be brought back under 'popular control' so as to make them cease to be obnoxious in that particular." ...

While the generosity and toleration shown by the government to the people lately in rebellion has not met with a corresponding generosity shown by those people to the government's friends, it has brought forth some results which, if properly developed, will become of value. It has facilitated the re-establishment of the forms of civil government, and led many of those who had been active in the rebellion to take part in the act of bringing back the States to their constitutional relations; and if nothing else were necessary than the mere putting in operation of the mere machinery of government in point of form, and not also the acceptance of the results of the war and their development in point of spirit, these results, although as yet incomplete, might be called a satisfactory advance in the right direction. . . .

But as to the moral value of these results, we must not indulge in any delusions. There are two principal points to which I beg to call your attention. In the first place, the rapid return to power and influence of so many of those who but recently were engaged in a bitter war against the Union, has had one effect which was certainly not originally contemplated by the government. Treason does, under existing circumstances, not appear odious in the south. The people are not impressed with any sense of its criminality. And, secondly, there is, as yet, among the southern people an *utter absence of national feeling*. . . . Hardly ever was there an expression of hearty attachment to the great republic, or an appeal to the impulses of patriotism. . . .

A belief, conviction, or prejudice, or whatever you may call it, so widely spread and apparently so deeply rooted . . . that the negro will not work without physical compulsion, is certainly calculated to have a very serious influence upon the conduct of the people entertaining it. It naturally produced a desire to preserve slavery in its original form as much and as long as possible —and you may, perhaps, remember the admission made by one of the provisional governors, over two months after the close of the war, that the people of his State still indulged in a lingering hope slavery might yet be preserved—or to introduce into the new system that element of physical compulsion which would make the negro work. . . . Here and there planters succeeded for a limited period to keep their former slaves in ignorance, or at least doubt, about their new rights; but the main agency employed for that purpose was force and intimidation. In many instances negroes who walked away from the plantations, or were found upon the roads, were shot or otherwise severely punished, which was calculated to produce the impression among those remaining with their masters that an attempt to escape from slavery would result in certain destruction. . . .

Cases in which negroes were kept on the plantations, either by ruse or violence, were frequent enough in South Carolina and Georgia to call forth from General Saxton a circular threatening planters who persisted in this practice with loss of their property, and from Major General Steedman, commander of the department of Georgia, an order bearing upon the same subject. At Atlanta, Georgia, I had an opportunity to examine some cases. . . . While I was there . . . several negroes came into town with bullet and buckshot wounds in their bodies. From their statements, which, however, were only corroborating information previously received, it appeared that the reckless and restless characters of that region had combined to keep negroes where they belonged. Several freedmen were shot in the attempt to escape, others succeeded in eluding the vigilance of their persecutors; large numbers, terrified by what they saw and heard, quietly remained under the restraint imposed upon them, waiting for better opportunities. . . . It is not on the plantations and at the hands of the planters themselves that the negroes have to suffer the greatest hardships. Not only the former slaveholders, but the non-slaveholding whites, who, even previous to the war, seemed to be more ardent in their pro-slavery feelings than the planters themselves, are possessed by a singularly bitter and vindictive feeling against the colored race since the negro has ceased to be property. . . . The number of murders and assaults perpetrated upon negroes is very great; we can form only an approximate estimate of what is going on in those parts of the south which are not closely garrisoned, and from which no regular reports are received, by what occurs under the very eyes of our military authorities. As to my personal experience, I will only mention that during my two days sojourn at Atlanta one negro was stabbed with fatal effect on the street, and three were poisoned, one of whom died. While I was at Montgomery, one negro was cut across the throat evidently with intent to kill, and another was shot, but both escaped with their lives. . . .

The consequence of the prejudice prevailing in the southern States is that colored schools can be established and carried on with safety only under the protection of our military forces, and that where the latter are withdrawn the former have to go with them. There may be a few localities forming exceptions, but their number is certainly very small. . . .

In a letter of General Kirby Smith . . . occurs the following statement referring to the condition of things in Mobile, Alabama: "Threats were made to destroy all schoolhouses in which colored children were taught, and in two instances they were fired. The same threats were made against all churches in which colored people assembled to worship, and one of them burned. Continued threats of assassination were made against the colored preachers, and one of them is now under special guard by order of Major General Woods." . . .

The general government of the republic has, by proclaiming the emancipation of the slaves, commenced a great social revolution in the south, but has, as yet, not completed it. Only the negative part of it is accomplished. The slaves are emancipated in point of form, but free labor has not yet been put in the place of slavery in point of fact. And now, in the midst of this critical period of transition, the power which originated the revolution is expected to turn over its whole future development to another power which from the beginning was hostile to it and has never yet entered into its spirit, leaving the class in whose favor it was made completely without power to protect itself and to take an influential part in that development. . . .

In my dispatches from the south I repeatedly expressed the opinion that the people were not yet in a frame of mind to legislate calmly and understandingly upon the subject of free negro labor. . . . It is, indeed, difficult to imagine circumstances more unfavorable for the development of a calm and unprejudiced public opinion than those under which the southern people are at present laboring. . . . Only a minority is trying to adopt the new order of things. . . .

As the most difficult of the pending questions are intimately connected with the status of the negro in southern society, it is obvious that a correct solution can be more easily obtained if he has a voice in the matter. In the right to vote he would find the best permanent protection against oppressive class-legislation, as well as against individual persecution. . . . It is a notorious fact that the rights of a man of some political power are far less exposed to violation than those of one who is, in matters of public interest, completely subject to the will of others. A voter is a man of influence. . . . Such an individual is an object of interest to the political parties that desire to have the benefit of his ballot. . . . The only manner in which, in my opinion, the southern people can be induced to grant to the freedman some measure of self-protecting power in the form of suffrage, is to make it a condition precedent to "readmission." . . .

As to the future peace and harmony of the Union, it is of the highest importance that the people lately in rebellion be not permitted to build up another "peculiar institution" whose spirit is in conflict with the fundamental principles of our political system; for as long as they cherish interests peculiar to them in preference to those they have in common with the rest of the American people, their loyalty to the Union will always be uncertain.

The Repentant South

The statements of Schurz to the press and to the public, even before his report to the President, were doubtless the cause of the "coldness" of Johnson's reception of Schurz. Perhaps, also, the unfavorable appraisal of the South by Schurz had something to do with the President's efforts to secure other opinions regarding conditions in the South. In September 1865, he requested Benjamin C. Truman to visit the South and submit a report to him.

In the first two years of the war Benjamin C. Truman had been a newspaper correspondent. In 1862 he became an aide on the staff of Andrew Johnson when the latter became the military governor of Tennessee. He held that position until the closing months of the war. In September he left on his special mission and visited Alabama, Georgia, Florida, Tennessee, Arkansas, Mississippi, Louisiana, and Texas. Although he frequently sent lengthy letters to *The*

New York Times during his sojourn in the Southern states, the President did not seem irate, and when Truman returned in April 1866, he was warmly received by the President. The Truman report describes the South as pacified and conciliatory, and Johnson needed no prodding to send it to the Congress. The portion of the report given below emphasized the willingness of the people of the South to accept the verdict of Appomattox and their fitness to manage their own affairs.[3]

If any general assertion can be made that will apply to the masses of the people of the South, it is that they are at the present time *indifferent* toward the general government. For four years of eventful life as a nation, they were accustomed to speak of and regard "our government" as the one which had its seat in Richmond; and thousands who at first looked upon that government with great suspicion and distrust, gradually, from the mere lapse of time and force of example, came to admit it into their ideas as their *government*. The great body of the people in any country always move slowly; the transfer of allegiance from one *de facto* government to another is not effected in a day, whatever oaths of loyalty may be taken; and I have witnessed many amusing instances of mistakes on the part of those of whose attachment to the government there could be no question. Ignorance and prejudice always lag furthest behind any radical change, and no person can forget that the violent changes of the past few years have left the ideas of the populace greatly unsettled and increased their indifference. Fully one-half of the southern people never cherished an educated and active attachment to any government that was over them, and the war has left them very much as it found them.

The rank and file of the disbanded southern army—those who remained to the end—are the backbone and sinew of the south. Long before the surrender, corps, divisions, brigades, and regiments had been thoroughly purged of the worthless class—the skulkers—those of whom the south, as well as any other country, would best be rid; and these it is that are now prolonging past bitternesses. . . . To the disbanded regiments of the rebel army, both officers and men, I look with great confidence as the best and altogether most hopeful element of the south, the real basis of reconstruction and the material of worthy citizenship. . . . I know of very few more potent influences at work in promoting real and lasting reconciliation and reconstruction than the influence of the returned soldier. . . .

It is my belief that the south—the great, substantial, and prevailing element—is more loyal now than it was at the end of the war—more loyal to-day than yesterday, and that it will be more loyal tomorrow than to-day. It would be impossible to present the numerous and scattered evidences upon which I base this belief; but I entertain it in all sin-

---

[3] 39th Cong., 1st Sess., *Senate Executive Document*, no. 43, 2, 5–6, 7–11, 13–14.

cerity, and believe it to be consonant with the facts. "No revolution ever goes backward" is a convenient but shallow truism; or, rather, expressive of no truth whatever, since every revolution has its ultimate revulsion, partially at least; and just as certainly as for four years the mass of popular sentiment in the south was slowly solidifying and strengthening in favor of the bogus confederacy, just so certain it is that from the date of its downfall that opinion has been slowly returning to its old attachments. . . . I record it as my profound conviction, gathered from hundreds of intimate and friendly conversations with leading men in the south, that there are not fifty respectable politicians who still believe in the "constitutional right of secession," though they are exceedingly slow to acknowledge it in public speeches or published articles. Our conversations generally ended with the confession—which to me was entirely satisfactory, as meaning much more than was intended—"Whatever may be said about the *right* of secession, the thing itself may as well be laid aside, for it is certainly *not practicable,* and probably *never will be."* . . .

There is a prevalent disposition not to associate too freely with northern men, or to receive them into the circles of society; but it is far from insurmountable. Over southern society, as over every other, woman reigns supreme, and they are more imbittered against those whom they deem the authors of all these calamities than are their brothers, sons, and husbands. It is a noteworthy ethnological fact, and one I have often observed, that of the younger generation the southern women are much superior to the southern men both in intellect and energy; and their ascendency over society is correspondingly great. . . .

But the stories and rumors to the effect that northern men are bitterly persecuted and compelled to abandon the country, I pronounce false. If northern men go south they must expect for a while to be treated with neglect, and sometimes with contempt; but if they refrain from bitter political discussions, and conduct themselves with ordinary discretion, they soon overcome these prejudices and are treated with respect. The accounts that are from time to time flooded over the country in regard to southern cruelty and intolerance toward northerners are mostly false. I could select many districts, however, particularly in northern Texas and portions of Mississippi, where northern men could not at present live with any degree of self-respect. There are also localities in many of the Southern states where it would be dangerous for a northern man to live, but they are exceptional, and are about equally unsafe for any man who possesses attractive property. . . .

Almost the only key that furnishes a satisfactory solution to the southern question in its relation to the negro, that gives a reasonable explanation to the treatment which he receives and the estimation in which he is held, is found in the fact—too often forgotten in considering this matter—that the people from their earliest days have regarded slavery as his proper estate, and emancipation as a bane to his happiness. That a vast majority of the southern people honestly entertain this opinion, no one who travels among them for eight months can doubt. . . . From the surrender of the rebel armies up to the Christmas holidays, and more especially for a few weeks preceding the latter, there was a nervousness exhibited throughout the south, in relation to their late slaves, that was little consonant to their former professions of trust in them. There were vague and terrible fears of a servile insurrection—a thing which the simple-minded negroes scarcely dreamed of. In consequence of this there were extensive seizures of arms and ammunition, which the negroes had foolishly collected, and strict precautions were taken to avoid any outbreak. . . . Since the holidays, however, there has been a great improvement in this matter; many of the whites appear to be ashamed of their former distrust, and the negroes are seldom molested now in carrying the firearms, of which they make such a vain display. . . .

Another result of the above-mentioned settled belief in the negro's inferiority and in the necessity that he should not be left to himself without a guardian, is that in some sections he is discouraged from leaving his old master. I have known of planters who considered it an offence against neighborhood courtesy for another to hire their old hands, and in two instances that were reported, the disputants came to blows over the breach of etiquette. . . .

As to the personal treatment received by the negro at the hands of the southern people there is widespread misapprehension. It is not his former master, as a general thing, that is his worst enemy, but quite the contrary. I have talked earnestly with hundreds of old slave-owners, and seen them move among their former "chattels," and I am not mistaken. The feeling with which a very large majority of them regard the negro is one of genuine commiseration, although it is not a sentiment much elevated above that which they would look upon a suffering animal for which they had formed an attachment. Last summer the negroes, exulting in their new-found freedom, as was to have been expected, were gay, thoughtless, and improvident; and, as a consequence, when the winter came, hundreds of them felt the pinchings of want, and many perished. The old planters have often pointed out to me numerous instances of calamity that had come under their own observation in the case of their former slaves and others. . . .

It is the former slave-owners who are the best friends the negro has in the south—those who, heretofore, have provided for his mere physical comfort, generally with sufficient means, though entirely neglecting his better nature, while it is the "poor whites" that are his enemies. It is from these he suffers most. In a state of slavery they hated him; and, now that he is free, there is no striking abatement of this sentiment, and the former master no longer feels called by the instincts of interest to extend that protection that he once did. On the streets, by the roadside, in his wretched hut, in the field of labor—everywhere, the inoffensive negro is exposed to their petty and contemptible persecutions; while, on the other hand, I have known instances where the respectable, substantial people of a community have united together to keep guard over a house in which the negroes were taking their amusement, and from which, a few nights before, they had been rudely driven by white vagabonds, who found pleasure in their fright and suffering. . . .

It is the result of my observation, also, not only that the planters, generally, are far better friends to the negro than the poor whites, but also better than a majority of northern men who go south to rent plantations—at least they show more patience in dealing with him. The northerner is practical, energetic, economical, and thrifty—the negro is slow, awkward, wasteful, and slovenly; he causes his new employer to lose patience, and to seize hold and attempt to perform, himself, what he sees so badly executed. The southerner is accustomed to the ways of slaves from his youth up; hence he is languidly and goodnaturedly indifferent; or, at most, vents his displeasure in empty fuming. . . .

The negro has far less to apprehend, in my judgment, from organized oppression by the courts than from sudden and violent outbursts of passion on the part of the employers, from the petty and malicious persecutions of mean whites. He has less to fear from the perversion of law than from the absence of it; and the same is true of the whites, and has always been. . . .

On the great question of negro suffrage I have seen no occasion, in presence of facts, to change materially the belief I entertained eight months ago. To say that the south is opposed to it, almost to a man, is simply to utter that of which every one is already aware; to say that it is simply a question of time, is to give it no satisfactory solution. . . . So general and so bitter is the opposition of the whites to this measure, that I am fully persuaded that to confer suffrage forcibly by national enactment, upon the blacks at this time, would result to their serious detriment. . . . The southern poor whites, conscious as they are of only a slight superiority over the negro, and knowing that the suffrage and a few minor factitious distinctions are the chief points of their superiority, are jealous over them accordingly. It is they that will resist most stubbornly the negroes' enfranchisement, as it will remove the most marked of the few slight barriers that separate them from the blacks, and it is they that will hail his advent to the polls with the most unrelenting and senseless abuse.

The proper avenues of approach to these unreasoning minds is through the wealthy and powerful landowners of the south—the politicians—who are lords and masters over the peasantry to almost as great an extent as they are over the negroes. Through these let the parallels be constructed upon this strong castle of prejudice. If the politicians of the south have the absolute certainty laid before them that in 1870 their representation in Congress will be diminished largely in consequence of the non-enfranchisement of the negro, they will see to it before that time that the proper reform is introduced. They will convince their constituents that it is necessary and proper to allow the negro to vote, and he will be allowed so to do. At present it seems to me that it would be a misfortune to the negro himself to thrust this privilege upon him. . . .

Regarding the military establishment [in the] south, I will respectfully submit a few words. Taking everything into consideration, there is every reason to believe that it would be extremely injudicious to remove from the south the force now stationed there. Troops are required in the Red river counties, in Texas, to protect loyal men who are being continually outraged by some thousand or more rebel refugees from Missouri and Arkansas, who, on account of their atrocities during the war, dare not return to their homes. Troops are also required in the loyal German counties in Texas, whose people are suffering considerably from the depredations of nomadic bands of Indians. Regarding the colored soldiers, I only agree with all of our officers in the south, including those connected with the Freedmen's Bureau, that they should be removed as speedily as possible. To a great extent they incite the freedmen to deeds of violence and encourage them in indolence. There has been a great improvement in this respect, however, during the past three months. . . .

In conclusion, I must say that I bespeak for the south a glorious future. I predict that peace, prosperity, wealth, and happiness will be her lot. Her rich lands will come rapidly under cultivation, and increase tenfold in value; her noble waters will be thronged with the appliances of commerce; population, such as she desires, will flow steadily into her borders; cities and villages will dot her landscapes; schools and churches and public institutions will be her boast, and a refined society will grace the land. What may we not expect of her, now that freedom is her guiding star?

White Southerners Speak Out

Perhaps white Southerners could speak for themselves better than others could speak for them. They had positive views regarding their plight and the various possible solutions to it. Rather generally they were of the opinion that outsiders, whatever sympathies they might have, could not describe with accuracy and understanding the various facets of the Southern problem. They lost no opportunity to make this clear; many of them had spoken directly to the President. And when the Joint Committee on Reconstruction looked into the problem in 1865 and 1866, white Southerners willingly testified before the Committee or its representatives. Among the numerous white Southerners offering testimony was James D. B. DeBow of New Orleans. As editor of the widely read and highly respected *Review*, DeBow was in a unique position to observe conditions in the South and to articulate his views with singular clarity. In March 1866, he appeared before the Committee and gave the testimony that follows.[4]

---

[4] *Report of the Joint Committee on Reconstruction, at the First Session, Thirty-Ninth Congress* (Washington, 1866), Part 5, 132–36.

There seems to be a general—you may say universal—acquiescence in the results [of the war]. There is a great deal of dissatisfaction [among the people] as to the course in reference to their condition pursued by the federal government. I think the people have fairly tried the experiment of secession and are perfectly satisfied with the result, and that there is no disposition in any quarter, in any shape or form, to embarrass the United States government, or to refrain from the most complete performance of all the duties of citizenship. . . . All parties, those who were opposed to the war and those who were in favor of war, are now agreed that it is for the best interest of the State to perform all the duties of citizenship, and to accept whatever the government has effected in reference to the negro, as well as in reference to other questions. . . . The Freedmen's Bureau is very largely complained of, and the delay in admitting their representatives. They confidently expected a very early restoration of their civil condition and political rights from the promises which were made. I think that feeling of hostility has grown up since the surrender. . . . I do not think it is very serious, but it still exists; it would be dissipated immediately on the passage of liberal measures, such as, for instance, an order restoring the States to their status under the Constitution, restoring their political rights, the removal of the Freedmen's Bureau, or some such regulations which would be fair to both parties. . . .

I think those parties who have remained in the State and who were assuming they were good Union men during the war, perhaps making more claims in that regard than they are entitled to, are received with hostility. I think those who went away honestly for those reasons, and have returned, are respected, and receive much consideration. . . . The secession men, the men who were in the war, are generally ruined, their families are destitute, and there is a great disposition to sustain them, if they undertake any business at all. . . . There is a disposition on the part of those who have been with the South during the war not to mix a great deal with those who have remained in the South (as they say) as Union men; and the feeling extends, more or less, to northern men, though very little towards the majority of northern people. Some who come there a little disposed to talk, etc., receive the cold shoulder; that is about all. . . .

I think there are a great many young men who might be tempted to fight against the flag, but take the country over, a vast majority of the people are sick of war, and I think they would sustain the United States beyond a doubt. I have not heard any young men say they would take a different course. . . . The southern people are Americans, republicans. . . . The country is so devastated, there is so much distress, so much want and suffering among the people of the south, that they have no time for politics. I think they are disposed to go to work to restore their broken fortunes.

I think if the whole regulation of the negroes, or freedmen, were left to the people of the communities in which they live, it will be administered for the best interest of the negroes as well as of the white men. I think there is a kindly feeling on the part of the planters towards the freedmen. They are not held at all responsible for anything that has happened. They are looked upon as the innocent cause. In talking with a number of planters, I remember some of them telling me they were succeeding very well with their freedmen. . . . The sentiment prevailing is, that it is for the interest of the employer to teach the negro, to educate his children, to provide a preacher for him, and to attend to his physical wants. And I may say I have not seen any exception to that feeling in the south. Leave the people to themselves, and they will manage very well. . . . I think there is a willingness to give them [the Negroes] every right except the right of suffrage. It is believed they are unfit to exercise that. The idea is entertained by many that they will eventually be endowed with that right. It is only a question of time; but the universal conviction is that if it ever be conceded, it will be necessary to prepare for it by slow and regular means, as the white race was prepared. I believe everybody unites in the belief that it would be disastrous to give the right of suffrage now.

The Voice of the Negro

It is not generally known that in the years immediately following the Civil War articulate Negroes did not hesitate to describe their plight and to call on the federal and state governments for assistance and protection. Several of them appeared before the Joint Committee on Reconstruction and told of the violent means that their white neighbors were using to maintain a semblance of the master-slave relationship. In colorful language they described the floggings and other forms of punishment and the efforts in some communities to drive the Negroes away. In each instance they insisted that federal troops were necessary to prevent the Negro from being annihilated.

Negroes also organized conventions and associations in their search for protection and a stable order. In 1865 and 1866 they held conventions in Raleigh, Charleston, Savannah, Alexandria, and in other cities. After exhaustive discussions regarding their plight, they usually adopted "Resolutions" or "Addresses" in which they solicited the interest, support, and protection of the people of the United States. In demanding the franchise, one group of Negro veterans declared that they could not understand how it could be withheld from those who had fought to save the Union, while it was freely given to those who had recently returned from four years of fighting to destroy the Union. The following is "An Address to the Loyal Citizens and Congress of the United States of America," adopted by a convention in Alexandria in August 1865.[5]

---

[5] *Proceedings of the Convention of the Colored People of Virginia, Held in the City of Alexandria, August 2, 3, 4, 5, 1865* (Alexandria, 1865), 21–22.

We, the undersigned members of a Convention of colored citizens of the State of Virginia, would respectfully represent that, although we have been held as slaves, and denied all recognition as a constituent of your nationality for almost the entire period of the duration of your Government, and that by *your permission* we have been denied either home or country, and deprived of the dearest rights of human nature: yet when you and our immediate oppressors met in deadly conflict upon the field of battle—the one to destroy and the other to save your Government and nationality, *we*, with scarce an exception, in our inmost souls espoused your cause, and watched, and prayed, and waited, and labored for your success. . . .

When the contest waxed long, and the result hung doubtfully, you appealed to us for help, and how well we answered is written in the rosters of the two hundred thousand colored troops now enrolled in your service; and as to our undying devotion to your cause, let the uniform acclamation of escaped prisoners, "whenever we saw a black face we felt sure of a friend," answer.

Well, the war is over, the rebellion is "put down," and we are *declared* free! Four fifths of our enemies are paroled or amnestied, and the other fifth are being pardoned, and the President has, in his efforts at the reconstruction of the civil government of the States, late in rebellion, left us entirely at the mercy of these subjugated but unconverted rebels, in *everything* save the privilege of bringing us, our wives, and little ones, to the auction block. . . . We *know* these men— know them *well*—and we assure you that, with the majority of them, loyalty is only "lip deep," and that their professions of loyalty are used as a cover to the cherished design of getting restored to their former relations with the Federal Government, and then, by all sorts of "unfriendly legislation," to render the freedom you have given us more intolerable than the slavery they intended for us.

We warn you in time that our only safety is in keeping them under Governors of the *military persuasion* until you have so amended the Federal Constitution that it will prohibit the States from making any distinction between citizens on account of race or color. In one word, the only salvation for us besides the power of the Government is in the *possession of the ballot*. Give us this, and we will protect ourselves. . . . But 'tis said we are ignorant. Admit it. Yet who denies we know a *traitor* from a loyal man, a gentleman from a rowdy, a friend from an enemy? The twelve thousand colored votes of the State of New York sent Governor Seymour home and Reuben E. Fenton to Albany. Did not they know who to vote for? . . . All we ask is an *equal chance* with the white *traitors* varnished and japanned with the oath of amnesty. Can you deny us this and still keep faith with us? . . .

We are "sheep in the midst of wolves," and nothing but the military arm of the Government prevents us and all the *truly* loyal white men from being driven from the land of our birth. Do not then, we beseech you, give to one of these "wayward sisters" the rights they abandoned and forfeited when they rebelled until you have secured *our* rights by the aforementioned amendment to the Constitution. . . .

Trusting that you will not be deaf to the appeal herein made, nor unmindful of the warnings which the malignity of the rebels are constantly giving you, and that you will rise to the height of being just for the sake of justice, we remain yours for our flag, our country, and humanity.

3. RADICAL RECONSTRUCTION

When the Thirty-Ninth Congress met in December 1868, it was determined to take complete charge of Reconstruction. Its leaders were impatient with the lenient programs of Lincoln and Johnson that were based on the theory that the Confederate states had never left the Union and that only minor adjustments were necessary for their full participation in federal affairs. In the Senate, Charles Sumner argued that by seceding the Southern states had committed suicide and could not be resurrected by Presidential proclamation. In the House, Thaddeus Stevens contended that, at best, the former Confederacy should be treated as a conquered province and that its future status could be determined solely by Congress. To those who were now called Radicals it was unthinkable that high-ranking officials of the Confederacy should be seated in Congress without being subjected to greater tests of loyalty than those required by Lincoln and Johnson.

Johnson held just as firmly to his view that the business of Reconstruction should proceed without engendering any more bitterness than the war had created and by assuming that Southerners who desired to participate in federal affairs were acting in good faith. He abandoned all Republican policies—even the moderate ones—and sought to build a political following that would support him against Congress. He vetoed the Freedmen's Bureau Bill of 1866 on the grounds that it was unconstitutional and that it proposed to do more for blacks than had ever been done for whites. In vetoing the Civil Rights Bill some weeks later he insisted that Negroes were not yet ready for the privileges of citizenship. He then condemned the proposed Fourteenth Amendment, which, among other things, embodied the main provisions of the Civil Rights Bill, and launched a bitter personal attack on the Radical leaders. Soon all the Southern states except Tennessee had rejected the Fourteenth Amendment, and Congress was in an angry mood. Members did not agree on several important economic questions, but an increasing number stood together against the President's Southern policy. The enactment of the Black Codes, the widespread disorder in the South, and the President's growing hostility to Congress convinced many members that a legislative program of Reconstruction must prevail.

It is interesting to observe that in the Reconstruction debates the view was advanced, as it was to be set forth in later years—even in the middle of the twentieth century—that society can be manipulated to obtain desired change. If the Radicals believed that change could be effected by legislative enactments, judicial decisions, and executive action, their opponents believed just as fervently that significant and lasting change could come about only quite gradually and through the actions of those whites who traditionally held the reins of political and economic power. If Northerners argued, as they were to argue in the middle of the twentieth century, that the problem of race was a Southern problem, their opponents would insist then as now that the egalitarian tradition in the North was more a verbal posture than a serious commitment. But the Radicals of the Reconstruction era had a strong platform from which to set forth their position.

A Leader of the Radicals

Among the Radicals in Congress, who included such persons as Charles Sumner, Benjamin F. Butler, George S. Boutwell, Benjamin F. Wade, Henry Winter Davis, and John A. Bingham, none was more uncompromising or more determined that the South should be treated as a defeated enemy than Thaddeus Stevens of Pennsylvania. From the close of the war to his death in 1868, Stevens was the dominant figure in the program of Radical Reconstruction. It was he who opposed any kind of amnesty for the people of the South and who insisted that the "rebels" pay the cost of the war. It was he, as we have seen, who suggested the confiscation of all public lands in the seceded states and the distribution of the land of the "rebels" among the former slaves. In the use of vituperative language in debate he was, perhaps, unsurpassed by any man in public life. The spirit of Stevens dominated every move that the Radicals made, and his point of view was a powerful determinant in the evolution of Radical policy. On December 18, 1865, he described in detail, in a speech in the House of Representatives, the role that Congress should play in the re-establishment of the Southern states. A portion of his address follows.[6]

The President assumes, what no one doubts, that the late rebel States have lost their constitutional relations to the Union, and are incapable of representation in Congress, except by permission of the Government. It matters but little, with this admission, whether you call them States out of the Union, and now conquered territories, or assert that because the Constitution forbids them to do what they did do, that they are therefore only dead as to all

---

[6] *Congressional Globe*, 39th Cong., 1st Sess., 72–74.

national and political action, and will remain so until the Government shall breathe into them the breath of life anew and permit them to occupy their former position. In other words, that they are not out of the Union, but are only dead carcasses lying within the Union. In either case, it is very plain that it requires the action of Congress to enable them to form a State government and send representatives to Congress. Nobody, I believe, pretends that with their old constitutions and frames of government they can be permitted to claim their old rights under the Constitution. They have torn their constitutional States into atoms, and built on their foundations fabrics of a totally different character. Dead men cannot raise themselves. Dead States cannot restore their existence "as it was." Whose especial duty is it to do it? In whom does the Constitution place the power? Not in the judicial branch of Government, for it only adjudicates and does not prescribe laws. Not in the Executive, for he only executes and cannot make laws. Not in the Commander-in-Chief of the armies, for he can only hold them under military rule until the sovereign legislative power of the conqueror shall give them law. . . . Unless the law of nations is a dead letter, the late war between two acknowledged belligerents severed their original compacts and broke all the ties that bound them together. The future condition of the conquered power depends on the will of the conqueror. They must come in as new states or remain as conquered provinces. Congress . . . is the only power that can act in the matter. . . . Congress must create States and declare when they are entitled to be represented. Then each House must judge whether the members presenting themselves from a recognized State possess the requisite qualifications of age, residence, and citizenship; and whether the election and returns are according to law. . . .

It is obvious from all this that the first duty of Congress is to pass a law declaring the condition of these outside or defunct States, and providing proper civil governments for them. Since the conquest they have been governed by martial law. Military rule is necessarily despotic, and ought not to exist longer than is absolutely necessary. As there are no symptoms that the people of these provinces will be prepared to participate in constitutional government for some years, I know of no arrangement so proper for them as territorial governments. There they can learn the principles of freedom and eat the fruit of foul rebellion. Under such governments, while electing members to the Territorial Legislatures, they will necessarily mingle with those to whom Congress shall extend the right of suffrage. In Territories Congress fixes the qualifications of electors; and I know of no better place nor better occasion for the conquered rebels and the conqueror to practice justice to all men, and accustom themselves to make and to obey equal laws. . . . They ought never to be recognized as capable of acting in the Union, or of being counted as valid States, until the Constitution shall have been so amended as to make it what its framers intended; and so as to secure perpetual ascendency to the party of the Union; and so as to render our republican Government firm and stable forever. The first of those amendments is to change the basis of representation among the States from Federal numbers to actual voters.... With the basis unchanged the eighty-three southern members, with the Democrats that will in the best times be elected from the North, will always give a majority in Congress and in the Electoral College.... I need not depict the ruin that would follow....

But this is not all that we ought to do before these inveterate rebels are invited to participate in our legislation. We have turned, or are about to turn, loose four million slaves without a hut to shelter them or a cent in their pockets. The infernal laws of slavery have prevented them from acquiring an education, understanding the common laws of contract, or of managing the ordinary business of life. The Congress is bound to provide for them until they can take care of themselves. If we do not furnish them with homesteads, and hedge them around with protective laws; if we leave them to the legislation of their late masters, we had better have left them in bondage.... If we fail in this great duty now, when we have the power, we shall deserve and receive the execration of history and of all future ages.

The Joint Committee on Reconstruction Speaks Its Mind

The principal agency for conceiving and developing the program of Congressional Reconstruction was the Joint Committee of Fifteen "to inquire into the conditions of the states which formed the so-called Confederate States of America." Among the six members from the Senate were Reverdy Johnson of Maryland and William P. Fessenden of Maine, while the House named, among others, Thaddeus Stevens of Pennsylvania, Roscoe Conkling of New York, and Henry T. Blow of Missouri. For months the Committee held hearings in Washington and in various parts of the South. It listened to every conceivable shade of opinion regarding conditions in the former Confederate states, and its findings were the basis for the program of Congressional Reconstruction that was launched on a full scale in 1867. That part of its report follows in which it sought to restate the "general facts and principles applicable to all the states recently in rebellion." The report is dated June 20, 1866.[7]

We now propose to re-state, as briefly as possible, the general facts and principles applicable to all the States recently in rebellion:

First. The seats of the senators and representatives from the so-called Confederate States became vacant in the year 1861, during the second session of the thirty-sixth Congress, by the voluntary withdrawal of their incumbents, with the sanction and by direction of the

---

[7] *Report of the Joint Committee on Reconstruction at the First Session, Thirty-Ninth Congress* (Washington, 1866), xix–xx.

legislatures or conventions of their respective States. This was done as a hostile act against the Constitution and government of the United States, with a declared intent to overthrow the same by forming a southern confederation. This act of declared hostility was speedily followed by an organization of the same States into a confederacy, which levied and waged war, by sea and land, against the United States. . . . From the time these confederated States thus withdrew their representation in Congress and levied war against the United States, the great mass of their people became and were insurgents, rebels, traitors, and all of them assumed and occupied the political, legal, and practical relation of enemies of the United States. . . .

Second. The States thus confederated prosecuted their war against the United States to final arbitrament, and did not cease until all their armies were captured, their military power destroyed, their civil officers, State and confederate, taken prisoners or put to flight, every vestige of State and confederate government obliterated, their territory overrun and occupied by the federal armies, and their people reduced to the condition of enemies conquered in war, entitled only by public law to such rights, privileges, and conditions as might be vouchsafed by the conqueror. . . .

Third. Having voluntarily deprived themselves of representation in Congress for the criminal purpose of destroying the federal Union, and having reduced themselves, by the act of levying war, to the condition of public enemies, they have no right to complain of temporary exclusion from Congress; but, on the contrary, having voluntarily renounced the right to representation, and disqualified themselves by crime from participating in the government, the burden now rests upon them, before claiming to be reinstated in their former condition, to show that they are qualified to resume federal relations. In order to do this, they must prove that they have established, with the consent of the people, republican forms of government in harmony with the Constitution and laws of the United States, that all hostile purposes have ceased, and should give adequate guarantees against future treason and rebellion—guarantees which shall prove satisfactory to the government against which they rebelled, and by whose arms they were subdued.

Fourth. Having, by this treasonable withdrawal from Congress, and by flagrant rebellion and war, forfeited all civil and political rights and privileges under the federal Constitution, they can only be restored thereto by the permission and authority of that constitutional power against which they rebelled and by which they were subdued.

Fifth. These rebellious enemies were conquered by the people of the United States, acting through all the co-ordinate branches of the government. . . . The authority to restore rebels to political power in the federal government can be exercised only with the concurrence of all the departments in which political power is vested. . . .

Sixth. The question before Congress is, then, whether conquered enemies have the right, and shall be permitted at their own pleasure and on their own terms, to participate in making laws for their conquerors;

whether conquered rebels may change their theatre of operations from the battle-field, where they were defeated and overthrown, to the halls of Congress, and, through their representatives, seize upon the government which they fought to destroy. . . .

Seventh. The History of mankind exhibits no example of such madness and folly. The instinct of self-preservation protests against it. . . .

Ninth. The necessity of providing adequate safeguards for the future, before restoring the insurrectionary States to a participation in the direction of public affairs, is apparent from the bitter hostility to the government and people of the United States yet existing throughout the conquered territory, as proved by the testimony of many witnesses and by undisputed facts.

Radical Reconstruction Condemned

When President Johnson saw that Congress was determined to take over the program of reconstructing the Southern states, he sought to thwart the Radicals by appealing to the people to elect Congressmen in 1866 who would support his position. His speeches in a number of important cities were miserable failures, and the bloody race riot in New Orleans in late July strengthened the argument of the Radicals that the President's policy was unwise. When the Radicals won a resounding victory in the elections, they interpreted the results as a mandate from the people, and in March 1867, they took complete charge of Reconstruction. In a series of sweeping measures, Congress declared that no lawful government existed in the South, except in Tennessee, divided the former Confederacy into five military districts to be commanded by generals, and stipulated the conditions upon which the states could return to the Union. Each state was required to call a constitutional convention elected by black and white voters, except the disfranchised former rebels; to frame a constitution acceptable to Congress and the electorate; and to establish Negro suffrage. The state legislature was to ratify the Fourteenth Amendment and enact laws to replace those enacted during the period of Presidential Reconstruction.

A thoroughly aroused Congress was now determined to get rid of the President; and for that purpose it passed the Tenure-of-Office Act, which the President violated in an effort to dismiss his Secretary of War. All these measures were vetoed by Johnson, but Congress had the votes to override his veto in each instance. In his veto messages the President set forth the argument supporting his view that Radical Reconstruction was subversive and unconstitutional. These views are cogently stated and adequately summarized in his Third Annual Message of December 3, 1867.[8]

---

[8] James D. Richardson, ed., *A Compilation of the Messages and Papers of the Presidents* (New York, 1897), 8:3760–62.

I would be unfaithful to my duty if I did not recommend the repeal of the Acts of Congress which place ten of the Southern States under the domination of military masters. If calm reflection shall satisfy a majority of your honorable bodies that the acts referred to are not only a violation of the national faith, but in direct conflict with the Constitution, I dare not permit myself to doubt that you will immediately strike them from the statute book.

To demonstrate the unconstitutional character of those acts, I need do no more than refer to their general provisions. It must be seen at once that they are not authorized. To dictate what alterations shall be made in the constitutions of the several States; to control the elections of State legislators and State officers, members of Congress and electors of President and Vice-President by arbitrarily declaring who shall vote and who shall be excluded from the privilege; to dissolve State legislatures or prevent them from assembling; to dismiss judges and other civil functionaries of the State and appoint others without regard to State law; to organize and operate all the political machinery of the States; to regulate the whole administration of their domestic and local affairs according to the mere will of strange and irresponsible agents, sent among them for that purpose—these are powers not granted to the Federal Government or to any one of its branches. Not being granted, we violate our trust by assuming them as palpably as we would by acting in the face of a positive interdict; for the Constitution forbids us to do whatever it does not affirmatively authorize. . . . If the authority we desire to use does not come to us through the Constitution, we can exercise it only by usurpation, and usurpation is the most dangerous of political crimes. By that crime the enemies of free government in all ages have worked out their designs against public liberty and private right. It leads directly and immediately to the establishment of absolute rule, for undelegated power is always unlimited and unrestrained.

The acts of Congress in question are not only objectionable for their assumption of ungranted power, but many of their provisions are in conflict with the direct prohibitions of the Constitution. The Constitution commands that a republican form of government shall be guaranteed to all the States; that no person shall be deprived of life, liberty, or property without due process of law, arrested without a judicial warrant, or punished without a fair trial before an impartial jury; that the privilege of *habeas corpus* shall not be denied in time of peace; and that no bill of attainder shall be passed even against a single individual. Yet the system of measures established by these acts of Congress does totally subvert and destroy the form as well as the substance of republican government in the ten States to which they apply. It binds them hand and foot in absolute slavery, and subjects them to a strange and hostile power, more unlimited and more likely to be abused than any other now known among civilized men. It tramples down all those rights in which the essence of liberty consists, and which a free government is always most careful to protect. It denies the *habeas corpus* and the trial by jury. Personal freedom, property, and life, if assailed by the passion, the prejudice, or the rapacity of the ruler, have no security whatever. It has the effect of a bill of attainder or bill of pains and penalties, not upon a few individuals, but upon whole masses, including the millions who inhabit the subject States, and even their unborn children. These wrongs, being expressly forbidden, can not be constitutionally inflicted upon any portion of our people, no matter how they may have come within our jurisdiction, and no matter whether they live in States, Territories, or districts.

4. THE SOUTH IN TRAVAIL

Radical Reconstruction is sometimes regarded as a period when a civilized people were subjugated by selfish, scheming white interlopers and their black, ignorant henchmen. Those persons holding this view emphasize the abuses of white citizens by members of the Negro militia, the "social equality" program of the Union League, and the excessive corruption of the Reconstruction governments throughout the South. They find no difficulty, therefore, in justifying the widespread resentment in the South to Radical Reconstruction and the resort to economic pressures and even to violence to overthrow it. In interpreting these years as the South's "darkest hour" they insist that they are adhering closely to the facts and are supported by an abundance of evidence contemporaneous with the period.

Others have regarded the period quite differently. They do not overlook the traumatic effects of the radical shift of political power or the social consequences of the rise of the Negro in politics. They deprecate the claim, however, that real Negro rule prevailed anywhere in the South, or that barbarism characterized the conduct of those Negroes who did occupy positions of responsibility and leadership. They point to the magnanimity of many Negroes who advocated the enfranchisement of the former Confederates and to the humility with which Negro leaders almost invariably deferred to their white colleagues. They insist that the idea that Negroes sought to enter the drawing rooms of Southern whites through the efforts of the Union League is as fantastic as was the idea that the Ku Klux Klan was necessary to protect the virtue of white womanhood.

The conflicting interpretations of Reconstruction merely reflect the struggles that ensued during the period itself. The misunderstandings then were deep and almost irreconcilable. The spectacle they created attracted world-wide attention. From Europe came a procession of observers and reporters. Numerous Northerners likewise made the journey and recorded their impressions in letters, articles, and books. They saw Negroes serving as lieutenant-governors, speakers of houses, superintendents of education, state treasurers, members of legislative bodies on the state and federal levels, and in numerous other capacities of public trust. Some thought the spectacle ludicrous; others thought it tragic; others praised the progressive legislation of the governments and regarded as necessary the intervention by the federal government.

The Southern Whites Protest

Although there were some scattered gestures in the South of acceptance of Radical Reconstruction, there was, from the beginning, a deep-seated resentment on the part of the vast majority of Southern whites to what they called the "barbarization of the South." They regarded the enfranchisement of the Negroes as more galling than the defeat on the battlefield. To them the Radical policy was vindictiveness compounded. They were distressed, moreover, by the obviously political motivation of many Northern Republicans in supporting measures designed to keep the Democratic party impotent, thereby rendering the Republican rule unassailable. But they brushed aside the humanitarian considerations that motivated many Northerners who worked in the South.

The Southern whites could not hold their collective tongue or temper. In the press and on the platform they vigorously attacked the Radical program. They derided the "Black and Tan Conventions" and the "Negro-dominated legislatures." They loudly deprecated the use of Negro troops in the South, and they warned the federal government that its Negro policy would make it impossible for the wounds of the war to heal. There were numerous protests directed to Washington. The following remonstrance of the South Carolina Democratic Central Committee, drawn up in 1868 and sent to the House of Representatives, is typical of the protests made by white Southerners.[9]

Section two of article eight enfranchises every male negro over the age of twenty-one, whether a convict, felon, or a pauper, and disfranchises every white man who has held office in South Carolina. Intelligence, virtue, and patriotism are to give place, in all elections, to ignorance, stupidity, and vice. The superior race is to be made subservient to the inferior. Taxation and representation are no longer to be united.

---

[9] *The American Annual Cyclopedia and Register of Important Events of the Year, 1868* (New York, 1869), 697.

They who own no property are to levy taxes and make all appropriations. . . . The consequences will be, in effect, confiscation. The appropriations to support free schools for the education of negro children, for the support of old negroes in the poorhouses, and the vicious in jails and penitentiary, together with a standard army of negro soldiers, will be crushing and utterly ruinous to the State. Every man's property will have to be sold to pay his taxes.

We have thus suggested to your honorable body some of the prominent objections to your adoption of this constitution. We waive all argument upon the subject of validity. It is a constitution *de facto,* and that is the ground upon which we approach your honorable body in the spirit of earnest remonstrance. That constitution was the work of Northern adventurers, Southern renegades, and ignorant negroes. Not one per cent of the white population of the State approves it, and not two per cent of the negroes who voted for it understand what their act of voting implied. The constitution enfranchises every male negro over the age of twenty-one and disfranchises many of the purest and best white men of the State. The negro being in a large numerical majority as compared with the whites, the effect is that the new constitution establishes in this State negro supremacy, with all its train of countless evils. A superior race—a portion, Senators and Representatives, of the same proud race to which it is your pride to belong—is put under the rule of an inferior race; the abject slaves of yesterday, the flushed freedmen of today. And think you that there can be any just, lasting reconstruction on this basis? The committee respectfully reply, in behalf of their white fellow-citizens, that this cannot be. We do not mean to threaten resistance by arms. But the white people of our State will never quietly submit to negro rule. We may have to pass under the yoke you have authorized, but by moral agencies, by political organization, by every peaceful means left us, we will keep up this contest until we have regained the heritage of political control handed down to us by an honored ancestry. This is a duty we owe to the land that is ours, to the graves that it contains, and to the race of which you and we are alike members—the proud Caucasian race, whose sovereignty on earth God has ordained, and they themselves have illustrated on the most brilliant pages of the world's history.

The Southern Whites Act

It would have been too much to expect that the South, known for its measures of direct action, would have been content with mere protests, however vigorously they might have been made. Observing that the Union League, an altruistic wartime organization, was welding the Negroes into a powerful Republican organization, many whites came to the conclusion that a program of action was necessary. Indeed, there were some Southerners who had immediately resorted to violent tactics upon the cessation of hostilities. Early in 1866 the head of the Freedmen's Bureau in Georgia complained that bands of men calling themselves Regulators, Jayhawkers, and the Black Horse Cavalry were committing "the most fiendish and diabolical outrages on the freedmen." These early groups set the pattern by which resistance was made to Radical Reconstruction in the South.

For ten years after 1867 there flourished the Knights of the White Camellia, the Constitutional Union Guard, the Pale Faces, the White Brotherhood, the Council of Safety, the '76 Association, and the Knights of the Ku Klux Klan.

Among the numerous local organizations were the White League of Louisiana, the White Line of Mississippi, and the Rifle Clubs of South Carolina. Armed with guns, swords, or other weapons, the members of those secret organizations patrolled portions of the South day and night. They used intimidation, force, ostracism in business and society, bribery at the polls, arson, and even murder to accomplish their deeds. Depriving the Negro of political equality became, to them, a holy crusade in which a "noble" end justified any means. State and federal laws failed to render them ineffective, and they succeeded in driving many Negroes from participation in politics.

The following sworn testimony of a Negro woman, Hannah Tutson of Clay County, Florida, before the Congressional committee investigating the Ku Klux conspiracy reveals the techniques of the terroristic organizations during the period.[10]

When they came to my house that night, the dog barked twice, and the old man got up and went out of doors and then came back and lay down; she flew out again, and I got up and went out of doors . . . but I could see nothing; I went back into the house, and just as I got in bed five men bulged right against the door, and it fell right in the middle of the floor, and they fell down. George McCrea was the first who got up . . . and he went where I had left all the children; went circling around the children's bed, and I said, "Who's that?" The old man had not spoke. George McCrea ran right to me and gathered me by the arm. . . . The old man threw his arm around my neck and held on to me. Cabell Winn catched hold of my foot, and then there was so many hold of me I cannot tell who they were. George McCrea and Cabell Winn were the first to take hold of me. He said, "Come in, True-Klux."

I started to scream, and George McCrea catched me right by the throat and choked me. I worried around and around, and he catched the little child by the foot and slinged it out of my arms. I screamed again, and he gathered me again. Then there were so many hold of me that they got me out of doors. After they got me out, I looked up and I saw Jim Phillips, George McCrea, and Henry Baxter. I looked ahead of me and they had the old man; and they tore down the fence the same as if you saw people dragging hogs from the butcher-pen. And they went to another corner of the fence and jerked me over, just as if you were jerking a dumb beast. The old man was ahead of me, and I saw Dave Donley stamp on him. I said, "Sam, give up; it is not worth while to try to do anything; they will try to kill us here." They said, "O, God damn you, we will kill you." I said, "I will go with you." George McCrea said, "Come right along." I said, "Yes, I am coming. . . ." After they carried me about a quarter of a mile from the house . . . they took me through a path to a field, and down

---

[10] *Testimony Taken by the Joint Committee to Inquire into the Condition of Affairs in the Late Insurrectionary States* (Washington, 1872), 13:59–62.

to the lower end of the field. When they got there, he said, "Come here, True-Klux." The True-Klux came there and stopped and whispered about as far from here to this gentleman. . . . Then he said, "Now, old lady, you pretend to be a good Christian; you had better pray right off." I cast my eye up to the elements and begged God to help me. George McCrea struck me over the head with a pistol, and said, "God damn you, what are you making this fuss for?" I said, "No." He said, "Where is the ropes?" They said they had lost the ropes. Now, I never saw any horses; I did not see any that night. They went off next to my field and came back with a handful of saddle-girths, with the buckles on them. They took and carried me to a pine, just as large as I could get my arms around, and then they tied my hands there. They pulled off all my linen, tore it up so that I did not have a piece of rag on me as big as my hand. They tied me, and I said, "Men what are you going to do with me?" They said, "God damn you, we will show you; you are living on another man's premises." I said, "No I am living on my own premises; I gave $150 for it and Captain Buddington and Mr. Mundy told me to stay here." He said, "God damn you, we will give them the same as we are going to give you." I quit talking to them, only as they asked me anything. They tied me to a tree and whipped me for awhile. Then George McCrea would say, "Come here, True-Klux." Then the True-Klux would come, and they would step off about as far as that gentleman and whisper; and then they would say that they would go off to where the saddles were. They would go, and then when they came back they would whip me again. Every time they would go off, George McCrea would act scandalously and ridiculously toward me and treat me shamefully. . . . They whipped me, and went off again to the horses, and got liquor of some kind and poured it on my head, and I smelled it for three weeks, so that it made me sick. . . . He asked me where was my ox. It was in the field, but I would not tell him. . . . They would go and hunt, and then come back. . . . Understand me, men, while they were going to hunt for that ox, George McCrea would make me sit down there, and try to have me do with him right there. They came back and whipped me. I said, "Yes, men, if you will stop whipping me, I will give way to you." . . . they whipped me from the crown of my head to the soles of my feet. I was just raw. The blood oozed out through my frock all around my waist, clean through, when I got to Captain Buddington's. After I got away from them that night I ran to my house. My house was torn down. I went in and felt where my bed was. It was along in the middle of the floor. I went to the other corner of the house and felt for my little children. . . . I could not feel my little children and I could not see them. . . . [The next day] They were there at my house, where the True-Klux had whipped me. Their father lay out in the middle of the night, and my children lay out there too. They said that when they got away from me they went out into the field and my little daughter said that as the baby cried she would reach out and pick some gooseberries and put them in its little mouth. When she could hear none of them any more she went up into the field to a log heap and staid there with her brother and the baby. . . . On Friday while I was eating my breakfast . . . Byrd Sullivan came to my house with Jake Winn and Dave Donley and George Mc-Crea. They went into the field and let down the fence; the old man was gone to the hammock. Old Byrd Sullivan came up to the house and said: "Aunty, these people are devilish people; they are determined to put you off this land. Now pay good attention to what I say. When you get your hand into a lion's mouth, you pull it out just as easy as you can. . . . You can tell your old man to give it up, or in a month's time, or such a matter they will come here, and the lot will push him out of doors and let you eat this green grass. . . ." I said, "Mr. Ashley, Mr. Rohan, and Mr. Swindell told me not to give it up; that if I let anybody else come on the land I could not get it back."

Negro "Domination" Condemned

One of the most persistent if specious arguments advanced by white Southerners against Radical Reconstruction was that it was a period of Negro rule. Even where Negroes were in the minority, which was the case in all former Confederate states except South Carolina and Mississippi, white Southerners contended that Negroes held the balance of power, and that this made them the dominant force in Southern politics. Added to this, the argument went, was the widespread and humiliating use of Negro troops to maintain order and to intimidate the former white rulers. There was no more basis of truth in this argument than in the one that claimed that there was Negro rule in the South. For many years after the overthrow, this argument was revived and used to warn Southern whites that they must be vigilant lest Negro domination, with all its evils, recur. Among those who lived through the period and later rose to a high position of influence was the Chief Justice of the Mississippi Supreme Court, H. H. Chalmers, who in 1881 reviewed the period and gave a moving description of the consequences of Negro domination.[11]

Thirteen years have elapsed since, by act of Congress, negro suffrage was established in ten States of the Union, and ten years since, by amendment of the Constitution, it was made universal throughout the nation. The enfranchisement of so large a mass of new electors, and the instant elevation of so much ignorance and pauperism to complete equality with wealth and intelligence, was never before, in the history of the world, wrought by a single legislative act. In several of the States it put the representatives of that race who alone knew anything of public affairs, or of private virtue, in a hopeless minority as

---

[11] H. H. Chalmers, "The Effects of Negro Suffrage," *The North American Review*, 132 (March 1881), 239-44.

compared with that race who had ever been barbarians save when they were slaves, and who were destitute alike of property, education, or morality. . . .

We are not yet sufficiently removed from the strife evoked by these measures to do impartial justice to the motives of their authors, but time enough has elapsed to enable us to see something of the practical workings of the hazardous venture. . . . The most superficial effect of the enfranchisement of the blacks has been to give them the balance of power in all our recent political struggles. There has been no presidential election, since the suffrage was conferred upon them, in which the result would not have been different if their votes had been eliminated from the contest. . . . But this is a mere surface view of the subject, and these are, it is to be hoped, only the temporary and accidental results of negro enfranchisement. Its deeper and more lasting effects are to be found in that demoralization of our politics, which has sprung from the debasement of the elective franchisement. It was madness to suppose that the body of electors could be swollen by the sudden injection into it of such an enormous mass of ignorance, pauperism, and immorality without debasing the value of the franchise in popular estimation, and without breaking down, in great measure, our reverence for the ballot box as the supreme arbiter of our disputes. . . .

The ballot indeed has won for the newly enfranchised every civil and legal right, but fearful has been the price which the country has paid for it, and direful the consequences. The reconstruction acts manifestly if not avowedly proceeded upon the theory that the whites were unfit to rehabilitate their upturned governments, and that this duty must be developed upon the negroes. While the whole of the latter were suddenly enfranchised, large classes of the former, embracing the most cultured and experienced, were disfranchised, and as the ingenuity of President Johnson's legal advisers sought to limit the number of the disfranchised classes, successive acts of Congress made them yet more sweeping. While the scheme was nominally submitted to the vote of the people of the States affected by it, no election was permitted to stand that did not result in its favor, and in some of the States repeated elections were ordered until the desired result was compelled. When negro domination had by these methods been established, there ensued a scene of incompetence, profligacy, and pillage, the like of which has never disgraced the annals of any English-speaking people.

It was wealth plundered by pauperism, intelligence dominated by ignorance, America ruled by Ethiopia. . . .

At length, when longer endurance became impossible, when taxes, already swollen a thousand per cent on former rates, were mounting still higher and threatening confiscation of all property; when, despite these enormous levies, the bonded indebtedness grew year by year more enormous, when millions of acres of land had already been forfeited for unpaid taxes, when all industries were paralyzed, and the very soil seemed reluctant to bring forth its accustomed fruits, the maddened whites burst their bonds—burst them under the forms of law and the guise of the ballot-box, since federal power would not otherwise permit, but by means in some instances, certainly which a firm believer in the efficacy of the ballot-box would find it difficult to defend. . . . Let not those who have not felt the bitterness of such tyranny judge the whites of the South too harshly. Let it be remembered that in no time or clime have the Caucasian race ever consented to live with the inferior ones *save as rulers.*

Negro "Domination" Denied

The claim of Negro domination did not go unchallenged. Republican leaders in the North and South denied it. Negroes also denied it, especially resenting the contentions that they were either the blind dupes of the Radical leaders or that in their inexperience they exercised a dominant and deleterious influence in Southern politics. Admitting that their votes were important to the Republicans, especially in towns and counties where they constituted a majority, they steadfastly argued that nowhere was there anything approaching "Negro rule." Among the Negroes who vigorously refuted the claim of Negro domination was John R. Lynch, former Speaker of the Mississippi House of Representatives and later a member of Congress from the famous "shoestring" district. In 1913 he made the following comment.[12]

It is claimed that in States, districts, and countries, in which the colored people are in the majority, the suppression of the colored vote is necessary to prevent "Negro Domination," to prevent the ascendency of the blacks over the whites in the administration of the State and local governments. This claim is based upon the assumption that if the black vote were not suppressed in all such States, districts, and counties, black men would be supported and elected to office because they were black, and white men would be opposed and defeated because they were white.

Taking Mississippi for purposes of illustration, it will be seen that there has never been the slightest ground for such an apprehension. No colored man in that State ever occupied a judicial position above that of Justice of the Peace, and very few aspired to that position. Of seven State officers only one, that of Secretary of State, was filled by a colored man, until 1873, when colored men were elected to three of the seven offices—Lieutenant-Governor, Secretary of State, and State Superintendent of Education. Of the two United States Senators and the seven members of the lower house of Congress not more than one colored man occupied a seat in each house at the same time. Of the thirty-five members of the State Senate, and of the one hundred and fifteen members of the House—which composed the total member-

---

[12] John R. Lynch, *The Facts of Reconstruction* (New York, 1913), 92–99.

ship of the State Legislature prior to 1874—there were never more than about seven colored men in the Senate and forty in the lower house. Of the ninety-seven members that composed the Constitutional Convention of 1868, but seventeen were colored men. . . . There was a slight increase in the colored membership [of the state legislature] as a result of the election of 1873, but the colored men never at any time had control of the State Government, nor of any branch or department thereof, nor even that of any county or municipality. Out of seventy-two counties in the State at that time, electing on an average of twenty-eight officers to a county, it is safe to assert that not over five out of one hundred of such officers were colored men. The State, district, county, and municipal governments were not only in control of white men, but white men who were to the manor born, or who were known as old citizens of the State—those who had lived in the State many years before the War of the Rebellion. There was, therefore, never a time when that class of white men known as Carpet-baggers had absolute control of the State Government, or that of any district, county, or municipality, or any branch or department thereof. There was never, therefore, any ground for the alleged apprehension of negro domination as a result of a free, fair, and honest election in any one of the Southern or Reconstructed States.

5. THE END OF AN ERA

Even while they complained bitterly of Radical Reconstruction, the Freedmen's Bureau, and other "encroachments" on their way of life, the whites of the South were making noticeable strides toward recovery. They had evolved a working relationship with the freedmen that left much to be desired, since the various forms of tenancy and sharecropping made the Negroes peculiarly dependent on the landlords. But it secured the labor desperately needed on the plantations. They had begun to stimulate interest on the part of the Northern capitalists in investing in new ventures in the South. They had begun to talk freely about the "New South" that was in the making. An increasing number of Northerners looked sympathetically upon the South, and some of them saw prospects for a real Southern renaissance.

Reconstruction did not end abruptly as the result of Congressional or Presidential action. Rather, it came to a gradual end as restraints were relaxed and stringent legislation repealed. Just as Reconstruction began long before the war was over, so it drew to a close long before the final withdrawal of troops from Southern soil. As early as 1865 many Southerners had resumed their places at home as respected citizens of their communities, and they entered public affairs on taking the oath of allegiance. Even during Radical Reconstruction others continued to return to the fold and to aid in restoring home rule. In 1869 the ex-Confederates of Tennessee were enfranchised. Within a few months large numbers of Southerners in other states reclaimed their citizenship through individual acts of amnesty. In 1871 the "iron clad" oath, which Congress had imposed to disqualify many ex-Confederates, was repealed. In the following year a general amnesty restored the franchise to all but about six hundred ex-Confederate officials. It then became possible for the south to take up where it left off in 1861 and to govern itself.

Gradually the Democratic Party was revived. In 1870 the border states began to go Democratic; and North Carolina and Virginia came under the control of Conservatives who outnumbered the Republican combination of Negroes, "Scalawags," and "Carpetbaggers." In the following year the Georgia Democrats returned to power. In 1874 and 1875 the Democrats gained control of Texas, Arkansas, and Alabama. By 1876 the only states that the Republicans could claim in the South were South Carolina, Florida, and Louisiana. By that time the cause of Democracy had gained such momentum that the overthrow of Republicanism was regarded by many as a crusade. Wherever Republicans attempted to resist the rise of the Democrats, riots and bloodshed ensued. There were times in the 1870s when it appeared as though civil war would break out anew. The intimidation of Negroes had become a fine art, and when they attempted to vote, punishment was swift and ruthless. The organized whites became bolder as they patrolled the voting places to guarantee "fair, peaceful, and Democratic" elections. More and more Negroes remained at home, and the change of political power from Republican to Democratic hands was hastened.

The North had grown weary of the crusade. Perhaps Stevens, Sumner, Butler, and the old anti-slavery leaders could have gone on with it, but younger people, with less zeal for reform and a greater interest in "stability," took their places. The assumption of Republican leadership by men like Hayes, Blaine, Conkling, and Logan was a signal for the party to turn to more profitable and practical pursuits. The indifference of many Republicans, the preoccupation of some with other matters, and the venality of still others set the stage for the final overthrow that came after the election of 1876.

A Traditional Interpretation

Opinions regarding the benefits of Reconstruction range all the way from those that view the period as the darkest blot on American political history to those that see it as a period in which considerable significant and salutary changes took place. In his *History of the United States,* James Ford Rhodes,

Northern industrialist turned historian, was distressed over the deleterious effects of Radical Reconstruction policy. Typical of the traditional interpretation of the era is the portion of his evaluation, written in 1906, that follows.[13]

No large policy in our country has ever been so conspicuous a failure as that of forcing universal negro suffrage upon the South. The negroes who simply acted out their nature were not to blame. How indeed could they have acquired political honesty? What idea could barbarism thrust into slavery obtain of the rights of property? Even among the Aryans of education and intelligence public integrity has been a plant of slow growth. . . . The scheme of Reconstruction pandered to ignorant negroes, the knavish white natives, and the vulturous adventurers who flocked from the North; and these neutralized the work of honest Republicans who were officers of State. . . . From the Republican policy came no real good to the negroes. Most of them developed no political capacity, and the few who raised themselves above the mass did not reach a high order of intelligence. . . . The negro's political activity is rarely of a nature to identify him with any movement on a high plane . . . he has been a political failure and he could not have been otherwise. . . .

The Congressional policy of Reconstruction was shortsighted even from the partisan point of view in that it gave the South a grievance. In that balancing of rights and wrongs, which must be made in a just consideration of a great human transaction, the North at the end of the war could appeal to Europe and to history for the justification of its beliefs that there was on its side a large credit balance. Some of this it has lost by its repressive, uncivilized, and unsuccessful policy of Reconstruction. Moreover the close sequence of events has led the South to regard negro rule as the complement of emancipation with the result that she has sometimes lost sight of the benefit of the great act which gave freedom to the slaves.

An avowed aim of the Congressional policy was to build up a Republican party at the South. Here was a failure complete and an opportunity missed. The nucleus of a Republican party was there in the old-line Whigs and Union-men-who-went-with-their-State. . . . At the end of the war they were ready to act in opposition to Democrats and fire-eaters . . . but the policy of Congress, which raised the race issue, consolidated all the white men into one party for self-protection. . . . No doubt can exist that, if negro suffrage had not been forced upon the South, a healthy and respectable Republican party would have been formed, attaining perhaps the power and influence which the Democrats have in New England and in contests like those of 1896 and 1900, furnishing electoral votes for the Republican presidential candidate. And so far as we can divine, had the matter been left to the States themselves suffrage by this time [1906] would have been fully

---

[13] James Ford Rhodes, *History of the United States* (New York, 1906), 7:168–72, 291.

accorded to the negroes on the basis of educational and property qualifications. . . .

The United States of 1877 was a better country than the United States of 1850. For slavery was abolished, the doctrine of secession was dead, and Lincoln's character and fame had become a possession of the nation. From 1877 on, is seen a growing marvel in national history: the reunion of hearts which gives to patriotism the same meaning at the South as at the North. Freedom and reunion were glorious achievements but in human affairs blessings do not come unmixed. Other legacies of the War and Reconstruction were an increase of governmental corruption and a more pronounced tendency towards bad administration. But there was clamour where there had been abuse; and the American people remained sound at the core.

A Revisionist Evaluation

In recent years several historians have undertaken to re-examine the Reconstruction period with a view to weighing more carefully the social and economic changes that occurred and studying these changes in the context of the larger picture of American history. This approach has resulted in some considerable revision of the evaluations of the period. Among the first persons to re-examine the period was W. E. B. Du Bois, who wrote the following in 1910.[14]

Undoubtedly there were many ridiculous things connected with Reconstruction governments: the placing of ignorant field-hands who could neither read nor write in the legislature, the gold spittoons of South Carolina, the enormous public printing bill of Mississippi—all these were extravagant and funny, and yet somehow, to one who sees beneath all that is bizarre, the real human tragedy of upward striving of down-trodden men, the groping for light among people born in darkness, there is less tendency to laugh and gibe than among shallower minds and easier consciences. . . .

Then too a careful examination of the alleged stealing in the South reveals much. First, there is repeated exaggeration. For instance it is said that the taxation in Mississippi was fourteen times as great in 1874 as in 1869. This sounds staggering until we learn that the state taxation in 1869 was only ten cents on one hundred dollars, and that the expenses of government in 1874 were only twice as great as in 1860, and that too with a depreciated currency. . . .

The character of the real thieving shows that white men must have been the chief beneficiaries. . . . The frauds through the manipulation of state and railway bonds and of banknotes must have inured chiefly to the benefit of experienced white men, and this must have been largely the case of the furnishing

---

[14] W. E. Burghardt Du Bois, "Reconstruction and Its Benefits," *American Historical Review*, 15 (July 1910), 781–99.

and printing frauds. . . . That the negroes led by astute thieves became tools and received a small share of the spoils is true. But two considerations must be added: Much of the legislation which resulted in fraud was represented to the negroes as good legislation, and thus their votes were secured by deliberate misrepresentation. . . .

Granted . . . that the negroes were to some extent venal but to a much larger extent ignorant and deceived, the question is: did they show any signs of a disposition to learn better things? The theory of democratic governments is not that the will of the people is always right, but rather that normal human beings of average intelligence will, if given a chance, learn the right and best course by bitter experience. This is precisely what negro voters showed indubitable signs of doing. First, they strove for schools to abolish ignorance, and, second, a large and growing number of them revolted against the carnival of extravagance and stealing that marred the beginning of Reconstruction, and joined with the best elements to institute reform. . . .

We may recognize three things which negro rule gave to the South:

1. Democratic government.
2. Free public schools.
3. New social legislation.

In South Carolina there was before the war a property qualification for officeholders, and, in part, for voters. The Constitution of 1868, on the other hand, was a modern democratic document . . . preceded by a broad Declaration of Rights which did away with property qualifications and based representation directly on population instead of property. It especially took up new subjects of social legislation, declaring navigable rivers free public highways, instituting homestead exemptions, establishing boards of county commissioners, providing for a new penal code of laws, establishing universal manhood suffrage "without distinction of race or color," devoting six sections to charitable and penal institutions and six to corporations, providing separate property for married women, etc. Above all, eleven sections of the Tenth Article were devoted to the establishment of a complete public-school system.

So satisfactory was the constitution thus adopted by negro suffrage and by a convention composed of a majority of blacks that the state lived twenty-seven years under it without essential change and when the constitution was revised in 1895, the revision was practically nothing more than an amplification of the Constitution of 1868. No essential advance step of the former document was changed except the suffrage article. . . .

There is no doubt that the thirst of the black man for knowledge . . . gave birth to the public free-school system of the South. It was the question upon which black voters and legislators insisted more than anything else and while it is possible to find some vestiges of free schools in some of the Southern states before the war, yet a universal, well-established system dates from the day that the black man got political power. . . .

Finally, in legislation covering property, the wider functions of the state, the punishment of crime, and the like, it is sufficient to say that the laws on these points established by Reconstruction legislation were not only different from and even revolutionary to the laws in the older South, but they were so wise and so well suited to the needs of the new South that in spite of a retrogressive movement following the overthrow of negro governments the mass of this legislation, with elaboration and development, still stands on the statute books of the South.

CONCLUSION

As Reconstruction drew to a close in 1877, the question could well have been raised as to whether it had solved more problems than it had created. The pattern of race relations had been greatly modified, but had Negroes and whites actually learned to live together peacefully by the time that the federal government bowed out of the picture? Had the "Negro Policy" of the Radicals, limited as it was in its objectives, accomplished enough to justify all the bitterness and opposition that it aroused? If bitterness and opposition were going to be aroused in any case, as the evidence of the Johnson governments could have indicated, should Congress' objectives have been broader, and its insistence upon obedience of the law more firm and long-lasting? Was it possible, that in giving so much attention to political problems and so little attention to pressing economic problems, the federal government might have been guilty of distorting values and of inadvertently directing an excessive amount of the South's attention to these problems? To what extent was the South's preoccupation with racial and political questions responsible for the economic conquest of the section by Northern and foreign capital? Regardless of where the responsibility lay, the new and complex economic developments greatly aggravated the South's problems and made all of them much more difficult to solve.

And what of the way in which the resort to violence and the disrespect for law came to be sanctified in the South? The tendency that was apparent in the ante-bellum period received the justification that gave it renewed vigor and vitality during the Reconstruction. As hooded, secret orders became synonymous with the righteous crusade for "home rule," the more responsible members of Southern communities could well have raised questions about the wisdom of some Reconstruction policies. Unwise Reconstruction policies, however, could hardly absolve the South of its guilt in resorting to lawlessness and barbarianism in resisting them. To what extent, then, did the reign of terror during Reconstruction provide an unsavory legacy for the South of a later day? Long after Reconstruction was over, the respectable people of the South continued to face the difficult task of trying to dissociate themselves from the odium of rule by force and violence. And they have not yet succeeded.

Finally, what of the feelings between the North and the South? Despite the fact that there were gestures of accord, such as the return of Confederate flags and the elimination of all disabilities on former Confederates, feelings of animosity persisted. These feelings were deep seated, and the waving of the "bloody shirt" and the cries of the threat of "Negro domination" kept them very much alive. As one views the aftermath, he cannot fail to raise questions regarding the wisdom of Reconstruction as it was carried out, the possible alternatives to it, and the way in which it could have been modified in order to achieve greater success than it did.